NINETEENTH-CENTURY CHORAL MUSIC

Nineteenth-Century Choral Music is an in-depth examination of the rich repertoire of choral music and the cultural phenomenon of choral music-making throughout the period. The book is divided into three main sections. The first details the attraction to choral singing and the ways it was linked to different parts of society, and the role of choral voices in the two principal large-scale genres of the period: the symphony and opera. A second section highlights ten choral–orchestral master-works that are a central part of the repertoire. The final section presents overview and focus chapters covering composers, repertoire (both small and larger works), and performance life in a historical context from over a dozen regions of the world: Britain and Ireland, the Czech Republic, France, Germany, Hungary, Italy, Latin America, the Philippines, Poland, Russia, Scandinavia and Finland, Spain, and the United States.

This diverse collection of essays brings together the work of twenty-five authors, many of whom have devoted much of their scholarly lives to the composers and music discussed, giving the reader a lively and unique perspective on this significant part of nineteenth-century musical life.

Donna M. Di Grazia is the David J. Baldwin Professor of Music and Choral Conductor at Pomona College in Claremont, California, and a recipient of the Wig Distinguished Professor Award for Excellence in Teaching.

NINETEENTH-CENTURY CHORAL MUSIC

Edited by Donna M. Di Grazia

Routledge
Taylor & Francis Group

NEW YORK AND LONDON

Senior Editor: Constance Ditzel
Editorial Assistant: Elysse Preposi
Production Editor: Sarah Hudson
Marketing Manager: Joon Won Moon
Copy Editor: Janice Baiton
Proofreader: Jacqueline Dias
Cover Design: Jayne Varney

First published 2013
by Routledge
711 Third Avenue, New York, NY 10017

Simultaneously published in the UK
by Routledge
2 Park Square, Milton Park, Abingdon, Oxon OX14 4RN

Routledge is an imprint of the Taylor & Francis Group, an informa business

Library of Congress Cataloging in Publication Data
    Nineteenth-century choral music / edited by Donna M. Di Grazia.
    pages cm – (Routledge studies in musical genres)
    Includes bibliographical references and index.
    1. Choral music–19th century. I. Di Grazia, Donna Marie, editor of
    compilation. II. Series: Routledge studies in musical genres.
    ML1505.N56 2012
    782.509'034–dc23   2012001083

ISBN: 978–0–415–98852–0 (hbk)
ISBN: 978–0–415–98853–7 (pbk)
ISBN: 978–0–203–11518–3 (ebk)

Typeset in Bembo
by Keystroke, Station Road, Codsall, Wolverhampton

CONTENTS

The Iberian World

North America

PREFACE

> Keep in mind that there are also singers, and that the highest in musical expression is achieved through the chorus and orchestra.
>
> *Robert Schumann (1849)*[1]

Whether one agrees with Robert Schumann's assessment or not, the broadly defined genre of choral art music, encompassing a vast amount of diverse material with and without accompaniment, continued to attract considerable attention from nineteenth-century composers even as instrumental music and opera took their place at the center of the cultural fabric of the day. This attraction was at least partly because choral music was the one genre pursued in five distinct performance venues: concert halls, churches and synagogues, theatres, salons, and schools. In these places, professionals and, more importantly, a growing army of amateurs, made music for an equally expanding middle-class audience. As William Weber and others have established, the so-called canon of Western classical music took shape during this time thanks to the rise of concert societies and subscription series in Europe's major capitals and in the United States. The availability and increased frequency of public orchestra concerts and opera propelled the emergence of the middle class as patrons of music most directly, of course. But even in these two arenas, the presence and influence of choral music can be seen throughout the century, not only in Germany and England, as is frequently cited in the literature, but also throughout much of Europe and the Americas.

Although the repertoire for choral forces from the nineteenth century has shaped modern listening experience at least as much as early music has, study of it and the cultural phenomenon of choral singing then has eluded recent in-depth examination. The literature that exists on the choral art in general is, for the most part, decades old; its relative age is significant because so much research has been done in the intervening years on many of the composers discussed here and on the environments in which they worked and their music initially came to life. This more recent work on individual composers, their music, and their cultural surroundings has influenced the way performers and researchers alike think and write about choral music now, and how they assess and interpret the musical works of the great Romantic age.

Compilation and Organization

Nineteenth-Century Choral Music, featuring the perspectives of twenty-five authors, most of whom have spent significant parts of their scholarly lives working with the composers and the cultures they write about here (and some of whom have performed large portions of the repertoire they discuss), aims to fill a gap in the literature on the choral art as it developed in the nineteenth century. As the volume began to take shape, answers to fundamental questions of how to manage the different strands of the repertoire, how much of it to cover, and how to cover it began to emerge.

A book on choral music from this period should address choral music-making as a cultural phenomenon, one that had an impact on multiple parts of society. Additionally, its coverage should extend beyond the major choral–orchestral works by the most prominent composers of the century to include short works for unaccompanied voices or for instruments other than orchestra, much of which is equally rich albeit on a smaller scale. This approach allows our view of the century to include the contributions of composers such as Fanny Hensel, Charles Villiers Stanford, and a host of others who did not compose symphonic literature or large-scale choral–orchestral works, or at least not enough of them for their music to have made it into the list of works regularly performed by civic and symphonic choruses.

The goal of this book, then, is to provide a distinctive resource, one that is inclusive of small and large works and not limited to or exclusive of the most well-known choral–orchestral works, and one that considers the subject of choral music as a coherent complex of topics that touch both on the repertoire itself and on the society for which it was created, performed, and heard. To foster this approach, we settled on a three-part organizational scheme.

Part I—indeed, the entire book—is anchored by Celia Applegate's wonderfully engaging essay on the fundamental attraction of choral singing in the nineteenth century, how it impacted the social, political, and economic scenes, who participated in it, and so on. The two chapters that follow offer perspectives on the changing and expanding role of the chorus in the century's two super genres: the symphony and opera.

In Part II, our attention shifts to ten of the century's masterworks for chorus and orchestra. Here D. Kern Holoman, a conductor as well as an eminent music historian, offers the insight of a performer–scholar, placing each work in its historical context and drawing out salient details from the music in elegant prose.

In Part III, we get to the heart of the matter, with chapters organized geographically. Here one will find a flexible approach within each section that reflects the disparate state of our understanding of nineteenth-century choral music in terms of both the repertoire and its practitioners. For those regions where scholarship and performance has been the most plentiful, introductory essays offer a critical overview of contemporary society and the role music played in it, followed by chapters on individual composers whose contributions either mark an important step in the development of the choral genre or highlight a composer whose choral output is significant within his or her *œuvre*. For the rest, we opted for a broader approach, so that authors might weave together these less-familiar stories of choral music-making more easily. Because most of the signature choral–orchestral masterworks from the period are dealt with in Part II, authors in Part III had the freedom to discuss a wider range of pieces and to a greater or lesser degree of detail. This approach made exhaustive coverage impossible, yet such a works-list-in-prose was never the aim of this book. Instead, the reader will get a reasonable sense of how choral music flourished throughout the century, and how the diverse repertoire was linked to different parts of society. Though every piece mentioned is not as inspired as the most familiar and universally recognized gems, this variability reflects the variety of the period, and is part of the story of choral music-making in the nineteenth century.

Scope

As with any volume on a topic as large as this one, there were limits to what we could include, and some may reasonably question certain decisions we made in terms of coverage. For example, how can a book on nineteenth-century choral music include a chapter on Luigi Cherubini and Augusta Holmès but not Franz Schubert—Ryan Minor mentions him in his overview for Germany and Austria, but he has no chapter of his own. Additionally, choral singing in nineteenth-century

Jewish communities in the synagogue and in secular circles is touched on briefly, but a satisfactory exploration of the subject still awaits future study,[2] and there is only slightly more coverage for spirituals, shape-note music, Moravian music, and so on. Regrettably, considerations of space and of breadth and balance of coverage forced hard decisions, and for these I take full responsibility.

If we're missing some great stuff, we hope we make up for it by revealing just how vast the choral landscape really was, including regions of the world where the growth of choral music and music-making has been difficult to assess outside of the "home" country. We are especially pleased in this regard to open a window onto the choral life and repertoire of Latin America, the Philippines, and Spain; of Scandinavia and Finland; and of the Eastern European capitals in Poland, Bohemia and Moravia, Hungary, and Russia. And no book on this subject would be complete without a summary of choral music-making in the United States, an emerging nation during this long century that went through perhaps the most profound growth of any country represented here, and where we see most clearly how the perceived natural boundaries between the sacred and secular performance worlds were often blurred. Indeed, in reading these chapters, one can see how often there is an overlap between civil and church singing, and, as Carlo Caballero put it, how genres easily traveled from the stage to the salon and to the concert hall in no particular order.

We hope this book will be something to which performer and non-performer scholars, cultural and music historians, conductors, and students can turn. Repertoire is certainly the focus, but so is the cultural life of each region. Understanding the link between them will revitalize performance and scholarship alike.

Donna M. Di Grazia
Claremont, California

Notes

1 Robert Schumann, *Musikalische Haus- und Lebensregeln* (pub. 1850), as quoted in John Daverio, *Crossing Paths: Schubert, Schumann, and Brahms* (Cambridge and New York: Oxford University Press, 2002), 184.

2 For a compact overview of Jewish choral music in the synagogue and in the community, see Joshua Jacobson, "Choirs," *Encyclopedia Judaica*, ed. Fred Skolnik and Michael Berenbaum (Detroit: Thomas Gale, 2007), 2nd ed., vol. 4, 658–64; this source is available on online as part of the Jewish Virtual Library at http://www.jewishvirtuallibrary.org/jsource/judaica/ejud_0002_0004_0_04266.html. See also Alexander Ringer, "Salomon Sulzer, Joseph Mainzer and the Romantic a cappella Movement," *Studia Musicologica*, 2 (1969), 355–70; Edwin Seroussi et. al., "Jewish Music," *Grove Music Online. Oxford Music Online*, http://www.oxfordmusiconline.com.ezproxy.libraries.claremont.edu/subscriber/article/grove/music/413 22 (accessed July 23, 2011); and various publications by Joshua Jacobson, including his "Franz Schubert and the Vienna Synagogue," *The Choral Journal*, 38:1 (Aug. 1997), 9–15, and "The Oldest Jewish Choir," *The Journal of Synagogue Music*, XX:2 (Dec. 1990), 24–7. According to Jacobson, secular Jewish choral societies that were not affiliated with a synagogue did not begin to appear until the latter part of the century, beginning with the Serbian-Jewish Vocal Ensemble (1879) in Belgrade, and later, the more well-known Hazomir Chorale (1899) in Łodz, Poland.

ACKNOWLEDGMENTS

This book is indebted first and foremost to my fellow contributors, twenty-four wonderful scholars whose work I greatly admire and without whom this book simply would not exist. No small amount of credit is due to R. Larry Todd, general editor of the series *Routledge Studies in Musical Genres*, who first approached me to take on the project and who was both incredibly receptive to my ideas and generous with his time and energy. I extend similar gratitude to Constance Ditzel, Senior Music Editor at Routledge, for her flexibility, support, and understanding at every turn; to the anonymous reviewers who supported the proposal, to Denny Tek and Elysse Preposi in New York; and to Sarah Hudson and the entire production team at Routledge.

Various colleagues, former teachers and mentors offered invaluable encouragement and advice along the way. The list is too long to name everyone individually here, but I would be remiss if I did not single out Ralph Locke, whose support for this and other projects has been constant, Hugh Macdonald, and D. Kern Holoman, who came to the rescue at a most critical time and whose contributions here literally kept the project alive when there was no more time to reconfigure things to meet the publisher's more than reasonable deadlines.

The following institutions and firms have graciously given permission to reproduce musical examples and illustrations: Bärenreiter-Verlag, Bayerische Staatsbibliothek, Carus-Verlag, Collection Médiathèque Musicale Mahler (Paris), Casa Ricordi (MGB Hal Leonard), Editorial Boileau, Tecla Editions, and the Philadelphia Orchestra Association. The remaining musical examples were drawn from sources in the public domain.

My home institution, Pomona College, has supported my musicological and performance-related work most generously for almost fifteen years. For this project specifically, the College's Research Committee provided funding for the index and for my undergraduate student assistant, Mollie McLaren, whose work on the production details and preliminary aspects of the index during the summer of 2009 was first rate. Acknowledgment is also due to Holly Gardinier, Performing Arts Librarian for the Claremont Colleges' Honnold/Mudd Library, for giving me special access to the collection that allowed me to push to the finish line while the semester's craziness swirled on. Thanks of a more personal sort are extended to my Department of Music colleagues, especially my dear friend Tom Flaherty, whose counsel, support and behind-the-scenes efforts on my behalf continue to go well beyond what any junior colleague could hope to have, and my fellow nineteenth-century historian Bill Peterson.

Over the years, the students in my two choral ensembles at Pomona College have graciously sung a rather surprising amount of this repertoire—large-scale masterworks and small octavos alike; in doing so, they have played a significant role in shaping my ideas about the book's coverage and in helping me discover through performance the true beauty embedded in many of the works discussed here. I am also grateful to Lucie McGee, who read part of my initial proposal for the book, and Katie Bent, who offered insightful feedback near the end. And it is with much gratitude that I mention Carrie Henderson, Beth Nitzan, and Katie Bent (again), each of whom made a point of finding various ways to keep me going and smiling, especially during the last few months of editing and writing.

Lastly but most importantly, I offer my most profound and everlasting thanks to my family, who have sustained me in and through everything.

DMD
January 2012

CONTRIBUTORS

Celia Applegate is Professor of History at the University of Rochester and Affiliate Faculty in the Department of Musicology at the Eastman School of Music. She is a scholar of modern German cultural, social, and political history. Her publications range from work on German and European nationalism and regionalism to a variety of topics in the history of German and European musical culture. She is the outgoing president of the German Studies Association.

Paul A. Bertagnolli is Associate Professor of Musicology at the University of Houston's Moores School of Music. His book *Prometheus in Music: Representations of the Myth in the Romantic Era* (Ashgate, 2007) investigates cultural and analytical contexts of Promethean works by composers ranging from Beethoven to Fauré. Other publications in *19th-Century Music*, the *Journal of Musicology*, the *Journal of the American Liszt Society*, and various volumes of conference proceedings focus on Franz Liszt's compositional process.

Carlo Caballero is Associate Professor of Music and Erma Mantey Faculty Fellow at the University of Colorado, Boulder. He received his B.A. from Pomona College and his Ph.D. from the University of Pennsylvania. He is the author of *Fauré and French Musical Aesthetics* and recently review editor of *The Journal of the American Musicological Society*. He is currently writing a book about continuities in French music from the *ancien régime* to the early twentieth century, with a special focus on ballet and comic opera.

Walter A. Clark is Professor of Musicology at the University of California, Riverside, and Director of the Center for Iberian and Latin American Music. He is the author of *Isaac Albéniz: Portrait of a Romantic* (Oxford, 1999/2002) and *Enrique Granados: Poet of the Piano* (Oxford, 2006/ 2011), and co-author of *Federico Moreno Torroba: A Musical Life in Three Acts* (Oxford, forthcoming). He is also series editor of Oxford's Currents in Latin American and Iberian Music.

Donna M. Di Grazia holds the David J. Baldwin Professorship of Music at Pomona College (Claremont, California), where she conducts its two auditioned choirs and teaches courses in music history. Her research on nineteenth-century concert life in Paris, and on early seventeenth-century English sacred music, has appeared in such journals as *19th-Century Music*, *Music and Letters*, *Early Music*, and elsewhere. She received her B.A. and M.A. degrees from the University of California, Davis and her Ph.D. from Washington University in St. Louis.

James Garratt is Senior Lecturer in Music and University Organist at the University of Manchester. Before moving to Manchester in 2002, he lectured at the National University of Ireland, Maynooth. He has written widely on nineteenth-century music, thought and culture, and his publications include *Palestrina and the German Romantic Imagination: Interpreting Historicism in 19th-Century Music* (Cambridge, 2002), and *Music, Culture and Social Reform in the Age of Wagner* (Cambridge, 2010).

Virginia Hancock is Professor of Music at Reed College (Portland, Oregon), directs the Chorus and Collegium Musicum, and teaches theory and history courses. She holds degrees in chemistry from Reed and Harvard and a doctorate in music history from the University of Oregon. She is the author of *Brahms's Choral Compositions and His Library of Early Music* (Ann Arbor, 1983) and a number of articles and book chapters on Brahms topics, particularly his study and performance of Renaissance and Baroque music, his choral music, and his songs.

Paul Hawkshaw is Professor of Music History at the Yale School of Music and Director of the Norfolk Chamber Music Festival. His publications on Anton Bruckner include seven volumes of the composer's Collected Works Edition (Vienna). He served as co-editor of *Bruckner Studies* (Cambridge, 1997) and *Perspectives on Anton Bruckner* (Ashgate, 2001), and wrote the Bruckner biography for *The New Grove Dictionary of Music and Musicians*. In 2011 he was awarded the Kilenyi Medal of the American Bruckner Society in recognition of his efforts on behalf of the composer's music.

Harald Herresthal is organist and professor at the *Norges musikkhøgskole* (the Norwegian Academy of Music) in Oslo. Writing in French, German, and Norwegian, he has published many books and articles on Norwegian music, most recently a biography in four volumes of the Norwegian violinist Ole Bull (1810–80). Herresthal holds an honorary doctorate from the Universität der Künste in Berlin, and is a member of The Norwegian Academy of Science and Letters in Oslo and The Academy of Europe (Academia Europeae).

D. Kern Holoman is Distinguished Professor of Music at the University of California, Davis, and conductor emeritus of the UC Davis Symphony Orchestra. Among his books are the first thematic *Catalogue of the Works of Hector Berlioz* (New Berlioz Edition, 1987), *Berlioz* (Harvard University Press, 1989), *The Société des Concerts du Conservatoire* (University of California Press, 2007), *Writing About Music* (2nd ed. University of California Press, 2008), *Charles Munch* (Oxford University Press, 2011), and *The Orchestra: A Very Short Introduction* (Oxford University Press, 2012).

Alan Houtchens is an authority on the life and times of Antonín Dvořák and focuses his research and publishing endeavors on topics concerned with Czech culture. On the faculty of the Department of Performance Studies at Texas A&M University since 1989, Dr. Houtchens maintains a broadly interdisciplinary perspective in both his teaching and his research endeavors. Currently he is engaged as chief editor of Dvořák's opera *Vanda,* which will be published by Bärenreiter as part of the *New Critical Edition of the Works of Antonín Dvořák.*

Steven Huebner is James McGill Professor of Musicology at McGill University and has written on French and Italian music of the nineteenth and early twentieth centuries, with a concentration on opera. His articles and reviews have appeared in such journals as *19th-Century Music, Journal of the American Musicological Society,* and many others, and in numerous collections of essays. Currently co-editor of *Cambridge Opera Journal,* he is the author of *The Operas of Charles Gounod* (Clarendon, 1990) and *French Opera at the Fin de Siècle: Wagnerism, Nationalism, and Style* (Oxford, 1999).

Francesco Izzo is Senior Lecturer in Music at the University of Southampton. His research focuses on nineteenth-century opera and culture. He has published articles in *Acta Musicologica,*

Cambridge Opera Journal, Journal of the American Musicological Society, Journal of Musicology, Nineteenth-Century Music Review, Studi Musicali, and in numerous books and congress proceedings. He is co-director of the American Institute for Verdi Studies and the editor of Giuseppe Verdi's *Un giorno di regno*, forthcoming with Ricordi and the University of Chicago Press.

Roe-Min Kok received her Ph.D. from Harvard University, and is an Assistant Professor of Music at McGill University. Co-editor of *Rethinking Schumann* (2011), and *Musical Childhoods and the Cultures of Youth* (2006), she has published numerous articles and reviews in German, Austrian, and Anglo-American journals. Current projects include a monograph about children's music, fairy tales and the private lives of nineteenth-century bourgeoisie.

David B. Levy is Professor of Music at Wake Forest University. His contributions to Beethoven scholarship include his book, *Beethoven: the Ninth Symphony* (rev. ed. Yale University Press, 2003), as well as articles and reviews in publications including *Beethoven Forum*, *19th-Century Music*, *NOTES*, *Berlioz Studies* (Cambridge University Press, 1992), and *Essays on Music for Charles Warren Fox* (ESM Press, 1979).

Judith Mabary received her Ph.D. in historical musicology from Washington University in St. Louis, Missouri and is Assistant Professor of Music at the University of Missouri, Columbia, where she teaches courses in music history and world music. Her research interests include Czech music of the nineteenth and twentieth centuries, with a focus on Czech melodrama and more broadly, on the life and works of Dvořák, Fibich, Martinů, and Kapralová.

Barbara Milewski is Associate Professor of Music at Swarthmore College. She earned a Ph.D. in Musicology from Princeton University. Her research focuses on nineteenth- and twentieth-century Polish music and music of the Nazi camps, and has been generously supported by fellowships awarded by the Fulbright Program, the American Musicological Society, the USHMM, the U.S. Department of Defense, the PIASA, and the Kosciuszko Foundation. She is presently writing a book on the musical-poetic activities of prisoners in Birkenau, Sachsenhausen and Buchenwald.

Ryan Minor is Associate Professor of Music at SUNY Stony Brook. He is the author of *Choral Fantasies: Music, Festivity, and Nationhood in Nineteenth-Century Germany* (Cambridge University Press, 2012), as well as essays on Brahms, Liszt, and Wagner. Current projects include a performance history of *Die Meistersinger* and a monograph on music and vitalism at the *fin-de-siècle*. He has received awards from the Alexander von Humboldt Foundation, the DAAD, and the Radcliffe Institute for Advanced Study at Harvard.

Dr. Vladmir Morosan is Founder and President of Musica Russica and one of the leading experts outside Russia in the fields of Russian choral music and Orthodox liturgical music. He is Editor-in-Chief of the series *Monuments of Russian Sacred Music*, and his book *Choral Performance in Pre-Revolutionary Russia* (1986) is considered the definitive study of this topic.

N. Lee Orr is Professor of Music at Georgia State University. He has written widely on nineteenth-century American music, including Dudley Buck, organ music, and choral music. His research has appeared in a number of journals, including *American Music*. He has also had books and editions published by University of Illinois Press, Greenwood Presses, AR Editions, and Routledge.

Clair Rowden's research deals mainly with opera and nineteenth-century France; her book *Republican Morality and Catholic Tradition at the Opera: Massenet's* Hérodiade *and* Thaïs was published in 2004. She is currently working on caricature and parody of opera in the French *fin-de-siècle* press, as well as editing an interdisciplinary volume entitled *Performing Salome, Revealing Stories* (Ashgate, 2013), for which she is the author of the chapter "Whose/Who's Salome? Natalia Trouhanowa, a dancing diva."

Mark Seto is Assistant Professor of Music at Connecticut College. He holds a Ph.D. in Historical Musicology from Columbia University, where his dissertation research focused on symphonic culture in *fin-de-siècle* Paris. An active conductor, he is Co-Artistic Director of the Chelsea Symphony and Music Director of Morningside Opera, both in New York City.

Jeffrey S. Sposato is Associate Professor of Musicology at the Moores School of Music, University of Houston. His most recent book, *The Price of Assimilation: Felix Mendelssohn and the Nineteenth-Century Anti-Semitic Tradition* (Oxford, 2006), was named a *Choice* magazine Outstanding Academic Title for 2006 and was a Royal Philharmonic Society Music Award finalist. He is currently working on a new book entitled *Leipzig After Bach: Musical Life in a German City, 1750–1850.*

R. Larry Todd is Arts and Sciences Professor of Music at Duke University and the author of *Mendelssohn: A Life in Music*, named Best Biography in 2003 by the Association of American Publishers. An expanded German translation appeared as *Felix Mendelssohn Bartholdy: Sein Leben, seine Musik*. He has also written *Mendelssohn Essays* and *Fanny Hensel: The Other Mendelssohn*, and serves as general editor of the Routledge Studies in Musical Genres.

Lesley A. Wright is Professor of Music (Musicology) at the University of Hawai'i at Mānoa, has centered her research on Bizet, Massenet, and others of their generation as well as the institutions and press of nineteenth-century France. She also serves as a member of the editorial board for a recent project to publish critical editions of Saint-Saëns' important works, and is preparing a critical edition of Massenet's *Werther* for Bärenreiter.

ABBREVIATIONS

A	alto
B	bass
Bar	baritone
C	contralto
CPDL	Choral Public Domain Library
D	dessus
H-c	haute-contre
IMSLP	International Music Score Library Project
Mez	mezzo soprano
Op.	opus
S	soprano
T	tenor

PART I

Cultural Influences

1

THE BUILDING OF COMMUNITY THROUGH CHORAL SINGING

Celia Applegate

UNIVERSITY OF ROCHESTER

Music-making in human society has always been a group activity. No other kind of music-making demonstrates this as simply and as fully as does choral singing, and no other century in recorded human history was so rich in forms of choral activity, so diverse in venues and sizes and purposes of choral activity, as was the nineteenth. Even though many of these forms have survived, in one way or another, into the twenty-first century and estimates of numbers of regular choral singers in the United States alone reach into the millions, the nineteenth century remains the choral century par excellence. We may be, as historian Suzanne Marchand put it, "embarrassed by the nineteenth century," suspicious of its officious energy, put off by its Eurocentric complacency, baffled by its sentimentality, its respectability, above all its earnestness, but we nevertheless continue to live off its work.[1] Its institutions and organizations, its rediscoveries and revivals, its compositions and publications created an enduring place for choral song in modern Western society.

Of course, one might attribute that endurance to the quality of the choral repertoire as a whole, which includes works that most would consider among the greatest in all of Western art music. And given that many of these greatest of works—the *St. Matthew Passion*, *Messiah*, *The Creation*—belong in some literal sense to the eighteenth century, what do we really owe to those singing masses of the nineteenth? Handel's and Haydn's choral works sailed straight on into our own times as though the winds of change themselves were behind them. Bach and Palestrina, to be sure, took a little extra effort on the part of their nineteenth-century admirers to be sung and heard again, and we would certainly want to credit the century with producing a significant, though not disproportionately large, number of works one still wants to sing or hear. But against all that, we should probably also weigh in the balance what Percy Young memorably dubbed "mediocrity in spate." "In the whole history of music," he observed in Churchillian cadences, rarely has "so much deplorable music by so many experienced composers" been written as in the second half of the nineteenth century.[2] Their compositional failures, moreover, he blamed on the public itself, whose insatiable demand for new choral works, combined with the pious tyranny of "good taste," bequeathed to posterity "great heaps of discarded choral compositions which represent almost the total output in this medium of practically every composer whether major or minor."[3]

Yet even if the first half of the nineteenth century were called in to redeem its second half, Mendelssohn's *Elijah*, perhaps, making up for Max Bruch's thirty-one choral works that have ended up on the discard pile, we would still be in no position to take the measure of this century by such means. The choral activity that formed so large a part of nineteenth century music-making should strike us fundamentally as a cultural phenomenon, that is, an expression of values and needs that were not merely or only musical. To approach the subject this way does not require dismissing the particularities of the music itself as mere surface noise that obscures a deep evolutionary history of singing as well as a shallower social and political history of change and modernization. It requires only that one find revelation in the rehearsal schedule of Leipzig's pioneering Choral Society for Sacred Music as well as in the key modulations of the *German Requiem*, in the musical understanding of Thomas Alsager as well as in that of Beethoven, whose *Missa solemnis* was performed in full in Alsager's Bloomsbury drawing room on Christmas Eve 1832.[4] The choral century mobilized tremendous numbers of people in formal and informal musical activities, in public, semi-public, and private music-making, in single-sex and same-sex singing, in sacred, communal, and national musical gatherings, and in all the varied combinations of these elements that one could devise.

For a decade or more, musicologists and historians have been going back and forth on the question of whether something happened to music in the course of the eighteenth century, something that perhaps had less to do with the transition from Bach to Mozart than with changes in attitudes regarding such people and their compositions. For some scholars, the "dominant conception" of music changed. People began to think about music "in terms of the production, performance, and preservation of works" and, as a result, to listen to music for its own sake.[5] Or as Ray Robinson and Allen Winold put it in their introduction to choral singing, "the very thought of a concert, at which large numbers of people would gather for the purpose of listening to a performance, would have seemed strange to the medieval mind."[6] For others, William Weber and Charles Rosen among them, one cannot assume that the absence of our musical behaviors—for example, silence at a performance—means, *ipso facto*, the absence of seriousness and attention to music as such.[7]

These debates have particular relevance for our explanations of the practices, places, and purposes of choral music that emerged in this same period of transition. Whether or not people began for the first time really to listen to music for its own sake in the eighteenth century, they most certainly began to hear it, see it, and perform it on an increasingly large and socially diverse scale. That new experiences would come out of new attitudes or that new attitudes would be prompted by new experiences seems commonsensical, yet connecting the two—attitude and activity—is by no means as straightforward as one might wish it to be. Why, for instance, did Prussian court composer Carl Friedrich Fasch take such interest in the early Italian Baroque composer Orazio Benevoli? And why did he shortly thereafter, in 1791, decide to found a choral group in Berlin, the Singakademie, that consisted largely of women and amateurs? And why did this choral group grow to some hundreds of singers, expanding to include men as well as women, within a decade and prove to be a model for other such groups all over central Europe and beyond? The first questions may admit of straightforward and limited answers: to the first, his friend Johann Friedrich Reichardt brought him a work of Benevoli from a trip to Italy and Fasch really liked it; to the second, he wanted to hear it sung, so he gathered some available singers together for that purpose. But the third question opens up a vast field of aesthetic, social, and political considerations to our consideration. In the case of music especially, the practice of which has always been as much diverse and dispersed as it has been congruent and concentrated, questions of cause and effect, context and substance, have multi-faceted answers. The only way to approach them, then, is to divide up the choral landscape into parts and hope thereby to find the characteristics and interconnections that made the nineteenth century distinctive.

Before turning to that landscape, we might take a moment to consider deep history with its intriguing potential to illuminate questions of why people make music together at all.[8] The capacity for what biologists call "behavioral synchrony," that is, in historian William McNeill's formulation, "keeping together in time," seems to be one of the few traits of living creatures unique to human beings. Chimpanzees make and use tools, manipulate and deceive, mourn and fall in love, understand relational syntax and numerical sequences, and appreciate the beauty of a sunset over a lake. But, as paleontologist Steven Mithen has written, they "cannot keep to a beat, even with training" and even alone, let alone with groups of their fellow chimps.[9] Certainly the contemplation of why several hundred people were willing and more or less able to sing the same thing "together in time," as they did in countless nineteenth-century choral festivals, or ten people for that matter, does indeed make one wonder if there is not something more going on than love of the music. McNeill, for his part, thinks that communal rhythmic activity, whether dancing or drilling together, does not derive from social bonds. It creates them and constantly re-animates them, thus making possible the very experience of society itself, which is one of "boundary loss" between individuals.[10]

But while McNeill makes his case on the basis of a lifetime of sweeping historical investigations, biologists have been looking for the physiological manifestations of this bonding. The evolutionary psychologist Robin Dunbar has suggested that music-making in groups releases surges of endorphins in the brains of participants, thus making them happy to be together. The neurobiologist Walter Freeman looks to the hormone oxytocin. The release of it, for instance while singing together, loosens certain kinds of synaptic connections in the brain through which we store knowledge we have already acquired. Once freed of these prejudices, the brain is apparently more able to acquire "new understanding through behavioral actions that are shared with others," in other words, to form groups.[11] Joan Oliver Goldsmith, in her quasi-memoir of the experience of choral singing, tells of how four women, strangers to each other, came practically to be able to read each other's thoughts in the course of a week of carpooling and singing in intensive choral rehearsals at the Aspen Music Festival. Although one might attribute this effect to the carpooling, Goldsmith prefers the musical metaphor of "quartet making," attributing the bonding, which has lasted ever since, to experiencing music together, whether listening, rehearsing, or performing.[12] The science would seem to back her up.

The Festive Century: Singing in Big Groups

Making music in groups, then, does not just express but enables our capacity for cooperative existence and action. Turning to the rise of large-scale choral singing in the eighteenth and nineteenth centuries, a period that by any measure saw major changes in the circumstances of people's lives and thus major challenges to traditional social bonds, we should, I think, remain conscious of such deeper undercurrents to this new form of social activity, even as we attend to the rich specificity of its effects. Henry Raynor's classic social history of music since 1815 suggested that "it would not be merely fanciful" to see the large orchestras of the nineteenth century as "an essential expression of the personality" of that age. Linking new conceptions of musical force and complexity to new methods of warfare and industry, with their "precise co-ordination of many disparate specialist functions," Raynor sees a reflective relationship between industrial civilization and the symphony orchestra.[13] In looking at the ever more multitudinous mixed-voiced choruses that began to proliferate from the last decades of eighteenth century on, one is tempted to link the mobilization of the choral crowd to the mobilization of crowds of a less musical sort in the era of the French Revolution. People making lots of noise together seemed consonant with the mood of the times, and once an organizer had gathered together 200 for a performance, then 300, then 500, little seemed to resist the notion of a chorus of 10,000 and orchestra of 1,000, such as gathered in Boston for the National Peace Jubilee and Musical Festival of 1869.

But just as the actual size of revolutionary crowds matters less than their place, mood, and the response to them, so too does the phenomenon of large choruses require further investigation than the inventory of their growing presence on the musical landscape can provide. The story of singing in big groups begins in Great Britain. The first large-scale choral performances, immediate ancestors of the sort that became so widespread in the nineteenth century, themselves grew out of a congeries of Anglican musical rituals, some dedicated to St. Cecilia's Day, some to charitable fund-raising (especially for clerical widows and orphans), and some to royal thanksgiving services. These all crystallized by the mid-eighteenth century in the Festival of the Sons of the Clergy in London and the provincial Three Choirs Festival, though that moniker, interestingly, was not used until much later, in the tradition-conscious nineteenth century. These gatherings in turn found an immediate heir in the Lenten performances of George Frideric Handel's newly composed oratorios. Already in 1784, with the enormous centenary commemoration of Handel in Westminster Abbey, the model received an early apotheosis, with choirs and choral societies from all over England assembling to sing *Messiah*.

The British, first to industrialize, thus developed in a short amount of time a "social and musical ritual" that, in the words of William Weber, "proved remarkably appealing and adaptable."[14] This model brought together large numbers of amateur as well as professional singers to perform revered older or serious newer works, with orchestral accompaniment and for purposes so broadly and loosely defined as to be non-exclusive. As the festival format grew in popularity, singers gathered from many places with their own small or large choruses and then returned to them, sometimes establishing their own regional Handel events, which drew on different groups of singers or stimulated the creation of new ones. Nor were these developments confined to the British Isles. In 1786, Johann Adam Hiller, the first director of Leipzig's soon famous Gewandhaus concerts, pulled off the first full performance of *Messiah* in German-speaking Europe. It took place in the Berlin Cathedral, with an orchestra and chorus numbering in the hundreds, and he followed it up with similarly large-scale performances in Leipzig in 1786 and 1787, then in Breslau in 1788.

The nineteenth century added a degree of institutionalization to the spread of choral festivals, with the proliferation of musical societies, each with their leading committees, membership lists, and statutes. By 1815, the United States had its Handel and Haydn Society in Boston, with many more to follow. France developed its own version of institutionalized mass singing. The Orphéon was founded in Paris in the 1830s as a quasi-educational society for school children and working-class men but grew into a mass choral movement with thousands of similar groups in the provinces by the end of the century.[15] Number, sizes, and purposes of festivals expanded apace, crowding the civic calendars of the nineteenth century with commemorative and contemporary celebrations of composers, monarchs, events, and inventions too numerous to recount. From the virtually round-the-clock oratorio performances at the London Great Exhibition of 1851, to the three thousand orphéonistes who descended on the English capital in 1860, to the exhibitions of "Welsh Choral prowess" displayed annually at the National Eisteddfod after 1880, nineteenth-century singers left behind an impression of constant motion and tireless (not to say tiresome) enthusiasm.[16]

What is not so clear to our retrospective gaze is the point of all this singing. Summary treatments of the phenomenon, like that in the previous paragraph, tend to conceal the great variety of reasons for coming together to sing and, by the same token, to assume the purchase of an explanatory model of innovation and imitation. In telling the story that way, we often give too much credit to those who appear to come first or take too literally their metaphors of seeds planted which then, randomly, grow. The model of innovation and imitation works well in the French case, with the pioneering work of a man like Guillaume-Louis Bocquillon Wilhem, father of singing instruction in the French primary school system and (not coincidentally) later founder of the Orphéon movement.[17] But in the Welsh case, early eisteddfodau at the end of the eighteenth century were local affairs and received no broader regional, let alone international, attention until almost a century later. Likewise, Hiller's Handel festivals in north Germany were more like a flurry of activity in a limited time and place than the first sprouts of a quickly spreading weed. Bringing Handel back to the Germans formed one part of an extremely varied career as composer, theorist, pedagogue, and impresario, working as much outside as inside the established niches for musicians in church and court. At various times in his life, he organized concert series, established musical societies for amateurs, ran a school for singers out of his own house, and founded a short-lived but pioneering musical periodical. His treatises on singing instruction were, in John Butt's estimation, "revolutionary," and his collections of songs for children and for household music-making reflected fresh, progressive ideas about the place of music in the German household and the enlightening sociability inherent to music-making as a whole.[18]

Perhaps had Hiller lived in Paris, and not Leipzig, his work would have spawned a movement. But even though all his efforts echoed far into the nineteenth century, suggesting them as a point of origin for a number of key transformations in the musical culture of Europe and North America (festivals, big groups, training regimens, printed music for amateurs, attention to national traits and traditions), his immediate impact was small to non-existent. Nor is it even clear that the later developments built on his initial work. That, certainly, was the gist of Friedrich Rochlitz's tribute to Hiller in the *Allgemeine Musikalische Zeitung*, shortly after his death in 1804. Following Lessing, Rochlitz noted that "some are famous, others deserve to be so."[19] Hiller, he thought, had been "an honest man, in the fullest, noblest sense of the word," and for this, rather than any lasting influence of his compositions or his pedagogical writings, he should be remembered. Rochlitz did not even think it worth mentioning what our more modern sensibilities would probably call his organizational genius. The idea that the mere organizing of people to make music could reflect genius would probably not have occurred to this man of the Enlightenment, and that in itself tells us something about the circumstances in which modern forms of choral singing developed. Unlike the new reading groups, patriotic societies, or secret fraternal organizations such as Masonic societies, the beginnings of choral societies did not mark a clear break from the past. While early founders, Hiller included, held similar aspirations to contribute to the improvement of mankind, they generally regarded their efforts as working *with* rather than *against* the grain of their times and its leading institutions of court, church, and local government. As William Weber has shown in the case of the Handel festivals, the social composition of festival organizers tended to get more rather than less elite as the festivals grew more popular, though he is also attentive to variations between, say, north and south England, Norwich and Hereford, Oldham and London. The Handel festival model, he argued, inhabited a civic space; it mediated between the institutions of the state (including the Church of England) and society and thereby stabilized both.[20]

The social, political, and cultural significance of large-scale singing gets more complicated, however, with the French Revolution and the growth of choral festivals on the Continent. Revolutionary and Napoleonic Paris was itself the site of many open-air festivals, the main purpose of which may not have been musical but which certainly recruited music to the cause of the new regimes. The *Fête de la Fédération* (July 14, 1790), the reburial of Voltaire's remains (July 11, 1791), and the *Fête de l'Etre Suprême* (June 8, 1794) included massed choral singers along with drums, trumpeters, and the whole array of military musicians. Composers, the Belgian François Joseph Gossec chief among them, wrote works with titles like "An Offering to Liberty" or "The Triumph of the Republic" to clarify the meaning of all this noise, and in what is surely the most audible continuity between revolutionary and Napoleonic France, the form of these musical festivals carried on after 1800 (celebrations of the victory at Marengo, the Concordat, Napoleon's coronation, and so on), with hardly a change even of musical personnel. While one might certainly regard these hordes of singers and instrumentalists as comparable in their regime-supporting role to those who gathered to sing *Zadok the Priest* in Westminster Abbey, their voices sounded differently after 1815 and not just in France itself. There the revolutionary overtones of massed song were ultimately tamed by the educational earnestness of the Orphéonistes. Mass choral singing became more an expression of patriotism than a call to arms. Choral performances embodied reformist, not revolutionary, impulses; at their most challenging, they were a call to fulfill the Revolution's promise of equality, here in the form of equal access of all to the civilizing effects of musical culture.[21]

In German-speaking Central Europe, and later in the century, in the Slavic parts of the Austrian Empire, the destabilizing potential of choral festivals was ever present, even if unrealized. The first large-scale festival with a lasting impact on musical activities in Germany took place in 1810 in the small Thuringian town of Frankenhausen. The festival was not overtly political, but its place and time sounded themes of a nationalizing consciousness that were to become louder over the next decades. Its organizer was an obscure local cantor and court musician named G. F. Bischoff. He was inspired by a performance of Haydn's *The Creation* in his native Frankenhausen to invite Louis Spohr, then conductor of the court orchestra in nearby Gotha, to direct a larger-scale festival in his hometown. Frankenhausen lies at the foot of the Kyffhäuser mountain, deep inside of which, according to German legend, the Emperor Frederick Barbarossa slept in a hidden chamber, waiting to arise and come to Germany's rescue in his country's hour of greatest need. This fanciful notion resonated among those Germans whose educational and occupational experiences had made them conscious of their nationality. The participants in the festival did not cry "Wach' auf!" to the emperor or to their fellow German, like the townspeople of Wagner's *Die Meistersinger of Nuremberg* some sixty years later. Still, hundreds of German musicians, both amateur and professional, did gather to perform Haydn's *The Creation* and Beethoven's Fifth Symphony. Five years later, even more of them gathered again in Frankenhausen, this time to commemorate the great victory over Napoleon two years earlier at the Battle of the Nations in Leipzig. They sang Gottfried Weber's *Te Deum* as well as Spohr's newly composed cantata *Das befreite Deutschland* (Germany Liberated). The emperor, it seems, had awoken.

In 1818, the first of what became the most musically ambitious of the German festivals, the Lower Rhine Festival, took place in Elberfeld, with large orchestra and chorus, all drawn from the surrounding Prussian Rhine Province.[22] The Lower Rhine Festivals featured oratorios and symphonies of composers whose German nationality the organizers and participants found deeply satisfying. The international significance of the compositions were to them truths they held to be self-evident, and hence the performance of such works asserted, in a very public fashion, the existence of a German nation among nations; they were a cultural declaration of national independence.

We can also regard the Lower Rhine Festivals, and others like them, as the most public face of the many respectable singing societies that had developed in central Europe since the founding of Carl Friedrich Fasch's Berlin Singakademie in 1791. It had begun without any public fanfare as the side project of Fasch, a harpsichordist and composer in the Prussian court, who set his circle of private music students, most of them women, to practice a sixteen-part mass he had composed and hoped one day to hear. The members soon established regular Tuesday evening rehearsals, recruiting a few professional singers. By 1800, the group had more than a hundred regular members; by 1815, more than two hundred. Under Fasch and his successor, Carl Friedrich Zelter, the group became known for its careful study of sacred choral music, much of it no longer regularly heard in either Catholic or Protestant churches. In January 1794, for instance, Fasch introduced J. S. Bach's double-chorus motet *Komm, Jesu, Komm* into rehearsals, setting the Singakademie off on its thirty-five-year journey to its celebrated revival of his *St. Matthew Passion* in 1829—an event, like the Lower Rhine Festivals, of profound national significance to performers and audiences alike.[23]

Music aficionados and musical visitors to Berlin, including Beethoven, were soon aware of the excellence of the Singakademie's work. Just as important, groups seeking a similar kind of musical experience began to appear all over Germany. Its first wave of imitators, starting with the Leipzig Singakademie (founded in 1800) included choral societies in Stettin (1800), Münster (1804), Dresden (1807), Weimar (1807), Potsdam (1814), Bremen (1815), Chemnitz (1817), and

Schwäbisch-Hall (1817), and soon extended all the way to Innsbruck in the south, Breslau in the east, Hamburg in the north, and Frankfurt in the west. At the same time, Hans Georg Nägeli in Switzerland embarked on a parallel, soon intersecting, process of encouraging musical improvement and historical revival, founding the Zürich Singinstitut (in 1805), publishing music for choral performance, and encouraging festival oratorio performances on the scale of the ones in England. The German festival movement, and the large mixed-sex choruses that constituted its musical and organizational heart and soul, did not challenge established authority directly, but part of its rapid spread across the German landscape reflected the satisfaction that Germans, men and women, found in doing something active in the public sphere. As Karen Ahlquist has argued, choruses all took great care, like their counterparts elsewhere in Europe and eventually in the Americas, with writing statutes, electing officials, and running themselves efficiently and even profitably, all the while proving themselves good citizens of their towns and states.[24]

The desire of people to assert themselves publicly was even more the case with a rowdier strand of the choral-festival movement, that of male choruses. Starting in 1809, with Carl Friedrich Zelter's founding in Berlin of a *Liedertafel*, a singing group for men only, hundreds of similar organizations sprang up all across German-speaking Europe. By the 1830s, these men's singing societies represented one of the most important outlets for the public participatory impulses of people whose political activism was virtually shut down by censorship laws and bans on political organizations. Gatherings of singers, increasingly frequent in the years preceding the outbreak of revolution in 1848, were occasions for cautious speech-making and unrestrained singing, both making a case for a single German nation, as well as celebrating German nature, German home life, and the German people.[25] Whether organized around the unveiling of a monument (Gutenberg in Mainz in 1840, Beethoven in Bonn in 1845), the restoration of a cathedral (two for the Cologne cathedral in 1842), or simply the patriotic fellowship of song itself, these events brought to a city several thousand singers and drew even larger audiences from the city itself and surrounding towns and villages. None of the festivals or groups contributed directly to the outbreak of the revolution, and they more or less ceased as a form of public activism in the revolutionary years themselves, thus making this kind of massed singing very different from its French predecessors. Nevertheless, the men's singing movement of the pre-1848 period had established its credentials as the supposedly authentic voice of the German nation.

The general tendency of the nineteenth century, no matter the country or the activity, was to consolidate and institutionalize, and singing was no exception. After the revolutionary period had faded away, massed singing events returned to central Europe more numerous than ever. In 1862, a German Singing Confederation (Deutsche Sängerbund) was formed to make more solid the fluid ties among different localities, and soon an annual Confederation Festival became a regular, ever larger, ever more staid event on the musical calendar of a soon-to-be-united German Empire. Yet the *Liedertafel* model, with its easily imitated combination of small local groups and periodic large festivals, had not simply become establishment. It proved influential, for instance, in showing eastern European nationalities a way to act out their sense of belonging together in ways that directly challenged the status quo in the Austro-Hungarian empire. Workers, students, and veterans also asserted their presence in public life, and their values, through men's singing groups. Workers' choruses in particular, which began to form in large numbers in the 1860s, took the middle-class *Liedertafel* as both model and counter-model, adopting its earlier method of using singing as a way to pursue politics and consciousness-raising through non-political means. After the new German Empire passed anti-socialist laws in the 1870s, massed singing became, once again, as much a way to evade authority as to celebrate it.[26] But regardless of the political valence of German men's singing groups, all of them in one way or another served the cause of nation-building. Germany and other modernizing nations became real to people because many thousands traveled around these nations, first by coach or horseback or on foot, later most often by train, meeting their fellow countrymen and singing together.[27]

The German model (choral singing in small and large groups that gathered at festivals to form even larger ones) had some purchase in countries to its east and a great deal in the United States, but very little in the British Isles, despite one or two organizations, such as Charles Hallé's St. Cecilia Society in Manchester, founded "in imitation of the German Gesangverein, which dwelt in my memories since the days of my childhood."[28] Liverpool had its Apollo Glee Club and its Cecilian Society, both amateur organizations that had grown directly out of the eighteenth-century Handel happenings, and London had a wealth of professional and ecclesiastical vocal talent for public performances. But in the rest of England, the major force behind the creation and spread of choral societies was neither Anglicanism nor Handel-mania nor Germanophilia but evangelical revival.[29] Perhaps part of the explanation for this phenomenon was the musicality of the Wesley family, but music in Methodism served a very clear end that transcended mere pleasure in tones. Choral societies emerged in the context of a broader educational mission of moral and practical uplift to the new industrial working class in the new centers of an industrializing society. They also emerged in a context of polite exclusion on the part of the Anglican musical establishment. As William Weber points out, when none of the Dissenting choirs were invited to sing in the 1834 Handel commemoration, "a group of them proceeded to stage their own festival."[30] The Sacred Harmonic Society, which was the lasting result of the counter-festival, became the single most important amateur chorus in London and the south of England. But the quintessential expression of non-conformist culture were the Mechanics' Institutes, the first of which were incorporated in Glasgow and London in late 1823. By mid-century more than 700 institutes existed in the British Isles and overseas in Australia, and almost every one of them had spawned a choral society. Their success in gathering members and public interest in turn begat related and sustaining phenomena, many in the publishing industry: cheap editions of most-loved works, instructional methods and manuals, music magazines, stories, and biographies, affordable pianos, soon affordable parlor organs—in short the whole panoply of self-improvement consumption that characterized society as a whole.[31]

The large numbers of choral societies also led to a lively, even maniacal interest in competition. By the latter half of the nineteenth century neither a year nor an exposition went by without a choral competition taking place. "I am requested by the Musical Committee appointed by the Executive Council of the International Inventions Exhibition," wrote John Stainer in *The Musical Times* in 1885, "to call the attention of Choral Societies to the fact that it is proposed to hold choral competitions on an extensive scale during the forthcoming Exhibition."[32] For the exhibition organizers, this was a winning proposition, promising to bring "music-lovers in all parts of the country" to the event; for singers, this pursuit of war by other means brought the satisfaction of otherwise possibly guilty pleasures (travel, the thrill of defeating others) enjoyed with a clear, even righteous conscience. For all the differences between the development of choral singing and festivals in Germany and Great Britain, if one simply closed one's eyes and listened, one would have been hearing the same thing, and that held true over a surprisingly long period of time. From Handel to Haydn to Mendelssohn and other lesser composers, these societies converged on a repertoire that was, from the outset, the joint creation of German-English musical interactions and cross-fertilizations, at the institutional and the compositional level. Indeed, probably the most notable difference between singing societies and choral festivals in England and in Germany was not the music but the absence of alcohol at the former and its overindulgence at the latter. In contrast to the teetotalling temperance activists who filled the English choral societies, German festivals of local *Liedertafeln* had already by 1844 earned the reputation of being, in the words of the *Allgemeine Musikalische Zeitung*, "drinking bouts with shouting and tobacco smoke."[33]

Across the pond, the cities and towns of the United States present, not surprisingly, a medley of all these traditions, the English, the German, the rowdy, the sober, the educational, the competitive, the transcendent. America's first great choral organization was the Handel and Haydn Society of Boston, and after its founding in 1815, it remained (and considered itself) the gold standard for serious music-making in the New World, even if the subsequent rise of symphony orchestras and opera companies and rival choral societies took away its near monopoly over impeccably high-brow music-making. Communities with German immigrants always had at least one men's *Liedertafel* and often a mixed-voice German chorus as well. After the end of the Civil War, large-scale festivals drawing choruses from many different places, a form of choral participation already so well-established in Europe, began to take hold. Americans also jumped onto the international exposition bandwagon, and these massive events—1876 in Philadelphia, 1893 in Chicago, 1901 in Buffalo, 1904 in St. Louis, 1915 in San Francisco, to name only the best attended—added the dimension of choral competition to the mix. In 1914, when George W. Stewart, musical director of the Panama-Pacific International Exposition of 1915 in San Francisco, declared that there would be no competitions and only one chorus at the eight-month-long extravaganza, it seemed like the end of an era even before the Americans joined the Europeans on the battlefields of France and Belgium.

The Sociable Century: Singing in Small Groups

The possibilities and pleasures of participation in the public world were the hallmark of singing in big groups and choral gatherings, but we should not allow the sometimes peremptory claims of publicity to blind us to the more intimate forms of singing that were just as important to music lovers in the nineteenth century. In many cases, small-group singing among amateurs formed the foundation of larger musical gatherings and directed itself toward them; in other cases, it existed for its own sake. Composers wrote for them; publishers catered to them; parents encouraged their older children to participate in them, likewise employers, their employees, and eventually all levels of schooling, from the elementary to the university, included them. Small-group singing was often, though not always, a single-sex activity. In Great Britain, the Noblemen and Gentlemen's Catch Club of London, founded in 1762, was the first of many small gentlemen's clubs devoted to singing "glees," or unaccompanied secular partsongs, which enjoyed a century or so of popularity from the mid-eighteenth to the mid-nineteenth centuries before giving way to larger and less elite choral societies. In Germany, the *Liedertafel* in Zelter's original formulation consisted of a small number (fifteen or so) of like-minded men, who would gather "with German gaiety (*Fröhlichkeit*) and conviviality (*Gemütlichkeit*)" for a "frugal repast" and the singing of songs that the members themselves had written. Within a decade of its founding, it had become stodgy enough that a rival organization, of *younger* like-minded men, had formed in Berlin. And so it went all across Germany and soon across America, with the English glee tradition forming a second, more collegiate (that is to say, in the nineteenth century, more socially elite) strand of men's singing groups. The logic of the diffusion of all such groups was that of sociability, of finding people with whom one wanted to spend time. Some societies organized themselves around certain genres—madrigals, motets— and thus considered themselves chiefly motivated by the work of historical recovery. Others grew out of the isolation of immigrants in foreign lands or small-towns-people in big cities and so affirmed regional and local identities in unfamiliar places. The whole superstructure of festivals, competitions, and national dreams grew out of this basic experience of "keeping together in time" and also creating together in time. As William McNeill put it, this togetherness constituted and re-constituted social bonds on a daily basis—it did not simply reflect the fact that society already existed.[34]

Take the Berlin Singakademie, for another instance. At the start of the century in which it became the model for so many other choruses, Zelter described it as "a kind of artistic corps" in which "every serious-minded friend of art" would find "as much satisfaction through serious art as is possible." Its gatherings encompassed "attentiveness without visible exertion, beauty without privilege, multiplicity of all estates, ages, and trades, without affectation; delight in a fine art without weariness; the young and the old, the aristocrat and the burgher; the joy and the discipline; the father and the daughter, the mother with her son, and every possible mixing of the sexes and the estates."[35] The musicologist Erich Valentin once wrote that groups of people singing in homes "formed the foundation on which public music life first began to constitute itself, radiating from within society to more outward forms."[36] Zelter's description, in which his group is a family, confirms the truth of this. Many a choral society in the nineteenth century, especially those that began almost casually as did the Singakademie, had their roots not in church practices or public, state-centered ceremonials, but in the semi-private and private settings of domestic music-making.

As a result, the organizational structures of this quasi-formal, quasi-private singing varied enormously, from occasional gatherings in someone's living room or—at the more prosperous end of the social scale—music room to highly organized groups with statutes, dues, membership lists, and annual reports. Women's choruses sometimes traced their activity to the singing that went on in the spinning rooms of pre-modern households, and the contemporaneous enthusiasm for folklore societies and amateur history meant that plenty of evidence for historical antecedents circulated among an increasingly literate European population.[37] Richard Wagner gave the theory his own distinctive blessing in the chorus of spinning women that opens Act II of *Der Fliegende Holländer*. In the way of such things, women's chorus versions of this much-loved scene in the opera circulated back into the women's chorus repertoire and not just in Germany. Singing and spinning did go together naturally, as did song and work of all kinds.[38] But both the women's choruses and the workers' choruses—and for that matter, any chorus that sang one of the many work-related songs that were to be found in nineteenth-century song anthologies—served fundamentally different purposes, none of which was the effort to make an onerous workday go by faster. For instance, Lowell Mason formed singing schools in the United States in the 1830s, which became the basis for practically all singing in American schools and from there for school choruses and many a small-town adult chorus. His purposes were pedagogical in the broad sense of devising instructional methods that would enable children and adults to reap the great moral and aesthetic harvest of European art and religious music. In this endeavor (from which he profited handsomely), he worked closely with the Handel and Haydn Society of Boston, compiling, arranging, and composing music for "tunebooks," which came out in new editions almost every year under the title *The Boston Handel and Haydn Society Collection*.[39] Edification, education, and moral improvement were essential also to the mission of the individual groups within the great network of Methodist-initiated singing in Great Britain and to the orphéonistes of France.

But so too was conviviality, with or without alcoholic lubrication. If one follows the yearly activities, for instance, of the University of Munich men's chorus (Münchener akademischer Gesangverein) in the late nineteenth century, one finds a group that maintained in its yearbook a list of all former members, honorary members, auxiliary members, and "philistines" (that is to say, community people who paid dues but did not sing along), thus constituting social bonds across time as well as in place. Rituals abounded in such groups. An annual party before Lent included elaborate shenanigans that usually involved cross-dressing: imagine a young Max Planck, future Nobel Prize winner in theoretical physics and one-time assistant director of this organization, writing an operetta about the unexpected arrival of a harem at the Vienna world's fair. An annual expedition took the group to some town in the surrounding countryside, where much wining, dining, and singing with the town men's chorus would take place, followed often by an early morning hike to the local promontory or castle ruin, accompanied by more wining and dining and lots more singing.[40] Nature itself was inscribed with social significance in such practices, and the combination of movement and music created vital bonds of belonging that could be mobilized in other settings and for other purposes as well.

What did such groups sing? In a few cases, a small singing group would be called into being by a composer, present in a place for whatever reason or for however long, to serve as a kind of live instrument for his compositional practice. The most famous instance of this was the Hamburg Frauenchor that Brahms founded in 1859 after his successful concerts there had produced something of a Brahms cult, especially among young unmarried women (this was when Brahms was still in his twenties—a golden-haired young man with beautiful blue eyes). The chorus consisted of about forty young women, and Brahms conducted them in works he wrote especially for them, including his *Marienlieder*, settings of folktales of the Virgin Mary. The surviving records of the group leave an impression of much jollity in the presence of a serious young man determined to bring some musical discipline to the proceedings. Directors of small mixed-sex choruses were not infrequently musicians with ambitions beyond these small-step beginnings, so they too would compose works for their groups, as well as encourage them to learn one or two more ambitious pieces, beyond the level of difficulty that characterized the countless collections of songs available for home and small group singing. Usually, these groups would learn *Messiah* or even the *St. Matthew Passion* as preparation for a larger gathering, a regional festival or commemorative performance such as those described in the previous section.

But what the groups actually sang was perhaps less important than we might think. Choristers had their favorites, to be sure, as did audiences, but I would argue that the key to the whole phenomenal success of choral singing in the nineteenth century was not performance at all but the humble vehicle of the weekly rehearsal. Choral singing consists, of course, of both. Performance and its repertoire have received the lion's share of attention, but we should attend to rehearsals as well. Seen in the context of the tremendous changes that marked the early decades of the nineteenth century, the creation of decidedly new ways for men and women to act in tandem in everyday contexts, to relate to each other and to the public world around them by means that quickly seemed unremarkable to them, should strike us just as forcefully as the big events that this everyday behavior occasionally produced. All the early records of the Berlin Singakademie concern rehearsals: attendance books, detailed accounts of when and where they were held, records of what they sang. Zelter's contribution to the Singakademie, after succeeding Fasch in 1800, was to increase rehearsal time and to secure semi-permanent rehearsal (not performance) space for the group. Similar patterns emerge in the development of singing groups elsewhere as well, wherever the influence of the European choral repertoire was to be found. Many of the founders of such groups, from Mason to Wilhelm to Brahms, were just as, if not more, interested in the process of learning and rehearsing than in actual performance. Their reasons to emphasize the rehearsal process certainly varied: for Brahms, the benefits to his compositional work played an important role; for directors of young people's choral societies, the beneficial effects of disciplined work tended to be foremost. People who write about their experiences as choristers tend to focus on the rehearsing process as well, often with more enthusiasm in their accounts than in the more formulaic descriptions of the thrill of performance. To invoke again the biological and the anthropological, rehearsing is work done together; rehearsing is the struggle to reach a common goal together; rehearsing is the synchronization of individual bodies: ears, minds, eyes, lungs, arms holding music, legs standing and sitting. With the warm-ups, the repetitions, the tea breaks with sweet cakes, the talking and exchanging of musical (and other) opinions and experiences, the coming together and leaving only to return again the next week, the choral rehearsal became a central experience of everyday life for hundreds of thousands throughout Europe and the Americas, made all the more memorable by the unconscious effects, so hard to measure, of the music itself.

The Pious Century: Singing in Choirs

One further aspect of rehearsing demands our attention and that is its evocation of the sacred. It is not mere metaphor to say that most choral societies rehearsed religiously. As this discussion has already suggested, nineteenth-century choral singing in both Europe and the Americas was so infused with religious sensibilities as to render any argument about the secularization of modern life seem altogether mistaken when applied to singing together in groups. Repertoire and rhetoric alike focused on religious texts, religious festivals, and religious experience. The Berlin Singakademie took as its mission the preservation of "religious and serious music until the arrival of better times";[41] the Hamburg Gesangverein described its purpose as the "communal [*gemeinschaftlich*, as compared here to liturgical or church-based] practice of religious singing"; the name of London's Sacred Harmonic Society speaks for itself; and the Mendelssohn Club of Philadelphia drew its original membership from William Wallace Gilchrist's church choir. It is hard to imagine that the respectable bourgeois parents of Brahms's young ladies would have been so sanguine about their daughters' participation had they not been practicing songs about the Virgin Mary with their bachelor conductor, and it is likewise hard to feel the particular *frisson* of the Munich University Academic Chorus's operetta high-jinks without the vast backdrop of earnest and pious oratorio. Their fun and games with choral singing took place, after all, during the pre-Lenten season of Carnival.

So rather than try to make any clear distinction between secular choral singing—there are those suspiciously pagan Apollo Clubs in such places as Boston and Chicago, not to mention many oratorios featuring Greek and Roman and barbarian heroes—and sacred choral singing, we should think instead of the nineteenth century as a time in which the boundaries between the religious and the profane, the sacred and the secular, church and society were renegotiated in what sometimes seemed like contradictory ways. On the one hand, the lines could become more distinct, as states sought both to separate religious influences from statecraft and to control them. But, on the other hand, cultural and social life outside of formal religious institutions developed new, modern forms of religious expression, from mass, commercialized pilgrimage sites like Lourdes to Christmas holiday rituals to oratorio performances. In European and American musical practices alone, we find evidence of a long-term transformation in the expressions and practices of religious belief. According to the historian Lucien Hölscher, the whole meaning of religious community had changed—dramatically and decisively—by the beginning of the nineteenth century. The powerful integration of church and society, the visible sign of which had been "a regular participation of all in church festivals and services," virtually disappeared, and a process of "de-churching [*Entkirchlichung*]" rendered religious community more metaphorical. Modern piety was widespread but less centered on churches as such. In the nineteenth century, belief became more individual and religious experience more domestic.[42] In this interpretation, the lives of modern people were marked not by the decline of religious belief but by the free-floating of their pious practices into places outside traditional sacred space. We can see this transformation at work in the decline and then re-invigoration of institutional church music within established Protestantism and Catholicism; we see it also in the development of new means by which sacred music was performed and maintained.

To take the question of means first, we might focus again on the matter of rehearsing. Most formal choral societies, regardless of size or country, maintained a limited core group of works that they rehearsed and regularly performed, and it consisted of the oratorios and sacred vocal works of

Bach, Handel, Haydn, Mozart, and Mendelssohn; other composers, from Palestrina on one end of the chronological spectrum to Verdi on the other, remained very much on the periphery. Year after year, groups would perform the same works; indeed, they were proud of this. It was a marker of qualities—stability, loyalty, constancy, continuity, quality—that the middle classes held dear, all the more so as the survival of such qualities became threatened by their own striving for progress and profit. But of course, one does not need to practice all year to sing pieces as familiar to these singers as was *Messiah*, *The Creation*, and other favorites. In light of this, the emphasis on regular practice without regard to how long it actually took to be ready for a performance suggests the importance simply of gathering and singing together, in something like devotional practice or spiritual exercises. Many nineteenth-century singing groups did not, in fact, perform often in public, sometimes only in the Christmas or Easter season or only in conjunction with a solemn event like a funeral. The downplaying of performance, which was nearly universal early in the century, speaks of a continuing ambivalence about the appropriateness of participation in a public world marked by commerce and publicity, critical judgment and intellectual debate. The early choral leaders in Germany, for instance, believed that the sacred music of the past should be preserved and even quietly celebrated, but never too assertively, never too publicly, never just for the sound of the music. As late as 1881, officials of the YMCA in the United States thought that the rehearsal and performance of "oratorios for amusement" were an improper use of young men's energies.

Meanwhile, the nineteenth century also saw many movements to reinvigorate and redefine the singing of church choirs and congregations in actual churches. These movements grew out of the same broad socio-cultural trends that shaped other kinds of singing, sometimes following along at a safe distance (as in the case of the more radical forms of Romanticism), sometimes shaping the essential nature of the tendency (as in the case of musical historicism). Differences among various branches of Protestantism, between Protestantism and Catholicism, among nations, regions, and even localities further complicate the picture, and if one attempts to include the situation in Jewish communities as well, one is mainly struck by the near complete absence of any sort of fiat from above, indeed very little leadership at all from above, in the matter of church music. In Russia, the recovery and reinvigoration of Russian sacred music traditions in the last decades of the nineteenth century drew its impetus from below: its starting point is usually considered the publication, against the explicit fiat of the central Church authorities, of Tchaikovsky's *Liturgy of St. John Chrysostom*.[43] Not until 1903 did Pope Pius X formally endorse the principles of the Cecilian movement, with its emphasis on *a cappella* singing; not until 1881 did the Church of England undertake anything like a systematic investigation of the state of music in Anglican churches (and this survey, carried out by Charles Box, concerned only the 125 London churches); and church matters in Germany, Scandinavian countries, and the United States remain decentralized to a greater or lesser degree to this day. Nevertheless, certain commonalities, deriving from a general movement from decline to reform, characterized most places and religions, at least those that saw any change at all.

One can loosely place these reforms in church music on a spectrum from a low degree of lay involvement to a high one. The distinction provides a rough measure of the extent to which developments outside the churches, particularly the growing numbers of amateur singers in secular choral groups, spilled over into sacred services themselves. In Catholic Europe, the principal movement to resuscitate church music took the form of the Cecilianism. Although it drew its musical inspiration almost entirely from fifteenth- and sixteenth-century Italian composers, Palestrina supreme among them, the movement centered in German-speaking Europe. A few eighteenth-century groups called Cecilian Leagues formed the foundation for many more such groups that were founded in the nineteenth century, culminating in the establishment in 1868 of the Allgemeine Cäcilienverein for Catholic Germany. They consisted for the most part of church musicians committed to the ideal of "pure" singing without instrumental accompaniment (what they came to call, not entirely accurately, *a cappella* singing). In the first half of the nineteenth century, a number of composer / performers (e.g., Michael Haydn, the Abbé Vogler, Johann Kaspar Aiblinger), writers (e.g., Anton Friedrich Justus Thibaut, Ludwig Tieck, E. T. A. Hoffmann), and historians (e.g., Guiseppe Baini, Carl Georg Winterfeld) not only created music in imitation of the admired Palestrina and his contemporaries but provided extensive and eloquent justifications for this return to allegedly simpler times, when art and religion were indissolubly fused. Their work was certainly a reaction—against elaborate music, operatic music, uninspiring music, in short, the "foolish vagaries of fashion"—but it was also a creative response to the increasingly tenuous place of music in churches, which were cutting back on their professional musical staff almost everywhere.[44] If instituted as its proponents imagined it could be, the music of a distant past required no instrumentalists, in a pinch not even an organist, and just a limited number of choristers as well as clergy who could at least intone a few pitches with some accuracy. All were male.

Cecilianist propagandizing led to the growing popularity of Gregorian chant, and it worked considerable influence on Protestant Europe as well. Thibaut, author of the celebrated pro-Palestrinian tract *Purity in Music*, was a Heidelberg law professor and a Protestant. But until the young Felix Mendelssohn showed up in Thibaut's study and delivered a passionate speech on the greatness of J. S. Bach, the jurist regarded Bach as an inferior composer to Palestrina: Bach had been capable, pontificated Thibaut, but he had composed "by mere ingenuity" as a "sort of mathematical exercise without any life."[45] Frederick William III of Prussia thought likewise. When he embarked on his great reform of Protestant church affairs in Prussia, bringing together Lutheran and Reformed branches into a single Union church, he made the bizarre musical choice to subordinate congregational hymn-singing (one of the most powerfully communal aspects of Protestant services and one that German Calvinists and Lutherans actually had in common) to responsive chanting between minister and *a cappella* male choir. This notion reflected both his admiration for Russian Orthodox chanting, which he had heard in military encampments during the wars against Napoleon, and his unpleasant memories of childhood subjection to instrumental chamber music at the court.[46] A similar aesthetic preference marked musical reform efforts in the Anglican Church in Great Britain, reinforced in that case by the Tractarian movement's strong sense of affinity with Roman Catholicism. The Society for Promoting Church Music emerged directly out of Oxford Tractarian circles and sought, in Bernarr Rainbow's words, "to heighten devotion in the church service by giving due attention to those rubrics in the Book of Common Prayer which provided opportunities for music to contribute to solemnity" and "to recover authentic versions of the ancient music associated in former times with the liturgy."[47] The results of these musical reform efforts were uneven, though they did establish many of the tropes we now associate with the music of the Anglican service, including significant amounts of chanting during the service and choirs in white surplices. Perhaps most importantly, they encouraged the production of floods of new hymnals for general use that over time did have the effect of increasing the amount of congregational participation in the music of the Anglican service. But the trouble with the romantic infatuation with medieval and Renaissance music was that, hymnals and hymnal reform aside, it mainly failed to engage the participation of amateur singers. Perhaps the aesthetic was too spare, the numbers required for performance too small, or the opportunities for travel and friendly competition too infrequent. Most nineteenth-century amateur singers found and exercised their voices instead in choral societies, glee clubs, and parlor musicales.

The reforming of church choirs into institutions that could adequately engage both women's and men's enthusiasm for religious song, turned out to be a long-term process involving far more negotiating among conflicting constituencies than it took to establish a reasonably good amateur oratorio group that would fulfill the same social and religious needs. Looking back on all this singing almost a hundred years after the long nineteenth century ended in violence and disillusionment, one is mainly struck by how porous were the boundaries separating the many different groups organized around the ability of human beings to sing together. Festivity, sociability, and piety came together and came separately. Men and women sang with each other and sang separately. People sang in parks and parlors, churches and concert halls, spas and restaurants, town halls and town squares. Its effects could be heard in the trenches and on the battlefields, running the gamut from the perhaps apocryphal story of young German troops, many of them university students, singing the *Deutschlandlied* as they were mown down at the First Battle of Ypres in 1914, to the British–German singing of "Silent Night" across the trenches in the Christmas truce of the same year. Much of the choral century's legacy indeed survived the Great War and the Second World War, its institutions both reflecting and concealing the toll those conflicts took on their members and on music itself.

Notes

1 Suzanne Marchand, "Embarrassed by the Nineteenth Century," in *The Consortium on Revolutionary Europe 1750–1850: Selected Papers, 2002* , ed. Bernard Cook, Susan V. Nicassio, Michael F. Favkovic, and Karl A. Roider Jr. (Tallahassee, FL: The Consortium on Revolutionary Europe, 2004), 1–16.

2 Percy Young, *The Choral Tradition* (London: Hutchinson & Co., 1962), 236.

3 Ibid., 237, 236.

4 Alsager (1779–1854) was a managing editor of the London *Times* and a highly cultivated amateur musician; an early champion of Beethoven in Great Britain, he founded the Beethoven Quartet Society and was also a founding member of the Philharmonic Society. Dilwyn Porter, "Alsager, Thomas Massa (1779–1846)," *Oxford Dictionary of National Biography* (Oxford University Press, 2004). Online: http://www.oxforddnb.com/view/article/41071 (accessed September 17, 2008).

5 Lydia Goehr, *The Imaginary Museum of Musical Works: An Essay in the Philosophy of Music* (New York: Oxford University Press, 1992), 203; the view also informs much of Richard Taruskin's six volume *Oxford History of Western Music* (New York: Oxford University Press, 2006).

6 Ray Robinson and Allen Winold, *The Choral Experience: Literature, Materials, and Methods* (New York: Harper's College Press, 1976), 11.

7 Charles Rosen believes the insistence on regarding people before the eighteenth century as incapable of "appreciating art for its own sake" or enjoying "music as music" is simply "foolishness." See his review of Taruskin: Rosen, "From the Troubadours to Frank Sinatra," *New York Review of Books*, 53:3 (February 23, 2006). See also William Weber, "Did people listen in the 18th century?" *Early Music* (November 1997), 678–91.

8 Daniel Smail's *On Deep History and the Brain* (Berkeley and Los Angeles: University of California Press, 2008), not itself a book about music, prompted a look at some of the extensive new work on music and the brain, especially from an evolutionary perspective.

9 Steven Mithen, *The Singing Neanderthals: The Origins of Music, Language, Mind, and Body* (Cambridge, MA: Harvard University Press, 2006), 206.

10 William H. McNeill, *Keeping Together in Time: Dance and Drill in Human History* (Cambridge, MA: Harvard University Press, 1997).

11 Dunbar and Freeman cited in Mithen, *Singing Neanderthals*, 214–17. For a fuller account of these arguments, see Robin I. M. Dunbar, *Gossip, Grooming, and the Evolution of Language* (London: Faber & Faber, 1996); and Walter Freeman, "A Neurobiological Role for Music in Social Bonding," in *The Origins of Music*, ed. N. L. Wallin, B. Merker, and S. Brown (Cambridge, MA: MIT Press, 2000), 411–24.

12 Joan Oliver Goldsmith, *How Can We Keep from Singing: Music and the Passionate Life* (New York: W. W. Norton & Company, 2001), 96–117.

13 Henry Raynor, *Music and Society Since 1815* (New York: Schocken Books, 1976), 100–1.

14 William Weber, *The Rise of Musical Classics in Eighteenth-Century England: A Study in Canon, Ritual, and Ideology* (Oxford: Clarendon Press, 1992), 101.

15 For a full discussion of the Orphéon in its historical context, see Donna M. Di Grazia, "Concert Societies in Paris and their Choral Repertoires *c.*1828–1880" (Ph.D. diss., Washington University in St. Louis, 1993 (Ann Arbor, MI: UMI, 1993)). See also Jane Fulcher, "The Orphéon Societies: 'Music for the Workers' in Second-Empire France," *International Review of the Aesthetics and Sociology of Music* 10 (June 1971): 47–56.

16 The first so-called National Eisteddfod took place in 1861, itself inspired by a big 1858 gathering; the next was not until 1880 and thereafter they took place annually. The modern history of the eisteddfod revival movement begins in the 1790s. Percy A. Scholes, *The Mirror of Music, 1844–1944: A century of Musical Life in Britain as Reflected in the Pages of the* Musical Times (London: Novello & Company, Ltd., 1947), vol. 2, 642.

17 On the career of Wilhem and the multitude of choral music-making that his influence produced, see Di Grazia, "Concert Societies."

18 John Butt, *Music Education and the Art of Performance in the German Baroque* (New York and Cambridge: Cambridge University Press, 1994), 177.

19 "Every epoch," suggested Rochlitz, "seems to begin suddenly, its preparation to take place only inwardly, and subsequent fame accrues only to those who make the epoch, not to those who prepared its way." Rochlitz, "Zum Andenken Johann Adam Hiller," *Allgemeine musikalische Zeitung,* (1804): 137, 158.

20 Weber, *The Rise of Musical Classics*, 127–41.

21 See Di Grazia, "Concert Societies," esp. Chapter IV on the Orphéon movement, 93–164.

22 See Cecilia Porter, "The New Public and the Reordering of the Musical Establishment: The Lower Rhine Music Festivals, 1818–1867," *19th-Century Music* 3 (1979–80): 211–24; idem., *The Rhine as Musical Metaphor: Cultural Identity in German Romantic Music* (Boston: Northeastern University Press, 1996), 169–77.

23 Celia Applegate, *Bach in Berlin: Nation and Culture in Mendelssohn's Revival of the* St. Matthew Passion (Ithaca, NY: Cornell University Press, 2005).

24 Karen Ahlquist, "Men and Women of the Chorus: Music, Governance, and Social Models in Nineteenth-Century German-Speaking Europe," in Karen Ahlquist, ed., *Chorus and Community* (Urbana and Chicago: University of Illinois Press, 2006), 265–93. An interesting recent affirmation of this civic activist aspect of choral societies came from Robert Putnam in his much-cited work on the contemporary crisis of civil society and democracy; Putnam links successful democracies to "strong traditions of civic engagement," including "membership in choral societies." See *Bowling Alone: the Collapse and Revival of American Democracy* (New York: Simon & Schuster, 2001), 345–46.

25 Dieter Düding, "Nationale Oppositionsfeste der Turner, Sänger und Schützen im 19. Jahrhundert," in Dieter Düding, Peter Friedemann, and Paul Münch, eds., *Öffentliche Festkultur: Politische Feste in Deutschland von der Aufklärung bis zum Ersten Weltkrieg* (Hamburg: Rowolt, 1988), 166–90.

26 Josef Eckhardt, "Arbeiterchöre und der 'Deutsche Arbeiter-Sängerbund,'" in Monica Steegmann (ed.) *Musik und Industrie: Beiträge zur Entwicklung der Werkchöre und Werksorchester* (Regensburg: Gustav Bosse Verlag, 1978), 45–106.

27 A representative of the Prussian cultural ministry in 1910, for instance, stated that the Germans had built their unity out of songs (and gymnastics): see Jessica Gienow Hecht, *Sound Diplomacy: Music and Emotion in Transatlantic Relations 1850–1920* (Chicago: University of Chicago Press, 2009), 243.

28 Charles E. and Marie Hallé, *The Life and Letters of Sir Charles Hallé* (London, 1896), 116.

29 Raynor, *Music and Society*, 93.

30 Weber, *The Rise of Musical Classics*, 161. The term "Dissenter" in the English and Welsh context refers to people and religious groups that separated from the Established Church, that is, the Church of England and Wales; such groups are also referred to as non-conformist.

31 One can see the whole intersection of singing, society, and publishing in Fiona Palmer's biography, *Vincent Novello (1781–1861): Music for the Masses* (Aldershot, England: Ashgate Publishers, 2006).

32 John Stainer, "Choral Competitions at the Inventions Exhibition," *The Musical Times*, 26:503 (January 1, 1885), 50.

33 Quoted in Porter, *Rhine as Musical Metaphor*, 129.

34 McNeill, *Keeping Together in Time*, ii–iv. A marvelous exploration of this truth is Louise Erdrich's novel about German immigrants in a small town in South Dakota, *The Master Butchers Singing Club* (New York: Harper Collins, 2003).

35 Carl Friedrich Zelter, *Selbstdarstellung*, ed. Willi Reich (Zurich, 1955), 71–72.

36 E. Valentin, "Chor und Hausmusik," *Jahrbuch des deutschen Sängerbund*, (1961), 80.

37 See Annette Friedrich, *Beiträge zur Geschichte des weltlichen Frauenchores im 19. Jahrhundert in Deutsch*land (Regensburg: Gustav Bosse Verlag, 1961), 7–9.

38 Nineteenth-century scholars were alert to the historical-evolutionary implications of this phenomenon. A flurry of writings about music in general characterized one of the less well-known achievements of early sociology in Europe. In Germany, see for instance, Karl Bücher, *Arbeit und Rhythmus* (Leipzig: B. G. Teubner, 1909).

39 Richard Crawford, *America's Musical Life: A History* (New York: W. W. Norton & Company, 2001), 139–55.

40 See, for instance, the *Jahresbericht des Münchener akademischen Gesangvereines*: XXVI. und XXVII. Vereins-Semester, November 1873 bis Oktober 1874 (Munich, 1874).

41   Zelter to Prussian Interior Minister Karl von Hardenberg (June 1, 1802), in Cornelia Schröder, ed., *Carl Friedrich Zelter und die Akademie: Dokumente und Briefe zur Entstehung der Musik-Sektion in der Preussischen Adademie der Künste* (Berlin, 1959), 69.
42   Lucien Hölscher, "The Religious Divide: Piety in Nineteenth Century Germany," in H. W. Smith, ed., *Protestants, Catholics, and Jews in Germany* (Oxford: Berg, 2001), 35; "Die Religion des Bürgers: Bürgerliche Frömmigkeit und Protestantische Kirche im 19. Jahrhundert," *Historische Zeitschrift* 250 (1990): 595–630.
43   Carolyn C. Dunlop, *The Russian Court Chapel Choir, 1796–1917*, Music Archive Publications (New York: Routledge, 2000), 98–99.
44   A. F. J. Thibaut, *Über die Reinheit in der Tonkunst* (Heidelberg, 1825), 18–19.
45   Thibaut, *Reinheit in der Tonkunst*, 37. It is worth noting that the famous sketch of Thibaut leading his singing circle from the harpsichord, drawn by Jakob Götzenberger (a member of the Nazarenes, the German romantic painters who are visual arts' counterparts to the Palestrina revival enthusiasts in musical life) around 1829, depicts a portrait of J. S. Bach, not Palestrina, on his wall. This sketch is widely reproduced in music history surveys and has even made its way onto Wikipedia, without anyone noting this obvious apostasy from the gospel of Palestrina. For Mendelssohn's conversion of Thibaut to Bach, see Applegate, *Bach in Berlin*, 25–27.
46   Ironically, just as Frederick William III was admiring what he took to be the authentic Russian sound of the chant, Russian sacred music was (in the retrospective view of Russian musical nationalist Balakirev and his circle) engulfed in the Western influences of Italian and soon German musical styles.
47   Bernarr Rainbow, *The Choral Revival in the Anglican Church (1839–1872)* (New York: Oxford University Press, 1970), 5.

Selected Bibliography

Ahlquist, Karen, ed. *Chorus and Community*. Urbana and Chicago: University of Illinois Press, 2006.

Applegate, Celia. *Bach in Berlin: Nation and Culture in Mendelssohn's Revival of the* St. Matthew Passion. Ithaca, NY: Cornell University Press, 2005.

Butt, John. *Music Education and the Art of Performance in the German Baroque*. New York and Cambridge: Cambridge University Press, 1994.

Crawford, Richard. *America's Musical Life: A History*. New York: W. W. Norton & Company, 2001.

Di Grazia, Donna M. "Concert Societies in Paris and their Choral Repertoires *c*.1828–1880." Ph.D. diss., Washington University in St. Louis, 1993. Ann Arbor, MI: UMI, 1993.

Drinker, Sophie Hutchinson. *Brahms and his Women's Choruses*. Merion, PA, privately published, 1952.

Düding, Dieter, Peter Friedemann, and Paul Münch, eds. *Öffentliche Festkultur: Politische Feste in Deutschland von der Aufklärung bis zum Ersten Weltkrieg*. Hamburg: Rowolt, 1988.

Dunlop, Carolyn C. *The Russian Court Chapel Choir, 1796–1917*. Music Archive Publications. New York: Routledge, 2000.

Eckhardt, Josef. "Arbeiterchöre und der 'Deutsche Arbeiter-Sängerbund,'" in *Musik und Industrie: Beiträge zur Entwicklung der Werkchöre und Werksorchester*, ed. Monica Steegmann. Regensburg: Gustav Bosse Verlag, 1978.

Friedrich, Annette. *Beiträge zur Geschichte des weltlichen Frauenchores im 19. Jahrhundert in* Deutschland. Regensburg: Gustav Bosse Verlag, 1961.

Fulcher, Jane. "The Orphéon Societies: 'Music for the Workers' in Second-Empire France." *International Review of the Aesthetics and Sociology of Music*, 10 (June 1971).

Gienow Hecht, Jessica. *Sound Diplomacy: Music and Emotion in Transatlantic Relations, 1850–1920*. Chicago: University of Chicago Press, 2009.

Goldsmith, Joan Oliver. *How Can We Keep from Singing: Music and the Passionate Life*. New York: W. W. Norton & Company, 2001.

Grotjahn, Rebecca, ed. *Deutsche Frauen, deutscher Sang—Musik in der deutschen Kulturnation*. Munich: Allitera Verlag, 2009.

Jackson, Myles W. *Harmonious Triads: Physicists, Musicians, and Instrument Makers in Nineteenth-Century Germany*. Cambridge, MA: MIT Press, 2006.

Klenke, Dietmar. *Der singende "deutsche Mann": Gesangvereine und deutsches Nationalbewusstsein von Napoleon bis Hitler*. Münster: Waxmann, 1998.

Marchand, Suzanne. "Embarrassed by the Nineteenth Century," in *The Consortium on Revolutionary Europe 1750–1850: Selected Papers, 2002*, ed. Bernard Cook, Susan V. Nicassio, Michael F. Favkovic, Karl A. Roider Jr. Tallahassee: The Consortium on Revolutionary Europe, 2004.

McNeill, William H. *Keeping Together in Time: Dance and Drill in Human History.* Cambridge, MA: Harvard University Press, 1997.

Palmer, Fiona. *Vincent Novello (1781–1861): Music for the Masses.* Aldershot, England: Ashgate, 2006.

Pieper, Antje. *Music and the Making of Middle-Class Culture: A Comparative History of Nineteenth-Century Leipzig and Birmingham.* Basingstoke, Hampshire: Palgrave Macmillan, 2008.

Porter, Cecilia. "The New Public and the Reordering of the Musical Establishment: The Lower Rhine Music Festivals, 1818–1867," *19ᵗʰ-Century Music* 3 (1979–80): 211–24.

——. *The Rhine as Musical Metaphor: Cultural Identity in German Romantic Music.* Boston: Northeastern University Press, 1996.

Rainbow, Bernarr. *The Choral Revival in the Anglican Church (1839–1872).* New York: Oxford University Press, 1970.

Raynor, Henry. *Music and Society Since 1815.* New York: Schocken Books, 1976.

Robinson, Ray and Allen Winold. *The Choral Experience: Literature, Materials, and Methods.* New York: Harper's College Press, 1976.

Weber, William. *The Rise of Musical Classics in Eighteenth-Century England: A study in Canon, Ritual, and Ideology.* Oxford: Clarendon Press, 1992.

Young, Percy. *The Choral Tradition.* London: Hutchinson & Co., 1962.

2

VOX HUMANA

Choral Voices in the Nineteenth-Century Symphony

D. Kern Holoman

Univerisity of California, Davis

In hindsight one wonders, so obvious is the concept, why the symphony-with-chorus did not emerge sooner than Beethoven's Ninth, in 1824. The means had been there all along. The oratorios of Handel and then Haydn coincide, after all, with the emergence of the public concert and the stand-alone symphony as its own genre. Any number of progressive composers—Spohr, Weber, Méhul—were concerned with subject and narrative, and might soon have discovered the same path. The pipe organ already had its *vox humana*.

Beethoven himself had got nearly there with his Fantasy in C minor for Piano, Chorus, and Orchestra, Op. 80, in 1808—the Choral Fantasy, famously premiered alongside three turning points in orchestral music: the Fifth and Sixth Symphonies and the Fourth Piano Concerto. That was the very year Daniel Steibelt (1765–1823) effected his move from Vienna, where some time earlier he had been the vanquished party in a piano duel with Beethoven, to St. Petersburg. There in 1820, well before the Ninth, he premiered his Eighth Piano Concerto with finale for male chorus—an idea cloned by Busoni in his Piano Concerto of 1903. Even before that, in 1814, Peter von Winter (1754–1825) composed a patriotic *Schlachtsinfonie* (Battle Symphony) with closing chorus on poetry of fatherland and nationhood. But Beethoven's work, located as it was at a philosophical, political, and poetic crossroads of the era, established the precedent.[1]

The institutions of European society were certainly ready for it. Whatever the embarrassments of its first performance, the Ninth was drunk thirstily into the canon, with a performance by the nascent London Philharmonic Society within the year, then Lower Rhine Festival performances and early success in the Leipzig–Dresden–Weimar corridor. The Paris Société des Concerts du Conservatoire, with its integral chorus, was established in 1828 principally to give the Beethoven cycle a hearing; they reached the Ninth in March 1831. By the time of the 1845 Beethoven celebration in Bonn, culminating Liszt's effort to erect a monument in the Münsterplatz on the occasion of the composer's seventy-fifth birthday, the finale of the Ninth had acquired its festival identity, called forth so often to celebrate the merits of social democracy as eventually to have been chosen as the Anthem of Europe (January 1972). The marriage of Schiller's text and Beethoven's music was the vehicle by which the least contrived of all the musical instruments, the human voice, entered the symphony orchestra.

The spectacle of a sea of singers rising architecturally and symbolically over the seated players, and the anticipation of what they might have to say, stirred the souls of many a concert-goer in the Age of Industry. For countless listeners the symphony-with-chorus was the ultimate reward of the philharmonic society: an assembling of all music's makers (eventually with organ, too) undiluted by costumes and moving processions, to celebrate a season's climax or its close. The photograph of Mahler conducting the Ninth at a Strasbourg festival of 1905 (Figure 2.1) evokes nineteenth-century concert music at its most powerful.

But as a model for composers, the finale of the Ninth was not so emancipating after all. One can dismiss the inevitable invective, as in Spohr's sense that the music was "so monstrous and tasteless and, in its grasp of Schiller's Ode, so trivial that I cannot understand how a genius like Beethoven could have written it."[2] But Beethoven's challenge, especially in terms of symphonic weight and balance, was all too real. Wagner, characteristically, found in the Ninth a monumental turning point toward his own bias, where music would be returned to its mistress, the text. It was the first stage in *Zukunftsmusik,* music of the future: a universal drama, with sung text, freeing music of its absolutist shackles. At the same time, he famously reasoned, by calling poetry to his assistance, Beethoven had sounded the "death knell" of the symphony in its pure, absolute form. Wilfrid Mellers suggested in the fifth edition of *Grove's Dictionary* that what was at issue was nothing less than to abandon the "sovereignty of instrumental music."[3]

The result was that while, during the rest of the nineteenth century, homage to the Ninth was plentiful, few composers had the courage, and fewer still the acuity of imagination, to advance the case of the four-movement symphony with choral finale. Anton Bruckner's music is permeated with the mysteries of the Ninth, yet consistently shies away from that particular solution. (Bruckner's Ninth Symphony, lacking a fourth moment, is sometimes performed with his Te Deum functioning as a choral finale.) By alluding to the *Ode to Joy* in the chorus-less finale of his much-anticipated First Symphony, Brahms seemingly "corrected the wrong turn Beethoven had taken" (in the formulation of Richard Taruskin).[4] Yet even Brahms, it seems certain, toyed with

FIGURE 2.1 Mahler conducting Beethoven's Ninth, Strasbourg, 22 May 1905. (Collection Médiathèque Musicale Mahler, Paris)

the idea as he conceived a "sonata-symphony" in 1854 on the occasion of Schumann's suicide attempt, a work that evolved into portions of the First Piano Concerto and the German Requiem.[5] Arnold Schoenberg had a Beethovenian / Mahlerian symphony-with-chorus and a "Jacob's Ladder" finale in mind; by 1916 *Die Jakobsleiter* had become an oratorio. If in the twentieth century the choral symphony went on to gain so firm a foothold in the repertoire as to be commonplace, in the nineteenth uncertainty was the norm.

The first theoretically substantial response to Beethoven's symphony-with-chorus was Berlioz's third symphony, *Roméo et Juliette* (1839), with its monumental closing tableau of Capulets and Montagues swearing eternal friendship upon Friar Laurence's holy crucifix. The effect, as Berlioz himself noted, "falls into the domain of opera or oratorio."[6] Still, the moment of reconciliation of hostile parties, the very notion of universal *amitié,* is not so far a cry from Beethoven-and-Schiller's brotherhood and canopy of stars beneath the gaze of a benevolent father. That conceit cannot have been absent from Berlioz's thinking.

But Berlioz was engaged in another Beethovenian dilemma, too: how to communicate a narrative program to the concert public. In this case he nominated a subsection of his hundred-plus singers as a "prologue chorus": telling the story, foreshadowing the musical organization, and tagging onto the cadences in the great *strophes* for mezzo-soprano, "Premiers transports." He summons a larger choral force twice before the finale: as the Capulet boys retreat from the ball, eliding into the love scene, and then more remarkably still in Juliette's *convoi funèbre,* the fugal "Jetez des fleurs."

Like Wagner, Berlioz grasped the conundrum of the Ninth, but he came to the opposite conclusion, leaving the most sublime material—not the reconciliation, but the young lovers in their ecstasy—to the instruments. In his celebrated Foreword, he assures us that "there can doubtless be no mistake about the genre of this work: . . . a choral symphony." His memorable conclusion:

> If, in the famous garden and cemetery scenes, the dialogue of the two lovers, Juliet's asides, and Romeo's passionate outbursts are not sung; if the duets of love and despair are given to the orchestra, the reason for this are numerous and easy to understand. First, and this reason alone would be sufficient, it is a symphony and not an opera. Second, since duets of this nature have been treated vocally a thousand times by the greatest masters, it was wise as well as unusual to attempt another means of expression. It is also because the very sublimity of this love made its depiction so dangerous for the musician that he had to give his imagination a latitude that the positive sense of the sung words would not have given him, resorting instead to instrumental language, which is richer, more varied, less precise, and by its very indefiniteness incomparably more powerful in such a case.[7]

This appropriation and redeployment of the choral symphony made sense to Berlioz, and he never returned to the four-movement, instruments-only model. His fourth symphony, the *Grande Symphonie funèbre et triomphale* of 1840, adds (in a revised version) a choral finale to the slow march for band on parade and recitative for trombone solo. And his most perfect symphonic work, *La Damnation de Faust*, tries to avoid the question of genre altogether, calling itself a *légende dramatique.* (Daniel Albright terms *Roméo et Juliette* and *Faust* "semi-operas."[8]) Here the chorus has changing dramatic roles: Easter pilgrims, denizens of a Rathskeller, students, soldiers, neighbors. The last tableau-pair becomes a sort of dual-closing-chorus: the males as demons and the damned, vacuuming Faust into their abyss, and the women (and finally all the singers) as the chorus of "celestial spirits" that offers Marguerite her apotheosis. The harps and the virginal tessitura of the Eternal Feminine are those of an idealized convent school choir from the composer's childhood;[9] but this mode of closing chorus—of transfiguration, apotheosis, and resurrection, in a sense the mirror image of Beethoven's earthbound humanity—becomes the norm.

For in engaging the Faust legend as subject of a hybrid symphonic work, Berlioz figures in another lineage that connects the Romantic program symphony back to the milieu of Beethoven, Schiller, and Goethe. His own *Huit Scènes de Faust* of 1828 had been born of intoxication with Gérard de Nerval's French translation of Goethe. What is probably the first reference to the *Symphonie fantastique* "fermenting" in the composer's mind concerns a "descriptive symphony on *Faust*."[10] Schumann's *Szenen aus Goethes Faust,* a work of the mid-1840s, follows generally the same mixed-media approach to Goethe's tableaux. More significantly Berlioz had introduced Liszt to Goethe's *Faust* in Nerval's French, presumably as early as their first encounter, in December 1830. The Faustian symphony-with-chorus is a direct descendant of the Ninth.

Two Berlioz protégés were later drawn to the choral symphony. Charles Gounod is known to have experimented with a symphony with soloists and chorus on the passion of Christ. Asger Hamerick (1843–1923), who claimed with some justification to be Berlioz's only pupil (having spent 1864–69, the last five years of Berlioz's life, in Paris), went on to compose seven symphonies, most of them at the Peabody Conservatory in Baltimore. The last of these, Symphony No. 7, Op. 40 ("Choral," 1906, with an unpublished version from 1898), is roughly contemporaneous with Mahler's Eighth.

Mendelssohn's choral symphony of 1840, the year after *Roméo et Juliette,* is only tangentially related to the Ninth. Symphony No. 2 in B-flat major, Op. 52, *Lobgesang* (Hymn of Praise) has a nine-movement cantata added as finale to a three-movement sinfonia. The occasion for the work was the 400th anniversary of printing, celebrated by all the cities that laid claim to Gutenberg: Mainz, Strasbourg, and Leipzig, where his statue was to be erected. Mendelssohn's "symphony-cantata," as he later agreed to call it, was premiered in June at the Leipzig Thomaskirche, Bach's church. At about 70 minutes, the length is about the same as the Ninth, but the proportion of finale to the rest is of a different order, and there is little by way of organic function and purpose connecting the two halves. The texts of praise to God—psalm-derived lines like "Praise the Lord with stringed instruments; extol Him with thy song," and the chorale *Nun danket alle Gott* ("Now Thank We All our God")—are of a simpler poetic thrust. People would have thought of Beethoven anyway, since the first performance followed a complete Ninth Symphony.

Mendelssohn, more even than Berlioz, is distracted by other precedents than the Beethovenian symphony, most obviously, under the circumstances, the Bach chorale cantata. Positioned halfway between Mendelssohn's oratorio *St. Paul* of 1836 and *Elijah* a decade later, the *Lobgesang* is in fact the fourth of his five mature symphonies. Thus it follows and constitutes a studied departure from the disappointments and dissatisfaction surrounding his purer symphonies: the "Scottish" was begun in 1829 but not premiered until 1842; the "Reformation" Symphony was performed in 1832 but not again; and both it and the "Italian" Symphony, premiered in 1833, were left unpublished at his death. It is as though, like Mahler after him, Mendelssohn felt this genre above all required a *Fassung letzter Hand* before being left to the ages. The looser *Lobgesang,* though a work of occasion, proved a welcome addition to the festival repertoire. That, too, gave it identity as a descendant of the Ninth. But in the end Mendelssohn was more comfortable with the text-driven structures and the dramatic roles afforded by the oratorio chorus.

It was thus Liszt, in the mid-1850s, who most originally drew together a new, psychologically enriched dramatic symphony. Liszt's most direct influence was Berlioz. Geographically he was positioned, by virtue of establishing residence in Weimar in 1847, in the fatherland of both Goethe and Schiller. He had taken a high profile in the Goethe centennial in 1849, conducting Schumann's *Scenes from Faust* on the occasion and helping to establish the Goethe Foundation. The Weimar Berlioz-Woche of November 1852 included parts I and II of *La Damnation de Faust,* and there was a complete performance, with the Weimar singers Berlioz had long admired, in March 1856. (He dedicated the orchestral *Les Nuits d'été* to them.) Liszt dedicated his own *Faust* Symphony to Berlioz at about the same time.

The *Dante* and *Faust* symphonies, centerpiece of Liszt's orchestral *œuvre*—he thought of these works as laying claim to the serious composer's highest ground—were simultaneously composed in the 1850s. Both offer versions with closing chorus. But where Berlioz's Marguerite-in-Heaven scene is, like the reconciliation finale in *Roméo et Juliette,* a Franco-Catholic amalgam, Liszt chooses a male chorus to confirm the redemption of Faust, his soul drawn heavenward by the Eternal Feminine—*das Ewigweibliche.*

CHORUS MYSTICUS	MYSTIC CHORUS
Alles Vergängliche	All that is transitory
Ist nur ein Gleichnis;	Is but an approximation;
Das Unzulängliche,	What was inadequate
Hier wird's Ereignis;	Is here fulfilled;
Das Unbeschreibliche,	The indescribable,
Hier ist's getan;	Is here accomplished;
Das Ewig-Weibliche	The Eternal Feminine
Zieht uns hinan.	Draws us upward.

This is the closing strophe of *Faust,* part II, not published until the year of Goethe's death, 1832, and well after Berlioz had absorbed the Nerval version. Part I concludes with Faust merely being snatched away by Mephistopheles (Berlioz fashions his scene in heaven from the words "Viens! Viens!" which are those of Méphistophélès, and Marguerite's last line, calling "Anges, entourez-moi, protégez-moi de vos saintes armées," and the response of "voices from on high": "Elle est sauvée.")

Liszt's setting seems, given the psychological intensity of what has come before, pedestrian: a male chorus chants Goethe's text in unisons and octaves, as a tenor soloist dwells obsessively on the word *Ewigweibliche.* Orchestration and texture are heavily coded with celestial device: arpeggios and tremolos, harp and organ, articulations of Valhalla-like brass, softly affirming. The key is C major. A revision of the *Dante* Symphony (Inferno, Purgatorio, Paradiso) embraces a similar choral coda, where a women's chorus intones the Magnificat text to an orchestration of high strings, two harps, and woodwind undulations. The score specifies that "the female or boys' choir is not to be placed before the orchestra, but is to remain invisible together with the harmonium, or in case of an amphitheatrical arrangement of the orchestra is to be placed right at the top. In rooms having a gallery above the orchestra, it [might be preferable] to have the choir and harmonium in that gallery."[11] (The harmonium organ keeps the singers on pitch, as in Berlioz's *L'Enfance du Christ.*) In both cases the chorus is used minimally, in conclusion, and with a view toward capping off a primarily orchestral argument. Liszt himself wondered as to the aesthetic success of such strategies.[12]

Mahler did not. If the more obvious *vox humana* is found in the ongoing cross-fertilization of symphony with Lied, Mahler nevertheless references Beethoven and the Ninth from the first bar of the First Symphony. By this time he was arguably the world's expert on the Ninth, having introduced his versions with *Retuschen* ("retouchings") in 1895 and in 1900 in Vienna (the so-called Gabrilowitsch / Detroit version, currently in vogue). Mahler based his approach on Wagner's arguments in "Concerning the Execution of the Ninth Symphony": that the work should be performed in modern terms "in order to conform as nearly as possible to the intentions of its creator," then (with Siegfried Lipiner) mightily defended this position in a leaflet distributed in conjunction with the performances of February 1900.[13]

Mahler introduces chorus in the Second and Third Symphonies (1903, 1906) and takes his ultimate stand on the matter in the Eighth Symphony, "Of a Thousand" (1907). His one-movement death-march, *Totenfeier* of 1888, grew into the Second Symphony when the composer heard a chorale setting of Klopstock's *Die Auferstehung* ("The Resurrection") at Hans von Bülow's funeral, suggesting a path out of *Totenfeier* to an affirmative, universal finale. Another germ was hallucinatory: Mahler's dream of von Bülow's catafalque surrounded by flowers and candles, thus embracing scent, warmth, and the music of unseen singers. The concluding conceit—the soul soaring heavenward, "with wings I have won for myself"—is the touching stuff of *fin-de-siècle* psychology, a strained but endearing effort to validate the world's rapidly evolving secularity, to say nothing of its threats to a person of Mahler's cultural ambiguities. The poetry is his own:

O Schmerz! Du Alldurchdringer!	O Sorrow, all-penetrating!
Dir bin ich entrungen!	I am rescued from you!
O Tod! Du Allbezwinger!	O Death, all-conquering!
Nun bist du bezwungen!	Now, you are conquered!
Mit Flügeln, die ich mir errungen	With wings I have won for myself
In heißem Liebesstreben	In passionate love-struggle,
Werde ich entschweben	I shall soar upward
Zum Licht, zu dem kein Aug' gedrungen!	To the light, where no eye has penetrated!
Sterben werd' ich, um zu leben!	I shall die in order to live!
Aufersteh'n, ja aufersteh'n wirst du,	Rise again, yes, you will rise again.
Mein Herz, in einem Nu!	My heart, in a moment!
Was du geschlagen	What you have endured
Zu Gott wird es dich tragen!	Will carry you to God!

His treatment of the finale—the long apocalypse, the hushed *Aufersteh'n* chorale rising from the rubble, the poetic observations of the soprano and mezzo soprano, then the grandest of all choral climaxes, with pipe organ, harps, percussion, and full fanfare brass, is the first that successfully grasped how the Ninth actually achieves its impact. Here, too, the form is out of balance, the choral finale end-heavy. But that, in a way, is its point. The real meaning of the universe includes humanity, thus the chorus, at once earthly and celestial.

In their striving for a simpler view of all this, a child's perception of heaven, the Third and Fourth Symphonies call for the voice in other ways. In the Fourth, there is merely the naive wonder of the soprano soloist in the closing movement. ("We dance and spring, skip and sing; Saint Peter looks on.") In the Third Symphony, voices appear in the fourth and fifth of six movements—a solemn maternal figure at midnight followed by the three angels and their "sweet song," a sort of slow introduction for mezzo followed by a lusty *Allegro, Es sungen drei Engeln,* for female choir with a boychoir chiming the *bim-bam* of the bells. Much of the imagery seems Wagnerian: the soloist a sort of Erda figure, and Lord Jesus and his twelve disciples at evening meal suggesting, doubtless inadvertently, the rather similar tableau at the end of *Götterdämmerung.* But here all is joy: the sinner is forgiven, and eternal bliss is achieved. This leaves the finale for reflection and apotheosis on the orchestra's own terms, with quadrupled and octupled winds, brass, and percussion but no chorus at all.

With the Eighth Symphony Mahler controls a symphonic ideal at once free of generic bonds and yet plump with allusion to the choral and choral-symphony traditions from which it grew. Here the two choruses and solo-chorus, strongly evoking Berlioz's forces for *Roméo et Juliette,* are full participants in the pair of mega-movements, settings of the tenth-century hymn *Veni Creator Spiritus* and of the nightmarishly complex final scene from *Faust,* part II, *Ewigweibliche* and all. ("Ewig . . . ewig . . ." is also how the mezzo-soprano soloist concludes Mahler's last symphonic work, *Das Lied von der Erde.*) The elements of the closing celestial chorus are now familiar to us, though there should be as many harps as possible, and piano along with the pipe organ, stentorian

FIGURE 2.2 American Premiere of Mahler's Symphony No. 8 ("Symphony of a Thousand"): the Philadelphia Orchestra, Leopold Stokowski conducting, Academic of Music, 2 March 1916. (Philadelphia Orchestra)

brass, and bold percussion. The "Symphony of a Thousand" became its own myth: seldom played yet universally understood as the choral symphony's endgame (see Figure 2.2).

By the onset of the 1914 War, the choral voice was common stock in orchestra concerts, and its guises were many. Rachmaninoff's choral symphony *The Bells,* Op. 35 (1913), to Edgar Allan Poe's poem, is thought by many his symphonic masterpiece. The English choral symphony proved especially fecund, beginning with Vaughan Williams's *Sea Symphony* to texts of Walt Whitman (1910) and continuing with such works as Gustav Holst's First Choral Symphony (1925, well after *The Planets*), establishing a trend that continued through Havergal Brian's First Symphony ("Gothic," 1927), and on to Benjamin Britten. French contributions ran from Fauré's lovely *Pavane,* Op. 50, of 1886—the voices were to be heard coming from the shadows of a torchlit Bois de Boulogne during one of Countess Greffuhle's revels—to Guy Ropartz's Third Symphony of 1905. In Scriabin's First Symphony, Op. 26 (1899–1900), a chorus of "peoples everywhere" joins the finale in praise of art.

American primitives had ideas of their own. George Frederick Bristow's *Niagara Symphony* (1893) uses Beethovenian soloists and choir while making reference to the "Hallelujah" Chorus and *Old Hundredth*. Perhaps the most original and successful American response to the Ninth was Charles Ives's Fourth Symphony of 1916, where the first movement calls for a large offstage chorus ("preferably without voices,"[14] in one reading of the manuscript) to sing the Lowell Mason hymn "Watchman, Tell Us Of the Night," setting in motion an allegory that references Schiller's starry-heavens, the coming of the Christ child, the 1910 visit of Halley's comet, and the wonder of a traveling Everyman. In the finale, the chorus returns with wordless reminiscence of the hymn-tune BETHANY, revolving in a slow fade into the ether.

The chorus-without-words had entered the symphonic repertoire most obviously with Debussy's *Nocturnes* of 1899, where in the last movement "the mysterious song of the Sirens as they laugh and pass on" is offered by a female chorus. This is the inspiration for "Neptune" in

Holst's *The Planets* (1914–16)—to say nothing of the bacchanale in Ravel's *Daphnis et Chloé* (1912). The wordless chorus—of sirens, bacchantes, icy spheres in their orbits—is another idea that makes one pause to wonder why it took so long. But the chronological moment of its emergence, just at turn of century, provides a useful punctuation mark: the substance of the *vox humana* had been fully incorporated into the post-Romantic orchestra.

In the twentieth century, the symphony chorus was reliable enough as an ally to foster an entire modernist school. This was especially true in the United States, where a significant precedent was set with Stravinsky's Symphony of Psalms, a 50th-anniversary commission for the Boston Symphony Orchestra. The American choral symphony went on to flourish, with salient contributions by Roy Harris, David Diamond, Robert Ward, Leonard Bernstein, and on to John Corigliano.

Halls are now routinely built to accommodate the choruses required for oratorios, wordless choruses, and other extended uses. But the configuration is universally called, and the pre-set switches labeled, "Beethoven's Ninth." It is said that the playing time of a compact disc, 74 minutes, was fixed (by Norio Ohga, CEO of the Sony Corporation) to accommodate Furtwängler's account of the Ninth. Even if traditional symphonists like Brahms, Dvořák, and Tchaikovsky moved forward successfully without the chorus, Wagner had something of a point. Adding a chorus did not void the symphony at all: it loosed the shackles of genre and tyranny of the absolute—some would say the artificial. In the end bringing chorus to the orchestra made concert music more human.

Notes

1   The *Wikipedia* articles "Choral Symphony" and "List of Choral Symphonies" treat several dozen works. A search of the same term in Oxford Music Online (*Grove Music Online, Oxford Dictionary of Music*, etc.) yields similar results.

2   Louis Spohr, *The Musical Journeys of Louis Spohr,* trans. and ed. Henry Pleasants (Norman: University of Oklahoma Press, 1961), 106.

3   Wilfrid Mellers, "Choral Symphony," in *Grove's Dictionary of Music and Musicians,* 5th ed., ed. Eric Blom (London: Macmillan, 1954), vol. 2, 268.

4   Richard Taruskin, "Resisting the Ninth," in *Text and Act: Essays on Music and Performance* (New York: Oxford University Press, 1995), 24.

5   See Christopher Reynolds, "A Choral Symphony by Brahms?," *19th-Century Music* 9 (1985), 3–25.

6   Hector Berlioz, "Avant-propos de l'auteur" in *Roméo et Juliette;* see New Berlioz Edition, vol. 10, ed. D. Kern Holoman (Kassel: Bärenreiter, 1990), 2.

7   Ibid.

8   See Daniel Albright, *Berlioz's Semi-Operas:* Roméo et Juliette *and* La Damnation de Faust (Rochester: University of Rochester Press, 2001).

9   See Berlioz, "My First Communion / First Musical Experience," in *Memoirs,* ch. 1, trans. and ed. David Cairns (New York: Alfred A. Knopf, 2002), 6.

10   Letter to Humbert Ferrand, 2 February 1829 (CG 113), in Hector Berlioz, *Correspondance générale,* vol. 1 (1803–1832), ed. Pierre Citron (Paris: Flammarion, 1972), 232.

11   Franz Liszt, *Eine Symphonie zu Dantes Divina Commedia,* ed. Peter Raabe, in *F. Liszts Musikalische Werke* I/7 (Leipzig: Breitkopf & Härtel, 1920), 116 ("Magnificat").

12   Kenneth Hamilton, "Liszt," in *The Nineteenth-Century Symphony,* ed. D. Kern Holoman (New York: Schirmer Books, 1997), 159 and n. 15.

13   Transcribed by Henry-Louis de La Grange, in *Gustav Mahler, vol. 2: Vienna: The Years of Challenge (1897–1904)* (New York: Oxford University Press, 1995), 235–36; also, following La Grange, in *Orchestration: An Anthology of Writings,* ed. Paul Mathews (New York: Routledge, 2006), 40.

14   Charles Ives, Symphony No. 4, ed. John Kirkpatrick (New York: Associated Music Publishers, Inc., 1965), 4 (movt. I, reh. 4).

Selected Bibliography

Bonds, Mark Evan. *After Beethoven: Imperatives of Originality in the Symphony*. Cambridge, MA: Harvard University Press, 1996.

Hamilton, Kenneth, ed. *The Cambridge Companion to Liszt*. Cambridge: Cambridge University Press, 2005.

La Grange, Henry-Louis de. *Gustav Mahler: Vienna: Triumph and Disillusion (1904–1907)*. Oxford: Oxford University Press, 1995.

Rushton, Julian. *Berlioz, Roméo et Juliette*. Cambridge: Cambridge University Press, 1994.

Taruskin, Richard. "Resisting the Ninth," in *Text and Act: Essays on Music and Performance*. Oxford: Oxford University Press, 1995, 235–46.

3

THE NINETEENTH-CENTURY OPERA CHORUS

Steven Huebner

McGill University

Professionalization

The history of nineteenth-century opera might be said to begin with the growth of the chorus "in size, in dramatic role, in institutional footing," wrote James Parakilas almost twenty years ago in a rich study focusing on associated political implications.[1] According to Parakilas, the chorus first emerged as a real protagonist in the opéra-comique repertory of the 1770s and 1780s, particularly the works of André-Ernest-Modeste Grétry and the corpus of French "rescue operas" (not a period expression, it is worth remembering, but a term of convenience devised by modern writers).[2] These included not only Grétry's *Richard Cœur de Lion* (1784), but also more explicitly political works such as Luigi Cherubini's *Lodoïska* (1791) and Pierre Gaveaux's *Léonore ou l'amour conjugal* (1798), which famously served as a source for Beethoven's *Fidelio* (1805/1814) in staging liberation from tyranny. For listeners today, *Fidelio* remains the primary example of the rescue opera type, largely because of the persuasiveness of readings in light of the French Revolution and the symbolic significance of Beethoven's heroic phase more generally.[3] Parakilas suggests that the demands made on the singing and acting abilities of chorus members in these politically charged works encouraged opera houses to put more choristers on the payroll. In turn, composers soon fed on the greater availability of choristers to use them in many different kinds of operas, including comic subgenres.[4]

It is difficult to gainsay that these factors played a role in the increasing prominence of choral writing, but this argument might be contextualized within a wider frame. The Paris Opéra, with its repertory that accentuated splendor and ballet, had a large standing chorus that fluctuated between twenty-five and thirty-five members in the first third of the eighteenth century and then increased to around forty later in the century.[5] In the regulated environment of French music theater, the company that performed *opéra comique* was explicitly prohibited from staging choruses as late as 1780.[6] This suggests that the inclusion of choruses—which implied larger spectacles—was a matter of institutional marketing and prestige in Paris. The move of the Opéra-Comique troupe to a larger new building in 1783 (the Salle Favart) occasioned much fanfare, including attendance by the queen and many notables of the regime.[7] By 1786, ten people appeared on its roster as choristers. Plots at the Opéra-Comique became more wide-ranging and incorporated serious elements. Grétry's *Pierre le Grand* (1790), an *opéra comique* written before most rescue operas and on a subject much less politically charged than them, involves the chorus in half of its sixteen numbers. One might well ask, then, whether the creation of the Opéra-Comique chorus resulted from the proliferation of political plots as much as from the increased cultural importance of the troupe.

Across Europe changes in choral culture were incremental. In the most complete study of opera choruses currently available (though overwhelmingly centered on Germany), Christoph-Hellmut Mahling notes that the period of gradual emergence of the professional chorus (*Berufschors*) extended from 1750 (that is, before rescue opera) to 1850, by which time most houses had one.[8] Before professionalization, actors often sang choral parts as opera in Germany frequently shared the same stage as spoken theater; so too did children, music students, military personnel, and music copyists. Sometimes poor musicianship among these recruits required draconian measures, as when choral numbers had to be cut from the Cologne premiere of Giacomo Meyerbeer's *Robert le diable* in 1832–33. Time beating on stage was common, as was signaling to friends in the audience. Small wonder that Carl Maria von Weber made a standing chorus a requirement in his plan to reorganize the Dresden theater in 1817. In Italy things appear to have been worse and a high proportion of amateurs, few of whom could actually read music, remained the norm until the last third of the century. As late as the early 1870s, Verdi complained about the level of choral singing in Italian houses and felt it necessary to stress the obvious, that choral excellence was integral to the success of an opera such as *Aida*—but with no fewer than 100 voices, he added.[9] Chorus members were "regarded as the working class of the opera world," writes the social historian of Italian opera John Rosselli, "thought of as rough, insubordinate, apt to drink, smoke, and gamble in their collective dressing room."[10] At the Turin premiere of Meyerbeer's *L'Africaine* in 1875, they actually appeared drunk onstage.

Pressure for improvement came from a number of places. The growth of amateur choral societies made listeners less tolerant of shoddy choral singing on stage. Many houses moved to seasons much longer than the traditional carnival periods that included a greater number of performances each week, so an investment in a permanent chorus that knew an increasingly standardized repertory became more feasible.[11] At the same time, scores became more difficult, and acting requirements more demanding in the context of the increasing naturalism of sets.

Politics

As the chorus grew in importance at opera houses, allegory masked politics. Following defeat of the Austrians, Rossini's *Guillaume Tell* (1829) concludes with a choral paean to liberty ("Liberté, redescend des cieux!") set in slow harmonic rhythm that brings Beethoven's heroic style to mind. One index of political sensitivities in Hapsburg-occupied northern Italy is that later Italian translations would replace "liberté" with a vague reference to general happiness.[12] Politically allusive Verdi examples are particularly famous: the blustery chorus of Spanish conspirators in *Ernani* (1844) ("Si ridesti il leon di Castiglia") or the plea of Scottish refugees in *Macbeth* ("Patria oppressa") followed later, after Macbeth's death, by a march-like affirmation of victory ("Macbeth, Macbeth ov'è").[13] These choruses bristle against oppression, but less as an independent agent than reflecting the dramatic situation and agency of individual characters (Silva and Ernani in the first instance, Macduff in the second). The Hebrew slaves in *Nabucco* (1842) act as a more independent choral persona with nationalist overtones, especially familiar in the lament "Va pensiero." When Toscanini conducted the chorus with 820 voices at the memorial service for Verdi's death in 1901, he affirmed its stature—and that of its composer—as an icon of Italian culture.[14]

A sense of the chorus as a modern collectivity emerges with a stronger political edge in Wagner's *Die Meistersinger von Nürnberg* (1868), which culminates in the endorsement of "German art" by the citizens of a town with deep cultural significance in German-speaking lands. Wagner's chorus also maps onto the generic norms of comedy because the union of artist and society at the end of the opera is coterminous with a communal celebration of the young couple Eva and Walther. Moreover, with additional metaphysical overtones, the chorus in *Die Meistersinger* participates in the collective riot at the end of Act II that embodies the chaos of unrestrained Schopenhaurian Will. The chorus also famously represents a national group in Musorgsky's *Boris Godunov* (rev. 1872), but now in the role of a tragic protagonist goaded into celebrating Boris at the beginning and manipulated by the Pretender at the end. Whereas Wagner uses chorale texture at the beginning of *Die Meistersinger* to produce national color, Musorgsky not only dips into folk song for many of the choruses in *Boris Godunov*, but also occasionally mimics the kind of Russian folk heterophony where the voices are closely spaced, each adhering to and deviating from the main melody in equal measure (a case in point is "Uzh i kakna Rusi tsariu Borisu" in the Coronation Scene, based on the folk song "Slava Bogu na nebe").[15] Musorgsky's depiction of the collective recalls the invitation of Meyerbeer's grand operas to reflect on the populace as a historical actor, a phenomenon well described by Anselm Gerhard.[16] But whereas most French historical operas accentuate the impact of State imperatives on individuals, or conflate the two, *Boris Godunov* describes the effect of powerful individuals on the masses.

Wagner targeted the chorus as one of the main blemishes on the face of modern opera in his essay *Opera and Drama* (1852).[17] Wistfully evoking its role as a mediator between genuine heroes and the public in a halcyon vision of Greek tragedy, he argued that the modern chorus had deteriorated into a mere projection of stick characters that highlighted their limited dramatic compass and alienation from the "folk." Real substance had disappeared, the core of the genre had been hollowed out, the inessential had become essential. The chorus functioned much like stage sets and props: "stage machinery set into motion and song, the dumb pageant of the coulisses translated into nimble noise."[18] Wagner's critique has resonated in later critical literature on the opera chorus. In his writing on seventeenth- and eighteenth-century opera, Hellmuth-Christian Wolff described choruses and ballets as "more or less moving parts of the scenery."[19] For Carl Dahlhaus, early nineteenth-century opera choruses "function as musical extensions of the stage décor."[20] Philip Gossett has characterized choruses in certain early *ottocento* operas as "decorative, subsidiary, musically neutral, with a function analogous to the stage set."[21] Dahlhaus and Gossett both made their remarks in the context of arguments that contrast early nineteenth-century pasteboard choruses with later kinetic ones that in some way had real political and even psychological significance in their day—but with respect to repertories (French grand opera, Italian *Risorgimento* opera) antithetical to Wagner's aesthetic program in *Opera and Drama*. Indeed, the only modern work that Wagner singles out in the passage is Meyerbeer's grand opera *Les Huguenots* (1836), which he lambastes for shallow populism and its alleged congruence with dark strategies of the modern State to sedate the masses.

The shallow, framing choruses of one critic are the substantive additions to dramaturgical or ideological fiber of another. Although such debates would still seem vital and artistically challenging today, they are served by a thin historiographical record. Even the merely "decorative" nature of scene-setting choruses—invocations to gods (Rossini, *Semiramide* [1823], "Belo si celebri"), villagers' celebrations (Boieldieu, *La dame blanche* [1825], "Sonnez, sonnez, cors et musette"), sailors' calls (Wagner, "Jo ho hoe!," *Der fliegende Holländer* [1843])—seems worth questioning. Along these lines, Parakilas has argued that introductory picturesque choruses often have inherent political significance because, more than acting as mere extensions of sets, they connect people to place.[22] A rhetoric of self-determination often hinges on the *particular* needs of local populations, on geographic specificity. Few would contest this for an opera such as Rossini's *Guillaume Tell* (1829): its introductory scene-setting chorus ("Quel jour serein le ciel présage") with open fifths and echo effects not only evokes the alpine space and the collective Swiss protagonist that inhabits it, but also sets the scene for the incursion of the Austrian oppressor into that space. To refine Parakilas's point: a definition of political stakes coexists with refractions of *mentalités* more generally defined. For as Benjamin Walton has suggested, Rossini's Swiss local color also strongly signifies nostalgia, a relatively unpoliticized lost paradise set against the realities of Parisian urban life.[23]

Ideological resonances are more difficult to hear in works that do not contain strong antagonisms between rival choral factions—just to stay with alpine operas, pieces like the introductory choruses of Bellini's *La Sonnambula* (1831), Donizetti's *Linda di Chamounix* (1842) or Verdi's *Luisa Miller* (1849), all with plots centered on the tribulations of a virgin heroine. Yet Emanuele Senici has traced the premise of these to French boulevard melodrama, where representations of assaults on virtue often end with a reconciliation of society (though this is hijacked to a tragic conclusion in *Luisa Miller*).[24] Senici argues that the symbiotic entwinement of alpine settings with innocence echoes Jean-Jacques Rousseau's construct of a prelapsarian natural state where a concordance of passions and conscience produced social harmony. *La Sonnambula* begins with a choral celebration of Amina's impending betrothal ("Viva Amina"). This sounds offstage as disembodied pastoral music emerging from behind the village square, tavern, and mill—a way of projecting the décor into a larger alpine ambience. Then, once on stage, the villagers sing a song that they have prepared, possibly even composed, for Amina ("In Elvezia non v'ha rosa / Fresca et cara al par d'Amina"). Their collective identity and harmony manifestly depend on the purity of its heroine, no less a binding force—and thus inherently political—than explicitly nationalist rhetoric (as in *Guillaume Tell*).

For another example of high public stakes vested in female purity one need look no further than Bellini's next opera *Norma* (1831). Now, once again, there are rival factions; within this politically charged atmosphere, civic duty gets subsumed into the purity of the virgin priestess. The chorus of Gauls joins Norma in her prayer to the chaste moon goddess ("Casta Diva") and implicitly draws power from her (supposed) sexual abnegation when she leads them against the Romans. Three decades later, Bizet transplanted the public consecration of virginity to a far-off location in *Les Pêcheurs de perles* (1863), one of several operatic titles that actually take account of the chorus (like *I Puritani*, *I Lombardi*, *I Masnadieri*, *Les Huguenots*, and *Les Troyens*). In a typical exoticist move, the threatening forces are nebulous hostile spirits against which the chorus, buttressed by their trust in the priestess Léïla's virginity, invokes "divin Brahma." As she weaves coloratura to attract her lover, the pearl fishers sing at cross-purposes about her purity. Her voice—a pure voice—becomes a fetishized object that shields them from danger ("Ah! Que ton chant léger / Loin de nous chasse tout danger"). It is an eminently operatic way to define a group of people. Verdi's *Rigoletto* (1851) provides a counterexample. The self-absorbed investment in purity on the part of one character, Rigoletto, who protects his daughter Gilda, highlights both his isolation and the decadence of society around him, a society where the chorus of courtiers—clearly not invested in purity—participate as a strongly articulated dramatic agent in Gilda's loss of innocence. Returning to *La Sonnambula*: the chorus does indeed "extend" the stage scenery, but it does much more than that—and both transcend the picturesque to engage with the ideology of the work.

Beyond Politics

Notwithstanding institutional lethargy in funding professional choruses, Parakilas writes of a pronounced change in the dramaturgical function of choruses in the nineteenth century, contrasting kinetic, political choruses with earlier ones that "fill[ed] in breaks" and "mark[ed] stages of the action with commentary and celebration."[25] Seeking to establish a sharp divide between eighteenth- and nineteenth-century operatic choruses, he downplays continuities. This seems of the same order as the ready equations of choruses with stage sets—to some extent true, but limited. That Wagner wrote in *Opera and Drama* "a mass can never interest, but only dumbfound us"[26] (notwithstanding *Die Meistersinger*) would seem to suggest that he felt many of his contemporaries regarded the amazement produced by large numbers of people on stage—*le merveilleux* had long been a privileged criterion in French opera—as sufficient reason for their inclusion. It is difficult to know what motivated Verdi's call for 100 choristers in *Aida*: probably the communication of epic historical forces in conflict, but also perhaps the attraction of monumental spectacle *tout court*. Liberal bourgeois democracies have been no less enamored of stage extravagance than Baroque monarchies. Witness the continuing popularity of today's gargantuan Arena di Verona productions, with their manifestly populist appeal in exploring the limits of lavishness. Politics (and nationalism) at some level, to be sure. But the aesthetic value that we might call "excess" does not necessarily march in lockstep.

Sets have an undeniable role in creating ambience, but choruses surely have a more direct, even visceral, role in the ebb and flow of affects relatively unmarked by politics and ideology. The projection of affect had been the traditional role of the operatic chorus in Baroque opera, as prevalent in French opera as it was rare in *opera seria*. For example, far more than merely "marking" a stage of action, the chromatic chorus of Spartan people ("Que tout gémisse") in Rameau's *Castor et Pollux* (1737) magnifies the emotion associated with the death of the eponymous protagonists. The key role of choruses in the landscape of affect naturally endured into the nineteenth century and beyond: one thinks of how it magnifies Roméo's distress when he is exiled in Act III of Gounod's *Roméo et Juliette* (1867), colors Alfredo and Violetta's insouciance in the drinking song of *La Traviata* (1853), and embellishes the happiness of the bridal couple in the choral appeal to the Slavonic god of love, Lel, in the finale to Act I of Glinka's *Ruslan and Lyudmila* (1842). The last named chorus offers a typical example of the difference in dramaturgical significance between "filling in" or "marking" action (suggesting a secondary role) and magnifying affect. Guests at the court of the grand prince of Kiev celebrate the marriage of the two protagonists with a folk song-like melody that is repeated often enough to produce a strong sense of disruption when the dwarf-sorcerer Chernomor interrupts it in midcourse with a flash of lightning to abduct the bride. The shock seems generated from the sheer volume of sound achieved in the celebration—much greater than had a single voice delivered the nuptial song—and the ensuing sudden change of affect. This is not to ignore political readings of the chorus at this moment (and in this opera more generally). An Italianate concertato with successive solo entries follows immediately after the abduction (a frozen moment literally produced by Chernomor's magic), so that the close juxtaposition between Russian-sounding choral writing and Italianate soloists succinctly reflects a liminal position between East and West.

In view of such continuities between the eighteenth and nineteenth centuries, root causes for the increased importance of the chorus in nineteenth-century opera seem difficult to pin down. Rescue operas proved popular, but it bears remembering that chorus-filled French operas by Rameau and especially Gluck—mostly with much more choral music than *Lodoïska* or *Fidelio*—were exported well before them, especially to German houses. Domenico Cimarosa's post-Metastasian *opera seria Gli Orazi ed i Curiazi* (1796) has a considerable role for chorus (mainly TTB) and includes chains of short arias, recitatives, and choral passages more typical of earlier French opera. Inspired by the ideals of the Revolution, Cimarosa's work celebrates republican virtue: Horatio kills his sister Horatia because she laments the death of her lover from the enemy camp. But this adaptation of Corneille cannot be understood as a rescue opera, for instead of centering on escape from the clutches of tyranny it shows the exigent demands of patriotic duty. Influenced by French trends rooted in the Baroque with respect to the chorus in works such as *Gli Orazi ed i Curiazi*, the Italian tradition absorbed an increased role for the chorus independent of rescue opera.

Rossini's first major success *Tancredi* (1813) would premiere a mere seventeen years after Cimarosa's *opera seria* and it too contains a sizeable role for chorus. The heroine Amenaide must marry the head of a rival family to cement an alliance, but remains enamored of the outlaw Tancredi instead. When she sings of her longing for Tancredi as an aside in the cabaletta of her entrance aria ("E tu quando tornerai"), the chorus produces contrast by continuing to celebrate the marriage alliance. As it so often does in the nineteenth-century repertoire, the public dimension of the plot expressed by the chorus has the dramaturgical function of throwing the private sphere into greater relief. A few years earlier, Spontini had produced a remarkable effect in Act I of *La Vestale* (1807): Julia and Licinius plot their assignation against the energetic choral writing of a grand triumphal scene, now anticipating the "strong curtains" of so many later operas where the action builds across an act to a sharp juxtaposition of private and public at the end. Rossini's difference from both Cimarosa and Spontini was that he mapped his choruses onto a set of effective musico-dramatic strategies that proved remarkably hardy in the nineteenth century, partly because they both managed kinetic and static phases of plot development and facilitated listener engagement with the sensuousness of the voice.[27] For example, choruses typically introduce multi-movement arias, duets and finales ("Più dolci e placide spriano" before Amenaide's cavatina), act as intervening players in kinetic *tempo di mezzo* sections (the choral "Sì, giuriam" in the Argirio-Orbazzano duet), and reinforce the vocal ensemble during the concertato or stretta sections of finales, from the end of Act I of *Tancredi* right through to Desdemona on her knees at Otello's feet in Act III of Verdi's *Otello* (1887)—and beyond in the Italian repertory.

Such representation of private feelings under the gaze of a crowd produces highly effective music drama, and the ubiquity of such scenes in nineteenth-century opera reflects a psychic condition that remains relevant today. The sociologist Richard Sennett described this condition in his influential study of the "fall" of public man and his argument goes briefly as follows.[28] Unlike their more open eighteenth-century peers, nineteenth-century urban dwellers hid their feelings behind an impassive mask: personal space protected, strangers repelled, self-revelatory gestures carefully regulated. The entrenchment of liberal capitalism played a significant role in articulating a strong sense of private space. Thus, the artifice of the earlier eighteenth-century public persona, the construct of the "public man," came to be rejected in favor of the authentic self. But that communication of authenticity took place within private interpersonal relationships, especially within the domestic sphere shielded from public eyes. At the same time, certain explicitly public players—politicians, artists, actors, musicians—operated as vessels of repressed subjectivity, radiating the very authenticity and expressiveness so carefully guarded by citizens. Sincerity became *expected* of them, a prerequisite for success. (Here one can do no better than to think of today's evaluation of politicians based on personal traits that have little bearing on public policy.) Thus, authenticity became publicly validated as a desirable human trait while remaining carefully managed by individuals in their day-to-day public lives.

It is this counterpoint that seems at play in nineteenth-century opera and where the chorus has a key role. Broadly speaking, within the frame of increasingly naturalistic acting styles, scenes where characters tread a line between, on the one hand, seeming to allow themselves to be overheard and, on the other, deliberately projecting outwards, cast nineteenth-century audiences into the position of voyeurs much more often than with earlier operatic repertory. These scenes inhabit works where characters *also* break down—or express remorse or express their love—before a mass of watchful eyes on the stage, in effect a mirror of the basic audience–performer relationship. That is, the reigning affect gets inflated as played out before "the crowd," drawing attention not only to itself, but also to the very act of self-revelation before strangers. Take Lucia's mad scene in Donizetti's *Lucia di Lammermoor* (1835): that it occurs before assembled wedding guests—the chorus—is vital to its impact. Without denying Susan McClary's identification of "sexual excess the nineteenth century ascribed to madwomen" in this scene,[29] we might add that Lucia's collapse provides an extreme case of an involuntary aperture to an inner world, a cautionary—albeit hyperbolic—note about showing too much.

The same anxieties might even be rearticulated in a tragic-comic mode, as when in Verdi's *Un Ballo in Maschera* (1859) a group of conspirators launches a laughing chorus upon discovering Renato in (what they think is) an amorous assignation with his own wife (who has just resisted the advances of Riccardo). Not only a laughing matter at that moment, the story will make the rounds of the entire city ("E che baccano sul caso strano, e che commenti per la città") and provide a lesson in the embarrassment of public exposure. Renato hastily sets up an appointment with the conspirators and sternly bids his wife to follow him as the chorus withdraws: the act actually ends with a bare stage and the chorus heard from the wings.

This striking curtain reminds us that a creative use of theatrical space accompanied the ubiquitous interweaving of the public and private in nineteenth-century opera, a far cry from mid-eighteenth-century practice where the chorus (mainly) ringed the edge of the stage at the Paris Opéra. As early as 1793 in *La Caverne*, Jean-François Le Sueur slowly steered a chorus of robbers offstage with a decrescendo to leave it bare for a *pianissimo* conclusion at the end of one scene. A romantic quest for authentic expression not only produced a naturalistic approach to acting, stage blocking, and sets, but also encouraged characteristic color and atmosphere, all of which fired the imaginations of composers and librettists when writing for the chorus. Public space could be made heterogeneous through the use of different choral groups: witness the combination of wedding guests, Catholic students, and Huguenot soldiers in the third act finale of Meyerbeer's *Les Huguenots*, the conglomeration of the Spanish populace, monks, and Flemish deputies in the *auto da fé* scene of Verdi's *Don Carlos* (1867), or (once again reaching much earlier in the Parisian repertory) the juxtaposition of two warring tribes shown on a split stage near the end of Le Sueur's *Ossian* (1804).

Offstage effects are legion, particularly in the music of ritual, such as in the *Miserere* scene of *Il Trovatore* (1853) where the chorus contributes to the morbid atmosphere surrounding Manrico's impending public execution while Leonora gives voice to her private anguish. In Act I of Halévy's *La Juive* (1835), two different kinds of public expression stand in ironic contrast: an offstage ceremonial "Te Deum" leads to an onstage chorus of resentment against the Jews Eléazar and Rachel. Offstage ritual creates a more extended impression of an ironic foil in the Easter Mass that takes place out of view during most of Mascagni's *Cavalleria rusticana* (1890). Here the private drama occurs in a public space (the village square shown on stage), while the public persona (the villagers) are relegated to the interior of the church. A similar uncoupling of public space and collective persona occurs in Act IV of Bizet's *Carmen* (1875) where the tragic denouement occurs on the street outside of a bullring from which emerge the shouts of the crowd. Offstage choruses serve disembodied effects as well, as in the chorus of invisible spirits in the Wolf Glen of Weber's *Der Freischütz* (1821) that explores the dark side of Max's private trauma. On a more symbolic level, the voices of the city of Paris sound from offstage in Act III of Gustave Charpentier's *Louise* (1900). This seems to sublimate the cries of the street vendors (who appear on stage in the previous act) into the collective voice of the city causing the two young protagonists to imagine a public endorsement for their love. In one of the most ambitious offstage choral effects of the nineteenth-century repertory, at the end of Act I of Berlioz's *Les Troyens* (1863), the Trojan public moves as a unit around Cassandra. The chorus sings from various places behind the scene to produce the effect of a slowly approaching mass; it appears onstage (although the fateful horse remains unseen) only to withdraw once again, leaving Cassandra alone—dark, brooding, unheeded.

In Act I of Wagner's *Lohengrin* (1850), the chorus is onstage, the approaching hero offstage and seen from a distance. Here mysticism abuts realism in the interaction of the public and private spheres. Elsa seems literally to will Lohengrin into existence: at the moment that she jacks the key up from A-flat to A major and calls out to him ("Wie ich ihn sah, sei er mir nah'!"), individual voices from a large, spatially separated double chorus cut in with brief exclamations ("Seht! . . .

Wie? Ein Schwann!"). The texture thickens as it culminates in a massive homophonic double chorus for the appearance of Elsa's savior, the opera's tenor. For all the psychic acuity and possible political reverberations of the moment, the sophistication of the operatic chorus in the nineteenth-century extends to sheer stagecraft. In *Lucia*, the chorus frames pyrotechnics; in *Louise*, it reinforces the climactic vocal moment in the lovers' duet; in *Lohengrin*, it produces an effective character entrance. Within the burgeoning star-oriented economy of the genre, then, the chorus engages the opera public in these more material ways. Some might want to dismiss this as a rather mundane function. But that is to discount the distinction between ordinary talent and gift, tutti versus solo, and the intoxicating attraction of the extraordinary voice, shown to be extraordinary against a chorus of other singing voices—for public adulation and private pleasure.

Notes

1 James Parakilas, "Political Representation and the Chorus in Nineteenth-Century Opera," *19th-Century Music* 16 (1992): 186. With a somewhat different slant, see also his "The Chorus," in *The Cambridge Companion to Grand Opera*, ed. David Charlton (Cambridge: Cambridge University Press, 2003), 76–92.

2 David Charlton, "Rescue opera," in *Grove Music Online. Oxford Music Online*. Online: http://www.oxfordmusiconline.com/subscriber/article/grove/music/23227 (accessed February 24, 2009).

3 For a review of the issues see Paul Robinson, "*Fidelio* and the French Revolution," *Cambridge Opera Journal* 3 (1991): 23–48.

4 Parakilas, "Political Representation," 185–86.

5 On Rameau's opera choruses and the chorus at the Opéra, see Mary Cyr, "The Paris Opéra Chorus during the Time of Rameau," *Music and Letters* 76 (1995): 32–51.

6 David Charlton, *Grétry and the Growth of Opéra-Comique* (Cambridge: Cambridge University Press, 1986), 209.

7 For an account, see Raphaëlle Legrand and Nicole Wild, *Regards sur l'opéra-comique: Trois siècles de vie théâtrale* (Paris: CNRS Éditions, 2002), 59–60.

8 Christoph-Hellmut Mahling, *Studien zur Geschichte des Opernchors* (Trossingen: Editio Intermusica, 1962), 249.

9 Letter to Vincenzo Torelli, August 22, 1872 in Gaetano Cesari and Alessandro Luzio, *I Copialettere di Giuseppe Verdi* (Milan: S. Ceretti, 1913), 681–82.

10 John Rosselli, *Singers of Italian Opera: The History of a Profession* (Cambridge: Cambridge University Press, 1992), 204.

11 Mahling, *Studien zur Geschichte*, 344.

12 Philip Gossett, "Becoming a Citizen: The Chorus in *Risorgimento* Opera," *Cambridge Opera Journal*, 2 (1990), 51.

13 "Patria oppressa" appears only in the 1865 revision of the opera. On precedents for these choruses in the work of Rossini and Donizetti, see Gary Tomlinson, "Italian Romanticism and Italian Opera: An Essay in their Affinities," *19th-Century Music* 10 (1986): 59.

14 Mary Jane Phillips-Matz, *Verdi: A Biography* (Oxford: Oxford University Press, 1993), 765. "Va pensiero" seems not to have had enormous patriotic resonance at first; for a review of its early reception history, see Roger Parker, *Leonora's Last Act: Essays in Verdian Discourse* (Princeton: Princeton University Press, 1997), 33–41.

15 See Vladimir Morosan, "Musorgsky's Choral Style: Folk and chant elements in Musorgsky's choral writing," in *Musorgsky: In Memoriam 1881–1981*, ed. Malcolm Brown (Ann Arbor, MI: UMI Research Press, 1982), 104–5.

16 This post-Revolutionary theme of the chorus as actor runs as a thread through Gerhard's *The Urbanization of Opera: Music Theater in Paris in the Nineteenth Century*, trans. Mary Whittall (Chicago: University of Chicago Press, 1998).

17 Richard Wagner, *Richard Wagner's Prose Works*, trans. William Ashton Ellis (1892–99; repr., New York: Broude Brothers, 1944), vol. 4, 61–63. For a perceptive discussion of this passage, see Ryan Minor, "Wagner's Last Chorus: Consecrating Space and Spectatorship in *Parsifal*," *Cambridge Opera Journal* 17 (2005): 11–12.

18 Wagner, *Prose Works*, vol. 4, 63.

19 Hellmuth-Christian Wolff, *Oper: Szene und Darstellung von 1600 bis 1900*, Musikgeschichte in Bildern, ed. Heinrich Besseler and Max Schneider (Leipzig: Deutsche Verlag für Musik, 1968), vol. 4/1, 15.

20 Carl Dahlhaus, *Nineteenth-Century Music*, trans. J. Bradford Robinson (Berkeley and Los Angeles: University of California Press, 1989), 66.

21 Gossett, "Becoming a Citizen," 44.

22 Parakilas, "Political Representation," 190.

23 Benjamin Walton, *Rossini in Restoration Paris* (Cambridge: Cambridge University Press, 2007), 284–90.

24 See Emanuele Senici, *Landscape and Gender in Italian Opera: The Alpine Virgin from Bellini to Puccini* (New York: Cambridge University Press, 2005).

25 Parakilas, "Political Representation," 184.

26 Wagner, *Prose Works*, vol. 4, 304.

27 For a very good study of how choruses were integrated into Italian operatic conventions, see Markus Engelhardt, *Die Chöre in den Frühen Opern Giuseppe Verdis* (Tutzing: Hans Schneider, 1988), 108–227.

28 Richard Sennett, *The Fall of Public Man* (1977; pbk., New York: Norton, 1992). Sennett's study is a substantial influence on Gerhard's *The Urbanization of Opera*.

29 Susan McClary, *Feminine Endings: Music, Gender, and Sexuality* (Minneapolis: University of Minnesota Press, 1991), 93.

Selected Bibliography

Cyr, Mary. "The Paris Opéra Chorus During the Time of Rameau," *Music and Letters* 76 (1995): 32–51.

Engelhardt, Markus. *Die Chöre in den Frühen Opern Giuseppe Verdis*. Tutzing: Hans Schneider, 1988.

Gossett, Philip. "Becoming a Citizen: The Chorus in *Risorgimento* Opera," *Cambridge Opera Journal* 2 (1990): 51.

——. "'Edizioni distrutte' and the Significance of Operatic Choruses During the Risorgimento," in *Opera and Society in Italy and France from Monteverdi to Bourdieu*, ed. Victoria Johnson and Jane Fulcher. Cambridge: Cambridge University Press, 2007, 181–242.

Mahling, Christoph-Hellmut. *Studien zur Geschichte des Opernchors*. Trossingen: Editio Intermusica, 1962.

Minor, Ryan. "Wagner's Last Chorus: Consecrating Space and Spectatorship in *Parsifal*," *Cambridge Opera Journal* 17 (2005): 1–36.

Parakilas, James. "The Chorus," in *The Cambridge Companion to Grand Opera*, ed. David Charlton. Cambridge: Cambridge University Press, 2003, 76–92.

——. "Political Representation and the Chorus in Nineteenth-Century Opera," *19th-Century Music* 16 (1992): 181–202.

PART II

Selected Masterworks from the Choral–Orchestral Repertoire

4

MASSES AND REQUIEMS

D. Kern Holoman

University of California, Davis

Introduction

This section of *Nineteenth-Century Choral Music* situates ten central works in the context of their composition, performance, and publication as these are generally understood today. It seeks to provide a unified frame of reference for familiar works to be encountered routinely across the rest of the volume, noting recent advances in historical and critical thinking and suggesting some avenues of approach to problems encountered in performance.

The short essays are not, strictly speaking, program notes, though several of them began that way. They typically begin by articulating why these compositions have come to occupy the place they do in the repertoire, then consider the circumstance of creation and first performance, and finally assess how they have evolved in our understanding. For even the central repertoire mutates: Rossini's *Petite Messe solennelle* might once have figured here, but now is peripheral. The Fauré Requiem is understood very differently now that we can grasp the progress of its versions. The Requiems of Berlioz and Verdi, and finally Beethoven's *Missa solemnis,* have impressive new modern editions.

Striking currents emerge from thinking about these ten works as a group: how greatly, for instance, England and its music festivals shaped this repertoire. All of these works were career-defining for their composers; half were end-of-career valedictories. More than half are about death. All these composers concern themselves with cosmic order and visions of paradise, whether they began from the Bible or *Faust*. Both Beethoven and Mahler reference the Holy Spirit as a dove descending. Mendelssohn and Brahms were both pressured by their librettists to Christianize their texts. Are there unspoken connections between the two non-standard Requiems: one Protestant (Brahms) and one Catholic (Fauré)?

We are consistently reminded, too, how much the success of these works rests with the composer's initial discovery and response to his text. Each of these compositions grows from a canonic text, but not one represents a solution that could be described as conventional.

In the tabular descriptions of first performances, I have not usually listed the vocal soloists, since they are for the most part tangential to the story of the work and can be found today with a few clicks on the Internet. As to suggestions for further reading, I begin with Michael Steinberg's ever-fascinating introductions (*Choral Masterworks: A Listener's Guide*, Oxford University Press, 2005) and with references to two handbooks: Robert J. Summer, *Choral Masterworks from Bach to Britten:*

Reflections of a Conductor (Scarecrow Press, 2007), and Jonathan D. Green, *A Conductor's Guide to Nineteenth-Century Choral–Orchestral Works* (Scarecrow Press, 2008). If there is a one-volume study since 1990, as for example a Cambridge Handbook, I cite (and often follow) it.

One performance note applies, but for Fauré's tiny Requiem, to all these works. Each belongs *by itself* on a concert program. The primary reason is obvious: the music warrants presenting in its own world. Far from feeling deprived of variety, in my experience, listeners are grateful for the opportunity to focus on one big question at a time.

Ludwig van Beethoven (1770–1827): *Missa solemnis* in D, Op. 123

1   Kyrie eleison
2   Gloria
3   Credo
4   Sanctus
5   Agnus Dei

Duration	About 90 minutes.
For	Soloists (SATB), chorus (SATB); violin solo (in the Sanctus); flutes I–II, oboes I–II, clarinets I–II, bassoons I–II, contrabassoon; horns I–IV, trumpets I–II, trombones I–III; timpani; organ; strings.
Text	The Roman Catholic Mass Ordinary.
Composed	1819–23
First Performed	April 7, 1824,[1] St. Petersburg, in a benefit concert organized by Prince Nikolai Galitzin. Beethoven oversaw the Kyrie, Credo, and Agnus Dei in Vienna on May 7, 1824, at the concert during which the Ninth Symphony was first performed.
Dedication	To Archduke Rudolph of Austria (1788–1831).
Scores	• First published Mainz: Schott, 1827, very shortly after Beethoven's death = IMSLP.
	• Standard edition Breitkopf & Hartel, 1864 ("old" Beethoven complete edition) = Dover, Kalmus, IMSLP; Eulenburg pocket score, ed. Willy Hess (*c.*1938, rpt. 1964, 1985) = IMSLP.
	• Scholarly edition: ed. Norbert Gertsch, New Beethoven Edition viii/3 (Henle, 2000). Beethoven's autograph score of the Kyrie has been published in facsimile (Tutzing: Schneider, 1965).
Further Reading	Steinberg, *Choral Masterworks*, 45–60. Summer, *Choral Masterworks from Bach to Britten*, 51–63. Green, *A Conductor's Guide*, 27–30. William Drabkin, *Beethoven: Missa solemnis*, a Cambridge Music Handbook (Cambridge University Press, 1991).
	Also Warren Kirkendale, "New Roads to Old Ideas in Beethoven's 'Missa Solemnis,'" *Musical Quarterly* 56 (1970): 665–701. Norman Del Mar, *Conducting Beethoven, vol. 2: Overtures, Concertos, Missa Solemnis* (Oxford University Press, 1993).

The tortuous history of Beethoven's second Mass revolves around the elevation of Archduke Rudolph, son of the Holy Roman Emperor Leopold II, brother of the Emperor Francis of Austria, to the rank of cardinal archbishop in the Catholic Church, a ceremony announced in 1819 for the following spring in Olmütz, Moravia.[2] Rudolph had been a piano and composition pupil of Beethoven since 1803, the year of the "Eroica," and their encounters continued for most of the rest of Beethoven's life. Rudolph was the most influential and in some ways personally the closest of Beethoven's many noble patrons. He had taken the lead in establishing the salary arrangement that kept Beethoven from leaving Vienna in 1809, and over two decades commissioned and received the dedications of the "Archduke" Trio (Op. 97), the Fourth and Fifth Piano Concertos (Opp. 58 and 73 respectively), the "Hammerklavier" Sonata (Op. 106), a violin sonata (Op. 96), and the Grosse Fuge (Op. 133). Rudolph, forced to leave town as Napoleon approached Vienna in 1809, is the friend referenced in the Piano Sonata, Op. 81a (*Lebewohl / Les Adieux*), with its movements representing farewell, absence, and joyous return.

It was Beethoven's own idea to proffer a Mass for the archduke's investiture, where he imagined it as the axis of the liturgical ceremony: "the most glorious day of my life," he wrote in anticipation. "God will enlighten me so that my poor talents may contribute to the glorification of that solemn day."[3] The intimacy of the personal connection and presumed spectacle of the event were at first energizing, but yielded soon enough to the realization that what he had undertaken was of grave intellectual consequence and could not be rushed. Only the first two movements were completed in time, and the music for Rudolph's investiture on March 20, 1820 was instead by Haydn (deceased) and Johann Nepomuk Hummel.

At this point Beethoven's second Mass, no longer destined for a specific occasion, followed a course all its own, sprawling of scale and intent. The (historically inaccurate) title *Missa solemnis*[4] expresses the seriousness of its purpose. It was a work of unprecedented size, Beethoven's longest except for the opera *Fidelio*. Just as the "Eroica" Symphony announces Beethoven's second, "Heroic" period, the *Missa solemnis* confirms the arrival of a third, late style. In the "Eroica," Beethoven confronts Fate—specifically, his hearing loss—while in the *Missa solemnis* he confronts God, that is, faces the end of life.[5]

The *Missa solemnis* is thus central to grasping Beethovenian thought in the period that goes on to yield the Ninth Symphony and late quartets. Nevertheless it is a problematic work both for the musicians who present it and for the individual listener. The ear and mind are so frequently challenged by the compositional tactics—ambiguities of the harmonic framework, wandering downbeats, matters defined in retrospect, surprises of melody—that the logic can seem confounding. The grounding principles of sonata form coexist, sometimes uncomfortably, with Beethoven's evocation of old church practice and with his own changing priorities. The five long movements describe very complex arguments. One senses the struggles—philosophical, psychological—of composition, and of Beethoven's brilliance in all its complexity.

Composition

What Michael Steinberg calls this "intensely lived-with welter of thoughts and feelings"[6] came together over the three years 1819–22. As he turned fifty, Beethoven had been completely deaf for half a decade. He just completed the great "Hammerklavier" Sonata for piano, Op. 106, and would be simultaneously composing the piano sonatas Ops. 109–11, the Ninth Symphony, and the quartets. He had the Latin text and its translation copied and explained to him, annotating it as he went. He researched sacred music practice back through the Renaissance, both in his own library and in collections of others. There is a palpable sense of his trying to reconcile his world view with his only vague notions of religious belief. At the top of autograph score he writes: *Von Herzen—möge es wieder—zu Herzen gehn!*, roughly: "Written from the heart, to the heart may it then return."

He worked more or less in order, undertaking the Kyrie in February or March 1819 and the Gloria over the rest of 1819. He had reached the Agnus Dei by mid-1821 and had the overall substance of the work settled by 1822, having filled four sketchbooks and dozens of loose pages with his scribbled thoughts. The enterprise of interpreting this often illegible complex remains in its early stages, although in recent years it has at least been properly catalogued and tentatively ordered.[7]

Meanwhile, in March 1820, he concluded negotiations with Nikolaus Simrock to publish the work. This did nothing to dissuade Beethoven, in a string of unseemly maneuvers, from offering the Mass, still unfinished, to competing publishers, nor from inviting some twenty-eight noble subscribers to purchase a manuscript copy in advance of publication. Ten orders were received.

By early 1823, the complete work was ready for distribution. Copyists prepared a master manu-script of the definitive musical text, the dedication copy for Archduke Rudolph, the subscriber copies, and the engraver's manuscript—in most of which Beethoven entered annotations of one kind or another. B. Schott's Söhne of Mainz ended up with the definitive contract in 1825, after the first performances. Work on the typography and proofreading occupied Beethoven and his representatives through the last weeks of his life.

Performance and Publication

Prince Nikolai Galitzin (1794–1866), representing one of great lineages of Russian aristocracy, was the music lover and amateur cellist who commissioned the late string quartets (Opp. 127, 132, and 130, sometimes called the Galitzin Quartets). Offered one of the purchase copies of the *Missa solemnis*, he took it upon himself to organize a complete performance in St. Petersburg, a benefit, as was the custom for such events, for the widows and orphans of the philharmonic society. Afterwards Galitzin reported to Beethoven that "for my part I have never heard anything so sublime"; another admirer, Prince Radziwill, "was enraptured with it," Galitzin wrote, "just like myself and all those present."[8]

A month later in Vienna, the Kyrie, Credo, and Agnus Dei were heard together with the Ninth Symphony and *Consecration of the House* overture. But owing to local prohibition of Catholic liturgy in secular venues, German texts were substituted for the Latin and the movements called simply "hymns," without being identified as excerpted from a Mass. The Kyrie was performed again two weeks later. These were Beethoven's last appearances, the occasions when he "assisted" in the task of conducting by beating time while reading a score onstage. The conductor had told his musicians to pay no attention.

Schott's published score was available in score and parts three years later, within days of Beethoven's death. It was full of mistakes.

Structure

The *Missa solemnis* grew naturally from its Viennese forebears, particularly the six late-career masses Haydn had composed for his patron Prince Nikolaus II Esterházy for the name day of the prince's wife. (Beethoven's Mass in C, Op. 86, had been composed for the same patron and occasion.) Handel's *Messiah* was well known to Beethoven and by that time broadly recognized as a *summa* of choral music (in a way that Bach's B-minor Mass was, so far, not). Mozart's Requiem was another important precedent. If Beethoven's experience in choral music was relatively limited,[9] his mastery of sonata form in its symphonic context, of the substance of Viennese Classicism, was by that time unrivaled. Some of his tactics are reminiscent of accomplished pages from previous work, notably the "Eroica" and "Pastoral" symphonies; others foreshadow both the ideals and the substance of the Ninth. He chooses a traditional key, D major, and ordinary means: four soloists, four-part chorus, and conventional orchestra with trombones. As in the Ninth, he urges the voices, soloists and chorus alike, into the further reaches of register and breath capacity, human consid-erations all but forgotten in the game afoot.

In essence, the Mass is through-composed by piecing together responses to the rigorously studied lines of text, which Beethoven assembled into large-scale episodes conditioned, but seldom controlled, by traditional sonata practice: symphony / concerto expositions, for instance, and recapitulations strongly sensed as inevitable. Particular words, like "ascendit" and "omnipotens" provoke typically imaged music, but they can also assume editorial bent, as when the emphatically dual "Credo, credo" insists on the promises of faith. With the extravagant fugues that conclude the Gloria and the Credo, Beethoven seeks to honor what was at the time often described as "archaic" or "ancient" music, that of his Baroque and Renaissance predecessors. One also senses, however imprecisely, other unities of thematic design, coaxed by some theorists into a "germinal motive."[10]

Beethoven takes care to leave the five liturgical elements of the Mass Ordinary as large movements. Their sections—the "sub-movements"—address the compelling issues of Classical practice, for instance the frequent conflict of verse structures in the Latin text with movement types in the symphonic style.

Mit Andacht, "reverently," advises Beethoven at the start of the Kyrie.[11] The grand dotted-rhythm opening at once establishes kingly rhetoric[12] and introduces familiar sonata designs, with the Christe eleison sensed as a theme II that presents the soloists, a new meter (3/2), and the new key of F-sharp minor. The second Kyrie recapitulates much of the opening one, the pedal point on A and tonic cadence yielding a long *pianissimo* dissolve. When, at the end, the sopranos fall from their cadential A to the F-sharp of the D-major tonic triad, the stage is set for the jubilant Gloria, which begins, as though completing previous business, on a tutti D.

The three big sections of the substantial Gloria (Gloria in excelsis Deo / Qui tollis peccata mundi / Quoniam tu solus Sanctus) are rich with rhetorical gesture: the upward sweep of the opening, for instance, which keeps asserting thematic authority as a sort of ritornello even as its tonal focus begins to be lost. At the center comes the exquisite Larghetto "Qui tollis" in slow eighth notes, with the kind of lyric exchange among solo winds and then the vocal soloists that evokes the clarinet-rich sounds of Mozart's last years. The chorus enters, at first reiterating the soloists, then leading the exploration of a heroic B-flat major at the words "qui sedes ad dexteram Patris" ("who sitteth at the right hand of God the father"), an atmosphere and key we will encounter again in the Agnus Dei. The tonality eerily wends its back toward D and a recapitulatory "Quoniam." This fixes the essence if not the specifics of sonata form. The great D-major fugue "In gloria Dei Patris. Amen," is stated formally, with dramatic *colla parte* trombones serving to announce its importance. Almost immediately it embarks on esoteric contrapuntal and tonal device: redistribution of the material in stretto, inversion, and the like, including a passage (mm. 428*ff.*) where the words "Cum Sancto Spiritu" return in long note-values, like a white-note cantus firmus. (Beethoven's secretary Anton Schindler describes the master's keyboard rendition of this fugue, with "singing, howling, stamping."[13]) The sudden *Poco più allegro*, m. 458, and unison dash draw the music to its apparently conclusive Amens, but then the initial "Gloria in excelsis Deo" recapitulates, driving it to plagal cadences at the close. The singers, in a gesture sometimes seen as analogous to the close of the "Hallelujah Chorus," have the last word: "Gloria!"

At 20 minutes, the Credo is the longest movement of the Mass and the most intricate of organization. The brassy proclamation at the start forces the key of B-flat, in which the bold motto for "Credo, credo" is heard (see Example 4.1). This sets in motion another large tripartite structure, in a resolute B-flat major thick with trombones. One effect is to return

EXAMPLE 4.1 Beethoven, *Missa solemnis*, Credo.

[Allegro ma non troppo]

the upward-looking contours of the Gloria back to an earthly present and a human profession of faith.

Yet "Et incarnatus" just as purposefully insists on the mysteries of the celestial realm, in a church-like mode and with flute obbligato representing the Holy Spirit as a dove. The chorus, chanting quietly in a low register, confirms the spatial setting. In a succession so rapid as to be disconcerting come the angst-ridden statement of the "Crucifixus"; an "Et resurrexit" (m. 188) announced, *parlando*, by unaccompanied chorus and enigmatic as to harmonic goal; the burst of rocketing scales at "et ascendit" (*Allegro*, m. 194); and the stern trombone of the Last Judgment at "judicare" (m. 221). "Credo, credo" (*Allegro*, m. 264) reasserts the anchoring motto. The 3/2 "Et vitam venturi" (m. 306) unleashes Beethoven's Jupiter-Symphony-like display of every device in his contrapuntal arsenal. The lurch forward at the end, *Allegro con moto* (m. 372) predicts tactics put to good use at the close of the Ninth.

The lugubrious opening of the Sanctus with trio of trombones is a Viennese soundscape familiar from passages in Mozart, Schubert, and later Brahms, with whispered recitatives in the chorus, again *mit Andacht*. An extended C-sharp tremolo as pedal point introduces the florid coloratura of "Pleni sunt coeli" followed by the "Osanna," as a fugue, *Presto*, in 3/4, beginning in the soprano. Here occurs Beethoven's most interesting response to the Mass text. For the moment of the elevation of the Host, he composes a Praeludium in rich tenor sonorities, suggesting the organ improvisations traditional at this point in a Mass. A *siciliana* with solo violin returns the listener to the pastoral realm of God, a point emphasized by the pair of flutes heard with the violin, then again as the music descends from its initial lofty place. The whole eventually becomes understood as a slow introduction to a sonata process recapitulating at m. 176. The concluding Osanna demanded by the Mass text is announced by the soloists at the tonic cadence of the recapitulation, treated contrapuntally by the chorus for a coda.

The Agnus Dei reflects on the words "miserere" and "pacem," with an ambiguous opening (B minor? D major?) followed by a Dona nobis pacem in gentle 6/8. In a blatantly theatrical turn of events, military trumpet-and-drum intrude, with all this has to say of Vienna and the Napoleonic adventure—and the experiences there of the composer and his patron. Ample trumpet-and-drum precedents in Haydn, and from Beethoven's own work, would have come to mind among the first listeners. (Mahler went on to make military incursions something of a signature protocol.) The trumpet calls are in B-flat major, which makes for a certain rivalry between D and B-flat major in what follows. Trombones join for the "Dona nobis pacem" fugue in G major. The perceived reference to the "Hallelujah Chorus" ("and He shall reign for ever and ever," m. 216) is more a function, I think, of the intervals in play than a purposeful allusion. The Presto (m. 265) returns to D and duple meter in what Beethoven terms his "plea for inner and outer peace." Again the military element asserts itself (m. 406), but this time at a distance, quietly, on a low B-natural, a distant but gnawing truth overlooked as the last D major gathers. But where the Ninth Symphony finishes in a panorama of the cosmos, the *Missa solemnis*, having left its trumpets behind, simply dissolves.

Editions and Performance

The *Missa solemnis* is one of those works where the composer's death before publication of an authoritative score has left posterity to sort out its dilemmas. Two readings are famously problematic for performers. The "Et incarnatus," otherwise for soloists, opens in the autograph score with chorus tenors (Credo, mm. 125–31). The copyist scores, owing to an apparent misunderstanding, give the passage to solo tenor, and that reading appears in the Schott published edition despite Beethoven's attempt to restore the original. Those measures thus should, on good authority, be returned to the chorus. More troublesome are the "Pleni sunt coeli" and "Osanna" (Sanctus, mm. 34–78), which call for soloists to hold their own over full-blown orchestra with trumpets, trombones, and drums. William Drabkin's suggested explanation is that, short of staff lines on his manuscript paper, Beethoven borrowed the "soloist" lines to notate music intended for chorus.[14] To Anton Schindler's query as to this apparent anomaly, Beethoven is said to have replied "Solo voices it must be"[15]—but Schindler went on to advocate for the chorus anyway. It remains the conductor's call. My own preference, at least in the "Pleni," is for the soloists, thus emphasizing the coloratura in the manner of the decorative soprano solos in Haydn and for that matter in the B-minor Mass. Adjusting the orchestra there is simple enough.

The technical and aesthetic challenges of this cerebral but impractical monster score are formidable. (Theodor Adorno called it a *verfremdtes Hauptwerk*, an "alienated magnum opus."[16]) Recordings, even by the great conductors of the Viennese and Berlin traditions, prove just how easy it is to overplay it, how quickly the supposedly delicate violin obbligato in the Benedictus turns elephantine. The *Missa solemnis* finds its proper place not so much by insisting on epic force as by savoring its pallet of sonority.

If the *Missa solemnis* has never been exactly popular, every serious thinker about music has sensed its importance. Writers dwell on how threatening the Beethoven symphony was to the Romantic generations, but the Mass weighed just as heavily on Mendelssohn and Brahms when they came to compose their masterpieces for orchestra and chorus. Adorno is not alone in thinking the *Missa solemnis* "something peculiar." But I find its challenge undeniable, the opportunity to discover Beethoven's path from heart to heart utterly compelling.

Hector Berlioz (1803–69): *Grande Messe des morts* (Requiem), H. 75

1 Requiem et Kyrie. Introit
2 Dies irae. Prosa
3 Quid sum miser
4 Rex tremendae
5 Quaerens me
6 Lacrymosa
7 Offertoire ("Chorus of Souls in Purgatory")
8 Hostias
9 Sanctus
10 Agnus Dei

Duration	About 90 minutes.
For	Tenor solo (Sanctus), chorus (SSTTBB); piccolo, flutes I–IV, oboes I–II, English horns I–II, clarinets I–II, bassoons I–IV; horns I–VI, cornets *à pistons* I–II (Sanctus), brass bands as below, eight pairs timpani, bass drum, cymbals, tam-tam; strings. Bands in movements 2, 4, and 6: band I: cornets à pistons I–II, trombones I–II, tuba; band II: trumpets I–II, trombones I–II; band III: trumpets I–II, trombones I–II; band IV: trumpets I–II, trombones I–II, ophicleides I–II.
Text	The Roman Catholic Requiem Mass Ordinary text, substantially altered by the composer.
Composed	Late March–June 1837 in Paris.
First Performed	December 5, 1837, at the church of St. Louis des Invalides, Paris, with a festival ensemble, François-Antoine Habeneck conducting. Gilbert Duprez (1806–96), the leading French tenor of his generation, sang the Sanctus.
Scores	• First published by Maurice Schlesinger (Paris, 1838). • Standard edition Breitkopf & Härtel, Berlioz complete edition vol. 7, ed. Charles Malherbe and Felix Weingartner, 1902 = Kalmus, Dover, IMSLP. • Scholarly edition: Bärenreiter, New Berlioz Edition vol. 9, ed. Jürgen Kindermann, 1978 (materials BA 5449).
Further Reading	Steinberg, *Choral Masterworks*, 61–67. Green, *A Conductor's Guide*, 41–45. Julian Rushton, *The Music of Berlioz* (Oxford University Press, 2001), 203–15.

Berlioz's role in the events of July 28–30, 1830—the three "glorious days" of revolution in and around Paris that resulted in the demise of Charles X and his replacement by the citizen-king Louis-Philippe—was limited to some breathless running about town in search of weapons and ammunition and, some time that summer, readying his altogether rousing orchestration of the *Marseillaise*. But confirming as it did his spiritual lineage with 1789 and the Napoleonic glories, the 1830 Revolution was every bit as formative an influence on Berlioz's art as his discovery of Shakespeare had been in 1827 and Beethoven in 1828. It established, in short, his patriotic fervor.[17] "The nation has the right," Berlioz wrote in regard to one last-minute request from the government, "to ask of each of its children an absolute commitment. And so I said to myself, *Allons, enfant de la patrie!*"[18]

A significant portion of Berlioz's œuvre, indeed, consists of ceremonial music of one sort or another. Not all his contributions in this style retain the meaning or sense of purpose they had in his day: the Napoleonic cantata *Le Cinq Mai* (1835), the *Hymne à la France* (1844), a *Chant des chemins de fer* for the inauguration of the Paris-Brussels railroad line (1846), and a Second Empire cantata, *L'Impériale* (1854), that figured prominently in the closing formalities of the Festival de l'Industrie of 1855—these today seem mostly curiosities. Three of Berlioz's ceremonial works are, however, to be numbered among his masterpieces: the Requiem of 1837; the *Grande Symphonie funèbre et triomphale* of 1840, which was his fourth and last symphony; and the *Te Deum* of 1848–55, which Berlioz was fond of characterizing as a younger sibling of the Requiem.

The central image of the Requiem is the *clangor tubarum* of the Day of Judgment, where four brass choirs sound the fanfares announcing the end of the world, and all humankind cries out from the earthquake-thunder of a dozen percussionists. The fanfare-with-drums effect had first occurred to Berlioz as he composed the "Et resurrexit" of an early *Messe solennelle* shortly after arriving in Paris. (He would have not have learned of Beethoven's near-contemporaneous *Missa solemnis* for several years.) A similar scenario occurred to him in mid-1835 as he began to draft plans for a colossal third symphony in seven movements tentatively titled *Fête musicale funèbre* but never completed. Whatever sketches and drafts there may have been were put aside pending the development of more appropriate circumstances.

On July 28, 1835 the Corsican anarchist Giuseppe-Maria Fieschi and his accomplices loosed his "infernal machine"—twenty guns, rigged to fire at once—upon King Louis-Philippe and his entourage as they progressed through Paris on the first of the holidays celebrating the *Trois Glorieuses*. Among the eighteen killed were the Maréchal de France Édouard-Adolphe Mortier, the king's commander-in-chief. (Louis-Philippe, slightly wounded but in full control of the royal sangfroid, commanded "*Messieurs, continuons.*") Months later, in March 1837, the national government invited Berlioz to compose a Requiem Mass for Mortier and Fieschi's other victims, to be ready for the July holidays and given at the church of St. Louis des Invalides, the official chapel of the French military services. Berlioz retained his composure long enough to demand five or six hundred musicians, then succumbed to a period of dizzying intoxication at the prospect. "My brain felt as though it would explode with the pressure of ideas."[19]

His intellectual powers were at their peak, and the previous ruminations had primed him for the challenge. "The outline of one movement," he writes, "was barely sketched before the next formed itself in my mind. It was impossible to write fast enough."[20] He reveled in the composition of the Tuba mirum, "the moment for tears and gnashing of teeth, where I threw in such a violent stroke of the tam-tam that the whole church quaked." By late May he had the end in sight; the autograph was dated June 29, 1837, leaving a full month for copying and lithography of hundreds of parts, contracting the players and singers, rehearsals, and construction of the scaffolding to accommodate it all.

And then, abruptly, the ceremony was canceled. The treasury, it was argued, had been depleted by the costs of a royal wedding. Berlioz, having like Robinson Crusoe (as he put it) built a canoe too large to launch by himself, was stranded. He had already incurred major expenses, and neither he nor his creditors saw much likelihood that the government would make good on its promises.

Performance and Publication

In October 1837, news reached Paris of a new occasion for national mourning. Charles, comte de Damrémont and governor-general of Algeria, had fallen during the French siege of Constantine. For his *pompes funèbres* the coffers of the Ministry of War could be tapped and Berlioz's Requiem at last presented—and paid for. The ceremony took place on December 5, 1837, at the Invalides. François-Antoine Habeneck, royal chapel-master and *chef d'orchestre* of the Société des Concerts—the Paris Conservatoire Orchestra—conducted, with Berlioz overseeing the percussion section and the bands. A more eventful first performance it is difficult to imagine. Habeneck indulged his fondness for a pinch of snuff just as the Tuba mirum broke loose, and the composer had to leap to the rescue. Shortly thereafter a member of the chorus fainted in the bleachers. One of the priests burst into tears and had to be led away; the bereaved wept, the clergy went on chanting the liturgy. Withal, the event was remembered as a magnificent success.

The Requiem, published by subscription a few months after the first performance, was the work with which many Europeans first became aware of the look of a Berlioz score. (Several passages in full score were also included in his orchestration treatise of 1843, which had wider circulation still.) Berlioz continued to refine details of declamation, scoring, and even formal organization, notably in the course of preparing complete performances in 1846, 1850, and 1852.[21] These changes were incorporated in a second edition of the score offered by Ricordi of Milan in 1853, with a few further refinements in Ricordi's reprinting of 1867. Altogether Berlioz was occupied with one aspect or another of his apocalyptic vision—Mass, *Fête musicale funèbre,* Requiem and its revisions and publications—for forty-three of the fifty years he wrote music. He says in the postscript to his *Memoirs* that of his own works, he most prefers the love scene from his dramatic symphony *Roméo et Juliette,* but in 1867 writes with equal passion: "If I were threatened with seeing my entire œuvre burned, less one score, it would be for the *Messe des morts* that I would beg mercy."[22]

Structure

Conscious for years of his heritage in the patriotic music of François-Joseph Gossec, Étienne Méhul, and other composers of the Revolution and First Empire, Berlioz was by the late 1830s in impressive command of the particulars of what he came to call architectural music: acoustic phenomena, the deployment of multiple forces, the critical issues of pacing and frame. With its chorus, double-sized orchestra, four brass choirs, and ranks of percussion, the Requiem is the benchmark of Romanticism's urge toward the colossal. Yet we now understand it additionally in terms of its finesse, its taut organization, and the nuance of its materials.

For instance, Berlioz freely reorders the traditional Latin text to suit his poetic or structural purpose, thus contriving to balance the shattering movements (Dies irae, Rex tremendae, and Lacrymosa) with those of introspection and promise (Quaerens me, Offertorium, and Sanctus). The Quid sum miser, constructed from verses 7, 9, and 17 of the medieval poem, quells the fiery phrases heard earlier in the Dies irae with a gentler prayer:

> What, then, shall I say, wretch that I am,
> What advocate entreat to speak for me?
> When even the righteous may hardly be secure?
> Remember, merciful Jesu,
> That I am the cause of thy pilgrimage;
> Do not forsake me on that day.
> I pray in supplication on my knees,
> My heard contrite as the dust,
> Take care of my end.

He combines the Introit and Kyrie of the Requiem Mass into a single movement (as do, later, Verdi and Fauré), but divides the Offertory with a freestanding Hostias. The Sanctus is set without its Benedictus, but with two Osannas, making it into a two-strophe form. The Agnus Dei conflates the closing elements of the service in order to accommodate reminiscences of previous passages and the concluding "Requiescat in pace, Amen." This, too, is a matter of architecture, where the givens of inherited texts and traditions—the recapitulatory last movement, for instance, which we encounter in Bach, Mozart, and Verdi—are reconciled with the implications of the emerging architecture. Like Beethoven, Berlioz takes time to illustrate in music the broader context of individual words: "promisisti," for instance, which prompts the sensational six-voice cadence that closes the Offertoire (no. 7, mm. 137–45).

The Berlioz Requiem follows a harmonic scheme that opens in G minor and closes in G major, like *Harold en Italie*.[23] Much of the long Dies irae is in the general area of A minor and its relations, gently suggestive of the church modes. We become aware of the motion from B-flat to A as a prominent reference, motivically and harmonically, and are certain of it by the time it becomes the oscillating choral ostinato on those two pitches in the Offertory: Domine, Jesu Christe. In subsequent hearings, we may grasp subtler ways the chromaticism is woven in, or how, in the first movement, the opening melody is inverted to become the countersubject of the choral exposition and then the subject of the coda (see Example 4.2).

EXAMPLE 4.2 Berlioz, *Grande Messe des morts*, Requiem et Kyrie, inversions of opening melody.

The achieving of heavenly space is at issue all along, never more so than in the Offertoire and Sanctus. The Offertoire, an orchestral march–fugue with the text declaimed in cold, distant ostinato, is meant to suggest souls in Purgatory. (Berlioz returns to the same idea of fugue-with-ostinato in the funeral march in *Roméo et Juliette*, "Jetez des fleurs.") In the Sanctus, David Cairns reminds us, Berlioz composes out a defining moment of his childhood, his first communion at a convent-school, surrounded by "charming" girls dressed in white:

> As I took the sacrament a chorus of virginal voices broke into a eucharistic hymn. . . . I thought I saw Heaven open, a Heaven of love and chaste delight, a thousand times purer and more beautiful than the one I had been told about.[24]

The atmosphere, with angelic tenor soloist and women's chorus over strings in harmonics, subdivided into thirteen parts, is an original solution to the fraught problem of that *mise-en-scène*, just avoiding the saccharine and allowing the Osanna choruses of earthly praise, marching forward with the rank of trumpets and horns, their deserved focus.

In the Agnus Dei, Berlioz draws his arguments to a close in a splendid display of Romanticism's fascination with reminiscence and recall, and with Beethovenian tactics. Opening with the strange trombones-and-flute chords of the Hostias, it turns to a prominent recapitulation of the "Te decet hymnus" from the first movement, in its original key of B-flat major. The conclusion recalls at "quia pius es" the "fons pietatis" cadence of the Rex tremendae and, at the last Amens, the closing bars of the Introit and Kyrie (see Example 4.3). The timpani choirs, now tame and assured, have become celestial.

EXAMPLE 4.3 Berlioz, *Grande Messe des morts*, parallels between endings of Requiem et Kyrie and Agnus Dei.

1. Requiem et Kyrie

10. Agnus Dei

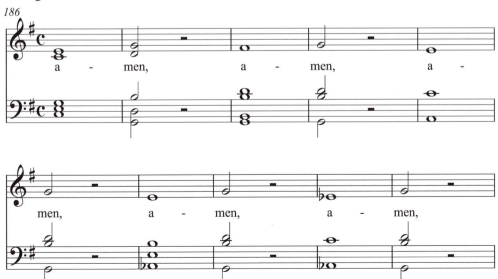

Be certain to note the delicacy; for instance, in the second strophe of the Sanctus with gentle punctuation of new strokes of the bass drum and cymbals, *pianissimo*. Berlioz's interest in how sound operates in its given space has been manifest from the first bars of the work, where the music seems to gather and rise from the venue itself. Each of the great climaxes is given the time and space to echo and clear. With the chords of trombones and flutes in the Hostias and Agnus Dei, the ear is drawn from the lowest orchestral register to the highest and back again. A more symbolic sort of space is at issue in the placement of the brass choirs around the perimeter of the force (north, east, west, and south, as specified in the score). This arrangement is particularly compelling in the Lacrymosa, where thrusts of brass from the compass points seem to give added momentum to an already grotesque dance of death.

Performance Considerations

Berlioz's performance materials ask for a chorus of at least eighty sopranos, sixty tenors, and seventy basses, with redoubled winds (hence 4–4–4–8 woodwinds, twelve horns, four trumpets, some dozen or more percussionists and more than 100 strings, 25–25–20–20–18)—plus the wrap-around brass groups. This makes for something like 200 each, chorus and orchestra, roughly doubling what was usually available in Paris for a big production. Even larger aggregations were possible, Berlioz imagined. In these cases the massed personnel would be reserved for the Dies irae, Rex tremendae, and Lacrymosa (movements 2, 4, and 6).

The central consideration for preparing the work, at least in the modern era of balanced four-part oratorio societies, is to achieve the necessary balance of two-thirds tenors and basses and one-third sopranos and altos. (The Sanctus has independent alto parts, for the angel-trio effects.) Use of the New Berlioz Edition materials, now twenty-five years old, corrects what was formerly the most common practical issue of offering the work: mismatched chorus and orchestra parts, with conflicting rehearsal numbers and letters. In the ubiquitous Schirmer vocal score of hallowed memory, prepared from the original Paris materials by Leopold Damrosch for his New York performances of the 1880s, the *a cappella* Quaerens me includes a passage Berlioz had deleted from the (slightly) revised second edition.

For what was often called the *concert monstre* Berlioz favored assistant conductors (sometimes pictured in newspaper illustrations from the era) as well as the *métronome électrique de Verbrugghen,* a giant pendulum controlled from the podium. Modern conveniences spare us both indignities, but often as not the placement of the bands has to be adjusted after the first general rehearsal owing to the realities of . . . architecture. Berlioz would have liked that.

What to make of Berlioz took a hundred years to sort out, as he predicted it might, and thus with the exception of Verdi's obvious reference to Berlioz,[25] the *Grande Messe des morts* served less as a model than a curiosity. The distinguished American theorist Edward T. Cone (1917–2004) laid the foundations for a comprehensive understanding of Berlioz's methods in work of the 1970s and 1980s, concurrent with the burst of musicological productivity that accompanied the 1969 centenary of the composer's death. Works like Julian Rushton's *The Music of Berlioz* (Oxford University Press, 2001) and Stephen Rodgers's *Form, Program, and Metaphor in the Music of Berlioz* (Cambridge University Press, 2009) have pretty well demystified matters. With Seiji Ozawa's dramatic programming of the Berlioz Requiem in the days after the terrorist attacks in September 2001, it achieved a talismanic stature. Having a reliable musical text and an increasingly sturdy performance history, it takes its place comfortably beside the *Missa solemnis* and "Symphony of a Thousand" as an ordinary part of the repertoire.

Johannes Brahms (1833–97): *Ein deutsches Requiem / A German Requiem, Op. 45*

nach Worten der Heiligen Schrift / on Words from Holy Scripture

1 Selig sind, die da Leid tragen ("Blessed are they that mourn") (Matthew 5:4. Psalms 126:5–6)
2 Denn alles Fleisch, es ist wie Gras ("For all flesh is like grass") (I Peter 1:24. James 5:7. Isaiah 35:10)
3 Herr, lehre doch mich ("Lord, make me to know mine end") (Psalms 39:5–8. Wisdom 3:1)
4 Wie lieblich sind deine Wohnungen, Herr Zebaoth! ("How lovely is Thy dwelling-place, O Lord of Hosts") (Psalms 84:2–3, 5)
5 Ihr habt nun Traurigkeit ("And ye now, therefore, have sorrow") (John 16:22. Ecclesiasticus 51:35. Isaiah 66:13)
6 Denn wir haben hie keine bleibende Statt ("For here have we no continuing city") (Hebrews 13:14. I Corinthians 15:51–55. Revelation 4:11)
7 Selig sind die Toten ("Blessed are the dead") (Revelation 14:13)

Duration	About 75 minutes.
For	Soloists (S., Bar.), chorus (SATB); piccolo, flutes I–II, oboes I–II, clarinets I–II, bassoons I–II, contrabassoon (*ad libitum*); horns I–IV, trumpets I–II, trombones I–III, tuba; timpani; harp (two players), organ (*ad libitum*); strings.
Text	In German from the Lutheran Bible; see below.
Composed	From 1865 to August 1866, mostly in Germany and Switzerland; autograph scored dated "Baden-Baden, summer [August 17] 1866." Revised May 1868 with the addition of no. 5, "Ihr habt nun Traurigkeit."
First Performed	April 10, 1868 (Good Friday), Bremen, by the Bremen Cathedral choir and orchestra; Brahms conducting. Earlier, the first three movements had been presented in Vienna: December 1, 1867, Gesellschaft der Musikfreunde, Johann Herbeck conducting. The new fifth movement was presented as a freestanding work in Zurich, September 17, 1868, Zurich Tonhalle Orchestra, Friedrich Hegar conducting. All seven movements first performed February 18, 1869, Leipzig Gewandhaus Orchestra and chorus, Carl Reinecke conducting.
Scores	• First published by J. Rieter-Biedermann (Leipzig, 1868). • Standard edition Leipzig: Breitkopf & Härtel, 1927 (Complete Works, vol. 17, ed. Eusebius Mandyczewski) = Dover, Kalmus, IMSLP. The vocal scores used most often by oratorio choruses are Peters Edition 3672, in continuous print since 1918 (after taking over Rieter-Biedermann), and G. Schirmer since 1877. For performances in English a vocal score edited by the legendary choral conductor Lara Hoggard (1915–2007) has gained currency (Chapel Hill: Hinshaw Music, 1984). • Scholarly edition: will be in series V of the Johannes Brahms Gesamtausgabe (Munich: G. Henle Verlag), the work of scholars led by Siegfried Oechsle at the musicology institute of the University of Kiel.
Further Reading	Steinberg, *Choral Masterworks*, 68–74. Summer, *Choral Masterworks from Bach to Britten*, 77–88. Green, *A Conductor's Guide*, 85–89. Michael Musgrave, *Brahms: A German Requiem,* a Cambridge Music Handbook (Cambridge University Press, 1996).

Also Leonard van Camp, *A Practical Guide for Performing, Teaching, and Singing the Brahms Requiem* (Lawson-Gould, 2002). Siegfried Ochs, "A German Requiem," etc., from *Der deustche Gesangverein* (1923–28) introduced and trans. Michael Musgrave, in *Performing Brahms,* ed. Musgrave and Bernard D. Sherman (Cambridge University Press, 2003), 155–69.

In its mastery of instrumental and choral sonority, clarity of declamation, pacing, and dense harmonic language, the *German Requiem* achieves a tautness of organization unparalleled in the literature for chorus and orchestra. Program notes commonly call this most familiar of all choral masterpieces Brahms's "largest." True enough, in terms of numbers of musicians summoned and minutes elapsed, but neither of those is especially large by the century's standards. Grandeur is hardly Brahms's purpose. Turning to his German bible and away from the fearsome Catholic "Dies irae," he assembles and then sets texts of reassurance, comfort to the living, trust in a heavenly resting place. The connotations of personal loss—his mentor Robert Schumann in 1856, his mother in early 1865—are sensed throughout the score. The success of the *German Requiem* at its Bremen premiere helped confirm Schumann's prediction of an heir to Beethoven and encouraged the composer along an ambitious trajectory of symphonic art. He was thirty-five.

Text

The poetic brilliance of the text as Brahms put it together redefined the concept of Requiem music, in no small measure by freeing it from the control of forms inherited with liturgy. His knowledge of Martin Luther's bible was thorough: his copy was at his bedside, read every day and copiously annotated. Choosing from gospels, psalms, prophecy, and apocrypha, Brahms linked sentiments separated by hundreds of pages, making them seem to grow naturally from one another. In the first movement, for instance, the themes of patience and promise are expressed with metaphors of sowing and reaping, one from the New Testament ("They that sow in tears shall reap in joy") and one from the Old ("He that goeth forth and weepeth, bearing precious seed, shall doubtless come again with rejoicing, bringing his sheaves with him").

As literature, the result is rich with nuance. Christ as a character goes unmentioned, but the first words are from the Sermon on the Mount. The hallucinatory images of apocalypse are generally avoided, but with an unmissable reference to the Last Trumpet (or trombone: *der letzten Posaune*) carefully positioned in the rhetoric. The dead go unmentioned, too, until the magnificent passage where the last movement opens "Selig sind die Toten," in response to the Beatitude heard at the very beginning. The words form a continuous libretto, with shape and sound that invite, though quietly acknowledging Requiem traditions, an altogether fresh musical response.

Composition and Performance

We first become aware of Brahms having undertaken a significant new project in April 1865, when he sends Clara Schumann a manuscript of the centerpiece movement, "Wie lieblich sind deine Wohnungen, Herr Zebaoth!," describing it as coming from "a kind of German Requiem."[26] Subsequent correspondence makes clear that the first two movements were also done. Completing the Requiem was the work of many more months, during which Brahms mentioned it only to his innermost circle of Clara and a very few others. It is as thought he sensed the intellectual turning point and needed to keep it to himself until its problems were identified and resolved.

Very much later, an acquaintance remembered how in the wake of Robert Schumann's suicide attempt in 1854 Brahms had begun a large instrumental work, a four-movement sonata for two pianos that then evolved into a symphony. This "sonata-symphony" in D minor was abandoned in the process of orchestration in 1856, the year of Schumann's death.[27] The first movement was diverted for the Piano Concerto No. 1 in D minor, Op. 15 (1857). The second, which he had variously described as a "slow scherzo" and a "sarabande," became the lugubrious dead-march of the Requiem: "Denn alles Fleisch," movement 2. Other friends (again, much later) drew a connection between the Requiem and the death of the composer's mother, Johanna Brahms, in February 1865: "we all think he wrote it in her memory," said Clara.[28]

Brahms reached the third movement in the spring of 1866 and that summer composed the last two movements of the six planned at the time, noting in his score its completion during "summer 1866, Baden-Baden"—where Clara Schumann had her villa. He presented her a finished manuscript vocal score on December 30.

Finished, that is, in its six-movement form. A new movement, "Ihr habt nun Traurigkeit" for solo soprano, was added (as no. 5) between the first performances and publication, its autograph manuscript dated May 24, 1868, in Hamburg. Brahms wrote Rieter-Biedermann to the effect that the new movement made the work "whole" (a truism in terms of balance alone).[29] When and why he chose this course of action involves a good deal of speculation. His handwritten text, on a single page, most likely comes from the summer of 1866 and possibly even earlier and seems to show that he had the "Traurigkeit" movement in mind all along.[30] But the order is different, and the correction to the Roman numerals that puts the fourth and fifth movements in their final position resists dating. One is inclined to accept the theory that Brahms had the full text in mind from the beginning, became reticent about setting these intimate and doubtless deeply felt verses, and was emboldened by the success of the first performances to go ahead with the original scheme.

The Requiem was a concert work, not in Latin and never intended for liturgical use. Brahms thus sought for the premiere a Protestant venue in north Germany. He found it at the Bremen Cathedral, in the region of his birth, where the chapelmaster Carl Reinthaler (1822–96) recognized exceptional achievement from the autograph score shown to him during the summer of 1867. But he urged Brahms to add at least some reference to a Christian's redemption in the crucifixion of Christ. (Brahms declined.) Reinthaler scheduled a Holy Week performance to benefit the widows and orphans fund and began rehearsals in February 1868.

Meanwhile the work had been sought out for performance in Vienna by the Gesellschaft der Musikfreunde under Johann Herbeck (1831–77). (Brahms would soon be president of this venerable philharmonic society.) Herbeck, who had premiered Schubert's "Unfinished" Symphony in December 1865, was unwilling to risk the whole work, instead putting three movements on a program with Schubert's *Rosamunde* music. At the performance on December 1, 1867, the timpanist, misreading the *fp* in his part, thundered through the closing fugue of the third movement, with which the concert ended. Brahms's appearance onstage was greeted with sustained applause from some quarters of the house, hisses from others. Joachim wrote his wife praising the "loftiness and originality" of the new work.[31]

Brahms arrived in Bremen for the last week of rehearsals, followed by Joachim and his wife, the singer Amalie Weiss. Clara came in during the dress rehearsal: "As I saw Johannes standing there, baton in hand, I could not help thinking of my dear Robert's prophecy, 'Let him but once grasp his magic wand and work with orchestra and chorus,' which is fulfilled today. . . . It was a joy such as I have not felt for a long time."[32] Since the occasion was a Good Friday *Geistliches Konzert,* a *concert spirituel,* the notable absence of references to Christ was corrected with the insertion of a Passion-themed segment of works featuring Joachim and Weiss. Among these was "I Know That

My Reedemer Liveth" from Handel's *Messiah*,[33] very possibly providing Brahms the stimulus to finish with the "Traurigkeit" movement. The noted baritone Julius Stockhausen (1826–1906) sang poorly owing to an indisposition. Public reception was nevertheless strong, and from this milepost the Brahms Requiem went on to claim an increasingly significant place in the standard concert repertoire.

"Ihr habt nun Traurigkeit" was offered in Zurich at the end of the summer, and the seven-movement definitive version of the whole work presented at a Leipzig Gewandhaus concert the following February. In this temple of European orchestra music the first piano concerto had failed a decade before. Now the Requiem was initially greeted with reserve (as "too contemplative") but not outright hostility. Within months it had gone on to earn Brahms a reliable Leipzig following.[34]

Structure

The Brahms Requiem leaves no doubt as to how *composed* a work it is. Its symmetries play out from several vantage points, most notably in the structural arch, with balanced solo movements (nos. 3 and 5), extravagant tableaux (2 and 6), and Beatitudes ("Selig sind," 1 and 7) around a conceptual centerpiece, "Wie lieblich sind deine Wohnungen" (no. 4). A clearly sensed root gesture, F–A–B-flat, sometimes called the "Selig" motive, permeates the work. Example 4.4 suggests some of the ways it operates.[35]

EXAMPLE 4.4 Brahms, *Ein deutsches Requiem*, selected uses of the "Selig" motive.

1. Selig sind, die da Leid tragen

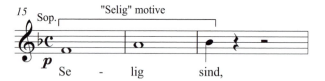

2. Denn alles Fleisch est ist wie Gras

3. Herr, lehre doch mich

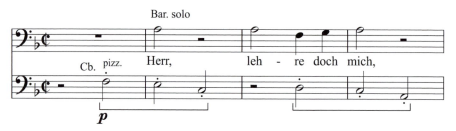

EXAMPLE 4.4 continued

dass ein En - de mit mir ha - ben muss.

4. Wie lieblich sind deine Wohnungen

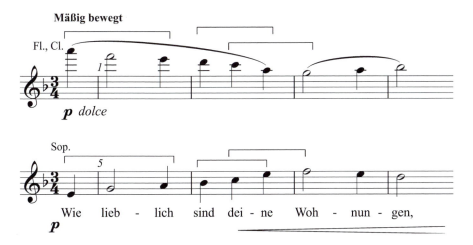

Wie lieb - lich sind dei - ne Woh - nun - gen,

6. Denn wir haben hie keine bleibende Statt

Herr, du bist wür - dig zu

neh - men Preis und Eh - re und Kraft.

Brahms brought to the project his affection for Baroque precedents: Heinrich Schütz and his German-language Requiem, the Lutheran chorale, and certainly the cantatas of J. S. Bach, which had been appearing in the Bach-Gesellschaft edition since 1851. The music also suggests its composer's knowledge of Cherubini's Requiem in C minor (1816, memorializing Louis XVI) as well as the *Missa solemnis*. Brahms hinted to a friend that the second movement and the first bars of the first movement were based on "a well-known chorale."[36] This has been taken to be "Wer nur den lieben Gott lässt walten" ("Whoever lets only dear God reign"), used by Bach in Cantata 27, also a reflection on death and resurrection: *Wer weiss, wie nahe mir mein Ende!* ("Who knows how near is my end!") (see Example 4.5).

EXAMPLE 4.5   Chorale melodies in Bach Cantata No. 27, *Wer weiss, wie nahe mir mein Ende!* and Brahms, *Ein deutsches Requiem*, "Denn alles Fleisch, es ist wie Gras."

Bach: Cantata 27, movt. 1

Brahms: Requiem, movt. 2

The matchless opening of the first movement, with violas and cellos divided into four parts over throbbing Fs in bass and French horns, introduces one of the Beatitudes of Christ ("Blessed are they that mourn, for they shall be comforted") sung at first unaccompanied in the chorus. The orchestration, without violins, is reminiscent of the Serenade No. 2 in A, Op. 16 of 1859, which likewise lacks violins (and is dedicated to Clara Schumann). The harps enter just before the end, and the chorus reiterates the important words "getröstet werden" through the short codetta, in ongoing reassurance.

Two bars of unison F–B-flat in bassoons and low strings draw away from F major and into the somber strains of the second movement. This unveils one of Brahms's most profound accomplishments: haunting of key (B-flat minor, five flats), violins and violas subdivided into three parts each, over a relentless tattoo in the timpani. It is the only movement to use the entire force, including contrabassoon, trombones, harps, and the organ. The chorus presents the chorale theme in unison, "Behold all flesh is as the grass": softly at first, then as the culmination of a magnificent crescendo. The dirge is offset at the center with the passage (G-flat major, six flats; m. 75) urging patience in the manner of a farmer awaiting the rain ("Morgenregen und Abendregen," evoked by the flute and harp), then recapitulates. The chorus, now stentorian of voice, reminds us that the Lord's word endures forever ("Aber des Herrn Wort bleibet in Ewigkeit"), and a jubilant fugal march in B-flat major celebrates the arrival of the chosen at a place of joy and gladness.

The baritone soliloquy (movement 3) returns to the D-minor key and duple meter in what amounts to another dark march, as the singer / psalmist contemplates his own end. It is a continuous train of thought: All is vanity; our only hope is in the Lord, where no harm can befall us. "Der Gerechten Seelen sind in Gottes Hand," proclaims the great choral fugue at the end (m. 173): "the souls of the righteous are in God's hands." Here eighteen pages, thirty-six bars of double fugue at multiple metric levels, play out over the single pitch D in the bass instruments, a musical symbol of the steadfastness of God's protection (see Example 4.6).

EXAMPLE 4.6 Brahms, *Ein deutsches Requiem*, "Herr, lehre doch mich," closing fugue subject.

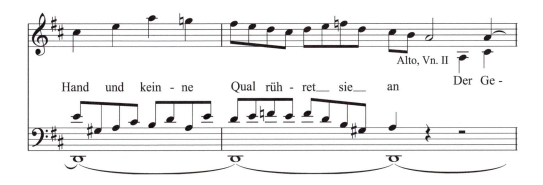

For most music lovers the fourth movement, with its beautiful English incipit "How Lovely is Thy Dwelling Place," is among the most perfect (and most familiar) miniatures in the choral repertoire. The rise from the prevailing D tonalities into E-flat major here defines a powerful change of scene. Despite the harp-like figurations, the harps remain silent; Brahms goes out of his way to assure that his evocation of the heavenly apartments is innocent, joyous, and above all dignified. We grasp spontaneously that we are at the center of a carefully crafted form, and become increasingly sensitive to elegance of the architecture as the work enters its second half.

The briefest and most intimate of the movements is the soprano aria (no. 5), in a G major that maintains the innocent character of the previous movement and a pristine A–B–A form. The sonority is unique to this movement, with muted strings and tender woodwind interplay; the principal melody is that of the muted violins at the beginning. At length, the soprano gathers this up, too (m. 62), over an augmentation of the same figure in the chorus beneath (see Example 4.7).

The huge movement that follows, another cortège of minor key (no. 6), nearly outweighs the second movement, with which it is paired in the structure. Here the baritone soloist recalls the mystery of resurrection ("all changed in a moment, in the twinkling of an eye") and references the

EXAMPLE 4.7   Brahms, *Ein deutsches Requiem*, "Ihr habt nun Traurigkeit."

last trumpet, thus introducing a diabolical dance of death for the full ensemble (m. 82). The great C-major cadence for "where is thy sting?," reached after a hair-raising journey from C minor through E major, introduces the long concluding fugue in slow note values, reminiscent of the white-note fugues of Bach and Handel.

Brahms closes the Requiem with the first-movement Beatitude transformed into the language of Revelation: "Blessed are the dead: they rest from their labors, and their work follows after them." Just toward the end comes a direct musical quotation from the first movement, momentarily disorienting in an E-flat major that sets up the long modulation to the celestial F-major close.

Performance

The words "ad libitum" for the contrabassoon and pipe organ must be ignored, since both instruments are vital to the argument. (There is evidence to support adding organ pedal to the prolonged D in the second-movement fugue.) Two harps playing one part is the custom of the time. Brahms left metronome markings for the six original movements but asked that they be removed from the published score, owing to his general distrust of the concept and because the work had achieved a proper performance tradition in short order.[37]

Predating the First Symphony, the Requiem calls for the fullest orchestra for which Brahms had so far composed. We have a general indication of the forces expected for the first performance in terms of the number of parts ordered: some 200 vocal scores and twelve of each string part, thus a relatively large conventional orchestra and concert-sized chorus. The materials used in the Vienna performances have been preserved,[38] along with commentary from Brahms and his contemporaries on what had been right and wrong in the concerts.

Americans typically encounter the Brahms Requiem in English, as sung by church choirs. The familiar English translation was prepared early on by E. (Elizabeth) M. Traquair, a British versifier of the 1870s, revised shortly afterward by the cleric R. H. (Hugh) Benson for the London Peters edition. It has long been respected as "close to the original, . . . close also to Brahms's placing of the syllables, and lastly it is good English and sings well."[39]

Tranquair / Benson:

How lovely is thy dwelling place, O Lord of hosts!
For my soul, it longeth, yea fainteth,
For the courts of the Lord.
My soul and body crieth out, yea for the living God.

King James version:

1   How amiable are thy tabernacles, O LORD of hosts!
2   My soul longeth, yea, even fainteth for the courts of the LORD:
    my heart and my flesh crieth out for the living God.

What irritates conductors about such translations is how they require altering the original note values to accommodate the English. Lara Hoggard argues (on behalf of his own translation) that Benson's subtle effort to Christianize the text is odious.[40] Influential conductors continue to insist that a work with this level of poetic intensity and spiritual importance profits from being offered in the language of the public, so the tinkering goes on.

The recorded performances document a wide latitude of approach, from old-school offerings in the Vienna–Berlin tradition (Wilhelm Furtwängler / Stockholm Philharmonic, live 1948; Otto Klemperer / Philharmonia, 1961, with Elisabeth Schwartzkopf and Dietrich Fischer-Dieskau; Bruno Walter / New York Philharmonic, 1954) to younger versions on older instruments, generally faster and seeking to shed weight (John Eliot Gardiner / Orchestre Révolutionnaire et Romantique and Monteverdi Choir, 1991; Roger Norrington / London Classical Players, 1992).[41] In America, the Robert Shaw legend is in a way capped by the Brahms Requiem, said to have been his favorite work and from whom we have a tender performance from Atlanta (Telarc, 1990). Shaw also chose the Brahms Requiem to inaugurate the Robert Shaw Choral Workshop series at Carnegie Hall, begun during the centennial season, 1990–91, and continuing to the present under Shaw's successor Norman Mackenzie.

Reception

Public and critical response to Brahms is a fraught, sometimes painful saga. It began that way, when Schumann penned his famous essay "Neue Bahnen" for the first number of his *Neue Zeitschrift für Musik,* announcing Brahms as successor to Beethoven.[42] The Brahms / Wagner opposition set in motion by the Viennese critic Edward Hanslick (1825–1904) was soft to begin with but has held sway anyhow, and on into the present. Already in his review of the Vienna performance, Hanslick associates Brahms with Bach and Beethoven at the pinnacle of sacred music. Audiences, however, often found Brahmsian argument abstruse and therefore difficult, and public resistance to Brahms carried into the mid-twentieth century. With the Franco-Prussian War and establishment of a German empire (1871), just as the Requiem was drawing international note, it inevitably became weighed down with the baggage of nationalism. With the word "German" in the title, it was easy to code as academic, wearying.

To George Bernard Shaw, for instance, the Requiem was "execrably and ponderously dull."[43] Michael Musgrave, scholarly author of the useful Cambridge companion, notes early on its reputation for "a certain stolidity and worthiness."[44] It is, for certain, a *German* Requiem, and that puts it squarely in the lineage that favors solemn, sometimes even stern pronouncements and purposefully seeks Gothic severities in high counterpoint. My colleague Kurt Rohde, a brilliant composer, confesses to losing sleep over Brahms, whose music he still finds enigmatic: over-argued but seductive, near-perfect after all, and the anchor of post-Beethovenian discourse.

Giuseppe Verdi (1813–1901): *Messa da Requiem*

for the anniversary of the death of Manzoni, May 22, 1874

1   Introit: Requiem—Kyrie eleison
2   Prosa: Dies irae
      Dies irae—Tuba mirum—Liber scriptus—Quid sum miser—
      Rex tremendae—Recordare—Ingemisco—Confutatis—Lacrymosa
3   Offertorium: Domine Jesu Christe
4   Sanctus
5   Agnus Dei
6   Communion: Lux aeterna
7   Absolution: Libera me

Duration	About 90 minutes.
For	Soloists (S Mez T B), chorus (SATB, divided into two choruses for the Sanctus); piccolo, flutes I–II, oboes I–II, clarinets I–II, bassoons I–IV; horns I–IV, trumpets I–IV, offstage trumpets I–IV, trombones I–III, ophicleide; timpani; bass drum; strings.
Text	The Roman Catholic Requiem Mass and Office responsory (Libera me).
Composed	Early 1874 for performance on the first anniversary of the death of Alessandro Manzoni in May. In November 1874 Verdi notified correspondents of his intent to rewrite the Liber scriptus, dispatching it to his publisher on February 6, 1875.
First Performed	In the Church of San Marco, Milan, on May 22, 1874, the composer conducting a festival ensemble; soloists Teresa Stolz, Maria Waldmann, Giuseppe Capponi, Ormondi Maini. Repeated at La Scala on May 25, 27, and 29, Verdi conducting the first of these. The first performance with rewritten Liber scriptus was May 15, 1875, in the Royal Albert Hall, London, Verdi conducting.
Scores	• First published, in vocal score, by Ricordi (Milan, 1874; as amended, 1875). The full score was available only on hire, hence not published. • Standard editions Eulenburg pocket score, ed. Fritz Stein (1910) = IMSLP; and Peters full score, ed. Kurt Soldan (1937). The standard vocal scores in use have been those of Peters, Novello (1956), and Ricordi. • Scholarly edition in *Works of Giuseppe Verdi,* series III, no. 1, ed. David Rosen (Ricordi / University of Chicago Press, 1990).
Further Reading	Steinberg, *Choral Masterworks,* 301–10. Summer, *Choral Masterworks from Bach to Britten,* 89–99. Green, *A Conductor's Guide,* 321–25. David Rosen, *Verdi: Requiem,* a Cambridge Music Handbook (Cambridge University Press, 1995).

Much as we never tire of Shakespeare's *Romeo and Juliet,* we savor repeated hearings of the Verdi Requiem, not only for its altogether human response to a terrifying text, but also for bringing serious Italian repertoire across the street, from the opera house to the concert hall. The sonic imagery—the bass drummer's infernal strokes, the contralto proffering a book in which everything is written, the soprano trembling in fear at the very end—is second to none.

A Requiem for Rossini

In the aftermath of Rossini's death (November 13, 1868, in Paris[45]) Verdi proposed that a Requiem Mass, a *Messa per Rossini,* be prepared by a collective of Italian composers and performed in Bologna on the first anniversary of his death, the traditional occasion in Europe for unveiling monuments and literary tributes. Verdi admitted the drawbacks of the scheme in his prospectus—"it will necessarily lack musical unity"—and proposed that after the memorial performance the manuscripts be sealed away in the archives of the local conservatory.[46] The score, with contributions by thirteen Italian composers (all of them reputable at the time, none but Verdi remembered today), was completed in due course. But the performance was abandoned owing to organizational and contractual dilemmas, an inept conductor (according to Verdi), and Verdi's own disinclination to attend. His contribution had been the Libera me, occupying the place of honor at the end.[47]

With *Aida* (1871) Verdi, approaching sixty, had meant to be done with the hurly-burly of composing operas and seeing them through to public productions. It was to take a conspiracy of his wife, his publisher, the composer–librettist Arrigo Boito, and Shakespeare to return him to the stage, with *Otello* (1887) and *Falstaff* (1893).

Alessandro Manzoni

Alessandro Manzoni (1785–1873) was author of the three-volume historical novel *I promessi sposi* (The Betrothed, 1827), widely deemed the great Italian novel. Manzoni's work shaped the modern language and, with its ongoing allusions to the scourge of Austrian empire, was seen—like Verdi's *Nabucco*—as a touchstone of the nationalist movement. On the occasion of his death, May 22, 1873, Verdi reacted as he had for Rossini five years before, the only way he knew how, by going back to his desk. At Manzoni's graveside he resolved to compose a full Requiem Mass to be ready in time for the first anniversary memorials a year later. "It is a heartfelt impulse, or rather a necessity," he wrote, "to do all in my power to honor this great spirit whom I valued so highly as a writer and venerated as a man."[48]

He adopted the same Latin text that had been prescribed for the Rossini Mass. His due diligence included reviewing precedent works from the Italian school: Requiems by Cherubini and Donizetti. Much of this was done in Paris, adopted home of Cherubini and Rossini, where the Verdis sojourned in the summer of 1873. With an unyielding deadline before him, Verdi composed in his typically focused, prodigious manner, drawing the Libera me for Rossini into his score, as well as, for the Lacrymosa, a duet cut from the French *Don Carlos* (1867: the Act IV duet of King Philip and Don Carlos, "Qui me rendra ce mort"). Once the singers were engaged, he nudged the music into place for their specific voices: a high C for Teresa Stolz (1834–1902; not to be confused with the French diva Rosine Stoltz), rich mezzo work for Maria Waldmann (1864–1920). Stolz and Waldmann had been Aida and Amneris in the Milan *Aida* and were Verdi's favorites at the time. (Waldmann was paid more for her participation than the bill for the entire orchestra.) Shortly after the premiere, he replaced the choral Liber scriptus with a solo for Waldmann, the finest vocal writing, I believe, in the long Dies irae.

Early Performances

Verdi was determined that the first performance would take place on the proper anniversary date, in Milan, and in a cathedral acoustic. The Milan cathedral was out of the question owing to its unwillingness to welcome the Roman text in the home of the Ambrosian rite.[49] Verdi ended up choosing the Chiesa San Marco, where there was a willing young priest to sponsor it. Even at St.

Mark's it was necessary to have the women "hidden by a grate work, off to one side, or something similar," and they were to be in long black dresses with head covered by "an ample mourning veil."[50]

The city council, asked to subvention the memorial event, questioned both the principle and the expense. "It is not a question of Masses or of ceremonies," replied the composer Boito in his capacity as member of the council, "but one of higher and greater importance: a matter of civic honor," and his argument carried the day.[51] The soloists assembled in Milan on May 2; the chorus began to work on the 3rd. The Requiem was ready on schedule three weeks later. Manzoni's commemoration at St. Mark's was a true church service: a celebrant sang Ambrosian plainchant between the movements of Verdi's composition.

The Milan performances cleared a profit, split between the city and Verdi's publisher Tito Ricordi, to whom he had sold the rights for a handsome sum and favorable royalty arrangement. Critical reception was for the most part positive. Ricordi, tightly controlling access to the work, sent Verdi to conduct it in Paris, where it earned multiple and hence lucrative performances, and arranged a New York premiere with an Italian conductor (Academy of Music, November 17, 1874). The next year Verdi toured with the Requiem to Paris again, then to London and Vienna; the rewritten Liber scriptus was introduced in London. He conducted the Requiem again in Paris in 1876, Cologne 1877 (for the popular Lower Rhine Music Festival), and one last time at La Scala in 1879.

Organization

One of the features shared by the Mozart, Berlioz, and Verdi Requiems is the last-movement reprise of material presented in the first. For Verdi this and several other forms of internal repetition are critical tactics, since he makes no effort to impose an overall key scheme on the seven movements. Witnessing his work in some ways brings the same pleasure as Mahler's Eighth: both examples reveal an acknowledged late-career master at his craft—a redoubled pleasure, in this case, since Verdi is unburdened by operatic offal such as getting the players on and offstage, providing the requisite hierarchy of materials for the stars, coping with the librettist. He seems thoroughly untroubled by the imposed text.

Like Berlioz, he begins by claiming the cavernous, silent venue for the music, the chorus murmuring in prayer while the orchestra states the primary material. The initial A minor lifts into A major for the tender violin lyric that emerges at the words "et lux perpetua." The psalm verse ("A hymn, O Lord, becometh Thee in Zion," m. 28) occasions a bold fugal statement from unaccompanied chorus, soon receding into the opening gestures. Verdi introduces the soloists in the Kyrie eleison and as the forces swell to the first huge climax, we begin to be aware of all the power pent up in the performing force and about to be fully unleashed.

The centerpiece of Verdi's conception of the Requiem text, and of this massive second movement that constitutes nearly half the work, is the apocalyptic image with which it begins: with bass-drum explosions and passagework fleeing it every direction—the Devil chasing you with a big stick, as David Cairns has it. Trumpets on and offstage introduce the Tuba mirum, Berlioz-fashion: Verdi almost certainly knew this passage from the excerpt that had been published in Berlioz's orchestration treatise.[52] The bass, like an emissary of death, has the first solo, at the words "Mors stupebit." Then comes the mezzo's chilling aria on the proffering of the Book of the Dead (Liber scriptus), in which all things are written, nothing hidden. At the center of the movement the soprano joins the mezzo-soprano for the Recordare, with its striking cello-dominated climax; there follow the big solos for tenor (Ingemisco, a plea to be numbered not with the goats but among the lambs) and bass (Confutatis maledictis, begging to be spared from the acrid flame of Judgment Day).

Fine trio and quartet passages are interspersed, and, in the profound chorus tuttis of the Salve me and Lacrymosa, spellbinding supplication and lament. The menu of fascinating ideas seems inexhaustible: the trio with bassoon obbligato, for instance, for Quid sum miser. Fine orchestra writing is to be found in the operas, too, but here we pay much closer attention.

A thorough change of atmosphere for the Offertory, Domine Jesu Christe, helps divert our attention from the immensity of the 30-minute tableau just concluded. This is a barcarolle for the soloist voices and cello, with the long-delayed soprano entry emphasizing the rise of tonality and wonderful image of the archangel Michael, God's standard bearer, leading the faithful toward eternal light. A surging minor-mode Quam olim Abrahae promisisti is introduced in close imitation, interrupted by the Hostias for tenor, *dolce* and in C major. Quam olim Abrahae recapitulates in the manner of the liturgical source, but since the movement cannot properly end in F minor, Verdi returns to close with the original barcarolle figure and key of A-flat.

An excited trumpet fanfare announces the Sanctus. Here the singers are redistributed into two choirs for a double fugue where the two subjects are treated simultaneously in the opposing choirs; in the counterpoint of rapid eighth-notes for strings (violin I, mm. 10–13, for example) is hidden the chromatic scamper that becomes (m. 127) the climax of the movement (see Example 4.8).

EXAMPLE 4.8 Verdi, Requiem, Sanctus, mm. 9–12.

Three of the four clauses of text (Sanctus, Osanna, Benedictus) come in the main statement; "Pleni sunt coeli," where the volume retreats and the note values augment into whole- and half-notes, uses the same melody. The second Osanna grows into dazzling unison chromatic scales at the end, with trombones and tuba.

The verse structure of the Agnus Dei implies for Verdi three delicately varied strophes, all soft, with choral responses and woodwind filigree. An atmospheric Lux aeterna, in B-flat major, strongly foreshadows the orchestral idiom of *Otello*—stars and moonlight in the opera, heavenly light here—with soft tremolo of strings divided into six voices and more. The bass intones the words "Requiem aeternam" as a death knell in B-flat minor, with divided timpani, four bassoons in their lowest register, three trombones, and ophicleide. This is softened by rain-like figuration in the upper octaves: note the descending chromatics, mirroring the rising ones at the end of the Sanctus.

The soprano has been left out of the Lux aeterna because the Libera me is to be hers. She is overcome with hellish presentiments, and the choir attempts to quell her frenzied parlando with *pianissimo* answers. But then her arioso is interrupted with a reprise of the Dies irae figure, bass drum and all, as she seeks her place among the saved. The image subsides, replaced by a return of the Requiem aeternam text and the orchestral opening of the first movement, now sung instead of played (m. 132). Her parlando breaks out again, met this time with the big closing fugue Libera me, in C minor, where the theme is a mirror of the Sanctus fugue. The grand *tutta forza* at the end dissolves away to a close in C major, leaving the soprano, at the bottom of her range, still atremble.

Think now about the fact that the substance of this Libera me had already been composed before Verdi came to write the rest. Chronologically, then, the opening bars of the work in fact started here, as did the bass-drum Dies irae, and the subject of the Sanctus fugue (inverted from Libera me). The mirror has two faces.

Performance

Verdi conducted the Requiem a total of nine times, by my count, always, after the first performance, as a concert work. Customarily there were 120–200 in the chorus and about 100 members in the orchestra (sixty strings: five sections of twelve). The sopranos and altos were grown women, as in an opera chorus. "I do not favor boys," Verdi had written.[53]

The Italian orchestra of the epoch remained in flux, especially in the low instruments. Four bassoons were customary, and among the splendid bassoon passages in the Requiem is a quartet of them in the Libera me.[54] Various models of trombones, including valved ones, were to be found in north Italy, and generally unsatisfactory instruments for the lowest brass line, here calling for ophicleide. Three-string double basses, stopping at low G, were still common. None of this (nor the call for a low piccolo in B-flat) adversely affects performance with modern orchestra, where ordinary solutions can account for all the required pitches. The question of cymbals is more nuanced. Italian opera practice of the time relied heavily on bass drum with attached cymbal played by a single player, so there is some possibility cymbals were heard in the early performances.

Verdi's metronome marks are authentic, but we also know that he was given to conducting with considerable rubato. He took an intermission after the Dies irae, and in proper nineteenth-century tradition granted movement encores during the performance. Among these was the Agnus Dei, played twice at the first performance.

Two generations of Verdi specialists, and the impressive Verdi edition co-published by Ricordi and the University of Chicago Press, have sharpened our understanding of his life and our appreciation for his work. The American scholar David Rosen, for instance, wrote his doctoral dissertation on the Verdi Requiem, prepared the heavy scholarly edition in three volumes, and wrote the Cambridge Handbook. In these resources may be found almost anything you would want to know, including the original Libera me for the Rossini Mass, and the choral Liber scriptus from 1874. Italian performance traditions are well documented in the several recordings left by Toscanini and in those of the more recent *maestri*: Claudio Abbado, Carlo-Maria Giulini, and Riccardo Muti.

Critique of the Requiem devotes inordinate time and space to the matter of genre, and to the distinctions implied by the words "dramatic," "theatric," and "operatic." Hans von Bülow, the distinguished conductor and great Wagnerian, put a memorable early spin on the work, describing it as "an opera in church clothes." (Much later he apologized to Verdi for so rash and juvenile a remark, to which Verdi responded to the effect that "he might have been right."[55]) To deconstruct the vectors between church and opera house, leaving out the concert hall, is in any event to miss the obvious. Verdi's principal store of compositional device was by definition operatic, with all that says of his awareness of the public and his ability to deploy a large force. Hanslick soon recognized that "usefulness to the church" was beside the point (and not just for Verdi). This was a work of "free art," crowning Verdi's greatness and putting him firmly in the company of the symphonists whose work peppers these pages: Mozart, Brahms, Berlioz, and Mahler.

Gabriel Fauré (1845–1924): Requiem, Op. 48

1   Introit et Kyrie
2   Offertoire
3   Sanctus
4   Pie Jesu
5   Agnus Dei et Lux aeterna
6   Libera me
7   In Paradisum

Duration	About 40 minutes.
For	Soloists (S, Bar.), chorus (SATB), and orchestra. The 1893 version (church version): divided strings (violas I–II, cellos I–II, basses), harp, organ, with horns I–II, trumpets I–II, timpani, and solo violin in the Sanctus. The 1900 version (concert version): flutes I–II, clarinets I–II, bassoons I–II; horns I–IV, trumpets I–II, trombones I–III; timpani; harps (one part, two players); organ; strings (violins, violas I–II, cellos I–II, basses).
Text	The Roman Catholic Requiem Mass, Office responsory (Libera me), and burial service (In Paradisum).
Composed	October 1887–89. January 1888 for church performance with small forces. The soprano solo Pie Jesu and baritone aria Libera me (first composed for baritone and organ, 1877) added by 1893. Re-orchestrated for publication with full orchestra, 1900.
First Performed	January 16, 1888, for a funeral at the Church of the Madeleine, Paris, Fauré conducting. The seven-movement smaller version first performed January 21, 1893 at the Madeleine, Fauré conducting. The concert version first performed in Liège (April 6, 1900) and Brussels (April 9, 1900), Eugène Ysaÿe, conducting; then July 2, 1900 at the Palais du Trocadéro by the Lamoureux orchestra and chorus, Paul Taffanel conducting.
Scores	• First published J. Hamelle (Paris, 1900 [vocal score] and 1901 [full score and parts]).
	• Standard edition of the "concert version": Hamelle 1900–01 = Kalmus, Dover, IMSLP. On the smaller versions and on John Rutter's edition of 1984, see below.
	• Scholarly editions. The foundational scholarship on the sources for Fauré's Requiem was that of the French musicologist Jean-Michel Nectoux, leading to publication of new scores by the original Paris publisher: church version, ed. Nectoux and Roger Delage (Hamelle, 1994); concert version of 1900 (Hamelle, 1998). The newest critical edition is that of Christina M. Stahl and Michael Stegemann, in *Gabriel Fauré: Œuvres complètes,* vol. I/2 (Bärenreiter-Verlag, 2011); includes facsimile of the autograph score.[56]
Further Reading	Steinberg, *Choral Masterworks,* 131–37. Summer, *Choral Masterworks from Bach to Britten,* 119–25. Green, *A Conductor's Guide,* 174–79.

Fauré's altogether unique Requiem was composed for no particular individual or event, but rather to express his view of death as a "happy deliverance, a yearning for the happiness of the beyond, rather than a distressing passing-on." He worked "for the enjoyment of it, if I may so express myself," and as antidote to a lifetime of "accompanying burial services on the organ. I couldn't stand it any longer!"[57] Fluently composed in the closing weeks of 1887 and first week of January 1888, the new Requiem was used for a funeral a week later, that of the Joseph Lesoufaché, on January 16, 1888. (Program notes always identify him as "an architect." He was considerably more than that: student of Charles Garnier, a noted city planner, and a great bibliophile, whose magnificent collection of books and prints is now in a room at the École des Beaux-Arts that bears his name.) In this form the work had four movements—Introit and Kyrie, Sanctus, Agnus Dei, and In Paradisum—offered by an all-male choir of about thirty, organ, and violas and cellos. He called it *mon petit Requiem*.[58] *Une berceuse de la mort,* "Death's lullaby," said a third party, in a formulation that caught on.[59]

From this simple basic form, the Requiem grew over the course of multiple church services, mutating in instrumentation and content as it aged, and in 1900 was converted at the publisher's suggestion into a concert version in full orchestral dress. This proved to have been an excellent idea, for the Requiem as published established Fauré's reputation in the world at large by claiming a space in the concert hall, where it tended to have better performances. One result of this genesis was to leave behind stacks of source materials, scores and parts, with conflicting readings. It is in the nature of church music to change as it goes: in that respect cantatas are not so different from Broadway shows. In the case of the Fauré Requiem, at least, there is an autograph score showing the various levels of the composer's work. But there is virtually no indication of Fauré's involvement in the published full score except for a copy of the proof marked in his hand *bon à tirer* ("good to go") but nevertheless rife with error.

For our purposes it makes sense to think in terms of two milepost conditions of the work: the finished smaller version of 1893 (called by Richard Langham Smith the "parish" version, "inflated" into seven movements[60]) and the concert version published in 1900–01.

Fauré's Requiem omits the Dies irae, molten core of the Requiem masses of Mozart, Berlioz, and Verdi. The imagery here is, instead, of untroubled slumber: that Fauré lingers again and again on the word "requiem," Latin for "rest," is no coincidence, nor is the predominance of movements with serene texts (Sanctus, Pie Jesu, Agnus Dei, In Paradisum). There's something personal, unpublic, about Fauré's accomplishment, a Requiem for everyman.

The Versions

The original four movements heard in 1888 were the Introit-Kyrie, Sanctus, Agnus, and In Paradisum, with organ and low strings; a solo violin appeared in the Sanctus. In subsequent performances, the horn-and-trumpet fanfare was introduced in the Hosanna, and horns, trumpets, and trombones for Libera me. There is evidence Fauré used two bassoons whenever they were available.

In early 1889, the baritone solo Hostias was added, followed by the O Domine; together these form the Offertoire—at least that is the inference of seeing the great baritone Numa Auguez (1847–1903) listed for a performance on February 13, 1889. Shortly thereafter Fauré wrote to the Countess Greffulhe that with its Hostias his Requiem was complete. But once having added a baritone soloist, it made sense to draw in a Libera me he had composed in 1877 for baritone and orchestra. The finished, seven-movement "smaller" version offered at the Madeleine in January 1893 indisputably represents the composer's "intent" as of the 1890s.

Julien Hamelle, who published the work, cultivated Fauré along with d'Indy, Lalo, and Widor as avatars of the future.[61] A contract for the Requiem was signed in September 1899 and the composer's pupil Jean Roger-Ducasse (1873–1954) put to the work of reducing a vocal score. Simultaneously Hamelle pushed for a larger, more commercial orchestration. It is now commonly accepted that Roger-Ducasse did some or all of the big orchestration, adding flutes, clarinets, and violins. In 1901, Ducasse wrote a friend that "Fauré has just come by with his orchestration,"[62] but by then the vocal score, reduced from some full orchestra score, now missing, had already appeared. The score and parts show mismatched bowings, dynamics, phrases, and slurs, and plenty of wrong notes.

The "concert version" as published got good exposure at turn-of-century festivals in Liège and Brussels in April 1900. On July 12, 1900, it figured in an official concert of the great Paris *Exposition universelle,* held in the Palais du Trocadéro, with its Cavaillé-Coll pipe organ, overlooking the Eiffel Tower across the river. There were 250 performers; admission went from 50 centimes to 2 francs. The following season it was premiered to the discriminating public of the Conservatoire concerts during the Good Friday *concert spirituel,* April 5, 1901. For a work to be included in a Conservatoire concert (on this occasion in the company of music by Handel, Beethoven, and Mendelssohn) was universally acknowledged in Paris, and had been since the 1830s, as the canonizing moment—the arrival in Music's Louvre.

Character and Structure

Fauré assembles a sound world as inviting as it is unprecedented in the major literature, gentle ("as I myself am," he said[63]) and purposefully naive. In voice it manages to convey our common smallness in the face of loss, the ordinary welling up of emotion in its search for the promises of faith. The effect is quite different from the one Brahms achieves in the *German Requiem,* though the underlying point of view is much the same. (You cannot help wondering whether Fauré had Brahms in the back of his mind as he composed.) Long unison lines, often in the tenors (the opening of the Agnus Dei, for instance), strike the ear as deeply personal, the prevailing instrumental sonority of two viola and two cello parts as humanizing. It is a soothing effect.

Nor are the other elements of composition especially complex. The work opens in D minor and closes in well under an hour by recalling the initial passage and lifting to conclude in D major, seldom having veered far afield. The movements follow rudimentary forms, mostly A–B–A; the phrase structures are neat. The score itself, with page after page of mostly empty staves, looks sparse. Full brass appear only to articulate a pair of turning points in the text; the harps, only in the "celestial" passages: Sanctus, Pie Jesu, and In Paradisum.

To be sure, there are funereal elements: the cold octaves of the first bars, for instance, and the hollow homophony of the chorus as it enters, evoking the rhythms and shape of liturgical chant. But the lyric hymn soon offered by the tenors dispels that atmosphere as it merges seamlessly with the Kyrie and Christe eleison. The Offertoire, O Domine Jesu Christe (no. 2), was the last music to be composed, and is the longest and by some measure the most complex. It opens in quasi-fugal imitation, and the duo of tenors and altos is canonic. At the center the baritone soloist intones the Hostias over pulsating strings, hovering around the dominant pitch A, in a triple meter with suggestions of lullaby. The chorus returns in a fuller statement of the imitative Domine Jesus Christe.

In the Sanctus, Fauré advances his particular notion of a heavenly choir with harp and viola arpeggiations, led by the sopranos and answered by tenors and basses, and the violin obbligato; for the Osanna, three simple horn calls, golden and martial. (Altos are tacet until the last cadence). By now we sense that not just the sonority but also the basic argument is quite different from the ordinary concerns of a funeral mass. The Pie Jesu says as much: minimal (even as we hear the woodwinds for the first time), serene, primitive in its perfection. Saint-Saëns famously remarked that just as there was only one *Ave verum corpus* (Mozart's), there was only one Pie Jesu.[64]

The Agnus Dei again brings the tenor section to the fore, with, toward the end, the recollection of the opening Introit. The baritone's Libera me, a gentle, then uplifting march with heartbeats in the low strings, at last reaches, at the center, reference to the flames and lava of judgment: at the metric shift to 6/4 and entry of the full brass. But this is short lived indeed, tamed by the words "et lux perpetua" and return of the march music, now with full chorus. The organ, joined later by harps, returns to arpeggiations for In Paradisum, as the soprano section, now overtly angelic, again sets out each phrase. In this part of the religious service, the casket is borne out of the church, led by angels, says the text, to the holy city of Jerusalem, there to rest with the soul of Lazarus, the beggar.

Performance

The score calls for "Chorus of Children: sopranos, altos; Chorus of Men: tenors, basses")—that is, an all-male choir. The constituency of the *maîtrise,* or choir school, at the Madeleine is well documented: thirty children and four or five each tenors and basses of professional caliber. Fauré wanted a "calm" baritone, *un peu chantre,* he said: "a little like a cantor."[65] The Pie Jesu was composed for boy soprano, though the concert performances always used a woman. Among the boys who sang it at the Madeleine was Louis Aubert (1877–1968), who went on to become a pupil of Fauré and a composer of note. Purists note that the Roman pronunciation of Latin now used in French churches was not adopted until 1904–05, hence Frenchified vowels and consonants are in order.[66]

The small Cavaillé-Coll organ in use for Madeleine choir in 1888 featured an 8' and two 4' reed ranks and a swell box. Both the full score and, more systematically, the published organ part give registrations ("Fonds et Anches Réc. Boîte fermée," for instance, at the start of the Sanctus.)

Fauré had a good deal to say about performing the work in his correspondence with the famous violinist Eugène Ysaÿe, who led the Belgian performances in 1900. It is clear that he enjoyed the orchestral version ("the more violas the better"), taking pride in the divided violin octaves and offering advice on mixing women and children in the choir. But since Fauré was negligent proof-reader, it fell to his successors to tidy up the score and parts of the concert version. Among these was Nadia Boulanger (1887–1979), who had been his student and who played organ in 1920 performances he attended. Her conducting copy of the published score, correcting pitches and reconciling dynamics and articulation, exists in the Bibliothèque Nationale in Paris and was consulted for the recent Hamelle full score.

It was three decades before the work achieved currency abroad. In the early 1960s, the Requiem was further popularized by two important recordings, Ernest Ansermet with the Orchestre de la Suisse Romande and two of the finest francophone soloists of all, Suzanne Danco and Gerard Souzay (Decca, 1961), and the very much superior recording of André Cluytens with the Société des Concerts du Conservatoire, Victoria de los Angeles, and Dietrich Fischer-Dieskau (EMI, 1962). The Nectoux-Delage "smaller" version, incidentally, is heard on Philippe Herreweghe's recording with La Chapelle Royale and Les Petits Chanteurs de St.-Louis (Harmonia Mundi, 1988).

In one of those incidents that makes professional music historians cringe, the composer John Rutter, following up on a remark by Robert Orledge in the preface to his *Gabriel Fauré* of 1979, visited the Bibliothèque Nationale in Paris to have a look at the sources for the early versions of the Requiem. To great fanfare, he published a score still widely heralded as "re-discovered by John Rutter" (*Gabriel Fauré / Requiem / 1893 Version,* Oxford University Press, 1989).[67] His recording with the Cambridge Singers and City of London Sinfonia effectively introduced the 1893 version to the world at large (Conifer CD, 1984; in mp3 from Naxos). In fact Fauré's autograph, the only source Rutter seems to have seen, had been in the library since 1925 and was no particular secret.[68] A generation of painstaking French scholarship was thus trumped, but the flaws of Rutter's too-hasty approach were soon evident ("do-it-yourself musicology," said one reviewer[69]) and his edition very soon supplanted in influence by the authoritative and carefully documented solutions summarized above.[70]

Which version is the more "authentic" is a question best left unasked. Fauré's early conception is, obviously, the more intimate and personal; the subsequent "big-orchestra" version won the Requiem its public—including Maurice Duruflé, who in 1947 composed a Requiem along the same lines. Nectoux finds the added violins in Hamelle's full score deplorable. Green seeks "the legitimate intention of the composer were he free of the influence of his publisher."[71] In fact the versions have equal authority, since it is reasonable to conclude from the evidence that Fauré approved of both. How could he not?

Whatever the version, the listener should try to picture the church of the Madeleine: its windowless darkness, all greys and blacks and flickering candles, warmed by the purity of the child-like voices and the sweetness of those particular ranks of the French church organ. Within that imposing though anachronistic edifice, Fauré spent much of his career. There he introduced and frequently thereafter repeated his Requiem. There, too, it was heard at his own funeral.

Notes

1 In the New System of the Russian calendar; Old System, March 26. This is often given as April 6, but see Boris Schwarz, "More Beethoveniana in Soviet Russia," *Musical Quarterly*, 49 (1963), 143–49.

2 Now Olomouc, Czech Republic.

3 Emily Anderson, *The Letters of Beethoven, 3 vols.* (London: Macmillan/New York: W. W. Norton, 1986), vol. 2, 814–15.

4 A true *missa solemnis* sets considerably more than the five movements of the Ordinary; see "The Mass in D as a 'missa solemnis,'" in William Drabkin, *Beethoven: Missa solemnis* (Cambridge: Cambridge University Press, 1991), 26–27.

5 Drabkin, *Beethoven: Missa solemnis*, 2.

6 Michael Steinberg, *Choral Masterworks: A Listener's Guide* (Oxford: Oxford University Press, 2005), 50.

7 See Douglas Johnson, Robert Winter, and Alan Tyson, *The Beethoven Sketchbooks: History, Reconstruction, Inventory* (Berkeley: University of California Press, 1985); see also Robert Winter, "Reconstruction Riddles: The Sources for Beethoven's *Missa Solemnis*," in *Beethoven Essays: Studies in Honor of Elliot Forbes,* ed. Lewis Lockwood and Phyllis Benjamin (Cambridge, MA: Harvard University Press, 1984), 217–50.

8 *Thayer's Life of Beethoven*, ed. Elliot Forbes (Princeton, NJ: Princeton University Press, 1964), vol. 2, 925 (April 8, 1824).

9 Previous works with chorus were *Christus am Ölberge* ("Christ on the Mount of Olives"), Op. 85 (1803), the Mass in C, Op. 86 (1807), and of course *Fidelio,* Op. 72 (1805).

10 Walter Riezler, *Beethoven,* trans. G. D. H. Pidcock (London, 1938), 190; Joel Lester, "Revisions in the Autograph of the *Missa Solemnis* Kyrie," *Journal of the American Musicological Society* 23 (1970): 420–38; summarized in Drabkin, *Beethoven: Missa solemnis,* 8. Drabkin's Cambridge Handbook on the *Missa solemnis,* which I follow closely, succinctly explains Beethoven's compositional strategies, with multiple charts and musical examples, an indispensable handbook to the work.

11 "Mit Andacht" occurs also at the head of the Sanctus, and in the Ninth Symphony at "Ihr stürzt nieder, Millionen" (Adagio ma non troppo, ma divoto).

12 Kirkendale, "New Roads to Old Ideas," 666–67, following Ursula Kirkendale, "The King of Heaven and the King of France: History of a Musical *topos,*" paper delivered at the annual meeting of the American Musicological Society, December 1969 (later published in Warren and Ursula Kirkendale, *Music and Meaning,* Florence: Leo S. Olschki, 2007).

13 Thayer/Forbes, vol. 2, 735.

14 Summarized in "Textual Problems," Drabkin, *Beethoven: Missa solemnis,* 23–26.

15 See Richard Kramer, rev. of *Missa Solemnis* by Ludwig van Beethoven, ed. Norbert Gertsch, *Notes* 59 (2003): 743–46.

16 Theodor Adorno: "Verfremdetes Hauptwerk: zur *Missa solemnis*" (1957), in English as "The Alienated magnum opus: On the *Missa solemnis*," in Adorno, *Beethoven: The Philosophy of Music,* ed. Rolf Tiedemann, trans. Edmund Jephcott (Stanford, CA: Stanford University Press, 1998), 142.

17 Portions of the essay are drawn from Holoman, *Berlioz* (Cambridge, MA: Harvard University Press, 1989).

18 Berlioz, *Mémoires* (Paris: Michel Lévy frères, 1870), ch. 46. The latest edition of David Cairns's celebrated

translation is New York: Knopf, 2002; of Pierre Citron's edition of the original French, Paris: Flammarion, 2010.

19 Berlioz, *Mémoires*, ch. 46.

20 Ibid.

21 Listed in Holoman, *Catalogue of the Works of Berlioz, New Berlioz Edition*, vol. 25 (Kassel: Bärenreiter, 1987), no. 75.

22 Letter to Humbert Ferrand, January 11, 1967, in *Berlioz: Correspondance générale* 7, ed. Hugh Macdonald (Paris: Flammarion, 2001), 517–18.

23 Julian Rushton presents the full scheme in *The Music of Berlioz* (Oxford: Oxford University Press, 2001), 204. See also Edward T. Cone, "Inside the Saint's Head: the Music of Berlioz," in *Music: A View from Delft; Selected Essays*, ed. Robert P. Morgan (Chicago: University of Chicago Press, 1989), 217–48.

24 Berlioz, *Mémoires*, ch. 1.

25 See David Rosen, *Verdi: Requiem* (Cambridge: Cambridge University Press, 1995), 8–9.

26 Letter Brahms to Clara Schumann, April 1865, in *Clara Schumann–Johannes Brahms Briefe aus den Jahren 1853–1896*, ed. Berthold Litzmann, 2 vols. (Leipzig: Breitkopf & Hartel) vol. 1, 504.

27 See Christopher Reynolds, "A Choral Symphony by Brahms?" *19th-Century Music* 9 (1985): 3–25.

28 Clara Schumann to Florence May, in May, *The Life of Johannes Brahms*, 2 vols. (London: Edward Arnold, 1905), vol. 2, 44.

29 Letter Brahms to Rieter-Biedermann, *Briefwechsel* XIV, 153; cited by Michael Musgrave, *Brahms: A German Requiem* (Cambridge: Cambridge University Press, 1996), 10.

30 Facsimile in Musgrave, *Brahms: A German Requiem*, 11.

31 Letter Joachim to his wife, Amelie, December 1, 1867, in English in *Letters from and to Joseph Joachim*, ed. Nora Bickley (London: Macmillan, 1914), 370.

32 Berthold Litzmann, *Clara Schumann: Ein Künsterleben nach Tagebüchern und Briefen*, 3 vols. (Leipzig: 1902–08), III, 218–19; cited by Musgrave, *Brahms: A German Requiem*, 9.

33 Also "Behold the Lamb of God" and "Hallelujah" from *Messiah*.

34 See "Reception," Musgrave, *Brahms: A German Requiem*, 60–71.

35 Full-page example in Steinberg, *Choral Masterworks*, 72.

36 Siegfried Ochs, preface to Eulenburg Edition no. 969 (*c*.1900).

37 These are presented in tabular form in Musgrave, *Brahms: A German Requiem*, 73. See also Musgrave, "Performance Issues in *A German Requiem*," in *Performing Brahms*, ed. Musgrave and Bernard D. Sherman (Cambridge: Cambridge University Press, 2003), 131–54.

38 Library of the Gesellschaft der Musikfreunde, Vienna.

39 Sc. G., brief review of a new organ-vocal edition (Oxford University Press), in *Music and Letters* 11 (1930): 419–20.

40 Lara Hoggard, "Afterword" to his edition (Chapel Hill: Hinshaw Music, 1984), i–vi.

41 Both recordings come with substantial liner-note essays.

42 Robert Schuman, "Neue Bahnen," in *Neue Zeitschrift für Musik*, October 28, 1953; as "New Paths," trans. Henry Pleasants, in *The Musical World of Robert Schumann: A Selection from his Writings* (London: Gollancz, 1965), 199–200.

43 George Bernard Shaw, rev. of Dvořák's Requiem, November 9, 1892, in *Bernard Shaw; Reviews and Bombardments*, ed. Louis Crompton (Berkeley: University of California Press, 1978), 39.

44 Musgrave, Brahms: *A German Requiem*, x.

45 He was exhumed from Père Lachaise cemetery in Paris on May 1, 1887 (a grizzly photograph of the open coffin was taken and published) and reinterred at the church of Santa Croce in Florence the next day. Verdi declined to participate.

46 *Gazetto musicale di Milano*, November 22, 1868.

47 The manuscript sources were recovered by David Rosen in 1970, edited for performance, and presented in concerts beginning in September 1988 in Stuttgart and Parma. See Philip Gosset, *Divas and Scholars: Performing Italian Opera* (Chicago: University of Chicago Press, 2007), 160–62.

48 Letter Verdi to the mayor of Milan, June 3, 1873, in D. Rosen, *Verdi: Requiem* (Cambridge: Cambridge University Press, 1995), 13.

49 The Catholic liturgy specific to the archdiocese of Milan, named for St. Ambrose, fourth-century bishop of Milan.

50 David Rosen, "Introduction," *Verdi: Requiem*, a Cambridge Music Handbook (Cambridge University Press, 1995), xxii. The girls were pretty, too, noted a reviewer after the La Scala performances, where they were allowed less restricted costume.

51 Ibid.

52 Hector Berlioz, *Grand Traité d'instrumentation et d'orchestration modernes* (Paris: Schonenberger, 1843).

53 Rosen, "Introduction," xxxi.

54 Mm. 15–19.

55 Hans von Bülow, "Musikalisches aus Italien," *Allgemeine Zeitung* (Munich), May 28 and June 1, 1874, p. 341. Verdi's reply to von Bülow's 1892 apology in Mary Jane Phillips-Matz, *Verdi* (New York: Oxford University Press, 1996), 712.

56 Additionally, Rigaudière has prepared modern editions for Carus-Verlag of Stuttgart: *version avec petit orchestre, 1889* (no. 27.311, 2011), and *version symphonique, 1900* (no. 27.312, 2005).

57 "Happy deliverance:" letter Fauré to Louis Aguettant in July 12, 1902; "enjoyment": letter Fauré to Maurice Emmanuel, March 1910, both cited by Nectoux, 1893 version, x.

58 Richard Langham Smith calls it a "parish mass" in his review of John Rutter's edition (Oxford University Press, 1989) in *Music & Letters* 71 (1990): 143–44.

59 Fauré to Aguettant, 1902.

60 Smith/Rutter, review, 143.

61 Éditions Hamelle was acquired by Éditions Alphonse Leduc publishing house in 1993; the imprint was retained.

62 Letter Ducasse to a friend, 1901, cited in Richard Langham Smith, review of Mutien-Omer Houziaux: *A la recherche des Requiem de Fauré* (see n. 18), in *Music and Letters* 84 (2005): 848–50.

63 Smith/Houziaux, review, 650.

64 Letter Saint-Saëns to Fauré, November 2, 1916, in *The Correspondence of Camille Saint-Saëns and Gabriel Fauré,* ed. Jean-Michel Nectoux, trans. J. Barrie Jones (Aldershot, England: Ashgate, 2004), 127.

65 Nectoux, 1893 version, xxii.

66 Nectoux lists these, 1893 version, xxiii.

67 Also: Chapel Hill, Hinshaw, 1984. See, for instance, *Wikipedia:* "John Rutter rediscovered Fauré's original manuscript . . . in the early 1980s."

68 The autograph is F-Pn mus. mss. 410–413, one number for each of the four original movements. Additionally wind parts and a manuscript score from the Madeleine had been at the BN since 1968, and their existence was common knowledge to regulars in the *salle de lecture* (including this author), where Nectoux was employed at the time.

69 Smith/Rutter, review, 144.

70 The quarter century spent in pursuit of the Fauré Requiem is documented in mind-numbing detail by Mutien-Omer Houziaux in *A la recherche des Requiem de Fauré* ("Tracking the Fauré Requiems," Liège and Paris, 2000). It includes a preface by Nectoux and a table of how the versions developed.

71 Nectoux, xii; Jonathan D. Green, *A Conductor's Guide to Nineteenth-Century Choral–Orchestral Works* (Lanham, MD: Scarecrow Press, 2008), 176.

5

WORKS WITH SECULAR AND NON-LITURGICAL TEXTS

D. Kern Holoman

UNIVERSITY OF CALIFORNIA, DAVIS

Hector Berlioz (1803–69): *La Damnation de Faust*, H. 111

Légende dramatique en 4 parties / Dramatic legend in four parts

PREMIÈRE PARTIE / PART I

Plaines de hongroie / the Hungarian plains

1 Introduction
2 Ronde de paysans / Peasants round dance
3 Marche hongroise / Hungarian march

DEUXIÈME PARTIE / PART II

Nord d'Allemagne / North Germany

4 Faust seul dans son cabinet de travail / Faust alone in his study
5 Chant de la Fête de Pâques / Easter hymn

La Cave d'Auerbach à Leipzig / Auerbach's Cellar in Leipzig

6 Chœur de buveurs / Drinking song
7 Chanson de Brander / Brander's song
8 Fugue sur le thème de Brander / Fugue on Brander's theme
9 Chanson de Méphistophélès / Mephistopheles's song

Bosquets et prairies du bord de l'Elbe / Thickets and meadows on the banks of the Elbe

10 Air de Méphistophélès / Mephistopheles's aria
11 Chœur de gnomes et de sylphes (Songe de Faust) / Chorus of gnomes and sylphes (Faust's dream)
12 Ballet des sylphes
13 Finale: Chœur de soldats; Chœur d'étudiants / Finale: Chorus of soldiers, chorus of students

TROISIÈME PARTIE / PART III

14 Tambour et trompettes sonnant la retraite / Drum and trumpets sound the retreat
15 Air de Faust dans la chambre de Marguerite / Faust's aria in Marguerite's bedroom
16 Le Roi de Thulé (Chanson gothique) / The King of Thule (Gothic song)
17 Evocation—Menuet des follets / Invocation—Minuet of will-o'-the-wisps
18 Sérénade de Méphistophélès avec chœur de follets / Mephistopheles's serenade with chorus of will-o'-the-wisps
19 Duo
20 Trio et Chœur

QUATRIÈME PARTIE / PART IV

21 Romance de Marguerite / Marguerite's romance
22 Forêts et cavernes: Invocation de Faust à la nature / Forests and caverns: Faust's invocation to Nature
23 Récitatif et Chasse / Recitative and Hunt
24 La Course à l'abyme: Duo / Ride to the abyss: Duo
25 Pandæmonium: Chœur de damnés et de démons / Pandemonium: Chorus of demons and the damned
26 Le Ciel: Chœur d'esprits célestes; Apothéose de Marguerite / In heaven: Chorus of heavenly spirits; Marguerite's apotheosis

Duration	About 2 hours and 30 minutes.
For	Faust (T), Méphistophélès (Bar. or B; "with alternatives for the two voices"), Brander (B), Marguerite (Mez); chorus (S I–II, T I–II, B I–II), children's chorus (S I–II, last scene); flutes I–III (piccolos I–III), oboes I–II (English horn), clarinets I–II, bassoons I–IV; horns I–IV, trumpets I–II, cornets *à pistons* I–II, trombones I–III, ophicleide and tuba; timpani (two pairs, four players), bass drum, cymbals, snare drum, triangle, tam-tam, bells; harps I–II, strings (15–15–10–12–9).
Text	By Gérard de Nerval, Almire Gandonnière, and Berlioz, after Goethe's *Faust,* part I.
Composed	November 1845–October 1846
First Performed	December 6, 1846, by a large ensemble assembled for the occasion, Paris Opéra-Comique (not staged), Berlioz conducting, Gustave Roger, tenor, as Faust.
Dedication	To Franz Liszt (published score).
Scores	• First published by S. Richault (Paris, 1854).
	• Standard edition: Breitkopf & Härtel, Berlioz complete edition, vols. 11–12, ed. Charles Malherbe and Felix Weingartner, 1901 = Kalmus, Dover, IMSLP.
	• Scholarly edition: New Berlioz Edition, vols. 8A–b, ed. Julian Rushton, 1979, 1986 (materials BA 5448).
Further Reading	Green, *A Conductor's Guide*, 50–55. Julian Rushton, *The Music of Berlioz* (Oxford University Press, 2001), 275–80. Daniel Albright, *Berlioz's Semi-Operas:* Roméo et Juliette *and* La Damnation de Faust (University of Rochester, 2006).

Synopsis

Part 1 takes place on the Hungarian plains. Faust, an aging scientist and professor, observes the dawn of spring. He is self-absorbed in post-middle-age crisis, unable to enjoy the simple pleasures that should be his: peasants in a springtide dance, a passing legion of virile young soldiers pursuing glory.

Part 2. North Germany: Leipzig and along the Elbe River. Alone in his study, Faust contemplates suicide; an Easter hymn is heard from pilgrims in the distance. Mephistopheles appears, mocking Faust's anguish and presenting some alternatives. He whisks Faust to Auerbach's Cellar, a Leipzig beer hall. Brander, a jolly patron, leads a drunken song of a poisoned kitchen rat; and to give the rat a decent funeral, the revelers sing an Amen fugue. Not to be outdone, Mephistopheles fashions a song about a flea and his relations, set to visit the royal court. When Faust disapproves of these unseemly goings-on, the scene morphs to a riverside meadow where, under Mephistopheles's spell, he dreams of the beautiful Marguerite. Another morph: Faust and Mephistopheles appear by dark of night outside Marguerite's house, as university students and soldiers encounter each other in the street, singing lustily of drinking and seduction. (Intermission.)

Part 3. Faust has hidden himself in Marguerite's room. Marguerite enters and absent-mindedly sings an old ballad, "The King of Thule." Mephistopheles and his will-o'-the-wisps cast their spell; Faust and Marguerite join destinies in their love duet. Mephistopheles interrupts, merrily, with news that the neighbors know there is a man in Marguerite's room and are fetching her mother. In the ensuing hubbub, Mephistopheles absconds with Faust.

Part 4. Marguerite's romance sets the same text as Schubert's *Gretchen am Spinnrade*: in erotic anguish she awaits his return, while the sound of soldiers and students in the street reminds her of the night of their tryst. But Faust has abandoned her, instead imploring Nature to assuage his anxiety. Mephistopheles materializes with more news: Marguerite, having killed her mother, is to be hanged next day. Faust signs a contract exchanging Marguerite's life for his own soul. They leap upon black horses, ostensibly to ride to her rescue. But instead the landscape grows ever more lurid as they race across it. The vortex to hell opens and they are swept into the pandemonium. In the aftermath, Marguerite arrives in heaven, welcomed by a chorus of celestial spirits.

La Damnation de Faust is, together with *Les Troyens*, Berlioz's most nearly perfect composition. No previous work of his fits together so effortlessly, goes by so quickly, or seems so lean and carefully wrought. No other *Faust,* for that matter, so successfully captures Goethe's spirit. Yet it must be taken on its own terms: respectful of its source but freely adapting it, Germanic in tradition but French in musical style. It is a refined product of Romance language, reason, embellishment, and above all sensitivity to *paysage* and *panorama*.

Composition

La Damnation de Faust probably began to take shape in the summer of 1845 as Berlioz planned his concerts for the 1845–46 season. He was in the habit of refashioning earlier material for concert use—as in the case, for instance, of the *Roman Carnival*, adapted in 1843 from the opera *Benvenuto Cellini* of 1838. Thus he at first considered a simple rewriting of his 1829 *Huit Scènes de Faust* (Eight Scenes from *Faust*), composed in a flush of excitement at discovering Gérard de Nerval's translation of Goethe's masterpiece. But Berlioz had grown immeasurably as a composer since the *Huit Scènes,* and on reflection he saw that they could only serve as the starting point for a new, much larger *Faust*. In September 1845, accordingly, he contracted with the librettist Almire Gandonnière to provide an expanded text; simultaneously he decided to set out for Vienna and its outlying cities to conduct concerts of his own music. Gathering up his notes, sketches, and texts, he left Paris on

October 22, 1845, in the company of his mistress, Marie Recio, for a concert tour that was to last more than seven months.

He worked on *Faust* during every leg of the journey: *en route* in stagecoaches, steamboats, and railroad trains; at night in the hotels of Passau, Vienna, Prague, Breslau, and Budapest. When he ran out of Gandonnière's text, he fashioned his own, beginning with the *Invocation à la nature* and its images of the *forêts* and *rochers* that had captivated him since his wanderings in the mountains of Italy. The chorus of rowdy students, *Jam nox stellata,* reflects an incident outside his window in the university town of Breslau. In Vienna, a Hungarian nobleman, presumably Casimir Bathyány (1807–54), suggested he orchestrate the Hungarian national march *Rákóczy* for his forthcoming concerts in Pest—because "the French know how to write revolutionary music."[1] (At the concerts of February 15 and 20, 1846, the public, perceiving the bass drum strokes as the cannon fire of revolution against the Austrians, became consumed in a riot of cheers and foot-stomping.) He completed the work during the late summer of 1846, in part at the country house in Normandy of a wealthy acquaintance. The autograph was finished and dated on October 19, 1846.

First Performance

Producing so massive a work as *Faust* entailed an enormous personal financial risk. Denied access to the Salle du Conservatoire, Berlioz was forced to take the Opéra-Comique, a hall to which the concert-going public was not accustomed to coming for Sunday afternoon concerts but the only one available that could accommodate the large performing force. He mounted a formidable publicity campaign, placing dozens of press releases on the conception of the work, its composition in Germany, its evocative color. He sent the published libretto to the king and queen, hoping that royal interest might draw attention to his new work.[2] Meanwhile the rehearsals went slowly, singers and instrumentalists alike finding the music of extreme difficulty. The premiere was postponed from late November until December 6, 1846.

The performances were apparently brilliant, and there were a few cries of *bis!* shouted from the audience. But *Faust* was an utter failure at the box office. At neither the premiere nor the second performance on December 20, 1846, was the house more than half full, and those who did come seemed bewildered by the unusual form and epigrammatic treatment of the story. By then it was clear that Berlioz had incurred a gross financial loss, the greatest of his career. The third performance was canceled: too much money had already been lost.

The performers and aristocratic patrons, anxious to assuage him, offered a subscription dinner on December 29, 1846, and arranged for the casting of a gold medal commemorating the work. Knowledgeable artists saw that *Faust* was Berlioz's best composition to date. But there was no erasing the pain of the worst failure he was ever to endure. "Nothing in my career as an artist wounded me more deeply that this unexpected indifference,"[3] he remembered in his *Mémoires.* Berlioz's morale was permanently affected, his urge to compose stifled for years. He was never again to have confidence in the Paris public, and would later risk his own purse again for only one new work, *L'Enfance du Christ.*

Well before Berlioz's death, Jules Pasdeloup (1819–87) began to popularize some of the orchestral excerpts in his mass-market Concerts Populaires from 1861, and Pasdeloup can be credited with the universal popularity of the so-called "Three Pieces from *La Damnation de Faust*": the Hungarian March, Ballet of Sylphs, and Minuet of the Will-o'-the-Wisps. Édouard Colonne (1838–1910), whose orchestra concerts began in 1873, premiered a complete, well-rehearsed *Faust* in February 1877, repeated it for six consecutive weeks, and over the long haul conducted more than 150 performances.

Genre

In organizational concept, *Faust* is not so different from Berlioz's third symphony, *Roméo et Juliette:* an evening's worth of symphonic music devoted to a single story. As in the dramatic symphonies (*Symphonie fantastique, Harold en Italie, Roméo et Juliette*), there is a series of related tableaux with relatively little connective tissue. From the beginning, Berlioz meant to incorporate elements of his first *Faust*. Three of the soloists (Brander, Mephistopheles, and Marguerite) and the chorus were predetermined by the use of the *Huit Scènes*. Berlioz added solo arias for Faust, a love duet, and the three big scenes at the end of the story. For the orchestra alone there were the march and the two ballets as well as the military music at the beginning of part III. For a time, Berlioz considered his work an *opéra de concert,* but in its finished form *Faust* had become a symphonic *légende dramatique,* a panoply of scenes assembled into four distinct parts.

Structure

The strong unity that informs *Faust* comes from recurring motives of orchestration, a pervasive tonality of D major inflected with B-flat, and the most pronounced control of thematic foreshadowing, transformation, and inter-movement recall that Berlioz ever practiced. The foreshadowing begins at the outset, where the pastoral calm of Faust's reverie is interrupted by presentiments of the *ronde des paysans* and military fanfares of the *Marche hongroise*—the latter a full forty pages before the march finally bursts forth. Méphistophélès first appears to a flashy trombone figure with an exclamation point in the flutes and piccolos. (This figure is a gloss on the main melodic gesture of the Mephistopheles's "Song of the Flea" in Auerbach's cellar, no. 9.) It occurs twice more to introduce Mephistopheles, after the "Amen" fugue and at the beginning of the scene in Marguerite's room. Mephistopheles is often supported by the deep brass, as in the rich trombone underpinning his unctuous aria *Voici des roses* (no. 10).

Thematic transformation is practiced on a grander scale as well. The drunken "Requiescat in pace, Amen" (no. 8) draws its fugue subject from the song of the rat just before (no. 7). Mephistopheles's silly serenade in part III—his "moral song, the better to mislead her" (no. 18)—is foreshadowed in the coda of the will-o'-the-wisps' sprightly minuet just before. The most sustained essay in thematic transformation is in the scene by the Elbe (nos. 10–12), which commences with *Voici des roses,* made up entirely of versions of the melody first fashioned for the chorus of sylphs. The concluding ballet, over a long-held D pedal, serves as a dissolution (see Example 5.1).

EXAMPLE 5.1   Berlioz, *La Damnation de Faust*, thematic transformation.

Sérénade de Méphistophélès

EXAMPLE 5.1 continued

Coda of the *Menuet des follets*

Chanson de Brander

BRANDER:

Cer - tain rat, dans u – ne cui - sine É - ta - bli,

Fugue sur le thème de la chanson de Brander

Chœur de sylphes

EXAMPLE 5.1 continued

Air de Méphistophélès

Ballet des sylphes

Though *Faust* is not one of the works Berlioz terms "architectural," he brings his sense of musical space to bear in a number of the scenes. When the paths of the soldiers and the university students cross, Berlioz composes a stylized *réunion des thèmes,* with the soldiers' march (in 6/8 and B-flat major) overlapping the students' Latin song (in a modal D minor and 2/4). Both texts celebrate women and the glories of seducing them, thus commenting indirectly on Faust and Marguerite. Then, in the inspired "Ride to the Abyss," Berlioz undertakes another masterly treatment of musical space. As Faust and Mephistopheles tear through the countryside with thundering hooves and an eerie oboe theme, we are presented with a succession of passing scenes: a litany of peasants at devotion by a roadside cross, hideous howling beasts, flapping night birds, and dancing skeletons—all in direct reference to the Wolf's Glen scene in Carl Maria von Weber's *Der Freischütz.* There is Faust's great cry and plunge into the abyss, to the delighted cries of demons and the damned in their "infernal" language—"Ha! Irimiru Karabrao: Has! Has!" and so on, followed immediately by Marguerite's apotheosis in Heaven, with (like the Sanctus of the Requiem and the final tableau of *L'Enfance du Christ*) high-pitched consonance, simple harmonic fabric, and chorale texture.[4]

Pause to compare *La Damnation de Faust* with other works of its decade. It is conceptually superior to Wagner's *Tannhäuser* (1845) and Glinka's *Ruslan and Lyudmila* (1841) and technically more secure than either; it makes Mendelssohn's *Elijah* (1846) seem a relic of the past, and Verdi's *Nabucco* (1842) and *Macbeth* (1847) longwinded. It surpasses anything presented on the Paris stage of that epoch. Yet *Faust,* though not Berlioz's last major work, is his last forward-looking one.

Performance

The critical challenge of *La Damnation de Faust* is for male singers in sufficient number to form two robust choirs, both TTBB: those of the university students and the soldiers at the end of part III—in some respects the focal point of Berlioz's work. Here some stagecraft is required, since the men's chorus was altogether in part I (Auerbach's cellar) but for the street scene at the end of part II needs splitting antiphonally into soldiers and students. The last scene, Marguerite's apotheosis, calls for children's chorus (200–300, in the composer's always extravagant imagination), which often appears at audience level in front of the orchestra platform, just after Faust and Mephistopheles have been swallowed up. Better still, of course, is to find them a lofty place above the main chorus.

The printed program needs to clarify the genre as symphonic, *not an opera*, and give the scene titles and other guideposts Berlioz leaves in the score. A certain number will have seen staged pageant-like productions of *La Damnation de Faust* by opera companies, a concept invented by the Monte Carlo Opera in 1893. But the conversation on Berlioz and genre grows quickly tedious. Mixed-genre entertainments are now common, after all, and the less said about "opera," in this case, the better.

Felix Mendelssohn (1809–47): *Elias / Elijah,* Op. 70

Oratorium nach Worten des Alten Testaments / Oratorio after Words of the Old Testament

PART I

ELIJAH'S CURSE

Introduction (Elijah): As God the Lord of Israel liveth (I Kings 17:1)

Overture

1   Chorus: Help, Lord! Wilt Thou quite destroy us? (Jeremiah 8:19–20)
    Recitative (chorus): The deeps afford no water (I Kings 17:7; Lamentations 4:4)
2   Duet with chorus: Lord, bow thine ear to our prayer! (Psalm 86:1; Lamentations 1:17)
3   Recitative (Obadiah): Ye people, rend your hearts (Joel 2:12–13)
4   Air (Obadiah): If with all your hearts ye truly seek Me (Deuteronomy 4:29; Job 23:3)
5   Chorus: Yet doth the Lord see it not (Deuteronomy 28:22; Exodus 20:5–6)
6   Recitative (an Angel): Elijah, get thee hence (I Kings 17:3–4)
7   Double Quartet: For He shall give His angels (Psalm 91:11–12)

ELIJAH RAISES THE WIDOW'S SON

8   Recitative (an Angel): Now Cherith's brook is dried up (I Kings 17:7, 9, 14)
9   Recitative, Air, and Duet (the Widow, Elijah): What have I to do with thee? (1 Kings 17:17–19, 21-24; Job 10:15; Psalms 38:6; 6:7; 10:14; 86;15–16; 88:10; 116:12; Deuteronomy 6:5; Psalm 128:1)
    Chorus: Blessed are the men who fear Him (Psalms 128:1; 112:1, 4)

THE CONTEST ON MOUNT CARMEL

10   Recitative (Elijah) and Chorus: As God the Lord of Sabaoth liveth (I Kings 18:1, 15, 17–19, 23–25)
11   Chorus: Baal, we cry to thee (I Kings 18:26)
12   Recitative and Chorus: Call him louder! For he is a god! (I Kings 18:27)
13   Recitative and Chorus: Call him louder! He heareth not (I Kings 18:28–30)
14   Air (Elijah): Lord God of Abraham, Isaac, and Israel (I Kings 18:36–37)
15   Quartet (Angels): Cast thy burden upon the Lord (Psalms 55:22; 16:8; 108:5; 25:3)
16   Recitative and Chorus: O Thou, who makest Thine angels (Psalm 104:4; I Kings 18:38–40)
17   Air (Elijah): Is not His word like a fire? (Jeremiah 23:29; Psalm 7:11–12)
18   Arioso (alto solo): Woe unto them who forsake Him (Hosea 7:13)

ELIJAH BRINGS RAIN

19   Recitative and Chorus: O man of God, help thy people! (Jeremiah 14:22; II Chronicles 6:19, 26, 27; Deuteronomy 28:23; Psalms 28:1; 106:1; I Kings 18:43–45)
20   Chorus: Thanks be to God! He laveth the thirsty land! (Psalm 93:3–4)

PART TWO

JEZEBEL ORDERS ELIJAH'S DEATH

21 Air (soprano): Hear ye, Israel (Isaiah 48:1, 18; 53:1; 49:7; 41:10; 51:12–13)
22 Chorus: Be not afraid, saith God the Lord (Isaiah 41:10; Psalm 91:7)
23 Recitative and Chorus: The Lord hath exalted thee (I Kings 14:7, 9, 15–16; 16:30–33; Jeremiah 26:9, 11; I Kings 18:10; 21:7)
24 Chorus: Woe to him! (Ecclesiasticus 48:2–3)

ELIJAH FLEES TO MOUNT HOREB

25 Recitative (Obadiah): Man of God, now let my words (II Kings 19:1, 3; Jeremiah 5:3; 26:11; Psalm 59:3; I Kings 19:3–4; Deuteronomy 31:6; Exodus 12:32; I Samuel 17:37)
26 Air (Elijah): It is enough (Job 7:16; I Kings 19:4, 10)
27 Recitative (tenor solo): See, now he sleepeth (I Kings 19:5; Psalm 34:7)
28 Trio (the Angels): Lift thine eyes to the mountains (Psalm 121:1–3)
29 Chorus (the Angels): He, watching over Israel (Psalm 121,4; 138,7)
30 Recitative (the Angel): Arise, Elijah (I Kings 19:7–8; Isaiah 49:4; 64:1–2; 63,17; I Kings 19:4)
31 Air (the Angel): O rest in the Lord (Psalm 37:1, 4, 7)
32 Chorus: He that shall endure to the end (Matthew 10:22)

ELIJAH IS SWEPT BY A WHIRLWIND TO HEAVEN

33 Recitative (Elijah): Night falleth round me (Psalm 143:6, 7; I Kings 19:11, 13)
34 Chorus: Behold! God the Lord passed by! (I Kings 19:11–12)
35 Recitative (quartet and chorus): Above Him stood the Seraphim (Isaiah 6:2, 3)
36 Chorus: Go, return upon thy way! (I Kings 19:15, 18; Psalms 71,16; 16:9)
37 Arioso (Elijah): For the mountains shall depart (Isaiah 54:10)
38 Chorus: Then did Elijah the prophet break forth (Ecclesiasticus 48:1, 6, 7; II Kings 2:1, 11)
39 Air (tenor solo): Then shall the righteous shine (Matthew 13:43; Isaiah 51:11)
40 Recitative (soprano): Behold, God hath sent Elijah the prophet (Malachi 4:5, 6)
41 But the Lord, from the north hath raised one (Isaiah 41:25) Quartet (SATB solo): O come ev'ry one that thirsteth (Isaiah 55:1–3)
42 Chorus: And then shall your light break forth (Isaiah 53:8; Psalm 8:1)

Duration	About 2 hours and 45 minutes.
For	Soloists (B [Elijah], T [Obadiah, Ahab], S I [the widow, an angel], S II, A [an angel, Jezebel], boy soprano); chorus (SATB, with some divided choruses, an angel trio, and a double quartet); flutes I–II, oboes I–II, clarinets I–II, bassoons I–II; horns I–IV, trumpets I–II, trombones I–III, ophicleide; timpani; organ; strings.
Text	From the book of Kings in the Old Testament, amplified by other passages from the Bible; assembled by Carl Klingemann in England, then Julius Schubring in Germany and; translated into English by William Bartholomew.
Composed	At the invitation of the Birmingham Music Festival, starting in 1845; completed August 11, 1846 (date in score); revised until April 1847.
First Performed	August 26, 1846, at the Birmingham Music Festival in Birmingham Town Hall, Mendelssohn conducting. After significant revisions, the definitive

version was premiered April 16, 1847, in Exeter Hall, London, with the composer conducting.

Scores
- First published by N. Simrock (Bonn, 1847) and Ewer (London, 1847) in full and vocal score. Mendelssohn prepared the piano reduction and, for one version of the Ewer vocal score, a two-piano version of the overture.
- Standard edition Breitkopf & Härtel, 1875, ed. Julius Rietz = Kalmus, Dover, IMSLP. Novello acquired Ewer in 1867, and from that point the Novello vocal score monopolized the market; the 1991 revision, ed. Michael Pilkington, has both English and German texts. The Schirmer vocal score comes from 1892.
- Scholarly editions: ed. R. Larry Todd, Stuttgart Mendelssohn Editions (Carus-Verlag, 1994; Carus 40.130); ed. Christian Martin Schmidt, Leipziger Ausgabe der Werke VI/11 (2009), materials Breitkopf & Härtel (Wiesbaden, 2008–09; Breitkopf 8649).

Further Reading   Steinberg, *Choral Masterworks*, 200–09. Summer, *Choral Masterworks from Bach to Britten*, 71–76 and 155–57; note especially "Suggestions for an abridged *Elijah*." Green, *A Conductor's Guide*, 196–201. Howard Smither, *The Oratorio in the Nineteenth and Twentieth Centuries,* vol. 4 of *A History of the Oratorio* (University of North Carolina Press, 2000), 166–84.

Also F. G. Edwards, *The History of Mendelssohn's Oratorio "Elijah"* (Novello, 1896). Jack Werner, *Mendelssohn's "Elijah": A Historical and Critical Guide to the Oratorio* (Chappell, 1965). Preface to the Novello vocal score cited above (ed. Pilkington, 1991).

Mendelssohn's Violin Concerto and "Italian" Symphony, however exemplary, cannot prepare us for the magnitude of his accomplishment in *Elijah,* his last major work. His response to the story of the great Old Testament prophet, defender of the faith of Jehovah against Ahab and Jezebel, worker of miracles, a demoralized desert hermit led to heaven by a whirlwind and fiery chariot, is as richly layered as the tale itself. On the one hand, a personal, often passionate statement of religious belief, it is on the other shrewdly contrived to please what is often described as the "burgeoning middle-class," consumers of musical culture in England and abroad, the core of support for the music festivals. In that respect, *Elijah* shows Romanticism's fascination with legend, autobiography, and the economic promise of the public at large. It is a cornerstone of the nineteenth-century colossal style.

Fashioning the Text

The Old Testament story of the prophet Elijah is told primarily in the first book of Kings. We have it on good authority that Mendelssohn was attracted in boyhood to the episode where God passes before Elijah: not in the earthquake, the wind, or the fire, but with a still, small, voice.[5] And we know for certain of developments in 1829, just as Mendelssohn was entering his twenties, that laid the foundation for an Elijah oratorio. One of these was the Berlin performance of J. S. Bach's *St. Matthew Passion* as organized and conducted by Mendelssohn in March, often characterized as the beginning of a modern "Bach revival." Another undertaking, just a few weeks later, was the first of his ten visits to England, where he absorbed the lore of two other German-speaking composers of English oratorios, Handel and Haydn, just as surely as the subject matter of *Fingal's Cave* and the "Scotch" Symphony.

In May 1836, Mendelssohn conducted his first oratorio, *Paulus / St. Paul,* at the Lower Rhine Music Festival in Düsseldorf. In the wake of its success, he began to consider options for a second, asking his friend Carl Klingemann (1798–1862), a German diplomat in London, to help him fashion a libretto from Elijah's story. He sought "an external impulse to urge me on,"[6] long on action scenes and short on narration. The following summer, while Mendelssohn was in England to conduct *St. Paul,* they met to rough out a plan.

Klingemann, never especially drawn to the idea, dallied too long and apparently talked too much. When an Englishman sent Mendelssohn an unsolicited Elijah libretto,[7] demonstrating to the composer how word had gotten out, he moved to reassert control, turning the choice of text over to the librettist of *St. Paul,* Julius Schubring (1806–89). The friendship between Mendelssohn and Schubring, a Protestant German pastor, was of long standing, but they hardly saw eye to eye. The composer wanted dramatic scenarios and a strong, worldly character for Elijah: "a prophet such as we might again require in our own day—energetic and zealous, but also stern, wrathful, and gloomy."[8] Schubring favored contemplative passages and insisted on developing the concept of Elijah as forerunner of the Messiah.

There the project lay unattended until the summer of 1845, when Mendelssohn was invited to conduct the triennial Birmingham Festival being organized for August 1846—premiering, it was hoped, a new work for chorus and orchestra. January and February 1846 find composer and librettist hard at work, but still arguing over the distribution of episodes, arias, and choruses. Declining one after another of Schubring's cherished ideas gave Mendelssohn an increasing courage of his own convictions.

The English translation, done in just a few weeks between the very late completion of the score and the first performance, was prepared by the English cleric William Bartholomew (1793–1867), closely following the King James Version. Bartholomew, too, was well known to Mendelssohn, having translated his other choral music for its English performances. With Bartholomew the correspondence was necessarily tedious, made all the more uncomfortable by the illegible and error-ridden German manuscript he was expected to work from—routinely sending him across London to the publishing house to copy out passages from the materials simultaneously being engraved. As with Schubring, Bartholomew's frustrations are obvious. But his tenacity and respectful enthusiasm paid off: Bartholomew successfully insisted on an orchestral introduction and went on to save "O rest in the Lord" from excision.

The text of *Elijah,* like that of *Messiah* and *The Creation,* consists largely of passages taken more or less directly from the Bible, the Elijah narrative from Kings supplemented by reflective arias and choral summaries, particularly from Psalms. The librettists' primary job has been to reduce each passage to its essence:

Aria, no. 31: O rest in the LORD; wait patiently for Him, and He shall give thee thy heart's desires. Commit thy way unto Him, and trust in Him, and fret not thyself because of evil doers. Psalm 37:1, 4, 7.

Chorus, no. 20: Thanks be to God! He laveth the thirsty land! The waters gather; they rush along; they are lifting their voices! The stormy billows are high, their fury is mighty. But the LORD is above them, and Almighty! Psalm 93:3–4.

There are also two short passages from the Gospel of Matthew in the New Testament.

Part I concerns Elijah's prediction of drought, the story of the widow's son, the contest on Mount Carmel, and the end of the drought. Part II recounts Elijah's flight from the wrath of Ahab's queen, Jezebel, his sojourn in the wilderness, and—for Mendelssohn, the climax of the story—the appearance of the Lord before the prophet. At the conclusion, Elijah is gathered, living, to Heaven in the whirlwind. There is, indeed, little narration, and several characters are portrayed by each of the soloists (except for Elijah himself)—making it necessary for listeners to follow a copy of the text during the performance.

Composition, First Performance, and Revision

Having already conducted his own works at the Birmingham Festivals of 1837 and 1840, Mendelssohn was well known to the organizing committee. He hesitated for weeks to accept their invitation, not wanting to conduct the entire festival but tempted by the notion of completing the oratorio he had so long had in mind. In September 1845 he took on the challenge, and by October was engrossed in the work, having the essentials of the text at hand and a harmonic plan for the order of movements. The English contralto Charlotte Dolby remembered a Leipzig evening at the end of that month when Mendelssohn arrived late for a dinner party with the music publisher G. C. Härtel and Robert and Clara Schumann, detained at his desk by the arias for *Elijah*. He tempted Dolby by describing her part, including Jezebel's appearance, as "half angel, half devil."[9] The soprano arias were composed for Jenny Lind, who sang in Leipzig that December, notably in a Liederabend with Mendelssohn at the piano. Whatever the details of their romance, her effect on his artistry was thoroughgoing.[10]

In December 1845 he was still uncertain he could complete the work in time for Birmingham. By April he had turned the corner, and in late May was able to dispatch Part I to London. The chorus parts arrived in the hands of the singers batch by batch, the last only nine days before the concert.

Mendelssohn himself reached London in mid-August, bringing orchestra parts that had been read through and corrected at home. He rehearsed the soloists individually, then led orchestra rehearsals with the London Philharmonic and opera players on Thursday and Friday of the week before the premiere. The London forces and members of the press traveled to Birmingham together by special train that Sunday, with full rehearsals in Birmingham Town Hall on Monday and Tuesday.

Mendelssohn looked "worn and nervous," but the musicians were captivated by the music and by the delicacy of his conducting even with so large a force.[11] At the premiere, Wednesday morning at 11:30 am, eight numbers were encored. Despite its length (and after *Elijah* had come two obligatory Italian sets and a Handel chorus), the oratorio was welcomed with a "unanimous volley of plaudits, vociferous and deafening."[12] He expressed deep satisfaction both from the stage and in written descriptions to family and friends, though that very afternoon was describing how he meant to change "Lift thine eyes" from a duet into a trio.[13]

Elijah had, after all, been rushed into shape. Mendelssohn spent the better part of the winter touching up the score for publication and the London performances set for the following spring: refashioning, among others, the opening sequence and "Cast thy burden," rewriting and transposing the widow's scene up a half-step.[14] (He also began to frame a third oratorio, *Christus,* much as he had begun to think about *Elijah* after the success of *St. Paul.*) He returned to England in April 1847, on his tenth and last visit, conducting four performances in London of what was to be the definitive version, then one concert each in Manchester and Birmingham. On May 14, he learned of the death of his beloved sister, Fanny, and collapsed with a frightful cry. He spent the summer of 1847 preparing for performances of *Elijah* in Berlin, Leipzig, and Vienna, but by October the combined trials of his personal and professional lives led to several nervous attacks that prevented further work. On the first day of November, he suffered a serious stroke, followed by a second on November 3. The next day, Mendelssohn died in his sleep. He never heard *Elijah* in German.

Structure

Mendelssohn's fecundity of compositional ideas keeps this very long work from seeming that way. At every turning point we encounter some new ravishment, finding a good half dozen individual movements that have since become stand-alone audience favorites (e.g., "Cast thy burden," "If with all your hearts," or the chorale in no. 19, "Open the Heavens," used as a choral response in Protestant church services). "Elijah's curse," at the opening, announces three different ideas referenced elsewhere in the work: the low-wind chords that evoke Elijah's seriousness of purpose, the upward arpeggio of the D-major triad, and the fateful interlocking pair of diminished fifths— a powerful Leitmotif (see Example 5.2).

EXAMPLE 5.2 Mendelssohn, *Elijah*, Introduction.

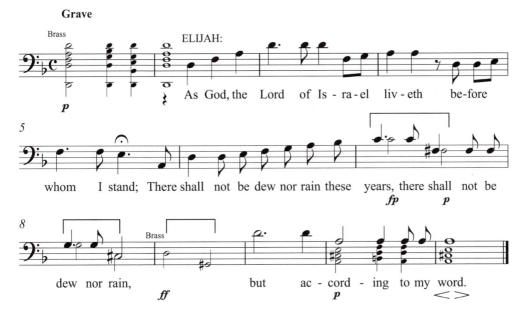

The orchestral introduction, with its anxiety-ridden character and highly chromaticized fugue, culminates in the parched misery of the general cry "Help, Lord! Wilt though quite destroy us?," followed by the recitative laments and duet—in sum, twelve of the most gripping minutes in the literature. The episodes themselves are strikingly different in character, as the soloists and chorus shift roles from incident to incident—not so different an organizational approach, in fact, from that of Berlioz in *La Damnation de Faust* (also of 1846). The contest on Mount Carmel between Elijah and the worshipers of Baal has strong precedent in passages from Bach and Handel, the chorus serving in much the same way as Bach's *turba* in the passions. Two of the arias have obvious Baroque forebears: Elijah's "Is not his word like a fire?" in "For He is like a refiner's fire" from Handel's *Messiah,* and Elijah's aria of despair, "It is enough" is, following Jesus's "Es ist genug" in the *St. John Passion*.

Writers like to characterize *Elijah* as embracing elements of "the opera Mendelssohn never wrote." That is to miss the enormous freedom of generic crossover as practiced by the Romantics. Still the through-composed scene with the widow (no. 8) seems prevailingly operatic in approach, as does the fine concluding tableau of part I (nos. 19–20), where after each verse of Elijah's prayer a boy runs to look for rainclouds. A great final chorus ensues, music of cloudburst and rushing torrents, rooted equally in the pictoral effects of *The Creation* and the Nature-scapes that define Romanticism.

Mendelssohn's keen ear for vocal color finds novel solutions in the antiphonal double quartet "For He shall give his angels charge over thee" and the angel trio "Lift thine eyes." What seems an effortless delineation of the multiple roles assigned to the soprano, alto, and tenor soloists is accomplished through sophisticated control of register and key. He considered removing the contralto aria "O rest in the Lord" for being unmotivated and "too sweet," but was convinced by admirers to leave it in place. The soprano aria that opens part II focuses on Jenny Lind's high F-sharp. She did not, in fact, sing the role until after Mendelssohn's death, and Madame Caradori-Allan, who did sing it, found it unladylike and asked the composer to take it down a step.[15]

To the orchestra is delegated the task of representing the particulars of the setting. It offers fire, flood, and whirlwind music, but also (and more impressively) the quietly undulating arabesques of "Blessed are the men who fear Him" (no. 9) and "He, watching over Israel" (no. 29), and clarinets mocking the priests of Baal at "hear and answer!"

Performance

The arguments for performing *Elijah* and *The Creation* in English are much the same. Both works were composed for and first presented in England, and both composers were acutely aware of their audience as they wrote. Mendelssohn, who spoke competent English, had the controlling hand in the final details of the English vocal score and thoroughly reviewed the proofs before his death: the musical text as published is essentially without error. The 1993 edition of the Novello score, incidentally, purposefully retained the pagination of previous editions, so choruses could use both old and newly acquired copies without needing a concordance.

Elijah is problematic in length. Mendelssohn wrote that he was aiming for two hours but instead came out with more like three, which stretches today's norms and practicalities. The schemes for shortening *Elijah* as collected from distinguished conductors by Robert J. Summer tend, in my view, to go too far. Trimming *Elijah* to 150 minutes can be accomplished with gentle excisions in part II.

Mendelssohn's first performance used just short of 400 musicians: some 125 in the orchestra with doubled winds and about 270 in the chorus (in round numbers 80, 60, 60, 70). His metronome marks are authentic. "Cast thy burden" calls for soloists in the full score but not the vocal score, and is typically sung by the entire chorus.[16]

Antonín Dvořák (1841–1904): *Stabat Mater*, Op. 58

1   Quartet, chorus: Stabat Mater dolorosa
2   Quartet: Quis est homo, qui non fleret
3   Chorus: Eja, Mater, fons amoris
4   Bass solo, chorus: Fac, ut ardeat cor meum
5   Chorus: Tui Nati vulnerati
6   Tenor solo, chorus: Fac me vere tecum flere
7   Chorus: Virgo virginum praeclara
8   Duo (soprano, tenor): Fac, ut portem Christi mortem
9   Alto solo: Inflammatus et accensus
10 Quartet, chorus: Quando corpus morietur

Duration	About 90 minutes.
For	Soloists (SATB), chorus (SATB); flutes I–II, oboes I–II (English horn), clarinets I–II, bassoons I–II; horns I–IV, trumpets I–II, trombones I–III, tuba; timpani; harmonium organ; strings.
Text	A thirteenth-century Roman Catholic hymn, usually attributed to Jacapone da Todi (d. 1306), a Franciscan poet working in north Italy.
Composed	1876–77: sketched February 19–May 7, 1876, for four soloists, chorus, and piano; full score completed on November 13, 1877.
First Performed	December 23, 1880, Prague: Association of Musical Artists, Adolf Čech conducting.
Dedication	To the Association of Musical Artists, Prague.
Note	By the composer's reckoning the composition was Op. 28. The publisher assigned the opus number 58 to suggest that it was recent work.
Scores	• First published Berlin: N. Simrock, 1881, as Op. 58.
	• Standard edition: in Dvořák, *Complete Works,* series 2, vol. 1, ed. Antonín Čubr (Prague, 1958) = Kalmus, Dover, IMSLP. Vocal score: Novello, ed. Michael Pilkington (2000).
	• Scholarly edition: as above, incl. Urtext study score (Bärenreiter 2004). A New Complete Dvořák Edition is underway (Prague: Bärenreiter Praha, 2008*ff.*).
Further Reading	Steinberg, *Choral Masterworks*, 113–18. Green, *A Conductor's Guide*, 151–53.

We hear Dvořák's *Stabat Mater* in the tragic context of the loss of all three of his children—a two-day-old daughter whose death prompted the composition, and two other children before the orchestration was completed. (Later, six children reached adulthood.) This working out of grief through one's art is an artist's natural response. The Brahms and Fauré Requiems both embrace elements of personal mourning; Mahler's *Kindertotenlieder* of 1904, setting Friedrich Rückert's haunting poems on the deaths of his children, acquired the same connotation when one of Mahler's daughters died of scarlet fever and diphtheria in 1907. This intimate, probing *Stabat Mater* spontaneously connects with listeners as genuine, heartfelt, and deep. People took note, and the composer's steady acquisition of international prestige rested in part on its beauties.

Text

The medieval poetic structure called the sequence—the most familiar is the "Dies irae," used in the Requiem mass—consists of three-line stanzas in the rhyme scheme AAB CCB, etc. Each line consists of four trochaic feet (STA-bat MA-ter DO-lo-RO-sa). Here there are twenty stanzas. Both the "Stabat Mater" and "Dies irae" are strongly visual, but where the "Dies irae" weaves a chaotic tapestry of Judgment Day, the "Stabat" text considers a single image, that of the Virgin Mary standing watch beside the crucified Christ. The Stabat Mater scene, often including St. John the Evangelist as well, is represented in hundreds of works of Marian art from the fifteenth century forward, one of the three common representations—with the weeping Mary, or *Maria dolorosa,* and the Pietà—of Our Lady of Sorrows. Her feast day, September 15, once again calls for the singing of the Gregorian sequence, which had been excluded from the liturgy by the Council of Trent in the sixteenth century.

From the central image, evoked in the first stanza, the poet construes a prayer wherein we share the bitter pain of Mary's loss, standing with her in grief as she will stand by us along the path to paradise. The short strophes and relentless singsong meter of the poetic form bothers composers, who sometimes break free of it by reordering or otherwise editing the lines. (Similarly, both Berlioz and Verdi refashion their "Dies irae" texts.) Dvořák's ten movements set the entire text in order, one to four strophes at a time, establishing variety by way of meter, key, and performing force: he seems to have no trouble with the pitfalls of the prosody. He follows Pergolesi and Rossini in adopting, toward the end, the alternative line "Inflammatus et accensus" ("Inflamed and set afire," . . . may I be protected by the Virgin on the Day of Judgment), the better to have the wonderful word "inflammatus" as the movement title.

Dvořák was, with the Czech majority, a devout Catholic. The Czech nationalist composers, including Dvořák in his *Hussite Overture* and related works, celebrated the pre-Reformation followers of the theologian Jan Hus, and lamented crushing defeat of the Bohemian Protestants at the hand of a Catholic confederation in 1612. In the nineteenth century, those events were interpreted less as a matter of religion than as the beginning of political domination by the Austrian empire. In this case, there are no political overtones, merely a grieving father finding solace in the traditional texts of his faith.

Composition and First Performance

Having chosen the text for his therapeutic project, Dvořák composed the entire work fluently in a little over ten weeks, and by spring 1876 had produced an essentially finished vocal score with piano accompaniment. His precedents were G. B. Pergolesi's *Stabat Mater* of 1736, for soprano and alto soloists and strings, and Rossini's of 1841, containing a famous "Inflammatus" for soprano. Both are celebrated compositions, with Pergolesi's said to have been the most frequently performed and reprinted work of its time. Dvořák may well have encountered them, since his own *Stabat Mater* is thick with passages in the Italian style.

Meanwhile his compositional career, having drawn the attention in Vienna of Brahms, the critic Eduard Hanslick, and the music publisher F. A. Simrock, was in the ascendant. Knee-deep in commissions and contracts, he set the *Stabat Mater* aside, not returning to orchestrate and tidy up the final version until the end of 1877. The Prague premiere on December 23, 1880, went unnoticed abroad. Leoš Janáček conducted a second performance to greatly more acclaim in Brno on April 2, 1882, after the Simrock publication. With a published score and enthusiastic champions, now including the peripatetic violin virtuoso Joseph Joachim, the *Stabat Mater* soon reached England. Dvořák's first extended composition for chorus with orchestra, it is thus part of the cluster of mid-career works, with the great Serenade for Winds, Op. 44 (1878), and the first orchestrated Slavonic Dances, Op. 46 (1878), that established his world celebrity.

Structure

The *Stabat Mater* opens, in B minor, with a profound and wrenching treatment of the miserable scene. The dominant pitch, F-sharp, tolls in the tenor-register horn, opening upward across three octaves in the woodwinds and strings—drawing our thoughts, it is usually held, toward the figure on the cross. As the spell takes hold, the F-sharps begin to fall, like tears, chromatically to the tonic B. Out of this is born a new line in contrary motion, then other curvacious interweaving voices as the rest of the orchestra enters. Gradually we discern the meter, a slow 3/2, and the throb of the timpani pedal point, planted firmly on the tonic B. The effect is something like that of a Baroque death passacaglia, its chromatic wiltings insisting on the melancholy scene before us. The huge climax and briefly Italianate lyric set up the entry of the chorus, when virtually all of what has come before is restated. At the halfway point of the 20-minute movement, the solo tenor at last approaches the second strophe of text, breaking the spell, and a central section for the four soloists takes its course, culminating in a reprise of the opening. The form is thus a broad A–B–A.

This first movement, symphonic in scope and redolent with the scent of Schubert and the other Viennese, dwarfs all the others. Much shorter vignettes follow, each unveiling a new perspective through re-combinations of the vocal and orchestral constituents. In truth, we lose track of the details of the poem, hearing instead a series of reflections on death and grieving. All are relatively slow and in rudimentary ternary forms. Gradually, as these simple movements unfold, the sea of melancholy that has all but consumed us begins to recede. Dvořák now seeks threads of solace.

The "Quis est homo, qui non fleret" ("Is there one who would not weep?" no. 2) is for the solo quartet alone, reaching G major when the text contemplates the "tender child"; listen for the plaintive English horn, the fine harmonic pairings (alto soloist with French horn, for instance, m. 8), and the bass soloist's cadential low E at the return of the first section. "Eja, Mater, fons amoris" (no. 3) is a C-minor dead march, its prevailing rhythm that of the nineteenth-century outdoor funeral parade, its several references to the "Eroica" funeral march innately sensed. The soothing turns to E-flat major, choral climaxes (on the word *fac,* "make me" . . . like the grieving mother, consumed in love), and the fragmented dissolution at the end place this wonderful movement in the company of the great processionals of the era.

The stirring bass solo "Fac ut ardeat cor meum" (no. 4), bringing the *Stabat Mater* to its midpoint, combines the familiar sound worlds of the stentorian bass aria (in Mozart and Verdi, for instance) and the distant angel chorus ("Holy Mother, grant that the wounds of the Crucified drive deep into my heart"), with harmonium organ and harp-like arpeggiations in the strings. The second of the chorus interjections has been raised from E-flat into E major, allowing a bolder climax than before and requiring a longer modulatory return to the tonic. This subsides into a low C pedal and a long, coda-like reprise and dissolution of the bass aria, much imbued, again, with references to the "Eroica" funeral march. The pastoral 6/8 meter, wind-band figures, and E-flat major of the choral "Tui Nati vulnerati" (no. 5), are those of the meadow dance, underscored by the woodwind centered scoring. The *forte* passages emphasize the word "poenas" (pains); the sterner center section repeats the single strophe of text in this short movement, on sharing the torments of the crucified Christ.

The chorus continues in the tenor aria, "Fac me vere tecum flere" (no. 6) repeating and resetting the tenor's simple proffers. Each phrase is decorated with different orchestral filigree; increasingly, and with bolder and bolder interjections from the brass and timpani, the focus is on the words "in planctu desidero": our desire to weep beside the grieving mother. The modulatory opening of

"Virgo virginum praeclara" (no. 7) settles in A major, introducing *a cappella* homophonic phrases, each joined at the end by the orchestra, and with climactic arrivals on the word "amara" (bitter). "Fac ut portem," the short duo for soprano and tenor (no. 8), affects a simple walking-bass style in dialogues shared with the solo winds; the principal thematic contour is very closely associated with themes in the earlier march-like movements. "Inflammatus" (no. 9) signals the beginning of the end of a "Stabat Mater," hardly aflame in this case but rather a Baroque-style ritornello aria for the alto soloist, with thematic reference to materials in the third movement.

Acute listeners will sense from the timpani roll and blossoming octaves, again F-sharps, that the closing movement, "Quandos corpus morietur" (no. 10), incorporates the materials of the first. We are sure of it when we reach the long crescendo and first climax. But here the goal is altogether different: arrival in D major, not B minor, for the words "paradisi gloria." While the body decays, says the poem, the soul arrives safely in paradise, there to dwell with Mary the mother. A jubilant Amen peels forth from all the forces, with metric displacements and harmonic jolts all but out of control for so formulaic an ending, and obviously responding to the similar passage in Beethoven's *Missa solemnis*. The chorus, unaccompanied, intones the poetic stanza once more, and in the fadeout the violin arpeggiations lift again and again to their topmost D-major triad.

The apparent simplicity of this *Stabat Mater,* too often described as having roots in "folk music," is an allusion. In fact, the compositional craft is by some measures decidedly advanced, with patches of real harmonic daring. One is struck especially by the changing character of the chorus: in no. 3, as mourners in a funeral march; in no. 4, as angel chorus; in no. 5, with the unmistakable lilt of the village green; in no. 7, as an *a cappella* church choir. Dvořák, gifted with a voice of his own, is well embarked on his mature style.

Dvořák in England

It was the *Stabat Mater* that first popularized Dvořák in England, where he went on to have much the same success as Haydn and Mendelssohn before him. The London conductor Joseph Barnby, who led the resident choral society of the new Royal Albert Hall (1871), had enjoyed such splendid reception of their performance on March 10, 1883, that he invited Dvořák to come the following season to conduct it himself. The concert of March 13, 1884, in the Albert Hall boasted 900 in the chorus and an orchestra of 150, offered to an audience of 10,000. The papers praised Dvořák's "calm, unostentatious yet firm manner" on the podium, while the promoters clamored for more. Dvořák himself was naturally overwhelmed with the size of things: "If you put together all the Czechs in the whole of Bohemia there would still be fewer of them than live in London. And if all the people of Kladno came into the huge hall where I conducted my *Stabat Mater,* there would still be room for them."[17] Wherever he went he saw his picture in the shop windows and was crowded for autographs. He took pleasure in being proclaimed the lion of the season.

Momentum gathered into a sturdy association of composer and empire. He returned in September 1884 to conduct the *Stabat Mater* for the Three Choirs Festival, that year celebrating the 800th anniversary of Worcester Cathedral. Among the orchestral musicians first encountering the work in Worcester was the young Edward Elgar. "I wish you could hear Dvořák's music," he wrote an acquaintance. "It is simply ravishing, so tuneful and clear and the orchestration is wonderful: no matter how few instruments he uses it never sounds thin. I cannot describe it, it must be heard."[18] Elgar often programmed Dvořák after that, and must surely have had his music in mind as he came to compose *The Dream of Gerontius* and his E-minor Cello Concerto, Op. 85.

Altogether Dvořák made nine trips to England, usually to present a new work, often choral: *The Spectre's Bride* for the 1884 Birmingham Festival; the wonderful Symphony No. 7 in D minor for the Royal Philharmonic Society in 1885; *St. Ludmilla* for the Leeds Festival in 1886; a Requiem for the Birmingham Festival in 1890. In 1896, after returning from his American sojourn, he visited London for the last time, bringing with him his new B-minor Cello Concerto.

From England the *Stabat Mater* had reached the United States with performances in New York and Pittsburgh as early as 1884, but the composer's American sojourn, 1892–95, inevitably drew attention to the works composed in the New World. The assimilation of the *Stabat Mater* into the standard repertoire of American orchestras and oratorio societies was gradual, and it has never quite achieved the stature it enjoys in England. It was nevertheless well represented in commemorative concerts during the Dvořák centenary in 2004. Robert Shaw's last recording in September 1999, a few weeks before his death, was of Dvořák's *Stabat Mater* (Atlanta Symphony Orchestra and Chorus, Telarc 1999). He had come to the work in late career, discovering then how "people are deeply, deeply moved by it and without expecting it or even knowing exactly why. It just happens. Sometimes music expresses the inexpressible."[19]

Edward Elgar (1857–1934): *The Dream of Gerontius*, Op. 38

Note: The work is through-composed without separate movements. It is customary to locate passages by reference to the rehearsal numbers in the Novello scores, which start over again for part II.

Part I:

Prelude—Jesu, Maria, I am near to death (Gerontius, reh. 22)—Kyrie eleison (chorus, 29)—Rouse thee, my fainting soul (Gerontius, 33)—Be merciful, be gracious (chorus, 35)—Sanctus fortis, sanctus Deus (Gerontius, 40)—I can no more (Gerontius, 57)—Rescue him, O Lord (chorus, 63)—Novissima hora est (Gerontius, 66)—Proficiscere, anima Christiana (bass, 68)—Go in the name of angels and archangels (chorus, 72).

Part II:

Andantino—I went to sleep (Soul of Gerontius, 4)—My work is done (Angel, 11)—It is a member of that family (Soul)—A presage falls upon thee (duo, 26)—Low born clods of brute earth (chorus of demons, 32)—I see not those false spirits (Soul, 55)—There was a mortal whose is now above (Angel, 58)—Praise to the Holiest in the height! (semi-chorus of Angelicals, 61)—We have now passed the gate and are within the House of Judgment (Angel, 71)—Double Chorus: Praise to the Holiest in the height! (chorus, 88)—Thy judgment now is near (Angel, 102)—Jesu! by the shuddering dread (Angel of the Agony, 106)—I go before my Judge (Soul, 114)—Take me away and in the lowest deep (Soul, after 120)— Lord, Thou has been our refuge (chorus of souls in Purgatory, 125)—Softly and gently, dearly-ransomed soul (Angel, 127).

Duration	About 90 minutes (part I: just over 30 minutes; part II: just under an hour).
For	Soloists (Mez [the angel], T [Gerontius in part I, the Soul of Gerontius in part II], B [priest, angel of agony]); chorus (semi-chorus, double chorus) [assistants, demons, angelicals, souls in purgatory]; flutes I–III (piccolo), oboes I–II, English horn, clarinets I–II, bass clarinet, bassoons I–II, contrabassoon; horns I–IV, trumpets I–III, trombones I–III, tuba; timpani; bass drum, cymbals, snare drum, triangle, tam-tam, jingle bells; harp (II ad lib.), organ; strings. The strings are often divided into more than a dozen lines.
Text	Extracted from *The Dream of Gerontius* by Cardinal Newman (1801–90), written and published in 1865.
Composed	1899–1900
First Performed	October 3, 1900, at the Birmingham Festival, Hans Richter conducting.
Dedication	At the head of the manuscript and published scores, "A. M. D. G.": *ad maiorem Dei gloriam,* "to the greater glory of God"—the motto of the Jesuits.
Scores	• First published London: Novello & Co. in vocal score (1900) with the heading "Composed expressly for the Birmingham Musical Festival, 1900." • Standard edition Novello (vocal score 1900, full score 1901–02), in continuous print since = IMSLP, Kalmus, etc. The German translation that appears below the English is by Julius Buths (1851–1920), the German conductor who introduced *Gerontius* to Europe in performances of 1901 and 1902. The Dover score is from a 1922 Novello rpt. with new introduction and text analysis by Stanley Appelbaum.

- Scholarly edition: Elgar Edition, series I, vol. 6 (1982). The 1992 study score (London and Sevenoaks) is essentially the same.

Further Reading   Steinberg, *Choral Masterworks*, 119–30. Howard Smither, *The Oratorio in the Nineteenth and Twentieth Centuries*, vol. 4 of *A History of the Oratorio* (University of North Carolina Press, 2000), 362–82. The first analysis remains valid: August Jaeger, *The Dream of Gerontius John Henry Newman & Edward Elgar analytical & descriptive notes* (Novello, rpt. 1974).

Also Andreas Friesenhage, *The Dream of Gerontius von Edward Elgar: das englische Oratorium an der Wende zum 20. Jahrhundert* (Dohr, 1994). A vibrant scholarship on Elgar has developed since Michael Kennedy's *Portrait of Elgar* (Oxford University Press, 1982). On the occasion of the centenary of *The Dream of Gerontius,* the Elgar Society published a reflection: Geoffrey Hodgkins, *The Best of Me: A Gerontius Centenary Companion* (Elgar Editions, 1999). The most accessible study of Elgar's compositional practice is Diana M. McVeagh: *Elgar, the Music Maker* (Boydell, 2007).

Gerontius, whose name comes from the Greek for "old man," is an everyman character at the end of his life. Cardinal Newman's radiant poetry opens unseen worlds—the passage from life to death, a soul's instant in the presence of God, the blissful wait for eternal afterlife.[20] Elgar's setting is to be understood in the context of English Catholicism in the Victorian era, a minority position shared by both poet and composer. Many think *The Dream of Gerontius* his masterpiece, and certainly it is the work of an assured, unique voice at the peak of its powers. In English choral circles, *Gerontius* is thought one of the big four, with *Messiah, The Creation,* and *Elijah.*

Synopsis

A 10-minute prelude evokes the agony of the deathbed and the footfall of the departing soul. Part I: On Earth. Gerontius is surrounded by his intimates and a priest, who has come to administer Last Rites. Acknowledging that death is near, Gerontius describes his sensations: "a new feeling, never felt before, . . . this strange innermost abandonment." He recognizes the dire summons of a visitor at his door and asks the friends assembled at his bedside to pray for him. These "assistants" reply with an amplified *Kyrie eleison,* the universally understood plea for God's mercy. Gerontius girds himself for the passage, briefly gaining strength as the assistants continue to pray for his salvation. He confirms his creed in the aria "Sanctus fortis, Sanctus Deus," continuing the pattern of quotations from the Roman rites of death. His agony returns, an ill that "flaps its hideous wings" prompting another cry to Jesus, Mary, and Joseph. The assistants respond a third time ("Rescue him, O Lord, in this his evil hour"), chanting their litany to the redeemed souls of Noah, Job, Moses, and David. "Novissima hora est," Gerontius announces: "It is the final hour." The priest intones "Proficiscere, anima Christiana, de hoc mundo!": "Depart, O Christian soul, out of this world." Priest, chorus, and orchestra escort the departing spirit in a solemn recessional.

Part II: Beyond Earth. The Soul of Gerontius, refreshed, becomes aware of a mystic singing ("I cannot of that music rightly say / Whether I hear, or touch, or taste the tones.") The guardian Angel—a male role sung by the mezzo-soprano—sings a threefold Alleluia, satisfied that his work is nearly done. Soul and Angel exchange greetings and a long dialogue as Gerontius seeks to understand the mysteries of his new situation. The Angel assures him that in the goodness of his life he has forestalled the agony of the damned, and that the bitterness of death has passed. "Already in thy soul the judgment is begun," the Angel says, and together they approach the seat of judgment. They come upon demons, assembled outside the judgment court ("Lowborn clods of brute earth"). For a fleeting moment the Soul will dwell in the presence of God, though the Angel cautions that, like the stigmata of St. Francis, "the flame of the Everlasting Love / doth burn ere it transform." The angels offer "Praise to the Holiest in the height" as Gerontius and his escort cross the threshold: "Thy judgment now is near, for we are come into the veiled presence of our God." Standing before the throne is the Angel of the Agony, suppliant of the dying and the dead. The soul is "consumed, yet quickened by the glance of God," which transpires on the downbeat of reh. 120. "For one moment," Elgar writes in the score, "must every instrument exert its fullest force." As the moment fades an ecstatic Gerontius exults "Take me away!," ready to await his entry to paradise. The Angel, in the most loving of all oratorio closes, lowers him, softly and gently, into the placid lake of Purgatory. The distant semi-chorus of angels continues its song of "Praise to the Holiest," while the chorus of souls below goes on in quiet prayer. "Farewell, but not for ever!" says the Angel. "I will come and wake thee on the morrow."

Text

John Henry Newman (1801–90) was born two years before Berlioz and died a decade before the first performance of Elgar's oratorio, thus dominating a century. As intellectual giants go, he was the real thing: a leading figure in social and religious thought, and an important figure in English university life. (Newman Centers at universities are named after him, as are many dozens of Catholic schools.) In 1845, after two decades of urging Victorian, secularized Anglicism to return to its medieval values, he converted to Roman Catholicism. Received into the Roman priesthood, he spent much of the rest of his life with a monastic brotherhood in Birmingham. *Gerontius* of 1865 precedes his elevation to cardinal in 1879.

Newman composed his long poem "by accident," he wrote, during three weeks in early 1865.[21] You need to brush up on your Catholicism to appreciate it, notably on the notion of Purgatory, here described not as a threatening place but (for the righteous) a restful way-station to the promised land. Newman interleaves dozens of references to the Last Rites, the Recommendation for the Departure of Souls, and the Requiem Mass. Any number of the lines are of spine-tingling beauty: the Soul of Gerontius, for instance, trying to understand his new condition, observes:

> How still it is!
> I hear no more the busy beat of time
> No, nor my fluttering breath, nor struggling pulse
> Nor does one moment differ from the next.

The guardian angel is said to characterize Fr. Ambrose St. John (1815–75), Newman's longtime companion. *Gerontius* was no less personal to Elgar and his wife, Lady Alice, who had received a copy of the poem as a wedding present in 1889. *The Dream of Gerontius* had also served to comfort the doomed General Charles Gordon (Gordon pasha) during the siege of Khartoum in 1884–85, and his annotated copy was brought back to England by a journalist. Together the Elgars had entered Gordon's annotations in their copy. "The poem has been soaking in my mind for at least eight years," Elgar told an interviewer in 1900.[22]

The Catholicity of Newman's poem made it a controversial choice for an oratorio text, certain to needle the English establishment. Good Anglicans wanted little of the Virgin Mary (the first words are Jesu! Maria!) and nothing at all of Purgatory. It was common, for too long, to substitute cleansed lines for passages deemed inappropriate for particular venues.

Composition and First Performance

Elgar grew up in the shadow of St. George's (Catholic) Church, Worcester, where his father was choir director and where he himself often served in apprentice capacities. Worcester Cathedral (with Gloucester and Hereford Cathedrals, all three Anglican) was also one of the sites of the Three Choirs Festival, for which Elgar played violin (see Dvořák, *Stabat Mater*, p. 94 above). He was thus steeped in the necessary traditions, and moreover had by that time completed a series of cantatas and oratorios through which he perfected his techniques of composing for soloists, chorus, and orchestra.

In short, Elgar was in top form when the governing committee from Birmingham invited him to compose a new festival work. The chair of the committee was a Catholic, and by the New Year 1900 had convinced Elgar to accept the commission. The score would need to be completed by summer, and so he abandoned a more ambitious plan for *The Apostles* and turned to Newman's text. (*The Apostles,* Op. 49, was completed in 1903; its sequel, *The Kingdom,* Op. 51, is from 1906.)

He worked with assurance, spurred on by the warm success of the "Enigma" Variations. He composed in short score, knowing that the vocal score would have to be published in order for the choirs to start work. The orchestration could be done as the vocal score was being prepared, and the orchestra parts could be copied at the very end.

A central influence on the final shape of *The Dream of Gerontius* was that of August Jaeger (1860–1909, portrayed as Nimrod in the "Enigma" Variations), the editor-in-chief at Novello & Co—a real editor, who worried about his works in progress and sought to affect their outcome. Their correspondence on *Gerontius* is especially lively with regard to the moment in God's presence. Elgar had wished to avoid the matter altogether, while Jaeger urged an orchestral climax: "a bewilderment of fear, excitation, and crushing overmastering hopelessness. . . . What is your gorgeous orchestra for?" When Elgar continued reticent, Jaeger pressed back, if only for "a few gloriously great and effulgent orchestra chords, given out by the whole force of the orchestra in its mostly glorious key, the momentary vision of the Almighty. A few chords!" Wagner or Richard Strauss, he prodded, would have had an easy time of it.[23] Elgar, accepting the challenge, returned the present reading a few days later.

The first performance was to be conducted by Hans Richter (1843–1916), who had led the very first *Ring* at Bayreuth in 1876 and since had established himself on a heroic scale in England. He had been principal conductor of the Birmingham Orchestra for fifteen years, and had just been called to the nearby Hallé Orchestra of Manchester. Beginning with the "Enigma" Variations, he became Elgar's leading international champion.

Elgar was late delivering the score and Novello later still in printing up the choral parts. The chorus master died and was replaced by a stand-in. The soloists were not especially well suited to their parts. All these factors contributed to the legendary failure of the first performance. "I always said God was against art," sulked the composer, "and I still believe it."[24] *Gerontius* fared better in subsequent seasons, and critical consensus in its favor gathered soon enough for Elgar to enjoy it.

Structure and Style

Though anchored in D major, the key in which the prelude and both halves conclude, *Gerontius* is perceived as a through-composed meditation, unified by more than a dozen motivic reference points in something like Wagnerian fashion. Much of the text is presented as free arioso, giving the more structured arias and set-pieces particular formal power. The hymn-march that follows the priest's "Go forth upon thy journey, Christian soul" (reh. 70), for instance, evokes the British imperial style, that of coronation marches, of Westminster Abbey and St. Paul's. Again and again we think of Wagner's *Parsifal,* a work Elgar is known to have admired in performance and to have studied in score.

In the prelude, seven melodic ideas devolve from the cornerstone "Judgment" motive, presented in the opening bars, in the contralto register (see Example 5.3). In contour and declamatory gesture,

EXAMPLE 5.3 Elgar, *Dream of Gerontius,* selected motives from the Prelude.

1. Judgment

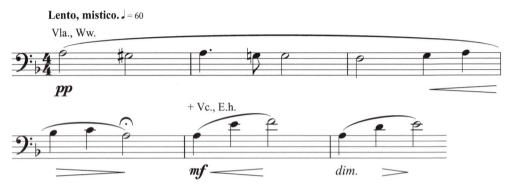

2. Fear

3. Prayer

EXAMPLE 5.3 continued.

4. Sleep

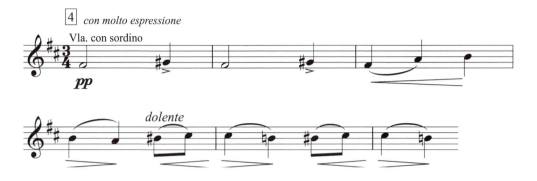

5. Miserere

6. Despair

7. Commital

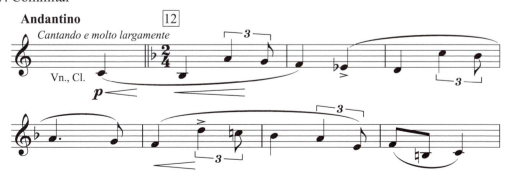

the motive evokes the Gregorian "Dies irae" chant. "Prayer" has the contour of the "Dresden Amen." All the motives have counterparts in Wagnerian thinking—compare the last one, "Committal," with the corresponding place in "Wotan's Farewell" from *Die Walküre*. Much of *Gerontius,* after all, concerns magic sleep.[25]

Elgar has become, with the "Enigma" Variations and *Gerontius*, a great symphonist. The extent of his imagination in deploying the orchestra is remarkable: nearly every word capable of musical reflection is painted, words like "pierce" and "agony" and "bitterness." As a work composed for the great choruses of the English festivals, it renders their pieces in high relief, as in the hissing "dispossessed" and witches-sabbath round dance of the chorus of demons (reh. 32). The transition to the celestial hymn "Praise to the Holiest" summons a web of filigree from arpeggiated flutes, harps, and upper strings, softly underlain by the full chords in the gamba rank of the pipe organ (reh. 60). It takes twenty-eight lines of score to notate the big double- and triple-choir climaxes. Yet *Gerontius* is not especially long—considerably shorter than *Messiah* and *Elijah,* and one-third the length of *Parsifal.*

The musico-poetic journey from agony to tranquility to rapture is so heavy with allusions, intended and spontaneous, that they threaten to overwhelm. Dante's *Purgatorio,* for instance, opens with reference to "kindly waters"; Virgil, with Dante as his guardian angel (as in Delacroix's famous painting of 1822), is a clear precedent for Gerontius. Pre-Raphaelite in aesthetic, *Gerontius* has something in common with Debussy's *La Damoiselle élu* (1889) and *Le Martyre de St-Sébastien* (1911). Christina Rossetti, in her poem "Cardinal Newman," writes "Long was thy sowing day, rest now and reap." Even Oscar Wilde comes to mind: he flirted with Catholicism for much of his adult life and was baptized into the faith on his deathbed in 1900, the year of *Gerontius.* (*De Profundis* of 1897 was published in 1905.) Then, too, there are strong predictors of the sound world later identified with Benjamin Britten and Peter Pears.

Gerontius was identified at the first performance, as a "sacred cantata," to which Elgar objected on reading Jaeger's analysis: "I say, *need* you call it a *Sacred Cantata?* . . . Don't perpetuate that dreadful term." He later told Jaeger to go ahead and "put Gerontius in [Novello's] Oratorio list: there's no word invented yet to describe it."[26] Elgar's notion was simpler: Newman's words "set to music." But Newman's words were not to everyone's taste. Sir Hubert Parry complained of "morbid priestcraft," and thought Newman's text "revolting."[27] Charles Villiers Stanford said, "It stinks of incense." The peculiarly English aspects were lost on Americans.

Those assessments were of little moment. More telling is a passage copied at the end of his manuscript score from the art critic and philosopher John Ruskin, amounting to Elgar's own *envoi:*

> This is the best of me; for the rest, I ate, and drank, and slept, loved and hated, like another: my life was as the vapour and is not; but *this* I saw and knew; this, if anything of mine, is worth your memory.[28]

Performance

Gerontius is probably the most difficult of the works considered in this chapter, by virtue of its chromatic language and freedom of phrase and period structure. The chorus, being divided into eight parts for the climaxes and up against a full "imperial" orchestra with pipe organ, needs numbering in the above-200 category, and to the extent that the English "cathedral sound" (or for that matter the "choral festival" sound) is implied, the sopranos need augmenting with a boychoir.

Gustav Mahler (1860–1911): Symphony No. 8 in E-flat Major

("Symphony of a Thousand")

Part I: Hymn: *Veni creator spiritus*
Part II: Closing scene from Goethe's *Faust*

Duration	About 90 minutes.
For	Eight soloists (SSSAATBarB, characters treated below); two choruses (SATB), boychoir; flutes I–IV, piccolos I–II (=flute V), oboes I–IV, English horn, clarinets I–III, E-flat clarinets (two), bass clarinet, bassoons I–IV, contrabassoon; horns I–VIII, trumpets I–IV, trombones I–IV, tuba; timpani (two groups), bass drum, cymbals (three pairs), tam-tam, triangle, bells, glockenspiel; organ, harmonium organ, piano, harps (two to four), celesta, mandolins (several); strings. At the conclusion, an extra band of brass: trumpets I–IV and trombones I–III.
Texts	The ninth-century Latin hymn *Veni Creator Spiritus* and the last scene of *Faust,* part II (1832, post.), by Johann Wolfgang von Goethe (1749–1832).
Composed	Maiernigg, summer 1906 (June 21–August 18)
First Performed	12 September, 1910, Munich, in a festival performance conducted by Mahler.
Dedication	"Meiner lieben Frau Alma Maria" / "to my dear wife Alma Maria."
Scores	• First published Vienna: Universal Edition, 1912.
	• Standard edition: descendants of the above. The study score published in 1977 (UE 13824), ed. Karl Heinz Füssl (1924–92), was prepared while Füssl was general editor of the Mahler complete edition (see below). The Dover score, 1989, is from a "pirate" Moscow edition of 1976.
	• Scholarly edition: to appear from the International Gustav Mahler Society, Vienna; see www.gustav-mahler.org.
Further Reading	Steinberg, *The Symphony: A Listener's Guide* (New York: Oxford University Press, 1998), 332–48. Summer, *Choral Masterworks from Bach to Britten,* 101–17 (includes an account of training choruses for Robert Shaw's performance with the Atlanta Symphony Orchestra for a Telarc recording, April 1991).
	Also the splendidly detailed accounts of composition and first performance in the biography by Henry-Louis de La Grange; see *Gustav Mahler, vol. 3: Vienna: Triumph and Disillusion, 1904–1907* (Oxford University Press, 2000) and *Gustav Mahler, vol. 4: A New Life Cut Short, 1907–1911* (Oxford University Press, 2008).

In the two decades before electricity changed everything, the orchestral mega-force of the kind used here—and in Schoenberg's *Gurre-Lieder*, Stravinsky's *The Rite of Spring*, and perhaps Holst's *The Planets*—seemed the ultimate in live performance. The common name "Symphony of a Thousand" is nothing more than a marketer's hook. But with two full choruses, children's chorus, extended orchestra with offstage players, and pipe organ, even a modest rendition demands some 600 souls and the venue to accommodate them. Mahler's Eighth lowers the curtain on the Long Century, its compositional priorities rooted thoroughly in Romanticism, from its fascination with literary masterpieces to the syrupy pre-modernism of a tonal system stretched to capacity.

Veni creator *and* Faust

Mahler's combination of a medieval hymn text with the cosmic allegories of *Faust,* part II, is at once a stroke of genius and problematic of burden. Two languages are in play, with the English renderings famously inadequate to express this nuanced vocabulary of love. (*Caritas,* for instance, often given as "Christian love" but here something a good deal more ecumenical.) Reconciling the disparate elements becomes music's function, a challenge the composer was happy to set for himself.

The Latin poem, usually attributed to the German bishop Raban Maure (*c.*780–856), concerns Pentecost, when the Holy Spirit descended over the gathered disciples in what Acts of the Apostles describes as "a sound from heaven, as of a rushing mighty wind."[29] The followers of Christ found tongues to speak in all the languages and hence to witness to all mankind. Seven rhymed quatrains here invite the Holy Spirit, likewise, to enter our own hearts and minds, in a vivid poetry that admirably describes the *creator spiritus* as a "font of life, of fire, of love"—*vivus, ignis, caritas.* (The last two quatrains are rhymed settings of the Gloria Patri.) What captivates Mahler is the first word-pair, *Veni creator,* which after all summarizes any composer's fundamental condition.

The *Faust* text bulges with symbol and metaphor. Understand from the outset that the "original" *Faust* of 1808 (Gretchen and her spinning wheel, the episodes in *La Damnation de Faust,* and so on) has become a thing of the past. Part II, completed in 1832 and published after Goethe's death, concerns the much older Faust after Gretchen: his alliance with Helen of Troy and its physical and metaphysical outcomes. Faust dies at 100. Now, following their infernal contract, Mephistopheles appears to collect his soul. But angels, recognizing a life corrected and well finished, trick the demon and abscond with Faust's spirit. Here begins our final scene.

Strongly alluding to Dante's *Divine Comedy* (where his muse, Beatrice, guides him toward paradise),[30] this scene describes a journey winding upward, begun in a veil of mystery and ending in eternal light. We encounter anchorites, wise and prayerful hermits who have retreated from life to await their own turn to enter Heaven. Though curiously named, these prove to be familiar character types: wise men (Pater Ecstaticus, Pater Profundis), once-sinful women who redeemed themselves in love (Magna Peccatrix, Mulier Samaritana, Maria Aegyptiaca), and toward the top a visionary (Doctor Marianus) able to perceive the Mater Gloriosa, the *Jungfrau*—the Virgin Mary in all her radiance. Among the supporting legions are Blessed Boys who have died before reaching adulthood, Angels, More Perfect Angels, and the Mystic Chorus of the spheres. Una Poenitentium—one of the penitents—is Gretchen herself.

Composition and First Performance

A typical summer for Mahler consisted of mornings spent composing, alone in a "composing hut" and often consumed in self-doubt, offset by afternoon promenades in the placid natural settings Austrians frequent for their vacations. Since 1901, the Mahlers had occupied a handsome lakeside villa in Maiernigg on the Wörthersee, with the master's custom-built *Komponierhäuschen* just up the hill behind. He arrived in 1906 fatigued and in the throes of writer's block, with nothing particular in mind for a new symphony. On entering his little workplace, however, he found his lethargy reversed by an onset of the *creator spiritus* and thoughts of a first movement on the *Veni creator* hymn. "I saw the whole piece before my eyes,"[31] he told an interviewer, feeling as if the music were being dictated to him, just as legend described Pope Gregory receiving the Roman liturgy and its chant tunes.

The first general plans for the new symphony reckoned a conventional four movements: after the *Veni creator* would come a scherzo ("Children at play on Christmas," in one iteration), slow movement on the concept of *caritas,* and a concluding hymn to erotic love. He composed the opening movement in a white heat, before the correct poem text had arrived from Vienna. (When it came, said his wife, it "fit the music exactly."[32]) But he abandoned the original plan when he realized the connection between the old hymn and *Faust,* part II: a kind of love that enters the heart, consumes it, and in the end transfigures. Ordinarily Mahler was a troubled composer. Now, hyper-stimulated and suffused with the very creative energy considered in his text, the only demon he encountered was the defeated Mephistopheles. In its keen sense of character and voice and its knack for orchestral scene-setting, the Eighth Symphony testifies to a career's worth of lessons learned as much in the opera pit as anywhere else.

Mahler was all but smugly satisfied about the result, certain that his new symphony outdistanced all that had come before in its evocation of metaphysical realms—the music of the spheres. He thought of it as a great bringer of joy. At the end of the last rehearsal, the innocent voice of one of the children in the chorus was heard from the top of the scaffold: "Herr Mahler, das Lied ist schön," reducing him to tears.[33]

Performances

Being well versed in the challenges of live production, Mahler had the very good sense to engage Emil Gutmann, a professional impresario, to produce the first performance. (It was Gutmann who coined the nickname.) A venue was found in the new Musik-Festhalle built on the fairgrounds of the Munich Exhibition, the Austellung München, of 1908. This barn-like pavilion, accommodating 3,000, was typical of the permanent–temporary structures of the era, with electric lighting and a "fearful stink" of automobiles depositing and collecting the concertgoers. The choral forces came from Munich, of course, and as far away as Leipzig and Vienna; the soloists, from great opera houses of Germany and Austria. Mahler's two young assistants were Bruno Walter and Otto Klemperer, both of whom went on to become *maestri.*

For those in the know it was a trip worth making. Among the composers who traveled to Munich were Richard Strauss, Anton Webern, Alexander von Zemlinsky, and the French master Camille Saint-Saëns. Other notables included the novelist Thomas Mann, Strauss's librettist Hugo von Hofmannsthal, and Siegfried Wagner. Heads of state, civic leaders, and conductors young and old flocked to hear. There was a "kingly" greeting when Mahler took the podium, and widespread appreciation of the clarity and energy of his conducting. At the conclusion came the salvos of a thoroughgoing success, the greatest of Mahler's lifetime, going on (according to some accounts) nearly an hour. Three boys from the children's choir made their way down from the rafters with the congratulatory wreath.

The atmosphere was charged for another reason: Mahler's obviously fragile state of health. Just after reaching Munich, he had taken to his bed with a sore throat. He had not been seen in Europe since the previous summer, having spent the 1909–10 concert season in New York. His associates were astonished at how he had aged, now seeing before them a yellowed little man who got about with difficulty. The soprano Lilli Lehmann was "overcome with emotion and unable to pull myself together," in part because of her presentiment of Mahler's demise.[34] It proved to be his last premiere. Shortly afterward he and his wife returned to New York, where his final decline accelerated.

Within a few years of Mahler's death, the Eighth Symphony had been heard in the major European capitals, notably in Amsterdam under Willem Mengelberg (1912, and again as part of the complete symphonic cycle in 1920). In 1916, the young Leopold Stokowski and Arthur Judson, the manager he had brought to the Philadelphia Orchestra, presented ten sold-out performances including a commute to the Metropolitan Opera House. Stokowski was elevated to stardom as though overnight, while Concert Management Arthur Judson, Inc. went on to dominate classical music as Columbia Artists Management, Inc.

Structure

The musical fabric of Mahler's Eighth is inviting, first of all, in its brilliant surfaces, with extra brass and pipe organ to take things over the top, multiple high-Cs for the soprano soloist, and consistently captivating orchestration. Architecture and content are clearly delineated, anchored strongly by E-flat major and the opening motto. With the central words "Accende lumen sensibus / Infunde amorem cordibus" ("Kindle our reason with light / Infuse our hearts with love") comes a second motive heard across both movements, Mahler's hint as to how closely the two seemingly disparate texts are connected (see Example 5.4). Mahler nudges this "Accende motive" into E major, the key in which it returns most obviously in the second movement.

EXAMPLE 5.4 Mahler, Symphony No. 8, part I, Hymnus: *Veni creator spiritus*

A Mahlerian sonata form is easily distinguished in the contours of the *Veni creator,* with the secondary thematic material, in D-flat, at "Imple superna gratia" (7, m. 46) and the ravishing texture of the seven soloists, followed by a brief subsidiary reprise of the *Veni creator* (15, m. 104) and closing material at the return of the choruses (19, m. 141). The Development has begun at the outbreak of the vaguely sinister nocturnal march over a tolling chime (23, m. 169), gathering into the "Accende" squarely at the middle point (38, m. 262) and an extravagant display of fugal device to establish maximum tension. Recapitulation comes with the strong return of the opening *Veni creator* (64, m. 413), and for a Coda the Gloria Patri, referencing procedures that opened the Development and ending *tutta forza,* with the head-motive sounding regally from the extra trumpet-and-trombone choir.

Part II, twice as long as the first, is controlled by the scenario, taking place in a setting described by Goethe as "mountain gorges, forest, cliff, desert; holy anchorites, scattered up the mountain-side, living in clefts of the rocks." Four principal sections are articulated: the introductory orchestral poem that describes the eerie setting, the episodes with the wise men, those with the three women, and a finale with the Mater Gloriosa and Chorus Mysticus. Remember to think vertically: characters materialize and evaporate during the course of the ascent to secure Faust's admission to paradise.

Mahler is very good at insisting on the critical words—most of them *Liebe*-constructs—so in this case (unusually) following every line of the libretto during the concert may be counterproductive. By contrast it makes good sense to read the entire text beforehand and re-read it just afterward, each time grasping a little more of Goethe's complicated poetic text.

The magnificent orchestral prelude that transports us into Goethe's world, nearly 15 minutes of music, evokes the lugubrious scene in a brooding essay on all that is pent up in the anchoring motives. After about 10 minutes the men of the chorus, as though from the darkness, describe the setting in words, with tenors and basses exchanging lines antiphonally, as though across the gorge. With the entry of the women singers, the wooziness is transcended; this is, they say, "love's holy hermitage," a *heiligen Liebeshort*.

Pater Ecstaticus, a baritone "floating above and below" the scene, describes the power of erotic love—burning, foaming, piercing, eternal—in an ecstatic passage rooted firmly in the home key of E-flat and alighting marvelously on the words *Liebebande* and *Gotteslust* (after 31, m. 219). Pater Profundis, a Wotan-like bass heard from the rocky chasm below, interprets the waterfalls and lightning around him as love's messengers, *Liebesbote*, there to release a man from the riot of his confused thoughts and into a higher realm (39, m. 266). This notion of a spirit chained to earth by the demands of daily life is not just Faust's agony but also Mahler's.

Angels bearing Faust gloat over rescuing his spirit from Mephistopheles (56, m. 385), in a superb example of Mahler's affection for the delighted nattering of children. The Blessed Boys join hands, circling above, and the girlish Younger Angels describe how strewing rose petals around Faust's lifeless body had caused the devil to draw back, allowing their escape (after 63, m. 443). More Perfect Angels (75, m. 540), in a sudden change of tone, pose the problem of separating the spirit of Faust from the earthly remains, a task accomplished by the Blessed Boys. Dr. Marianus, a heroic tenor close to the top of the metaphorical mountain / pyramid, gazes on the Mater Gloriosa above (84, m. 604). The Blessed Boys (85, m. 612), then Dr. Marianus, and finally all the men extol the purity of the Queen of Heaven (89, m. 639; 100, m. 738). Mater Gloriosa materializes (106, m. 774), to the stunning accompaniment of harps and piano, as the approximate midpoint of the movement is reached.

What has been a predominantly masculine focus becomes increasingly feminine as penitent women plead for Faust's admission to the sacred mysteries. The marvelous scene of the three women who have sinned and loved (Mary Magdalene, who dressed Christ's wounds, at 117, m. 868; the Samaritan woman who gave him water for Abraham's well, 121, m. 906; and Mary of Egypt, who repented of her life as a camp follower and became a saintly desert hermit, 128, m. 970), concludes with a trio in canon (136, m. 1022). Gretchen, to the accompaniment of mandolins, steps forward from among the penitents (148, m. 1096), asking to bring Faust into heaven. The Blessed Boys support her petition by arguing that the rejuvenated, virile young Faust can serve as their mentor. "Komm," the Mater Gloriosa invites Gretchen (172, m. 1249): "if he is aware of you, he will follow." The Chorus Mysticus continues: "Komm! Komm!"

Dr. Maurianus's ecstatic "Blicket auf" ("Look upward," 176; m. 1277) leads to the great mystic chorus ("Alles Vergängliche ist nur ein Gleichnis," roughly, "earthly things are all transitory"; after 52, m. 1449). This begins *ppp* "in a whisper," gathering by the end into a wholesale phantasmagoria of sound and spectacle much along the lines of the *Auferstehen* hymn that concludes the Second Symphony. The auxiliary brass choir shouts the *Veni creator* motive from the beginning of the work. The great essay on *Liebe* and *Liebeslust*, having treated the mysteries of masculine and feminine, Latin and French, real and imagined worlds, concludes as it had opened: celebrating the creative enterprise.

Reception

It hardly mattered what the newspaper journalists might write, given the caliber of the intellectuals who had heard the first performance and the clout they carried across Europe. Webern wrote to Schoenberg, who had been unable to make the trip: "So beautiful."[35] The music critic Julius Korngold and his prodigiously gifted eleven-year-old son, Erich, were at the dress rehearsal and both performances, Erich "strangely excited" and Julius struck by "Mahler's transfiguration, and . . . his ascent—like another Dr. Marianus—into the highest and purest cell of musical creativity."[36] Wittier minds made jokes: "What if the Holy Spirit doesn't come?"

In Mahler's case redemption in the Eternal Feminine was already distorted by truer facts of life. The Eighth Symphony, with its fulsome dedication to his beautiful young wife, Alma, had also been a soul-baring personal statement. As the premiere approached, Mahler learned of her spa romance with the architect Walter Gropius. (She had felt trapped in the conditions of her marriage, she said, and was in a deep depression following the death of their daughter at Maiernigg in the summer of 1907.) So to the many other levels of our perception of the Eighth we must add the uncomfortable awareness of love's capacity for failure, as Mahler surely sensed while leading it.

The transparency of Mahler's approach in the Eighth, his disinclination to poke further into the implications of *fin-de-siècle* thought, is sometimes held in the critical literature to be a step backward. But the works that follow—the Ninth Symphony and unfinished Tenth, along with *Das Lied von der Erde*—go precisely there, and to the concert-going public the relief from darker concerns was altogether welcome. As was the dazzle of the biggest work anyone was likely ever to hear.

Notes

1 Berlioz, *Mémoires*, Travels in Germany II, letter 3.
2 Kent W. Werth, "Dating the 'Labitte Catalogue' of Berlioz's Works," *19th-Century Music* 1 (1977), 137–41.
3 Berlioz, *Mémoires*, ch. 54.
4 The idea of the language of the damned, incidentally, was first used in the "ancient Nordic" of the Chorus of Shades in the *mélologue, Le Retour à la vie,* Berlioz's strange sequel to the *Fantastique* (H. 55, 1831 and 1855). I think it is also a souvenir of the many languages Berlioz had heard around him but failed to understand in the months just preceding.
5 I Kings 19:11–12.
6 Letter Mendelssohn to Klingemann, August 12, 1836, in F. G. Edwards, *The History of Mendelssohn's Oratorio "Elijah"* (Novello, 1896), 3.
7 Ibid., 6–9.
8 Letter Mendelssohn to Schubring, November 2, 1838, in ibid., 12.
9 Ibid., 35.
10 An affadavit by Lind's husband Otto Goldschmidt, concerning their affair, now housed at the Mendelssohn Scholarship Foundation at the Royal Academic of Music, London, was the subject of a press brouhaha in January 2009. See for instance Jessica Duchen, "Conspiracy of Silence: Could the release of secret documents shatter Felix Mendelssohn's reputation?" *The Independent,* January 12, 2009.
11 Edwards, *Mendelssohn's Oratorio "Elijah,"* 77.
12 Ibid., 83.
13 Ibid., 85.
14 The autograph score reached the Birmingham Central Library in 1996.
15 Edwards, *Mendelssohn's Oratorio "Elijah,"* 76.
16 Promotional pieces for Elijah often adopt the fine frontispiece engraving by Julius Hübner for Simrock's first edition, where an imposing bearded Elijah looks heavenward, arms widespread, with one bare foot planted on the ruins of the altar to Baal.
17 Letter, Dvořák to his father, March 1884, in Kurt Honolka, *Dvořák,* trans. Anne Wyburd (London: Haus, 2004), 60–61.
18 Letter Elgar to Charles William Buck, 28 September, 1884, in *Edward Elgar: Letters of a Lifetime,* ed. Jerrold Northrup Moore (London: Oxford University Press, 1990), 12.

19 Robert Shaw, interview with Martin Goldsmith of NPR, included on the Telarc CD (Telarc 2CD-80506).
20 Gerontius may be pronounced with either form of *g*, hard or soft, and in any event the name is not spoken in the composition.
21 Letter Newman to Lady Thynne, October 29, 1865, in *The Letters and Diaries of John Henry Newman*, vol. 22, ed. Charles Stephen Dessain (London: Nelson, 1972), 86.
22 *Musical Times*, October 1, 1900.
23 Letters August Jaeger to Elgar, "gorgeous orchestra": June 27, 1900; "a few chords": June 30, 1900, in Jerrold Northrop Moore, *Edward Elgar: A Creative Life* (New York: Oxford University Press, 1984), 318, 321.
24 Letter Elgar to August Jaeger, October 9, 1900, in Moore, *Edward Elgar*, 334.
25 On the motivic connections, see Diana M. McVeagh, *Elgar the Music Maker* (Woodbridge: Boydell, 2007), 60–62.
26 Letters Elgar to Jaeger, July 4, 1901 and August 23, 1904, in Jerrold Northrop Moore, *Elgar and His Publishers* (London: Oxford University Press, 19087), vol. 1, 292–93 and vol. 2, 580.
27 Splendidly summarized by Byron Adams, in "Elgar's Later Oratorios: Roman Catholicism, Decadence, and the Wagnerian Dialect of Shame and Grace," *Cambridge Companion to Elgar*, ed. Daniel Grimley and Julian Rushton (Cambridge: Cambridge University Press, 2004), 89.
28 John Ruskin, "Of King's Treasuries," in *Sesame and Lilies: Three Lectures* (New York: Thomas Y. Crowell, 1865), 48.
29 Acts 2:2.
30 See above, concerning *The Dream of Gerontius* and its suggestions of Dante and Beatrice.
31 Richard Specht, in the *Tagespost*, Vienna, June 14, 1914; given in full (in English) in Donald Mitchell, *Gustav Mahler, Songs and Symphonies of Life and Death: Interpretations and Annotations* (Berkeley: University of California Press, 1986), 519.
32 Alma Mahler's account is considered and documented in Mitchell, *Gustav Mahler*, 521–24 and notes.
33 Henry-Louis de La Grange, *Gustav Mahler, vol. 4: A New Life Cut Short, 1907–1911* (Oxford: Oxford University Press, 2008), 961.
34 Ibid., 972.
35 Ibid., 967.
36 Ibid., 971–72.

PART III

The Choral Repertoire Large and Small

Germany and Austria

6

CHORAL MUSIC AND CHORAL SINGING IN GERMANY AND AUSTRIA

An Overview

Ryan Minor

SUNY Stony Brook

On Sunday, July 5, 1885, members of the Cäcilien-Verein chorus in Hamburg went on an outing. They boarded a special train headed for Hausbruch, a hilly suburb south of the city, where coffee and cake awaited them at a local inn. The singers and their families then headed for the forest. They sang among the trees and enjoyed the running spring water. Back in Hausbruch, they ate some more, and they sang some more; speeches were given, glasses were raised. The chorus returned to Hamburg that night wishing that every day could be a Sunday such as this.[1]

The Cäcilien-Verein's trip to the woods is difficult to place within existing musicological accounts of nineteenth-century music, not only because the social world of music-making has typically been forced to take a back seat to compositional histories, but also because choral music in general is often overshadowed by the prominence accorded nineteenth-century instrumental music. Put another way, both the genre of choral music itself as well as its intensely social milieu run afoul of musicology's traditional obsession with pure, "absolute" music. But as musicologists have begun to focus more on the social and political world of music-making (both amateur and professional), and simultaneously have questioned the very possibility of the "purely musical," anecdotes such as the Hamburg chorus's woodsy excursion begin to look more like the substance of music history, rather than a merely charming supplement to it.

For one thing, Hamburg's Cäcilien-Verein was hardly an insignificant organization within German musical culture. Although mixed-voice choral societies proliferated throughout Germany in the nineteenth century, from small towns to big cities—they were the virtual embodiment of the German bourgeoisie and its allegiance to the high arts and education—relatively few attained the status of the Hamburg organization.[2] Renowned for the strength and training of its voices, and particularly its *a cappella* abilities, the Cäcilien-Verein performed frequently with the likes of Brahms, Joachim, and Hans von Bülow; in this sense, the chorus's trip to the forest cannot be taken as a compensatory gesture, an exercise in sociability substituting for actual musical talent or seriousness.[3] But perhaps more importantly, a distinction between the social and musical would have made no sense to the Hamburg choristers in the first place; unlike today, acknowledging that music had social roots would not have amounted to a fall from grace. In fact, for bourgeois German choral societies such as the Cäcilien-Verein, it was precisely the educational and communal rewards that choral singing offered that made it so attractive in the first place. Perhaps more so than any other medium in nineteenth-century Germany, the world of choral music demonstrated that musical seriousness and social interaction were not mutually exclusive. As we will see, the choristers' outing to the woods illustrates in miniature the interdependence between musical and social values that fueled choral music—and choral singing—throughout the century.

Institutional Foundations

To account for the astonishing variety of choral music in nineteenth-century Germany is simultaneously to account for the wide array of institutions and spaces in which Germans came into contact with each other. From the *Liedertafel* (the tavern) comes an impressive supply of group drinking songs for men's chorus (*Männerchor*); from the huge choral festivals along the Lower Rhine, a large stock of oratorios; from advanced bourgeois choruses such as the Cäcilien-Verein, an ambitious flow of polyphony; and from choruses both in- and outside of the church, a steady stream of sacred music on both sides of the confessional aisle. Moreover, even within relatively narrow social circles the sheer number of choruses that flourished is deeply impressive. In Hamburg, for instance, the Protestant bourgeoisie was not limited to the Cäcilien-Verein, which had emerged as the town's preeminent mixed chorus by the end of the century; at least half a dozen other choruses drew from similar swaths of Hamburg society.[4]

These choruses' importance reached beyond the music written for them. In most towns in nineteenth-century Germany, choruses provided the main institutional anchor for music-making and concert-going outside the opera house. Indeed, for most of the century it was not the orchestra but the choral society that served as the chief institutional home for serious music. In an exact inversion of the situation today, a mixed-voice choral society offered the preeminent series of subscription concerts in many cities; if an orchestra was needed for a work such as an oratorio, one would be hired, or even put together from the ground up for the occasion. Only by the end of the century, and with the increasing prestige and institutional power of groups such as the Berlin Philharmonic or the Hofkapelle in Meiningen, did orchestras begin to eclipse choral societies as permanent musical agents on both a local and a national level—but even this was a gradual process, and hardly applicable across the country. In Hamburg, for instance, the Philharmonische Gesellschaft was the city's main orchestral institution, but it was more a society of subscribers than it was an orchestra unto itself; for performances, players were generally borrowed from the opera house's orchestra (and dependent on the opera house's largesse in doing so), and the number of performances was relatively rare.[5] Indeed, it was more often choral societies that performed—or, rather, organized performances of—orchestral music. Hamburg's Cäcilien-Verein included quite a few orchestral works in its repertoire, although it is not clear from concert programs or internal documents who the orchestral musicians were. The absence of that information, in direct contrast to the minutely detailed rosters of the chorus members who ran the organization, is a telling distinction.

What makes this institutional prominence of the chorus all the more surprising were the humble, and in many ways strikingly unambitious, beginnings of the choral movement in Germany. The first notable choral society, the Berlin Sing-Akademie, was initially formed by Carl Friedrich Christian Fasch in 1791 out of informal gatherings of educated bureaucrats and minor nobility. They met in members' living rooms, and their evenings together seem to have consisted of equal parts *kaffeeklatsch* and earnest attempts to sing sacred polyphony. Gradually the group outgrew these spaces, in terms of both size and aspiration, and in 1827, under the leadership of Carl Friedrich Zelter, the Sing-Akademie moved into a building all of its own. It was from this new, public position that Zelter's Sing-Akademie attracted so much attention two years later with its famous performances of the *St. Matthew Passion*, under the baton of Felix Mendelssohn.[6] This movement out of the domestic sphere and into the public one was both the result of, and a catalyst for, the increasing prominence of choral institutions and choral singing throughout German society: not only in taverns, churches, schools, and choral societies, but also events such as the Lower Rhine festivals, which drew tens of thousands of singers and spectators.[7] Indeed, we might view Mahler's Eighth Symphony (1907), whose expansive incorporation of large multiple choruses sought to encompass the entirety of both earthly and heavenly realms, as the supreme telos of the chorus's transition out of its sequestered domesticity and into German public and intellectual life. Particularly in light of the bourgeois ensemble's demure beginnings, this trajectory was not only a move up in prestige, but it was also a move out (into the wider public realm) and outwards (encompassing increasingly larger numbers of amateur singers).

In this sense, we can see the burgeoning success of the choral movement as both a reflection and an agent of monumentalism, that increasing propensity of nineteenth-century German culture to eschew the personal and intimate in favor of the cosmic and overwhelming.[8] But we must be careful here, for there are notable exceptions. Schubert's many partsongs, for instance, were written for small domestic get-togethers, and even if one accepts that these intimate gatherings were a political necessity in light of Foreign Minister Metternich's harsh control over public assembly in Vienna, they nonetheless produced a delightful corpus of works that would suffer at the hands of larger performing forces. Similarly, much of the music stemming from the Cecilian movement— the pan-European attempt to reanimate church music through the careful emulation of counter-Reformation polyphony—was rather pointedly *not* written for performance in the concert hall, even if that is where some of it, like Bruckner's motets, has frequently ended up.[9]

Rather, what bound together the intimate and the monumental, and religious music as well as a religion *of* music, was the participatory ethos of choral singing. Although participation itself was a catchword of political liberalism, emphasizing democracy and reform "from below," the appeal of choral participation reached beyond the largely Protestant and bourgeois milieu of liberal politics.[10] Choral singing worked hand in hand with a fervent investment in the promise of *Bildung*—the moral and social edification ascribed to education—that enjoyed a wide appeal across class, confessional, and regional lines.[11] (Hamburg's Cäcilien-Verein, for instance, focused on musical education and voice training as an integral part of its mission.[12]) And even if individual choruses tended to consist of one particular social stratum, it was certainly the case by the end of the century that the massive proliferation of choruses throughout all realms of German society enabled a degree of participation among the general public that would have been unimaginable for those early members of Fasch's Singakademie, gathered in each other's elegant parlors.

Compositional Issues

Not surprisingly, the music written for this wide array of German choral institutions is as diverse as the institutions themselves; a standard-issue *Männerchor* drinking song and the searing chromatic austerity of Liszt's *Via Crucis* (1879) are about as far apart compositionally as two works from the same century could be. Still, one can point to some general similarities across the century and across genres. For one thing, creative uses of timbre were arguably as unimportant for choral composition as they were integral to orchestral music. There was relatively little innovation in the division and grouping of voices; choral music was almost exclusively written for mixed chorus, men's chorus, or women's chorus. Put another way: natural adult voices sang in their normal ranges, and they did so in tried-and-true ensembles. (An exception is Schubert, who occasionally scored his choral works for STB, TTBBB, or other unusual combinations.) And as far as the voices themselves are treated, there is little if anything in the German repertoire to compare with the French use of the closed mouth effect (*bouche fermée*), which had been featured for much of the century across the Rhine. Compared to France, and even more so the extended ranges and innovative instrumental groupings explored in contemporaneous orchestral composition, German choral timbres remained fairly conservative.

This relative lack of interest in non-traditional choral timbres most likely has its roots in the idealization of amateur music-making that underlay the choral movement. In fact, the sound of average, untrained voices was not an unavoidable or lamentable byproduct of the choral movement; it was precisely the point.[13] Moreover, this notion that the (imagined) voice of the *Volk* should provide an aesthetic model for choral composition was not only a key factor in the general avoidance of more cultivated timbres, but it also helped sustain the influence of the chorale—as melody, as texture, and as the participatory ideal of group singing *par excellence*—well beyond its specifically theological aims.[14] In both cases, the goal was the naturalization of song, indeed of singing itself. What Germans saw in the chorale was nothing less than, in Richard Wagner's words, "the character of German art . . . the inclination of the people to song."[15] In other words, choral music as exemplified by the chorale was not simply music written *for* a chorus; it was also, in some idealized (if highly mediated) sense, music stemming *from* the *Volk* and its natural propensity to sing. And this naturalization of song also extended far beyond the chorale to encompass the most advanced counterpoint. After all, one of the guiding principles of the choral movement was the promise of education and self-betterment through musical participation; to sing a fugue was to inhabit the edifying structures of music itself, to take part directly in the very craft of musical composition at its most rarified. (It is most likely this gratifying social component, rather than some blind adherence to tradition, that accounts for the large quantity of fugues in works such as Mendelssohn's oratorios, which were explicitly written for bourgeois choral societies.)

Choral music thus thrived at the juncture of nature and nurture, of the uncultivated human voice on the one hand and the highly cultivated compositional skill of counterpoint on the other. And it is important to note that just as composers sought to "vocalize" advanced compositional techniques for the chorus, they simultaneously came to rely more and more on choral textures in their instrumental works. Indeed, for a century that is said to have jettisoned vocal music in favor of purely abstract instrumental music, choral textures retained a remarkably persistent presence: the repeated reliance on brass and wind chorales in the symphonic works of Brahms, Liszt, Bruckner, and Mahler—and of course their hymnic correlates in Beethoven's piano and chamber music— suggest that an idealized communal voice attained an increasingly privileged compositional presence even outside actual choral music. Thus if some of Bruckner's motets seem at moments to be mere vocalizations of his symphonic works, it is worth remembering that his symphonic language was itself built around a vocabulary of choral textures. Indeed, the popular cliché that Bruckner's symphonies evoke the space of a cathedral is an implicit acknowledgment of the fundamental correspondence between the choral and the instrumental (as well as the sacred and the secular) that is not easily parsed into signifier or signified, naive or sentimental. To be sure, we might attribute this confluence to Bruckner himself: the devout Catholic organist-cum-symphonist. But we can observe much the same amalgamation on the other end of the German musical world as well— with Johannes Brahms and the Protestant, north German heritage that suffuses both his choral and his instrumental music. Here the most obvious example, of course, is his *German Requiem*, whose symphonic textures and instrumental forms meld seamlessly with idiomatic choral writing that both references its sacred past (Bach and Schütz most notably) and substantially moves beyond it in its exploration of a new, non-liturgical form.[16]

Jewish choral music also participated within the larger world of German composition—starting with the very notion of a modern chorus, which in many synagogues began to replace the *meshorerim*, the solo or small groups of solo singers. In fact many Reform congregations began to incorporate elements from the broader world of German music: prayers sung in German, the introduction of the organ, and perhaps most surprisingly the singing of chorales with Jewish texts to Protestant melodies. This broadening out can be seen stylistically as well in works by com-posers such as Louis Lewandowski and Salomon Sulzer—the latter of whom was responsible for commissioning Schubert's 92nd Psalm (1827), written in Hebrew for baritone solo and mixed chorus, and probably the most famous German example of a "Jewish" choral work written by a canonical composer in the nineteenth century.

Schubert's choral works can also be seen as a link to yet another segment of German composition, and that is, of course, the *Lied*. Most of Schubert's choral music shares with his *Lieder* the same unmistakable lyricism, and in terms of both poets and subject matter many of the texts are interchangeable with those of his solo songs. Indeed, this link to solo singing is often exploited in the works themselves, particularly the large number of part songs composed for small choruses. Schubert was also fond of juxtaposing solo and choral singing—as, for instance, in his famous *Ständchen* (1827) for alto solo and men's voices, as well as the *Nachthelle* (1826) for tenor solo and men's voices, which is also notable for the stratospheric heights of the tenor line. As many critics have noted, these *Männerchor* works remain underperformed—perhaps because of the punishing tessitura, and perhaps because the *Männerchor* as a social institution is virtually extinct—but Schubert's sacred music has not had a much easier time. Aside from some of the Latin masses, his large catalogue of motets, the *Deutsche Messe* (1827), and *Lazarus*, an unusual (and unfinished) oratorio-cantata hybrid that even has stage instructions, all await popular discovery.

A Case Study

All of these links between choral music and the other genres of "classical" composition in nineteenth-century Germany—the *Lied*, the symphony, even chamber music—might appear not to play much of a role in the Cäcilien-Verein's outing to the Hamburg woods that Sunday in 1885. But as I have suggested above, the communal aspects of choral singing hardly precluded an engagement with "high" art music. There is, unfortunately, no documentation of what the nature-loving choristers sang in the forest. We can, however, make some educated guesses about the kind of music they might have sung, all of which lead us to Brahms—not simply because the chorus shared a hometown with the composer, but because it performed almost all of his choral works (and even premiered his Op. 109, the *Fest- und Gedenksprüche*).[17] What is more, the previous December Brahms had conducted his new Third Symphony under the aegis of the organization, and in the following season he would bring them his still-unpublished Fourth Symphony.[18] (The orchestra for these performances is entirely unclear from the Cäcilien-Verein's account of the occasions as well as Sittard's 1890 history of Hamburg's musical life; as I have suggested above, this ambiguity is in keeping with the primacy of choral over orchestra institutions in much of nineteenth-century Germany). Moreover, the chorus's tie to Brahms was not limited to the composer's visits; performances of his choral music made up a substantial portion of its public concerts throughout the latter part of the century.[19]

Thus of the many forest-themed choral works in its repertory the Cäcilien-Verein might conceivably have sung on this outing—and the list is surprisingly large, including examples by Schubert, Schumann, both Fanny and Felix Mendelssohn, and Franz Wüllner, as well as the chorus's own conductor, Julius Spengel—let us focus on one woodsy composition by Brahms as a potential candidate: "Waldesnacht" (Forest Night), written to a text by Paul Heyse in 1874 and published as part of Brahms's *Sieben Lieder* Op. 62.[20] Easily the most famous of the opus—and possibly of his *a cappella* choral works *tout court*—"Waldesnacht" has long been noted for its evocative beauty, particularly in the way that it pairs a highly atmospheric, and typically Romantic, praise of nature with strict contrapuntal underpinnings.[21]

The double canon at a fifth in mm. 12–16 (see Example 6.1) is the most obvious manifestation of this contrapuntal orientation, but the fact that the canon is sung *pianissimo* to a text praising a dream-like fusion with nature helps remove any trace of pedantry or self-consciousness from the strict counterpoint.[22] Indeed, it is a good deal more productive to view the counterpoint in this

EXAMPLE 6.1 Brahms, "Waldesnacht," Op. 62/3.

EXAMPLE 6.1 continued.

EXAMPLE 6.1 continued.

work as the dynamic interaction of various musical agents than simply as a top-down exercise in compositional control. That is at least the message behind Johann Gottfried Herder's impassioned description of choral singing, issued in 1800, just as the choral movement was getting underway:

[The voices] are one and not one; they leave, search, follow, contradict, fight, strengthen, destroy each other, and awaken and animate and console and flatter and hug each other again, until they finally give way [*ersterben*] to one tone. There is no sweeter image of searching and finding, of amicable dispute and reconciliation, of loss and yearning, of doubting and full recognition, at long last of utterly sweet unification and merging as these two- and multiple-voiced tone-movements [*Tongänge*].[23]

Following Herder, we might consider Brahms's wrenching dissonances in mm. 11, 15, and 22 of "Waldesnacht" not just as contrapuntal by-products, or text-setting alone, but also as the forces of "dispute and reconciliation." Along similar lines, the frequent syncopations (mm. 3, 8, 9, and 21) function as assertive gestures, much as the fluid and ever-changing pairings of voice parts help explore the processes of "unification and merging."

Thus just as the Romantic subject in Heyse's poem seeks to merge himself with nature (a desire replicated in the Hamburg choristers' trip to sing in the woods), we might also speak of a more communal desire—located within Brahms's "Waldesnacht" as well as the choral movement for which it was written—both to merge with and to distinguish oneself from the community. It was a desire both musical and non-musical, both individual and collective. And it arguably found no better means of fulfillment than the culture of choral singing in nineteenth-century Germany.

Notes

1 These details come from an occasional poem entitled "Caecilien-Verein." The chorus's documents are not all catalogued; they are located at the Brahms-Institut an der Musikhochschule Lübeck. My thanks to Wolfgang Sandberger and Stefan Weymar for their generosity in sharing the chorus's documents with me.

2 For a relatively complete list of the main choral societies and when they were founded, see Georg Knepler, *Musikgeschichte des 19. Jahrhunderts. Band II Österreich—Deutschland* (Berlin: Henschelverlag, 1961), 713–14.

3 On the Cäcilien-Verein, and particularly its relationship with Johannes Brahms (who praised its strength), see Annemari Spengel, ed., *Johannes Brahms an Julius Spengel. Unveröffentlichte Briefe aus den Jahren 1882–1897* (Hamburg: Gesellschaft der Bücherfruende zu Hamburg, 1959).

4 Also noteworthy were the Hamburgische Musikverein, the Sing-Akademie, the Deppe'sche Sing-Akademie, the Bach-Gesellschaft, Euthymia, the Gesang-Verein, and the Altonaer Sing-Akademie. On Hamburg's musical life in the nineteenth century, see Josef Sittard's 1890 *Geschichte des Musik- und Concertwesens in Hamburg vom 14. Jahrhundert bis auf die Gegenwart* (New York: Georg Olms, repr. 1971).

5 Sittard, *Geschichte*, 304–38.

6 The Sing-Akademie's building is now the Maxim Gorki Theater, an amusing irony given the thoroughly bourgeois character of the hall's original purpose. An excellent history of the Sing-Akademie through its watershed performances of the *St. Matthew Passion* is Celia Applegate, *Bach in Berlin: Nation and Culture in Mendelssohn's Revival of the* St. Matthew Passion (Ithaca, NY: Cornell University Press, 2005).

7 On the Lower Rhine festivals, see Cecilia Hopkins Porter, "The New Public and the Reordering of the Musical Establishment: the Lower Rhine Music Festivals, 1818–67," *19th-Century Music* 4 (1980): 211–24.

8 See Alexander Rehding, *Music and Monumentality: Commemoration and Wonderment in Nineteenth-Century Germany* (Oxford: Oxford University Press, 2009).

9 For a recent account of the Cecilian movement in Germany, see James Garratt, *Palestrina and the German Romantic Imagination* (New York: Cambridge University Press, 2002).

10 See James J. Sheehan, *German Liberalism in the Nineteenth Century* (Chicago: University of Chicago Press, 1978).

11 On the idea of *Bildung*, see Hermann Glaser, *Bildungsbürtertum und Nationalismus. Politik und Kultur im Wilhelminischen Deutschland* (Munich: Deutscher Taschenbuchverlag, 1993).

12 Sittard, *Geschichte*, 339–56.

13 For a fascinating look into the pedagogy and aesthetics behind amateur choral singing, see David Gramit, *Cultivating Music: The Aspirations, Interests, and Limits of German Musical Culture, 1770–1848* (Berkeley: University of California Press, 2002).

14 On the chorale, see Glenn Stanley, "Bach's *Erbe*: The Chorale in the German Oratorio of the Early Nineteenth Century," *19th-Century Music* 11, no. 2 (1987): 121–49.

15 Richard Wagner, *Sämtliche Schriften und Dichtungen* (Leipzig: Breitkopf & Härtel, 1912), vol. 1, 158.

16 See most recently Daniel Beller-McKenna, *Brahms and the German Spirit* (Cambridge: Harvard University Press, 2004).

17 On the Op. 109 performances, see my "Occasions and Nations in Brahms's *Fest- und Gedenksprüche*," *19th-Century Music* 29, 3 (2006): 261–88.

18 The chorus also boasted in its annual report that Brahms had offered them a "new series of choral songs," a promise Brahms only partially honored; several years later, the Cäcilien-Verein gave the premieres of two of the five numbers in his Op. 104 (the entirety of the opus was first performed in Vienna), "Nachtwache II" and the popular "Im Herbst."

19 See the "Jahresbericht des Cäcilien-Vereins in Hamburg für das Vereinsjahr 1884–85," marked "108–111" in "box 1" of the chorus's documents at the Brahms-Institut an der Musikhochschule Lübeck.

20 "Cäcilien-Verein. Katalog," at the Brahms-Institut an der Musikhochschule Lübeck.

21 Virginia Hancock, "Brahms and Early Music: Evidence from his Library and his Choral Compositions," in George S. Bozarth, ed., *Brahms Studies: Analytical and Historical Perspectives* (Oxford: Clarendon Press, 1990), 29–48, here 39.

22 See also Joachim Geiger, "J. Brahms: 'Waldesnacht' Op. 62/3. Ein Beitrag zu Analyse, Interpretation und Probentechnik," *Musik und Bildung* 22, 2 (1990): 90–95.

23 Quoted in Erich Valentin, ed., *Aussprüche über Chorgesang. Berichte und Bekenntnisse* (Köln-Bayenthal: Verlags- und Vertriebsgesellschaft für Chorbedarf, 1965), 39.

Selected Bibliography

Applegate, Celia. *Bach in Berlin: Nation and Culture in Mendelssohn's Revival of the* St. Matthew Passion. Ithaca, NY: Cornell University Press, 2005.

Beller-McKenna, Daniel. *Brahms and the German Spirit*. Cambridge, MA: Harvard University Press, 2004.

Beuerle, Hans Michael. *Johannes Brahms. Untersuchungen zu den A-cappella-Kompositionen. Ein Beitrag zur Geschichte der Chormusik*. Hamburg: Karl Dieter Wagner, 1987.

Donakowski, Conrad L. *A Muse for the Masses: Ritual and Music in an Age of Democratic Revolution 1770–1870*. Chicago: University of Chicago Press, 1977.

Elben, Otto. *Der volksthümliche deutsche Männergesang. Geschichte und Stellung im Leben der Nation; der deutsche Sängerbund und seine Gleider*. 2nd edition. Tübingen: H. Laupp, 1887.

Fellerer, Karl Gustav. "Das deutsche Chorlied im 19. Jahrhundert," in *Gattungen der Musik in Einzeldarstellungen. Gedenkschrift Leo Schrade*, ed. Wulf Arlt, Ernst Lichtenhahn and Hans Oesch. Bern: Francke, 1973, 785–812.

Garratt, James. *Palestrina and the German Romantic Imagination*. New York: Cambridge University Press, 2002.

Gramit, David. *Cultivating Music: The Aspirations, Interests, and Limits of German Musical Culture, 1770–1848*. Berkeley: University of California Press, 2002.

Gutsche, Susanne V. *Der Chor bei Beethoven. Eine Untersuchung zur Rolle des Chores in den Orchesterwerken von den Bonner Cantaten bis zur 9. Symphonie*. Kassel: Gustav Bosse Berlag, 1995.

Hancock, Virginia. "Brahms and Early Music: Evidence from his Library and his Choral Compositions," in *Brahms Studies: Analytical and Historical Perspectives*, ed. George S. Bozarth. Oxford: Clarendon Press, 1990, 29–48.

Kirsch, Winfried. "Religiöse und liturgische Aspekte bei Brahms und Bruckner," in *Religiöse Musik in nicht-liturgischen Werken von Beethoven bis Reger*, ed. Walter Wiora et al. Regensburg: Gustav Bosse, 1978, 143–55.

Klenke, Dietmar. "Bürgerliche Männergesang und Politik in Deutschland," *Geschichte in Wissenschaft und Unterricht* 40 (1989): 458–85 and 534–61.

Kross, Siegfried. *Die Chorwerke von Johannes Brahms*. Berlin: Max Hesses Verlag, 1963.

Minor, Ryan. *Choral Fantasies: Music, Festivity, and Nationhood in Nineteenth-Century Germany*. Cambridge: Cambridge University Press, forthcoming.

Porter, Cecilia Hopkins. "The New Public and the Reordering of the Musical Establishment: The Lower Rhine Music Festivals, 1818–67," *19th-Century Music* 4 (1980): 211–24.

Rosen, Charles. "Mendelssohn and the Invention of Religious Kitsch," in *The Romantic Generation*. Cambridge, MA: Harvard University Press, 1995, 569–98.

Sposato, Jeffrey. *The Price of Assimilation: Felix Mendelssohn and the Nineteenth-Century Anti-Semitic Tradition*. New York: Oxford University Press, 2006.

Stanley, Glenn. "Bach's *Erbe*: The Chorale in the German Oratorio of the Early Nineteenth Century," *19th-Century Music* 11, no. 2 (1987): 121–49.

Valentin, Erich, ed. *Aussprüche über Chorgesang. Berichte und Bekenntnisse*. Köln-Bayenthal: Verlags- und Vertriebsgesellschaft für Chorbedarf, 1965.

7

LUDWIG VAN BEETHOVEN

David B. Levy

WAKE FOREST UNIVERSITY

Beethoven's fame rests primarily on his instrumental works. Consequently, most paradigms that have evolved to define his style have also been derived from instrumental models. Only a handful of his pieces that use choral forces can be said to have exerted much influence on subsequent composers, even if they served as models of how *not* to write for chorus. The most frequently performed of these works—the "Choral" Fantasy, Op. 80 (1808), the *Missa solemnis*, Op. 123 (1823), and the finale of the Ninth Symphony, Op. 125 (1824)—are the most problematic examples of Beethoven's choral writing because of their often high tessitura and extraordinary technical demands. Beethoven's largest and most striking choral piece, by far, is the *Missa solemnis*. Yet, as Tovey observed nearly a century ago, the 20 minutes of choral writing in the finale of the Ninth Symphony proves more exhausting than the hour and a half of the *Missa solemnis*.[1] Almost as popular as the works listed above, and far less problematic from the singers' standpoint, is the final chorus "Welten singen Dank und Ehre / Preiset Ihn ihr Engelchöre" from Beethoven's 1803 oratorio, *Christus am Ölberg*, Op. 85. This chorus, loosely translated as "Hallelujah unto God's Almighty Son / Praise the Lord," has become a favorite of church and high school choirs in the English-speaking world.

Among Beethoven's less frequently performed significant choral works are the Mass in C major, Op. 86 (1807), the *Elegischer Gesang*, Op. 118 (1814), a cantata written for the Congress of Vienna, *Der glorreiche Augenblick*, Op. 136 (1814), and the choral setting of Goethe's poetic pair, *Meerestille und glückliche Fahrt*, Op. 112 (1814–15). Even less frequently performed are two youthful cantatas of 1790: the *Trauer-Kantate auf den Tod Kaiser Josephs des Zweiten*, WoO 87, and the *Kantate auf die Erhebung Leopolds des Zweiten zur Kaiserwürde*, WoO 88. Beethoven also penned other works involving choral forces, including some impressive moments from his only opera, *Fidelio* (1814, originally presented as *Leonore*, 1804–05, rev. 1805–06), and numbers in his incidental music for the stage: *Die Ruinen von Athen*, Op. 113 (1811), *König Stephan*, Op. 117 (1811), and two choral pieces from *Die Weihe des Hauses* ("Wo sich die Pulse," WoO 98 and a March with Chorus, Op. 114, adapted from *Die Ruinen*). Our list is rounded out by some isolated works, including settings of Carl Bernard's *Chor auf die verbündeten Fürsten*, WoO 95 (1814), Anton Joseph Stein's *Hochzeitslied*, WoO 105 (1819), Friedrich von Matthisson's *Opferlied* for soprano and chorus, Op. 121b (1822, rev. 1824), and Goethe's folksy *Bundeslied*, Op. 122 (1823–24). Choruses are also indicated for some of Beethoven's folk-song settings created for George Thompson of Edinburgh, and for a few isolated Lieder (such as at the end of the humorous setting of Mephisto's *Flohlied* from Goethe's *Faust*, Op. 75, no. 3).[2]

The Bonn Cantatas

Of the two early cantatas composed in 1790, the one lamenting the death of the Austrian Emperor Joseph II contains the most interesting choral writing. The author of the texts of both cantatas—works commissioned by the University *Lesegesellschaft*—was Severin Anton Averdonk, a theology student at the University of Bonn whose family was close to the Beethoven clan. This group of intellectuals was an offshoot of the Masonic Order of the Illuminati founded in Bavaria in 1776. The Bonn *Lesegesellschaft* began in 1787 and did not usually engage in musical activities, although Beethoven's earliest teachers, Christian Gottlob Neefe, Nikolaus Simrock, and Franz Ries, among other musical colleagues, were active members.[3]

The Funeral Cantata's opening and closing movements, "Todt! Todt!," frame the entire work in an impressively somber C minor (the first movement eventually moves to the relative E-flat major at the end, a feature that does not recur in the final movement). It is hard to identify where Beethoven may have found a precedent for its sorrowful choral outbursts, but these anguished cries certainly resonate with even greater effectiveness fourteen years later in the instrumental introduction to Act II of *Leonore / Fidelio*, wherein we experience in sound the sufferings of the unjustly imprisoned Florestan. Yet another, and more direct precursor of Beethoven's opera is found in the cantata's aria with chorus (no. 3), "Da stiegen die Menschen," whose arching melody was reused by the composer in the finale of Act II with the words, "O Gott, Welch ein Augenblick!"[4]

The second cantata, for Emperor Leopold II's accession, opens with a recitative with chorus ("Er schlummert"), but contains only one purely choral movement, the rousing "Heil! / Stürzet nieder, Millionen / Erschallet Jubelchöre" that brings the work to a jubilant conclusion. The text's obvious paraphrase from Schiller's 1785 "An die Freude" (the source for the text of the finale of the Ninth Symphony) has drawn some attention from scholars, although it is unfortunate that they have missed an important distinction: Schiller's text and Beethoven's setting in the Ninth is an interrogative ("Ihr stürzt nieder, Millionen?") rather than Averdonk's imperative in which the "millions" are exhorted to bow down in praise of their new ruler.[5] Nevertheless, this suite of choruses is impressive for its clear declamation and fugal writing. While it demands that the sopranos sustain some high As (not nearly as strenuous as we shall see in his later works), it does not present insuperable difficulties for most choirs and deserves to be heard more often.

It is believed that Haydn was shown one or both of these impressive works either in 1790 while en route to London, or in July of 1792 upon his return. What is significant is the fact that the elder master agreed to accept the young Rhinelander as his pupil. Unfortunately, neither work was performed or published during Beethoven's lifetime and are heard only rarely today. Perhaps this is the fate of any *pièce d'occasion* that is linked too specifically to a political event. Upon reading Eduard Hanslick's enthusiastic words in 1884, no less a figure than Johannes Brahms recognized that the works were "Beethoven through and through," noting also of the Joseph Cantata its "noble pathos . . . its feeling and imagination, the intensity, perhaps violent in its expression, also the voice-leading and declamation, and, in the two outer sections, all the features that we may observe in and associate with his later works."[6]

Christus am Ölberg (Christ on the Mount of Olives), Op. 85

Composed in 1802 and first performed on April 5, 1803 at an *Akademie* held in Vienna's Theater an der Wien, *Christus* has been from the start a work rife with problems. The libretto is attributed to a minor Austrian (Czech-born) author, Franz Xaver Huber, but Barry Cooper has argued that Beethoven played a major role in shaping the text and its dramatic structure.[7] The composer revised *Christus* for another performance that took place on March 27, 1804 but it went unpublished until

October 1811. Beethoven himself recognized its uneven nature and problematic libretto, although in responding to criticism from the work's publishers (Breitkopf und Härtel), he begged indulgence for a piece that was "my first work of that kind and, moreover, an early work . . . written in a fortnight during all kinds of disturbances and other unpleasant and distressing events in my life (my brother happened to be suffering from a mortal disease.)"[8] Biographers have drawn parallels between Christ's sufferings, as depicted in *Christus*, with the composer's own, as revealed in his Heiligenstadt Testament. While this may be true, one can't help but sense that Beethoven found as much empathy in the suffering of Leonore's husband, Florestan, as he did in Jesus.

But what kind of work is *Christus am Ölberg*? Beethoven called it an oratorio and Cooper, among others, has suggested that the composer was influenced by the great oratorios of Haydn—*The Creation* and *The Seasons*—which had recently been performed in Vienna in 1798 and 1801 respectively. But if this is so, the only true resemblance lies in the final chorus. The incidental choral episodes, representing variously the *turba*-like Roman soldiers and the utterances of Jesus's disciples, cannot be performed apart from the context of the dramatic *scena* that shapes the entire work. A critic for the *Allegemeine musikalische Zeitung*, much to Beethoven's consternation, called the work a "cantata," but in fact its shape more closely resembles that of a passion oratorio than anything else.

For whatever weaknesses one may find in *Christus*, its tripartite final chorus sung by the Angelic Choir mentioned above rises to our popular notion of Beethovenian nobility and has become (in its English translation) a favorite concert work of church and amateur choirs, making it the "other" Hallelujah chorus. Unlike the *Missa solemnis* or the finale of the Ninth Symphony, its ambitus places relatively little strain on the singers' voices.

Mass in C Major, Op. 86

As is well known, Beethoven's study with Haydn bore considerable fruit, even if their pupil–teacher relationship was occasionally attenuated. Haydn's continuing connection to the Esterházy family led to a significant opportunity in 1807 for the young composer to try his hand at a major sacred work: the Mass in C major. The commission for the Mass came from Prince Nikolaus Esterházy for the name-day (September 8) of his wife, née Marie von Liechtenstein. Haydn had written his last six masses for the same occasions between 1796 and 1802; these, along with his famous *Te Deum* in C major and final two oratorios (*The Creation* and *The Seasons*) represent some of the elder master's finest music. There can be no question that Haydn's own settings of the Mass had a significant impact on Beethoven's Mass in C major. Another composer, Johann Nepomuk Hummel, also figures into the mix, as he had followed in Haydn's footsteps by composing several masses for the Esterházy court.[9] Beethoven's challenge, therefore, was to arrive at something both appropriate and original for this important patron. That Beethoven may have failed in this regard is evidenced by Prince Esterházy's haughty dismissal of it: "But, my dear Beethoven, what is this that you have done again?" Indeed, the Prince subsequently described the work as "unbearably ridiculous and detestable."[10]

Today's audience has good reason to be puzzled by the Prince's overwhelmingly negative reaction to the Mass in C major. Beethoven himself acknowledged the "inward looking" nature of the piece. "Gentleness," he wrote to the publisher in 1811, "is the fundamental characteristic of the whole work." In this sense, it leans far more strongly toward the ethos of the *Pastoral* Symphony, than the driven qualities of the Fifth Symphony, both of which were being composed at the same time.

It is not surprising to find excerpts from Haydn's "Creation" Mass (*Schöpfungmesse*) among the sketches for Beethoven's Mass in C. Nor should we be surprised to find direct musical paraphrase from Haydn's Mass in Time of War (*Missa in tempore belli* or *Paukenmesse*), also in the key of C major, at certain points in Beethoven's Mass. The opening of the Agnus Dei from the *Paukenmesse* and Beethoven's Sanctus bear striking melodic and harmonic similarities, as well as sharing the similar effective use of the kettledrum. The more war-like aspects of Haydn's Agnus Dei will resonate, of course, with even greater force in Beethoven's second setting of the Mass—the more famous *Missa solemnis* of 1819–20.

William Kinderman's observation that "Beethoven's dynamic and richly contrasting musical characterization of the text [of the Mass in C] departs from Haydn's more restrained, unified approach; this is presumably what displeased the Prince."[11] Beethoven's approach to the liturgy certainly was different from Haydn's in many respects, as was his preference for finding suitable musical material for smaller textual details, rather than using self-contained forms (sonata form, canon) within a movement.[12] Perhaps it was Beethoven's self-consciousness of this difference that compelled him to bring back the music of the opening Kyrie at the end of the Agnus Dei, thus creating an external musical unity that might otherwise be perceived as missing.[13]

What strikes me as more important, however, is the way in which Beethoven invented a kind of devotional tone throughout the Mass in C major, a tone that he would identify in the Kyrie of the *Missa solemnis* as *Andacht*, a word that has no direct English equivalent, but contains within it elements of devotion, contemplation, and piety.[14] It is music that seeks the soul of its text. This quality of *Andacht* bespeaks many of the most poignant moments in Beethoven's subsequent instrumental and vocal works: think not only of the Sanctus and Benedictus of the *Missa solemnis*, but also of the heavenly slow movements such as the second movement of the "Emperor" Concerto, the third movement and Adagio ma non troppo ma divoto section from the finale of the Ninth Symphony ("Ihr stürzt nieder, Millionen?"), not to mention the slow movements from the late piano sonatas and string quartets. The generations of composers that came after Beethoven would draw upon this sentiment as well.

Chorfantasie (Choral Fantasy), Op. 80

Beethoven's notorious four-hour *Akademie* of December 22, 1808 gave occasion to this short, but impressive addition to the choral repertory. As is well known, this concert mixed improvised solo piano music together with the premiere of Symphony Nos. 5 and 6, the Fourth Piano Concerto, and excerpts from the Mass in C major. To tie up the loose ends and to give the program an appropriately celebratory conclusion, Beethoven hastily put together the Choral Fantasy with a text attributed to Christoph Kuffner to create a grand finale. The poem, "Schmeichelnd hold" (Coaxing, fair), may be viewed as an ode to the beneficial nature of music, a gift of the gods.

While the published work (1811) begins with a quasi-improvisatory and searching solo for piano, this may not have been the same music that Beethoven actually improvised at the premiere.[15] The principal tune of the finale, however, was not even new, but was a recycled version of his 1794–95 song, *Gegenliebe*, WoO 118 ("Wüsst ich, dass du mich lieb.") Much has been made about the parallels in overall structure between the finale of the Choral Fantasy and that of the Ninth Symphony: a tuneful melody that undergoes instrumental variations before the entry of solo voices and chorus. The obvious surface similarities between the *Gegenliebe* tune and that of the "An die Freude" may suggest to those unfamiliar with Beethoven chronology that the Choral Fantasy was conceived as a model for the finale of the Ninth Symphony, when in fact Beethoven, although long interested in setting Schiller's poem, was not engaged with it when he composed the Choral Fantasy. What is true, however, is that after the Ninth Symphony's premiere in 1824, Beethoven referred to the earlier work by way of comparison, although hastening to add that the finale of the Ninth was executed "on a far grander scale."[16]

Any challenges that the Choral Fantasy presents to singers are ameliorated somewhat by the work's brevity. Like the finale to Act Two of Beethoven's *Fidelio*, the energy of the Choral Fantasy's finale generates considerable excitement without overly taxing the voices.

Elegischer Gesang, Op. 118

This short and moving work composed in 1814 (published 1826) is dedicated to Beethoven's friend and patron, Baron Johann von Pasqualati, in whose home on the Mölkerbastei the composer had taken up residence at various points between 1804 and 1815. This lofty apartment was located near the wall that surrounded Vienna in Beethoven's time—the building still exists as one of Vienna's Beethoven museums. The occasion for *Elegischer Gesang* was the third anniversary of the death of the Baron's second wife, Eleonore (née von Fritsch). The authorship of its text, "Sanft, wie du lebtest hast du vollendet" (Gently, as you lived, have you died) is unknown—an attribution to Ignaz Franz von Castelli is unsubstantiated. While it is likely that the work, which was first performed privately at the Pasqualati residence, was initially conceived for four vocal soloists accompanied by string quartet, the published version is marked "Chor," indicating its suitability for choral performance.

Elegischer Gesang's principal theme, a triple-meter hymn in sarabande rhythm, bears close kinship with the third movement of the more famous Piano Trio, Op. 97 ("Archduke").[17] Its overall serenity is briefly interrupted by a few *forte* outbursts (e.g., "für den Schmerz!" in mm. 29 and 32–3) prompted by Beethoven's tendency, seen also in the Mass in C, for localized text painting. One encounters some challenging chromatic passages in the middle section ("Kein Auge wein'") but the work's smooth voice-leading and range makes it approachable for any competent amateur choir and worthy of more frequent performance.

Der glorreiche Augenblick, Op. 136

Only Beethoven's Battle Symphony (*Wellington's Victory*) has had more scorn heaped upon it than the cantata *Der glorreiche Augenblick* (The Glorious Moment). Lewis Lockwood, for one, damned it as a "grotesque parody of his serious style," while Maynard Solomon condemned it, along with works by Beethoven associated with the Congress of Vienna as "the nadir of Beethoven's artistic career."[18] This fact is ironic insofar as it was written during a high water mark in Beethoven's popularity. Composed to a text by Aloys Weissenbach, the cantata was published posthumously in 1837 as Op. 136. Its first performance, along with *Wellington's Victory* and the Seventh Symphony, took place before an enthusiastic audience of gathered heads of state in Vienna's Redoutensaal on November 29, 1814. The enthusiasm, unfortunately, was insufficient to guarantee a full house at a repeat performance and a third scheduled performance was canceled. No wonder, then, that this work has fallen by the wayside.[19]

The result is that, until recently, choral directors have either shied away from performing *Der glorreiche Augenblick* or remained totally unaware of its existence.[20] This is a shame because it contains flashes of Beethoven at his best, and even most inspired. Indeed, it features several passages that anticipate the most exalted moments of the *Missa solemnis* and Ninth Symphony finale. The thrilling registral leaps from low to high, echoed by the orchestra, in the opening chorus of the cantata ("Europa steht!"), for example, anticipate an analogous gesture at the onset of the Credo of the *Missa solemnis*.[21] For all its shortcomings, this *piece d'occasion* merits more frequent hearings, not only because it represents an important document in Austrian / Viennese history, but also for the glimpse it provides into Beethoven's development as a choral composer.

Meeresstille und glückliche Fahrt, Op. 112

This 1814–15 setting of Goethe's pair of poems, *Meeresstille und glückliche Fahrt* (Calm Sea and Prosperous Voyage) has been deemed by Beethoven scholars and critics to be far superior to *Der glorreiche Augenblick* of the same period.[22] Nevertheless, this mini-cantata / choral scenario dedicated to the great German poet remains to this day a relatively unknown work to most audiences and choral singers. Indeed, Beethoven's choral and orchestral setting has been eclipsed by Felix Mendelssohn's 1828 (rev. 1834) purely instrumental concert overture of the same title. Beethoven's setting was evidently intended to be used for a concert planned for February of 1815, but it had to wait until December 25 for its premiere at a benefit concert in Vienna. The work remained unpublished until 1822.

Beethoven inserted a quotation from the eighth canto of Homer's *Odyssey* (translated by Voss) on the verso side of the title page, no doubt intended as a tribute to Goethe:

> Alle sterblichen Menschen der Erde nehmen die Sänger
> Billig mit Achtung auf und Ehrfurcht; selber die Muse
> Lehrt sie den hohen Gesang, und waltet über die Sänger.
> (From all who walk the earth our bards deserve
> esteem and awe, for the Muse herself has taught them
> paths of song. She loves the breed of harpers.) [23]

The smooth voice leading and essentially homophonic texture of the vocal lines in *Meeresstille* present few difficulties for most choirs. The wide leap in the sopranos from e^1 to a^2 on the words "ungeheurern Weite" in mm. 27–28 and 35–36 as well as the speed of the *Allegro vivace* of *Glückliche Fahrt* provide the most challenging moments in an otherwise quite singable and satisfying choral experience.

Choral Finale of Symphony no. 9, Op. 125

Earlier in this chapter I mentioned Tovey's observation that although the *Missa solemnis*—a work that is choral from start to finish—is longer than the entire Ninth Symphony, the Choral Symphony's finale "is more exhausting in 20 minutes than the whole Mass in an hour and a quarter." Regarding the difficulties presented by the choral (and solo vocal) writing, he added that "whatever may be said against Beethoven's choral writing . . . [he] is completely at ease in accompanying the voice."[24] Wherein then, does the problem lie? While there are some uncomfortable changes of register for the altos and sustained high a^2s for the tenors and sopranos, there is no reason to assume that these, and other passages, are to be sung loudly throughout. Any chorus that attempts to sing the finale of the Ninth Symphony from start to finish at full throttle is doomed to fail. Indeed, a sensitive and nuanced performance of the movement should not ask the singers to sustain a high level of volume without offering the level of contrast that makes for a truly musical performance of the work (strict observance of *szforzandi, diminuendos,* and other dynamic markings). A bigger problem lies in the unrelenting high tessitura of many of the passages, especially for the sopranos, whose stamina is challenged by long stretches of singing between e^2 and a^2. Interestingly, the decision to supplement the soprano (and alto) section of the chorus with boys at the premiere in Vienna on May 7, 1824 may be taken as evidence that Beethoven was cognizant of this problem.[25]

Despite its challenges, the finale of the Ninth Symphony still offers vocalists one of the most exciting and satisfying experiences in all choral singing. The artful folksiness of Beethoven's tune for Schiller's "An die Freude" and the lofty humanistic message resulting from his reworking of the original poem appeals to singers and audiences of all nations, races, colors, and creeds.[26] The legacy of the Ninth Symphony's finale as progenitor of subsequent choral symphonies can be said to extend at least from Mendelssohn's *Lobgesang* (Symphony No. 2) to Mahler's Eighth Symphony.[27] Its wider impact on the development of Western art music in the nineteenth century, however, is far too broad to be treated adequately here.

Missa solemnis, Op. 123[28]

Beethoven originally intended the *Missa solemnis* to be performed at the coronation of his friend and pupil, Archduke Rudolph, to the post of Archbishop of Olomouc (Ölmutz), an ecclesiastical seat now located in Moravia in the Czech Republic. Rudolph, the nephew of the Emperor, was Beethoven's only direct connection to the Habsburg monarchy. Beethoven did not complete the work in time for Rudolph's installation, however, and its first performance took place in a concert setting in St. Petersburg. Three "Hymns" (Kyrie, Credo, and Agnus Dei) from the *Missa solemnis* were performed in Vienna on May 7, 1824 in the same concert that marked the premiere of the Ninth Symphony.

Joseph Kerman has identified the *Missa solemnis* as a work more "respected, one senses, rather than loved," and Warren Kirkendale, among others, has examined the debt of gratitude that Beethoven owed to sacred music of the Renaissance and Baroque masters (Palestrina, Handel, and Bach in particular) in creating it.[29] Whether respected or loved, old or new, the *Missa solemnis* remains along with Bach's B-minor Mass, one of the epic settings of the Roman Catholic liturgy that, while not at home in a normal ecclesiastical ritual, in its finest moments gets inside the meaning of its text in profoundly moving ways. While one may thrill at the blazing explosion of praise that opens and closes the Gloria, or be awed by the majesty of the "Et vitam venturi" fugue at the end of the Credo, the quieter, more reflective, moments such as the Kyrie and the Sanctus embody that spirit of devotion (*Mit Andacht*) that Beethoven indicates in the tempo indications at the beginning of both movements, and the Praeludium that connects the first "Osanna in excelsis" with the "Benedictus." Like Haydn's *Missa in angustiis* (Nelson Mass) and *Paukenmesse*, warfare serves as a backdrop that is brought forcefully to the forefront in the Agnus Dei and Dona nobis pacem movements. In this sense, the political canvas upon which Beethoven's career was painted is placed in high profile.

For all its tremendous vocal challenges for choirs and SATB soloists (high tessitura, uncomfortable leaps, and complex rhythms), the *Missa solemnis* represents the summit of the composer's achievements in the choral realm—a true representative of "late" Beethoven that pointed the way toward even grander scale choral works that emerged in the later nineteenth century and beyond. Even more, it is, along with the finale of the Ninth Symphony, a public statement of personal faith—not in political philosophy or orthodox religiosity—but in a higher power and music's role in addressing that deity.

Notes

1 Donald Francis Tovey, *Essays in Musical Analysis* 2 (Oxford: Oxford University Press, 1935), xv.

2 For a complete list of Beethoven's works for chorus, see the works list from the New Grove. A complete list is also included in Eliot Forbes, "Beethoven as a Choral Composer," *PRMA* 97 (1970–71): 69–82.

3 See Maynard Solomon, *Beethoven*, 2nd rev. ed. (New York: Schirmer, 1998), 50ff.

4 This tune was later given the sobriquet "Humanitätsmelodie."

5 See Maynard Solomon, "Beethoven's Ninth Symphony: The Sense of an Ending," *Critical Inquiry* 17 (1991): 303–04 and Forbes, "Beethoven as a Choral Composer," 75. See also David Benjamin Levy,

Beethoven: The Ninth Symphony, rev. ed. (Yale University Press, 2003), 16–17. Lewis Lockwood, *Beethoven: The Music and The Life* (New York: W. W. Norton, 2003), 65 correctly acknowledges the difference in tone between the two texts.

6   See Solomon, *Beethoven,* 68f, *Thayer's Life of Beethoven,* ed. Elliot Forbes (Princeton, NJ: Princeton University Press, 1964), 120, and Lockwood, *Beethoven,* 65.

7   Barry Cooper, "Beethoven's Oratorio and the Heiligenstadt Testament," *Beethoven Journal* 10 (1995): 19–24.

8   *Briefwechsel,* no. 523 (October 9, 1811).

9   See D. G. Brock, "The Church Music of Hummel," *Music Review* 31 (1970): 249–54.

10 Quoted in Barry Cooper, *The Beethoven Compendium* (London: Thames and Hudson, 1991), 256.

11 William Kinderman, *Beethoven* (Berkeley, CA: University of California Press, 1995), 122.

12 Such as found in the Kyrie and Credo, respectively, of Haydn's *Missa in angustiis* (*Nelsonmesse*).

13 Beethoven may have gotten the idea for this thematic recall from Mozart's "Coronation" Mass, K. 317. The dramatic contexts of the two instances, however, are quite different in their effect.

14 Lewis Lockwood, *Beethoven: The Music and The Life* (New York, 2003), 273, calls it *stille Andacht.*

15 Owen Jander, in an unpublished paper, "The Artists and his Muse" delivered at the Pepsico Summerfare on August 6, 1989, proposed an elaborate scenario for the entire Choral Fantasy, likening the passage for solo piano as an artist in search of his muse. For another point of view, see Steven Moore Whiting, "Hört ihr wohl: Zu Funktion und Programm von Beethovens 'Chorfantasie'," *Arkiv für Musikwissenschaft* 45, 2 (1988): 132–47.

16 See Levy, *Beethoven: The Ninth Symphony,* 46.

17 See Paul Nettl, *The Beethoven Encyclopedia* (New York, 1956), 165.

18 Lockwood, *Beethoven,* 340 and Solomon, *Beethoven,* 287.

19 At least two attempts were made to rescue the cantata from oblivion. The first one was a revised version of the text prepared by Friedrich Rochlitz and published in 1837 under a new title: *Preis der Tonkunst.* Hermann Scherchen prepared another version in 1956, with the original title restored but with a much altered text (in German and English) that expunges the specific political and topical nature of Weissenbach's original words to create an "ode to peace" (Friedenskantate). This edition is published by Ars Viva Verlag, Mainz.

20 Two excellent CD recordings of the work were released in 1997. One is a taken from a live performance in Carnegie Hall with the St. Luke's Chamber Orchestra, Collegiate Chorale, and a fine group of soloists headed by Deborah Voigt under the baton of Robert Bass (Koch International Classics). The other features the Roma Orchestra dell'Accademia Nazionale di Santa Cecilia conducted by Myung-Whun Chung included in vol. 19 of the Complete Beethoven Edition (Polygram).

21 For additional comparisons, see Forbes, "Beethoven as Choral Composer," 73–74.

22 Donald Francis Tovey preferred translating the title "Becalmed Sea and Prosperous Voyage." See Tovey, *Essays in Musical Analysis* 5 (London, 1937), 193.

23 Homer, *The Odyssey,* trans. Robert Fagles (Viking, 1996).

24 Tovey, *Essays* 2, 11.

25 For more information, see David Benjamin Levy, "Early Performances of Beethoven's Ninth Symphony: A Documentary Study of Five Cities" (Ph.D. diss., University of Rochester, 1979). One rarely encounters modern performances that include boys' voices. Interestingly, in Leipzig boy sopranos and altos were used to the exclusion of female singers, until Felix Mendelssohn's performance on February 21, 1839 (see Levy, "Early Performances," 388–90).

26 For more on this aspect of the Ninth Symphony, see, *inter alia,* Levy, *Beethoven: The Ninth Symphony,* Nicholas Cook, *Beethoven: Symphony No. 9* (Cambridge, 1995), and Esteban Buch, *Beethoven's Ninth. A Political History,* trans. Richard Miller (Chicago, 2003).

27 See also D. Kern Holoman on choral forces in the nineteenth-century symphony in Chapters 4 and 5 of this volume.

28 A more detailed study of this work may be found in Chapter 4 of this volume.

29 Joseph Kerman, CD booklet for *Missa solemnis,* John Eliot Gardiner, conductor, Archiv CD 429 779-2, and Warren Kirkendale, "New roads to old ideas in Beethoven's Missa solemnis," *Creative World of Beethoven* (New York, 1971), 163–99. See also Martin Zenck, *Die Bach-Rezeption des späten Beethovens: zum Verhältnis von Musikhistoriographie und Rezeptionsgeschichtsschreibung der "Klassik"* (Stuttgart, 1986), *passim.*

Selected Bibliography

Buch, Esteban. *Beethoven's Ninth. A Political History*. Translated by Richard Miller. Chicago, University of Chicago Press, 2003.

Cook, Nicholas. *Beethoven: Symphony No. 9*. Cambridge: Cambridge University Press, 1995.

Cooper, Barry. "Beethoven's Oratorio and the Heiligenstadt Testament." *Beethoven Journal* 10 (1995): 19–24.

Del Mar, Norman. *Conducting Beethoven*. Volume 2: Overtures, Concertos, Missa solemnis. Oxford: Clarendon Press; New York: Oxford University Press, 1993.

Fillion, Michelle. "Beethoven's Mass in C and the Search for Inner Peace," *Beethoven Forum* 7 (1999): 1–15.

Fiske, Roger. *Beethoven's Missa Solemnis*. New York: C. Scribner's Sons, 1979.

Forbes, Eliot. "Beethoven as a Choral Composer," *PRMA* 97 (1970–71): 69–82.

Gutsche, Susanne V. *Der Chor bei Beethoven: eine Untersuchung zur Rolle des Chores in den Orchesterwerken von den Bonner Cantaten bis zur 9. Symphonie*. Kassel: Gustav Bosse, 1995.

Kinderman, William. "Beethoven's Compositional Models for the Choral Finale of the Ninth Symphony," in *Beethoven's Compositional Process*, ed. William Kinderman. Lincoln, NE: University of Nebraska Press, 1991, 160–88.

——. "Beethoven's Symbol for the Deity in the Missa solemnis and the Ninth Symphony," *19th-Century Music* 9, 2 (Fall 1985): 102–18.

Kirkendale, Warren, "New Roads to Old Ideas in Beethoven's Missa solemnis," in *Creative World of Beethoven*. New York: W. W. Norton, 1971, 163–99.

Levy, David Benjamin, *Beethoven: The Ninth Symphony*. Revised edition. New Haven: Yale University Press, 2003.

——. *Early Performances of Beethoven's Ninth Symphony: A Documentary Study of Five Cities*. Ph.D. diss., University of Rochester, 1979.

Lodes, Birgit. "'When I try, now and then, to give musical form to my turbulent feelings': the human mind and the divine in the Gloria of Beethoven's Missa solemnis," [translated by Glenn Stanley] *Beethoven Forum* 6 (1998): 143–79.

Mainka, Jürgen. "Beethovens Bonner Kantaten," *Bericht über den Internationalen Beethoven-Kongress* (Berlin, 1971): 315–26.

Platen, Emil, "Kaiser-Kantaten WoO 87 and WoO 88," *Beethoven: Interpretationen seiner Werke* 2 (Laaber, 1994): 488–93.

Schneider, Frank. "Kantate, Der glorreiche Augenblick' op. 136," in *Beethoven: Interpretationen seiner Werke*. Laaber: Laaber-Verlag, 1994, vol. 2, 364–69.

——. "'Meeresstille und glückliche Fahrt' für gemischten Chor und Orchester op. 112," in *Beethoven: Interpretationen seiner Werke*. Laaber: Laaber-Verlag, 1994, vol. 2, 182–84.

Solomon, Maynard. "Beethoven's Ninth Symphony: The Sense of an Ending," *Critical Inquiry* 17 (1991).

Tovey, Donald Francis. *Essays in Musical Analysis* 2. Oxford: Oxford University Press, 1935.

Whiting, Steven Moore. "Hört ihr wohl: Zu Funktion und Programm von Beethovens 'Chorfantasie'." *Arkiv für Musikwissenschaft* 45, 2 (1988): 132–47.

8

FANNY HENSEL

R. Larry Todd

DUKE UNIVERSITY

"Had Madame Hensel been a poor man's daughter, she must have become known to the world by the side of Madame Schumann and Madame Pleyel, as a female pianist of the very highest class."[1] Thus the English music critic Henry Chorley assessed the rare case of Fanny Mendelssohn Hensel (1805–47), an "amateur *pianiste* and composer of no ordinary force and feeling," and a virtuoso who successfully vied with her celebrated brother in rendering intractable passages from the fantasies of Friedrich Kalkbrenner, Chopin's teacher. To the extent Hensel is remembered today, she is usually anthologized as a composer, dependent on the piano, who produced attractive, finely nuanced piano pieces and *Lieder*, several of which her brother regarded as among exemplars of the genre. Considerably less well known is her lifelong engagement with choral music, a genre to which she made significant contributions, even if most were forgotten until their rediscovery late in the twentieth century. Because of her gender and social standing—the Mendelssohns ranked among the wealthiest members of Berlin society—Hensel did not pursue a public career as a composer until very late in life. Choral music, which she performed at the family residence in a music room that could accommodate upwards of one hundred guests, provided a crucial musical outlet that successfully bridged the private and public, and juxtaposed in a semi-public venue the contrasting institutions of domestic music making and fashionable concert life.

Like her brother, Hensel acquired practical experience in choral music early on. As children, the siblings sang in the Berlin Singakademie, founded in 1797 by C. F. C. Fasch to promote the study of sacred music. Within two years it boasted a membership of 148 amateur musicians who were rehearsed well enough to "execute the most difficult polyphonic vocal works with a purity and precision beyond all belief."[2] In 1800, the directorship passed to Carl Friedrich Zelter, who began rehearsing the motets of J. S. Bach, and exploring portions of the *St. Matthew Passion*, then viewed as an imponderable work in an obsolete Baroque style (and by the young theologian Julius Schubring as a "dry, arithmetical sum"[3]). In 1819, Zelter became Fanny and Felix's composition instructor, and led them through a rigorous (and Bachian) course of figured bass, chorale harmonizations, canon and fugue. One year later the siblings joined the alto section of the Singakademie, Fanny at age fourteen, Felix, at age eleven.

Here, she encountered a conservative, eighteenth-century repertoire of Fasch, C. H. Graun, Handel, Mozart, and especially J. S. Bach, to whom, like her brother, she was decidedly partial. When, in 1829, the twenty-year-old Felix resurrected the *St. Matthew Passion* at the Berlin Singakademie, some one hundred years after its Leipzig premiere, Fanny sang in the chorus, and there is every reason to believe that she was intimately involved in the preparations leading up to this landmark performance, generally thought to have triggered the modern Bach revival. Not without reason did Felix affectionately label Fanny his Thomaskantor; and in 1830, on the birth of her son, she named him Sebastian.

In 1821, Fanny's parents began fortnightly Sunday concerts at the family residence, initially described by her mother as "Sonntags Uebungen" ("Sunday Practices").[4] Fanny participated in these concerts, though their primary purpose was to showcase the astonishingly precocious compositions of her brother. In 1831, two years after marrying the court painter Wilhelm Hensel, she decided to reorganize the series, and began programming what she viewed as the best of German music, with a preference for J. S. Bach, Handel, Gluck, Mozart, Beethoven, and her brother. In these concerts, Fanny found an outlet for her own music. Only on rare occasions did she engage an orchestra, and preferred instead to lead from her piano. We have a brief account of her conducting from the composer Johanna Kinkel, who sang in the chorus:

> It was an immersion into the innermost fibers of the composition's spirit, and its most powerful radiation into the souls of the singers and audience . . . When one watched Fanny Hensel performing a masterpiece, she seemed to become larger. Her forehead lightened, her features became noble, and one believed in seeing the most beautiful forms.[5]

Fanny's repertoire featured solo piano and chamber works, concerti, *Lieder*, arias, cantatas, operas (in concert versions), and oratorios. Among major choral works she performed were cantatas of Bach (BWV 8, 102, 103, 104, 105, and 106) and oratorios, either complete or excerpted (Handel's *Samson*, *Messiah*, and *Judas Maccabeus*; Mozart's *Davidde Penitente*; and Mendelssohn's *St. Paul*). The concerts were private affairs, with admission by invitation only; nevertheless, they quickly became a coveted meeting place of musicians, literati, nobility, and Berlin society. Among musical celebrities who attended or participated were Franz Liszt, Clara and Robert Schumann, Clara Novello, Niels Gade, Joseph Joachim, Henri Vieuxtemps, and, of course, Fanny's brother. With relatively few interruptions—Fanny traveled to Italy in 1839–40 and 1845—she sustained the yearly concert series until May 14, 1847. On that day, after beginning to rehearse Felix's cantata *Die erste Walpurgisnacht*, she suffered two strokes and died.

Apart from minor compositions,[6] Hensel's choral music comprises *Nachtreigen* of 1829 for *a cappella* eight-part chorus; three substantial sacred cantatas, all clustered in 1831; *Zum Fest der heiligen Cäcilia*, for soloists, mixed chorus and piano, for St. Cecilia's Day in 1833; the still unpublished *Einleitung zu lebenden Bildern* of 1841, for speaker, mixed chorus, and piano; a setting of a scene from Goethe's *Faust*, for soloists, chorus and piano, composed in 1843; and seventeen part-songs for mixed chorus, all concentrated in 1846, and of which six appeared as her Op. 3. All of her other choral works remained in manuscript when she died, and unknown until their rediscovery and revival late in the 1980s and 1990s (for editions, see the Selected Bibliography).

Fanny composed *Nachtreigen* as a surprise for her fiancé, Wilhelm Hensel, the amateur poet of its text. It celebrates nature and an overarching deity that brings individuals together into a group to share experiences. Fanny designed her setting to alternate between four-part female and male choruses, which then join together in "unified" eight-part harmony; the composition concludes with a culminating eight-part fugato that in its chromatic severity is distinctly reminiscent of Bach (Fanny may have had in mind Bach's antiphonal, eight-part motets). On the other hand, the second entrance of the female chorus, marked by a simple, block-chordal passage moving in quarter notes, resembles the principal theme of Beethoven's Choral Fantasy, often heard as a harbinger of the "Ode to Joy" finale of the Ninth Symphony. And Fanny thickens the web of allusions by paraphrasing in the opening of *Nachtreigen* the principal theme from the first movement of her brother's String Quartet in E-flat major, Op. 12 (1827).[7]

If *Nachtreigen* is an unusual occasional work, the three cantatas of 1831 mark a response to her brother's embrace of sacred choral music between 1828 and 1832, when he produced several Bachian chorale cantatas, like so many preliminary studies for *St. Paul*, the oratorio that in 1836 established his broad, international fame. Fanny began with *Lobgesang*, written for Sebastian's first birthday, and drawing on verses from Psalm 62, John 16, and Johann Mentzer's hymn *O daß ich tausend Zungen hätte*. A work for mixed chorus and orchestra, its five movements include an introductory orchestral *Pastorale* in G major, chorus ("For God alone my soul waits in silence"), alto recitative ("When a woman is in labor, she has pain"), soprano aria ("O that I had a thousand tongues"), and *Schlußchor* ("I will sing of God's goodness"). Not infrequently Fanny's Bachian proclivities come to the fore. Thus, the pedal points and gentle trochaic rhythms of the *Pastorale* trace their lineage to Bach's Cantata No. 104 (*Du Hirte Israel, höre*) and *Christmas Oratorio*, and celebrate Sebastian's birth by placing it in the context of Christ's Nativity. If the following chorus, with its deliberate harmonic pacing and compact points of imitation, suggests Handel, the central aria, a neo-Baroque conception in A major with obbligato violin part, initially seems to recall the Laudamus te from Bach's Mass in B minor. And the last movement draws upon a Bachian cantus-firmus technique—here J. B. König's chorale melody for *O daß ich tausend Zungen hätte* is introduced phrase by phrase in the altos, with freely composed interludes, all animated by a bustling bass line.

As a first essay, *Lobgesang* was not without blemishes; Felix, for one, criticized its orchestration and selection of texts. Fanny's next cantata, *Hiob* (Job), marked a considerable advance. In three movements (chorus, Arioso for four soloists, and concluding chorus), it drew on six verses from Job 7, 13, and 10 to confront the central issue of theodicy—the reconciling of evil with divine goodness. "What are human beings," the opening chorus asks, in four angular entries prefaced by a short orchestral introduction in G minor reminiscent of the opening of Felix's Psalm 115, Op. 31 ("Non nobis Domine" / "Nicht unserm namen, Herr"). Tonally, too, *Hiob* suggests a series of searching questions, including a dramatic half cadence at the end of the first movement on G major. Inspired by a passage from Bach's funeral cantata, the *Actus Tragicus* (BWV 106), this half cadence in turn introduces another question in the middle movement, "Why do you hide your face," set against pulsating tremolos in the orchestra, a texture reminiscent of the "Et incarnatus est" from Bach's Mass in B minor. The answer—"You have granted me life and steadfast love, and your care has preserved my spirit"—then comes in the buoyant finale in G major, constructed on four subjects introduced one by one in the tenor, alto, bass, and soprano. The first of these is a reworking of the opening motive of the first movement. Through the course of the movement Fanny leads the subjects through several harmonic excursions before restating the original subject, now revived over a pedal point. Wind fanfares then introduce the final cadential gesture, presented in a stately *Lento* as it secures the tonic G major, the ultimate musical answer.

Closely related to *Hiob*, premiered on Fanny's second wedding anniversary in October 1831, is her choral masterpiece, the *Cholera Cantata*, finished two months later and premiered in December on her father's birthday. Both begin in a somber G minor, and both concern the tribulations of mankind, as evidenced in 1831 by the rapid advance of the Asiatic cholera that ravaged Berlin. The expanded dimensions of the third cantata—thirteen movements requiring four soloists, chorus (*a* 4 and *a* 8), and orchestra buttressed by trombones—encouraged its twentieth-century editor to describe the untitled work as an oratorio. But in her diary Fanny alluded to her *Choleramusik*, and the discovery of some parts in 1996 finally revealed the title, *Cantata nach Aufhören der Cholera in Berlin, 1831* (Cantata after the Cessation of the Cholera in Berlin, 1831).

Prefacing the composition is a dark orchestral overture in Fanny's most dissonant style, with plaintive entries in the oboe and clarinet, grating chromatic lines, and the descending chromatic tetrachord, emblem of a lament. Fanny culled the texts for her cantata largely from the Psalms, Job, Isaiah, and the New Testament, and shaped them into a proto-narrative that unfolds roughly in three parts: God's calamitous judgment on his people (Nos. 1–5), the tribulations of the living and dead from the collective and individual viewpoints (Nos. 6–10), and reconciliation with God (Nos. 11–13). The highlights include several fine choruses—the dramatically charged No. 3, recalling J. S. Bach's *turba* choruses; No. 6, in which Fanny superimposes the chorale *O Traurigkeit, O Herzeleid* above verses from Psalm 84 and Isaiah 9, as if reflecting on "O Mensch, bewein dein' Sünde groß" in the *St. Matthew Passion*; No. 9, an eight-part *Trauerchor* in which the living lament the dead, withered like grass and scattered like flowers (Isaiah 40); No. 10, for which Fanny created an imaginary, freely composed *a cappella* chorale of the departed on 2 Timothy 4 ("I have fought the good fight"); and No. 13, the celebratory finale of praise ending with a verse from Psalm 150, "Alles was Odem hat, preiset den Herrn," used by Felix in his *Lobgesang* Symphony, Op. 52 in 1840.

With the *Choleramusik*, about a half hour in duration, Fanny embraced choral composition on a large scale. Its taut succession of recitatives, arias, and choruses, many through-composed and connected, anticipate similar techniques in her brother's *St. Paul*, and show Fanny to have understood issues of macro tonal design. Underscoring her conception is an overarching progression from the dissonant, unstable G minor (Nos. 1, 3, and 9) to the stable, diatonic C major (No. 13), prepared by the major form of the dominant in the imaginary chorale (No. 10). The work thus describes a large-scale motion from the minor, then major form of the dominant to the tonic, so that an elementary musical progression underlies the universal, epic message of the composition.

None of Fanny's remaining choral works aspired to the monumentality of the *Cholera Cantata*. The *Einleitung zu lebenden Bildern* (Introduction to Tableaux vivants), which survives in an incomplete manuscript, was an unusual experiment combining spoken text, music for chorus and piano, and a series of *tableaux vivants* in which actors assumed fixed poses, and applied what Fanny described as the "double counterpoint" of music and painting—her life with her husband. Similarly, *Zum Fest der heiligen Cäcilia*, Fanny's "versets" for St. Cecilia's Day, blended visual and musical elements. Scored for soloists, chorus, and piano, the work used texts from the introit, gradual, and collect of the Mass for November 22, and featured a prominent part for the soprano Pauline Decker, who appeared in a robe designed after Raphael's famous altarpiece of 1516 (Pinacoteca Nazionale, Bologna), and with a prop suggesting the portative organ associated with the saint's ecstatic musicality. Fanny cast the music, her only setting of a Catholic text, in a *stile antico* style that emulated Palestrina's careful handling of dissonances.

Her remaining choral work with piano accompaniment was the setting of the opening scene from *Faust*, Part II, in which Faust, having abandoned Gretchen to her fate at the end of Part I, lies asleep in a "charming landscape." Attending him are Ariel and a chorus of elves, who serenade and restore him before his awakening to a new life. This disembodied spirit music, which alternates between Ariel, soloists, and a female chorus, is stitched together by the piano, which performs solo interludes, and also depicts in the accompaniment by means of luminous arpeggiations in the high register Goethe's Aeolian harps. The composer gave some thought to orchestrating the work and having it performed in Vienna, but like the cantatas it fell into oblivion after her death, and did not emerge until 1998.

Standing quite apart are Fanny's final works to be considered, the seventeen partsongs of 1846, composed the last year of her life, when she decided to begin publishing her music. Intended for open-air performance, they are celebrations of nature, shared as communal experiences rather than private, intimate expressions of her solo piano pieces and *Lieder*. Pervading the texts—principally by Eichendorff, followed by Wilhelm Hensel, Goethe, Geibel, Uhland, and Lenau—is the omnipresent rustling (*Rauschen*) of nature and contemplation of springtime renewal. Four-part writing is the norm, but Fanny expands the complement to eight-part writing in *Schweigend sinkt die Nacht* (Hellwig-Unruh 439, text by W. Hensel), and in *Ariel* (H-U 435, on verses from the

Walpurgisnachtstraum scene of *Faust*, Part I) she begins with an ethereal duet, while in another Goethe setting, *Wer will mir wehren zu singen* (H-U 447), she scores for soprano, alto, and baritone. Stylistically the partsongs are close to those of her brother, who between 1838 and 1843 published eighteen examples in his Opp. 41, 48, and 59. There are occasional echoes of these works in Fanny's music, but her partsongs clearly show the hand of a seasoned choral musician, and display any number of original, well-turned phrases, harmonic progressions, and variations in texture. Chordal homophony predominates, but she does not hesitate to introduce compact points of imitation, use pairings of voices or austere octave doublings, or apply judicious examples of word painting.

The *Gartenlieder*, published late in 1846 by Bote & Bock as Op. 3, brought together six of Fanny's best choral *Lieder* into a miniature cycle that progresses textually from night to day, from a dream-like recollection of spring to the eruption of the season in full force. Musically, the opus describes a taut tonal scheme that first descends through the chain of fifths from B major to E major / minor, A major, and D major, and then reverses direction to A minor and A major. At every turn, the music is fraught with the stirrings of nature, and calculated to convey a sense of romantic expectation and yearning, even when, in the third *Lied*, we encounter a harmonically mercurial passage for Uhland's wistful verses, which might be taken as a metaphor for Fanny's art: "Ahnest Du, O Seele wieder / sanfte, süsse Frühlingslieder? / Sieh' umher die falben Bäume, / ach, es waren holde Träume!" ("Do you sense again, O soul, those gentle, sweet songs of spring? / Look around at the faded trees, / Ah, they were lovely dreams.")

The *Gartenlieder* were among the few works of Fanny Hensel that enjoyed an afterlife. Robert Schumann and Johanna Kinkel rehearsed and performed them in Dresden and Bonn, in the United States they appeared in transcriptions for brass band, and in England they were still being issued in the 1860s and 1870s. But few who sang them could have suspected the full range and depth of their composer's choral music, of the "other" Mendelssohn.

Notes

1 Henry F. Chorley, "Mendelssohn's Sister and Mother," in W. A. Lampadius, *Life of Felix Mendelssohn Bartholdy* (London, 1877), 185.
2 *Allgemeine musikalische Zeitung* 2 (1799), col. 576.
3 Schubring, "Reminiscences," repr. in R. Larry Todd, *Mendelssohn and his World* (Princeton: Princeton University Press, 1991), 221–36 (quotation at 227).
4 See Klein, *Fanny Hensels Sonntagsmusiken*, 11.
5 "Aus Johanna Kinkel's (1810-1858) Memoiren," cited in Klein, *Fanny Hensels Sonntagsmusiken*, 68.
6 For a complete list, see the comprehensive thematic catalogue in Renate Hellwig-Unruh, *Fanny Hensel geb. Mendelssohn Bartholdy*.
7 Christopher Reynolds, *Motives for Allusion: Context and Content in Nineteenth-Century Music* (Cambridge, MA: Harvard University Press, 2003), 94–95.

Selected Bibliography

Borchard, Beatrix and Monika Schwarz-Danuser, ed. *Fanny Hensel geb. Mendelssohn: Komponieren zwischen Gesellligkeitsideal und romantischer Musikästhetik.* Kassel: Furore, 1999, 223–34.
Citron, Marcia, ed. *The Letters of Fanny Hensel to Felix Mendelssohn.* Stuyvesant, NY: Pendragon, 1987.
Gundlach, Willi. "Die Chorlieder von Fanny Hensel—eine späte Liebe?" *Mendelssohn Studien* 11 (1999): 105–30.
——. "Fanny Hensels geistliche Kantaten," *Forum Kirchenmusik* 6 (1997): 219–24.
Hellwig-Unruh, Renate. "Die 'Cholerakantate' von Fanny Hensel," *Musica* 50 (1996): 121–23.
——. "'Eigentlich sollte das Stück wohl für Orchester gesetzt seyn . . .': Fanny Hensels *Faust*-Szene," in *Fanny Hensel geb. Mendelssohn Bartholdy: Das Werk*, ed. Martina Helmig. Munich: text + kritik, 1997.

——. *Fanny Hensel geb. Mendelssohn Bartholdy: Thematisches Verzeichnis der Kompositionen*. Adliswil: Edition Kunzelmann, 2000.

Hensel, Fanny. *Faust: Part II of the Tragedy: Act I—A Pleasant Landscape*, ed. Suzanne Summerville. Kassel: Furore, 1998.

——. *Hiob*, ed. Conrad Misch. Kassel: Furore, 1992.

——. *Lobgesang*, ed. Conrad Misch. Kassel: Furore, 1992.

——. *Nachtreigen*, ed. Ulrike Schadl. Stuttgart: Carus-Verlag, 1995.

——. *Oratorium nach Bildern der Bibel*, ed. Elke Mascha Blankenburg. Kassel: Furore, 1999.

——. *Tagebücher*, ed. Rudolf Elvers and H.-G. Klein. Wiesbaden: Breitkopf und Härtel, 2002.

——. *Weltliche a-cappella-Chöre von 1846*, ed. Elke Mischa Blankenburg. Kassel: Furore, 1988, 5 vols.

——. *Zum Fest der heiligen Cäcilia*, ed. Willi Gundlach. Kassel: Furore, 1998.

Heymann-Wentzel, Cordula, "Ein ungewöhnliches Geburtstagsgeschenk: Fanny Hensels 'Lobgesang,'" in *Musik und Biographie: Festschrift für Rainer Cadenbach*, ed. Cordula Heymann-Wentzel and Johannes Laus. Würzburg: Königshausen & Neumann, 2004, 462–71.

Hinrichsen, Hans-Joachim, "Kantatenkomposition in der 'Hauptstadt von Sebastian Bach': Fanny Hensels geistliche Chorwerke und die Berliner Bach-Tradition," in Helmig, 115–29.

Huber, Annegret, "In welcher Form soll man Fanny Hensels 'Choleramusik' aufführen?" *Mendelssohn Studien* 10 (1997): 227–45.

Kellenberger, Edgar, "Fanny Hensel und die Cholera-Epidemie 1831," *Musik und Kirche* 67 (1997): 295–303.

Klein, Hans-Günter. *Das verborgene Band: Felix Mendelssohn Bartholdy und seine Schwester Fanny Hensel*. Wiesbaden: Reichert Verlag, 1997.

——. ". . . mit obligater Nachtigallen- und Fliederblütenbegleitung": Fanny Hensels Sonntagsmusiken*. Wiesbaden: Reichert Verlag, 2005.

Nubbemeyer, Annette, "Zweifel und Bekenntnis: Fanny Hensels Kantate 'Hiob'—Entstehungsgeschichte und Werkanalyse," *Musik und Kirche* 67 (1997): 286–95.

Todd, R. Larry. *Fanny Hensel: The Other Mendelssohn*. New York: Oxford University Press, 2010.

——. *Mendelssohn: A Life in Music*. New York: Oxford University Press, 2005.

Wallace, S. M. H. "The *Gartenlieder* Op. 3, by Fanny Mendelssohn Hensel (1805–1847)," D.M.A. diss., Michigan State University, 2000.

Wolitz, Stefan. *Fanny Hensels Chorwerk*. Tutzing: Hans Schneider, 2007.

9

FELIX MENDELSSOHN BARTHOLDY

Jeffrey S. Sposato

University of Houston

Of the canonic early nineteenth-century German composers who engaged in choral writing, Mendelssohn stands apart due both to the copious amount of choral music he composed and to the degree to which his reputation relied upon such music. The vast majority of these pieces fall into the category of what Mendelssohn and later generations would call sacred music; his predecessors, on the other hand, might have seen things differently. For unlike the sacred music of only a few decades earlier, the bulk of which was composed for use in the church liturgy, much of Mendelssohn's sacred music was (as paradoxical as it might seem) composed expressly for the new emerging temple of secularism, the concert hall. For Mendelssohn, however, no paradox existed. Rather, his music demonstrates his conviction that while church and concert hall each required their own nuances in terms of musical style, there should be little or no differentiation in devotional content. Indeed, creating a devotional atmosphere in music for the concert hall was so central to Mendelssohn's aesthetic that it could not help but occasionally find its way into his secular works as well.

Sacred Music and the Concert Hall

In 1974, Carl Dahlhaus coined the term "imaginary church music" to describe Mendelssohn's first oratorio, *Paulus*, Op. 36,[1] a concert work designed to rouse devotional feelings among its German Protestant listeners through its use of congregational song (chorales).[2] Mendelssohn's efforts to instill religiosity in other concert works (including instrumental ones) led Charles Rosen to a less flattering assessment, dubbing the composer "the inventor of religious kitsch in music."[3] But while we may take issue with the disdain and dismissiveness inherent in Rosen's tone, his fundamental premise, like Dahlhaus's, holds: "Mendelssohn's evocation of religion . . . is designed to make us feel that the concert hall has been transformed into a church. The music expresses not religion but piety."[4] Neither of these observations is anything new, however. Contemporary reviewers of *Paulus*, for instance, remarked frequently upon the work's ability to turn the listener's mind to thoughts of faith.[5] But while these kinds of observations are common to Mendelssohn's oratorios and other large-scale works, the implications of the rise of the concert hall for his smaller sacred works remain underappreciated, as do the circumstances that led to the use of this new venue for them.

    The authenticity and depth of Mendelssohn's Protestant faith is affirmed by many of his letters, the memoirs of his colleagues, the confessional statement he wrote for his religion instructor, and, most notably, his inscription of one of two prayer anagrams—"L.e.g.G." (*Laß es gelingen, Gott* ["Let it succeed, God"]) and "H.D.m." (*Hilf Du mir* ["Help Thou me"])—on the bulk of his manuscripts (sacred and secular).[6] But Mendelssohn's relationship with the church itself appears to have been distant, with no evidence to suggest that he ever attended services regularly.[7] This separation of steadfast faith from church attendance exemplified a trend that had been building steadily since the German Enlightenment in the mid-eighteenth century. Mendelssohn and his siblings were part of an increasing number of people who confessed to belief in God and even, as in Mendelssohn's case, to allegiance to a particular Christian church, but did not feel that church attendance was a component of faith. Early nineteenth-century commentators developed numerous theories for this group's growth, which ranged from problems with the service itself (e.g., bad preaching), to politics (e.g., Prussian King Friedrich II's disdain for the church), to competition from the ever-increasing number of secular diversions (e.g., coffee houses).[8]

Factors such as these, combined with an Enlightenment-inspired desire to eliminate everything from the service not oriented toward reverence and devotion,[9] led to a streamlining of the liturgy in most parts of Protestant Germany in the late eighteenth and early nineteenth centuries. In part, this meant shortening the service as a whole, often by eliminating many sung elements, as well as drastically reducing the number of services held in a given week. Many German states also demanded less elaborate celebrations of major feast days and the merging of minor ones into the following Sunday's service (such celebrations had traditionally been prime opportunities for the performance of elaborate concerted music).[10] In the Berlin of Mendelssohn's youth, for example, the liturgy of the newly unified Prussian church, which merged the Lutheran and Reformed churches in 1817, made the inclusion of elaborate music extremely difficult. With the exception of the opening and closing chorales, the service was never supposed to last more than an hour, with the liturgy and sermon equally dividing the time. More significant, any choral music performed by the church choir was supposed to "in general be sung without organ accompaniment."[11] Furthermore, the music had to be in keeping with the devotional character of the service, meaning relatively simple, with clear melodies, little or no complex counterpoint, and German (as opposed to Latin) text.[12] Restrictions such as these, combined with the subsequent decline in the prestige and quality of church choirs and competition from public concerts, led to the church's diminished role in public music life in most parts of Germany and to the need for new outlets for sacred music performance. Stepping in to fill that need in Berlin was the Singakademie, among whose stated goals was "the cultivation of serious and sacred music, especially for music in contrapuntal style."[13]

It was through the Singakademie and its director, Carl Friedrich Zelter, that Mendelssohn—along with his sister Fanny—received his earliest training in composition, and it was there (as well as at a similar society in Frankfurt, the Cäcilien-Verein) that several of his early sacred works received their first performances. Among the most substantial of these pieces was a multi-movement setting of Psalm 19, which Zelter had the Singakademie read through on September 18, 1821.[14] Like so many of the small sacred works of Mendelssohn's student years, the psalm revolves around fugues. And while fugal composition certainly formed an important part of his education, it cannot be coincidental that by writing the psalm in a "contrapuntal style," Mendelssohn had composed a work that was in keeping with the Singakademie's charge and, consequently, was inappropriate for Prussian church usage.[15] The same holds true for his early works based on liturgical texts, such as the 1822 Gloria in E-flat major (his first large-scale piece for chorus and orchestra), the 1822 Magnificat, the 1823 Kyrie in C minor, and the rich and highly underappreciated 1825 Kyrie in D minor that he wrote at Cherubini's request while in Paris.[16] Despite their liturgical nature, none of these works appears to have ever been performed in the Prussian church. Indeed, the C-minor Kyrie was written for and performed by the Frankfurt Cäcilien-Verein,[17] again demonstrating Mendelssohn's understanding that the concert hall was the appropriate venue for these compositions.

On March 11, 1829, Mendelssohn revived J. S. Bach's *St. Matthew Passion* at the Singakademie, igniting the "Bach revival." For Mendelssohn himself, the years of fascination with Bach's work, the performance itself, and its aftermath all had a tremendous impact on his own sacred compositions. Throughout the early 1820s, Felix and Fanny sang through numerous Bach works both at the Singakademie and at Zelter's private gatherings,[18] and on or around his fifteenth birthday (1824) Felix received a copy of the Passion score from his grandmother.[19] At this point, Mendelssohn's knowledge of Bach's repertoire—choral and otherwise—was considerable for the time, and also included the chorale cantata *Ein feste Burg*, BWV 80 and some or all of Bach's motets.[20] No doubt inspired by such works, Mendelssohn began that same year to set his own chorale-based pieces, starting with a multi-movement motet, *Jesus, meine Zuversicht,* and ending in 1836 with *Paulus*, a work that would eventually solidify his reputation both at home and abroad. In between, Mendelssohn composed a series of energetic and often dramatic chorale cantatas, as well as some shorter chorale-inspired pieces, including the now frequently performed *Verleih' uns Frieden* (1830), a lush work that borrowed its text from Luther, but used a new melody.

Despite their obvious debt to Bach, the cantatas reflect the realities and expectations of their age, and appear, in many instances, to have been designed with their new performance venue in mind. Among the more fundamental changes from the Bachian model is a lack of sermonizing in the works, which frees them from attachment to any specific feast, with the possible exceptions of the Christmas cantata *Vom Himmel hoch* (1831) and the passion-tide *O Haupt voll Blut und Wunden* (1830). Musically, too, the works separate themselves from church use by removing the possibility—or even the illusion—of congregational involvement. While it remains uncertain whether the congregation sang along during the chorales that close most of Bach's cantatas, their stylistic simplicity suggests that such participation was at least possible (an impression Bach may well have wanted to convey, even if he never intended the congregation to sing).[21] Not so with Mendelssohn: the chorale at the end of *Ach Gott, vom Himmel sieh' darein* (1832), for instance, modulates strikingly after the first of the two normally identical *Stollen*,[22] while the phrasing and melodic variants in similar movements of other cantatas likewise lack the predictability necessary for congregational involvement. More significant, Mendelssohn often imbued the works with symphonic—and thus concert-associated—characteristics: *Ach Gott,* for instance, is cyclical (the final chorale closes with a quotation from the first movement), while *Wer nur den lieben Gott lässt walten* (1829) opens with a simple presentation of the chorale, creating the effect that much of the remainder of the cantata is a set of variations on that theme. In addition, Mendelssohn closes all of the multi-movement cantatas in a manner reminiscent of a triumphant symphonic finale.

This blending of sacred and symphonic is epitomized in Mendelssohn's *Lobgesang* (Symphony No. 2, Op. 52), a "symphony-cantata," as he labeled it, that begins with three purely instrumental movements (all performed *attacca*), followed by a series of vocal and choral ones, a structure that clearly recalled Beethoven's Ninth Symphony.[23] The piece was composed for Leipzig's 1840 celebration of the 400th anniversary of Johannes Gutenberg's invention of movable type. Despite the apparent secularity of the event, the celebration, like the *Lobgesang* itself, had strong Protestant overtones. Indeed, the festivities were as much a celebration of the Reformation as of Gutenberg, since the printing press was in many ways instrumental in Luther's success. This dual meaning found its way into the *Lobgesang* in part through its text, in which light emerging from darkness—a metaphor both for the spread of knowledge through the printed word and for the Reformation— serves as a recurrent theme. The Reformation is further suggested through repeated presentation of the work's opening chorale-like theme, which is later set to the words "Alles was Odem hat, lobe den Herrn" ("All that hath breath, praise the Lord"), and through the clear, triumphant presentation toward the end of the piece of one of the most familiar of Lutheran chorales, *Nun danket alle Gott.*[24]

Bach's music and the chorale genre as a whole would remain potent forces for Mendelssohn throughout his lifetime, influencing his sacred, secular, choral, and instrumental works alike, including his unfinished third oratorio, *Christus*, Op. 97. Although the evidence is fragmentary, Mendelssohn originally intended this oratorio to be a three-part work entitled *Erde, Hölle und Himmel* (Earth, Hell and Heaven). As it stood at the time of his death in 1847, the work consisted of a short Epiphany-themed scene from a Christmas section (from which the frequently performed chorus "Es wird ein Stern aus Jakob aufgehn" ["A star shall come forth out of Jacob"] stems), and a slightly longer passion segment, both of which likely belonged to the *Erde* part of the oratorio.[25] Remarkably, in their narrative structure and their use of chorales and *turba* choruses, these surviving fragments bear a stronger resemblance to Bach's *St. Matthew Passion* than any work Mendelssohn had previously composed—one reason why they deserve to be heard more often.

Several of the earlier chorale-inspired works were written while Mendelssohn was on his so-called Grand Tour of Europe from 1829 to 1832, a result, in part, of his having received a gift of a collection of Luther hymns while in Vienna.[26] But Mendelssohn also found himself stimulated by his surroundings, particularly in Italy, where his exposure to the Catholic liturgy inspired the composition of a small handful of Latin motets (the sublime *Ave Maria*, Op. 23/2 being a notable highlight). Of particular significance, however, was the composition in 1830 of his first large-scale psalm-cantata, Psalm 115, Op. 31 (*Non nobis Domine,* more commonly performed as *Nicht unserm Namen, Herr*). Not only a delightful work in itself, this Psalm opened up a whole new genre for Mendelssohn, which he would take up again shortly after assuming the directorship of the Gewandhaus in Leipzig in 1835. The psalm-cantata had become a particularly popular genre for concert performance in that city, leading Mendelssohn to compose three more such works for performance there: Psalm 42, Op. 42 (*Wie der Hirsch schreit*, 1837–38), Psalm 95, Op. 46 (*Kommt, laßt uns anbeten*, 1838–41), and Psalm 114, Op. 51 (*Da Israel aus Ägypten zog,* 1839–40).[27] All four psalm cantatas were published during Mendelssohn's lifetime and can be counted among his most masterful and popular works.

Following the first English-language performance of *Paulus* (*St. Paul*) in 1836, Mendelssohn's growing reputation in England led to a surge of commissions from that country. Beginning in 1839, Mendelssohn began composing psalm settings (including, in 1844, his beloved *Hear My Prayer*)[28] that were based on new, non-canonical English translations, and thus were not suitable for the liturgy. It would also be from England—or, more specifically, the Birmingham Festival—that the commission for Mendelssohn's most well-known sacred work, *Elijah*, Op. 70, would come in 1845, and where it would be premiered the following year. (*Elijah* is discussed in greater depth in Chapter 5 of this volume.)

Compositions for Church Services

Despite his focus on the concert hall, Mendelssohn did write a sizable number of pieces for church services, although most of these works were on commissions from traditions other than his own. Mendelssohn was exceptionally non-denominational in accepting such projects, possibly a product, as R. Larry Todd has speculated, of the filtering down of his grandfather Moses Mendelssohn's own advocacy of religious tolerance.[29] But while commissions were offered from a total of four traditions—Catholic, Anglican, French Reformed, and Jewish (the last of which he apparently never fulfilled)—the first two received by far the most attention.[30]

Mendelssohn began composing for the Catholic Church while still on the Grand Tour, presenting a series of three motets (*Veni, Domine*, Op. 39/1; *O beata et benedicta*; and *Surrexit pastor bonus*, Op. 39/3) to the nuns' choir at Trinità dei monti in Rome.[31] More Catholic works came in the years that followed, including the 1833 *Responsorium et Hymnus*, Op. 121 for the men's choir at the church in Düsseldorf (for which he also likely composed the *Zwei geistliche Chöre*, Op. 115), and the magnificent 1846 *Lauda Sion*, Op. 73 for the Church of St. Martin in Liège. Notations on Mendelssohn's manuscripts show that most of these works were written with specific services in mind (e.g., Vespers for the twenty-first Sunday after Trinity, in the case of the *Responsorium*), a fact that appears to have influenced his approach to the music. For when presented with the possibility of a performance of the *Lauda Sion* in London, Mendelssohn all but declared that his works for the liturgy and the concert hall were not interchangeable: "it would hardly do to use it without the Catholic Church and its ritual."[32]

The Grand Tour also sparked commissions for Anglican works, the first of which, a *Te Deum* for the morning service (sometimes referred to as the *Te Deum à 4*) written in the style of an English cathedral anthem, came during or shortly after his spring 1832 stay in England.[33] Mendelssohn followed this up early the next year with a Kyrie (*Lord Have Mercy Upon Us*), and in 1847 with another set of service pieces, what would posthumously become the *Drei Motetten*, Op. 69. In a letter to English publisher Edward Buxton discussing publication of the *Te Deum*, Mendelssohn again demonstrated his distinction between liturgical and non-liturgical (as well as Anglican and Lutheran) music, adamantly declaring, "There must not be a German translation made of this piece, for I do not wish to have it published in this country, as it is written for yours and for your Service. . . . [K]eep it for yourself and England."[34] As Todd points out, we will never know if Mendelssohn would have similarly prohibited the publication of the 1847 pieces in Germany, but Breitkopf & Härtel's elimination of the organ accompaniment (likely in an attempt to align the pieces with contemporary German service music, which, as noted earlier, was mostly *a cappella*) reaffirms that all of these works were written with a very specific audience and purpose in mind.[35]

Mendelssohn finally had the opportunity to compose music for a German Protestant liturgy shortly after accepting an appointment in Berlin as Kapellmeister to Friedrich Wilhelm IV's court. In 1842, the king had ordered the revision of the Prussian liturgy, with one of his goals being "the revival and advancement of singing in the Evangelical Church." He planned on placing Mendelssohn "in charge of all Evangelical Church music in the monarchy" through a position akin to Leipzig's *Thomaskantor*, in which he would not only compose, but also supervise singers, choirmasters, and organists, and create a singing school.[36] Mendelssohn had no interest in such administrative duties and attempted to decline the position. The king was persuasive, however, and Mendelssohn took up his new post in the fall of 1843. He then immediately began composing psalms, chorale harmonizations, and other liturgical pieces for the all-male cathedral choir (*Domchor*) and small orchestra that had been assembled specifically for him.[37]

Although Mendelssohn had access to this orchestra, most of his *Domchor* works are *a cappella*, including most of the psalms written to open the service; the set of six *Sprüche*, Op. 79 to be sung before the Alleluia; and the *Deutsche Liturgie*, which includes a Kyrie, Gloria (*Ehre sei Gott in der Höhe*), the now frequently performed Sanctus (*Heilig*), and several choral responses.[38] Having been charged with revitalizing music in the Prussian church, Mendelssohn no doubt felt free to redefine the liturgical style, and indeed, this breathtakingly beautiful music is generally more adventurous than that for either the Catholic or Anglican services. Nevertheless, he still attempted to show respect for the past. This blend of old and new is readily apparent in works such as Psalm 2 (*Warum toben die Heiden*, Op. 78/1), where, for the last verse, most of the double chorus chants in unison while four members of Chorus I sing in harmony. But tributes to older traditions did little to assuage the concerns of a clergy skeptical of the new reforms, who found Mendelssohn's music insufficiently liturgical in style.[39] No doubt such conflicts further soured Mendelssohn in his new position and were a factor in his resignation less than a year later.

Secular Music, Sacred Overtones

As with his sacred music, Mendelssohn's secular choral music and the aesthetic that shaped it began with Carl Zelter. In December 1808, Zelter, drawing from the ranks of the Singakademie, organized the *Liedertafel*, "[a] society," as he described it, "of 25 men who meet monthly at an evening meal . . . and amuse themselves with pleasant German songs."[40] While such recreational singing was already common by this point, even within the Singakademie, and had led to the composition of a fair amount of repertoire (known variously as *Chorlieder*, choral-songs, and partsongs), Zelter's ensemble was one of the first to be formally organized, and soon became a model for other groups throughout the German-speaking world.[41] The depth of Mendelssohn's association with the *Liedertafel* remains unclear, but given his level of involvement with Zelter's other musical endeavors and the renown of the ensemble itself, it seems impossible that he did not, at the very least, attend an occasional rehearsal or concert. In any case, Mendelssohn composed several works for men's chorus under Zelter's supervision, some or all of which may have been performed by the *Liedertafel*.[42] Mendelssohn continued to write individual settings and collections of *Chorlieder* over the course of his life, roughly half of which were for men's chorus (including Opp. 50, 75, 76, and 120), with the rest being for mixed voices (including Opp. 41, 48, 59, 88, and 100). Indeed, the *Chorlieder* account for the majority of Mendelssohn's secular choral output. Limited mostly to quality, timeless (i.e., ones with no political or other dateable content) poems, these works enjoyed extraordinary popularity in Germany throughout the nineteenth century and into the early twentieth, to the point that some of their melodies were included in published collections of German folk songs. Strangely, however, the *Chorlieder* have experienced a slower recovery from the Nazi era and its prohibition of Mendelssohn's music than have his works in other genres.[43] Given their unconventional melodic contours, their innovative use of counterpoint (something generally avoided by most partsong composers), and their flexibility of form in the service of the text,[44] these are works that clearly deserve more attention from scholars and performers alike.

That same call could be made for Mendelssohn's other secular works, which include several occasional cantatas and the choral movements of his incidental music. Fortunately, the most substantial choral work of Mendelssohn's secular *œuvre*, *Die erste Walpurgisnacht*, Op. 60, has finally begun to enjoy the attention it so richly deserves.[45] Set to Goethe's poem of the same name, the piece depicts the Druids' attempt to celebrate their sacred rites in a predominantly Christian world now hostile to them. In depicting both the rite and the Druids' efforts to frighten away what Goethe called the "dimwitted, gullible Christians," Mendelssohn brings his full programmatic talents to bear, particularly through the use of his signature "fairy" scherzo style, employed most famously in the *Midsummer Night's Dream* overture, Op. 21 (see Examples 9.1a and 9.1b).[46]

It is, perhaps, telling that the masterpiece of Mendelssohn's secular output should have sacred overtones; for while he no doubt found secular choral composition enjoyable, sacred composition was a personal imperative, one that periodically required expression. One such moment was the summer of 1831, when he noted to Eduard Devrient, "That I have lately written only sacred things was a necessity to me, just as one feels sometimes an irresistible impulse to read one certain book— it may be the Bible—and finds happiness only in reading it."[47] Indeed, so strong was this imperative that, as Rosen implied, the sacred occasionally seeped into the secular, either through hymn-like passages (as in *Die erste Walpurgisnacht*) or actual chorale quotation (as in the partsong *Der frohe Wandersmann*, Op. 75/1). But no doubt equally responsible for this crossover was the fact that for Mendelssohn, the sacred was something equally at home in the church and the concert hall.

EXAMPLE 9.1A Mendelssohn's "fairy" scherzo style in *A Midsummer Night's Dream*, Overture, mm. 8–15.

EXAMPLE 9.1B Mendelssohn's "fairy" scherzo style in *Die erste Walpurgisnacht*, no. 7, mm. 13–19.

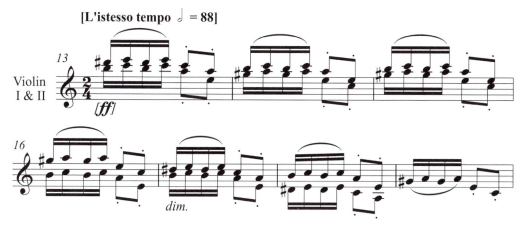

Notes

1 Mendelssohn's opus numbers are included here when available, but are not a reliable indicator of chronology, in part because they were assigned (when assigned at all) according to date of publication, not composition. To confuse matters further, Opp. 72 to 121 were ascribed posthumously to those pieces published between 1848 and 1873. Works published since then have not been assigned numbers. For more on this issue, see John Michael Cooper, "Knowing Mendelssohn: A Challenge from the Primary Sources," *Notes* 61, 1 (2004): 38–39.

2 Carl Dahlhaus, "Mendelssohn und die musikalischen Gattungstraditionen," in *Das Problem Mendelssohn*, ed. Carl Dahlhaus (Regensburg: Gustav Bosse Verlag, 1974), 58. (All translations throughout this chapter are mine, unless otherwise indicated.) See also Jeffrey Sposato, "Saint Elsewhere: German and English Reactions to Mendelssohn's *Paulus*," *19th-Century Music* 32, 1 (Summer 2008): 28–32.

3 Charles Rosen, *The Romantic Generation* (Cambridge, MA: Harvard University Press, 1995), 590–98 (quotation from 590).

4 Ibid., 594.

5 See Sposato, "Saint Elsewhere," 29–32.

6 Jeffrey Sposato, *The Price of Assimilation: Felix Mendelssohn and the Nineteenth-Century Anti-Semitic Tradition* (New York: Oxford University Press, 2006), 33–34.

7 While it is tempting to attribute this apparent lack of visible piety to Mendelssohn's birth into a Jewish family and the delay of his baptism until age seven, there is nothing to suggest that he was immersed in Judaism at an early age. See ibid., 14–37.

8 Paul Graff, *Geschichte der Auflösung der alten gottesdienstlichen Formen in der evangelischen Kirche Deutschlands*, 2 vols. (Göttingen: Vandenhoeck & Ruprecht, 1937–39), vol. 2, 71–72.

9 Georg Feder, "Decline and Restoration," in *Protestant Church Music: A History*, ed. Friedrich Blume (New York: W. W. Norton, 1974), 323–24.

10 Ibid., 334; Graff, *Geschichte der Auflösung* 2:43–51, 89–97, 109–13, 161–64.

11 *Kirchen-Agende für die Hof- und Domkirche in Berlin*, 2nd ed. (Berlin: Dieterici, 1822), 25–26 (quotation from 26). See also Mendelssohn's letter of January 12, 1835 to Pastor Albert Bauer, in Paul and Carl Mendelssohn Bartholdy, eds., *Letters of Felix Mendelssohn Bartholdy from 1833 to 1847*, trans. Lady Wallace (Boston: Oliver Ditson and Co., 1863), 62.

12 Feder, 323–31; Elizabeth A. Kramer, "The Idea of *Kunstreligion* in German Musical Aesthetics of the Early Nineteenth Century" (Ph.D. diss., University of North Carolina at Chapel Hill, 2005), 224.

13 Feder, 321–23 (quotation, taken from the 1816 Singakademie statutes, from 322).

14 Rudolf Werner, "Felix Mendelssohn Bartholdy als Kirchenmusiker" (Ph.D. diss., Universität Frankfurt am Main, 1930), 8–10; R. Larry Todd, *Mendelssohn: A Life in Music* (New York: Oxford University Press, 2003), 53–56.

15 Psalm 19 or one of Mendelssohn's other motets may have been performed at the Thomaskirche in Leipzig in late 1821 or early 1822. Susanna Großmann-Vendrey, *Felix Mendelssohn Bartholdy und die Musik der Vergangenheit* (Regensburg: Gustav Bosse Verlag, 1969), 17. Leipzig was not subject to the kind of liturgical streamlining seen elsewhere in Germany, however, and, as a result, several of Mendelssohn's sacred works intended for the concert hall were eventually performed in churches there.

16 Werner, "Felix Mendelssohn Bartholdy," 12, 17, 25, 30; Todd, *A Life*, 141–42.

17 The performance took place in 1825. Todd, *A Life*, 116.

18 Felix Loy, *Die Bach-Rezeption in den Oratorien von Mendelssohn Bartholdy* (Tutzing: Hans Schneider, 2003), 21.

19 R. Larry Todd and Peter Ward Jones have recently dispelled the myth that Mendelssohn received the Passion score as a Christmas gift in 1823 (see Todd, *A Life*, 122–24). The Singakademie performances and rehearsals of Bach that Mendelssohn heard or took part in are chronicled in Loy, *Die Bach-Rezeption*, 164–66.

20 Loy, *Die Bach-Rezeption*, 160–62.

21 Daniel R. Melamed, "Cantata Choruses and Chorales," in *The World of the Bach Cantatas*, vol. 1, ed. Christoph Wolff (New York: W. W. Norton, 1997), 164.

22 Chorales that are in bar form (AAB) consist of a melody (*Stollen*) that is repeated, followed by a second melody (*Abgesang*).

23 For more on the parallels between Mendelssohn's and Beethoven's choral symphonies, see Mark Evan Bonds, *After Beethoven: Imperatives of Originality in the Symphony* (Cambridge, MA: Harvard University Press, 1996), 73–108.

24 Ibid., 81–83.

25 Sposato, *Price of Assimilation*, 163–70.

26 Letter of October 16, 1830 to Carl Friedrich Zelter. Paul Mendelssohn Bartholdy, ed., *Reisebriefe aus den Jahren 1830 bis 1832 von Felix Mendelssohn-Bartholdy* (Leipzig: Hermann Mendelssohn, 1864), 41. See also Sposato, *Price of Assimilation*, 109.

27 My assessment of Leipzig concert trends is based on Alfred Dörffel, "Statistik der Concerte im Saale des Gewandhauses zu Leipzig," in *Geschichte der Gewandhausconcerte zu Leipzig vom 25. November 1781 bis 25. November 1881* (Leipzig: [n.p.], 1884), 1–79.

28 *Hear My Prayer* is more frequently recorded and published under its German title, *Hör mein Bitten*.

29 R. Larry Todd, "On Mendelssohn's Sacred Music, Real and Imaginary," in *The Cambridge Companion to Mendelssohn*, ed. Peter Mercer-Taylor (Cambridge: Cambridge University Press, 2004), 169.

30 For more on the commission Mendelssohn was offered from the New Israelite Temple in Hamburg, see Todd, *A Life*, 468–69. Mendelssohn composed only a single hymn, the 1846 *Cantique pour l'Eglise wallonne de Francfort*, for the French Reformed church.

31 When Mendelssohn decided to publish the set as opus 39, he replaced *O beata et benedicta* with *Laudate pueri* (Op. 39/2). Todd, *A Life*, 242.

32 Letter of January 19, 1847 to Karl Klingemann. Karl Klingemann, Jr., ed., *Felix Mendelssohn-Bartholdys Briefwechsel mit Legationsrat Karl Klingemann in London* (Essen: G. D. Baedecker, 1909), 319, quoted and translated in Todd, "On Mendelssohn's Sacred Music," 185.

33 For a comparison of the *Te Deum* with anthems by Croft and Boyce, see Todd, *A Life*, 265–66.

34 Letter of February 13, 1846 to Edward Buxton. "Mendelssohn and His English Publishers: Some Unpublished Letters," *Musical Times* 46 (1905): 168.

35 Todd, *A Life*, 558–59.

36 Cabinet order of Friedrich Wilhelm IV to Minister of Religious Affairs, Health, and Education J. A. F. Eichhorn, quoted in David Brodbeck, "A Winter of Discontent: Mendelssohn and the *Berliner Domchor*," in *Mendelssohn Studies*, ed. R. Larry Todd (Cambridge: Cambridge University Press, 1992), 3.

37 Ibid., 3–6; Todd, *A Life*, 450.

38 Two of the *Sprüche* and the *Deutsche Liturgie* were commissioned by Friedrich Wilhelm IV for the *Domchor* in 1846, two years after Mendelssohn's departure from Berlin. Todd, *A Life*, 529–31.

39 For more on this conflict, see Brodbeck, "Mendelssohn and the *Berliner Domchor*," 20–23.

40 Ludwig Geiger, ed., *Briefwechsel zwischen Goethe und Zelter in den Jahren 1799–1832* (Leipzig: P. Reclam, 1902), vol. 1, 245, quoted and translated in Mark A. Henderson, "The German Part-Song in the First Half of the Nineteenth Century" (D.M.A. thesis, University of Illinois at Urbana-Champaign, 1989), 27. See also Karl Gustav Fellerer, "Das Deutsche Chorlied im 19. Jahrhundert," in *Studien zur Musik des 19. Jahrhunderts*, vol. 1, *Musik und Musikleben im 19. Jahrhundert* (Regensburg: Gustav Bosse Verlag, 1984), 230–31.

41 Henderson, "The German Part-Song," 27–41.

42 R. Larry Todd attests to the first two of these works ("Einst ins Schlaraffenland zogen" and "Lieb und Hoffnung," both still available only in manuscript) as being in Zelter's *Liedertafel* style. Todd, *A Life*, 581, n. 45.

43 Lars Ulrich Abraham, "Mendelssohns Chorlieder und ihre musikgeschichtliche Stellung," in *Das Problem Mendelssohn*, 79–84.

44 Henderson, "The German Part-Song," 163–85; Abraham, "Mendelssohns Chorlieder," 84–87.

45 This attention includes John Michael Cooper, *Mendelssohn, Goethe, and the Walpurgis Night* (Rochester, NY: University of Rochester Press, 2007).

46 Sposato, *Price of Assimilation*, 111–13.

47 Letter of July 13, 1831 to Eduard Devrient. Eduard Devrient, *My Recollections of Felix Mendelssohn-Bartholdy and His Letters to Me*, trans. Natalia Macfarran (London: Richard Bentley, 1869), 114–15.

Selected Bibliography

All of the sacred works and partsongs for mixed chorus have been published in Urtext editions by Carus Verlag; most of these are also available through Breitkopf und Härtel, as is *Die erste Walpurgisnacht*. Although some of the partsongs for men's chorus have been reprinted in recent decades, they are most easily available in the nineteenth-century complete edition of Mendelssohn's works edited by Julius Rietz. The edition was reprinted in the twentieth century by a variety of publishers, including Breitkopf und Härtel, Gregg Press, and Belwin Mills. Most of the choral works have been recorded on CD, with complete sets of the sacred works available on the Carus Verlag and Brilliant Classics labels.

Clostermann, Annemarie. *Mendelssohn Bartholdys kirchenmusikalisches Schaffen: neue Untersuchungen zu Geschichte, Form und Inhalt*. Mainz: Schott, 1989.

Dinglinger, Wolfgang. *Studien zu den Psalmen mit Orchester von Felix Mendelssohn Bartholdy*. Köln: Studio, 1993.

Seaton, Douglass, ed. *The Mendelssohn Companion*. Westport, CT: Greenwood Press, 2001.

Sposato, Jeffrey S. *The Price of Assimilation: Felix Mendelssohn and the Nineteenth-Century Anti-Semitic Tradition*. New York: Oxford University Press, 2006.

Todd, R. Larry. *Mendelssohn: A Life in Music*. New York: Oxford University Press, 2003.

Werner, Rudolf. "Felix Mendelssohn Bartholdy als Kirchenmusiker." Ph.D. diss., Universität Frankfurt am Main, 1930.

10

ROBERT SCHUMANN

Roe-Min Kok

McGill University

Introduction and Overview

> One beautiful summer's day, we boarded a steamship on the River Elbe, bound for Pillnitz
> and the nearby Porsberg mountains. Under flowering chestnut trees in the castle restaurant
> we ate lunch. Then, singing music by Schumann, Mendelssohn and Hauptmann, we formed
> a caravan that, laughing, headed off to climb the mountain.
>
> . . . On a return journey of another trip to Meissen, again we had to sing for [Schumann]
> his song *Mich zieht es nach dem Dörfchen hin.*[1]

Vivid and illuminating, Emil Naumann's memoirs describe a day trip with the Dresden Chorverein.
We glimpse Schumann, its co-founder and director, at his convivial best. We learn of activities
jovially undertaken with people from different walks of life. We sense communal warmth in their
rendition of Schumann's Op. 55/3. As we shall see, the ability of vocal polyphony to encapsulate
and communicate collective opinion, as well as its potential for dramatic expressivity, defined
Schumann's engagement with choral genres over the course of his career.[2]

About a third of Schumann's forty (or so) choral works originated before November 1847;
he composed most of the rest over the next seven years.[3] His sojourn in Dresden, between
November 1847 and September 1850, was particularly fruitful (see Figure 10.1), clearly a result of
collaborating with the mixed-voice Chorverein and other groups.[4] After the Schumann family
moved to Düsseldorf, where the composer took the job of municipal music director, his choral
output shifted noticeably toward large-scale pieces with orchestral accompaniment (see Figure
10.2). This trend aligned with his directorship, under which the Düsseldorf Gesangverein performed at least one large-scale oratorio per season, in addition to choral–orchestral works with the
municipal orchestra.[5]

The sheer variety, quality, and quantity of Schumann's choral output belie his checkered career
as a choral conductor.[6] He wrote for all-female and all-male as well as mixed-voice choirs; a
significant number of his choral works are unaccompanied, while others feature orchestral, keyboard, or chamber accompaniment (some *ad libitum*). While some of his later works are difficult
to classify in terms of traditional genres—not least because Schumann himself deliberately experimented with these—his output includes large pieces for solo, chorus and orchestra, sacred works,
and partsongs.[7]

Unaccompanied Unless Otherwise Indicated

Drei Gesänge, Op. 62 (TTBB, 1847)

Ritornelle, Op. 65 (TTBBB, 1847)

Drei Freiheitsgesänge, WoO 4 (TTBB, *Harmoniemusik* ad lib.: winds, brass, percussion, 1848)

Romanzen und Balladen, Op. 67 (SATB, 1849)

Romanzen, Op. 69 (SSAA, piano ad lib., 1849)

Romanzen und Balladen, Op. 75 (SATB, 1849)

Romanzen, Op. 91 (SSAA, piano ad lib., 1849)

Motette Verzweifle nicht im Schmerzensthal, Op. 93 (TTBB/TTBB, organ ad lib., 1849)

Fünf Gesänge aus H. Laubes Jagdbrevier, Op. 137 (TTBB, 4 horns ad lib., 1849)

Vier doppelchörige Gesänge, Op. 141 (SATB/SATB, 1849)

Der Handschuh, original *a cappella* version of Op. 87 (SATB, 1849)

Romanzen und Balladen, Op. 145 (SATB, 1849–51)

Romanzen und Balladen, Op. 146 (SATB, *Das Schifflein* with fl., hn., 1849–51)

With Orchestral Accompaniment

Adventlied, Op. 71 (soli SATB/chorus SATB, 1848)

Requiem für Mignon, Op. 98b (soli SSAAB/chorus SATTBB, 1849)

Nachtlied, Op. 108 (SSAATTBB, 1849)

Neujahrslied, Op. 144 (soli SAB/chorus SATB, 1849–50)

In Dramatic Works

Genoveva, Op. 81 (incl. chorus SATB, 1847–48)

Manfred (dramatic poem), Op. 115 (incl. soli SATBBBB, chorus SSATB, 1848–49)[1]

1 All titles and opus or catalog numbers follow those in Margit McCorkle, *Robert Schumann: Thematisch-Bibliographisches Werkverzeichnis* (Munich: G. Henle, 2003).

FIGURE 10.1 Choral works composed (or begun) in Dresden between November 1847 and September 1850.

With Orchestral Accompaniment

Der Rose Pilgerfahrt, Op. 112 (originally with piano; soli SMsATB, chorus SSAATTBB, 1851)

Der Königssohn, Op. 116 (soli ATBarB, chorus SATTBB, 1851)

Motette Verzweifle nicht im Schmerzensthal, Op. 93 (TTBB/TTBB, version with orchestra, 1852)

Des Sängers Fluch, Op. 139 (soli SATB, chorus SATTBB, 1851–52)

Vom Pagen und der Königstochter, Op. 140 (soli SATB, chorus SATTBB, 1852)

Requiem, Op. 148 (soli SATB, chorus SATB, 1852)

Missa Sacra, Op. 147 (soli STB, chorus SATB, 1852–53)

Fest-Ouvertüre mit Gesang, Op. 123 (soli SATB, chorus SATB, 1853)

Das Glück von Edenhall, Op. 143 (soli TB, chorus TTBB, 1853)

Szenen aus Goethes Faust, WoO 3 (soli SATBarB, chorus SSAATTBB, 1844–53)

FIGURE 10.2 Choral works composed in Düsseldorf (after September 1850).

Schumann's choral music has been variously discussed elsewhere.[8] In this chapter, I seek to highlight aspects of his compositional practices from different points in his career through snapshots of four splendid (if relatively unknown) choral works. Op. 33 (partsongs for men), Op. 55 (partsongs for mixed voices), Op. 108 (a large choral–orchestral work), and Op. 112 (a "fairytale" oratorio) represent a cross-section of his musical styles and ideas, as well as the types of vocal ensembles for which he wrote. Before turning to these works, I shall briefly discuss the issue of performing forces in Schumann's choral music, a topic rarely mentioned, but which may be helpful for modern-day performers.

Performing Forces

Little is known with certainty about the size of performing forces Schumann envisioned for his works. Although he left the occasional instruction, on the whole he seems to have entrusted this decision to groups that sang his music, and to the performance practices of his day. Indications on his scores might be understood in context of the ensembles with which he worked.[9] According to Thomas Synofzik, Schumann differentiated between relative sizes of groups, rather than number of voices per part. The word *Chor* (choir, chorus) often referred to a large group; for instance, the three partsongs Op. 62 (1847) were written for a Dresden *Männerchor*. The words *vierstimmige* (four-part voices) and / or *mehrstimmige* (multiple-part voices) in titles pointed to smaller forces: possibly Mendelssohn's Leipzig *Liedertafel* for the six partsongs Op. 33 (1840), and Schumann's Dresden *Liedertafel* in the case of *Ritornelle in canonischen Weisen* (Op. 65, 1847). Membership numbers give us an idea of the relative sizes of *Chor* and *Liedertafel*. In 1849, Schumann reported that the Dresden Chorverein numbered sixty to seventy, while at the height of their popularity, five Dresden men's choruses around 1847 had a combined membership of 220.[10]

Occasionally, Schumann specified the number of voices in his scores. In Op. 65, nos. 1 and 5 call for one singer per part; no. 2, four singers; and nos. 4 and 6, full chorus. Four soloists (SATB) alternate with a mixed choir in nos. 1, 4 and 5 of Op. 55, while three measures for "four bass voices" are included in Op. 108 (mm. 192–94), a work about nine minutes long for mixed-voice choir and orchestra. Overall, however, the composer seems to have maintained the flexible attitude of a practical, practicing musician, recognizing that his works might be sung by groups of different sizes and combinations of voices, as well as varying levels of ability.[11]

Sechs Lieder für vierstimmigen Männergesang Op. 33 (1840)

Along with solo Lieder, Schumann turned to writing vocal polyphony in 1840, his "Year of Song."[12] Among the fruits of his pen were the six partsongs Op. 33 for four-part *Männergesang*, an all-male ensemble then popular in German musical life whose prominence has since declined (rather like its English counterpart, gentlemen's glee clubs).[13] Filled with musical charm and lively wit, they were dedicated to his friend Gustav Keferstein, an influential theologian and a contributor to the *Neue Zeitschrift für Musik* (*NZfM*). Keferstein had helped Schumann secure a doctorate from the University of Jena early in 1840, thus strengthening his legal bid to marry Clara Wieck despite vigorous opposition from her father. Accordingly, Op. 33 celebrates topics more cultivated than those found in typical *Liedertafel* texts (student life, drinking, and war).[14] A sense of fragility and loneliness underlies "Der träumende See" (The dreaming lake), for instance; darkly erotic, "Die Lotosblume" (The lotus flower) finds a playful counterpart in "Frühlingsglocken" (Spring Bells), a paean to the season of rebirth. The set features piquant chromaticism and harmonies to an extent unusual for *Männergesang* music in general, perhaps because Schumann composed them in the wake of a debate over the value of men's choruses; he was probably siding with F. A. Gelbcke's rebuttal of Eduard Krüger's uncharitable comments about the limitations of the genre and its performers.[15]

"Der träumende See" (Op. 33/1) gently warms up performers and listeners alike, with its moderate tempo, straightforward harmonies, and quiet dynamics; staggered vocal entries add subtle lilt, highlighting the wistful quality of the text. In setting Heine's "Die Minnesänger" (The Minnesingers, Op. 33/2), Schumann unleashed his skill at musical characterization. Couched in a modified barform (ABA'B'/AC) in an obvious nod to the medieval Minnelied, the song is a breathtaking play on speed, articulation and texture: swaggering swains, bejeweled women and flying flags swirl in this strange tournament ("seltsames Turnei"). "Die Lotosblume" (Op. 33/3) features sinuous phrasing and a striking approach to an augmented sixth chord (see Example 10.1).

Slyly tucked deep in the set is the humorous "Der Zecher als Doktrinär" (The tippler as doctrinaire, Op. 33/4) by Julius Mosen.[16] It is a through-composed homage, in true *Liedertafel* tradition, to male companionship, complete with a description of broken hearts, sung "with somewhat trem-

EXAMPLE 10.1 R. Schumann, "Die Lotosblume" (H. Heine), Op. 33/3, mm. 15–21. Source: *Robert Schumann's Werke*. Ed. Clara Schumann. Leipzig: Breitkopf & Härtel (1880s).

EXAMPLE 10.2 R. Schumann, "Frühlingsglocken" (R. Reinick), Op. 33/6, mm. 1–8. Source: *Robert Schumann's Werke*. Ed. Clara Schumann. Leipzig: Breitkopf & Härtel (1880s).

bling voices" and call-and-response sections. Last in the set, "Frühlingsglocken" (Op. 33/6) is the longest and most virtuosic. In this onomatopoeic showcase, Schumann calls for bell sonorities brilliant and delicate alike—clanging, ringing, and tinkling in different registers—above folk-like drones (see Example 10.2).

Fünf Lieder nach Robert Burns für gemischten Chor, Op. 55 (1846)

A constructed "folk" style characterizes Op. 55, settings for mixed voices dedicated to Mendelssohn's Leipzig *Liederkranz*.[17] Already in 1842, *NZfM* critics "W.Z." and "12"—probably Schumann himself—had opined that Robert Burns's poetry seemed animated by old folk melodies, rendering it naturally suited to "true folk songs."[18] Indeed, "folk" music characteristics appear in almost every piece in the set. For instance, homophonic declamation dominates all five songs, with three in either strophic or modified strophic form. Solo-tutti sections appear in "Das Hochlandmädchen" (The highland maiden, Op. 55/1), "Die alte, gute Zeit" (The good old times, Op. 55/4), and "Hochlandbursch" (Highland laddie, Op. 55/5), all of which also feature much stepwise and triadic motion. Both "Hochlandmädchen" and "Mich zieht es nach dem Dörfchen hin" (I am drawn to the little village, Op. 55/3) make prominent use of pedal points. Folk-like elements are abandoned, however, in the madrigal-like "Zahnweh" (Toothache, Op. 55/2). Marked "With humor" and sung throughout by the entire choir, this partsong is technically challenging, featuring tortuous chromaticism and awkward intervallic leaps (see Example 10.3), along with divisions of inner parts later in the work.[19]

EXAMPLE 10.3 R. Schumann, "Zahnweh" (R. Burns), Op. 55/2, mm. 20–28. Source: *Robert Schumann's Werke*. Ed. Clara Schumann. Leipzig: Breitkopf & Härtel, [1880s].

EXAMPLE 10.3   continued.

Nachtlied für Chor und Orchester, Op. 108 (1849)

Nachtlied is one of Schumann's most beautiful (if neglected) choral works with orchestral accompaniment.[20] Spare and elegant, the poem by Friedrich Hebbel describes the dying protagonist's keen awareness of approaching fate, telescoped into just twelve lines (see Figure 10.3). Schumann's through-composed, bipartite setting divides the poem unequally, with the first two stanzas taking up roughly half the work's duration (Section A, poem lines 1–8, mm. 1–88, 4 minutes 40 seconds, D minor). The third and final stanza occupies the remainder of the music (Section B, mm. 89–227, 4 minutes 20 seconds, D major). Clearly the composer wanted the poetic message in these last four

Quellende, schwellende Nacht,	Swelling, expanding night,
Voll von Lichtern und Sternen:	Filled with lights and stars:
In den ewigen Fernen,	into eternal distances,
Sage, was ist da erwacht?	Speak, what has there awakened?
Herz in der Brust wird beengt,	The heart in the breast feels cramped,
Steigendes, neigendes Leben,	Life rising, falling,
Riesenhaft fühle ich's weben,	I sense the enormous weaving
Welches das meine verdrängt.	of things that repress my own.
Schlaf, da nahst du dich leise	Sleep, you softly come near
Wie dem Kinde die Amme,	as a nurse would approach a child,
Und um die dürftige Flamme	and around the meager flame
Ziehst du den schützenden Kreis!	you draw the protective circle!

FIGURE 10.3 *Nachtlied*, Op. 108 (1849; text by Friedrich Hebbel).

EXAMPLE 10.4a R. Schumann, *Nachtlied* (F. Hebbel), Op. 108, mm. 1–6, Section A, Motif X (with melodic reduction). Source: *Robert Schumann's Werke*. Ed. Clara Schumann. Leipzig: Breitkopf & Härtel (1880s).

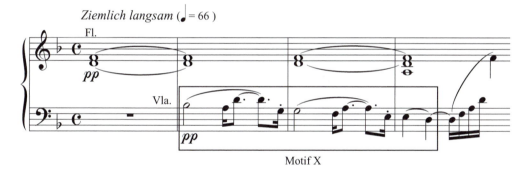

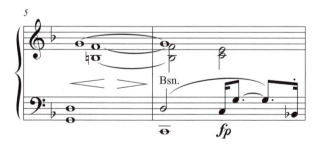

Melodic reduction

lines, depicting a trusting, child-like figure looking forward to death (in the guise of slumber), to outweigh the fears expressed in the earlier part of the poem.[21]

Among the tools he used to shape his musical take on the poem are two motifs, X and Y. Found almost exclusively in Section A, motif X (see Example 10.4a, mm. 2–6) is couched in dark timbres and imparts a sense of uncertainty: it emerges in the minor mode in the violas, before restlessly moving into an applied dominant, where it elides with a second entry in the bassoon and violoncellos. Rhythmically, the first three note values seem to allude, albeit in inversion, to the opening of Mendelssohn's song "Frage" (Question, Op. 9/1; see Example 10.4b). Reversed, *Frage's* potentially existentialist question "Is it true?" might be affirmed "It is true" by *Nachtlied's* opening.[22] Interestingly, Mendelssohn quotes "Frage" in the Adagio of his String Quartet in A minor, Op. 13, a gesture perhaps referring to the "Muss es sein?" (Must it be?) motif in Beethoven's String Quartet Op. 135 (see Example 10.4c).[23] In *Nachtlied,* motif X, whose initial contour resembles the Beethoven and Mendelssohn motifs, descends from the flat sixth to the first scale degree, and is played solely by orchestral instruments. Musically, it embodies the protagonist reluctantly acknowledging the end of life as described in Hebbel's first two stanzas.

EXAMPLE 10.4b   Felix Mendelssohn, "Frage" (G. Droysen), Op. 9/1, anacrusis into m. 1. Source: Bayerische Staatsbibliothek, Musikabteilung, Signatur: 2 Mus.pr. 2643-18,137/19,157; used with permission.

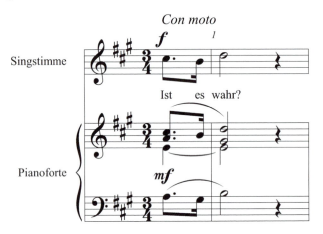

EXAMPLE 10.4c   Beethoven, String Quartet in F major, Op. 135, "Muss es sein?" Source: *Ludwig van Beethoven's Werke: vollständige kritisch durchgesehene überall berechtigte Ausgabe. Quartett für 2 Violinen, Bratsche und Violoncell. Zweiter Band.* Leipzig: Breitkopf & Härtel (1860s).

DER SCHWER GEFASSTE ENTSCHLUSS
[The resolution, reached with difficulty]

EXAMPLE 10.4d   R. Schumann, *Nachtlied* (F. Hebbel), Op. 108, mm. 96–98, Section B, Motif Y (with melodic reduction). Source: *Robert Schumann's Werke*. Ed. Clara Schumann. Leipzig: Breitkopf & Härtel, [1880s].

Melodic reduction

In contrast, Y, sung first by bright-toned sopranos at the opening of Section B, begins and ends in the major, with a straightforward 5–4–3–2–1 descent in stately rhythm on the words "you softly come near" (see Example 10.4d, mm. 96–98). From m. 140 onwards, Y appears increasingly frequently, as if intensifying the message of this last stanza, already augmented musically in relation to its text. Y, then, is the "true answer" to questions about the unknown. In the final eighty-seven measures of *Nachtlied*, Y is not only prominent, it is inclusive, sung by voices and played by instruments (for instance flute, mm. 146–148) so that by the very end, X's disquiet and doubts seem but distant, isolated memories. Other features of note in the work include antiphonal passages between male and female voices (mm. 18–21, 121–24, 165–68) which recall Schumann's liturgical choral works; homophonic declamation, text repetitions in different sonic colors (mm. 31–43, 96–104), and tasteful word painting (for example, violins, mm. 30–32, with violas, 51–88).[24]

Der Rose Pilgerfahrt, Märchen nach einer Dichtung von Moritz Horn für Soli, Chor und Orchester, Op. 112 (1851)

Often bypassed by performers and scholars alike for its older, larger sibling *Das Paradies und die Peri* (Op. 50, 1843), *Der Rose Pilgerfahrt* was based on a text written and sent by the amateur poet Moritz Horn to Schumann, who requested certain changes in agreeing to set it.[25] With its quasi-religious references to pilgrimage and heaven, and as a non-staged dramatic work, Op. 112 is often called an oratorio, although critics note that it is only superficially related to traditional oratorio, and should instead be regarded as a hybrid bringing together elements of piano-accompanied *Liederspiel*,[26] song cycle, and oratorio—an example of Schumann's genre experimentation in his late choral works.[27] Schumann himself called it *Märchen* (fairytale), defending this unusual term by arguing it was a "more rustic, more German" folk-like work accessible to all: he would eschew complicated contrapuntal art for a simple, moving musical language achieved through rhythm and melody.[28]

The plot recalls those of *Undine* (1811) by Friedrich de la Motte Fouqué and *Little Mermaid* (1836) by H. C. Andersen. A non-human being (here a rose) aspires to become human in order

Part I

No. 3	Elves' Chorus, "Elfenreigen" (SSA)
No. 4	Elves' Chorus, "Wir tanzen, wir tanzen" (SSA from No. 3)
No. 8	"Wie Blätter am Baum" (SATB)
No. 10	Elves' Chorus, "Schwesterlein!" (solo S, chorus SA)

Part II

No. 15	"Bist du im Wald gewandelt" (TTBB)
No. 18	"O sel'ge Zeit" (SATB)
No. 21	"Was klingen denn die Hörner" (solo S, chorus SATTB),
	"Den Bund der treuen Herzen" (SA)
No. 22	"Im Hause des Müllers" (SATB)
No. 24	Angels' Chorus "Röslein!" (solo SSAA, chorus SSAA)

FIGURE 10.4 Choral numbers in *Der Rose Pilgerfahrt* (M. Horn), Op. 112.

to experience love. Turned into a maiden by the Queen of Elves, who also gives her a protective rose talisman, Rose endures many trying encounters before being adopted by a miller and his wife. Her "pilgrimage" ends a year after she weds a gamekeeper's son. Explaining that her mission—to experience human love and happiness—has been accomplished, she disappears, leaving the talisman with her newborn, and a chorus of angels welcomes her into their ranks.[29]

Women's voices feature prominently in *Der Rose Pilgerfahrt*, with its female protagonist, Marian symbols (the rose, heavenly ascent), and cast of supernatural secondary characters.[30] Like Schubert, Schumann could draw diverse sounds out of sopranos and altos, and in Op. 112 he created for them a sonic showcase ranging from haunting, pearly shimmer and ethereal transparency to sharp, focused sounds, sweet lyricism, and warm maturity.[31] As mentioned earlier, Schumann envisioned an accessible work. Probably as a result of his experiences with the largely amateur choirs of Düsseldorf, technical demands are relatively modest: the ensemble numbers of Op. 112, for instance, are well within reach of solid chorus singers.[32] Of the twenty-four musical numbers in *Der Rose Pilgerfahrt,* nine include choruses: four combine sopranos and altos, four are for SATB, and one, for tenors and basses (see Figure 10.4).

Choral numbers have several functions in *Der Rose Pilgerfahrt*. All are integrated into the dramatic action, and serve either to describe or further the narrative. They delineate structurally important points: Parts I and II end with choruses (nos. 10 and 24, respectively). No. 10 is an example of the fluid arioso style and continuous musical action favored by Schumann in works such as *Peri* and *Requiem für Mignon* (Op. 98b, 1849). Featuring Rose and an Elves' Chorus (SA), it initially portrays the young girl drifting to sleep in the Gravedigger's home. Her graceful, declamatory prayer in D-flat major and triple time soon tapers into a twilight zone between human and supernatural realms: a twelve-measure passage in C-sharp minor and simple duple (mm. 20–31; see Example 10.5, here in the original piano version). Wondering if the elves—her former playmates—remember her, she asks half-dreamingly in the last four measures (mm. 28–31), "Are they thinking of me?" In trips the elves' chorus at a brisk pace (mm. 32ff.), with the performance indication "Very lively," deftly accompanied by *tremolo* and *pizzicato* in the strings as well as woodwinds playing high, *staccato* eighth-note chords (see Example 10.5). This is a clear reference to Mendelssohn's "fairy music" style, perhaps most famously embodied in his *A Midsummer Night's Dream Overture*, although in this minor-mode strophic number the elves are all fluttering anxiety as they try to persuade Rose to give up her quest and return to their fold.

Schumann cleverly draws out an entirely different character from a combination of sopranos

EXAMPLE 10.5 R. Schumann, *Der Rose Pilgerfahrt* (M. Horn), Op. 112/10, mm. 18–35. Source: *Robert Schumann's Werke*. Ed. Clara Schumann. Leipzig: Breitkopf & Härtel, (1880s).

EXAMPLE 10.5   continued.

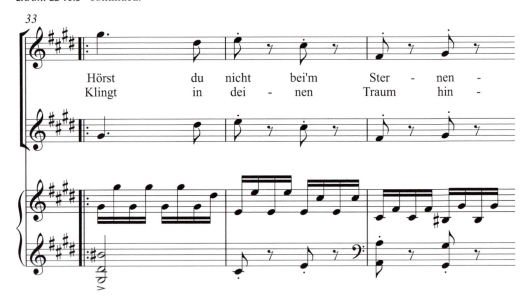

and altos he would use again, albeit *divisi*, in no. 24 (SSAA). In several ways, this concluding number of the work is the musical incarnation of the third and final stage of Rose's transformative journey from flower to human to angel. The contrasts between no. 10 (when Rose was still human) and no. 24 are masterfully deployed. Where the elves had squeaked and fretted in C-sharp minor, mirroring the girl's subconscious fears, the angels sing, calm and self-assured, in mid-range and C major as befitting their dignified status, one Rose herself has implicitly earned by her persistent, heartfelt endeavors. No longer the humble little sister (*Schwesterlein*), she is hailed by her own name (*Röslein*, mm. 1–2) and soars, borne ever upward by celestial music. Where the elves' chorus had been strophic, no doubt a reference to their folksy nature, the angels sing a through-composed number in four-part chorale texture (see Example 10.6, mm. 3ff.).

Contributing to the quiet, reflective mood are a lullaby-like triplet motif in the accompaniment, and slow harmonic rhythm throughout. Spiritual peace and calm reign; even an unexpected harmonic shift from C major (m. 9) to E minor at the second iteration of "raise you aloft" (mm. 10–11), and an unprepared move from the dominant (with B-natural, m. 18) to the dominant seventh of IV (with B-flat, m. 19), barely stir the stream of soft sound. Strategically placed, this chorus musically—and psychologically—resolves the story of Rose and her journey. Despite its earnest, sentimental cast that many criticized,[33] it in fact reveals not a weak, naive maid, but a striving heroine who successfully initiates, plans, and carries through her ambitions from beginning to end, finally gaining redemption through her perseverance and the support of human and supernatural beings alike.

Conclusion

As illustrated in the four works above, Schumann's approach to choral composition was as engaging as it was wide-ranging. From musical characterization in Op. 33, to evoking musical traditions such as "folk" and madrigal styles (Op. 55), from musically bending a poetic message to his will in the case of Op. 108—he is well known for this practice in his solo Lieder—to rendering boundaries of established genres flexible and fluid (Op. 112; the earliest precedents for this practice may be

EXAMPLE 10.6 R. Schumann, *Der Rose Pilgerfahrt* (M. Horn), Op. 112/24, mm. 1–12. Source: *Robert Schumann's Werke*. Ed. Clara Schumann. Leipzig: Breitkopf & Härtel, (1880s).

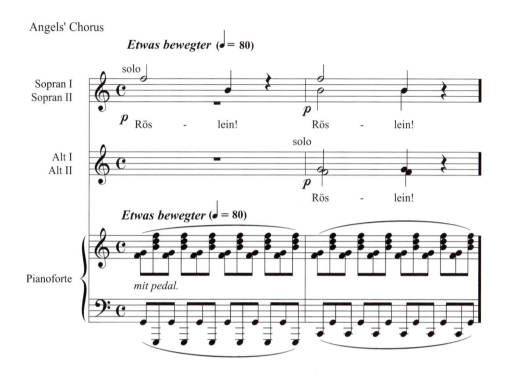

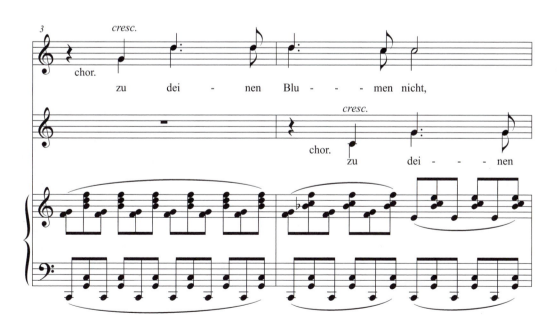

EXAMPLE 10.6 continued.

EXAMPLE 10.6 continued.

found in his piano music), Schumann revealed how highly he valued choral music as an outlet for his creativity throughout his career. Close study of his manifold endeavors in this field carries the potential for many rich rewards.

Notes

I thank Donna Di Grazia and Peter Schubert for their detailed, helpful comments on this chapter. Eric Lo, Evan Campbell, Mikaela Miller and Rodolfo Moreno prepared the musical examples. All translations are mine unless otherwise indicated.

1 Hermann Erler, ed., *Robert Schumann's Leben. Aus seinen Briefen geschildert von Hermann Erler.* 2nd edition. Berlin: Ries & Erler, 1887, vol. II, 54.
2 Schumann also touted choral music's pedagogical value for composition, advising aspiring composers to write music for choirs as often as possible. See Gustav Jansen, ed., *Robert Schumann, Briefe. Neue Folge* (Leipzig: Breitkopf & Härtel, 1904), 257, 289. Also see *Neue Zeitschrift für Musik* 12/42 (May 22, 1840), 267, hereafter *NZfM*; and Martin Kreisig, ed., Robert Schumann, *Gesammelte Schriften über Musik und Musiker*, vol. I (Leipzig: Breitkopf & Härtel, 1914), 472. Bernhard R. Appel details Schumann's engagement with renaissance polyphony in "Schumann und die klassische Vokalpolyphonie," in *Der späte Schumann*, ed. Ulrich Tadday (Munich: edition text + kritik, 2006), 117–32.
3 Susanne Popp estimates forty, while Louis Halsey counts fifty (he includes chamber vocal works—duets, trios, small ensembles—in the figure). See Popp, *Untersuchungen zu Robert Schumanns Chorkompositionen* (Bonn: Rheinische Friedrich-Wilhelms-Universität, 1971), 8–12; and Halsey, "The Choral Music," in *Robert Schumann: The Man and His Music*, ed. Alan Walker (London: Barrie & Jenkins, 1973), 350–89.
4 The Chorverein was co-founded with his wife Clara in January 1848, at a time when he was losing interest in the *Liedertafel*, his first choral conducting appointment in Dresden. By October 1848 he had given up the latter: "there was simply too little real musical effort involved—and I felt I didn't fit in." See Irmgard Knechtges-Obrecht, "Critical Notes," in *Romances for Female Voices Op. 69 and 91. Robert Schumann: New Edition of the Complete Works*, ed. Irmgard Knechtges-Obrecht and Matthias Wendt (Mainz: Schott, 1991), 62–63. Also see Jansen, *Robert Schumann, Briefe*, 294, 302.
5 John Daverio, *Robert Schumann: Herald of a "New Poetic Age"* (New York: Oxford University Press, 1997), 441–42.
6 Halsey, *Robert Schumann*, 351–52.
7 On Schumann's genre experiments in choral works, see my discussion of Op. 112 later in this chapter, including note 27. He may have invented the "chorale ballade"; see Hansjörg Ewert, "Die großbesetzten vokal-instrumentalen Werke," in Ulrich Tadday, ed., *Schumann Handbuch* (Stuttgart and Weimar: J. B. Metzler, and Kassel: Bärenreiter, 2006), 513.
8 Abraham (1952) and Cooper (1973), for example, included commentary on Schumann's choruses in their work on his dramatic music, while Probst (1975) and Harwood (1991) analyzed them in dissertations on the oratorios and liturgical works, respectively. Schumann's music for women's voices is the focus of Paul (1984). General surveys of the choral works by Fellerer (1981), Halsey (1973), Popp (1971), Godwin (1967), and Horton (1952) offer observations of varying depth. Paley (2007) and Ewert (2006) consider choruses in dramatic works and the large-scale compositions for soloists, chorus and orchestra, respectively. The most detailed study of Schumann's *a cappella* works to date is Synofzik (2006).
9 The discussion in this section is mainly drawn from Thomas Synofzik, "Weltliche a capella-Chormusik," in Ulrich Tadday, ed., *Schumann Handbuch* (Stuttgart and Weimar: J. B. Metzler, and Kassel: Bärenreiter, 2006), 458–59. See also Siegfried Kross, *Die Chorwerke von Johannes Brahms* (Berlin and Wunsiedel: Max Hesse, 1963), 273–76 in which he shows Brahms was sometimes vague about performance forces for his small vocal works, which could range from one or more than one voice per part to a "small chorus" (Klein-Chor).
10 Knechtges-Obrecht, "Critical Notes," 62–63.
11 In an April 16, 1849 letter to his publisher regarding the twelve *Romanzen* of Opp. 69 and 91 "for women's voices," for example, Schumann suggested, "may also be sung by [women's] chorus." Synofzik, "Weltliche a capella-Chormusik," 459.
12 "Now I am writing only songs, large and small, also quartets for male voices, which I would like to dedicate to [you] . . . I can hardly tell you what a treat it is to write for the voice compared with instrumental composition, and what a ferment I am in as I sit at work. *I have been inundated with new ideas*, and I am even considering an opera." Letter to Gustav Keferstein, February 19, 1840. Emphasis in the original.

This translation modified by the present author from May Herbert, *The Life of Robert Schumann told in his Letters* (London: Richard Bentley and Son, 1890), vol. 1, 247–48.

13 This set deserves far more attention than it has received, as noted by Joachim Draheim, "Robert Schumann—Liederfrühling 1840–1847," liner notes to *Schumann: The Secular Choral Works*, Werner Pfaff and Studio Vocale Karlsruhe, Brilliant Classics 92148, c2001, compact disc, p. 3.

14 As described by Eduard Krüger, "Ueber Liedertafeln," *NZfM* 11, 36 (November 1, 1839): 142.

15 The debate was published in *NZfM*. See Thomas Synofzik, "Mendelssohn, Schumann und das Problem der Männergesangskomposition um 1840," in *Schumanniana nova: Festschrift Gerd Nauhaus zum 60. Geburtstag*, ed. Bernhard R. Appel, Ute Bär, and Matthias Wendt (Sinzig: Studio-Verlag, 2002), 739–66.

16 On the genesis of this text, see Synofzik, "Weltliche a capella-Chormusik," 461.

17 Originally an all-male *Liedertafel* that began welcoming women members in February 1846, at which point it was renamed. Synofzik, "Weltliche a capella-Chormusik," 463.

18 Synofzik, "Weltliche a capella-Chormusik," 464. Schumann set two Burns texts in 1840; these were not published in his lifetime. See Kazuko Ozawa, "Robert Burns, der Jakobitismus und die *Gerstenmehlbrode*," in Bernhard Appel, Ute Bär and Matthias Wendt, ed., *Schumanniana nova: Festschrift Gerd Nauhaus zum 60. Geburtstag* (Sinzig: Studio-Verlag, 2002), 539–68.

19 Apparently these technical challenges led reviewer August F. Riccius to predict that *Zahnweh* would be sung less often than the rest of the set, despite its ingenuity. *NZfM* 31 (1849): 36, 190.

20 John Daverio calls the work "a miniature masterpiece," and observes, "it is difficult to say why the *Nachtlied* is hardly known; indeed it has never before been recorded." Liner notes, Schumann/Gardiner, Deutsche Grammophon Archiv Produktion 289 457 660-2, 1997/99, compact disc, p. 13.

21 This is the second Hebbel poem on Death as Sleep that Schumann set that year. See Roe-Min Kok, "Falling Asleep: Schumann, Lessing and Death in a *Wunderhorn* Lullaby," *Studien zur Wertungsforschung* 48 (2007): 236–72.

22 The rest of the poem describes a young couple's romantic love, unlike Hebbel's text. The poet of Mendelssohn's song remains unclear: it may have been the composer himself, or Gustav Droysen. See R. Larry Todd, *Mendelssohn: A Life in Music* (Oxford: Oxford University Press, 2003), 176.

23 Beethoven's quartet was composed in 1826, and published the following year; Mendelssohn wrote the song, followed by the quartet, in 1827.

24 In a letter to P. August Strackerjan dated January 17, 1854, Schumann wrote that he had always been especially attached to *Nachtlied*, for whose performance he recommended a "nocturnal" sound quality and coloring. See Jansen, *Robert Schumann, Briefe*, 391. On Schumann's performance directions, which he rarely made, see letters to C.v. Bruyck of December 17, 1852 and Friedrich Hebbel, March 14, 1853, in Jansen, *Robert Schumann, Briefe*, 363, 367. For examples of how poetic meaning, voices, and instrumental parts are interlaced throughout the work, see Ewert, "Die großbesetzten vokal-instrumentalen Werke," 487 and Popp, *Untersuchungen*, 67.

25 The work exists in two versions: the original with piano accompaniment first performed in July 1851, and an orchestrated version completed in November. On the textual genesis of the poem, see Gerd Nauhaus, "Der Rose Pilgerfahrt, Op. 112: Schumanns Abschied vom Oratorium," in *Schumann in Düsseldorf: Werke—Texte—Interpretationen*, ed. Bernhard Appel (Mainz and London: Schott, 1993), 181–84.

26 *Liederspiel* (song-play) was an early nineteenth-century dramatic entertainment in which songs were introduced into a play. See Peter Branscombe, "Liederspiel," in *Grove Music Online. Oxford Music Online*, http://www.oxfordmusiconline.com/subscriber/article/grove/music/16619 (accessed January 28, 2011).

27 See, for instance, Popp, *Untersuchungen*, 62ff; Karl Gustav Fellerer, "Schumanns Chorlied," in *Robert Schumann: Universalgeist der Romantik*, ed. Julius Alf and Joseph A. Kruse (Düsseldorf: Droste, 1981), 91ff.; Daverio, *Robert Schumann*, 439–47; and Ewert, "Die großbesetzten vokal-instrumentalen Werke."

28 Letter of August 9, 1851 to Emanuel Klitzsch, in Erler, *Robert Schumann's Leben*, vol. II, 157. See also Jansen, *Robert Schumann, Briefe*, 460. On Schumann's title, Margit McCorkle, *Robert Schumann: Thematisches-Bibliographisches Werkverzeichnis* (Mainz: Schott, 2003), 477–78.

29 Schumann specially asked the poet to elevate Rose to angelhood. In Horn's original, Rose expires shortly after her husband dies in a hunting accident. Nauhaus, *Schumann in Düsseldorf*, 182.

30 Nauhaus, *Schumann in Düsseldorf*, 186. The rose remains a Marian symbol today.

31 Schumann admired Schubert's choral music for women. See, for example, his review of Schubert's Opp. 134, 135, 136 and 139 in Kreisig, *Gesammelte Schriften*, vol. II, 336.

32 Handpicked members of the chorus sang ensemble numbers in the work's first private performance. See McCorkle, *Robert Schumann*, 475.

33 See Nauhaus, *Schumann in Düsseldorf*, 196 for examples.

Selected Bibliography

Abraham, Gerald. "The Dramatic Music," in *Schumann: A Symposium*, ed. Gerald Abraham. London: Oxford University Press, 1952, 260–82.

Benjamin, William. "Hypermetric Dissonance in the Later Works of Robert Schumann," in *Rethinking Schumann*, ed. Roe-Min Kok and Laura Tunbridge. New York: Oxford University Press, 2011, 206–34.

Burger-Güntert, Edda. *Robert Schumanns "Szenen aus Goethes Faust": Dichtung und Musik*. Freiburg i. Br.: Rombach, 2006.

Cooper, Frank. "Operatic and Dramatic Music," in *Robert Schumann: The Man and His Music*, ed. Alan Walker. London: Barrie & Jenkins, 1973, 324–49.

Daverio, John. "*Einheit—Freiheit—Vaterland*: Intimations of Utopia in Robert Schumann's Late Choral Music," in *Music and German National Identity*, ed. Celia Applegate and Pamela Potter. Chicago: University of Chicago Press, 2002, 59–77.

——. "Schumann's Ossianic Manner," *19th-Century Music* 21, 3 (1998): 247–73.

Ewert, Hansjörg. *Anspruch und Wirkung: Studien zur Entstehung der Oper Genoveva von Robert Schumann*. Tutzing: Hans Schneider, 2003.

Godwin, Robert C. *Schumann's Choral Works and the Romantic Movement*. D.M.A thesis, University of Illinois, 1967.

Harwood, Gregory W. *The Genesis of Robert Schumann's Liturgical Works and A Study of Compositional Process in the Requiem, Op. 148*. Ph.D. diss., New York University, 1991.

Horton, John. "The Choral Works," in *Schumann: A Symposium*, ed. Gerald Abraham. London, New York, Toronto: Oxford University Press, 1952, 283–99.

Jacobsen, Heike. *Robert Schumanns Chorballaden nach Texten von Ludwig Uhland*. Ph.D. diss., Ruprecht-Karls-Universität Heidelberg, 2002.

Koch, Armin. "'In holde Träume einsingen'. Zu Schumanns Nachtlied für Chor und Orchester op. 108," in *Schumann und Dresden. Bericht über das Symposion Robert und Clara Schumann in Dresden—Biographische, kompositionsgeschichtliche und soziokulturelle Aspekte in Dresden vom 15. Bis 18. Mai 2008*, ed. Thomas Synofzik and Hans-Günter Ottenberg. Cologne: Christoph Dohr, 2010, 197–218.

Kok, Roe-Min. "Who Was Mignon? What Was She? Popular Catholicism and Schumann's *Requiem*, Op. 98b," in *Rethinking Schumann*, ed. Roe-Min Kok and Laura Tunbridge. New York: Oxford University Press, 2011, 88–108.

Mintz, Donald. "Schumann as an Interpreter of Goethe's Faust," *Journal of the American Musicological Society* 14 (1961): 235–56.

Nauhaus, Gerd. *Robert Schumann: Scenen aus Goethes "Faust."* Zwickau: Kulturhaus, 1981.

——. "Schumanns Das Paradies und die Peri: Quellen zur Entstehungs-, Aufführungs- und Rezeptionsgeschichte," in *Schumanns Werke*, ed. Akio Mayeda and Klaus-Wolfgang Niemöller. Mainz: Schott, 1987, 133–48.

Paley, Elizabeth. "Dramatic Stage and Choral Works," in *The Cambridge Companion to Schumann*, ed. Beate Perrey. Cambridge: Cambridge University Press, 2007, 195–219.

Paul, Sharon June. *Robert Schumann's Choral Music for Women's Voices*. D.M.A. thesis, Stanford University, 1984.

Probst, Gisela. *Robert Schumanns Oratorien*. Wiesbaden: Breitkopf & Härtel, 1975.

Sams, Eric. "Schumann and Faust," *The Musical Times* 113 (1972): 543–46.

Schaarwächter, Jürgen. "Sublimierte Dramatik oder Klassizismus. Zu Schumanns Vokalkompositionen mit Orchester ab 1846." *Archiv für Musikwissenschaft* 54, 2 (1997): 151–70.

Zanoncelli, Luisa. "Von Byron zu Schumann oder Die Metamorphose des 'Manfred'." *Musik-Konzepte Sonderband: Robert Schumann I*, ed. Heinz-Klaus Metzger and Rainer Riehn. Munich: edition text + kritik, 1981, 90–104.

11

ANTON BRUCKNER AND THE AUSTRIAN CHORAL TRADITION

His Mass in F Minor

Paul Hawkshaw

YALE UNIVERSITY

> Bruckner's Mass [in F minor] is . . . a most laudable testament to the ingenuity and excep-
> tional craft of its composer. With poetic appreciation he has immersed himself in the
> challenges of setting the Mass text, and his enormous contrapuntal artistry enables him to
> solve the most difficult problems easily . . . He has allowed himself to be seduced by the
> dramatic content of the text, striving now and then for the theatrical, as . . . in the Credo
> where, at one point, one has the impression of being in the middle of a Christian wolf glen.
> But on the whole, Bruckner's Mass is a work that inspires great respect for the expertise and
> craft of the composer.[1]

The Viennese critic Ludwig Speidel wrote this review of Anton Bruckner's F-minor Mass after its
premiere in the *Augustinerkirche* on June 16, 1872.[2] For a spontaneous first impression of such an
original and monumental work, the critique contains some perceptive observations. While Speidel
was one of many early writers to admire the composer's contrapuntal prowess, he was one of the
few to comment on the expertise and sensitivity with which Bruckner set sacred texts.[3] "Poetic
appreciation" infused with religious fervor and an extensive acquaintance with eighteenth-century
musical-rhetorical practices is evident in much of the composer's mature sacred music.[4] And, while
Speidel's reference to the Wolf's Glen scene from Weber's *Der Freischütz* may have caught even
Bruckner by surprise, there is little question the composer would have acknowledged that he had
attempted to fuse avant-garde Wagnerian theatrical style with the Viennese Mass tradition he
had inherited from Haydn, Mozart, Beethoven, and Schubert. Eduard Hanslick's comment about
the Mass in F minor "Albrechtsberger arm in arm with Wagner," though pejorative in intent, had
a basis in truth.[5]

   The 1872 performance of the F-minor Mass was Bruckner's first public appearance as a
composer in Vienna after moving to the imperial city four years earlier.[6] Although subsequent
generations have come to know him primarily as a symphonist, Bruckner's contemporaries would
not have been surprised to encounter him as a composer of sacred choral music. Up to that point,
he was known to the Viennese as a superb organist who had come to the Court Chapel after twelve
years at the Cathedral in Linz. His modest reputation as a composer was based on one symphony
(the first in C minor), a handful of motets and male chorus pieces, and the Masses in D minor
(1863–64) and E minor (1866).[7] Composed in Linz between September 14, 1867, and September
9, 1868, the Mass in F minor proved to be his final contribution to the genre.[8] During Bruckner's

lifetime, it was the most often performed of his major works in Vienna and was chosen to celebrate his seventieth birthday in the *grosse Musikvereinsaal* in 1894.[9] Along with its predecessors in D minor and E minor, it must be included among the nineteenth century's most important contributions to the choral repertoire.

––––––––––––––

Bruckner brought more than two decades of professional experience as a choral composer, singer and conductor to the composition of his three great masses. He became acquainted with the musical traditions of the Austrian Catholic Church early in his career. His formative years were spent entirely within the pastoral orbit of the Upper-Austrian Monastery of Saint Florian where he lived from 1837 to 1840 and again from 1845 to 1855.[10] The origins of his devout Roman Catholicism, his legendary skills as an organist, his extensive knowledge of eighteenth-century church music, and many elements of the style and rhetoric of his own sacred music have all been traced to the Baroque halls of the monastery.[11] During the first half of the nineteenth century, the performance of liturgical music at Saint Florian was the responsibility of a fine semi-professional establishment, consisting of a chorus of men and boys, small orchestra, organist and soloists, which performed an orchestral Mass, a Gradual and an Offertory every Sunday and major feast of the Church year.[12] Bruckner's responsibilities throughout his time at the monastery included singing and playing the violin or organ on all or most of these occasions. The liturgical repertoire was selected from an archive of roughly 30,000 pieces of Austrian church music from Caldara and Lotti, through Eybler, Michael Haydn and Albrechtsberger, to Josef Haydn and, of course, Mozart.[13]

Prior to 1855, composition for Bruckner meant imitating and following in the footsteps of these composers within the confines of the monastery walls. He wrote liturgical works including hymns, motets, a Magnificat, and masses, as well as occasional pieces and psalm settings in the vernacular for evening concerts and special events.[14] His two largest works from the Saint Florian years are a Requiem (1849) commemorating the passing of his friend Franz Sailer and the *Missa solemnis* for the investiture of the new Prelate Friedrich Mayr in 1855.[15] Formally and stylistically these works imitate and include direct citations from eighteenth-century models that Bruckner observed every day in the musical life of Saint Florian.[16] The Requiem in D minor, for example, is so reminiscent of Mozart's that Elizabeth Maier has called it an hommage to the eighteenth-century master.[17] The structure of the exposition of its Quam olim Abrahae double fugue is modeled directly on another Mozart work, the "In te Domine speravi" fugue from the *Te Deum* in C major, K. 141.[18]

Much of Bruckner's choral writing during his early years is homophonic with the orchestra weaving figurations around it in the style of eighteenth-century chorale preludes.[19] Also conservative are rhetorical gestures such as the use of trombones with texts associated with death (m. 41 of Psalm 114, for example: "I am cloaked in the pains of death"). His Latin text setting, while awkward at times, can be effective as at the word *lux* ("let eternal light shine upon them") in bar 23 of the Agnus Dei of the Requiem (see Example 11.1).[20] Almost all his early works and their individual movements employ repeat structures or are through-composed. Only late in his second Saint Florian period, as in the cantata *Heil, Vater! Dir zum hohen Feste* or the enigmatic Psalm 146, did Bruckner begin to experiment with an organic motivic process that would become central to later compositions like the Mass in F minor.[21] Psalm 146 is an enormous work and represents an important stage in Bruckner's maturation as a composer. It deserves to be heard more often than it is today.

In 1855, after years of ambivalence, Bruckner took the decision to leave the monastery, give up school teaching, and pursue a career exclusively as a professional musician. He assumed his first

EXAMPLE 11.1 Bruckner, Requiem in D minor, Agnus Dei, mm. 22–23. Piano reduction by Hans Jancik.

full-time musical position as Cathedral organist in Linz just before Christmas of that year. The Bruckner who arrived in Linz was a world-class performer and a talented, self-taught composer unknown outside Saint Florian. Aware of his shortcomings, he stopped composing, with some minor exceptions, for a period of almost eight years to solidify his technical knowledge.[22] He studied counterpoint with the great theorist Simon Sechter from 1856 to 1861, and then form and orchestration with the conductor of the Linz Theater Orchestra, Otto Kitzler, from the end of 1861 to the summer of 1863.[23] Under Sechter, Bruckner became a master of the counterpoint he had learned through his self-study of Marpurg in Saint Florian. With Kitzler, he investigated the organic processes of the Beethoven piano sonatas, studied modern orchestration techniques, and became infatuated with the music of Richard Wagner to whom he referred for the remainder of his life as the "Master of all Masters."

Even Bruckner's most ardent admirers in Saint Florian could not have envisaged the composer who emerged from this study period and finished his first major masterpiece, the Mass in D minor, completed between June and 29 September 1864. The strings of parallel thirds and sixths in the fledgling counterpoint of earlier works such as Psalms 22 and 114 were transformed into the imposing fugue at the end of the Gloria. And however effective the earthquake in *stile agitato* at the "Et resurrexit" ("and he rose to judge the living and the dead,") in the Credo of the *Missa solemnis* may have been, it paled in comparison with the Wagnerian eruption at the corresponding place in his new Mass (mm. 113ff, see Example 11.2). Here woodwind (or organ) and brass chorales

EXAMPLE 11.2 Bruckner, Mass No. 1 in D minor, Credo, mm. 113–146. Piano reduction by Ferdinand Löwe.

EXAMPLE 11.2 continued.

EXAMPLE 11.2 continued.

EXAMPLE 11.2 continued.

respond to the plaintive *a cappella* "passus et sepultus est" ("and he died and was buried") before the strings propel a tremendous *crescendo* to a triumphant reentry of the chorus proclaiming the Resurrection.[24] The falling half steps are derived from the opening measures of the Kyrie, which provides motivic cells for the entire work. Throughout the Mass the orchestra plays a prominent role developing material and intensifying the dramatic impact. Instrumental figurations are integrated with the motivic fabric and drive the waves of *crescendo* evident in all of Bruckner's subsequent orchestral work.

It is no surprise that Bruckner regarded the winter of 1863–64 as the beginning of his career as a professional composer.[25] The F-minor Mass, completed four years later, is the pinnacle of his achievement as a choral composer.[26] Very much a product of its time with its extended chromaticism and orchestration in choirs of like instruments *alla* Wagner, the work is also part of the Austrian Mass tradition that Bruckner had known since his earliest days in Saint Florian. Hanslick was the first to recognize Beethoven's *Missa solemnis* as a model.[27] Specifically, Bruckner almost certainly had Beethoven's Benedictus in mind when he composed the extraordinary "Et incarnatus est" ("And he was born of the virgin Mary," Credo, mm. 117ff.) with the solo violin and viola woven around one of his most beautiful melodies in the vocal parts.[28]

Despite the Wagnerian treatment, the instrumentation of the Mass is classical: strings, double woodwinds, horns and trumpets, three trombones and timpani.[29] The overall tonal and formal plan is also conservative. The outer movements are in F minor; the others are in the dominant and relative or parallel major. The Kyrie is tripartite with the middle "Christe" sung by soloists in the classical tradition. The Gloria is also in A–B–A' form, the slower B section beginning at "Qui tollis peccata mundi" ("Who takes away the sins of the world," m. 116), and the varied reprise, again in classical tradition, in the tonic of C major at "Quoniam tu solus sanctus" ("For you alone are holy," m. 179). There are two nineteenth-century formal modifications in this movement: the A section is extended to the point where Max Auer describes it as the closing of a Brucknerian sonata exposition (mm. 76–115), and the thematic material is reversed in the reprise with the celebratory opening subject reserved for the "Cum Sancto Spirito" ("and with the Holy Spirit," m. 215).[30]

Again in classical tradition, both the Gloria and the Credo end with fugues—two of Bruckner's finest. The double fugue at the end of the Credo, "Et vitam venturi saeculi" ("And the life of the world to come") punctuated with outbursts of "Credo, credo" ("I believe," mm. 437–end) is one of the nineteenth century's technical tours de force. The Credo also has a slower middle section (mm. 117ff.) and a modified reprise in the tonic at "Et in Spiritum Sanctum" ("And in the Holy Spirit," m. 327). Bruckner reserved his most expressive rhetorical gestures—both Wagnerian and Baroque—for the middle section of this movement. Christ's suffering ends in the death chorale of trombones and horns (mm. 186), followed by an unprecedented upheaval (Speidel's Christian Wolf's Glen) at "Et resurrexit." The subsequent accented octaves and fourths at "judicare vivos et mortuos" ("to judge the living and the dead," mm. 260ff.) must have been calculated to instill a healthy respect for the Lord's justice in even the most casual church-goer. During the reprise, at "Et unam sanctam catholicam" ("and one holy, catholic and apostolic church," m. 399ff.), Bruckner reverts to another old-fashioned rhetorical device: choral octaves that he had used as early as the *Missa solemnis* in the analogous passage (m. 80).

The Sanctus and Benedictus with identical "Hosannas" are separate movements performed before and after the consecration respectively. In the Sanctus, one wonders whether Bruckner might be reminding us once again (as in the "judicare" section of the Credo) of the ominous power of the Lord with the sudden and unexpected tonic minor chord at the word "Sabaoth" (m. 14).

Early reviewers cited the poignant Benedictus as the most beautiful moment in the Mass.[31] To this day it remains, along with the *Adagio* of the Seventh Symphony, one of Bruckner's most popular movements. In the Agnus Dei, the second and third petitions are variations of the first. The "dona nobis pacem" ("grant us peace," mm. 67ff.) is the occasion for an extended coda where Bruckner yields to his post-Beethovenian symphonic impulses with explicit references to the opening measures of the Kyrie and the fugue theme from the end of the Gloria.

Three musical elements that have been present in Bruckner's choral works since the 1840s are evident again throughout this Mass: the fugue, chorale-like passages (perhaps better categorized as a homophonic hymn in his Latin church compositions), and Gregorian chant. The two magnificent fugues have already been mentioned, as has the death chorale in the Credo. Bruckner often used chorales such as this one to serve as musical punctuation—to end one major section of a work and prepare the listener for the contrast that follows. A similar chorale-like passage occurs at the *a cappella* "in gloria Dei Patris" ("in the glory of God the Father," Gloria, mm. 231ff.) before the triumphant fugue that closes the movement.[32]

Specific references to chant and melodies imitating chant had been building blocks for Bruckner since his earliest effort in the genre, the so-called Windhaag Mass of 1842.[33] Hans Ferdinand

EXAMPLE 11.3a *Gloria cunctipotens genitor Deus (Liber Usualis, p. 26)*

EXAMPLE 11.3b Bruckner, Mass No. 3 in F minor, Gloria, mm. 1–4. Piano reduction by Hans Jancik.

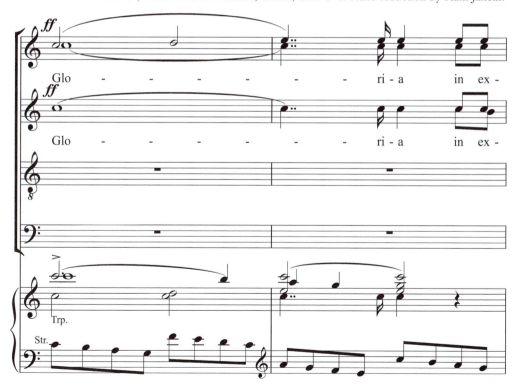

EXAMPLE 11.3b   continued.

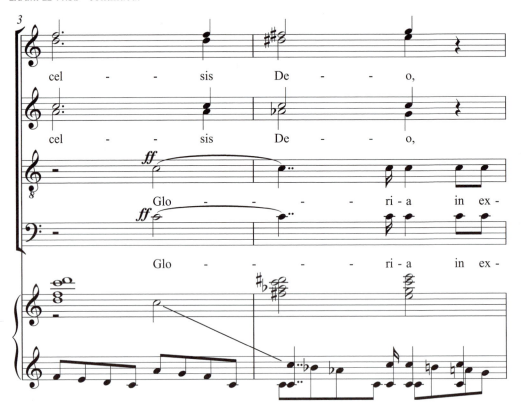

Redlich pointed out how important chant continued to be in Bruckner's motivic thinking and melodic construction in the F-minor Mass:

> The thematic . . . is fertilized by plainsong to an even greater extent than that of the two pre-ceding Masses [in D minor and E minor]; it is also closely organized by virtue of a common root-motive of unmistakably liturgical flavor: a falling or ascending fourth that determines the subject matter in all parts of the work, thereby assuring symphonic coherence.[34]

Redlich traced the fourth motive to the intonation of the *Gloria cunctipotens genitor Deus* (*Liber usualis*, p. 26) that serves as the seed for the opening phrase of Bruckner's Gloria and is modified, for example, at the beginning of the Credo (see Example 11.3a–b). In a penetrating essay, the great Bruckner scholar Ernst Kurth suggested that one of Bruckner's major accomplishments as a composer was a successful blend of romantic melodic style with plainchant in his church music.[35] For confirmation, one need look no further than the Benedictus where the beautiful principal theme outlines Redlich's fourth in the soprano while the alto descends stepwise before an expressive leap of a major ninth (mm. 18–23).

The opening measures of the Kyrie will illustrate more details of Bruckner's choral com-positional style (see Example 11.4). In addition to numerous iterations of Redlich's fourth, the passage contains two figures that recur throughout the Mass: the Baroque sigh motive of the falling half step in mm. 10–12 (as in the D-minor Mass) and the innocuous (at first) trills in the cellos and double basses in mm. 22 and 24.[36] That all these motives are presented first in the orchestra is an

EXAMPLE 11.4 Bruckner, Mass No. 3 in F minor, Kyrie, mm. 28–32. Piano reduction by Hans Jancik.

EXAMPLE 11.4 continued.

EXAMPLE 11.4   continued.

EXAMPLE 11.4 continued.

indication of the extent to which Bruckner adopted Wagner's approach to vocal composition. The accompaniment figures in the violin, mm. 20, 22, and 24, that leave an almost casual impression of filigree between vocal phrases are also important. Apart from outlining the local harmony, such passages often contain motivic references, such as the falling half steps, and grow into an integral part of the contrapuntal fabric.[37] They are also used to propel Bruckner's extended *crescendi* (as in the second Kyrie, mm. 77–100 and 101–121). This quasi-improvisational referential instrumental writing is probably an outgrowth of Bruckner's legendary ability as an organist to extemporize on a given theme.

The vocal writing in Example 11.4 typifies the craft of post-Sechterian Bruckner with contrary motion between the outer voices and conjunct voice-leading in all parts. Such homophonic writing is contrasted throughout the Mass with the intricate contrapuntal passages, as in the Gloria "Qui tollis peccata mundi, miserere nobis" ("Who takes away the sins of the world, have mercy upon us," mm. 116–40) that Speidel and others have praised since the first performance. For an illustration of Bruckner's motivic processes at work in relation to the text throughout the Mass, compare this passage from the Gloria with two derivations from it setting the same text in the Agnus Dei, mm. 22–26 and 41–45. One idiosyncratic feature of Bruckner's mature vocal writing can be seen in another passage from the Gloria: the series of parallel first inversion chords, mm. 291–99 (derived in this case from the falling half steps of the opening measures of the Kyrie). This chromatic *fauxbourdon* quality was a favorite of Bruckner's and is found again both in the *Te Deum*, mm. 129ff., and in Psalm 150 (1892), mm. 211ff. (see Example 11.5).

The kernel for Bruckner's organic chromatic process is also found in the opening measures of the Kyrie (Example 11.4). The Neapolitan flavor in mm. 4–10 (highlighted with a *crescendo*, accent and *sf* in m. 4) foreshadows important secondary and transitional tonalities of the Mass: G-flat–C-flat–F-flat or their enharmonic equivalents, and provides much of the chromatic color throughout the work.[38] The climax of the second Kyrie *crescendo* on C-flat (mm. 113–20) is a good example. The C-flat root of the triad in the bass is respelled as B-natural in m. 121 before being subject to

EXAMPLE 11.5 Bruckner, Mass No. 3 in F minor, Gloria, mm. 291–99. Piano reduction by Hans Jancik.

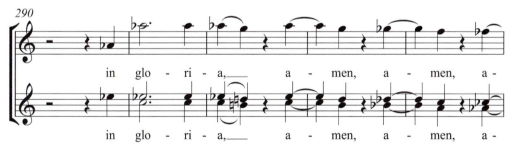

the very Schubertian gesture of becoming the third of the subsequent G-major triad (m. 122). After a further Neapolitan excursion (another of Bruckner's punctuation chorales), mm. 124–30, it becomes clear that the G-major triad is V/V preparing for the return to F minor in m. 135.[39]

One of the ironies of Bruckner's career is that, after obtaining a post in the Imperial Chapel in 1868, the most prestigious and sophisticated church music establishment in Austria, perhaps in the world at the time, he composed almost nothing for it. With the exception of *Christus factus est* of 1873, the relatively few sacred pieces that date from after he moved to Vienna were all written for other constituencies.[40] The great motets *Locus iste* (1869), *Tota pulchra es* (1878), *Virga Jesse* (1885), and *Ecce sacerdos magnus* (1885), for example, were all composed for Linz.[41] Leopold Nowak's observation that Bruckner was something of an outsider at the chapel, perhaps due to his modernist leanings, is almost certainly correct.[42] Bruckner's loyalty to the new music of his "Master of all Masters" also kept him apart from the most important aesthetic movement in Church music in the middle of the century. He could never accept the anti-avant-garde stance of his Cecilian contemporaries even though some of his choral works—specifically the Mass in E minor and the motet *Os justi* (1879)—are often mentioned in this connection.[43] The motet was composed in the older style for his friend, Ignaz Traumihler, who was a confirmed Cecilianist. The consciously retrospective Palestrina-style counterpoint and chant-like melodies of the Mass in E minor must be attributed to a desire to provide a musical parallel to the neo-Gothic aesthetic of the new cathedral for which it was written, rather than to any empathy with Franz Xaver Witt and his followers.[44]

The Mass in F minor, of course, has no such architectural analogue. Here Bruckner wears his modernism—his Wagnerism—on his sleeve. At the same time, as Speidel pointed out in the review quoted at the beginning of this chapter, his respect for and knowledge of the Austrian Mass tradition is evident in almost every measure. Twenty-one years later, after its first concert performance, Speidel reviewed the Mass again.[45] He reiterated his opinion that the work is an extraordinary fusion of the traditional with the modern achieved in the hands of an artist who truly believed in and understood his text:

> [In the F-minor Mass] Bruckner takes liberties. But the freedom he allows himself is the original expression of a man who is full of imagination and faith, of an artist who believes. He interprets dogma as a modern artist. When he utilizes forms he has inherited, rather than mechanically copying the past, he reshapes them in his unique way.

Notes

1 [Ludwig Speidel], *Fremdenblatt*, June 20, 1872, 6. The review is reprinted in Paul Hawkshaw, ed. *Anton Bruckner Sämtliche Werke*, 18. *Messe F-moll Revisionsbericht* (Vienna: Musikwissenschaftlicher Verlag, 2004), 243–44. Scores for all the works mentioned in this chapter can be found in the collected works edition (general editor Leopold Nowak), which will be cited as *BrSW* throughout. The Mass is catalogued as No. 28 in Renate Grasberger, *Werkverzeichnis Anton Bruckner* (Tutzing: Hans Schneider Verlag, 1977), referred to as *WAB* for the remainder of the chapter.

2 The composer himself conducted the performance which featured the chorus, orchestra, and soloists of the Viennese Imperial Chapel.

3 Even the redoubtable Eduard Hanslick admired Bruckner's "artful contrapuntal and fugal technique." Hanslick wrote two reviews of the Mass: a short favorable critique with this comment about counterpoint in 1872 and an extensive negative feuilleton in response to a concert performance of the work in the *grosse Musikvereinsaal*, Vienna, on November 4, 1894. *Neue Freie Presse*, June 29, 1872, 29; and November 13, 1894, 1–2. Reprinted in Hawkshaw, *BrSW*, 18, *Revisionsbericht*, 244–45 and 254–56 respectively.

4 Othmar Wessely, "Vergangenheit und Zukunft in Bruckners Messe in D Moll," *Österreichische Musikzeitschrift*

29 (1974): 412–18, discusses Bruckner's rhetorical gestures in a historical context. Wessely connects the falling semitones that permeate the Mass in D minor, for example, to the Baroque figure of the *passus duriusculus.*

5 *Neue Freie Presse,* November 13, 1894. Hawkshaw, *BrSW*, 18, *Revisionsbericht*, 254.

6 Bruckner came to Vienna in 1868 to succeed Simon Sechter as counterpoint teacher at the Conservatory and to serve as an unpaid organist in the Imperial Chapel. For detailed biographical information on the composer, see Franz Scheder, *Anton Bruckner Chronologie,* 2 vols. (Tutzing: Hans Schneider, 1996).

7 The symphony (*WAB* 101, *BrSW* 1) and the Mass in E minor (*WAB* 27, *BrSW* 17) had been performed in Linz on May 9, 1868 and September 29, 1869 respectively. The Mass in D minor (*WAB* 26, *BrSW* 16) received its premiere in Linz on November 20, 1864 and was repeated in Vienna on February 10, 1867. The 1860s saw the composition of some memorable motets including the *Ave Maria* a 7 (1861, *WAB* 6, *BrSW* 21), *Afferentur regi* (1863, *WAB* 1, *BrSW* 21), his last *Pange lingua* (1868, *WAB* 33, *BrSW* 21) and *Locus iste* (1869, *WAB* 23, *BrSW* 21). By 1872 Bruckner had also completed the *Nullte* Symphony (1869, *WAB* 100, *BrSW* 10) that never received a performance during his lifetime.

8 The dates are found in the autograph score, Austrian National Library, Music Collection Mus. Hs. 2106.

9 The concert took place on November 4, 1894. This is the concert that Hanslick reviewed. See note 3.

10 He came to Saint Florian as a boy soprano in 1837 and returned as assistant school teacher in 1845. He was appointed singing teacher to the boy choristers in October 1849 and, in 1850, provisory organist. For information on Bruckner's activities at St. Florian, see Walter Schulten, "Anton Bruckners künstlerische Entwicklung in der St. Florianer Zeit" (Ph.D. diss. Mainz, 1956); Walter Pass, "Studie über Bruckners ersten St. Florianer Aufenthalt," in *Bruckner-Studien. Festgabe der Österreichischen Akademie der Wissenschaften zum 150. Geburtstag von Anton Bruckner,* ed. Othmar Wessely (Vienna: Österreichische Akademie der Wissenschaften, 1975), 11–51; and Franz Linninger, "Orgeln und Organisten im Stift St. Florian," *Oberösterreichische Heimatblätter,* 9 (1955): 171–86.

11 See for example, Augustinus F. Kropfreiter, "Zu Anton Bruckners 90. Todestag," in *Stift St. Florian 1686–1986 "Welt des Barock,"* In Unum Congregati 33, 2/4 (1986), 80.

12 Paul Hawkshaw, "Anton Bruckner's Counterpoint Studies at the Monastery of Saint Florian," *The Musical Quarterly* 90, 1 (Spring 2007), 94–97, describes the church music activities at St. Florian during the first half of the nineteenth century.

13 Walter Pass, "Bruckners ersten St. Florianer Aufenthalt," 11–51 and Walter Schulten "Bruckners künstlerische Entwicklung," 40–53, contain excellent synopses of the repertoire. Bruckner also encountered and copied from two major Beethoven choral works at St. Florian: *Christ on the Mount of Olives* and the Mass in C major, Hawkshaw, "Bruckner's Counterpoint Studies," 109–10. The tradition of secular music performance was equally rich at the monastery, and the repertoire was more *au courant.* Evening concerts at which Bruckner sang and played the piano included songs, operatic overtures and arias, chamber music, and secular and sacred choral music in the vernacular that had no place in the Roman Catholic liturgy. Dozens of uncatalogued, handwritten programs survive from the 1840s and 1850s for evenings in the monastery music room. See, for example, Andreas Lindner, "Josef Eduard Seiberl (1836–1877): Leben und Werk des Florianer Stiftsorganisten und Nachfolgers Anton Bruckners," *Oberösterreichische Heimatsblätter,* 56 (2002): 179. These concerts acquainted Bruckner with secular music of Schubert and sacred music of Mendelssohn. The Prelate Michael Arneth, who was Bruckner's first important patron, was also one of the first people outside Vienna to recognize Schubert's genius; he purchased 126 Schubert first editions and invited the composer to the monastery in 1825. Friedrich Buchmayr, "Arneth, Michael v.," in *Biographisch-Bibliographisches Kirchenlexikon* (Nordhausen: Verlag Traugott Bautz, 1998), vol. 14, 720–723. See also Elizabeth Maier and Franz Zamazal, *Anton Bruckner und Leopold von Zenetti,* ed. Franz Grasberger. *Anton Bruckner: Dokumente und Studien* 3 (Graz: Akademischer Druck- und Verlagsanstalt, 1980), 146–50. For more on Bruckner's knowledge of Mendelssohn, see "Bruckners Mendelssohn-Kenntnis," in *Festgabe zum 150. Geburtstag,* 81–112. The monastery owned scores and parts, for example, to Mendelssohn's Psalms 22 and 114. Bruckner's own Psalms 22 and 114 (*WAB* 34 and 36, *BrSW* 20/1–2), both in the vernacular, were almost certainly composed as a response to these works of Mendelssohn. Paul Hawkshaw, "Die Psalmkompositionen Anton Bruckners," in *Bruckner-Tagung Wien* 1999, ed. Elizabeth Maier, Andrea Harrandt and Erich Wolfgang Partsch (Vienna: Musikwissenschaftlicher Verlag, 2000), 8–10.

14 Perhaps the most significant motet from the early years is the *Libera me* (1854, *WAB* 22, *BrSW* 21) that he composed for the funeral of his patron Prelate Michael Arneth. An example of one of the secular cantatas is *Auf, Brüder, auf die Saiten zu Hände* for male chorus and winds (*WAB* 60, *BrSW* 22/1) composed for the name-day celebrations of the new Prelate, Friedrich Mayr. For more on Bruckner's motets and male chorus settings, see A. Crawford Howie, "Bruckner and the Motet" and "Bruckner and Secular Vocal Music," in *The Cambridge Companion to Bruckner,* ed. John Williamson (Cambridge: Cambridge University Press, 2004), 54–63 and 64–76.

15 Both the *Requiem* (*WAB* 39, *BrSW* 14) and *Missa solemnis* (*WAB* 29, *BrSW* 15) continue to receive performances. Bruckner himself declared the *Requiem* "not bad" when he returned to it very late in his life. August Göllerich and Max Auer, *Anton Bruckner: ein Lebens- und Schaffensbild*, 9 vols. in 4 (Regensburg: Gustav Bosse Verlag, 1924–37) vol. II/1, 70. There are also three very early masses for meager forces in the *Landmesse* tradition (*WAB* 9, 25 and 146, *BrSW* 21) written for Windhaag and Kronstorf where Bruckner served brief periods (1841–43 and 1843–45 respectively) as assistant school master. In Upper Austria at the time, the school master or his assistant also served as organist and choir director for the local church.

16 For more on Bruckner's early choral music, see Karl Gustav Fellerer, "Bruckner und die Kirchenmusik seiner Zeit," in *Anton Bruckner: Studien zu Werk und Wirkung*, ed. Christoph-Hellmut Mahling. *Mainzer Studien zur Musikwissenschaft* 20 (Tutzing: Hans Schneider Verlag, 1988), 41–62; and Paul Hawkshaw, "Bruckner's Large Sacred Compositions," in *Cambridge Companion*, 43–8. Direct citations in the *Missa solemnis* include the "Recordare" from Mozart's *Requiem* at the beginning of the Credo and the Gloria (m. 219) of Haydn's St. Bernard Mass at the "Quoniam tu solus sanctus" ("For you alone are holy."). Göllerich and Auer, *Anton Bruckner*, vol. II/1, 156

17 Elisabeth Maier, "Requiem in d-Moll (*WAB* 39)," in *Bruckner Handbuch*, 350.

18 Hawkshaw, "Bruckner's Counterpoint Studies," 104–05.

19 As in the Agnus Dei of the *Requiem* for example.

20 Paul Hawkshaw, "The Enigma of Anton Bruckner's Psalm 146," in *Musica Conservata: Günter Brosche zum 60. Geburtstag*, ed. J. Gmeiner et al. (Tutzing: Hans Schneider Verlag, 1999), 115–16.

21 *WAB* 61 and 37, *BrSW* 22/1 and 24 respectively. Nothing is known about the genesis or early history of Psalm 146. Hawkshaw, ibid., 105–11.

22 A brief compositional flurry in 1861 included *Afferentur regi* and the *Ave Maria* a 7, two miniatures often regarded as Bruckner's first masterpieces. See note 7.

23 For more on Sechter and Kitzler, see Ernst Schwanzara, *Anton Bruckner: Vorlesungen über Harmonielehre und Kontrapunkten der Universität Wien* (Vienna: Österreichischer Bundesverlag, 1950) and Paul Hawkshaw, "A Composer Learns his Craft: Anton Bruckner's Lessons in Form and Orchestration with Otto Kitzler 1861–63," in *Perspectives on Anton Bruckner*, ed. Crawford Howie et al. (Aldershot: Ashgate, 2001), 3–29.

24 It was standard practice in nineteenth-century Austrian church establishments, including the Imperial Chapel, to have the organ playing *basso seguente* with the orchestra throughout performances of such works. In this instance, the woodwind chorale in modern editions was first written for the organ in the autograph score in the Music Collection of the Austrian Library, Mus. Hs. 19.483. Bruckner did the reorchestration himself, probably because he realized that, in most performance situations, the pitch of the orchestra had risen above that of most church organs by the 1860s. See his letter to Rudolf Weinwurm of January 21, 1865. Andrea Harrandt, ed. *BrSW*, 24/1. *Briefe 1852–1886* (Vienna: Musikwissenschaftlicher Verlag, 2004), 59.

25 See Bruckner's letter of September 7, 1862 to Rudolf Weinwurm. Harrandt, *BrSW*, 24/1, 32. The Mass has since come to be identified as Mass no. 1 in the composer's repertoire (those in E and F minor being nos. 2 and 3 respectively).

26 The composer himself might have disagreed with this assessment. Later in his life he is reported to have referred to his *Te Deum* (*WAB* 45, *BrSW* 19), begun in 1881 and completed in 1884, as the pride of his career. Göllerich and Auer, *Anton Bruckner*, vol. IV/2, 143.

27 See note 3. Schubert's Masses in A-flat major, D. 678, and E-flat major, D. 950, may also have been on Bruckner's mind while composing the Mass in F minor. It is not known when Bruckner heard either of these works or the *Missa solemnis* for the first time.

28 Bruckner would return to this texture in his *Te Deum* (mm. 191–204) and Psalm 150 (*WAB* 38, *BrSW* 26, mm. 109–42).

29 The first edition (Vienna: Doblinger, 1894) is scored for four horns. The addition of the two horns and many other orchestration changes were editorial aberrations of Josef Schalk who tried to make the Mass more Wagnerian.

30 Max Auer, *Anton Bruckner als Kirchenmusiker* (Regensburg: Gustave Bosse Verlag, 1927), 38. It is not uncommon in the older German literature to find analyses of these Mass movements using the terminology of sonata form. See, for example, Horst-Günther Scholz, *Die Form der reifen Messen Anton Bruckners* (Berlin: Merserburger, 1961).

31 Max Graf, *Musikalische Rundschau* 8, 1893, 7, p. 59, describes the Benedictus as "a melodic wonder that . . . sounds as though it is coming from another world." Cited in Hawkshaw, *BrSW*, 18, *Revisionsbericht*, 250.

32 To the best of this writer's knowledge, none of these passages is borrowed from a preexistent chorale or hymn.

33 *WAB* 25, *BrSW* 21. Elisabeth Maier, "Der Choral in den Kirchenwerken Bruckners," in *Bruckner-*

Symposion: Anton Bruckner und die Kirchenmusik, ed. Othmar Wesselly (Linz: Akademische Druck- und Verlagsanstalt, 1985), 119.

34 Hans Ferdinand Redlich, ed. *Mass in F Minor* (London: Ernst Eulenberg, 1967), Foreword, 31.

35 Ernst Kurth, *Bruckner*, 2 vols. (Berlin, 1923; repr. Hildesheim and New York: G. Olms, 1971), vol. 2, 1201.

36 Bruckner was an inveterate reviser of his own music. He appears to have become less sanguine with the trill figure as he got older. The two versions of the Mass published in *BrSW* 18 and performed today date from 1883 and 1893. In both of these scores, the trill motive is less prominent, particularly in the Credo, than in the first version of 1868. Hawkshaw, *BrSW* 18, *Revisionsbericht, Beispiele* 6–8, 285–295.

37 The violin and viola solos of the above-mentioned "Et incarnatus est" in the Credo are a wonderful example.

38 For more on Bruckner's use of enharmonicism in his sacred music see, Timothy L. Jackson "Schubert as 'John the Baptist to Wagner-Jesus': large-scale Enharmonicism in Bruckner and his Models," *Bruckner-Jahrbuch* 1991/92/93 (1995): 61–107.

39 Further examples of extended passages in the C-flat (B)–E areas are the above mentioned "in gloria Dei Patris" (Gloria, mm. 231ff.) and the Credo "Et incarnatus est" (mm. 117ff.).

40 *WAB 10, BrSW* 21.

41 *WAB 23, 46, 52* and *13; BrSW* 21.

42 Leopold Nowak, *Anton Bruckner: Musik und Leben* (Linz: R. Trauner Verlag, 1973), 70. The chapel continued to serve as an occasional performance outlet after the premiere of the Mass in F minor of 1872. Theophil Antonicek, *Anton Bruckner und die Wiener Hofmusikkapelle,* ed. Franz Grasberger. *Anton Bruckner: Dokumente und Studien,* I (Graz: Akademischer Druck- und Verlagsanstalt, 1979), 142–44.

43 *Os justi* is *WAB 30, BrSW* 21.

44 The Mass was commissioned by Bruckner's Linz patron, Bishop Rudigier, for the cornerstone ceremony of the Votive Chapel of the new Linz cathedral in 1869. Franz Xaver Witt was founder of the German Cecilian Society that saw Gregorian chant and the music of Palestrina as models for a church music renaissance. Karl Gustav Fellerer, "Bruckners Kirchenmusik und die Cäcilianismus," *Österreichische Musikzeitschrift* 29 (1974), 404–12.

45 *Fremdenblatt*, April 23, 1893, 5. Cited in Hawkshaw, *BrSW* 18, *Revisionsbericht*, 252. The concert performance was conducted by Josef Schalk in the *Musikverein* on March 23, 1893.

Selected Bibliography

Works List and Music

Grasberger, Renate. *Werkverzeichnis Anton Bruckner.* Tutzing: Hans Schneider, 1977.

Nowak, Leopold et al., eds. *Anton Bruckner Sämtliche Werke*, 14–23. Vienna: Musikwissenschaftlicher Verlag, various years. Scores, piano vocal scores, octavo and performing parts.

Biography and General Information

Antonicek, Theophil. *Anton Bruckner und die Wiener Hofmusikkapelle,* ed. Franz Grasberger. *Anton Bruckner: Dokumente und Studien*, 1. Graz: Akademischer Druck- und Verlagsanstalt, 1979.

Hawkshaw, Paul and Timothy L. Jackson, eds. *Bruckner Studies.* Cambridge: Cambridge University Press, 1997.

Howie, A. Crawford, Timothy L. Jackson and Paul Hawkshaw, eds. *Perspectives on Anton Bruckner.* Aldershot, England: Ashgate, 2001.

———. *Anton Bruckner: A Documentary Biography.* Lewiston, New York: Edwin Mellen Press, 2002.

Scheder, Franz. *Anton Bruckner Chronologie,* 2 vols. Tutzing: Hans Schneider, 1996.

Williamson, John. *The Cambridge Companion to Bruckner.* Cambridge: Cambridge University Press, 2004.

Letters

Harrandt, Andrea and Otto Schneider†, eds. *Anton Bruckner Sämtliche Werke,* xxiv/1–2. Vienna: Musikwissenschaftlischer Verlag, 2010 and 2004.

Church Music

Fellerer, Karl Gustav. "Bruckners Kirchenmusik und die Cäcilianismus," *Österreichische Musikzeitschrift* 29 (1974): 404–12.

——. "Bruckner und die Kirchenmusik seiner Zeit," in *Anton Bruckner: Studien zu Werk und Wirkung*, ed. Christoph-Hellmut Mahling. *Mainzer Studien zur Musikwissenschaft* 20. Tutzing: Hans Schneider, 1988, 41–62.

Hawkshaw, Paul. "An Anatomy of Change: Revisions to the Mass in F Minor," in *Bruckner Studies*, ed. Timothy L. Jackson and Paul Hawkshaw. Cambridge: Cambridge University Press, 1997, 1–31.

——. "Anton Bruckner's Counterpoint Studies at the Monastery of Saint Florian," *The Musical Quarterly* 90, 1 (Spring 2007): 94–7.

——. "Bruckner's Large Sacred Compositions," in *The Cambridge Companion to Bruckner*, ed. John Williamson. Cambridge: Cambridge University Press, 2004, 41–53.

——. "The Enigma of Anton Bruckner's Psalm 146," in *Musica Conservata: Günter Brosche zum 60. Geburtstag*, ed. J. Gmeiner et al. Tutzing: Hans Schneider Verlag, 1999, 105–119.

——. "Die Psalmkompositionen Anton Bruckners," in *Bruckner-Tagung Wien 1999*, ed. Elizabeth Maier, Andrea Harrandt and Erich Wolfgang Partsch. Vienna: Musikwissenschaftlicher Verlag, 2000, 8–10.

Howie, A. Crawford. "Bruckner and the Motet," in *The Cambridge Companion to Bruckner*, ed. John Williamson. Cambridge: Cambridge University Press, 2004, 54–63.

——. "Bruckner and Secular Vocal Music," in *The Cambridge Companion to Bruckner*, ed. John Williamson. Cambridge: Cambridge University Press, 2004, 64–76.

Jackson, Timothy L. "Schubert as 'John the Baptist to Wagner-Jesus': Large-scale Enharmonicism in Bruckner and his Models," in *Bruckner-Jahrbuch* 1991/92/93 (1995), 61–107.

Maier, Elisabeth. "Der Choral in den Kirchenwerken Bruckners," in *Bruckner-Symposion: Anton Bruckner und die Kirchenmusik*, ed. Othmar Wessely. Linz: Akademische Druck- und Verlagsanstalt, 1985, 119.

Wessely, Othmar. "Vergangenheit und Zukunft in Bruckners Messe in D Moll," *Österreichische Musikzeitschrift* 29 (1974): 412–18.

12

JOHANNES BRAHMS

Virginia Hancock

Reed College

The earliest choral compositions by Brahms were two pieces he wrote for a small men's chorus that he conducted on a summer holiday in 1847 (at age fourteen); one is said to have shown "a feeling for independent part writing."[1] Until he was thirty years old, he wrote choral music primarily for the choirs he himself conducted—the court choir at Detmold (1857–59), the Hamburg Frauenchor (1859–62), and the Vienna Singakademie (1862–63).[2] Beginning with *Ein deutsches Requiem* (completed 1868–69), however, he appears to have produced choral works not on commission or for a choir of his own, but because he was stimulated by a text or an event.[3]

Before 1983, the 150th anniversary of Brahms's birth, there was little published scholarship on his choral music beyond Siegfried Kross's dissertation, and almost none was in English.[4] But the continuing popularity of all Brahms's music has stimulated research in previously neglected areas, particularly the choral music and songs. Although the principal purpose of this chapter is to try to describe many of the choral works in such a way as to illuminate their steady appeal to performers and audiences, another is to provide information on the literature for those who would like to investigate further.[5]

Works for Women's and Men's Voices

During his years with the Frauenchor, Brahms wrote a significant amount of music for women's voices; he later published some of these pieces in other arrangements, most for mixed voices.[6] Those most often performed today are the four *Gesänge für Frauenchor* (Op. 17, for SSA, two horns and harp) and the twelve *Lieder und Romanzen* (Op. 44). The three sacred choruses (Op. 37), *Ave Maria* (Op. 12), and Psalm 13 (Op. 27) have not worn nearly as well.[7]

Brahms's charming setting of Eichendorff's "Der Bräutigam" (Op. 44/2) exemplifies his style in these outwardly simple works. Each of the four voice parts has its own melodic interest, and exchanges between voice pairs lend textural and rhythmic variety. In the third and fourth stanzas, a Romantic depiction of the forest includes whispering breezes and horn calls;[8] harmonic interest in the final stanza is provided by an apparent common-tone modulation to the flat sixth key before the tonic is regained.

Brahms wrote relatively little for men's chorus; the reason may have been, as Kross suggests, that he felt the earlier proud *Männerchor* tradition had declined.[9] Until the discovery in 2010 of two early pieces,[10] the *Fünf Lieder* (Op. 41) were thought to be his only surviving *a cappella* works in this medium. They are rarely performed today not only because of the scarcity of men's choruses but because the texts of nos. 2–5, by Carl Lemcke, are too militaristic for contemporary taste.[11] Two additional works for accompanied male chorus, *Rinaldo* and the *Alto Rhapsody*, will be discussed later in this chapter.

Folk-song Arrangements

Brahms's long involvement with folk song is well documented, beginning years before 1857, when he made SATB arrangements for the Detmold choir of texts and tunes primarily from his favorite source, Kretzschmer and Zuccalmaglio's *Deutsche Volkslieder mit ihren Original-Weisen*.[12] Many arrangements also appear in the partbooks of the Frauenchor.[13] For the Singakademie, Brahms composed several new SATB settings, mainly of sacred texts and melodies he found and copied in Viennese libraries; he published them in 1864, together with some of those probably written earlier (WoO 34).[14] His last arrangements of folksongs for mixed chorus were two more from Kretzschmer and Zuccalmaglio (WoO 35, nos. 7 and 8), written for the Singverein in 1874 but unpublished until they were included in the complete works (vol. 22) with a number of the Detmold settings (WoO 35).

The majority of Brahms's SATB arrangements are primarily homophonic; the melodies are in the soprano, and the lower voices accompany chordally, with occasional touches of melodic interest or rhythmic independence. However, several of the Singakademie settings and the last two from Kretzschmer and Zuccalmaglio are more elaborate, with extensive imitation.[15] An example is "Es flog ein Täublein" (WoO 34 no. 5), a song of the Annunciation. The opening phrase of each of the three identical strophes is introduced by the three lower voices in imitation, with the tenor and alto singing an inversion of the first notes of the tune; the remainder is imitative polyphony, with all parts sharing equally in the rhythmic and melodic activity. Even in a popular idiom like the folk song, Brahms could not restrain his instinct for contrapuntal games.

Vocal Quartets with Piano

Brahms intended his vocal quartets for performance by four soloists, but regardless of what might have been his preference in the matter, the deservedly popular *Liebeslieder* (Op. 52), *Neue Liebeslieder* (Op. 65), and *Zigeunerlieder* (Opp. 103 and 112 nos. 3–6) are frequently and successfully sung by choirs. Far less often heard but equally adaptable and as enjoyable to sing are most of the quartets Opp. 31, 64, 92, and 112 nos. 1 and 2, although a few with more individual "characters" (e.g., the couples in "Wechsellied zum Tanze" Op. 31/1) or virtuoso solo lines (the tenor of "Fragen" Op. 64/3) are less suited to choral performance.

The *Liebeslieder* have relatively easy four-hand piano parts, but the other quartets require a single pianist, usually one with considerable technical prowess. Simpler than most for the pianist is "Abendlied" (Op. 92/3), on a text by Friedrich Hebbel. Here the singers will, as in so much of Brahms, take pleasure in expressive accented dissonances—chromatic in the first half and diatonic in the tranquil concluding section, where the text is "kommt mir das Leben ganz wie ein Schlummerlied vor" ("life seems to me just like a lullaby").[16]

A Cappella Works with Sacred Texts

The history of Brahms's *a cappella* pieces with sacred texts begins with several canons he wrote in 1856 while studying counterpoint in correspondence with Joseph Joachim.[17] The very first, a Benedictus, became part of the "Warum" motet (Op. 74/1) many years later (as did transformations of two additional mass movements), and a five-voice augmentation canon resurfaced as the opening of the motet Op. 29/2.

The earliest unaccompanied sacred pieces not deriving from this exchange were the *Marienlieder* (Op. 22), which were written for the Frauenchor in summer 1859 (except for no. 3), and later arranged for SATB when they were published in 1862.[18] The texts are traditional poetic versions of Marian legends, but unlike the folk-song arrangements Brahms was writing at about the same time, these settings contain frequent imitation, meter changes, and musical illustrations of pictorial texts. The most sophisticated is no. 5, "Ruf zur Maria," where the melody in the soprano—diatonic except for one expressive passing tone—is harmonized with remarkable chromaticism, wide leaps in alto and tenor, exchange of parts among accompanying lines, and even a contrapuntally derived, inverted German augmented sixth chord at the climax of each stanza, "pray for us, Mary!"[19]

As Beller-McKenna writes, the two motets Op. 29 "established . . . the parameters for [Brahms's] later motets Opp. 74 and 110. All three groups . . . bring together pieces of apparently diverse origin and juxtapose settings of chorale texts with settings of Lutheran biblical texts."[20] *Es ist das Heil uns kommen her* (Op. 29/1) dates from a period in 1860 when Brahms and Joachim were studying chorale settings in the style of Bach.[21] The opening section is a chordal setting of the chorale melody (also set several times by Bach), and the much longer final section is a line-by-line setting of the same text, with the melody in long notes in bass 1. Each phrase is introduced by pre-imitation[22] and elaborately accompanied by the other four voices, who in the final phrase indulge in an extravaganza of motivic interplay and chromaticism that culminates in one of Brahms's most memorable cadential extensions.

The history of *Schaffe in mir, Gott, ein rein Herz* (Op. 29/2) is even less clear than that of its counterpart except for its opening section, a lushly harmonized augmentation canon between soprano and bass 2, which appears early in the 1856 counterpoint exchange with Joachim. The remaining three sections are disparate in style and tone, although they share contrapuntal intricacy. The long second section, more obviously modeled on the style of Bach than the others, is a chromatic fugue.[23] Strict canon reappears in the third section, where a canon at the seventh is sung in the outer voices of a three-voice texture (TBB), repeated exactly (SAA); the free middle voice must accomplish dramatic leaps in order to complete the harmonies. The final passage feels like an afterthought, tacked on to bring the piece to a rousing conclusion.[24]

The two motets Op. 74, although not published until 1878, both have origins in earlier periods of Brahms's career: *Warum ist das Licht gegeben dem Mühseligen?* (Op. 74/1) from the canonic mass movements of 1856, and *O Heiland, reiß die Himmel auf* (Op. 74/2) from Vienna in 1862–63, when he explored the local libraries and copied a quantity of German Renaissance music. The latter work illustrates Brahms's close study of these earlier models. It consists of five variations on verses of the chorale, the last of which is canonic and concludes with a double–canonic Amen.[25]

Brahms's motivation for writing the "Warum" motet—and particularly for including the concluding chorale in the style of Bach—has given rise to endless, diverse, and occasionally creative speculation.[26] The work as we know it was probably composed in 1877 and was certainly finished by summer 1878, when Brahms offered both motets to his publisher.[27] The sensitivity he showed in selecting and setting its biblical texts is even more remarkable in view of the fact that most of the motet is a recomposition in varying degrees of three of the canonic mass movements of 1856.[28] It seems almost miraculous that Brahms could have so perfectly matched the text of its opening movement (following the initial ritornello-like "Warum") with the searching, anxious quality of the chromatic fugue subject—one he had already written for the Mass's Agnus Dei some two decades earlier. The other transformed mass movements are equally suited to their German texts. Brahms provided his own evaluation of "Warum" when he sent it to Otto Dessoff in July 1878: "I am enclosing a trifle in which perhaps my knowledge of the Bible is to be praised. Besides that, it probably preaches better than my words. I've gone walking with it a lot!"[29]

Brahms's last choral works, composed in 1888 and 1889, were the *Fest- und Gedenksprüche* (Op. 109) and *Drei Motetten* (Op. 110), each containing three motets and all but Op. 110/2 for double choir.[30] The impetus for the composition of Op. 109 may have been an historical event, the *Dreikaiserjahr* of 1888, during which the old Kaiser Wilhelm I died and was rapidly succeeded, first by his ill son Friedrich and then his grandson, Wilhelm II. More than simply the "hurrah in tones" that Brahms described in a letter to Theodor Billroth in April 1889, the work was intended to speak to and for the nation. In Beller-McKenna's view, "events in German politics [had] colored [Brahms's] previously chauvinistic attitude . . . with a feeling of urgency bordering on despair"; the selection of biblical texts demonstrates "his opposition to the *Volk*-dominated religious nationalism of the right."[31] In gratitude for being awarded the honorary citizenship of Hamburg, Brahms offered the first performance for a trade fair in the city and dedicated the work to its mayor.[32]

The *Fest- und Gedenksprüche* are among Brahms's most frequently performed choral pieces. One obvious reason is their sheer beauty—the final canonic Amen is one of his most sublime cadential passages, comparable to the Amen that concludes the *Geistliches Lied* (Op. 30). Furthermore, they are enormously enjoyable to sing: the "ein Haus fallet" section of no. 2, with its rapid modulations and rhythmic disintegration, is a choral tour de force.[33] The texts are not at all jingoistic; rather, they have a timeless, universal quality suitable for many occasions.

The first mention of the Op. 110 motets is in a June 1889 letter Brahms wrote to his publisher about Op. 109, saying he had also composed some "much better" motets. The text for Op. 110/1—a combination of selected verses from Psalm 69 and Exodus 34—came from his notebook of biblical quotations, which also contains the texts of Opp. 74 and 109.[34] The motet's musical style partakes strongly of the music of Schütz in its through-composition, use of responsive psalmody, rhythmic irregularity, and chromaticism that includes cross relations and unexpected melodic leaps and harmonies, all in service of the text.[35]

The other two motets in Op. 110 both employ strophic chorale texts. No. 2, "Ach, arme Welt" (SATB) is a more realistic option for smaller choirs than the others, but it has its own difficulties, notably an intense and up-to-date chromaticism.[36]

Secular *A Cappella* Works (*Chorlieder*)

One reason Brahms stands out among nineteenth-century composers of choral music is that his secular works for unaccompanied choir are fully equal in quality to his settings of sacred texts—that is, many are distinguished by varied and often adventurous harmonies, intriguing counterpoint, and a close relationship between text and music. (They are also equally difficult.) Although a few were composed for specific choirs, in general his reasons for writing them seem to have been similar to those that inspired him to write *Lieder*: a poem appealed to him and would not let him rest until he had set it to music. For reasons that are unclear, these pieces have attracted much less scholarly attention than those with sacred texts or the works with orchestra.[37]

The three *Gesänge* (Op. 42), composed in 1859–61, have a relatively late opus number because Brahms had difficulty finding a publisher—a problem that would disappear after the success of the Requiem (Op. 45). Each perfectly conveys the atmosphere of its poem and shows Brahms already at his best as a composer for choirs. All are for six voices, SAATBB, a bottom-heavy combination that he also favored in later works (Op. 62/5, parts of Op. 74/1, Op. 104 nos. 1–3), but in each they are deployed differently. The outer sections of No. 3, "Darthula's Grabesgesang" (Herder's translation of a poem by the fake bard Ossian), alternate groups of higher and lower voices in funeral-march rhythm, with archaic modal scales and open fifths. In contrast to the opening and the diatonic central section of the piece, a transitional passage is so chromatic that Philipp Spitta commented on its "enharmonic difficulties."[38] Each of the other pieces is more unified and

Romantic in mood and setting. The first, "Abendständchen," on a poem by Clemens Brentano, evokes the sound of a distant flute heard at night; it is the first of Brahms's truly great lyric choral pieces. No. 2, "Vineta," is a lush, largely homophonic setting of a poem by Wilhelm Müller that tells of a drowned city. Its only moment of contrast appears with the text "Aus des Herzens tiefem Grunde" ("out of the heart's utmost depths"), set in descending unison octaves.

Of the seven Lieder for mixed chorus (Op. 62) published in 1874, two originated much earlier (versions of nos. 6 and 7 are found in the Frauenchor partbooks), while the rest were composed in 1873–74 when Brahms was music director of the Gesellschaft der Musikfreunde; three of these later five (nos. 2, 3, and 4) were first performed in one of the concerts he conducted there. All seven lieder have strophic structures and folk or folk-like texts. The three settings of texts from Heyse's *Jungbrunnen*, a collection of "fairy tales" that was one of Brahms's favorite sources, exemplify the sophistication he could bring to outwardly simple material.[39] No. 3, "Waldesnacht," with its peaceful mood and discreetly canonic counterpoint, is probably the most often performed of all the *Chorlieder*. No. 5, "All meine Herzgedanken," sung by someone separated from a lover, is heart-tugging because of its rich texture (SAATBB) and surprising but effective chromaticism. And no. 4, "Dein Herzlein mild," contains a wealth of contrapuntal and harmonic invention, particularly in the overlapping hemiolas that, at the end of the final stanza, compare the opening of a heart to love to the opening of a flower.

The texts of the six *Lieder und Romanzen* (Op. 93a), all for SATB, represent a variety of sources and sentiments, from the cheerful folk poetry of "Der bucklichte Fiedler" and "Das Mädchen," through the wistfulness of "O süßer Mai," "Der Falke," and "Fahr wohl," to Goethe's sententious "Beherzigung." Musical features of these settings, even those that seem simplest on the surface, show the kind of conciseness, motivic unity, and contrapuntal complexity that also characterize Brahms's instrumental music at this time,[40] along with details that stem from his long study of counterpoint and folk music. For example, the short middle section of "Der bucklichte Fiedler," the witches' dance, packs in an amazing number of illustrative features: beginning with the tuning fifths of the violin, it is in the Lydian mode and accompanied by a drone, both characteristic of much European peasant music. Both sections of "Beherzigung" begin with canons, the first in D minor and highly chromatic to illustrate the uncertainty described in the text, the second in a determined D major. "Das Mädchen" uses irregular meters typically found in eastern European folk music. In "O süßer Mai," Brahms employs one of his favorite rhythmic strategies—overlapping hemiolas that obscure the meter—to exemplify confusion. "Der Falke" is one of Brahms's most beautiful choral songs. Leaps in the bass line perhaps illustrate the falcon's wide-ranging flight; when the falcon at last speaks, its mysterious utterances are accompanied by chromatic harmonies and changes of key. Brahms's strophic setting of Friedrich Rückert's gentle, bittersweet "Fahr wohl," though outwardly simple, contains brief canons by inversion in its middle section. In 1897, as Brahms's funeral procession went by the Gesellschaft der Musikfreunde, its choir sang this piece.

Brahms's last set of secular choral works, the five *Gesänge* (Op. 104), are unified by what is often called his autumnal mood, but they vary in other ways, including the number of voices required for performance. The first three are for six voices (again SAATBB): "Nachtwache I" and "Nachtwache II" (both Rückert texts) and "Letztes Glück," on a poem by Brahms's biographer Max Kalbeck. "Verlorene Jugend" (no. 4), for five voices (SATBB), is a setting of a traditional Bohemian text, and "Im Herbst" (no. 5) is on a poem by Brahms's north German friend Klaus Groth. Its first two stanzas, set identically, describe melancholy events in nature and the human spirit. In the final stanza, which turns from C minor to the parallel major, the poet sees the sun set and compares the end of the year to the end of life; however, "in his tears flows the heart's most blessed outpouring." The intense chromaticism of this stanza features a series of brief modulations to distant keys, many accomplished by augmented sixth progressions.[41]

Each of the three six-voice pieces in this opus is, in its own way, perfect. The Rückert settings were much admired by Brahms's friends, although the virtues of the first were overshadowed by those of the second. In "Nachtwache I," a loving heart sends its music out into the night, hoping to find a receptive listener; the trios of upper and lower voices echo and embellish one another's lines in gently chromatic and subtly contrapuntal exchanges, coming together only briefly. In "Nachtwache II," horn calls sound in perfect fourths; anxious hearts are admonished to listen for "the whispering voices of angels" and to "extinguish your lamps with confidence" (in a brief appearance of the key of the flat sixth degree, in contrast to the otherwise diatonic setting). A beautiful cadence illustrates "peace" in the last line.

"Letztes Glück" preserves only some of the division of the six voices into upper and lower trios. In the first two lines of the poem ("lifelessly glides leaf upon leaf / quietly and sadly from the trees"), they echo one another at the time interval of just one beat; the passage is immediately repeated with the trios inverted. The next two lines, however, are in full six-part texture, fading away to four voices as "spring dreams" are recalled. A glorious and unexpected key change brings back all six voices; a gleam of sunshine lights a late wild rose as the texture thins again, and a return to opening material for the last two lines leads to a quiet conclusion. This beautiful piece is perhaps overlooked because of Kalbeck's reputation as an inferior poet, but it is fully worthy of its place alongside the others.

Accompanied Works

The *Begräbnisgesang* (Op. 13) is the only piece for mixed voices with instrumental accompaniment from the early years of Brahms's career. Composed during his second season at Detmold for SATB, wind band, and timpani, it is accessible, rewarding, and should be performed more often.[42]

The choral–orchestral work for which Brahms is best known, is, of course, the next he completed, *Ein deutsches Requiem* (Op. 45);[43] it begins the series of large works that fulfilled the "extravagant prophecy" made by Robert Schumann in his famous essay "Neue Bahnen."[44] Before settling down to finish it, however, Brahms had already composed all but the final chorus of *Rinaldo* (Op. 50), intending to enter it in a competition for men's choirs (he missed the competition deadline). This *Cantate von Goethe*, as the title page identifies it, is based on an episode that Goethe took from Tasso's sixteenth-century epic *Gerusalemme liberata*. Scored for tenor solo, four-part men's chorus (double in the finale), and large orchestra, it is the closest Brahms came to writing an opera. The rarity of performances today reflects the decline in the *Männerchor* tradition; furthermore, the tenor soloist must have a Wagnerian range and endurance.[45] There are beautiful moments in the score, especially in lyric passages for the soloist, and the dramatic climax, when Rinaldo sees his own degraded reflection in the diamond shield, is particularly effective. But in general the writing in the two choruses that frame the work is uninteresting compared with Brahms's usual choral style.

The *Alto Rhapsody* (Op. 53) has attracted more attention than any vocal work except the Requiem partly because of its role in Brahms's personal history. He wrote it in response to Julie Schumann's engagement, describing it as his "bridal song" to Clara, who had been unaware of Brahms's infatuation with her daughter.[46] It is more an orchestral *Lied* than a choral piece, with the four-part male chorus entering only in the final section to provide a hymn-like, consolatory response to the passionate sorrow expressed by the soloist.

Brahms began the *Schicksalslied* (Op. 54) in 1868, setting an interpolated poem in Hölderlin's *Hyperion*. Its composition was interrupted by the beginning of the Franco-Prussian War in 1870, when he was seized by a fit of patriotic enthusiasm and, choosing biblical texts from Revelation 19, embarked on the *Triumphlied*, which he completed and published as Op. 55 in 1872. Although it was popular for a time, the *Triumphlied* is almost never performed now; its bombastic sentiments are problematic in view of twentieth-century events, and its massive scale makes it impracticable.[47]

Writers on Brahms often group the *Schicksalslied* with his last two works for chorus and orchestra, *Nänie* (Op. 82) and the *Gesang der Parzen* (Op. 89), because they share themes from classical antiquity in poems by great modern writers—Hölderlin, Schiller, and Goethe respectively. The orchestral postlude of the *Schicksalslied*, a recasting of the prelude, cost Brahms a good deal of effort, and it has stimulated so much commentary that the work's other features are often overlooked.[48] Daverio's analysis of the prelude, which he calls "one of Brahms's most sumptuous opening paragraphs," describes how chromatic pitches, accented non-chord tones, and the timpani's triplets contribute to its coherence; these features return in the chorus's first two stanzas, which depict the blissful realm of the gods.[49] The abrupt shift in the third stanza to the human plane is shocking: the chorus declaims in unison "Doch uns ist gegeben / Auf keiner Stätte zu ruhn" ("But to us [suffering humanity] is given / to find rest nowhere") against a violent accompaniment of rushing strings and screeching woodwinds. Pounding hemiolas and successive diminished seventh chords contribute to the sense of dislocation, and the poem—though not the piece—ends with a descent into the unknown.

The ten years that separate the *Schicksalslied* and *Nänie* saw the appearance of the choral collections Opp. 62 and 74 and much instrumental music, including the first two symphonies, the violin concerto, and the second piano concerto. Brahms seems not to have been motivated to write large choral works, although he was musical director of the Gesellschaft der Musikfreunde from 1872 to 1875 and conducted his own Requiem, *Triumphlied*, *Alto Rhapsody*, and *Schicksalslied* with that institution's large and capable chorus and orchestra. He returned to choral–orchestral composition in 1880 on the occasion of the death of a friend, the neo-classical painter Anselm Feuerbach.[50] As a memorial, Brahms set Schiller's threnody *Nänie*, publishing it in 1881 with a dedication to the painter's stepmother.

Schiller's poem is a lament on the passing of beauty. Both its form (seven couplets in a meter traditionally used for elegies) and content (the deaths of Eurydice, Adonis, and Achilles and the mourning of their survivors) are classical. Brahms's setting is an asymmetric ternary form, which begins with an introduction for oboe solo and wind band reminiscent of the opening of the slow movement of the violin concerto. The chorus's fugal entry elaborates the oboe's melody with the text "Auch das Schöne muß sterben" ("even the beautiful must die"). The poem's meaning is that the dead live forever on the lips of those who loved them, and Brahms emphasizes it by returning to the first line of the final couplet—"Auch ein Klaglied zu sein im Mund der Geliebten ist herrlich" ("Even to be an elegy in the mouth of the beloved is glorious")—and ending with gentle repetitions of the word "herrlich."[51]

The *Gesang der Parzen* (Op. 89) followed *Nänie* by just a year. The poem, from Goethe's *Iphigenie auf Tauris*, is Iphigenie's reflection on the curse the gods placed on her family to punish her ancestor Tantalus.[52] In six stanzas of varying length, she describes how the gods can turn on one whom they loved but now reject, indifferent to the fate of his descendants. The orchestra is nearly Brahms's largest; the chorus is in the familiar SAATBB configuration, often divided with the three upper parts against the three lower. Chordal homophony predominates; there are only brief passages of imitative counterpoint, although other features suggest the influence of Bach. These include the organ-like orchestral introduction and passages reminiscent of the *St. Matthew Passion*, which Brahms had conducted in 1875 in his last performance as music director of the Gesellschaft der Musikfreunde.

The most striking feature of the *Parzenlied*, as Brahms called it,[53] is its tonal instability. Beginning with the second bar of the orchestral introduction, distant minor keys are juxtaposed, and contrasting passages in major describe the gods "feasting at golden tables." In the last stanza, Iphigenia tells her hearers "So sangen die Parzen" ("thus sang the Fates"): this is the song heard by the aged outcast in Hades. Brahms's setting of this stanza forms the coda, a monotonous choral chant,[54] at first accompanied by a quiet, tonally settled version of the introduction. However, as the orchestra slows toward the conclusion, stability vanishes: dominant sevenths, respelled as augmented sixths that resolve to tonic six-four chords, form a circle of enharmonic major thirds and finally come to rest on a desolate open fifth.[55] The work's text has the same meaning as that of the *Schicksalslied*, but here Brahms offers no comfort.

After the *Gesang der Parzen*, Brahms wrote no more for chorus and orchestra. Indeed, his entire output for these forces spans a relatively short period of his career. Leaving aside the *Begräbnisgesang* and preliminary efforts on the Requiem and *Rinaldo*, he completed all seven works between 1868 and 1882. One wonders why he wrote them at all, when during the same period he had found his symphonic voice, and when there are obvious technical limitations in writing for singers that do not exist in instrumental music. Was he trying to meet Schumann's expectations as expressed in "Neue Bahnen"? Did he anticipate lucrative sales, especially after the success of the Requiem? Rather, it seems most likely that he was motivated by poetic or biblical texts, as was true for the smaller choral works and *Lieder*, and—perhaps even more in these larger works—by events in his life and the lives of nations. Singers may be more limited than instruments, but they *can* articulate words, and Brahms's care in choosing and setting texts demonstrates that he valued what voices could express in his music.

The qualities that have made Brahms's choral works so valued by performers and audiences alike are surely the same as those cherished by players of his chamber music. One is his effortless command of counterpoint; every singer has rewarding melodic lines. The harmonic language is rich and varied, the rhythms sometimes unpredictable but always logically related to the texts, which are themselves worth attention. The works are formally interesting; there is always more to find in the ways in which structures and musical ideas are developed and changed. Our pleasure in this music is both sensual and intellectual; the sound itself is sufficient reward, but the rewards are even greater for those who explore the deeper levels of Brahms's music.

Notes

1 Florence May, *The Life of Johannes Brahms*, rpt. 2nd ed. (Neptune City, NJ: Paganiniana, 1981), 75–76, 80. On whether one might have survived, see note 10 below.

2 See "Brahms the Conductor" in Michael Musgrave, *A Brahms Reader* (New Haven and London: Yale University Press, 2000), 136–47, and summaries in Virginia Hancock, "Brahms's Performances of Early Choral Music," *19th-Century Music* 8, 2 (Fall 1984): 125–28, and Daniel Beller-McKenna, "The Scope and Significance of the Choral Music," in *The Cambridge Companion to Brahms* (Cambridge and New York: Cambridge University Press, 1999), 172–73. Sophie Drinker's book *Brahms and His Women's Choruses* (Merton, PA: by the author, 1952) is the principal source of information on the Frauenchor.

3 The repertoire of the Singverein of the Gesellschaft der Musikfreunde in Vienna, which he conducted from 1872 to 1875, included performances of his works, but he composed only a few *a cappella* pieces during that time: two folk-song settings, and Op. 62 nos. 2, 3, and 4 (May, *The Life of Johannes Brahms*, 466–67, 468–69, 482, 484, 489–90, 492–93, 495).

4 Dissertations by Hans Beuerle and Virginia Hancock were completed in 1975 and 1977 respectively.

5 Kross included all information available in the early 1950s from the published correspondence and other sources. Both he and Beuerle provide sometimes lengthy analyses. Beller-McKenna, "Choral Music," has brief accounts of selected choral works, and several authors' contributions to Botstein's volume cover all of them (plus the vocal quartets) in varying amounts of detail. Of the "life and works" volumes, MacDonald and Musgrave are the most recent and useful.

6 These include the *Marienlieder* (Op. 22), Op. 62 nos. 6 and 7, and perhaps Op. 41/1 and Op. 42/2. For works lists, see biographies and reference works including *Grove Music Online*.

7 See the descriptions of these works by Beller-McKenna and Botstein in Leon Botstein, ed., *The Compleat*

Brahms: A Guide to the Musical Works of Johannes Brahms (New York: W. W. Norton, 1999), 338–42 (Op. 37), 347–49 (Op. 44), 366–67 (Op. 12), and 370–73 (Opp. 17 and 27).

8 In Beller-McKenna's description of Op. 44 (Botstein, *The Compleat Brahms*, 347–49), he stresses the independence and musical necessity of the *ad libitum* piano part.

9 Siegfried Kross, *Die Chorwerke von Johannes Brahms*, 2nd ed. (Berlin-Halensee: Max Hesse, 1963), 149.

10 "Postillons Morgenlied" and "Goldne Brücken," on texts by Wilhelm Müller and Emanuel Geibel respectively; it has been suggested that the first could date back to Brahms's experience at age fourteen, while the second was composed for the Celle Liedertafel, an ensemble that Brahms wished to thank for its hospitality when he and Eduard Reményi performed in that city in May 1853. The two pieces, edited by their discoverer, Helmut Lauterwasser, have been published by Breitkopf & Härtel.

11 Beller-McKenna, *Brahms and the German Spirit* (Cambridge, MA and London: Harvard University Press, 2004), 149–151; Beller-McKenna in Botstein, *The Compleat Brahms*, 342–44.

12 August Kretzschmer and Anton Wilhelm von Zuccalmaglio, *Deutsche Volkslieder mit ihren Original-Weisen*, 2 vols. (Berlin: Vereins-Buchhandlung, 1838, 1840); see Hancock, *Brahms's Choral Compositions and His Library of Early Music* (Ann Arbor: UMI Research Press, 1983), 80–81, and Hancock, "Brahms: *Volkslied, Kunstlied*" in *The Nineteenth-Century German Lied*, 2nd ed. (New York: Routledge, 2009), 147–48, 172 n. 12.

13 See the edition by Gotwals and Kepler. Margit McCorkle describes the Frauenchor sources (569–79) and lists the arrangements (WoO 36–38, 604–9) in *Johannes Brahms: Thematisch-Bibliographisches Werkverzeichnis* (Munich: Henle, 1984).

14 Folk-song arrangements stemming from this copying project appear in WoO 34 and 35; see McCorkle, *Johannes Brahms*, 598–604, for an account of contents, sources, and chronology. Brahms's principal new source was David Gregor Corner, *Gross' Catolisch Gesangbuch*. 2 vols. (Nürnberg: Gregor Ender der Jünger, 1631). See George S. Bozarth, "Johannes Brahms und die Liedersammlungen D. G. Corners, K. S. Meisters, und F. W. Arnolds," *Die Musikforschung* 36 (1983): 177–99, for a thorough discussion of these sources (and for the origin of the best-known of the folksong settings, "In stiller Nacht"); also see Hancock, *Brahms's Choral Compositions*, 15–17, 82.

15 Brahms made two arrangements of "Wach auf, mein Kind." For the later setting (WoO 35/7) and its sketches and resemblances to German Renaissance music, see Hancock, "Brahms's Links with German Renaissance Music: A Discussion of Selected Choral Works," in *Brahms 2: Biographical, Documentary and Analytical Studies*, ed. Michael Musgrave (Cambridge: Cambridge University Press, 1987), 105–06.

16 See Stark for texts, translations, and analytical comments on the quartets.

17 See David Brodbeck, "The Brahms-Joachim Counterpoint Exchange; or, Robert, Clara, and 'the Best Harmony between Jos. and Joh.,'" *Brahms Studies 1*, ed. David Brodbeck (Lincoln, NE: University of Nebraska Press, 1994), 35–37, for a summary. Other canonic choral pieces stemming from the correspondence are the openings of "O bone Jesu" and "Adoramus te" for women's voices (Op. 37, nos. 1 and 2; no. 3, "Regina coeli," also canonic, was composed in 1863 in Vienna), and the *Geistliches Lied* ("Lass dich nur nichts nicht dauern," Op. 30) for mixed voices and organ. A double canon at the ninth with an independent organ part, this work is much more convincing musically than the pieces with Latin texts.

18 See Hancock in Botstein, *The Compleat Brahms*, 332–34, for composition and publication. Also see Hancock, "Brahms's Links," 99–100, for no. 2 ("Marias Kirchgang"), and Beller-McKenna, *Brahms and the German Spirit*), 12–17, for Op. 22 and German Romantic nationalism.

19 The description of no. 5 by Hancock (Botstein, *The Compleat Brahms*, 334) as "three identical stanzas" is wrong. The third stanza begins differently and includes exchange of parts between alto and tenor.

20 Beller-McKenna in Botstein, *The Compleat Brahms*, 335.

21 The autograph manuscript is dated July 1860. Beller-McKenna, "Brahms's Motet *Es ist das Heil uns kommen her* and the 'Innermost Essence of Music,'" in *Brahms Studies 2*, ed. David Brodbeck (Lincoln: University of Nebraska Press, 1998) attributes its composition to Brahms's desire to assert his place in German tradition; he provides a detailed analysis, primarily of motivic relationships. Hancock, *Brahms's Choral Compositions*, 117, links it to Cantata 4, *Christ lag in Todesbanden*, which Brahms had conducted in Detmold, and specifically to its fourth stanza, "Es war ein wunderlicher Krieg." The motets Op. 29 were not published until 1864, when Brahms wanted printed copies of no. 1 for a Singakademie concert featuring his works.

22 The German term is *Vorimitation*, a technique where the principal subject enters imitatively, but in shorter note values, before it appears as a cantus firmus.

23 Beller-McKenna (Botstein, *The Compleat Brahms*, 337) follows Hans Michael Beuerle, *Johannes Brahms: Untersuchungen zu den A-cappella-Kompositionen* (Hamburg: Karl Dieter Wagner, 1987), 173, and Hancock, *Brahms's Choral Compositions*, 117–18, in suggesting Bach's Cantata 21, "Ich hatte viel Bekümmernis," as a possible model for this section. Hancock also cites Andreas Hammerschmidt's setting of the same text as a work that Brahms probably knew.

24 The *animato* coda includes a seven-bar pedal high G for the soprano. Brahms's friend Julius Otto Grimm, who conducted a women's choir in Göttingen, complained about the low range of the alto parts in the canonic mass movements. Brahms could be equally brutal to sopranos and tenors.

25 The traditional text and melody are part of the copying project, primarily traditional sacred texts and tunes, described in note 14 above. Some version of the motet had been written by 1870, when Brahms mentioned it to Max Bruch. See Hancock in Botstein, *The Compleat Brahms*, 352–54, for the history and descriptions of both Op. 74 motets. For an analysis of no. 2 and its connection with German Renaissance music that Brahms studied and performed, see Hancock, "Brahms's Links," 105–09.

26 Beller-McKenna, "The Great *Warum?*: Job, Christ, and Bach in a Brahms Motet," *19th-Century Music* 19, 3 (Spring 1996): 254, argues that the chorale shows Brahms's continuing self-doubt, an "inability to define himself as an individual artist without evoking another, more authoritative artistic figure." Robert Pascall, "Brahms's *Missa Canonica* and its Recomposition in his Motet *Warum* op. 74, no. 1," in *Brahms 2: Biographical, Documentary and Analytical Studies*, ed. Michael Musgrave (Cambridge: Cambridge University Press, 1987), 135, concludes that after "the impassioned, original subjectivity of the opening, . . . the poise and universality of traditional forms" are needed at the close.

27 In his description of the motet's texts in Brahms's Bible and his notebook of biblical quotations, Beller-McKenna, *Brahms and the German Spirit*, 51–56, assumes a date of 1877, as does Pascall, "Brahms's *Missa Canonica.*"

28 See Pascall, "Brahms's *Missa Canonica*," for the transformation of the mass movements and for an analysis of the motet; unlike other writers, he stresses unity and overall shape in the result.

29 Quoted by Kross, *Die Chorwerke von Johannes Brahms*, 364, who describes it as "[Brahms's] own mixture of half-ironic skepticism and steady self-consciousness with respect to his own creations": "Ich lege eine Kleinigkeit bei, an der vielleicht—meine Bibelkenntnis zu loben ist. Zudem aber predigt es wohl besser als m[eine] Worte. Ich bin viel spazieren gegangen damit!"

30 He may have been inspired to write for double chorus by the recent start of publication of the complete works of Heinrich Schütz, edited by Spitta; Brahms copied a number of fragments from the first volume of the polychoral *Psalmen Davids* (1619). See Hancock, *Brahms's Choral Compositions*, 30–33, and Hancock, "Brahms and Early Music: Evidence from his Library and his Choral Compositions," in *Brahms Studies: Analytical and Historical Perspectives*, ed. George S. Bozarth (Oxford: Clarendon Press, 1990), 40–41.

31 Beller-McKenna, *Brahms and the German Spirit*, 136, 147. Ryan Minor, "Occasions and Nations in Brahms's *Fest- und Gedenksprüche*," *19th-Century Music* 29/3 (Spring 2006): 269–71, describes how the "texts were carefully chosen, even recontextualized, to convey a parable of national memory that often altered the texts' original meanings." Brahms himself proudly called attention to the "jesuitical" distortion of meaning he imposed on the text of no. 2 (Kross, *Die Chorwerke von Johannes Brahms*, 445–46, and many other authors).

32 Op. 109 was completed before Brahms was notified of the honor; it was not composed as a response, and is not, therefore, an "occasional" piece. Minor, "Occasions and Nations," 262–64, lists the authors who have mistakenly assumed that it was.

33 Both Beller-McKenna, *Brahms and the German Spirit*, and Minor, "Occasions and Nations," provide extended and perceptive analyses.

34 See Beller-McKenna, *Brahms and the German Spirit*, 54–57. Beller-McKenna, "Brahms, the Bible, and post-Romanticism: Cultural issues in Johannes Brahms's later settings of biblical texts, 1877–1896," Ph.D. diss. (Harvard University, 1994) includes photographs of the notebook pages, transcriptions, and translations. Hancock discusses Brahms's manipulation of the biblical texts in "Inspiration and Obfuscation in Brahms's Choices and Settings of Biblical Texts," *Ars Lyrica* 19 (2010): 115–29.

35 See Hancock, "Brahms and Early Music: Evidence from His Library and His Choral Compositions," in *Brahms Studies: Analytical and Historical Perspectives*, ed. George S. Bozarth (Oxford: Clarendon Press, 1990), 40–48, for an analysis of the motet and parallels in works of Schütz that Brahms copied from or marked in the complete works.

36 Its opening gesture is a four-note ascending whole-tone scale in the soprano, reminiscent of the chorale "Es ist genug," which Brahms had conducted in 1873. See Hancock, "Brahms's Performances," 138–40, for his performance decisions in this and other works, and Hancock, *Brahms's Choral Compositions*, 137–41, for an analysis of the motet.

37 Compare the number of entries for Opp. 42, 62, 93a, and 104 with the other works listed in Platt's and Quigley's bibliographies. Kross and Beuerle have sometimes lengthy analyses; and all the pieces are described at least briefly in Botstein.

38 The most striking of these "enharmonische Schwierigkeiten" is a German augmented 6th chord, used in the reverse of the usual progression to shift in a single measure between B-flat-minor and B-minor six-four chords. This is a rare move for Brahms; see Hancock, "Brahms: *Volkslied, Kunstlied*," in *The Nineteenth-Century German Lied*, 2nd ed., ed. Rufus Hallmark (New York: Routledge, 2009), 161.

39 They illustrate a discussion of Brahms's use of techniques from German Renaissance music in Hancock, "Brahms and Early Music," 35–40.

40 Both Kross and Beuerle emphasize this point. Beller-McKenna writes (Botstein, *The Compleat Brahms*, 354–57) that their "sophisticated style" must have been influenced by the "mastery of larger forms" that Brahms had acquired in the ten years since the publication of Op. 62.

41 "Im Herbst" was first performed by the Hamburg Cäcilien-Verein in an early version in A minor/major that has been published (see the Selected Bibliography). The modulations and musical climax are more effective and singable in Brahms's revision.

42 See Hancock, "Brahms and Early Music," 30–35, for comparison with works of Bach that Brahms conducted.

43 A detailed study of this work may be found in Chapter 4 of this volume.

44 McCorkle, "The Role of Trial Performances for Brahms's Orchestral and Large Choral Works: Sources and Circumstances," in *Brahms Studies: Analytical and Historical Perspectives*, ed. George S. Bozarth (Oxford: Clarendon Press, 1990), 296. See also her description of the circumstances of composition, early performances, and publication of these works.

45 Daverio (Botstein, *The Compleat Brahms*, 380–84) cites critical comparisons to *Tannhäuser* and attributes the scarcity of performances partly to audiences' ignorance of the background of the text.

46 Garlington emphasizes the biographical context of Goethe's poem and describes how Brahms manipulated the text. See also the analyses by Wallace Berry, "Text and Music in the *Alto Rhapsody*," *Journal of Music Theory* 272 (Fall 1983): 239–53, and Allen Forte, "Motive and Rhythmic Contour in the *Alto Rhapsody*," *Journal of Music Theory* 27, 2 (Fall 1983): 255–71.

47 Beller-McKenna, *Brahms and the German Spirit*, 123, in a sympathetic account, nevertheless describes it as "full-throttle writing" and lacking the "long-breathed, elegiac lines" that characterize Brahms's other large works.

48 John Daverio, "The *Wechsel der Töne* in Brahms's *Schicksalslied*," *Journal of the American Musicological Society* 46, 1 (Spring 1993): 84–113 (p. 104); see also for a summary, including Brahms's own contradictory statements. Relating the musical setting to Hölderlin's own writings, Daverio concludes that the work "mediates these phases" in Brahms's life: "the peripatetic composer of confessional lyrics [such as the *Alto Rhapsody*] was settling down as a bourgeois symphonist" (p. 111).

49 Writers going back to Kalbeck have commented on the resemblance of the orchestral writing at the chorus's entrance to the Air from Bach's Third Orchestral Suite.

50 Feuerbach began a portrait of Brahms, but when a painting with which he had hoped to establish his reputation in Vienna was ridiculed by the critics, he found it impossible to work for a time; the Brahms project was left unfinished and eventually destroyed. (One wonders how the sloppy and rough-edged Brahms would have looked in a treatment by Feuerbach, whose subjects were usually ideally beautiful.)

51 *Nänie*'s resemblance to the outer movements of the Requiem has often been noted. See Hancock, "Inspiration and Obfuscation in Brahms's Choices and Settings of Biblical Texts," for Brahms's alteration of the sense of the final couplet.

52 As Rosemarie Mauro explains (14), Brahms ignored the fact that the poem represents a turn toward a positive outcome in the drama. See Mauro, "The *Gesang der Parzen* of Goethe and Brahms: A Study in Synthesis and Interpretation" (M.A. thesis, University of Washington, 1986).

53 Jan Swafford (Botstein, *The Compleat Brahms*, 196–97) calls this title, and the entire work, a "negation" of the *Triumphlied*. He attributes its hopelessness partly to "what a later age would call middle-age crisis" and partly to Brahms's despair "not only for the future of society and of music in general but for the future of his own work."

54 Mauro's analysis shows how the work's entire harmonic and motivic plan culminates in the chorus's lines in the coda.

55 Anton Webern, in *The Path to the New Music*, famously cited this conclusion as "already . . . far away from tonality" (Mauro, "A Study in Synthesis and Interpretation," 50). Mauro describes the entire tonal cycle as an "expanded 'tonic'."

Selected Bibliography

Editions

Brahms, Johannes. *Sämtliche Werke*, ed. Eusebius Mandyczewski and Hans Gál. Leipzig: Breitkopf & Härtel, 1926–28. Reprint ed., Ann Arbor: J. W. Edwards, 1949.

XVII. *Chorwerke mit Orchester* I: Op. 45 (also in Dover reprint)

XVIII. *Chorwerke mit Orchester* II: Opp. 55, 50.

XIX. *Chorwerke mit Orchester* III: Opp. 53, 54, 82, 89, 12, 13, 17 (Opp. 53, 54, 82, 89 also in Dover reprint).

XX. *Mehrstimmige Gesänge mit Klavier oder Orgel*: Opp. 27, 30, 31, 64, 52, 65, 92, 93b, 103, 112, "Kleine Hochzeits-Kantate" (WoO 16).

XXI. *Mehrstimmige Gesänge ohne Begleitung*: Opp. 22, 29, 74, 109, 110; 42, 62, 93a, 104; 37, 41, 44, 113; *Deutsche Volkslieder* (WoO 34); "Dem dunkeln Schoß der heilgen Erde" (WoO 10); canons "Töne, lindernder Klang" (WoO 28) and "Zu Rauch" (WoO 30).

———. *"Alto Rhapsody," Opus 53, for Contralto, Men's Chorus, and Orchestra. Text from Goethe's "Harzreise im Winter."* Facsimile edition of the autograph manuscript, ed. Walter Frisch. New York: New York Public Library, 1983.

———. *Der Herbst—Erste Fassung von 1886 / Im Herbst—Zweite Fassung von 1888*. Ed. Kurt Hofmann. Kassel: Bärenreiter, 1983.

———. *Folk Songs for Women's Voices, arranged by Johannes Brahms*. Ed. Vernon Gotwals and Philip Keppler. Northampton, MA: Smith College Music Archives, vol. 15, 1968. *Four Songs for Three Voices* published as no. 47 in series From the Choral Repertoire. New York: Broude, 1987.

———. *Geistliche Chormusik: Gesamtausgabe der motettischen Werke*. Ed. Günter Graulich. Stuttgart: Carus-Verlag, 1983.

———. *Messe für vier- bis sechsstimmigen gemischten Chor und Continuo (Orgel)*. Ed. Otto Biba. Vienna: Doblinger, 1984.

Piano-vocal scores of the larger works, collections of the *a cappella* works and vocal quartets, and a variety of octavos of individual pieces are widely available.

Books, Articles, Etc.

Beller-McKenna, Daniel. *Brahms and the German Spirit*. Cambridge, MA and London: Harvard University Press, 2004.

———. "Brahms, the Bible, and post-Romanticism: Cultural issues in Johannes Brahms's later settings of biblical texts, 1877–1896." Ph.D. diss., Harvard University, 1994.

———. "Brahms's Motet *Es ist das Heil uns kommen her* and the 'Innermost Essence of Music,'" in *Brahms Studies 2*, ed. David Brodbeck. Lincoln and London: University of Nebraska Press, 1998, 31–61.

———. "The Great *Warum?*: Job, Christ, and Bach in a Brahms Motet," *19th-Century Music* 19, 3 (Spring 1996): 213–51.

———. "The Scope and Significance of the Choral Music," in *The Cambridge Companion to Brahms*, ed. Michael Musgrave. Cambridge and New York: Cambridge University Press, 1999, 171–94.

Berry, Wallace. "Text and Music in the *Alto Rhapsody*," *Journal of Music Theory* 27, 2 (Fall 1983): 239–53.

Beuerle, Hans Michael. *Johannes Brahms: Untersuchungen zu den A-cappella-Kompositionen*. Hamburg: Karl Dieter Wagner, 1987.

Botstein, Leon, ed. *The Compleat Brahms: A Guide to the Musical Works of Johannes Brahms*. New York: W. W. Norton, 1999.

Bozarth, George S. "Johannes Brahms und die Liedersammlungen D. G. Corners, K. S. Meisters, und F. W. Arnolds." *Die Musikforschung* 36 (1983): 177–99.

Brodbeck, David. "The Brahms-Joachim Counterpoint Exchange; or, Robert, Clara, and 'the Best Harmony between Jos. and Joh.,'" *Brahms Studies 1*, ed. David Brodbeck. Lincoln and London: University of Nebraska Press, 1994.

Daverio, John. "The *Wechsel der Töne* in Brahms's *Schicksalslied*," *Journal of the American Musicological Society* 46, 1 (Spring 1993): 84–113.

Drinker, Sophie. *Brahms and His Women's Choruses*. Merion, PA: by the author, 1952.

Forte, Allen. "Motive and Rhythmic Contour in the *Alto Rhapsody*," *Journal of Music Theory* 27, 2 (Fall 1983): 255–71.

Garlington, Aubrey S., Jr. "*Harzreise als Herzreise*: Brahms's *Alto Rhapsody*," *Musical Quarterly* 69, 4 (Fall 1983): 527–42.

Geiringer, Karl. *Brahms: His Life and Work*. 2nd ed. New York: Oxford University Press, 1947.

Hancock, Virginia. "Brahms and Early Music: Evidence from His Library and His Choral Compositions," in

Brahms Studies: Analytical and Historical Perspectives, ed. George S. Bozarth. Oxford: Clarendon Press, 1990, 29–48.

——. "Brahms: *Volkslied, Kunstlied*," in *The Nineteenth-Century German Lied*, 2nd ed., ed. Rufus Hallmark. New York: Routledge, 2009, 142–77.

——. *Brahms's Choral Compositions and His Library of Early Music*. Ann Arbor: UMI Research Press, 1983.

——. "Brahms's Links with German Renaissance Music: A Discussion of Selected Choral Works," in *Brahms 2: Biographical, Documentary and Analytical Studies*, ed. Michael Musgrave. Cambridge: Cambridge University Press, 1987, 95–110.

——. "Brahms's Performances of Early Choral Music," *19th-Century Music* 8, 2 (Fall 1984): 125–41.

——. "The Growth of Brahms's Interest in Early Choral Music, and Its Effect on His Own Choral Compositions," in *Brahms: Biographical, Documentary and Analytical Studies*, ed. Robert Pascall. Cambridge: Cambridge University Press, 1983, 27–40.

——. "Inspiration and Obfuscation in Brahms's Choices and Settings of Biblical Texts," *Ars Lyrica* 19 (2010): 115–29. Cambridge, MA: Lyrica Society for Word-Music Relations.

Hess, Carol A. "'Als wahres volles Menschenbild': Brahms's *Rinaldo* and Autobiographical Allusion," in *Brahms Studies 2*, ed. David Brodbeck. Lincoln and London: University of Nebraska Press, 1998, 63–89.

Ingraham, Mary I. "Brahms's *Rinaldo*, op. 50: A Structural and Contextual Study." Ph.D. diss., University of Nottingham, 1994.

Kross, Siegfried. *Die Chorwerke von Johannes Brahms*. 2nd ed. Berlin-Halensee: Max Hesse, 1963.

MacDonald, Malcolm. *Brahms*. New York: Schirmer, 1990.

Mauro, Rosemarie P. "The *Gesang der Parzen* of Goethe and Brahms: A Study in Synthesis and Interpretation." M.A. thesis, University of Washington, 1986.

May, Florence. *The Life of Johannes Brahms*. 2nd ed. London: Wm. Reeves [1948]; reprint ed., Neptune City, NJ: Paganiniana, 1981.

McCorkle, Margit. *Johannes Brahms: Thematisch-Bibliographisches Werkverzeichnis*. Munich: Henle, 1984.

——. "The Role of Trial Performances for Brahms's Orchestral and Large Choral Works: Sources and Circumstances," in *Brahms Studies: Analytical and Historical Perspectives*, ed. George S. Bozarth. Oxford: Clarendon Press, 1990, 295–328.

Minor, Ryan. "Occasions and Nations in Brahms's *Fest- und Gedenksprüche*," *19th-Century Music* 29, 3 (Spring 2006): 261–88.

Musgrave, Michael. *A Brahms Reader*. New Haven and London: Yale University Press, 2000.

——. *The Music of Brahms*. 2nd ed. Oxford: Clarendon Press, 1994.

Pascall, Robert. "Brahms's *Missa Canonica* and its Recomposition in his Motet *Warum* op. 74, no. 1," in *Brahms 2: Biographical, Documentary and Analytical Studies*, ed. Michael Musgrave. Cambridge: Cambridge University Press, 1987, 111–36.

Platt, Heather. *Johannes Brahms: A Guide to Research*. New York and London: Routledge, 2003.

Quigley, Thomas. *Johannes Brahms: An Annotated Bibliography of the Literature through 1982*. Metuchen, NJ and London: Scarecrow, 1990.

——. *Johannes Brahms: An Annotated Bibliography of the Literature from 1982 to 1996, with an Appendix on Brahms and the Internet*. In collaboration with Mary I. Ingraham. Lanham, MD, and London: Scarecrow, 1998.

Stark, Lucien. *Brahms's Vocal Duets and Quartets with Piano*. Bloomington: Indiana University Press, 1998.

Webster, James. "The *Alto Rhapsody*: Psychology, Intertextuality, and Brahms's Artistic Development," in *Brahms Studies 3*, ed. David Brodbeck. Lincoln and London: University of Nebraska Press, 2001, 19–45.

France

13

CHORAL MUSIC AND MUSIC-MAKING IN FRANCE

Clair Rowden

CARDIFF UNIVERSITY

In the wake of the French Revolution, the government's banning of public religious practices deeply affected religious music-making and cathedral choirs in France. Yet the dissolution of many *maîtrises*—singing schools for church choirs—during that time did not bring choral singing and the composition of choral music to a halt. While France's choral tradition may not present as linear a development from the mid-eighteenth century onward as that perceived in the English and German traditions, the French made concerted efforts throughout the century to develop choral singing and repertories, from the revival of Palestrinian polyphony to the creation of a modern oratorio repertoire. Choral activity was drawn along many societal lines, most notably Catholic and Protestant, aristocratic and working class, and particular repertories became associated with different groups whose motivations varied from religious devotion, to self-improvement, and to the advancement of the nation's identity.

When Napoléon Bonaparte signed the Concordat with Pope Pius VII in 1801 that reinstated the official relationship between the French state and the Vatican, there was a return to religious music that drew on earlier traditions of the *Ancien régime*. Nearly seventy-five years earlier, Anne Danican Philidor's *Concert spirituel*, established as one of Europe's first concert series, had provided a new context for eighteenth-century sacred and instrumental music away from the court at Versailles, and by the end of the 1770s, it had become a platform for hearing oratorios.[1] In the 1780s, Jean-François Le Sueur (1760–1837) began to alter the oratorio genre, transforming it into a quasi-liturgical work intended to be heard during Mass.[2] Le Sueur's efforts for the chapel at the Tuileries Palace, where French sacred music enjoyed its most rapid rebirth after the Concordat, attempted to stimulate Romantic spiritual and artistic imaginations in the age of Chateaubriand's influential *Le Génie du Christianisme* (1802).[3] Religious texts began to drive compositional genres and processes in the same way that programmatic impetuses would inspire the orchestral music of Berlioz, Liszt, and others. Le Sueur's generation had been fed the anti-clerical aesthetic diet of Rousseau and Diderot, who argued for the supremacy of melody and for music as an imitative art, and against counterpoint as a cacophony of voices. As many French composers of the period lacked rigorous training as polyphonists, they rejected counterpoint in favor of dramatization in their religious choral music that aided the rechristianization process that took place after the Concordat.[4]

The revival of sacred music that began in 1801 came about in various ways. Le Sueur's appointment as director of the Tuileries Chapel in 1804 provided him an opportunity to write a considerable amount of sacred music—masses, motets, cantatas, and oratorios, the latter including four on the subjects of Old Testament women: *Ruth et Booz, Ruth et Noémi* (both written before 1811), *Debbora*, and *Rachel*.[5] Although his oratorios were significant at the time, they had little influence on the genre's further development in France, as new approaches paralleled characteristics found in opera instead. Indeed, the French oratorio evolved throughout the rest of the century as a dramatic genre with considerable variation in concept and design, as illustrated by such diverse genre categorizations as *églogue biblique, trilogie sacrée, mystère*, and *drame sacré*.

Sacred genres other than oratorios were slow to develop in the first half of the century due to the suppression of religious institutions and the general dechristianization of the society in the 1790s. After the Concordat, however, important changes began to take place, as once again there was a need to train church musicians and to compose music for the church. Throughout the period of Napoleon's Empire (to 1814) and the subsequent Restoration of the monarchy (1815–30), the Tuileries Chapel was the most important institution for sacred music. The chapel grew steadily in size during Le Sueur's directorship, and by 1814 it had nearly 100 instrumentalists and singers (men and boys only).[6] Two years later, Luigi Cherubini became Le Sueur's co-director; his choral works written for the chapel reflect the high quality of the music-making there.[7] His two requiems of 1816 and 1836, for example, show both his considerable attention to instrumentation, a characteristic also found in contemporary French opera, and the influence of Renaissance polyphony (more so than in other sacred works from the period).

While the music of the Tuileries Chapel exploited the large-scale genres of the oratorio and mass, Alexandre Choron argued in 1810 for a more austere form of religious music: less theatrical, *a cappella* music, comprising elements and techniques such as plainchant, *fauxbourdon*, counterpoint, and fugue.[8] Choron was indeed a champion of Renaissance polyphony and a key player in launching the early music revival in France, beginning with his work for the Ecole primaire de chant (known after 1825 as the Institution royale de musique religieuse).[9] Although the school achieved a certain success and by 1827 boasted a 200-strong mixed choir, it did not survive the financial cuts made by Louis-Philippe in the 1830s. Yet interest in *musique ancienne* itself had become unstoppable. François-Joseph Fétis started his *Concerts historiques* in 1832; the following year Dom Prosper Guéranger restored the Benedictine community at Solesmes Abbey (which had been closed since 1791) and spearheaded the movement for the revival of liturgical Gregorian chant.

In the post-Concordat period, ultramontane Catholicism—Catholics swearing direct allegiance to the Vatican and its traditions rather than to the French Gallic Church and bishops—grew in popularity. The Prince de la Moskova, Joseph Napoléon Ney (the son of Napoléon's Maréchal Ney), an ultramontane Catholic and member of the St. Cecilia Society of Rome, looked to regenerate Catholic church music in Europe by reviving works composed by the masters of the Sistine Chapel.[10] To accomplish this goal, he founded the Société des Concerts de musique vocale classique in 1843. (Louis Niedermeyer and Jean-Baptiste Weckerlin were Moskova's assistants; each would go on to promote early music on their own later in the century.) In its three-year existence, Moskova's elite, aristocratic choir concentrated on the *a cappella* or organ-accompanied repertoire of the sixteenth and seventeenth centuries, most notably works by Palestrina, Lassus, and Victoria, much of which Moskova himself published.[11] Ten years later, Niedermeyer established the École de musique religieuse (est. 1853)—later known as the École Niedermeyer—not only as an alternative to the Paris Conservatoire for the training of singers, organists, choir directors, and composers, but also as the natural successor to Choron's earlier efforts.[12]

It is important to note here that the revival of early music during the Second Empire was not a purely Parisian phenomenon, although little has been written to date on early music in the provinces. The cathedrals in Autun, Moulins, Langres, and Rouen, for example, stand out for their singing of Renaissance polyphony à la Palestrina and Gregorian chant. They sang this repertoire rather than the French grand motets and other sacred genres written for the church by Michel-Richarde de Lalande, André Campra and others from the Gallican tradition. Indeed, although there is evidence that the native Gallican repertoire was sung in some locales such as Carpentras and Aix-de-Province, it remained virtually forgotten or ignored by Niedermeyer (and later, the Schola Cantorum), as it had been by Choron, who vilified it openly.[13]

While most cathedral choirs were disbanded during the Revolutionary period of the 1790s, church musicians at the time found work in the emerging secular arena, especially with its most conspicuous musical manifestation, the grand Revolutionary festivals and pageants, where massed voices symbolizing the brotherhood of humanity or the will of "le peuple" would sing patriotic songs and choral hymns written to glorify the new Republic. Between 1789 and 1803, over 1,300 such works were written, many with such period-revealing titles as *Hymne à la fraternité* (Luigi Cherubini, 1794), *Hymne à l'Etre suprême* (François-Joseph Gossec, 1794), and *Hymne à l'Agriculture* (Xavier Lefèvre, 1796). Especially notable was Étienne Méhul's rousing *Le Chant du départ* (1794), a work that has remained popular in the canon of military hymns.[14] The ceremonial works of the Napoleonic Empire were built on the grandeur of Revolutionary and Republican spectacles, reflecting a new, yet familiar breed of pomp and circumstance. Influential in this regard were works such as Méhul's *Chant national du 25 messidor* (1800) and Le Sueur's *Chant du Ier Vendémiaire an IX* (1800), which involved as many as four separate choirs and three full orchestras, as well as small ensembles of trumpets and harps positioned around the performance space. Such works served as models for the kind of spatial experimentation that reappeared on the French music scene in the later 1830s and 1840s, the most obvious examples being the larger choral–orchestral works of Berlioz (see Chapters 4 and 15 in this volume). Due to the acoustics of performance venues such as the Invalides for these mammoth works, their compositional style tended to remain simple, with few modulations, little contrapuntal writing, and the deliberate use of basic harmonies with octave doublings.

As the 1820s came to a close, France witnessed the birth of one of the most significant concert societies in all of Europe: the Société des Concerts du Conservatoire (1828–1967). Much has been written about this influential ensemble from the perspective of its instrumental offerings, and the considerable impact it had both on the emerging school of French symphonists (from Berlioz on) and on the creation of an orchestral canon that shaped the modern concept of a subscription series.[15] But a less-known part of the society's history involved choral music. From its first concert in 1828, almost every concert offered by the society included at least one choral piece (and often more than one). Indeed, from the year of its founding to 1880, nearly 40% of its repertoire was choral, including masses, motets, choral–orchestral works (the fourth movement of Beethoven's Ninth Symphony figured most prominently), madrigals, partsongs, and selections from oratorios and opera—it was a body of music that represented the most consistently challenging works written for choral forces to be offered in Paris during the period.

During the July monarchy of Louis-Philippe (1830–48), funding for official and ceremonial music-making was cut as resources for the Chapelle royale, the Musique du Roi, the royal bands, and for cathedral choirs was withdrawn. Nevertheless, the Republican tradition of popular massed choirs found various outlets during this period, the most significant of which was the Orphéon, a movement started by Guillaume-Louis Bocquillon Wilhem in 1833. Wilhem had been experimenting with a new singing method based on the fundamentals of music notation and solfège since the mid-1810s.[16] By the early 1830s, this method was adopted widely for use in Parisian schools, providing a whole generation of the middle class with a musical education and a love of choral singing. Its success inspired Wilhem to establish the first Orphéon choir, initially created to give his former students an opportunity to keep singing after they finished their schooling. Within three years, he expanded his efforts by offering free evening classes, initially including women and girls, but from 1838 on for men only.[17]

As it developed in these early years, the Orphéon's purpose was to provide structured leisure activity for the working and artisan classes, encouraging "disciplined learning through art under the banner of brotherhood and in the . . . spirit of association."[18] From the first Orphéon concert in 1838, the movement quickly grew and eventually spread all over France; by the early 1860s, 3,000 provincial Orphéon choirs were active, involving about 140,000 singers. Wilhem's nine-volume collection of Orphéon repertoire illustrates the range of works performed by these groups. Not surprisingly, most were composed in a non-contrapuntal and homorhythmic style with slow-moving harmonies.[19] Such stylistic traits not only reflected the ability of many (perhaps even most) Orphéon choirs and sociétés chorales, but they were also the result of composers who knew that Orphéon events catered to huge numbers of performers often held (by necessity) in the open air or in large venues with dreadful acoustics.[20]

By the 1850s, the Orphéon movement was a fixture in Parisian life, engaging the efforts of some of the capital's most active composers, including Fromenthal Halévy, Adolphe Adam, Ambroise Thomas, and most notably Charles Gounod, who directed the Orphéon de Paris from 1852 to 1859.[21] Under Gounod's leadership, the reputation of the Orphéon grew in terms of its overall competence and the quality of its performances.[22] By the beginning of the 1860s, the movement was at its peak. Following the first "grande réunion des orphéonistes de France" in 1859, which brought together some 6,000 voices representing over 200 Orphéon and sociétés chorales from all over France, a Franco-British massed meeting took place in London (1860); 3,000 French singers traveled to the Crystal Palace specifically for the occasion. A second joint festival planned for 1861 turned out to be an all-French affair held in Paris, with 8,000 orphéonistes taking part in six days of competitions and concerts.[23] The Orphéon de Paris, now split into Left Bank and Right Bank divisions (the latter conducted by the young, dynamic Jules Pasdeloup until 1873), also participated in the *Expositions universelles* held in Paris in 1867 and 1878.[24]

By mid-century, the French dramatic oratorio began to emerge, moving out of its traditional sacred sphere and into the concert hall; nevertheless, attendance of such performances was increasingly perceived as a popular public act of devotion. Berlioz's triptych *L'Enfance du Christ*, for example, a work of true warmth and pastoral simplicity, and César Franck's *Ruth* both owe much to Le Sueur's sacred oratorios; yet unlike those older models, neither of these works was conceived as part of a liturgy.

An influential pedagogue of students who would make an important mark on French music later in the century (and early in the next), Franck is often under-represented in the history of French music. Yet his choral output of over forty masses, oratorios, motets, and smaller-scale cantatas is significant with regard to his contemporaries. His contribution to the genre of oratorio in particular provided models for those by Gounod and Saint-Saëns, which contrasted sharply with the later, more operatic oratorios of Massenet.[25] *Ruth* (1846), a biblical eclogue in three parts, uses no fugato or polyphonic writing, sticking instead to homophonic choral textures, sober melodic gestures, and instrumental timbres to provide simple pastoral shading. One noteworthy example of Franck's choral writing in this work is the "Chœur des moissonneurs" (Chorus of reapers) from the beginning of Part II, which featured dance rhythms and orientalist coloring, the latter characteristic perhaps a direct result of the success enjoyed by Félicien David's popular orientalesque ode-symphony *Le Désert* (1844).[26]

As the second half of the century took shape, middle-class choral societies, many modeled on the larger oratorio societies in England and Germany, began to replace the more elitist choral societies that had been dedicated almost exclusively to sixteenth-century music. Parisian ensembles such as Pasdeloup's Concerts populaires (1861–84, whose programs regularly featured choral works) and his shortlived Société des Oratorios (1868), Louis-Albert Bourgault-Ducoudray's Société Bourgault-Ducoudray (1869–74), and Charles Lamoureux's Société de l'harmonie sacrée (1873– 75) brought a wide variety of choral music before the public, including small pieces, oratorios, and other large-scale works. These ensembles provided audiences with an opportunity to hear repertoire that was more diverse than any from earlier in the century, such as extended excerpts from Bach's *St. Matthew Passion* and from selected cantatas; complete (or nearly so) performances of Handel's *Judas Maccabeus*, *Alexander's Feast*, *Acis and Galatea*, and *Messiah*; Part I from Mendelssohn's *Elijah*; Rossini's *Stabat Mater*; and five movements from Brahms's Requiem.[27] Despite this influx of oratorio-style ensembles, a number of societies emerged in the 1860s that continued to focus significant attention on sixteenth-century music. Most notable in this vein were Weckerlin's Société Sainte-Cécile (1864–68, reviving François Seghers's society of the same name from 1850–55), Charles Vervoitte's Société académique de musique sacrée (est. 1861; concerts from 1863–72), and Antonin Guillot de Sainbris's Société Chorale d'Amateurs (1866–1914).[28] The Société académique was the successor to Moskova's group from the 1840s, though its repertoire was much more diverse than its precedessor's had been, including a small number of works by Beethoven, Rossini, Mendelssohn, Bortniansky, and Cherubini. Like Moskova two decades earlier, Vervoitte drew his members from ultramontane Catholic circles, the clergy, the aristocracy and the elite artistic community, thereby cementing the perceived connection between *a cappella* polyphony and elitism.[29]

Following the French surrender to the Prussians in early 1871 and the ensuing civil uprising (the Paris Commune),[30] French musicians and composers formed the Société Nationale de musique for the creation and performance of a national repertoire of symphonic and chamber music to rival the Austro-Germanic symphonic tradition. Given that stated goal, it is perhaps surprising to note that the Société Nationale's concerts included a steady (albeit comparatively small) stream of choral music. These works were written exclusively by French composers until the 1890s when, under Vincent d'Indy's direction, the society's choral offerings contentiously included early music by both foreign and native composers.[31]

Additional efforts to promote the performance of choral music, especially large-scale choral-orchestral works from Bach and Handel as well as new works, included renewed attempts by Pasdeloup, who secured a government grant in 1878 specifically to program choral music; by Lamoureux, whose previously mentioned Société de l'harmonie sacrée was modeled after the similarly named England-based Sacred Harmonic Society directed by Michael Costa; and by a new ensemble, the Protestant, high society La Concordia founded in 1879 by the soprano Henriette Fuchs and her husband Edmond.[32] One of the most significant endeavors created at the time specifically to champion new music were Édouard Colonne's Easter concerts given in 1873. Modelled on Philidor's *Concert spirituel*, Colonne's Concert national and the chorus of the Société

Bourgault-Ducoudray premiered Franck's new "poème symphonie" (with chorus) *Rédemption*, followed the next day by Massenet's "drame sacré" *Marie-Magdeleine*.[33]

The chapters that follow focus on a handful of nineteenth-century French composers whose output included a healthy amount of choral music, and whose efforts in this arena reveal the diversity of musical styles that were heard in Paris's various sacred and secular spaces, from the straightforward partsongs of the Orphéon movement to the dramatic oratorios that emerged during the second half of the century. Out of the religious and ceremonial works of the Napoleonic Empire came sacred and liturgical compositions infused with non-sacred, descriptive, and sometimes openly dramatic elements that reflect their creators' training at the Paris Conservatoire. Because that training was specifically geared to composing opera,[34] the choral music of the period abounds in lyrical themes and dramatic musical gestures. Indeed, much like the performers themselves, many of whom worked in the various Parisian opera houses in addition to singing (or playing) in the thriving community of concert societies, this native repertoire had features that blurred the lines between music for the theatre, concert hall, and church, and created a pervasive dramatic style that is a distinctive feature of nineteenth-century French choral music. At the same time, the ultramontane influence of Choron, Niedermeyer, and their late-century successor, d'Indy (who founded the Schola Cantorum in 1894 with Alexandre Guilmant and Charles Bordes), promoted a more traditionally religious idiom through the revival of plainchant and Renaissance polyphony. As a result, they often appropriated the works of former masters from all over Europe to create a revisionist canon of French musical heritage in an increasingly nationalist political and social climate.[35] These developments, combined with the renewed interest in the choral works of Bach and Handel, the formation of large middle-class oratorio societies from the 1860s onwards, and the strength of the popular Orphéon movement, resulted in a vibrant century of choral music-making from which survives a rich tapestry of sacred and secular choral repertoires and idioms.

Notes

1 Howard E. Smither, *The History of the Oratorio*, vol. 3 (Chapel Hill, NC, and London: University of North Carolina Press, 1987), 541–42. According to Smither (vol. 4, 507), these works were typically 20 to 30 minutes in length.
2 Ibid., vol. 3, 579–81. For a discussion of the way the term "oratorio" was used in nineteenth-century France, see ibid., vol. 4, 507–10.
3 Ibid., vol. 4, 508, 513.
4 For a more detailed discussion of this phenomenon, see Jean Mongrédien, *La Musique en France des Lumières au Romantisme 1789–1830* (Paris: Flammarion, 1986), 167–74.
5 According to Smither, *The History of the Oratorio* (vol. 4, 519), Le Sueur's oratorio output stopped in 1815. For a detailed discussion of *Ruth et Booz* and *Ruth et Noémi*, see ibid., vol. 3, 582–601.
6 Ibid., vol. 3, 581. Women were specifically forbidden to perform in church.
7 Mongrédien referred to the Tuileries Chapel under Le Sueur and Cherubini as an institution that "shone with exceptional brilliance." See Mongrédien, "Le Sueur" in *Grove Music Online*. For details about Cherubini's music, see Chapter 14 in this volume.
8 Jean Mongrédien. *La Musique en France des Lumières au Romantisme 1789–1830* (Paris: Flammarion, 1986), 193.
9 Many of the ideas expressed in this paragraph are further developed in Clair Rowden, "French *a cappella* Chanson and its *fin-de-siècle* Regeneration" (M.A. diss., City University, London, 1996).
10 Katharine Ellis, *Interpreting the Musical Past: Early Music in Nineteenth-Century France* (Oxford: Oxford University Press, 2005), 31. No doubt Moskova was inspired by Choron concerts, which he had attended regularly.
11 *Recueil des morceaux de musique ancienne exécutés aux concerts de la Société de musique vocale, religieuse et classique* . . . 12 vols. (Paris: Pacini, 1843–?). For a description of the collection and a list of its contents, see Donna

M. Di Grazia, "Concert Societies in Paris and their Choral Repertoires *c.*1828–1880," 2 vols., (Ph.D. diss., Washington University in St. Louis, 1993), 191–96.

12 Di Grazia, "Concert Societies," 205.

13 Ellis, *Interpreting the Musical Past*, 74, 113–14. For more on the Palestrina revival, see also pp. 179–207.

14 For an overview of music and music-making in the Revolutionary period, see Ralph P. Locke, "Paris: Centre of Intellectual Ferment," *The Early Romantic Era. Between Revolutions: 1789 and 1848*, ed. Alexander Ringer (London: Macmillan Press, 1990), 32–83.

15 For the most recent account of the society's long history, see D. Kern Holoman, *The Société des Concerts du Conservatoire, 1828–1967* (Berkeley: University of California Press, 2004).

16 The information in the next three paragraphs relies heavily on Di Grazia, "Concert Societies," 93–163.

17 The term *orphéon* originated with Wilhem's classes and was initially reserved specifically for groups that used Wilhem's singing method. Other working-class choral societies that did not use the method typically called themselves *sociétés chorales*, not *orphéons*, and were referred to as such in the contemporary literature. Eventually, the term *orphéon* came to be used more generically to indicate any amateur French choir (or band in the latter part of the century) made up of working-class and artisan men.

18 Ellis, *Interpreting the Musical Past*, 224.

19 *Orphéon. Répertoire de musique vocale sans accompagnment à l'usage des jeunes élèves et des adultes; composé de pièces inédites et des morceaux choisis à voix seules ou à plusieurs parties.* Ed. G-L-B Wilhem. 9 vols. (Paris: Perrotin et Hachette, 1833–51). For a summary of this collection's contents, see Di Grazia, "Concert Societies," 413–14; for selected lists of works performed specifically by the Orphéon de Paris, see pp. 157–59; for scores of selected works frequently sung by ensembles involved in the movement, see pp. 528–680.

20 For an engraving of one such event, see Di Grazia, "Rejected Traditions: Ensemble Placement in Nineteenth-Century Paris," *19th-Century Music* 22, 2 (Fall 1998): 202.

21 Perhaps not surprisingly, the famous soldier's chorus from Act IV of Gounod's *Faust* was an Orphéon staple.

22 Ellis (*Interpreting the Musical Past*, 224, n. 55) notes that under Gounod's direction (as well as that of his successors Jules Pasdeloup and François Bazin) the Orphéon de Paris' repertoire was "unusually experienced in the 'classique.'"

23 Berlioz's only work written specifically for the Orphéon movement, *Le Temple universel* for double chorus, was planned for the 1861 Franco-British event, but he withdrew it after several rehearsals (and just one day before its scheduled performance); for details, see Di Grazia, "Concert Societies," 154–55.

24 François Bazin conducted the Left Bank division. The Orphéon de Paris had also appeared at the 1855 *Exposition universelle* during Gounod's tenure as director.

25 Jules Massenet was present at the revival of *Ruth*, which inspired his more operatic *Marie-Magdeleine*. (See my Chapter 16 on David, Gounod, and Massenet in this volume.)

26 Franck's oratorio was heavily revised (including a new "Chœur des moissonneurs") during the 1860s to strengthen the dramatic design and reinforce the orientalist style; it enjoyed great success at its revival in 1871. For further reading on Franck's *Ruth*, see Joël-Marie Fauquet, *César Franck* (Paris: Fayard, 1999), 170–86.

27 For more details on these ensembles and their repertoires to 1880, see Di Grazia, "Concert Societies," 267–97, and 328–55.

28 All three ensembles presented both *ancienne* and *contemporaine* repertoire. See Di Grazia, "Concert Societies," 220–40, 297–314, and 314–27 for more information on these societies and their specific repertoires.

29 Ellis, *Interpreting the Musical Past*, 63–64.

30 For further reading on music making during this period, see Delphine Mordey, "Music in Paris, 1870–1871" (Ph.D. diss., University of Cambridge, 2006).

31 D'Indy took over running the Société Nationale de musique in 1886, ousting Saint-Saëns as president, who objected to the increasing inclusion of foreign music on the society's programs. Repertoire early on included works by Franck, Massenet, Saint-Saëns, Dubois, Marie de Grandval (née de Reiset), Fauré, and others. For more information on the choral repertoire of the Société Nationale prior to 1880, see Di Grazia, "Concert Societies," 361–66; see also Michael Strasser, "*Ars Gallica*: The Société Nationale de musique and its Role in French Musical Life, 1871–1891" (Ph.D. diss., University of Illinois, Urbana-Champaign, 1998).

32 Ellis, *Interpreting the Musical Past*, 98, 232

33 For more information on the premieres of these two works, see Fauquet, *César Franck*, 415–47. Massenet's more operatic oratorio appealed immediately to the concert audience and completely overshadowed Franck's work, which was given a dreadful performance. *Rédemption* only achieved success in a remodeled version performed posthumously in 1896.

34 Fugue, choral, and three-solo-voiced cantata writing were part of the coveted annual Prix de Rome competition from 1803, but the acquisition of these techniques was seen as preparatory to the writing of opera—the ultimate goal and mark of distinction and prosperity for French composers—rather than ends in themselves. See David Grayson, "Debussy on stage," in *The Cambridge Companion to Debussy*, ed. Simon Tresize (Cambridge: Cambridge University Press, 2002), 61–83. Debussy's *La Damoiselle élue* (1887–8, premiered 1893), his "little oratorio in a mystic, slightly pagan vein" (Grayson, "Debussy on stage," 70), was his third Prix de Rome *envoi* from the Villa Medici, and uses a female chorus as narrator, syllabically declaiming the text of Gabriel Sarrazin's translation of Dante Gabrieli Rossetti's poem, combined with typically (early) Debussyian harmonies and orchestral sound world.
35 Catrina Flint de Médicis explores the discourses linking the early music revival and nationalism, both associated with the Schola Cantorum and d'Indy, himself an aristocrat with far-right political leanings, in her article "Nationalism and Early Music at the French *Fin-de-Siècle*: Three Case Studies," *Nineteenth-Century Music Review* 1, 2 (2004): 43–66. For more on the Schola generally, see Ellis, *Interpreting the Musical Past*, 100, 105–11.

Selected Bibliography

Cooper, Jeffrey. *The Rise of Instrumental Music and Concert Societies in Paris, 1828–1871*. Ann Arbor, Michigan: UMI Research Press, 1983.

Di Grazia, Donna M. "Concert Societies in Paris and their Choral Repertories, *c.*1828–1880." Ph.D. diss., Washington University in St. Louis, 1993.

D'Indy, Vincent. *César Franck*. Paris: F. Alcan, 1906.

Ellis, Katharine. *Interpreting the Musical Past: Early Music in Nineteenth-Century France*. New York & Oxford: Oxford University Press, 2005.

Fauquet, Joël-Marie. *César Franck*. Paris: Fayard, 1999.

Flint de Médicis, Catrina. "Nationalism and Early Music at the French *Fin-de-Siècle*: Three Case Studies, *Nineteenth-Century Music Review* 1, 2 (2004): 43–66.

Fulcher, Jane. *French Cultural Politics & Music: From the Dreyfus Affair to the First World War*. New York & Oxford: Oxford University Press, 1999.

Holoman, D. Kern. *Société des Concerts du Conservatoire 1828–1967*. Berkeley & London: University of California Press, 2004.

Kelly, Barbara L., ed. *French Music, Culture, and National Identity, 1870–1939*. University of Rochester Press, 2008.

Kelly, Barbara L. and Murphy, Kerry, eds. *Berlioz and Debussy: Sources, Contexts and Legacies. Essays in Honour of François Lesure*. Aldershot, England: Ashgate, 2007.

Langham Smith, Richard and Potter, Caroline, eds. *French Music Since Berlioz*. Aldershot, England: Ashgate, 2006.

Locke, Ralph. "Paris: Centre of Intellectual Ferment," in *Man and Music: The Early Romantic Era. Between Revolutions: 1789 and 1848*, ed. Alexander Ringer. London: Macmillan Press, 1990, 32–83.

Mongrédien, Jean. *La Musique en France des Lumières au Romantisme 1789–1830*. Paris: Flammarion, 1986.

Mordey, Delphine. "Music in Paris, 1870–1871." Ph.D. diss., University of Cambridge, 2006.

Rowden, Clair. "French *a cappella* Chanson and its fin-de-siècle Regeneration." M.A. thesis, City University, London, 1996.

Smither, Howard E. *A History of the Oratorio*, vols. 3 and 4. Chapel Hill, NC: University of North Carolina Press, 1987 and 2000.

Strasser, Michael. "Ars Gallica: The Société Nationale and its role in French Musical Life 1871–1891." Ph.D. diss. University of Illinois, Urbana-Champaign, 1998

———. "The Société Nationale and Its Adversaries: The Musical Politics of *L'Invasion germanique* in the 1870s," *19th-Century Music* 24, 3 (Spring 2001): 225–51.

Thomson, Andrew. *Vincent d'Indy and His World*. Oxford: Clarendon Press, 1996.

Trezise, Simon, ed. *The Cambridge Companion to Debussy*. Cambridge: Cambridge University Press, 2002.

14

LUIGI CHERUBINI AND AUGUSTA HOLMÈS

Mark Seto

Connecticut College

Although Augusta Holmès (1847–1903) was born five years after the death of Luigi Cherubini (1760–1842), their careers were parallel in several respects. The two enjoyed considerable renown in their lifetimes and were esteemed by their peers: Beethoven called Cherubini the greatest living composer, and Holmès was championed by Saint-Saëns as France's muse. Both had international credentials and were French by choice. A native of Florence, Cherubini moved to Paris in the 1780s, took French citizenship, and led the Paris Conservatoire from 1822 until his death. Holmès, born in Paris of Irish parentage, became naturalized French and added the accent to her name as a young adult. In their choral music, they responded to the political exigencies of the day: the Revolution and the Restoration for Cherubini, nationalist movements and a renewed interest in the Revolutionary era for Holmès. Their reputations suffered posthumously, but for different reasons. Cherubini did not fit neatly into a national school or a historiographic periodization. Much of Holmès's music, despite its vitality and beauty, was too closely bound to the cultural milieu of the Third Republic to have lasting appeal. Yet both composers left a profound impression on their contemporaries, and their choral works shed revealing light on musical life in nineteenth-century France.

Luigi Cherubini

Observers have traditionally divided Cherubini's career into two periods, the first focused on opera, the second on sacred music, but he wrote choral music throughout his lifetime.[1] His earliest compositions include three Kyrie and Gloria settings for solo voices, chorus, and orchestra (1773, 1774, 1775) and the cantata *La pubblica felicità* (1774), performed at the Florence Cathedral in honor of Duke Leopold of Tuscany. From 1778 to 1781 he apprenticed with Giuseppi Sarti, to whom Cherubini attributed much of his knowledge about counterpoint and dramatic composition. During this period he composed about twenty unaccompanied antiphons and litanies in the style of Palestrina. Although written "for my study," Cherubini recopied his antiphon *Petrus Apostolus* (1778), based on the Gregorian plainchant fragment of the same name, in 1839—a testament to the esteem in which he held this early work.[2] He also composed the antiphonal motet *Nemo gaudeat* (1781) for double chorus and two organs, and two exemplars of restrained architectonic beauty, the madrigals *Udite, lagrimosi spirti* and *Ninfa crudel* (1783).

Cherubini devoted most of his attention to secular music for the next two decades. One of his earliest works for Paris was the cantata *Amphion* (1786) for tenor soloist, chorus, and orchestra, the first of several pieces he wrote for the Loge Olympique. The subject befits Cherubini's association with the masonic lodge; the title character, along with his twin brother Zethus, built the walls of Thebes through the magical sounds of his lyre, which Cherubini represents with extended passages of violin *pizzicati*. Cherubini would later rework material from this cantata in his overture to *Anacréon, ou l'amour fugitif* (1803).

In the 1790s, Cherubini was appointed a teaching inspector of the newly formed Conservatoire Nationale de Musique, along with Gossec, Méhul, Grétry, and Le Sueur. In this capacity he was responsible for producing choral music for national festivals and commemorations, from the state funeral of General Hoche[3] (*Hymne et marche funèbre*, 1797) to the opening of a saltpeter mine (*Le Salpêtre républicain*, 1794). Some of these settings were simple enough to be performed by large crowds of amateurs. The *Hymne pour la fête de la reconnaissance* (10 Prairial 1799) and *Hymne pour la fête de la jeunesse* (10 Germinal 1799), for example, are syllabic, diatonic songs that alternate strophic verses sung by a soloist or a small choir with a unison refrain for the whole chorus.[4] Others, like the *Hymne à la victoire* for four-part chorus and band (1796), feature greater textural variety and unusual instruments like the tuba curva.[5]

Cherubini returned to sacred composition in 1806, when he completed the monumental eight-part *Credo* for two *a cappella* choruses.[6] He published and analyzed the concluding fugue, a marvel of polyphonic craft, in his *Cours de contrepoint et de fugue* (1835).[7] Around the time he finished the *Credo*, Cherubini fell into a deep depression—a condition that afflicted him at intervals throughout his life—and composed little for the next two years. In 1808, he took an extended stay at the castle of the Prince of Chimay along the Franco-Belgian border, where he indulged in long walks and cultivated an interest in botany. When locals asked if he would provide music for a St. Cecilia's day service, Cherubini first declined, but then produced a Kyrie and Gloria for three-part chorus (STB) and orchestra for the occasion. His creativity reawakened, Cherubini completed the Mass (in F major, known as the "Mass of Chimay") upon returning to Paris in 1809. The influential critic François-Joseph Fétis, recalling the first complete performance of the work that March, marveled at Cherubini's genius in combining "the severe beauties of fugue and counterpoint with the expression of dramatic character and richness of orchestral effects."[8]

Thus began a remarkable and fruitful period of choral writing. In hopes of becoming Haydn's successor at the Esterházy court, Cherubini dedicated his first *Litanie della Vergine* (1810) and the *Messe solennelle* in D minor (1811) to Prince Nikolaus II. The D-minor Mass is much more expansive and boldly conceived than Cherubini's later essays in the genre, which were intended for liturgical use. The work rivals Beethoven's *Missa solemnis* in scope; the Gloria alone, cast in five sections that alternate between chorus and soloists, requires half an hour to perform. Cherubini includes dramatic touches throughout the piece. In the "Crucifixus," the four-part chorus, accompanied by a sinuous violin line and rhythmic orchestral punctuations, intones the text on a repeated E for fifty-one measures—an arresting evocation of stillness and death (see Example 14.1).

Cherubini's output in 1814–15 is a testament to tumultuous political events: he wrote music for the Napoleonic Garde nationale, brass works for the Prussian regiment, and a cantata and several shorter works in honor of the returning Bourbon monarch, Louis XVIII. Upon Louis's definitive return to the throne in July 1815 following the Hundred Days of Napoleon, Cherubini became *Surintendant de la musique* at the Royal Chapel, a position he shared with Le Sueur. During his tenure, he composed six masses, including one commissioned for the coronation of Louis XVIII (which never took place); a second set of *Litanies de la Vierge* (1820); a dozen choral motets, most with orchestral accompaniment; and numerous shorter works. Many of these pieces, including all of Cherubini's complete Mass settings, have been published in modern editions; thanks to the efforts of Riccardo Muti and other conductors, this repertoire has rightly begun to find a wider audience in recent decades.

EXAMPLE 14.1 Cherubini, D-minor Mass, Et incarnatus, mm. 78–82.

The crowning achievements of Cherubini's choral output are his two settings of the Requiem Mass. He wrote the four-voice Requiem in C minor (1817) for a memorial service commemorating the death of Louis XVI—a testament to Cherubini's political adaptability, since he had conducted music for a 1796 celebration of the monarch's execution.[9] The work was one of the most popular requiems of nineteenth century: Berlioz considered it the composer's "masterpiece" because of its wealth of ideas and stylistic grandeur, and it was performed at the funerals of

Beethoven, Méhul, and many luminaries.[10] Cherubini includes the Graduale and Pie Jesu, relative rarities, in both of his settings. In contrast to his usual practice, he omits vocal soloists.

Cherubini establishes a somber mood in the C-minor Requiem by scoring the Introitus and Kyrie for low instruments only: bassoons, horns, muted timpani (*timbales voilées*), and strings without violins. The string texture, with divided violas, divided celli, and independent double basses, recalls his heartfelt *Chant sur la mort de Haydn* (inspired by a false report of Haydn's death in 1805) and foreshadows the similarly dark scoring that characterizes the opening of Brahms's *Ein deutsches Requiem*. The austere choral writing in these sections, alternating between homophony and discreet imitation, rarely ventures above *pianissimo*. Cherubini reserves the full ensemble for the Dies irae, which opens with a stentorian brass fanfare on octave Gs followed by a *fortissimo* tam-tam stroke. (While the use of the tam-tam had precedents in Gossec's *Marche lugubre* (1790) and in Cherubini's own Revolutionary-era pieces, its appearance in a liturgical context was unusual and creates a thrilling effect.[11]) For the most part, however, Cherubini eschews the theatricality that one customarily finds in Dies irae settings in favor of subtle illumination of the text. In the ethereal C-major prayer "Salva me," for example, he offers a respite from the images of the Last Judgment, and he intones the "Lacrimosa" in poignant, dissonant homophony.

Cherubini concedes to musical tradition in the Offertorium, when he sets the passage "Quam olim Abrahae" in a boisterous, elaborate triple fugue. The Pie Jesu presents an unsettling contrast between gestural restraint and plaintive, unpredictable chromaticism; the chorus's final statement of "Pie Jesu," for example, moves from a dominant pedal to an unexpected IV sonority (see Example 14.2).

EXAMPLE 14.2 Cherubini, C-minor Requiem, Pie Jesu, mm. 47–54.

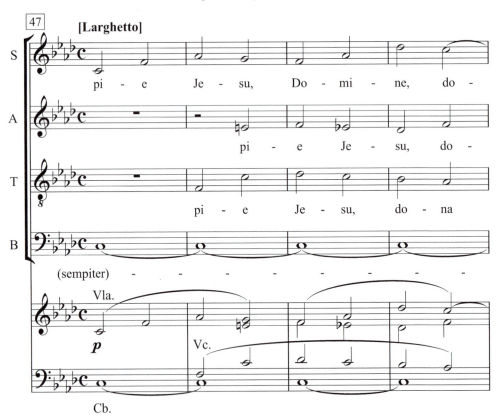

EXAMPLE 14.2 Cherubini, C-minor Requiem, Pie Jesu, mm. 47–54.

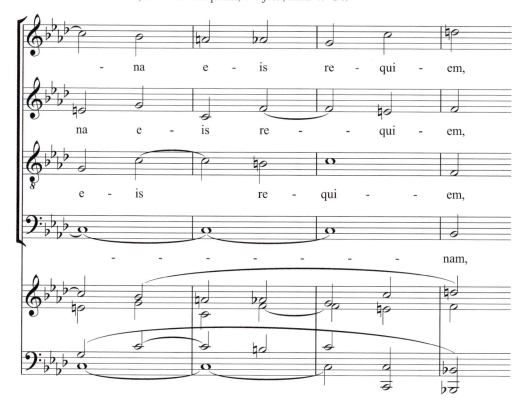

Cherubini saves the most striking moment in the work for the end. Against an orchestral ostinato derived from the opening of the Agnus Dei, the chorus exchanges monotone recitations of the closing lines ("Requiem aeternam dona eis, Domine, et lux perpetua luceat eis") in a slow, haunting *diminuendo* that caused Berlioz to marvel, "[it] surpasses everything that has been attempted in this genre."[12]

Cherubini composed the Requiem in D minor (1836), his last major choral work, under very different circumstances. After Louis-Philippe dissolved the Royal Chapel in 1830, the composer devoted most of his energy to directing the Conservatoire. Without a regular outlet for composition, his creativity seemed to have flagged and he produced little besides the unsuccessful opera *Ali-Baba* (1833). He wrote this second requiem, for men's voices and orchestra, for use at his own funeral: the archbishop of Paris had opposed the performance of the earlier C-minor Requiem at the funeral of Cherubini's colleague François-Adrien Boieldieu (1775–1834) because it included women's voices.

The D-minor Requiem is a more introspective work than its predecessor. The three-part male chorus gives the music an intense tone color, made more so by the high tessitura of the first tenor

EXAMPLE 14.3a Gregorian Requiem Mass, opening phrase.

EXAMPLE 14.3b Cherubini, D-minor Requiem, Introitus and Kyrie, mm. 12–22.

EXAMPLE 14.4 Cherubini, D-minor Requiem, Dies irae, mm. 145–51.

part. Compared to the C-minor Requiem, Cherubini includes more *a cappella* writing here, notably in the harmonically adventurous Graduale and the Pie Jesu, and the vocal parts are more chromatic, melismatic, and sinuous. These qualities are evident in the first vocal entrance, whose upper neighbor motion on "Requiem" and stepwise ascent on "aeternam" echo the beginning of the Gregorian Requiem Mass (see Example 14.3). The adjoining Kyrie begins in B-flat major and the last choral phrase cadences on a D-major chord, but the orchestral postlude reverts to minor—a foretaste of the work's despondent ending. The Dies irae is looser in structure than its counterpart in the C-minor Requiem, with numerous changes in tempo, meter, and key. At the "Recordare," Cherubini sets the lower two voices in canon while the first tenors sing in free counterpoint (see Example 14.4).[13] The movement ends with an uplifting "Pie Jesu" in D major, but again the orchestra negates the major resolution. The Offertorium and Sanctus, in F major and B-flat major, respectively, provide the longest stretch of sunny, diatonic harmonies. The conclusion of the piece rivals that of his C-minor Requiem for dramatic effect. For eighteen bars, the singers quietly intone an open fifth on D and A, accompanied by funereal timpani rolls and two-note sighing figures in the strings. On the last statement of "luceat eis," the first tenors surge up to a high A and the chorus cadences in D major, suggesting a glimmer of light for the deceased. But the sighing figures return and the orchestra collapses for the third time in minor. The final D-minor chords, sparse and *pianissississimo*, are a singularly pessimistic expression of grief by a man whose reputed last words were "I do not want to die."[14]

Augusta Holmès

Although Holmès is best remembered today for a handful of songs and symphonic pieces, some of her greatest music appears in her large-scale works for chorus and orchestra. These choral compositions—the cornerstones of Holmès's nineteenth-century reputation—were a vital part of the soundscape of Third Republic France and were performed by some of the most important musical organizations in Paris. The Société Nationale de musique, a leading forum for French composers, presented her psalm *In exitu Israel* in 1872. The Société Philharmonique de Paris repeated the work the following year; two years later they performed an excerpt from *Astarté*, a *poème musical* for soloists, choir, and orchestra.[15] Holmès wrote her first major work, *Lutèce*, for the inaugural City of Paris competition in 1878. Entrants for the biennial prize were required to submit a "symphony with soloists and chorus" on a subject that would take advantage of "the most complete developments of their art" and "address feelings of the highest order."[16] Théodore Dubois and Benjamin Godard tied for first prize after a series of votes failed to produce a single winner. Holmès placed second.

A *symphonie dramatique* in the tradition of Berlioz's *Roméo et Juliette*, *Lutèce* is cast in three parts and scored for four soloists, narrator, divided SATB chorus, children's chorus, and large orchestra. As with almost all of her vocal compositions, Holmès wrote the text. Lutetia, the Gallic forerunner of modern Paris, is under attack and falls to the Romans—a scenario that alludes to the recent siege of Paris and the country's defeat in the Franco-Prussian War (1870–71).[17] The piece exhibits a duality between sensual lyricism (in the love duet between two young Gauls) and patriotic virility; as many critics have noted, this juxtaposition also characterizes many of Holmès's later works.[18]

Although *Lutèce* sometimes employs hackneyed gestures to depict battle and strife—chromatic runs, diminished and augmented chords, and extended sequences—the piece foreshadows Holmès's mature style. Reflecting her Wagnerian sympathies, she employs a system of leitmotives, including a pungent figure with clashing minor and augmented seconds that underscores the image of Gaul "sous le pied lourd de l'étranger" ("under the heavy foot of the foreigner"). The vocal writing is demanding: the chorus sings for extended periods near the top of its range. In the final chorale, Holmès calls for the tenor section to sing a high B, first softly (she indicates "voix de tête"), then *fortissimo*. The parts for the children's chorus include rapid chromaticism and challenging leaps, with a range spanning nearly two octaves.

Holmès's next large-scale composition, *Les Argonautes* (1880), features sharply gendered choral writing. A dramatic symphony in four parts, the work recounts Jason's quest for the Golden Fleece. In addition to five vocal soloists and orchestra, Holmès employs a mixed chorus to portray towns-people and the guardians of the Fleece, a men's chorus of Argonauts, and a women's chorus that represents the Sirens and Medea's attendants. In Part One, Jason sings of his desire for glory, encouraged by his men and the people of Iolcos. At a climactic moment, Holmès builds excitement by ascending through a series of chromatic mediants (F major, A-flat major, B major, and D major) while using texture to differentiate the characters. The townspeople urge the Argonauts on in imitative polyphony while the sailors sing in unison, "Rompez les cordages! Arrachez l'ancre! En mer!" ("Sever the ropes! Pull up the anchor! To sea!"). Above both choirs, Jason (a solo tenor) proclaims his desire for the Fleece (see Example 14.5).

The second section, "Le Voyage," depicts the Argonauts' struggle with the rough sea and the Sirens' attempt to seduce them. The Sirens sing in lyrical stepwise motion, a sharp contrast to the rhythmic, disjunct melodies of the Argonauts. Part Three opens with a "danse magique" by Medea's attendants. As they perform the rites of Hecate (the goddess of witchcraft), the contraltos sing in sinuous, chromatic lines marked by exotic altered scale degrees (see Example 14.6). Medea's first solo entrance, in contrast, features assertive declamation, sharp dotted rhythms, and angular leaps; as Jann Pasler observes, this aggressive music suggests that Medea and Jason are similar in character.[19] Medea's initial suspicion of Jason turns to desire, and she offers to betray her people to help Jason in his quest. Holmès changes the myth in the concluding section. Rather than escaping with Medea and the Golden Fleece, Jason must choose between love and renown. Spurning Medea, he declares, "Je n'aime que la gloire! . . . Je vaincrai l'amour de la femme!" ("I love only glory! . . . I will conquer woman's love!")

When Holmès entered *Les Argonautes* in the 1880 City of Paris competition, the work impressed everyone on the jury. Many were surprised when it only placed second, but Holmès was able to parlay the ensuing "scandal" into performances at Jules Pasdeloup's Concerts populaires and the Société des Concerts du Conservatoire.[20] Critics were generous in their praise. Charles Darcours of *Le Figaro* claimed it was "definitely one of the most original and most interesting compositions produced in several years."[21] Several reviewers were struck by Jason's renunciation of love, and Saint-Saëns drew attention to Holmès's gender in his comments on this scene. Invoking Wagner, he noted that to obtain the Golden Fleece, "as to seize the *Rhinegold*, one must damn love. . . . it has been almost a rule in poetic works to sacrifice everything for love. It is peculiar that a woman has done the opposite."[22]

Holmès returned to nationalistic subjects in her next two choral works, *Ludus pro patria* (1888) and the *Ode triomphale* (1889). *Ludus pro patria* was inspired by a mural painting of the same name by Puvis de Chavannes depicting games for the glorification of the fatherland. Holmès's subtitle, "ode-symphonie pour chœurs et orchestre avec récit en vers," suggests a kinship with Félicien David's pioneering essay in the genre, *Le Désert* (1844).[23] The Société des Concerts, the most prestigious and conservative orchestra in Paris, gave the premiere of *Ludus*—the first time a woman was so honored; celebrated actor Jean Mounet-Sully recited the poetry.

Like many of Holmès's compositions, *Ludus* features striking contrasts between masculine and feminine idioms. Compared to *Lutèce* and *Les Argonautes*, however, the choral writing is simpler, with a greater emphasis on homophonic textures, syllabic declamation, and diatonicism. In the first section, a lively G-major Allegro in 2/4 time, the chorus proclaims in rapid-fire anapests: "Écoutez!

EXAMPLE 14.5 Holmès, *Les Argonautes*, part I (vocal score, p. 58).

EXAMPLE 14.5 continued.

EXAMPLE 14.5   continued.

EXAMPLE 14.5 continued.

EXAMPLE 14.6   Holmès, *Les Argonautes*, part III (vocal score, p. 104).

une voix a parlé de patrie et de gloire et d'amour!" ("Listen! a voice has spoken of country, glory, and love!") Holmès reinforces the patriotic effect through use of a choral unison, with many voices expressing one sentiment. While *Ludus* contains moments of great beauty—notably the charming orchestral interlude "La Nuit et l'amour"—on the whole the piece is less noteworthy than the composer's other major works.[24]

Holmès's most high-profile performances took place the following year, when she composed the *Ode triomphale en l'honneur du centenaire de 1789* for the 1889 Paris *Exposition universelle*. The Commission des fêtes du centenaire had sponsored a competition for a cantata to celebrate the Revolution. After the committee rejected the initial group of submissions as unsatisfactory, they accepted Holmès's proposal for a staged, hour-and-a-half long spectacle for 300 instrumentalists and 900 singers. The committee allocated an astonishing 300,000 francs for the production. Holmès wrote the text and music, designed the sets and costumes, and helped with the casting. Three free performances were given on September 11, 12, and 14, all to capacity crowds in the 22,500-seat Palais de l'Industrie; two paying performances were added to benefit charity.

The *Ode triomphale* shares much in common with the musical spectacles of the Revolutionary era. Annegret Fauser and Jann Pasler have linked the piece to works by François-Joseph Gossec, notably his *Offrande à la Liberté* (a dramatization of the *Marseillaise*, 1792) and *Le Triomphe de la République* (1793).[25] The *Ode* begins with a fanfare played by four trumpets positioned through the hall, followed by a triumphal march for the orchestra in D major. Ten different choral groups, representing wine growers, soldiers, workers, and the like, enter the stage, each one preceded by a mute allegorical figure. The singers for the premiere, drawn from Parisian schools and amateur choruses, performed their parts from memory.[26] Holmès's vocal writing is almost exclusively homophonic—perhaps a concession to the singers' limited abilities and the poor acoustics of the Palais. Composer and Wagnerian acolyte Victorin Joncières called the music "sagely written," but preferred the more adventurous choral writing in *Lutèce*, *Les Argonautes*, and *Ludus pro patria*.[27] Once each chorus has sung, the hall darkens and the orchestra intones a funeral march. A blond woman in a black veil and chains, personifying the country's grief, slowly proceeds to a central altar. Another figure representing the Republic "appears in a flash of light" (une clarté fulgurante). La République, portrayed at the premiere by the contralto soloist Mathilde Romi, encourages her people to take heart. Ripping off her veil and chains, the figure in mourning emerges in the three French colors, and the chorus proclaims the Republic's glory in a valedictory chorale.

The stirring patriotism of the *Ode* inspired critics to champion Holmès as the country's "muse" and a musical "Marianne," the allegorical symbol of the Republic.[28] Holmès also fostered an image as an advocate of other nations' causes through her non-choral works: her symphonic poem *Irlande* (1882) was written during a time of political upheaval in her ancestral country, and *Pologne* (1883) was inspired by Tony Robert-Fleury's painting of the 1861 Warsaw Massacres.[29] Thus when the philologist and poet Angelo de Gubernatis organized a festival in Florence to celebrate Italian women and commemorate the 600th anniversary of the death of Dante's Beatrice, Holmès was a natural choice to write the music.[30] Her *Hymne à la paix* (*Inno alla pace in onore della Beatrice di Dante*) for soloists, orchestra, and an SATB chorus of 300 premiered at the Politeama ampitheater in May 1890. The crowd of 4,000 spectators cheered Holmès for eighteen curtain calls. It was her greatest triumph, and she marveled to a friend that a queen would not have been received better.[31]

Although Holmès was best known in her lifetime as a composer of ambitious, patriotic works—a reputation she herself did much to foster—her shorter choral pieces and solo songs reveal a more intimate musical idiom. *Au Pays bleu* (begun *c.*1888 and premiered in 1891), a symphonic suite for orchestra and voices, presents a picturesque journey through Italy. In the second movement, "En mer," a fisherman sings from offstage and the chorus hums discreetly, imitating the movement of waves. *La Vision de la reine* (1895), a lovely scene for women's chorus, piano, harp, and cello, is a gentle benediction for the newborn child of a queen. The chorus, representing heavenly voices, offers its blessings, and then a succession of solo voices imparts bits of wisdom. The mood turns martial for a brief moment as one of the voices urges the child, "Plus que tout, aime la Patrie!" but quickly reverts to dreamy lyricism.[32] *Fleur de Néflier* (1901), one of Holmès's final works, seems disarming in its simplicity: the tenor soloist, echoed by a two-part men's chorus with piano accompaniment, describes his beloved as "plus douce que la fleur du néflier" (sweeter than the flower of the medlar tree). But the charming setting belies a poignant, possibly autobiographical subtext. The medlar fruit, which must decay before being eaten, symbolized premature destitution in Elizabethan and Jacobean literature. Holmès may well have been making an ironic commentary on her own fate: her health and reputation declined precipitously after the failure of her opera *La Montagne noire* at the Paris Opéra in 1895, and she spent her final years in relative obscurity. Her final choral work is an ambiguous coda to a career dominated by bold, unambiguous gestures.

Notes

1 See, for example, Edward Bellasis, *Cherubini: Memorials Illustrative of his Life and Work* (London, 1874; revised edition, Birmingham: Cornish Brothers Limited, 1912); and Basil Deane, *Cherubini* (London: Oxford University Press, 1965). More recent studies have focused on one genre. See Michael Fend, *Cherubinis Pariser Opern (1788–1803)* (Stuttgart: Franz Steiner Verlag, 2007); Christine Siegert, *Cherubini in Florenz: Zur Funktion der Opera in der toskanischen Gesellschaft des späten 18. Jahrhunderts* (Laaber: Laaber-Verlag, 2008); and Oliver Schwarz-Roosmann, *Luigi Cherubini und seine Kirchenmusik* (Köln: Verlag Christoph Dohr, 2006).

2 Pietro Spada, preface to Luigi Cherubini, *Antifona sul canto fermo 8° tono (1778)* (Rome: Boccaccini & Spada Editori, 1978). The copying of older works was a common pedagogical tool during this time, and a practice that Cherubini endorsed in his *Cours de contrepoint et de fugue* (1835): "I would induce the pupil who aims at becoming a composer, to read, and even to copy out, with attention, and with reflection, as much as he can of the works of the classical composers particularly, and occasionally those of inferior composers, with the view of learning from the former what mode he is to pursue for composing well, and from the latter, in what way he may avoid the contrary." Published in English as *A Treatise on Counterpoint and Fugue* (Melville, NY: Belwin Mills, n.d.), 7.

3 Lazare Hoche (1768–97) was a general of the Revolutionary army who briefly served as the French minister of war.

4 Much of this repertoire was reconstructed and first published in the late nineteenth century. See, for example, Constant Pierre, *Musique exécutée aux fêtes nationales de la Révolution française* (Paris: Alphonse Leduc, 1893). For a discussion of music in Revolutionary festivals and the political utility of the Conservatoire, see Jann Pasler, *Composing the Citizen: Music as Public Utility in Third Republic France* (Berkeley and Los Angeles: University of California Press, 2009), 107–34 and 141–49. See also David Charlton, "Revolutionary Hymn," in *The New Grove Dictionary of Music and Musicians*, 2nd ed., ed. Stanley Sadie (New York: Grove, 2001), www.oxfordmusiconline.com (accessed October 21, 2010).

5 The tuba curva was a wind instrument created during the French Revolution for use in outdoor music. Its curved "G" shape was inspired by brass instruments from Roman antiquity.

6 In his autograph catalogue, Cherubini noted that he began the work in Italy in 1778–79 during his studies with Sarti. See Cornelia Schröder, "Chronologisches Verzeichnis der Werke Luigi Cherubinis unter Kennzeichnung der in der Musikabteilung der Berliner Staatsbibliothek erhaltenen Handschriften," *Beiträge zur Musikwissenschaft* 3, 2 (1961), 41.

7 *A Treatise on Counterpoint and Fugue*, 96–115. Cherubini also includes an analysis of an eight-part fugue by Sarti, 116–23. A new edition of the *Credo*, edited by Oliver Schwarz-Roosmann, has been published by Carus (Stuttgart, 2010).

8 "La réunion des beautés sévères de la fugue et du contrepoint avec l'expression d'un caractère dramatique, et la richesse des effets d'instrumentation, met ici le génie de Cherubini hors de pair." Fétis, *Biographie universelle des musiciens*, 2nd ed. (Paris: Librairie de Firmin Didot Frères, 1867), vol. 2, 269.

9 Pierre, "Les anniversaires du 21 janvier sous la Révolution," *L'Art musical* 33 (1894): 42, referenced in Michael Fend, "Luigi Cherubini," in *The New Grove Dictionary of Music and Musicians*.

10 Hector Berlioz, "Berichte aus Paris: Cherubini," *Neue Zeitschrift für Musik* 16, 31 (15 April 1842): 123.

11 Pierre, "Musique exécutée aux fêtes nationales de la Révolution française," 45. Berlioz's Requiem employs tam-tam strokes with similar effect.

12 "Das *Agnus* mit seinem Decrescendo überflügelt alles, was man in dieser Gattung versucht." Berlioz, "Berichte aus Paris: Cherubini," 123.

13 According to Oliver Schwarz-Roosmann, this is the only passage in Cherubini's religious music where each voice declaims a separate text. *Luigi Cherubini und seine Kirchenmusik*, 221.

14 "Je ne veux pas mourir." Bellasis, *Cherubini: Memorials Illustrative of his Life and Work*, 284 n. 14.

15 A number of organizations with this name existed in nineteenth-century Paris, including a group directed by Berlioz in the 1850s. The ensemble in question was founded in 1872 under the honorary direction of Félicien David. Saint-Saëns conducted the concerts, which took place in the Salle Erard. Édouard Colonne became the conductor in 1874. See Elisabeth Bernard, "Le Concert symphonique à Paris entre 1861 et 1914: Pasdeloup, Colonne, Lamoureux" (Ph.D diss., Université Paris I, 1976), vol. 1, 33.

16 "Nouvelles de Partout," *Journal de musique*, November 4, 1876. For a discussion of the City of Paris prize, see Jann Pasler, "Deconstructing d'Indy, or the Problem of a Composer's Reputation," *19th-Century Music* 30, 3 (Spring 2007): 235–39. For more on French symphonic writing at this time, see Ralph P. Locke, "The French Symphony: David, Gounod and Bizet to Saint-Saëns, Franck, and Their Followers," in *The Nineteenth-Century Symphony*, ed. D. Kern Holoman (New York: Schirmer, 1997), 163–94; Brian Hart, "The French Symphony after Berlioz: From the Second Empire to the First World War," in A. Peter Brown, *The Symphonic Repertoire*, vol. 3 part B: The European Symphony from ca. 1800 to ca. 1930:

Great Britain, Russia, and France (Bloomington, IN: Indiana University Press, 2008), 529–725; Andrew Deruchie, "The French Symphony at the Fin de Siècle: Style, Culture, and the Symphonic Tradition" (Ph.D diss., McGill University, 2008); and Mark Seto, "Symphonic Culture in Paris, 1880–1900: The *Bande à Franck* and Beyond" (Ph.D diss., Columbia University, 2012).

17 The narrator connects past and present at the piece's outset, imploring: "O fils des défenseurs de la vieille Lutèce, écoutez-les, pour vivre et pour mourir comme eux" ("O sons of the defenders of old Lutetia, listen to them, to live and die like them").

18 See Gérard Gefen, *Augusta Holmès, l'outrancière* (Paris: Pierre Belfond, 1987), 163; and Jann Pasler, "The Ironies of Gender, or Virility and Politics in the Music of Augusta Holmès," *Women and Music* 2 (Fall 1998): 9–17, reprinted in idem., *Writing through Music: Essays on Music, Culture, and Politics* (Oxford and New York: Oxford University Press, 2008). Holmès's negotiation of gender stereotypes has been a central theme in recent studies of the composer. See also Karen Henson, "In the House of Disillusion: Augusta Holmès and *La Montagne noire*," *Cambridge Opera Journal* 9, 3 (1997): 233–62; and Annegret Fauser, "The Republic's Muse: Augusta Holmès's *Ode triomphale*," in *Musical Encounters at the 1889 Paris World's Fair* (Rochester: University of Rochester Press, 2005), 103–38.

19 Pasler, "The Ironies of Gender," 18.

20 Pasdeloup premiered *Les Argonautes* in 1881 and the Société des Concerts performed part three of the work in 1885. See discussions by Jann Pasler in "The Ironies of Gender," 17–19, and in *Composing the Citizen*, 363–64. For more on the Société des Concerts, see D. Kern Holoman, *The Société des Concerts du Conservatoire, 1828–1967* (Berkeley: University of California Press, 2004). Holoman has also compiled a list of all the Société's programs, available online at http://hector.ucdavis.edu/SdC/default.html (accessed 10 January 2010).

21 Charles Darcours [Charles Réty], "Notes de musique," *Le Figaro*, April 27, 1881.

22 "Pour la [the Golden Fleece] conquérir comme pour s'emparer de l'*Or du Rhin*, il faut maudire l'amour. . . . il était presque de règle, dans les œuvres poétiques, de tout sacrifier à l'amour. Il est singulier qu'une femme ait fait le contraire." Camille Saint-Saëns, "Les Argonautes," *Le Voltaire*, March 26, 1881, clipping in *Recueil d'articles de journaux sur Augusta Holmès, 1866–1888*, 4 B 391, Bibliothèque nationale, Paris, reprinted in idem., *Harmonie et mélodie* (Paris: Calmann Lévy, 1885), 225–39.

23 For more on French orchestral works involving speech and song, see Angelus Seipt, "Vokale und symphonische Sprachebene in der französischen Programmsymphonik des 19. Jahrhunderts," in *Die Sprache der Musik: Festschrift Klaus Wolfgang Niemöller zum 60. Geburtstag*, ed. Jobst Peter Fricke (Regensburg: Bosse, 1989), 513–26.

24 A number of Holmès's contemporaries expressed similar opinions. See, for example, Adolphe Jullien, "Revue musicale," *Journal des débats*, February 16, 1895, evening edition.

25 Fauser, *Musical Encounters*, 121–26; Pasler, *Composing the Citizen*, 561–62.

26 Three of the choruses were from Belleville, a working-class neighborhood. The other choruses included Les Amis de la rive gauche, Le Choral des amis réunis, Le Choral Chevé Polytechnique de Montmartre, Le Choral du Louvre, L'École Galin-Paris-Chevé, Les Enfants de Paris, L'Union chorale française, L'Union chorale néerlandaise, and the chorus of the Association artistique du Châtelet.

27 Victorin Joncières, *Feuilleton de La Liberté*, September 16, 1889.

28 Saint-Saëns declared, "the French Republic has found what it lacked: a Muse!" *Le Rappel*, September 23, 1889, quoted in Fauser, *Musical Encounters*, 129 n. 90, and in Henson, "In the House of Disillusion," 239.

29 Gefen, *Augusta Holmès, l'outrancière*, 169–70. Holmès's opera *La Montagne noire* may also have been inspired by debates about Montenegrin independence in the 1880s. See Henson, "In the House of Disillusion," 241–42.

30 Gefen notes that by commissioning a Frenchwoman, Gubernatis could "thumb his nose" at Prime Minister Francesco Crispi, who had broken off negotiations for a Franco-Italian commercial treaty and entered the Triple Alliance with Germany and Austro-Hungary in 1882. Ibid., 15.

31 Michèle Friang, *Augusta Holmès ou la gloire interdite: Une femme compositeur au XIXe siècle* (Paris: Éditions Autrement, 2003), 78. See also Gefen, *Augusta Holmès, l'outrancière*, 199.

32 Literally, "More than all, love your country!" In the English version of the work, published by Schirmer in 1899, the heavenly voice speaks of loyalty in a more general sense: "More than all, like a son be loyal / To the realm to which thou dost owe thy life most royal."

Selected Bibliography

Cherubini

Bellasis, Edward. *Cherubini: Memorials Illustrative of his Life and Work.* London, 1874. Revised edition, Birmingham: Cornish Brothers Limited, 1912. Reprint, New York: Da Capo Press, 1971.

Deane, Basil. *Cherubini.* London: Oxford University Press, 1965.

Fend, Michael. *Cherubinis Pariser Opern (1788–1803).* Stuttgart: Franz Steiner Verlag, 2007.

Gerber, Gary George. "A Conductor's Analysis of the Sacred Choral Music of Luigi Cherubini." D.M.A. diss., Southwestern Baptist Theological Seminary, 1993.

Hohenemser, Richard. *Luigi Cherubini. Sein Leben und seine Werke.* Leipzig: Breitkopf & Härtel, 1913. Reprint, Weisbaden: M. Sändig, 1969.

Pougin, Arthur. "Chérubini: sa vie, ses œuvres, son rôle artistique," *Le Ménestrel*, September 4, 1881 to January 15, 1882; March 26 to December 17, 1882.

Schwarz-Roosmann, Oliver. *Luigi Cherubini und seine Kirchenmusik.* Köln: Verlag Christoph Dohr, 2006.

Siegert, Christine. *Cherubini in Florenz: Zur Funktion der Oper in der toskanischen Gesellschaft des späten 18. Jahrhunderts. Analecta Musicologica* 41. Laaber: Laaber-Verlag, 2008.

Spada, Pietro. "Aspekte von Cherubinis Schaffenskraft," in *Luigi Cherubini & Georg Schumann: Beiträge zur Musikforschung*, ed. Wolfgang Schult and Henrik Verkerk. München: Jahrbuch der Bachwochen Dillenburg, 2001, 32–38.

White, Maurice L. "The Motets of Luigi Cherubini." Ph.D. diss., University of Michigan, 1968.

Holmès

Fauser, Annegret. "The Republic's Muse: Augusta Holmès's *Ode triomphale*," in *Musical Encounters at the 1889 Paris World's Fair.* Rochester: University of Rochester Press, 2005, 103–38.

Friang, Michèle. *Augusta Holmès ou la gloire interdite: Une femme compositeur au XIXe siècle.* Paris: Éditions Autrement, 2003.

Gefen, Gérard. *Augusta Holmès, l'outrancière.* Paris: Pierre Belfond, 1987.

Harwood, Ronald. *César and Augusta.* London: Secker & Warburg, 1978.

Henson, Karen. "In the House of Disillusion: Augusta Holmès and *La Montagne noire*," *Cambridge Opera Journal* 9, 3 (1997): 233–62.

Olivier, Brigitte. *Les mélodies d'Augusta Holmès: C'est son âme que l'on montre.* Arles: Actes sud, 2003.

Pasler, Jann. *Composing the Citizen: Music as Public Utility in Third Republic France.* Berkeley and Los Angeles: University of California Press, 2009.

——. "The Ironies of Gender, or, Virility and Politics in the Music of Augusta Holmès," *Women & Music: A Journal of Gender and Culture* 2 (1998): 1–25. Reprinted in *Writing through Music: Essays on Music, Culture, and Politics.* Oxford and New York: Oxford University Press, 2008.

Seto, Mark. "Symphonic Culture in Paris, 1880–1900: The *Bande à Franck* and Beyond." Ph.D. diss., Columbia University, 2012.

15

HECTOR BERLIOZ

Donna M. Di Grazia

Pomona College

In the last three decades or so, the life and music of Hector Berlioz (1803–69) have received considerable attention through the publication of countless articles and monographs, a handsome thematic catalogue, eight volumes of letters, a complete new critical edition of his works, and many of his writings. The attraction is not just to his music, but also to the colorful life and personality of the man himself, extravagantly documented in his *Mémoires*—it is a fascinating and entertaining read. Discussions and performances of his music parallel those for most nineteenth-century composers, with an emphasis on orchestral works and operas. Several extended works with choral forces have also remained in public view, most notably his *Grande Messe des morts* (Requiem), which is perhaps best remembered for the large numbers of performers involved and for its massive sonic presence. This repertoire has shaped the commonly held view that Berlioz's music is always louder and requires more performers than other works from the period—too frequently a programming deterrent. Yet there are a number of pieces, many including choral forces, that do not conform to these characteristics. The following passage, Berlioz's response to remarks made by the famous German poet (and critic) Heinrich Heine, shows just how long this stereotype has influenced the reception of his music.

> But in any case, why did you behave like a critic and let yourself make a categorical statement about an artist when you only know part of his work? You are always thinking of the Witches' Sabbath and the March to the Scaffold from my Fantastic Symphony, and the Dies irae and Lacrymosa from my Requiem. Yet I think I have done and can do things that are quite different.[1]

That there is still some truth in Berlioz's complaint some 150-plus years later suggests that our knowledge of his music is still fairly narrow. The goal of this chapter is to refine our perspective by revealing a broader picture of his output and the techniques he used in writing for choral forces.

Overview

Given that very few of Berlioz's works with chorus are performed today with any frequency, it may be surprising to learn that over forty of his 143 extant titles require choral forces (see Figure 15.1); another dozen works for chorus are lost.[2] Most of the mixed-choir pieces composed prior

Works with Orchestra

Messe solennelle (H.20)[1]

Scène héroïque (H.21A; H.21B w/ military band)

La Mort d'Orphée (H.25; final chorus only)

Huit Scènes de Faust (H.33)

Hélène (H.40B)

La Belle Voyageuse (H.42D)[2]

Chant sacré (H.44B)

Sardanapale (H.50)

Hymne des Marseillais (H.51A)

Chant du neuf Thermidor (H. 51*bis*)

Le Retour à la vie (H.55A; H.55B as *Lélio*)[3]

Méditation religieuse (H.56B)[4]

Quartetto e coro dei maggi (H.59)[5]

Sara la baigneuse (H.69C)[4]

Le Cinq Mai (H.74)[4]

Grande Messe des morts (H.75)

Roméo et Juliette (H.79)

Grande Symphonie funèbre et triomphale (H.80B)

La Mort d'Ophélie (H.92B)[4]

Hymne à la France (H.97)[4]

Marche funèbre pour la dernière scène d'Hamlet (H.103)

Chant des chemins de fer (H.110)[4]

La Damnation de Faust (H.111)

Le Menace des Francs (H.117)[4]

Te Deum (H.118)

L'Impériale (H.129)

L'Enfance du Christ (H.130)

Works with Keyboard (piano unless otherwise noted)

Amitié reprends ton empire (H.10)

Le Ballet des ombres (H.37)

Chant guerrier (H.41)

Chanson à boire (H.43)

Chant sacré (H.44A [2 versions])

Hymne des Marseillais (H.51B)

Le Chant des Bretons (H.71A; revised ver. H.71B)

Grande Symphonie funèbre et triomphale (H.80C)

La Belle Isabeau (H.94)[6]

Prière du matin (H.112)

Hymne por la consécration du nouveau tabernacle (H.135 for organ or piano)

Le Temple universel (H.137A for organ)

Tantum ergo (H.142 for organ)

Invitation à louer Dieu (H.143 for organ)

Unaccompanied Works

Le Temple universel (H.137B)

Veni Creator (H.141)

1   H numbers refer to Holoman's numbering of Berlioz's works in his *Catalogue of the Works of Hector Berlioz*; I've included them because many of these works exist in more than one version, often involving different configurations of choral voices. This list excludes choruses from Berlioz's operas, lost works, and works preserved in incomplete form (with the exception of *Sardanapale*). Choral works reissued in Berlioz-sanctioned collections—*Tristia, Vox Populi, Feuillets d'album, Fleurs des landes*, and *Collection de 32 [33] mélodies*—are included, but his arrangements of two Latin hymns by Dmitri Bortniansky are not.

2   A version for male quartet and orchestra (H.42B) is lost. As with *Hélène* and *Sara la baigneuse*, versions of *La Belle Voyageuse* also exist for solo rather than choral voices.

3   Includes *Ouverture de La Tempête* (H.52, for chorus and orchestra) as its final musical number.

4   See Macdonald, ed., *Miscellaneaous Works and Index. NBE* vol. 21 (Kassel: Bärenreiter-Verlag, 2005) for versions with piano for *Méditation Religieuse, Le Cinq Mai, La Mort d'Ophélie, Hymne à la France, Chant des chemins de fer*, and *Le Menace des Francs*. These reductions were published in Berlioz's lifetime in *Collection de 32 [33] mélodies* (H.139, 1863 and c.1864). The reduction for *La Mort d'Ophélie* is from the song version of the work (H.92A) rather than from the orchestral version (though transposed to A major to match the original choral work); the reduction of *Le Cinq Mai* was not included in the collection until it was reissued as *Collection de 33 mélodies*. Another work to appear in the 1863 *Collection, Sara la baigneuse*, appeared there in a version for two voices and piano with a reduction by Berlioz's friend Auguste Morel; it is published in Ian Rumbold, ed. *Songs with Piano. NBE* vol. 15 (Kassel: Bärenreiter-Verlag, 2005), 139–52.

5   Given the absence of a solo quartet in this work (despite its title), Rushton's suggestion that this chorus may actually be the lost *Chœur d'anges* (H.58) rather than the *Quartetto* is interesting. (See Rushton, *NBE* 12a, xii, for the reasons behind his hypothesis.) If Professor Rushton is right, the piece titled *Quartetto* would be the lost work.

6   The chorus part in *La Belle Isabeau* is optional.

FIGURE 15.1   Berlioz's Works with Choral Voices

to 1850 call for the three- or six-way division of voices (STB) that was fairly common in nineteenth-century French choral music, especially in the first half of the century, rather than the four-way division (SATB) typically used elsewhere in Europe.[3] The music from his last two decades, however, shifts to four-part writing (with alto) almost exclusively.[4]

Perhaps reflecting the prevalence of male choirs in Paris and elsewhere in France throughout his life, Berlioz's choral output includes a significant amount of music for men's voices alone, usually (but not always) scored TTBB. Male voices are featured not only in self-contained works such as *Le Temple universel* (1861; rev. 1867–68), which was written specifically for a massive, planned gathering of orphéonistes from France and England,[5] but also in many of his large-scale works for mixed chorus, where Berlioz often wrote for them in a chordal style reminiscent of that same popular Orphéon repertoire: the Hostias and Agnus Dei of the *Grande Messe des morts*, the Capulet men leaving the ball in *Roméo et Juliette*, the chorus of students and soldiers that closes Part II of *La Damnation de Faust*, and the Pandemonium scene near the same work's conclusion, are all examples of this approach. More surprising given the paucity of women's choruses in Paris are the handful of works for women's voices alone. These include the Prix de Rome cantata *La Mort d'Orphée* (1827) and versions of *La Mort d'Ophélie* (1848) and *La Belle Voyageuse* (1851), all three of which use two-part female chorus. Finally, there are a few works for children's voices (though they can be successfully performed by women) including the *Prière du matin* (two equal voices, 1846) and three late works for three-part treble voices written in 1860s for Prosper Saint d'Arod's *Livre choral*: *Veni creator spiritus*, *Tantum ergo*, and *Invitation à louer Dieu*.

Multi-movement Works with Chorus and Orchestra

The discovery in 1991 of Berlioz's lost *Messe solennelle* (1824) allows us to see the first appearance of numerous familiar melodies and musical gestures that we know from important later works such as the *Symphonie fantastique*.[6] What we see in this Mass, the product of a mere twenty-one-year old, are the ideas of someone with an imagination that outstripped his still-raw technical gifts, and with an exceptional sense of the dramatic. Indeed, although it was his first attempt at writing a large-scale work, the Mass has many of the signature features that one associates with his mature compositional style: elegant melodies, electric rhythmic gestures, startling juxtapositions of unprepared harmonies, bold use of orchestral timbres, dramatic settings of texts, and a clear sense of how to exploit the acoustical space of the performance venue. All this from an untested young man who had come to Paris just three years earlier (to study medicine) and who had not yet enrolled at the Conservatoire, though he was studying privately with Jean-François Le Sueur. The response to the work from critics and from those in attendance at its premiere in 1825 was overwhelmingly positive, and it was after this performance that Le Sueur made his famous pronouncement, "Come, let me embrace you. Surely, you will be neither a doctor nor an apothecary but a great composer; you have genius, I tell you because it is true."[7] Despite the praise, Berlioz grew to have doubts about the Mass's quality, and his initial euphoric response was tempered as he refined his grasp of the creative process. The work enjoyed a successful second performance in 1827, but by 1838 he reported he had burned the score.

Influenced by the sacred works of Cherubini and Le Sueur, the Mass consists of fourteen movements: ten that present the usual Ordinary text, three that set non-liturgical Latin texts, and one orchestral introduction.[8] Clearly Berlioz's command of writing for choral voices at this stage is far from polished. The most obvious concern has to do with his unreasonable expectations of human wind instruments who, after all, need places to breathe and to place consonants.[9] One wonders, for example, how he expected his sopranos to sing the long passages of fast-paced sixteenth-note figures like the ones shown in Example 15.1a, which are more suited to untexted

EXAMPLE 15.1a   Berlioz, *Messe solennelle*, Gloria (choral parts only), mm. 132–42. Source: *Hector Berlioz: New Edition of the Complete Works*, vol. 23; used with permission, Bärenreiter-Verlag.

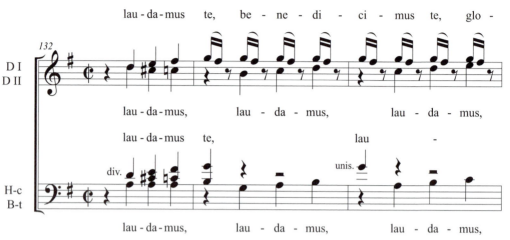

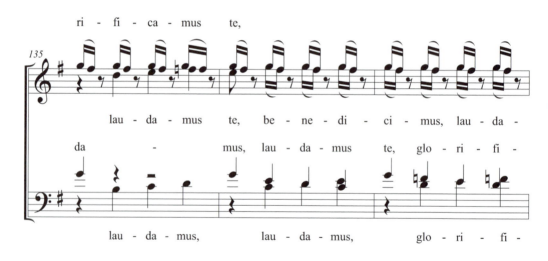

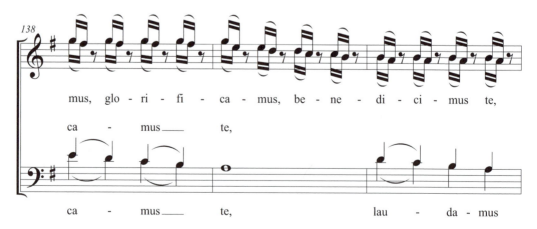

EXAMPLE 15.1a continued.

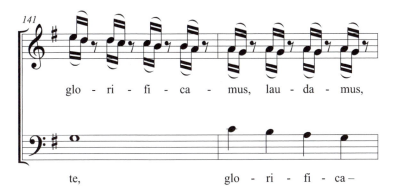

EXAMPLE 15.1b Berlioz, *Messe solennelle*, Gloria (choral parts only), mm. 61–70. Source: *Hector Berlioz: New Edition of the Complete Works*, vol. 23; used with permission, Bärenreiter-Verlag.

EXAMPLE 15.1c Berlioz, *Messe solennelle*, Gloria (choral parts only), mm. 172–93. Source: *Hector Berlioz: New Edition of the Complete Works*, vol. 23; used with permission, Bärenreiter-Verlag.

EXAMPLE 15.1c continued.

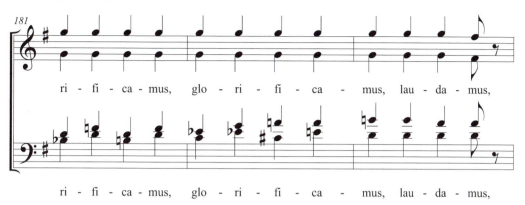

winds or strings. Yet there is something endearing about this movement, even this inelegant passage. Perhaps its appeal comes from the jaunty bassline that precedes and follows the quoted excerpt, which is more characteristic of music from *opéra comique* than sacred music (see Example 15.1b), or at the end of the Gloria, where Berlioz shifts from the unrelenting quarter-note patter, which prattles on without rests for twelve bars with sopranos on high Gs, to a final ten bars where sopranos float high Gs *pianissimo*, one whole note per bar, above a gentle harmonization (see Example 15.1c). If Berlioz's sopranos created anywhere near the effect John Eliot Gardiner's sopranos do on their 1993 recording, it is no wonder that those in attendance at the 1825 premiere were floored.[10]

In the remaining multi-movement works with chorus and orchestra, we encounter the core of what most people associate with Berlioz: the *Grande Messe des morts* (1837), *Roméo et Juliette* (1839), the *Grande Symphonie funèbre et triomphale* (1840; ver. with chorus,1842), *La Damnation de Faust* (1846), the *Te Deum* (1849, rev. 1855), and *L'Enfance du Christ* (1854). To these we can add two little-known works: *Huit Scènes de Faust* (1829) and *Le Retour à la vie* (1831). *Huit Scènes* was an early attempt to set portions of Goethe's great work as translated into French by Gérard de Nerval. Only a single scene was performed during Berlioz's lifetime (the "Concert de Sylphes"), and though it was received well by the critics, he had a different opinion, saying the piece as a whole had "many and grave defects" and was "crude and badly written."[11] Still, he thought highly enough of the music to absorb all eight scenes into *La Damnation de Faust* some seventeen years later.

Le Retour à la vie (renamed *Lélio* in 1855) is the most unconventional work in Berlioz's output in terms of its overall content. Originally subtitled a "mélologue," a word he borrowed from Thomas Moore after having read a French translation of the Irish writer's *On National Music, A Mélologue*,[12] Berlioz intended *Le Retour* to be played immediately after performances of the *Symphonie fantastique*, "of which . . . it is its 'conclusion' and its 'complement.'"[13] The work calls for an actor–narrator, whose spoken monologues alternate with musical numbers. The monologues, authored by Berlioz himself and containing details one should understand as being autobiographical, touch (at times only by implication) on subjects most on his mind at the time; in particular, Shakespeare, love, and the power of music.[14] As the *Symphonie fantastique* told the story of "the artist's" obsession with his beloved (a not-so-veiled reference to himself and the Irish actress Harriet Smithson, who was the object of his affection at the time but not yet his wife), so too *Le Retour* continued to deal with his pursuit of an elusive beloved—in this case, Camille Moke. The connection between the two works is unmistakable even in musical terms, as the famous *idée fixe* from the *Symphonie fantastique* reappears in *Le Retour*'s opening and closing movements.

Of its six musical numbers, three call for choral forces with orchestra; two others require vocal soloists, one with piano rather than orchestra; the penultimate movement is for orchestra alone. The music itself is not new; each selection had been written separately sometime earlier before being pulled into *Le Retour*. Of the numbers with choral voices, the dark "Chœur d'ombres" (No. 2; STB)[15] reuses music from Cléopâtre's passionate "Méditation" in the 1829 Prix de Rome cantata of the same name. In what is the first of several instances where imaginary languages appear in Berlioz's music, the singers here use an invented text Berlioz called an "ancient dialect from the north."[16] The next number, one well worth performing on its own, is the delightfully boisterous "Chanson de brigands" for baritone soloist and TTB choir, which calls to mind the energy and bravado of other choruses Berlioz wrote for men's voices. The movement perhaps most deserving of revival, however, is the finale, which Berlioz originally composed in 1830 as an independent piece titled *Ouverture de La Tempête* for SSATT chorus (singing in Italian) and orchestra;[17] Berlioz adjusted the name to "Fantaisie sur 'La Tempête'" before *Le Retour*'s premiere in 1832.[18] In thirteen or so minutes of music, the Fantaisie displays splendid, inventive orchestral writing (including four-hands piano), with delightful Rossinian touches along the way.

The extended works of the late 1830s and 1840s mark a highpoint in Berlioz's compositional career. With the *Grande Messe des morts* and *La Damnation de Faust* (discussed at length in Chapters 4 and 5 respectively in this volume), Berlioz explored two different genre types: a Requiem Mass and what he would call a "légende dramatique" that is, for all intents and purposes, a concert opera.[19] With *Roméo et Juliette*, however, we see both Berlioz's progression as a dramatic symphonist—appropriately, he called the work a "symphonie dramatique"—and his expansion of Beethoven's symphonic legacy, though as Mark Evan Bonds notes, achieved by a different route.[20]

Labeled a choral symphony by Berlioz himself, the work is a masterpiece of storytelling in music.[21] Consisting of seven titled movements, each is a tableau that focuses on (and in some instances recreates) specific parts of Shakespeare's play as Berlioz knew it through the English playwright David Garrick, whose version he had seen performed in Paris in 1827 (with his beloved Harriet in the title role).[22] The passions of the two title characters, who are the most directly represented in the "Scène d'amour" (movement 3) and "Roméo au tombeau des Capulets" (movement 6), are reserved for specific instrumental colors: dark lower strings and winds (bassoon, English horn, and French horn) for Romeo, and high woodwinds (especially clarinet) and violins for Juliet. In choosing to reserve the music of human passion for the orchestra alone, we see an important aspect of Berlioz's philosophy regarding the power of instrumental music, which he writes, "is richer, more varied, less precise, and by its very indefiniteness incomparably more powerful."[23] That the orchestra carries the most passionate music in this work—that of love as well as despair—

is not surprising given this view. Nevertheless, choral voices play an important role in the symphony, from foretelling the story in the prologue (for twelve-voice chorus [ATB] plus two soloists)[24] to offering the distant sounds of departing party-goers at the beginning of movement 3 (for two offstage men's choirs), the heaviness of Juliet's funeral procession in movement 5 (STB divisi), and the powerful final confrontation and reconciliation of the two families, Capulet and Montague, in movement 7 (for bass soloist [Friar Laurence], two STB divisi choirs, and the prologue chorus).

From a choral perspective, several features in *Roméo et Juliette* illustrate characteristics found throughout much of Berlioz's output. Perhaps the most important of these appears in the "Convoi funèbre de Juliette" (movement 5), which the Hungarian composer and pianist Stephen Heller remarked to Robert Schumann, "exudes deep feeling, unutterable sorrow."[25] The sopranos and tenors of the Capulet chorus sing a one-note ostinato on octave E-naturals for the text's opening phrase, "Jetez des fleurs pour la vierge expirée!," sounded over an extensive orchestral fugue. The approach here is similar to the Offertoire (Domine Jesu Christe) of the Requiem, where a two-note oscillating figure in the chorus is repeated forty times over a similarly slowly unfolding orchestral fugue. In Juliet's funeral procession, however, this technique is taken a step further than what we see in the Offertoire, as halfway through the movement the chorus and orchestra reverse roles, with the orchestra taking over the ostinato while the chorus assumes the fugal subject and the imitative development. The use of ostinato figures and of repeated phrases reminiscent of plainchant psalmody are a signature of Berlioz's style, and one can see various manifestations of this technique elsewhere in his choral music as well as in his non-choral works.[26]

In the *Te Deum* and *L'Enfance du Christ*, we see two very different sides of Berlioz's compositional voice. A work for two choirs and orchestra,[27] the *Te Deum* is one of several extroverted choral–orchestral works commonly referred to as "architectural," a label applied to it and three others (by the composer's own count) in contemporary reviews of his music: the Requiem, the *Grande Symphonie funèbre et triomphale*, and the patriotic cantata *L'Impériale*. Unlike those critics, though, who almost single-mindedly emphasized the enormity of the forces and the sound alone, Berlioz described this music with more subtlety, noting "it is above all the scale of the movements, the breadth of style and the formidably slow and deliberate pace of certain progressions, whose final goal cannot be guessed, that give these works their peculiarly 'gigantic' character and 'colossal' aspect."[28]

The vastness of scale to which Berlioz refers here has everything to do with the interplay he creates between his performers—voices and orchestra together or separately—and the physical space in which they perform. Nowhere in Berlioz's output other than in the Requiem is this so clearly seen as in the *Te Deum*, with the organ positioned in the back of the church (as was typical in most large Parisian churches in the nineteenth century) to create a true antiphonal effect for the listeners.[29] As in the Requiem, however, the *Te Deum*'s most expansive movements would not have the same impact were it not for the contrasts in sound and the power generated from the work's more intimate moments, and for his careful and purposeful use of silence, points Berlioz himself emphasized in his orchestration treatise:

> But in the thousand combinations available to a monumental orchestra . . . would reside a wealth of harmony, a variety of timbre and a series of contrasts comparable to nothing ever yet done in music, and, moreover, incalculable melodic, expressive and rhythmic power, an unequalled force of impact, and prodigious sensitivity in nuances of detail and ensemble. Its repose would be as majestic as the ocean's slumber; its agitation would suggest a tropical hurricane, its explosions the fury of a volcano. . . . The very solemnity of its silences would inspire fear, and the most rebellious beings would tremble to watch its crescendo swell and roar like an enormous, sublime conflagration![30]

Berlioz's calculated use of silence in the Requiem, in the first movement's opening measures in particular, is critical to the impact of the work as a whole. There, the care with which he paced out the opening two dozen bars or so is worth noting: three melodic fragments, each offered with different orchestral coloring, and each suspended and eventually swallowed into the space itself as dictated by his precisely notated silence, force the listener to follow the sounds of the orchestra (and eventually the chorus) as they travel through the reverberant acoustics of the performance space (see Example 15.2a).[31] Also at work here is a clever obfuscation of the movement's prevailing

EXAMPLE 15.2a Berlioz, *Grande Messe des morts*, Requiem et Kyrie, mm. 1–21 (orchestral reduction). Source: *Hector Berlioz: New Edition of the Complete Works*, vol. 9; used with permission, Bärenreiter-Verlag.

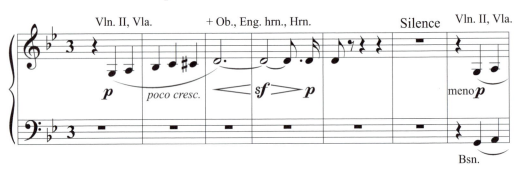

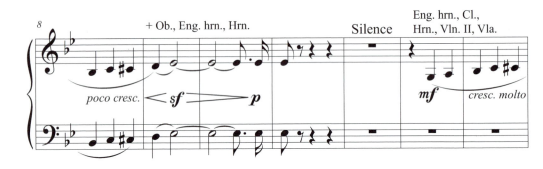

triple meter. With each fragment beginning on the second beat of the bar rather than the first or third, Berlioz creates uncertainty and dramatic tension that is increased by a number of details, not the least of which is the silence that punctuates each phrase.

We see a wholly different approach in the *Te Deum*. Like the Requiem, its first movement also features the contrast of sound and silence, but in a way not nearly as imaginative or integrated. The movement begins with a series of *forte* chords that alternate at regular intervals between the orchestra and chorus. Each is separated by silence of indeterminate length: a single empty bar with a fermata—quite different from the carefully and precisely paced out beats of silence in the Requiem example above (see Example 15.2b). From this point on the movement proceeds with much aesthetic fanfare, but with little drama other than the sheer volume of it all.

Berlioz's use of chant-like writing is another technique that appears regularly in his large choral–orchestral works. In the "Dignare, Domine" (movement 3), for example, the entire movement features the choral basses (supported by cellos) intoning short phrases below contrapuntal writing in the rest of the choir and orchestra; the basses seem fairly oblivious to the thickening texture and slowly increasing crescendo around them, shifting the pitch level of their chant only as necessary to keep up with the changing harmony (see Example 15.3a). Instances of this same kind of writing can be found elsewhere in Berlioz's œuvre, notably in the Quaerens me and Lacrymosa of the Requiem (see Examples 15.3b and 15.3c).

EXAMPLE 15.2b Berlioz, *Te Deum*, Te Deum laudamus, mm. 1–12 (orchestral reduction). Source: *Hector Berlioz: New Edition of the Complete Works*, vol. 10; used with permission, Bärenreiter-Verlag.

EXAMPLE 15.3a Berlioz, *Te Deum*, Dignare, Domine (choral parts only), mm. 46–66. Source: *Hector Berlioz: New Edition of the Complete Works*, vol. 10; used with permission, Bärenreiter-Verlag.

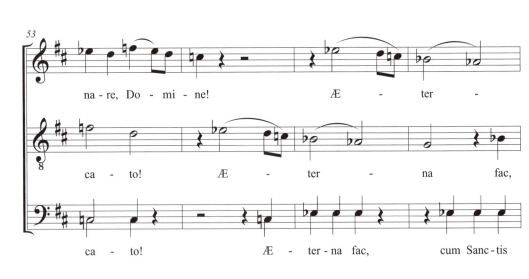

EXAMPLE 15.3a continued.

EXAMPLE 15.3b Berlioz, *Grande Messe des morts*, Quaerens me, mm. 42–57. Source: *Hector Berlioz: New Edition of the Complete Works*, vol. 9; used with permission, Bärenreiter-Verlag.

EXAMPLE 15.3b continued.

Of all the *Te Deum*'s movements, the "Judex crederis" (movement 6) has rightly been judged to be among Berlioz's best efforts; the composer himself considered it to be "unquestionably the most imposing thing I have produced."[32] Those who know the Requiem well will surely note the striking conceptual resemblance with that work's Lacrymosa. It is perhaps no coincidence, for example, that Berlioz sets up the "Judex crederis" with an extended passage at the end of the preceding movement ("Te ergo quaesumus") for the two choirs singing unaccompanied and *sotto voce*; this juxtaposition parallels the Requiem's placement of the *a cappella* Quaerens me just before the explosive Lacrymosa. Breaking into this most intimate, hushed sound are the organ's opening

EXAMPLE 15.3c   Berlioz, *Grande Messe des morts*, Lacrymosa (choral parts only), mm. 74–82. Source: *Hector Berlioz: New Edition of the Complete Works*, vol. 9; used with permission, Bärenreiter-Verlag.

trumpet blasts, echoed quickly by brass interjections, that launch the "Judex crederis"—it is an utterly thrilling moment. As in the Lacrymosa, the similar, prevailing 9/8 meter of the "Judex crederis" opening fugue, legendary for its unorthodox modulating subject, is interrupted by a contrasting section, here in 3/4 beginning in Bb minor for sopranos alone, and scored mostly for winds and upper strings at first, though the brass edge their way back in before too long with the return of the men's voices at "Per singulos dies." Even the layered orchestral textures and insistent orchestral ostinato, lasting some twenty-six bars, are reminiscent of the Lacrymosa. Yet for all of its energy and exhilarating sounds, one has the sense that the ideas here are less fully developed and polished than they are in the Lacrymosa. Considering the clues here and elsewhere in the work, one wonders if Hugh Macdonald's suggestion is on the mark that the genesis of the *Te Deum* may in fact be closer to 1835, which would have it predate the Requiem by two years.[33]

L'Enfance du Christ, Berlioz's greatest triumph among the critics during his lifetime, and a work Howard Smither calls "the most important French oratorio of the nineteenth century,"[34] is a unique piece in the composer's choral–orchestral output, more "naive and gentle," as Berlioz himself described it, as fitting the subject matter.[35] The work was composed in stages, starting with "La Fuite en Égypte," which received its premiere in 1853 before becoming the centerpiece of this "trilogie sacrée," framed by two additional parts: "Le Songe de Hérode" (Part I) and "L'Arrivé à Saïs" (Part III). *L'Enfance* requires soloists to cover seven specific roles, including one for a narrator as was customary in contemporary French oratorios. The chorus is also assigned various roles, and subsets of it are frequently heard singing from offstage. The orchestra is small by Berlioz's standards: double winds, double upper brass with three trombones (all used sparingly and only for two-thirds of Part I), harp, timpani, organ (orgue mélodium;[36] again all used sparingly), and strings.

Throughout *L'Enfance du Christ* one finds extensive writing for orchestra alone and much operatic writing for the soloists. Unlike Berlioz's other large-scale works, it has a greatly reduced role for the chorus, and a sizable amount of its music is written in a declamatory style that is void of extensive musical development. This type of choral writing reflects an approach more frequently used in opera choruses than in the choral oratorios of Berlioz's German and British contemporaries, and to a certain extent, even those written in France by Saint-Saëns, Franck, Gounod, and Massenet, all of whom use a chorus much more extensively than Berlioz does here. Of special note from a choral perspective is the tender four-part "L'Adieu des bergers à la Sainte Famille" with oboe, clarinet, and strings from Part II, and the oratorio's extraordinary unaccompanied choral finale, "O mon âme, pour toi que reste-t-il à faire?," which is unlike anything else in Berlioz's choral output. A "chœur mystique" for four-part choir, two-part chorus (for eight women) and the tenor narrator, this concluding number contains over six minutes of gentle, yet searching music written in the style of sixteenth-century polyphony. Although Berlioz was not a practicing believer, some aspects of his early Roman Catholic upbringing never completely left him, and one senses here a certain authentic reverent spirituality that captures the wonder of Christ's birth. Recalling his philosophy that instruments alone were the best conveyors of human love, it seems the purity of human voices alone, a sound Berlioz held dear from various religious experiences early in life, were best reserved for expressing spiritual passion.[37]

Shorter Works for Chorus with Orchestra

Among the most neglected compositions in Berlioz's choral output are his shorter works for chorus and orchestra. One of the best is *Sara la baigneuse* (1849), a work that evolved from two earlier versions, both now lost. The text is the sensual ballad from Victor Hugo's *Les Orientales* that tells in great detail the story of a young woman who, oblivious to the world around her, lays swaying in a hammock *au naturel* above a pond frittering the day away daydreaming and eventually dipping herself into the water. The work calls for three choruses—one STBB, another SA, and a third TTBB—however, the orchestral writing throughout is light enough that one could imagine a successful performance using a moderately sized ensemble divided into appropriately balanced choirs. Almost from the start one gets the sense that the choruses are playing the role of nosy neighbors, and when Sara leans over to see her own image in the water ("qui se penche pour se voir"), the singers see it too and are more than happy to describe the scene. Throughout the work, the writing for the chorus as well as the orchestra is exquisite, full of delightful touches that show Berlioz at the height of his powers as a storyteller in music, and even the smallest detail does not escape his attention, from the swaying hammock, captured in the music from the outset (see Example 15.4a), to the delicate tap of Sara's foot on the water (see Example 15.4b). This is a wonderful, playful work that deserves to be heard.

Berlioz's patriotic works each have memorable moments that aptly reflect the revolutionary spirit of the times, from the stirring *Hymne des Marseillais* (1830, rev. 1848) and the *Hymne à la France* (1844) to the unselfconsciously boisterous *L'Impériale* (1854) with its talk of imperial destiny and the virtues of the emperor. The strongest work in this group other than the Marseillaise arrangement is *Le Cinq Mai* (1835, subtitled "Chant sur la mort de l'Empereur Napoléon") for bass soloist and (principally) men's chorus (TB divisi)—sopranos are only needed for the last ten measures. The text is a five-stanza poem by Pierre-Jean de Béranger (1780–1857), the well-known writer of politically infused texts.[38] Unlike other patriotic works where Berlioz sets each stanza strophically, he takes a through-composed approach with Béranger's poem, though the last two lines of each stanza are used as a recurring refrain. If the work is a bit uneven—David Cairns calls it "competent but unmemorable,"[39]—it shows, like the *Messe solennelle* of the previous decade, flashes of innovation and originality that emerged more clearly and more thoroughly developed in the music from the later 1830s and 1840s.

Included in the works with orchestra listed in Figure 15.1 are two cantatas written for the famous Prix de Rome competition, which Berlioz entered on five separate occasions, winning only on his fifth attempt with *Sardanapale* (1830). The lone extant section of this prize-winning work, "Air final—Incendie," includes a minimal amount of choral writing for men's voices (TTBB) used in a supporting role.[40] Of the other four competition pieces, *La Mort d'Orphée* (1827) is the only one to include choral voices, employed here for the bacchanal for tenor soloist (Orpheus) and two, two-part women's choruses. This cantata as a whole is an astonishing work, from its moving orchestral introduction and the lyrical passion of Orpheus's opening monologue, through the frenetic bacchanal, to the magical final scene, a "Tableau musical" scored for orchestra alone.[41] Although there is an awkwardness in spots that reveals a composer who still had much to learn, it is a pity the work has not yet found a place in the concert literature.[42]

A similar lament can be registered for a trio of works Berlioz combined for publication purposes rather than musical or programmatic ones under the title *Tristia* (2nd version, 1852): the hymn-like *Méditation religieuse* (by 1849) for SSTTBB chorus based on a French translation of Thomas Moore's "This world is all a fleeting show"; *Le Mort d'Ophélie* (1848), a lyrical ballad in modified strophic form for two-part women's chorus; and *Marche funèbre pour la dernière scène d'Hamlet* (1848) which calls for an offstage wordless chorus—"femmes et hommes"—singing in octaves throughout.[43] The funeral march is in many ways the most interesting of the three, bringing together several influences that served as tremendous inspiration for Berlioz's music throughout his life: the ceremonial music of the French Revolution and Shakespeare, whose works had long captivated him. The *Marche funèbre* is a powerful piece, not only in the way Berlioz paces it, building a long dramatic crescendo that ultimately explodes in an impassioned cry from the chorus and a volley of gunfire (shot from offstage), but also in how the music slowly picks itself up from this wrenching interruption (see Example 15.5). Throughout the work, the intermittent choral "ahs" serve as a

EXAMPLE 15.4a Berlioz, *Sara la baigneuse*, mm. 1–17 (orchestral reduction). Source: *Hector Berlioz: New Edition of the Complete Works*, vol. 12a; used with permission, Bärenreiter-Verlag.

EXAMPLE 15.4a continued.

EXAMPLE 15.4b Berlioz, *Sara la baigneuse*, mm. 61–6 (orchestral reduction). Source: *Hector Berlioz: New Edition of the Complete Works*, vol. 12a; used with permission, Bärenreiter-Verlag.

EXAMPLE 15.4b continued.

plaintive mantra: they are the first sound one hears, *a cappella*, when the march begins, and they are the last sound remaining when the orchestral wailing has faded away.[44] Like *Le Mort d'Orphée*, this work deserves a fresh hearing.

Works for Chorus with Keyboard

Sprinkled throughout Berlioz's output are little-known choral works with keyboard accompaniment (almost always piano) that await wider discovery. Most of these are strophic settings by an eclectic group of authors, ranging from the famous (including Alphonse de Lamartine, Thomas Moore, and Thomas Aquinas) to the unknown. One of the earliest, *Le Ballet des ombres* (1829), is an inspired setting of a text by Albert Du Boys, a little-known writer and lawyer, based on Herder's

EXAMPLE 15.5 Berlioz, *Marche funèbre pour la dernière scène d'Hamlet*, mm. 84–101 (orchestral reduction). Source: *Hector Berlioz: New Edition of the Complete Works*, vol. 12b; used with permission, Bärenreiter-Verlag.

EXAMPLE 15.5 continued.

EXAMPLE 15.6a Berlioz, *Le Ballet des ombres*, mm. 92–109. Source: *Hector Berlioz: New Edition of the Complete Works*, vol. 14; used with permission, Bärenreiter-Verlag.

EXAMPLE 15.6b Berlioz, *Le Ballet des ombres* (1st strophe), mm. 71–90. Source: *Hector Berlioz: New Edition of the Complete Works*, vol. 14; used with permission, Bärenreiter-Verlag.

EXAMPLE 15.6b continued.

Der Schattentanz. Each strophe is set to the same music, an approach uncharacteristic of Berlioz's writing for chorus with orchestra rather than piano, where he is much more apt to vary the material on successive repetitions. Despite the strophic repetition here, the work is alive with energy as Berlioz uses ever-changing accompanimental figures, as well as silence as a tension builder (see Example 15.6a), to tell a dramatic story.

Berlioz withdrew the work shortly after it was printed, yet it is packed with good ideas, some of which found their way into later, more well-known works. This tendency to self-borrow is one Berlioz frequently relied on throughout his life, and as others have noted, he was especially adept at recognizing when an idea—melodic, rhythmic, or otherwise—was a good one, but could be used to greater effect elsewhere.[45] The most recognizable music in *Le Ballet* is the passage that presages the harp harmonics and antique cymbals made famous some ten years later in the Queen Mab scherzo of *Roméo et Juliette* ("La Reine Mab, ou la fée des songes"), though without the canonic writing we see here (see Example 15.6b). The basic outline of the song, too, is a model of sorts for the Queen Mab scherzo: the driving triple meter (3/4, *Allegro scherzando*, dotted half = 120 in *La Ballet*; 3/8, *Prestissimo*, dotted quarter = 138 in the scherzo); the opening introduction, with its simple, twice-stated melody (beginning with a pickup to propel it forward) that each time arrives on similar unexpected harmonies; and the use of swirling chromatic accompaniment that lends itself naturally to depictions of a brewing storm (in *Le Ballet*) or a flighty fairy (in Queen Mab) (see Example 15.6c). The Queen Mab scherzo is greatly expanded, of course, and so much more fully explored and developed, but many of the seeds for it were planted in this little gem from 1829.

The other short, stand-alone works for chorus and piano are of variable quality, yet several stand out, most notably three spirited strophic choruses for men's voices and various soloists: *Chant guerrier* (1830), *Chanson à boire* (1830), and *Hélène* (TTBB version, 1844).[46] Each is a vibrant example of Berlioz's writing for male chorus, and would work well on concert programs. Of the remaining works with keyboard, the strongest are the delicate *Prière du matin* (SS[47]) on a text by Alphonse de Lamartine, and *Le Chant des Bretons* (TTBB, 1835; rev. 1849), which shares a common spirit with *Chant guerrier* and *Chanson à boire* (as well as the "Chanson de brigands" from *Lélio* mentioned earlier). *Le Chant des Bretons* offers an exhilarating presentation of Auguste Brizeux's three stanzas extolling the virtues of being a son of Brittany, each slightly varied and tinged with small harmonic details that give it an unmistakable Berliozian stamp.[48]

Some of the most sublime and innovative moments in Berlioz's musical *œuvre* lie in his purely orchestral works and in his operas. Yet something continually drew him to write for the human voice, and more specifically, for choral voices. From early models, not only Gluck, the music of the French Revolution, and his teachers, but also contemporary French grand opera—the spectacles of Spontini and Meyerbeer in particular—he could see how choral forces could be an integral part of the stories he wanted to tell. Throughout his works, he repeatedly returned to this sound and explored it, leaving us with a rich and utterly original corpus of music that shows a varied approach to writing for choral voices, one that is just as often intimate and delicate as it is, at other times, overwhelming in its size and sonic power.

EXAMPLE 15.6c Berlioz, *Le Ballet des ombres* (1st strophe), mm. 39–54. Source: *Hector Berlioz: New Edition of the Complete Works*, vol. 14; used with permission, Bärenreiter-Verlag.

[Allegro scherzando]

EXAMPLE 15.6c continued.

Notes

1 Berlioz's reaction to Heinrich Heine's criticism of his music, as reported by the composer in his memoirs on the occasion of the latter's more positive response to the premiere of *L'Enfance du Christ* (1854) in David Cairns, ed. and trans., *The Memoirs of Hector Berlioz* (New York, W. W. Norton, 1975), 479. (All page numbers in this and subsequent citations of the *Memoirs* refer to this edition of Cairns's translation. Editions issued by publishers other than W. W. Norton have different pagination.)

2 D. Kern Holoman, *Catalogue of the Works of Hector Berlioz. Hector Berlioz: New Edition of the Complete Works*, vol. 25 (Kassel: Bärenreiter-Verlag, 1987). Subsequent references to volumes of this edition of the complete works, under the general editorship of Hugh Macdonald (as opposed to the old edition produced by Malherbe and Weingartner, Breitkopf und Härtel, 1900–07), will use the standard abbreviation *NBE*.

3 Eighteenth-century French sacred music was typically scored for five parts without altos: soprano (dessus), divisi tenor (haute-contre/haute-taille and taille), and divisi bass (basse-taille and basse-contre); the six-part SSTTBB commonly found in nineteenth-century French choral music is simply an extension of this tradition. Contemporary treatises, including François-Joseph Fétis's *Traité du chant en chœur* (1837), Georges Kastner's *Traité générale d'instrumentation* (1837 and 1844) and Berlioz's own *Grande Traité d'instrumentation et d'orchestration modernes* (1843 and 1855), conclude that the contralto voice was more of an Italian phenomenon than a French one. A few of Berlioz's works use the older (eighteenth-century) terminology including the *Messe solennelle* (1824) and *Huit Scènes de Faust* (1829).

4 Macdonald suggests that this change to four-part writing with altos was the result of his exposure to choirs in Germany and England; see Hugh Macdonald, *Berlioz's Orchestration Treatise: A Translation and Commentary* (Cambridge: Cambridge University Press), 248.

5 Donna M. Di Grazia, "Concert Societies in Paris and their Choral Repertoires *c.*1828–1880" (Ph.D. diss., Washington University in St. Louis, 1993), 154–55.

6 See Macdonald, "Berlioz's 'Messe solennelle,'" *19th-Century Music* 16, 3 (Spring 1993): 267–85, for a discussion of the work's discovery and an analysis of the music, including the material that would find its way into prominent spots in the *Symphonie fantastique*, the *Grande Messe des morts*, *Benvenuto Cellini*, the *Grande Symphonie funèbre et triomphale*, the *Le Carnival roman*, and the *Te Deum*.

7 *Correspondance générale de Hector Berlioz, I: 1803–1832*, ed. by Pierre Citron (Paris: Flammarion, 1972), 97.

8 The three non-liturgical movements set the texts "Quis similis tui, Domine," "O Salutaris," and "Domine salvum." According to Macdonald ("Berlioz's Messe solennelle," 278), this division of the text places the work closer to the masses of Cherubini than those of Le Sueur. On some specific influences from Le Sueur, especially the Kyrie, see Julian Rushton, "Ecstacy of Emulation: Berlioz's *Messe solennelle* and his debt to Lesueur [*sic*]," *Musical Times* 140, 1868 (Autumn 1999): 11–18.

9 Berlioz took a casual approach to setting texts, frequently ignoring natural word stresses, as well as rearranging, omitting, and adding words and phrases even to traditional texts. This habit was one he may have learned from Le Sueur, whose music frequently shows a similar loose approach. For a general discussion of the subject of words and music in Berlioz's output, see Rushton, *The Music of Berlioz* (Oxford: Oxford University Press, 2001), 84–97, especially 88–89. One might add a note about the famously misaccented Kyrie eleisons in the first movement of the Requiem—Ky–ri–E e–le–i–SON—which reflects the natural accentuation of a native-French speaker. On the extensive text changes in the Requiem, see Edward T. Cone, "Berlioz's Divine Comedy: The *Grande Messe des morts*," *19th-Century Music* 4, 1 (Summer 1980): 3–16.

10 *Berlioz: Messe solennelle*, John Eliot Gardiner, conductor (London: Philips 442 137-2, 1994)

11 Cairns, *Memoirs*, 125. For details of the critical reception, see Cairns, *Berlioz: Volume One: The Making of an Artist 1803–32* (London: Cardinal/Sphere Books Ltd., 1989), 299–300.

12 Peter Bloom, ed., *Lélio ou Le Retour à la vie. NBE,* vol. 7 (Kassel: Bärenreiter-Verlag, 1992), ix. By 1855 Berlioz began to use the term "monodrame" instead.

13 Ibid., viii.

14 Bloom, "A Return to Berlioz's *Le Retour à la Vie*," *Musical Quarterly* (July 1978): 362–63. For a full discussion of the work, see Bloom's complete article (pp. 354–85) or his preface to the work in *NBE,* vol. 7.

15 Although the score specifies "Contraltos" as well as "Sopranos" on the top vocal line, there is only one real part for female voices; three divisi notes are provided for range purposes only.

16 Ibid., 364, n. 32. Berlioz replaced this text with a French one in 1855. The most famous instance of Berlioz inventing a language is in the utterly extraordinary Pandemonium scene for men's chorus near the end of *La Damnation de Faust*, but there are several other examples in his output as well, including the chorus of Nubian slaves in Act IV scene 2 of *Les Troyens*, and the incomplete four-part *Chœur de 402 voix en langue celtique inconnue* (H.93).

17 This is one of the few pieces composed prior to the 1850s for which Berlioz writes a part specifically for altos.

18 Ibid., 370.

19 By using the term "concert opera" here, I do not mean to negate the significant symphonic aspect of this work. As Holoman rightly notes in Chapter 5 in this volume, *Faust* is *not* an opera and it should not be staged (despite current trends to the contrary).

20 Mark Evan Bonds, *After Beethoven: Imperatives of Originality in the Symphony* (Cambridge, MA and London: Harvard University Press, 1996), 60. Both Bonds (on p. 59) and Cairns, "Berlioz and Beethoven," in *The Cambridge Companion to Berlioz,* ed. by Peter Bloom (Cambridge: Cambridge University Press, 2000), 227, translate a passage from a letter Berlioz wrote to Edouard Rocher in 1829, where the composer reports (here in Bonds's translation), "Now that I have heard that terrifying giant Beethoven, I know exactly where musical art stands; the issue now is to take it from there and push it farther . . . not further, that is impossible—he has reached the limits of the art—but as far along another route."

21 In the forward to the printed score, Berlioz writes, "There can doubtless be no mistake about the genre of this work. Even though voices are often used, it is neither a concert opera nor a cantata, but a choral symphony." See Holoman, ed., *Roméo et Juliette. NBE,* vol. 18 (Kassel: Bärenreiter-Verlag, 1990), 383. Nevertheless, there are certainly parts of this work that draw directly on the French operatic tradition, not the least of which being the seventh movement, which closely resembles an operatic finale. For a discussion of this aspect of the work, see Jeffrey Langford, "The 'Dramatic Symphonies' of Berlioz as an Outgrowth of the French Operatic Tradition," *Musical Quarterly* 69, 1 (Winter 1983): 85–103.

22 Berlioz knew the play from Pierre Letourneur's French translation of Garrick, as well as having seen the play. According to Rushton, *Roméo et Juliette* (Cambridge: Cambridge University Press, 1994), 18, when Berlioz and Émile Deschamps came to work on the libretto, they consulted Garrick's full text as well as the original Shakespeare. The most significant differences in Garrick's version from Shakespeare's are Juliet's funeral procession (movement 5) and the inclusion of the Tomb scene (movement 6), where the two lovers share one last exchange.

23 Berlioz, *Avant-propos,* as translated by Holoman, ed., *Roméo et Juliette,* 383.

24 According to Berlioz's own prescription, the prologue chorus could include up to twenty voices.

25 Rushton, *Roméo et Juliette,* 65.

26 Examples of these gestures are plentiful; see, for instance, movement 2 of *Harold in Italy,* "Sur les lagunes" from *Les Nuits d'été,* the famous septet with chorus, "Tout n'est que paix et charme autour de nous!," in Act IV of *Les Troyens,* and the two passages from the Requiem and *Te Deum* quoted in Examples 15.3a–c. For an example of a orchestral ostinato without the reference to psalmody, see the beginning of the Requiem's Lacrymosa (see Di Grazia, "Volcanic Eruptions: Berlioz and his *Grande Messe des morts,*" *The Choral Journal* 43, 4 (November 2002): 47–48).

27 In 1853, Berlioz added an optional third chorus of children's voices to the first and last movements after hearing the sound of 6,500 children singing in unison during a concert in St. Paul's Cathedral (London) two years earlier.

28 Cairns, *Memoirs,* 479.

29 See Denis McCaldin, ed. *Te Deum. NBE,* vol. 10 (Kassel: Bärenreiter-Verlag, 1973), x, for Berlioz's "Notes regarding performance," where the composer stipulates that the choirs and orchestra must be placed "at the extreme ends of the church opposite the organ." Macdonald (*Orchestration Treatise,* 156) notes that Berlioz did not advocate for the use of the organ and orchestra simultaneously. Rather, he said the organ's sound coming from such a distance "would not fully blend with the other instruments; it would respond to them, it would pose them questions; there would simply be an alliance between the two rival powers . . . Every time I have heard an organ playing at the same time as an orchestra it has struck me as a detestable noise, detracting from the orchestra rather than adding to it" (Macdonald, *Orchestration Treatise,* 157).

30 Macdonald, *Orchestration Treatise,* 335.

31 Di Grazia, "Volcanic Eruptions," 36–38.

32 Cairns, *Memoirs,* 479.

33 Macdonald, "Berlioz's Napoleonic *Te deum,*" *The Choral Journal* 43, 4 (November 2002): 15–16. For an insightful and detailed structural and harmonic analysis of the *Te Deum,* as well as a complete list of Berlioz's alterations to the traditional text, see Rushton, *The Music of Berlioz,* 220–36.

34 Howard E. Smither, *A History of the Oratorio,* vol. 4 (Chapel Hill, NC, and London: University of North Carolina Press, 2000), 552. See David Lloyd-Jones, ed., *L'Enfance du Christ. NBE,* vol. 11 (Kassel: Bärenreiter-Verlag, 1998), ix, and Cairns, *Berlioz Volume Two: Servitude and Greatness 1832–1869* (Berkeley: University of California Press, 1999), 550–51, for additional insight on the work's success. As Cairns points out (p. 551), while the enthusiasm generated by *L'Enfance du Christ* was "immensely gratifying" to Berlioz, it was also disappointing that "he was judged to have made progress, [and] was

extolled for the very qualities he had always been told he lacked: charm, gentleness, economy of means, simplicity, melodiousness—all this thanks to a work which, fond though he was of it, was in his view not in the same class as *Romeo* or *Faust.*"

35 Cairns, *Memoirs*, 474.

36 Holoman, *Berlioz* (Cambridge, MA: Harvard University Press, 1989), 314. According to Holoman, the *orgue mélodium* was "a portable, foot-pumped harmonium" built by the firm Alexandre *père et fils* in the early 1840s.

37 On the subject of expression in his music, Berlioz wrote in his memoirs (Cairns, *Memoirs*, 478), "The predominant features of my music are passionate expression, inward intensity, rhythmic impetus, and a quality of unexpectedness. When I say passionate expression, I mean an expression bent on reproducing the inner meaning of its subject, even when that subject is the opposite of passion, and gentle, tender feelings are being expressed, or a profound calm—the sort of expression that people have claimed to find in *The Childhood of Christ* and, even more, in the scene in Heaven in *The Damnation of Faust* and the Sanctus in the Requiem."

38 Ralph Locke notes that Béranger was "[t]he uncrowned national bard of France and, in particular, the voice of the liberal and republican opposition during the Bourbon restoration, . . . [whose] works [drew] praise and in some cases imitation from Goethe, Heine, Thackeray, Garibaldi and many of the progressive Russian writers." See Ralph P. Locke, "Béranger, Pierre-Jean de," in *Grove Music Online. Oxford Music Online*, http://www.oxfordmusiconline.com/subscriber/article/grove/music/42940 (accessed August 11, 2011). If Berlioz can be taken at his word, however, Béranger's words were not among his favorites: "I did indeed use those bad verses by Béranger, because the *feeling* of this quasi-poetry seemed musical to me." (Letter to Humbert Ferrand as quoted in Rushton, ed., *Choral Works with Orchestra I. NBE* vol. 12a (Kassel: Bärenreiter-Verlag, 1991), xiii.)

39 Cairns, *Servitude*, 92.

40 This surviving fragment was not added to the cantata until after Berlioz had been announced as the competition winner, but before it was performed publicly. Eventually, Berlioz destroyed most of *Sardanapale*, but some of the music in this final scene reappeared in later compositions, including in the offstage chorus of men leaving the Capulet ball in *Roméo et Juliette* (movement 2), and as the first principal theme in *L'Impériale*.

41 That *La Mort d'Orphée* did not win the prize had mostly to do with Berlioz's disregard of the instructions and conventions expected of a prize-winning cantata. The problems were varied. According to David Gilbert, ed., *Prix de Rome Works. NBE*, vol. 6 (Kassel: Bärenreiter-Verlag, 1998), x, his "transgressions" included omitting huge chunks of the assigned texts and rearranging lines at will, adding the movement for chorus (for which he wrote his own new text), writing idiomatic orchestral music that could not be easily reduced at the piano (as was the custom during the judging portion of the competition), and generally ignoring the proper "decorum" expected for such a piece. David Cairns summed up the situation best: "[Berlioz] set about his delicate task with fatal enthusiasm, behaving not like an examination candidate but like an established dramatist with full authority over the text and the right to adapt it to his own convention" (Cairns, *Making of an Artist*, 205–06). The charge that it was "unperformable" was made after the pianist assigned the task of reducing the score gave up in frustration.

42 Berlioz recycled a significant portion of *La Mort d'Orphée* in *Le Retour à la vie*, but the oddities of the latter work makes it is even less likely to receive performances today (though the Chicago Symphony Orchestra performed *Lélio* properly, following the *Symphonie fantastique* as Berlioz intended, in September 2010). For a full discussion of *La Mort d'Orphée* and its reuse in *Le Retour*, see Bloom, "Orpheus' Lyre Resurrected: A *Tableau Musical* by Berlioz," *Musical Quarterly* 61, 2 (April 1975): 189–211.

43 For a summary of the publication history of this collection and explanation of the title *Tristia*, see David Charleton, ed., *Choral Works with Orchestra II. NBE*, vol. 12b (Kassel: Bärenreiter-Verlag, 1993), ix–xii. *La Mort d'Ophélie* also exists in a version for solo voice and piano.

44 In *The Life of Berlioz* (Cambridge: Cambridge University Press, 1998), 116, Peter Bloom notes several similarities between the march and the famous second movement of Beethoven's Seventh Symphony, including their shared key, tempo marking, and rhythmic ostinato.

45 See, for example, Rushton, *The Music of Berlioz*, 3–4, and Macdonald, "Berlioz's Self-Borrowings," *Proceedings of the Royal Musical Association* 92 (1965–1966): 39.

46 All three pieces come from the collection titled *Neuf mélodies* (1830; also known as *Mélodies irlandaises*) on French translations of texts by Thomas Moore. The set includes a fourth work for choral voices: *Chant sacré* (later orchestrated). *Le Belle Voyageuse*, originally published in *Neuf mélodies*, was published separately for female chorus and orchestra in 1851; *Chant sacré* also appeared separately in 1843 in a version for oboe, four horns, timpani and string quintet.

47 "Chœur d'enfants."

48 The revised setting of *Le Chant des Bretons* is the stronger of the two versions published in the *NBE* (vol.

14). Holoman's catalogue (p. 150) notes the existence of an orchestration in J.-B. Weckerlin's hand, "but it is not known whether [it] is by Berlioz."

Selected Bibliography

Albright, Daniel. *Berlioz's Semi-Operas:* Roméo et Juliette *and* La Damnation de Faust. Rochester, NY: University of Rochester Press, 2001.

Barzun, Jacques. *Berlioz and the Romantic Century*. 2 vols. Boston: Little, Brown and Company, 1950; revised edition, New York: Columbia University Press, 1969. A one-volume revision appeared in 1956 under the title *Berlioz and his Century*. Cleveland: World; rpt. Chicago: University of Chicago Press, 1982.

Bloom, Peter. "A Return to Berlioz's *Le Retour à la Vie*," *Musical Quarterly* (July 1978): 354–85.

——. "Berlioz and the 'Prix de Rome' of 1830," *Journal of the American Musicological Society* 34, 2 (Summer 1981): 279–304.

——. *The Life of Berlioz*. Cambridge: Cambridge University Press, 1998.

——. "Orpheus' Lyre Resurrected: A *Tableau Musical* by Berlioz," *Musical Quarterly* 61, 2 (April 1975): 189–211.

——, ed. *Berlioz Studies*. Cambridge: Cambridge University Press, 1992.

——, ed. *The Cambridge Companion to Berlioz*. Cambridge: Cambridge University Press, 2000.

——, ed. *Grand Traité d'instrumentation et d'orchestration modernes*. Vol. 24 of *Hector Berlioz: New Edition of the Complete Works*. Kassel: Bärenreiter-Verlag, 2003.

——, ed. *Lélio ou Le Retour à la vie*. Vol. 7 of *Hector Berlioz: New Edition of the Complete Works*. Kassel: Bärenreiter-Verlag, 1992.

Cairns, David. *Berlioz: Volume One: 1803–1832: The Making of an Artist*. London: A. Deutsch, 1989; 2nd rev. ed., Berkeley: University of California, 2000.

——. *Berlioz: Volume Two: 1832–1869: Servitude and Greatness*. London: Allen Lane The Penguin Press, 1999. Berkeley: University of California Press, 2000.

——, trans. and ed. *The Memoirs of Hector Berlioz*. (*Mémoires*, completed 1865; published 1870). New York: W. W. Norton, 1975.

Charlton, David, ed. *Choral Works with Orchestra II*. Volume 12b of *Hector Berlioz: New Edition of the Complete Works*. Kassel: Bärenreiter-Verlag, 1993.

Cone, Edward T. "Berlioz's Divine Comedy: The *Grande Messe des morts*," *19th-Century Music* 4, 1 (1980): 3–16. Reprinted in *Music: A View from Delft*, ed. Robert Morgan. Chicago: University of Chicago Press, 1989, 139–57.

——. "Inside the Saint's Head: The Music of Berlioz," in *Musical Newsletter* 1, 3 (1971), 3–12; 1, 4 (1971), 16–20; and 2, 1 (1972), 19–22. Reprinted in *Nineteenth Century Music*, Garland Library of the History of Western Music, 1–19. Vol. 9, New York: Garland, 1985; and in *Music: A View from Delft*, ed. Robert Morgan, 217–48. Chicago: University of Chicago Press, 1989.

Correspondance générale de Hector Berlioz. 8 vols. Pierre Citron, general editor. Paris: Flammarion, 1972–2003.

Di Grazia, Donna M. "Volcanic Eruptions: Berlioz and his *Grande Messe des morts*," *The Choral Journal* 43, 4 (November 2002): 27–55.

Gilbert, David, ed. *Prix de Rome Works*. Vol. 6 of *Hector Berlioz: New Edition of the Complete Works*. Kassel: Bärenreiter-Verlag, 1998.

Haar, James. "The Operas and the Dramatic Legend," in *The Cambridge Companion to Berlioz*, ed. Peter Bloom. Cambridge: Cambridge University Press, 2000, 81–95.

Holoman, D. Kern. *Berlioz*. Cambridge, MA: Harvard University Press, 1989.

——. "Berlioz," in *The Nineteenth-Century Symphony*, ed. D. Kern Holoman. New York: Schirmer Books, 1997, 108–41.

——. "Performing Berlioz," in *The Cambridge Companion to Berlioz*, ed. Peter Bloom. Cambridge: Cambridge University Press, 2000, 173–96.

——, ed. *Catalogue of the Works of Hector Berlioz*. Vol. 25 of *Hector Berlioz: New Edition of the Complete Works*. Kassel: Bärenreiter-Verlag, 1987.

——, ed. *Roméo et Juliette*. Vol. 18 of *Hector Berlioz: New Edition of the Complete Works*. Kassel: Bärenreiter-Verlag, 1990.

Kemp, Ian. "Romeo and Juliet and *Roméo et Juliette*," in *Berlioz Studies*, ed. Peter Bloom. Cambridge: Cambridge University Press, 1992, 37–79.

Kindermann, Jürgen, *Grande Messe des morts*. Vol. 9 of *Hector Berlioz: New Edition of the Complete Works*. Kassel: Bärenreiter-Verlag, 1978.

Lloyd-Jones, David, ed. *L'Enfance du Christ*. Vol. 11 of *Hector Berlioz: New Edition of the Complete Works*. Kassel: Bärenreiter-Verlag, 1998.

Locke, Ralph. "The Religious Works," in *The Cambridge Companion to Berlioz*, ed. Peter Bloom. Cambridge: Cambridge University Press, 2000, 96–107.

Macdonald, Hugh. *Berlioz*. London: J. Dent, 1982 (and subsequent reprints, including Oxford University Press, 2000).

——. "Berlioz's *Messe solennelle*," *19th-Century Music* 16, 3 (Spring 1993): 267–85.

——. "Berlioz's Napoleonic *Te deum*," *The Choral Journal* 43, 4 (November 2002): 9–17.

——. "Berlioz's Self-Borrowings," *Proceedings of the Royal Musical Association* 92 (1965–66): 27–44.

——, ed. *Berlioz's Orchestration Treatise: A Translation and Commentary*. Cambridge: Cambridge University Press, 2002.

——, ed. *Messe solennelle*. Vol. 23 of *Hector Berlioz: New Edition of the Complete Works*. Kassel: Bärenreiter-Verlag, 1994.

——, ed. *Miscellaneous Works*. Vol. 21 of *Hector Berlioz: New Edition of the Complete Works*. Kassel: Bärenreiter-Verlag, 2005.

McCaldin, Denis, ed. *Te Deum*. Vol. 10 of *Hector Berlioz: New Edition of the Complete Works*. Kassel: Bärenreiter-Verlag, 1973.

O'Neal, Melinda. *Berlioz's L'Enfance du Christ: trilogie sacrée, Op. 25: A Conductor's Analysis for Performance*. D.Mus., Indiana University, 1987.

Reeve, Katherine Kolb. "*The Damnation of Faust*: The Perils of Heroism in Music," in *Berlioz Studies*, ed. Peter Bloom. Cambridge: Cambridge University Press, 1992, 148–88.

Rushton, Julian. "Ecstasy of Emulation: Berlioz's *Messe solennelle* and his Debt to Lesueur," *Musical Times* 140, 1868 (Autumn 1999): 11–18.

——. "The Genesis of Berlioz's *La Damnation de Faust*," *Music and Letters* 56 (1975): 129–46.

——. *The Music of Berlioz*. Oxford: Oxford University Press, 2001.

——. *The Musical Language of Berlioz*. Cambridge: Cambridge University Press, 1983.

——. *Roméo et Juliette*. Cambridge: Cambridge University Press, 1994.

——, ed. *Choral Works with Orchestra I*. Vol. 12a of *Hector Berlioz: New Edition of the Complete Works*. Kassel: Bärenreiter-Verlag, 1991.

——, ed. *La Damnation de Faust*. Vol. 8a/b of *Hector Berlioz: New Edition of the Complete Works*. Kassel: Bärenreiter-Verlag, 1979 and 1986.

——, ed. *Huit Scènes de Faust*. Vol. 5 of *Hector Berlioz: New Edition of the Complete Works*. Kassel: Bärenreiter-Verlag, 1970.

Rumbold, Ian, ed. *Choral Works for Keyboard*. Vol. 14 of *Hector Berlioz: New Edition of the Complete Works*. Kassel: Bärenreiter-Verlag, 1996.

16

FÉLICIEN DAVID, CHARLES GOUNOD, AND JULES MASSENET

Clair Rowden

Cardiff University

When we think of the choral repertoire from nineteenth-century France, few are likely to mention the names of at least two of the composers studied here. The diverse outputs of Félicien David, Charles Gounod, and Jules Massenet, however, offer a view of the broad range of choral music composed in France from the 1830s to the end of the century, a time when choral music-making was linked to a wide range of social, political, religious, and educational experiences.

Félicien David

Félicien David (1810–76) is probably best remembered for his ode-symphonie *Le Désert* (1844), a musical tale of a caravan moving through the Arabian desert, comprising purely instrumental numbers, a tenor solo, male chorus, spoken and declaimed text. Through this work, David brought to musical exoticism a new authenticity, having traveled to Turkey and Egypt with a group of fellow Saint-Simonians between 1833 and 1835. After the success of *Le Désert* in France and elsewhere (including in the United States, where it was performed repeatedly from 1846 to 1849), he went on to write three other large-scale works all involving chorus: *Moïse au Sinaï* (1846), *Christophe Colomb, ou la découverte du nouveau monde* (1847), and *L'Eden* (1848). Of these, only *Christophe Colomb* enjoyed a successful public reception.

David's output as a composer of choral music were bound up with Saint-Simonianism, a utopian Christian social movement with which he was associated from 1832 on. He wrote much of the ceremonial and ritual music for the daily lives of the group's "apostles," who lived together in a celibate male community just east of Paris. The Saint-Simonians believed in the idea of using art as a "lever" to "stir the heart of humanity." The choral works David wrote for the twenty (or so) voices that made up the Saint-Simonian men's choir fell into three categories: strophic ideological songs (with verses sung by a soloist or unison voices, and the chorus sung in four-part homophony), propagandistic choruses or choruses keyed to events in the daily ritual—these followed a structure similar to the strophic songs—and works composed for specific, often ceremonial occasions.[1] Of these categories, the first type found immediate and continuing popular success.

The most well-known ceremonial chorus David composed was *Le Retour du Père* (later known as *Salut*), which was sung frequently by the Saint-Simonians and their supporters during the early 1830s. Its structure closely follows that of the prose text written by fellow Saint-Simonian Achille Rousseau. It is divided into several sections distinguished by constrasting tempos, moods, and keys:

opening and closing acclamations of "le père"—a reference to their leader, Prosper Enfantin—followed by sections reflecting the suffering of the people, the return of the Messiah, and new hope.[2] Another occasional work, *La Danse des astres*, was written shortly before the Saint-Simonian apostles dispersed in 1833, following a long period of government surveillance and harassment that led to significant legal action.[3] This piece displays slightly more varied choral textures than *Le Retour du Père*, and takes on the character of a pastoral dance with its extensive use of pedal points; it also includes some novel harmonic shifts.[4] One could imagine that the male-voiced Orphéon choirs made use of this repertoire, especially as both the Orphéon movement and Saint-Simonianism espoused the belief that music could foster socially progressive behavior in the masses. Surprisingly, it seems that only David's *Chant du Soir* figured in the Orphéon repertoire.[5]

David's large-scale works of the 1840s, following his return from the Middle East, were not written for performance by the Saint-Simonian apostles, but continued, in various ways, to serve both the ideological ends of the movement and Enfantin's self-aggrandizement within it.[6] For example, Enfantin harnessed the furthering of his cause in Germany for the building of the Suez Canal to the success of *Le Désert*. Similarly, the unsuccessful oratorio *Moïse au Sinaï* was planned as propaganda to further Enfantin's efforts in Sinai, and the ode-symphonie *Christophe Colomb* was a thinly veiled allusion to Enfantin and the creation of a Saint-Simonian "new world."[7]

The male-voice choral writing in *Le Désert* recalls the hymn-like style of many of his earlier Saint-Simonian choruses, but with more variation of choral textures, using voices paired or in alternation with the tenor soloist. The picturesque story of *Christophe Colombe*, however, includes a four-part mixed chorus that David featured in a much more dramatic, gender-specific and operatic way. In Part I, for example, a chorus of sailors swear allegiance before leaving for the Americas; after a choral prayer, the women bid farewell as the men depart.[8] Likewise, in Part II the "Chœur mysterieux des génies de l'océan," a reworking of the orientalist chorus *Les Étoiles* (1833) for men's voices, is a wordless, melismatic siren song (SSAA) that evokes the sailors' response. A rousing sailors' chorus (also in Part II) leads into the musical depiction of a storm on the high seas with fine expressive orchestral writing.

Charles Gounod

While David's choral works were largely the manifestation of his adherence to Saint-Simonian ideals and lifestyle, Charles Gounod's (1818–93) choral music stemmed from three different aspects of his life: his involvement with the Orphéon de Paris from 1852 to 1859 (as director and resident composer of sorts), his strong ties to the Catholic Church,[9] and his success in the world of opera, the choruses from which merged the needs of the stage with techniques he had absorbed while conducting the Orphéon.

Gounod's in-depth involvement with both the Orphéon and the Catholic Church resulted in a large output of sacred and secular choral music, including nearly two dozen masses, three oratorios and some 200 or so small-scale works—cantatas, motets, partsongs and other secular works.[10] His *Messe solennelle de Sainte Cécile* (1855), written for Baron Taylor's Association des Artistes musiciens and their annual celebratory concert at Saint-Eustache on the feast of Saint Cecilia is perhaps Gounod's most well-known mass.[11] Scored for SATB chorus and soloists, orchestra, and organ, the work employs the full chromatic harmonic palette typical of music from the mid-nineteenth century, though the choral writing tends to be predominantly homophonic and homorhythmic.[12]

Gounod's choral works composed during his years as director of the Orphéon de Paris also included pedagogical collections such as *La Prière et l'étude* (1853–55), comprising seventeen simple three- and four-part choruses for children's voices—"aux orphéonistes enfants"—designed to reinforce religious and educational ideas.[13] Short works with titles such as "Le Catéchisme,"

"L'Histoire sainte," "L'Arithmétique," and "La Géographie" are set homophonically, with simple diatonic harmony and stepwise motion.

Two more adventurous short works provide a good insight into Gounod's choral writing during this period. *Près du fleuve étranger* (1861), a paraphrase of "Super flumina Babylonis" (Psalm 137) with a text by A. Quételart, enjoyed huge success as a concert piece, and figured as a staple in the repertoires of many choral ensembles including that of the Société des Concerts du Conservatoire.[14] This highly attractive work opens with a long introduction in C minor for piano or organ alone. The four-part mixed chorus enters *a cappella* and *pianissimo*, with discreet accompaniment gradually added as they sing of weeping for Sion. As in much of Gounod's sacred music, the harmonic coloring is inspired by plainsong harmonizations, here with steps of a descending third between chords, thus emphasizing chords on the sixth and fourth, second and flattened seventh degrees of the scale. Several contrasting passages follow, including a rather static Adagio section in E-flat major (now in 4/4 meter) whose choral texture remains homophonic and conservative in its use of accidentals and small intervals; a brief *fortissimo* passage marked *Moderato maestoso* featuring a more expansive unison melody; a short three-voice fugal passage (*Allegro moderato*); and a broadly modulating peroration with much chromatic motion in the voices (doubled in the keyboard for ease of execution) that adds significant harmonic color and interest. The final section recalls the tempo of the third (here marked *Moderato maestoso assai* but now in 3/4 like the opening) and establishes C major, though with brief inflections of the minor mode. In a little over five minutes of music, this work makes a strong impression with its archaic, yet sophisticated harmony allied to varied vocal colors and textures, and one can only lament its disappearance from the active repertoire.

La Cigale et la fourmi (TTBB *a cappella*), written specifically for the Orphéon in 1856, is fairly indicative of the music Gounod wrote for the movement.[15] The choice of text, by the famous seventeenth-century fablist Jean de La Fontaine, illustrates the growing influence of early music at the time.[16] As briefly discussed in the overview chapter on France, there was a small but somewhat constant stream of Renaissance and Baroque vocal music performed in the capital by a surprising number of choirs throughout the century, both working class and high society, Catholic and Protestant. This corpus of music not only included sacred works by Palestrina, Victoria and others, but also Janequin's chansons *La Bataille de Marignan* and *Le Chant des oiseaux*. It was natural, therefore, for Gounod to set a seventeenth-century text that was a cornerstone of French literary heritage—La Fontaine's fable—in the style of Janequin, France's most popular Renaissance composer.

La Fontaine's tale recounts the story of the lazy and hungry grasshopper who, after singing all summer is left with no food stocks for the winter; on asking the industrious ant to give him some of his food, he is told by his ungenerous friend that he may have sung all summer but now will dance all winter. As in *Près du fleuve étranger*, the music of *La Cigale* is divided into short sections (following the text), beginning with a delicate but lively four-part fugal passage to set the scene. The grasshopper's dilemma and appeal to the ant (presented in the relative minor) again uses fugato entries and some imitation between the voice parts. The wary ant's response provokes a dramatic change of texture, including a witty musical effect gleaned from Janequin: the second tenor and first bass voices hum sustained notes while the second basses hum a rapid staccato walking bassline (tinged with chromaticism) before the first tenors voice the ant's suspicions.[17] The grasshopper's explanation of his lyrical outpouring comes in a homophonic full-voiced *forte* passage beginning in D minor that recalls Russian folk dance. But it is for the ant's condemnation of the grasshopper to dance all winter that a delicate *pianissimo* dance and drum rhythm is struck up in the lower three voices to a repeated "la la la la la," as the first tenors once again take on the voice of the ant, with a *crescendo* to a *forte* and the reuniting of all voices for the final command, "maintenant, dansez" ("now, dance"). As an unaccompanied work with more varied choral textures and vocal lines comprising less stepwise motion and larger intervals, this chorus must have posed serious challenges to some of the Orphéon groups who attempted to sing it. But due to its lively nature and effective character painting in the vein of the Janequin chansons, it has remained a firm favorite with male-voiced choirs in France.

Gounod's masses from the 1870s and 1880s show the composer's developing choral style, from the austere, white-note style of the organ-accompanied *Missa angeli custodes* (1873) to the archaic flavor of the *Messe solennelle sur l'intonation de la liturgie catholique* (1888), where Gounod weaves chant throughout the Mass as a cantus firmus, and moves his choral textures seamlessly between homophony and points of imitation.[18] During this later period in his career, Gounod continued to compose in other choral genres as well. Two late works were the result of commissions from the Birmingham Choir Festival to write large-scale religious oratorios of popular appeal: *La Rédemption* (not to be confused with Franck's work of the same name) received its premier in 1882 by a 270-strong chorus, and *Mors et vita*, conceived as a sequel to *La Rédemption* and first performed in 1885, with a royal command performance given in London's Royal Albert Hall the following year.[19] Both works are triptychs, with sections corresponding to Calvary, The Resurrection and Pentecost in *La Rédemption*, and Requiem, Judgment and Eternal life in *Mors et vita*.

Following Le Sueur and Berlioz as models, Gounod exploited the spatial separation of and dialogue between different performing forces in *Mors et vita*, which include a large SATB chorus with soloists, full orchestra and organ, a small twenty-four-voice chorus, and four harps. The "petit chœur" and accompanying harps were placed in front of the main ensemble at the start of the work, but later moved to either side of the organ loft for "Vita," thus symbolizing the elevation of the redeemed to heaven.[20] The piece abounds with recurring musical elements, the most characteristic being a whole-tone descent through a tritone to represent the implacability of divine justice and the suffering of the condemned. Indeed, the omnipresence of the tritone—the Renaissance *diabolus in musica*—saturates the oratorio's harmonic palette, especially in the first two parts of the oratorio, and highly colors the vocal lines with chromaticism.[21] Both the prologue and the "Confutatis maledictis" (Part I, No. 7) use the descending tritone theme sung by unison chorus three times; in the prologue, each repetition is a semitone higher, with prominent diminished seventh brass chords, ominous timpani rolls and tamtam strikes—a similar diabolical language to that used for *Faust*—to invoke the suffering in hell. Also in Part I, however, is "A custodia matutina" (Part I, No. 1b), a white-note double chorus in sixteenth-century pastiche style reminiscent of Palestrina's *Stabat Mater* and some of Gounod's masses mentioned above. The Dies irae (Part I, No. 2) is in C minor and includes the descending tritone at the heart of the ominous fugal subject, sung *pianissimo* and slowly building in dynamic and menacing. The "Quam olim Abrahae" section of the Offertorium (Part I, No. 9) also culminates in a grand choral fugue, following the chilling effect created by the slow build up through the vocal parts of chromatic chords, alleviated by the reassuring major key and resolutely diatonic soprano solo.

Part II ("Judicum") is dominated by brash brass fanfares and squalling piccolos, which use the descending whole-tone scale outlining the tritone sequentially, in ascending chromatic shifts to evoke hell and damnation. Indeed, rising sequences pervade the vocal writing throughout the work, as well as much of Gounod's choral *œuvre*. In Part III ("Vita"), the Sanctus (No. 3) first deploys angelic voices (SA), accompanied by harps and a lyrically serene solo violin melody, before the full choral entry. "Ego sum Alpha et Omega" (Part III, No. 7), with its bare fifth harmony and monotone intonation for unison chorus creates an almost medieval sound world before reverting to the joyously diatonic eternal realm (at "et ero illi Deus"), again using harps and a soaring violin melody worthy of Massenet, and alternating between the small chorus situated in the organ loft and full chorus below. This majestic work ends with a resounding fugal Hosanna (Part III, No. 9) in the best oratorio tradition.

Jules Massenet

Through its varied and subtle uses of solo voices and choral combinations, as well as its chromatic harmonic language, Gounod's *Mors et vita* is a work that is highly dramatic in tone. Nevertheless, it remains within the realm of religious oratorio, as opposed to the theatrical oratorios of Jules Massenet (1842–1912). As France's leading opera composer during the last two decades of the nineteenth century, Massenet managed to reconcile (for wide-ranging audiences at least) operatic form with religious content for the concert hall in a way unlike any other composer. While Gounod retained his allegiance to Catholic teachings and practice, Massenet was a disciple of the former cleric turned anticlerical theologian and positivist philosopher Ernest Renan and his "relativizing" retellings of the Gospels. In Renan's controversial book *La Vie de Jésus* (1863), Jesus and his entourage were placed squarely in their historical and geographical context, but stripped of their divinity.[22] In the Scriptures, Renan was interested in the biographical and psychological aspects of the protagonists. The same was true, but in the interests of drama and theatre, for Massenet and his librettist Louis Gallet in their "sacred drama" *Marie-Magdeleine* (1873).[23] In an attempt to express the human sentiments of the Gospel "characters," Massenet and Gallet reworked the traditional oratorio formula in *Marie-Magdeleine*, pushing it much further toward opera in terms of both its structure and its content.[24] The action unfolds in three acts (and includes stage directions as in opera), with passages of more traditionally religious music alternating with operatic arias, duets, and ensembles. The two protagonists—Mary Magdalene and Jesus—are assigned the voice types of typical opera lovers (soprano and tenor), and the duets written for them tread a fine, ambiguous line between chaste intimacy and open passion, as in much of Massenet's operatic and religious music. In a similar vein to David's ode-symphonies, Berlioz's *L'Enfance du Christ*, and Franck's oratorios *Ruth* and *Rébecca*, this work has pastoral and exotic musical coloring, although the musical orientalization of the prostitute Mary Magdalene and the women around her (before Christ's death and after his resurrection) immediately evokes the West's fixation on harem culture, and emphasizes the erotically alluring character of the repentant sinner and the potentially blasphemous portrayal of Christ.

Yet despite its operatic character, *Marie-Magdeleine* is a true choral work, but one where a Renan-derived realism is applied equally to the chorus. Rather than reflecting on the story in a more traditional oratorio manner, chorus members are required to act as full participants in the unfolding drama, appearing in various voice groupings with sharply characterized and differentiated musical styles that reflect multiple dramatic roles.[25] Short fugato passages tend to be reserved for belligerent haranguing of the protagonists, while some of the most serene chant-like choruses are reserved for the disciples. In Act II, the largely unaccompanied prayer for the twelve disciples in alternation with the full male chorus (singing passages of the Lord's Prayer) successfully combines a modern chromatic idiom with hymn-like plagal harmonic motion and points of imitation in a sublime meditation.

The crux of the oratorio from a choral perspective is the "Chœur du supplice" in Act III (No. 12), as the assembled groups (including children) taunt Jesus on the cross. This is a purely choral dramatic scene; apart from one short utterance from Jesus himself, no other solo characters are present. In the first section, all condemn the crucified in a D-minor, swift tempo, homophonic and homorhythmic rant. The *Andante con moto* section begins in B-flat major with unison basses (designated as Docteurs et Princes des Prêtres) ironically taunting Jesus. The unison tenors (Pharisiens) take up their lead, insulting Jesus, followed by a full *Allegro* chorus during which Jesus is incited to save himself, and where the chorus's aggression and mockery are suggested by copious diminished seventh chords. After Jesus's words "Forgive them Father, for they know not what they do," the first section is repeated with an added coda comprising some colorful harmonic resolutions. The oratorio's finale, the "Chorus of Christians" (No. 15), unites the organ, the disciples, full chorus and the children's "chœur invisible"—who interject from the depths of heaven ("dans les profondeurs du ciel") singing Gloria in excelsis Deo—in an E-major, joyous affirmation of the living Christ. The homophonic texture is varied only by a short passage of bell-like fugato entries: as in the "Chœur du supplice," the peroration of the movement contains some unexpected harmonic shifts before the final establishment of the tonic key.

The success of *Marie-Magdeleine* in April 1873 completely overwhelmed that of Franck's *Rédemption*, given the previous day by Édouard Colonne and the Concert national, and it went on to be one of two works that firmly established Massenet's national and growing international reputation.[26] Massenet repeated the success of *Marie-Magdeleine* in 1875 with the "mystère en trois parties" *Eve*, again with a libretto by Gallet.[27] This work is less operatic in style; the chorus is assigned a narrative function and is divided into less elaborate dramatic characters, although the piece nevertheless alternately deploys small and full choruses characterized as "les voix du ciel" and "les voix de la nuit," or "les voix de la nature" and "les esprits de l'abîme." Perhaps the most dramatic section of the work is "Eve dans la solitude" (Part II) in which the various choral groups entice Eve to taste the forbidden fruit. The opening number for small chorus is one of Massenet's finest examples of choral writing, as the lower three voices accompany with often surprising harmonies the lilting soprano melody.

A similar design is used for *La Vierge* (1880), a "sacred legend" in four scenes with a libretto by Charles Grandmougin that describes important episodes in the life of the Virgin Mary, from the Annunciation to the Assumption. The chorus is again used in different permutations as various characters, from heavenly angels to guests at the wedding in Cana. The third scene, "Good Friday," is of particularly successful dramatic design with the chorus acting as the people and soldiers—with aggressive taunts and spat insults—who accompany Christ's march to Calvary. The last scene, "The Assumption," contains some of the most moving music Massenet ever wrote. The hushed orchestral prelude "Le dernier sommeil de la Vierge" for muted strings quickly became a staple on concert programs while the Virgin's final rapturous aria of mystical ecstasy is on a par with the famous "Méditation religieuse" from Massenet's 1894 opera *Thaïs*.[28] As Mary ascends into heaven, an angel chorus, previously sung by women, is given to children placed in the loft next to the organ, who sing the Magnificat text (in Latin). In this section, Massenet, like Gounod and his predecessors, also exploits spatialization and dialogue techniques harnessed to theological doctrine. The female chorus sings of roses, Cherubim, and Seraphim while the male chorus sings of the Virgin's glory; the culmination of the work sees all choral voices unite in chanting the Magnificat in "pure" and "godly" C major.

Massenet's choral repertoire is far less extensive than that of the devout Gounod or of many other contemporaries who held posts as organists. His small-scale religious works that include a chorus number in the single digits. His secular choruses number around twenty, a dozen of which were written for unaccompanied men's chorus, along with his TTBB opera choruses, which were popular with Orphéon groups.

The theatrical qualities of the three large-scale oratorios, written over a period of seven years, were eschewed to a certain extent in favor of something closer to Handelian tradition for his last oratorio, *La Terre promise* (1900).[29] Soprano, tenor, and baritone soloists sing (in turn) in one universal voice rather than as different characters, while the chorus provides the voice of Israel. As the least operatic of Massenet's oratorios, it is the one that contains the most fugal passages, although the chorus is called upon to "act" in the narration of the fall of the walls of Jericho. Especially memorable are the chorus's four-fold cries of "Jahvé" at the top of their vocal and dynamic ranges, which are followed by a "terrible, high-pitched, powerful and prolonged scream" as the walls tumble; it is a moment that recalls the unpitched yet timed cry of horror from the people as Christ expires on the cross in *Marie-Magdeleine*.

Massenet's very human Christ and Gounod's traditional vision of Christian redemption present two complementary faces of religious beliefs, and of choral music, that gained immense popularity in nineteenth-century France. David's choral efforts, perhaps most notably *Christophe Colomb*, seem to bridge the gap between the sacred and the secular with their connection to the quasi-religious Saint-Simonian movement, and in *Christophe Colomb* with its portrayal of a Messianic figure who will lead to a better world within a social utopian framework. Despite the varied subject matter and choral approaches used by David, Massenet, and especially Gounod, all three composers managed to exploit the dramatic possibilities of their chosen choral genres—from *ode-symphonie* to *drame sacrée*—each developing formal procedures to enhance the role of the chorus and its identification with quasi-operatic individual characters on the one hand, and large collective, reflexive bodies on the other. One might argue, however, that it was Gounod who did more than any other French composer in the second half of the nineteenth century to keep choral singing in the foreground of France's musical culture. Through his diverse involvement with the Parisian choral scene, from his direction of the working-class Orphéon to his honorary presidency of the aristocratic Concordia choral society (founded in 1879),[30] and through his vast compositional output of liturgical music, large-scale works for the concert hall, and popular and operatic choruses, Gounod helped to ensure that by the turn of the twentieth century, choral singing remained part of everyday musical life for large sectors of the French public.

Notes

1 Ralph P. Locke, *Music, Musicians and the Saint-Simonians* (Chicago and London: The University of Chicago Press, 1986), 124–31.
2 *Le Retour du Père/Salut* was eventually revised with new opening and closing sections, and turned into the far more successful *Le Chant des moissonneurs* (see ibid., 253).
3 See ibid., 145–48 for details. Scores for a selection of David's Saint-Simonian choruses including *Le Retour du Père* and *La Danse des astres* can be found in ibid., 279–327.
4 David later expanded the piece and published it as *Chant du soir* (1846) with a text by Sylvain Saint-Etienne; an orchestrated version of the revised work appeared in 1867. Indeed, thirty of David's Saint-Simonian choruses were republished by Saint-Etienne (all with alternative texts by Charles Chaubet) and issued in a collection titled *La Ruche harmonieuse* (1853).
5 Donna M. Di Grazia, "Concert Societies in Paris and their Choral Repertoires *c.*1828–1880," 2 vols., (Ph.D. diss., Washington University in St, Louis, 1993), 411–12.
6 Locke, *Music, Musicians and the Saint-Simonians*, 142, 209–12.
7 On the conception and realization of *Christophe Colomb*, see Annegret Fauser, "'Hymns of the Future': Reading Félicien David's *Christophe Colomb* (1847) as a Saint-Simonian Symphony," *Journal of Musicological Research* 28 (2009): 1–29.
8 This section of *Christophe Colombe* was a reworking of the Saint-Simonian chorus *Le Nouveau Temple* (1833); see Locke, *Music, Musicians and the Saint-Simonians,* 135–6, and 254–55.
9 He took minor orders before realizing his true vocation as a musician, but he remained close to the Papal nuncio in Paris, and translated the Pope's sermons in an official capacity; his *Marche ponitificale* (1869) was adopted as the hymn of the Vatican City State in 1950.
10 This number includes several dozen unaccompanied works for children's voices.
11 Di Grazia ("Concert Societies," 418) affirms that Orphéon singers were almost certainly involved in the première of this work.
12 For a summary of this Mass, see Steven Huebner, "Gounod," in *Grove Music Online. Oxford Music Online* (accessed August 2010).
13 See Di Grazia, "Concert Societies," 416–19 for a list of Gounod's compositions written during this time.
14 Ibid., 47; a score of *Près du fleuve étranger* is reproduced on pp. 504–14.
15 Ibid., 534–41 shows a reprint of the score.
16 Gounod set several other La Fontaine texts as well, including *Le corbeau et le renard* (1857), also for unaccompanied men's voices.
17 Humming (*bouche fermé*) is an effect seen regularly in Orphéon repertoire.
18 Huebner, "Gounod," *Grove Music Online* (accessed August 2010).
19 Gounod also composed the Latin motet *Gallia* for the opening of the Royal Albert Hall in 1871.

20 Richard Langham Smith, "Gounod *Mors et vita*," liner notes (EMI Classics 7544592, Barbara Hendricks, Nadine Denize, John Aler, José Van Dam, Christoph Kuhlmann, Orféon Donostiarra, Orchestre du Capitole de Toulouse, Michel Plasson, 1992), 10–18, at 14.

21 Huebner argues that Gounod's insistence on the tritone also implies tonal dissolution and confusion in post-Wagnerian terms, and its later use in opposition to the perfect fifth (which produces harmonic stability), as a metaphor for faith (Gounod," *Grove Music Online*, accessed August 2010).

22 For further discussion of Renan's influence on the religious context within which Massenet wrote his oratorios and operas, see Clair Rowden, "L'Homme saint chez Massenet: l'amour sacré et le sacre de l'amour" in Jean-Christophe Branger and Alban Ramaut (eds.), *Opéra et religion sous la IIIe République* (Saint-Etienne: Publications de l'Université de Saint-Etienne, 2006), 257–84.

23 Erik W. Goldstrom also writes on Massenet's and Gallet's Renan-influenced oratorios in *A Whore in Paradise: The Oratorios of Jules Massenet* (Ph.D. dissertation, Stanford University, 1998).

24 *Marie-Magdeleine* was given in fully staged version at the Opéra-Comique in 1903.

25 The chorus's multiple roles include generic women, Holy women, Christians, Pharisees, Scribes, Young Magdalene men, Doctors and Princes of the Priesthood, Roman soldiers and executioners, as well as a small chorus of disciples (the role of Judas is taken by a bass soloist), and children's angelic voices.

26 The other work to establish Massenet's reputation was incidental music for Leconte de Lisle's play *Les Erinnyes*, also conducted by Colonne at the Théâtre de l'Odéon three months previously.

27 *Eve* was premiered by Charles Lamoureux and his Société de l'harmonie sacrée.

28 This music is used in instrumental version for the death of Manon Lescaut in Lucas Leighton's score of the popular ballet *Manon*, originally commissioned by Kenneth Macmillan for the Royal Ballet, Covent Garden in the 1970s, which constitutes a collage of pre-existing music by Massenet skillfully knitted together.

29 Demar Irvine, *Massenet: A Chronicle of His Life and Times* (Portland, OR: Amadeus Press, 1994), 227.

30 Katharine Ellis, *Interpreting the Musical Past: Early Music in Nineteenth-Century France*. New York and Oxford: Oxford University Press, 2005, 98.

Selected Bibliography

Di Grazia, Donna M. "Concert Societies in Paris and their Choral Repertories, *c.*1828–1880." Ph.D. diss., Washington University in St. Louis, 1993.

Ellis, Katharine. *Interpreting the Musical Past: Early Music in Nineteenth-Century France*. New York and Oxford: Oxford University Press, 2005.

Fauser, Annegret. "'Hymns of the Future': Reading Félicien David's *Christophe Colomb* (1847) as a Saint-Simonian Symphony," *Journal of Musicological Research* 28 (2009): 1–29.

Goldstrom, Erik W. *A Whore in Paradise: The Oratorios of Jules Massenet*, Ph.D. diss., Stanford University, 1998.

Irvine, Demar. *Massenet: A Chronicle of His Life and Times*. Portland, OR: Amadeus Press, 1994.

Langham Smith, Richard. "Gounod *Mors et vita*." Liner notes (EMI Classics 7544592, Barbara Hendricks, Nadine Denize, John Aler, José Van Dam, Christoph Kuhlmann, Orféon Donostiarra, Orchestre du Capitole de Toulouse, Michel Plasson, 1992), 10–18.

Locke, Ralph P. *Music, Musicians and the Saint-Simonians*. Chicago and London: The University of Chicago Press, 1986.

Rowden, Clair. "L'Homme saint chez Massenet: l'amour sacré et le sacre de l'amour," in Jean-Christophe Branger and Alban Ramaut (eds.), *Opéra et religion sous la IIIe République*. Saint-Etienne: Publications de l'Université de Saint-Etienne, 2006, 257–84.

17

CAMILLE SAINT-SAËNS

Lesley A. Wright

University of Hawai'i Mānoa

Though he is acknowledged for contributions to every major nineteenth-century genre, general opinion tends to rate Camille Saint-Saëns (1835–1921) as most successful in pieces that are "based on traditional Viennese models, namely sonatas, chamber music, symphonies and concertos."[1] During his lifetime, of course, he continued to seek out success in the theater, but choral music, too, both sacred and secular, acted as an important outlet for his prodigious creativity. He churned out canticles, motets, cantatas, and oratorios for soloists and choirs of varying abilities. He wrote partsongs for assorted vocal combinations and demanding *a cappella* pieces for the *orphéon* societies and their singing competitions.[2] For decades official organizers turned to him for grandiose *pièces d'occasion* that glorified the nation and Republican values, or that commemorated the heroes of French culture like Corneille or Victor Hugo. Undeniably well crafted, these inflated scores are often too much tied to their original purpose to speak readily to today's audience. But in both large and small choral genres, Saint-Saëns has also left gems, some well known and others much less so. To treat such a substantial repertory, this chapter surveys Saint-Saëns's connection with choral music throughout his long life and continues with focused commentary on several works that stand out in the principal genres mentioned above.

Saint-Saëns's choral music spans a good seventy years, from student efforts *c.*1850 until 1921, the last year of his life. His earliest sacred choral work is a fragment of an oratorio (*Les Israëlites sur la montagne d'Oreb*, *c.*1848). Early cantata manuscripts and secular choral pieces (like *Les djinns* and *La rose*, both from *c.*1850) probably stem from his preparation for the coveted Prix de Rome.[3] Immediately after losing in that 1852 competition, he entered another, sponsored by the Société Sainte-Cécile, and won top honors with his *Ode à Saint-Cécile*, for soloists, mixed chorus and orchestra.[4] At its public performance on December 26, 1852, the critic for the *Revue et Gazette musicale* greeted it as "honorable and reasonable," but disparaged its lack of youthful spirit or flashes of genius.[5] Saint-Saëns may have written his first large-scale sacred work, the *Messe* (Op. 4, for soloists, mixed chorus, orchestra and two organs) for an 1855 competition in Bordeaux, where the jury seems to have awarded it an honorable mention.[6] If this is so, it seems possible that he decided to take on a genre that would have served as his *envoi de Rome* had he won the Rome prize in 1852. In the end, the first performance of his Mass took place in 1857 at Saint-Merri, where he served as organist from 1853 to 1857.[7]

Successor in 1858 to Lefébure-Wély in the well-paid organist's post at the Madeleine in Paris, Saint-Saëns stayed on there for nearly twenty years. In this position, he produced large- and small-scale sacred choral works in substantial numbers and often very quickly;[8] among these were some two dozen motets and canticles (for soloist(s) or chorus) that repeatedly set texts like "O Salutaris," "Ave verum," or "Ave Maria." When he took the trouble to publish shorter works of this sort, he dedicated them to prominent members of his circle, like famed singer Pauline Viardot or Romain Bussine (co-founder with Saint-Saëns of the Société Nationale de musique), or even "Abbé" Franz Liszt. Choral pieces from these years range from concise, well-crafted homophonic settings such as the quietly effective *Ave verum* in E-flat major (*c*.1860),[9] to extended scores like the *Oratorio de Noel*, Op. 12 (1858) or the impressive Psaume XVIII (*Coeli enarrant*, 1865).[10]

Initially conceived as an oratorio, Saint-Saëns's most performed opera, *Samson et Dalila* (finally completed in 1873–77), gives important choral numbers to both Hebrews and Philistines.[11] In the same period he also completed his remarkable *poème biblique* based on Genesis: *Le Déluge*, Op. 45 (1875), for soloists, mixed chorus and large orchestra. Its most memorable section features an orchestral storm sequence (with choral recitation), equally as effective but considerably more complex than the better-known Bacchanale.[12] Other passages highlight the orchestra as well, such as the opening prelude with a meditative fugue for strings followed by an expressive violin solo and, opening Part III, a passage of utter peace and subtle harmonies followed by the charming illustration of the dove's flight from Noah's ark. Louis Gallet, the librettist, acknowledged the hybrid nature of *Le Déluge* by calling it a *drame symphonique*, while some critics of its March 1876 premiere called it a *symphonie dramatique*, linking this important piece to Berlioz in both its genre and its masterful orchestration.[13]

Saint-Saëns left the Madeleine in 1877 because his burgeoning career as composer and performer required too many absences. Just after this, his friend Albert Libon, head of the French post office, bequeathed him 100,000 francs to free him from the drudgery of frequent church services. Though a codicil in Libon's will (added on May 19, the day before his death) released Saint-Saëns from any obligation to compose a Requiem in his memory, Saint-Saëns nonetheless wrote his consoling score (for soloists, mixed chorus and orchestra) during a week in early April 1878 in order to commemorate the first anniversary of his friend's passing. On May 28, 1878, less than a week after the first performance of the Requiem, Op. 54 at Saint-Sulpice, Saint-Saëns's two-year-old son died in a tragic fall from an open window; on July 7 his other son, an infant, fell ill and also died.[14] In 1879, no doubt still affected by a father's grief, he wrote and published his setting of Psalm 136, the lament "Super flumina Babylonis."[15] After that, his production of sacred music slowed to a trickle for the next two decades. Barely more than a half dozen pieces, most of them brief, precede *The Promised Land,* Op. 140 (1913), a late number oratorio in the Handelian tradition.[16]

When in 1914 a young military priest asked Saint-Saëns about his own religious ideas, the composer described himself as a believer who had become a complete non-believer. He maintained that this conversion had given him peace; even so, he recognized the importance of religion to the evolution of Humanity, saying "I know how to respect what is respectable."[17] He proceeded to show this respect with a half dozen more short sacred pieces, composed principally during the First World War. For his state funeral at the Madeleine on December 24, 1921, some 250 performers presented the Kyrie, Rex tremendae, and Oro supplex from his own Requiem.

In contrast to the sacred choral music, Saint-Saëns's secular choral output is concentrated in the second half of his life. Before his departure from the Madeleine, he had published only a handful of secular choral works.[18] Among those we find his grandiose cantata *Les Noces de Prométhée*, Op.

19 (1867), winner of a government-sponsored competition for that year's Paris Exposition.[19] Saint-Saëns once again represented the nation in the 1900 Exposition, with his cantata, *Le Feu céleste*, Op. 115, which acknowledged nineteenth-century progress with a tribute to electricity (the word highlighted by eight trumpets at its first appearance). But, with slightly malicious humor, he revealed to conductor Paul Taffanel how little stock he placed in the work: "Electric wires could be placed under the listeners' seats to give them a violent shock at each stroke of the tam-tam: think about it! I'm afraid you are going to find this effect a little too advanced and *fin de vingtième siècle*."[20] With more sincerity he expressed the hope that another *pièce d'occasion*, the *Hymne à Victor Hugo* (1881), could be resurrected, since he had written this score, too, with the acoustics of the Trocadéro hall in mind.[21]

From the late 1870s to 1900, Saint-Saëns published more than a dozen fine secular choral works in addition to the occasional pieces mentioned above. Based on a Victor Hugo poem opposing Christian and pagan values, *La Lyre et la harpe*, Op. 57 (1879), a 50-minute score for soloists, mixed chorus and full orchestra, stands among his finest works in any genre. Effective shorter pieces also come from this time: *Chanson de grand-père*, Op. 53/1 (1878), its folk-like tune and constantly varying accompaniment for female chorus and orchestra; the magical *Calme des nuits*, paired in Op. 68 (1882) with the charming *Les fleurs et les arbres*, for unaccompanied mixed choir;[22] and a half dozen partsongs for male chorus such as "Les Marins de Kermor," Op. 71/1 (1884).[23]

With his short choral pieces after 1900, Saint-Saëns sometimes overtly supports the Republic and its ideals, as in his *a cappella* partsongs for men that pay tribute to French workers (*Aux mineurs*, Op. 137, *c*.1912), the virtues of work itself (*Hymne au travail*, Op. 142, 1914), and male patriotism (*À la France*, Op. 121, 1903).[24] Others, however, are more subtle pieces that would do well on choral programs today, like the mildly chromatic *Romance du soir*, Op. 118 (1902) or the exquisite Lento madrigal *Des pas dans l'allée*, Op. 141/1 (1913), both for *a cappella* mixed choir. *Salut au Chevalier Printemps*, Op. 151/2 (1917), a stylish SSA chorus with piano, would have marked a more graceful exit to choral composition than the unremarkable *Aux conquérants de l'air*, Op. 164, and *Le Printemps*, Op. 165, from 1921, the last year of Saint-Saëns's life; despite their date, all three of these partsongs for women remain squarely within the nineteenth-century tradition.

Several of Saint-Saëns's most important choral works are liturgical or biblical, an apparent paradox for one who turned so emphatically against religion. Even so, he allowed that music had its place in the church:

> What music, then, ought there to be in the Church? Music of a grand style, in accord with the elevated sentiments expressed in the liturgy. But the grand style is rare. Where unattainable, one may be content with correctness in the writing and gravity in the expression—a gravity which does not exclude sentiment but prevents it from turning into sentimentality. There being no intention, in the Church, of exciting applause, one should not strive after effect.[25]

For his first noteworthy sacred work, Saint-Saëns produced a remarkably assured *Messe* (Op. 4), serious in expression and devoid of sentimentality.[26] This 40-minute *missa longa* employs cantus firmus technique in the Kyrie, Credo and O Salutaris.[27] A weighty Kyrie, along with a striking Gloria, make up more than half the length of the Mass. In 1869, Liszt compared it to a "magnificent Gothic cathedral" where Bach would have felt at home; but he diplomatically urged Saint-Saëns to consider major cuts in the Christe eleison so the celebrant would not have to remain immobile at the altar for an inordinate amount of time.[28] Some fifty years later Louis Vierne, organist at Notre Dame de Paris, remarked that this cut in the Kyrie had become the norm, but praised the score as an important one in Saint-Saëns's sacred *œuvre*. Like Liszt, Vierne stresses its homage to Bach: "Against the old *O Salutaris* of Duguet, the composer has woven a counterpoint between harps and bassoons worthy of old Bach.[29] Its *Amen* is incomparably elegant. Finally the Agnus Dei, so reminiscent of Bach, ends in B major with an utterly seraphic dialogue between two organs."[30]

Using Part II of J. S. Bach's *Christmas Oratorio* as his model, Saint-Saëns dashed off the 40-minute score of his most popular large choral piece, the *Oratorio de Noël*, Op. 12, for a Christmas 1858 performance at the Madeleine. Its Latin texts from the Gospel of Luke (up through "Glory to God" in no. 2), psalms and other contemplative biblical passages are expressed in ten brief numbers, five with chorus.[31] A serene 12/8 *siciliano* ("dans le style de Seb. Bach") opens the work and later returns to generate no. 9, a quintet and chorus ("Consurge Filia Sion"); a maestoso chorale ends the work. Serious, even vehement in tone, the choral centerpiece (no. 6 "Quare fremuerunt") recalls the Baroque in its orchestral figures and choral writing. Surrounding this, however, Saint-Saëns places two ingratiating numbers for soloists, harp, and organ (no. 5 "Benedictus" (S, Bar) and no. 7 Trio "Tecum principium" (S, T, Bar)). Tuneful and unaffected, the *Oratorio de Noël* retains its appeal today not only for aesthetic and affective reasons but also for practical ones. As Howard Smither suggests, the "brevity and the simplicity of its choral parts place it within reach of an average church choir."[32]

Yet another sacred work stands out in Saint-Saëns's choral output, his Requiem, Op. 54. Until recently obscured by Fauré's Requiem, this concise score compares well with his former student's work. Vierne praised Saint-Saëns's "deep penetration" of the text and suggested that: "Thrilling in effect, it should be sung, like Fauré's marvellous Requiem, at important funerals."[33] However thrilling it is in spots, Saint-Saëns frequently opts for effects that are subdued, consoling, and restrained in dynamic levels. To this end, he omits trumpets, timpani, and clarinets, but specifies quadruple woodwinds, horns, and harps, plus strings, a great organ and an accompanying organ. He withholds the four trombones until the Tuba mirum, where they portentously sound an upward fifth answered by *tutta forza* chords in the great organ; the chorus replies, supported by the horns and accompaniment organ, declaiming the text on the tonic pitch. In the Agnus Dei, he introduces his expressive principal melody with woodwinds, then with vocal quartet and orchestra, and finally a choral tutti colored with harp arpeggios.

The most effective pieces open the Requiem (Introit / Kyrie, Dies irae, Rex tremendae, and Oro supplex) and close it (Agnus Dei). Reinforcing a sense that Saint-Saëns planned the outer movements as bookends is the return of two ideas in the Agnus Dei: the three-note sobbing figure from the opening of the Introit and the drooping motif from the Quid sum miser (see Examples 17.1 and 17.2). The brief Hostias, Sanctus, and Benedictus, though attractive, verge on the perfunctory; still, the strong outer movements more than make up for this. Notable are the beginning of the Dies irae (monophonic like the medieval sequence it quotes and alternating between soloists and chorus over a string tremolo that enhances the fearsome text), and the Oro supplex, for soloists and mixed chorus.[34] The latter movement is particularly moving, with its halting, descending, and chromatic principal idea, so suitable for an expression of submissive contrition.[35] Duple and triple meter alternate until consistent triple meter takes hold when the supplicant pleads to be spared ("Huic ergo parce Deus"), and finally bows his head in a *pianissimo,* unaccompanied Amen. Sometimes grand and sometimes touching, the score grapples thoughtfully with the liturgical texts. Even those who accused Saint-Saëns of dryness admitted that he had been able to "pull away from the scholastic formulas that make certain passages of his oratorios so cold."[36]

EXAMPLE 17.1 Saint-Saëns, Requiem, Agnus Dei, mm. 1–6.

Among the large secular works one score stands out, *La Lyre et la harpe*, Op. 57, an extended cantata commissioned by the Birmingham Festival in England and first performed there in August 1879 with a 350-voice choir and a 150-member orchestra led by Saint-Saëns himself. As noted earlier, it is based on Victor Hugo's 1822 ode, which juxtaposes pagan and Christian viewpoints. Jacques Langlois asserts that Saint-Saëns put more psychological depth in this piece than in many of his operas, including *Samson et Dalila*, which also explores pagan and Christian themes.[37] While critic Georges Servières would later tout this score as one of Saint-Saëns's most remarkable,[38] English critics of the premiere were not so enthusiastic and predicted that the intellectual demands of the text would prevent true success despite the graceful music.[39] Indeed, the piece has never achieved broad popularity, but the orchestral prologue and twelve contrasting vocal numbers have much to recommend them, especially in the sections of *La Lyre*, which are associated with antique wisdom and pagan pleasures. Particularly compelling is the choral lullaby (no. 1), which begins with a striking succession of quiet chords alternating with arpeggios. The Harp, symbolizing Judeo-Christian teachings, takes turns with the Lyre in speaking to the poet. In the end, the artist decides to reconcile their messages and "say to Pindus's echo Carmel's hymn." Stephen Studd has pointed out that instruments are not used "in any literal sense to denote the conflicting cultures: the harp, indeed often accompanies the ancient muse, while the organ is associated with Christian values."[40] The structure of the text itself guarantees some variety: five movements for the Lyre (four of them involving chorus), five for the Harp (one involving chorus[41]), a piece for both Lyre and Harp (no. 7) to open the second half of the work, and a choral epilogue for the poet. Saint-Saëns omitted only five of Hugo's verses—where the Harp asks for prayer to the true God.[42] Two deeply contrasted recurring motifs from the prologue, plus other subtle resemblances, add musical unity. The more solo-oriented second half opens with a soprano solo, its jagged, noble line evoking the pagan eagle; then a tender melody characterizing the Christian dove descending from heaven is decorated

EXAMPLE 17.2 Saint-Saëns, Requiem, Agnus Dei, mm. 98–102.

with a sensuous flute gesture vaguely reminiscent of the figures in Act II of *Samson et Dalila* that illustrate Dalila's anticipation of Samson's arrival. In nos. 9 and 10 Saint Saëns emphasizes deep contrast, for a charming alto-tenor duet praising Christian marital bliss (its turning woodwind figures reminiscent of Bizet) leads to the baritone's frenetic 3/8 paean to pleasure. Though the epilogue provides merely an adequate conclusion, the score as a whole makes a strong impact.

Two entirely secular works, one with orchestra and one with piano accompaniment, hint at the diversity and beauty of Saint-Saëns's shorter choral works. *La Nuit*, Op. 114 (1900), an evocative 10-minute cantata for soprano soloist, women's chorus, and Mozart-sized orchestra (with added harp), probably served the composer as a sort of antidote to the bombast of *Le Feu céleste* of the same year; Gérard has drawn attention to stylistic elements reminiscent of the early Debussy cantatas and an aesthetic similar to Fauré's.[43] Saint-Saëns described *La Nuit* to his publisher August Durand as suitable for "everywhere there is a light soprano—very light—a women's chorus and a flutist, things that are not rare, as you know."[44] In ternary form, it opens with strings in sinuous lines, refined harmonies, murmuring chorus, and an expressive violin solo, but in the middle section, inspired by the text's reference to the nightingale, the soloist and flutist duet with one another. At the end of the cantata, the women's chorus hums dreamily under the soprano's line. She closes with a *pianissimo* high B-flat, the choral line quietly descends, singing of sleep and the mystery of night, and finally, in the orchestra, the principal motive slows and merges with silence.

With its mostly diatonic harmonies, periodic phrasing and mildly archaic charm, "Madrigal tiré de *Psyché* (Molière)" contrasts nicely with the more modern language of *La Nuit*. This unassuming piece for lyric tenor, male chorus, and piano is not at all "athletic" in its choral parts. Its tender, triple meter Allegretto draws text from the third *intermède* of Molière's *tragédie-ballet* (1671). Saint-Saëns, commissioned to write this piece for the inauguration of the Molière monument in Pézenas (August 8, 1897), brought to the task his experience with editing and adding music to Marc-Antoine Charpentier's score for Molière's *Le Malade imaginaire* just three years earlier.[45] In "Madrigal" the tenor leads in both strophes (A A'), and floats above the chorus to close each large section, touching on a high C near the end of the piece.

On both large scale and small, in sacred and secular genres, Saint-Saëns has left substantive choral pieces well worth exploring. Remaining true to a French Romantic style infused with the harmonies of the 1870s and 1880s, his contribution to this repertory shows his lyricism, masterful command of sonority, craftsmanship and clarity of form, and, in so many instances, a beauty that is truly French.[46]

Notes

1 Sabina Teller Ratner, "Saint-Saëns, Camille," in *The New Grove Dictionary of Music and Musicians*, ed. Stanley Sadie (London: Macmillan, 2001). The worklist there, prepared by Daniel Fallon and Ratner, has served as the basis for comments on Saint-Saëns's choral output. All dates for the choral pieces are dates of composition taken from this source, which will gradually be displaced by *Camille Saint-Saëns (1835–1921). A Thematic Catalogue of his Complete Works*, published by Oxford University Press: *Volume I: The Instrumental Works* (2002), ed. Sabina Teller Ratner; *Volume II: The Dramatic Works* (2012), ed. Sabina Teller Ratner; *Volume III: The Vocal Works* (in preparation), ed. Yves Gérard.

2 On the earlier history of the *orphéon* movement in France, see Jane Fulcher, "The Orphéon Societies: 'Music for the Workers' in Second-Empire France," *International Review of Aesthetics and Sociology of Music* 10/1 (1979): 47–56. See also: Donna M. Di Grazia, "Concert Societies in Paris and their Choral Repertoires *c.*1828–1880," 2 vols. (Ph.D. diss., Washington University in St. Louis, 1993), especially Chap. 4 "The Orphéon movement and Sociétés Chorales du Département de la Seine," 93–163.

3 The chorus from Saint-Saëns's 1852 attempt at the prize survives at the French national library. He competed in the cantata round as no. 1, an indication of the jury's satisfaction with his fugue and chorus in the preliminary round. Indeed, his 6/8 *Chœur des sylphes* (BnF, Musique MS 535), for mixed chorus and orchestra, has a lyricism and accomplished orchestration that suit the text nicely. Saint-Saëns's Prix

de Rome pieces (with some of the early sacred works) were recorded in 2010 for a two-CD set (Flemish Radio Choir, Brussels Philharmonic, Hervé Niquet, Glossamusic GCD 922210) with accompanying essays by Alexandre Dratwicki and Yves Gérard.

4 Founded in 1850 by Charles de Bez (with François Seghers, conductor) to promote new and unknown repertory, the Société would dissolve in 1856 shortly after Seghers's departure. See Katharine Ellis, *Interpreting the Musical Past: Early Music in Nineteenth-Century France* (Oxford: Oxford University Press, 2005), especially the chapter "Patterns of Revival," 43–80.

5 Henri Blanchard, "Auditions musicales: Société Sainte-Cécile," *Revue et Gazette musicale* 20, no. 1 (January 2, 1853): 5.

6 See Daniel Fallon, "Saint-Saëns and the Concours de composition musicale in Bordeaux," *JAMS* 31, 2 (Summer 1978): 309–25. For a discussion of regulations controlling recipients of the Prix de Rome, see Alexandre Dratwicki, "Les 'Envois de Rome' des compositeurs pensionnaires de la Villa Médicis (1804–1914)," *Revue de musicologie* 91, 1 (2005): 99–193. An oratorio and a *Messe solennelle*, *Requiem* or *Te Deum* were considered appropriate envois for the first two years of the stipend (ibid., 108).

7 From 1853 to 1877 Saint-Saëns supported himself in Paris as a church organist, first for a few months at the Latin Quarter's Saint-Séverin in 1853, then from 1853 to December 1857 at the sixteenth-century Gothic church of Saint-Merri (on the right bank between Châtelet and the Centre Beaubourg), and finally at the high society church of the Madeleine. At Saint-Merri, the organ was in poor condition during the first two years Saint-Saëns was there, and under renovation for the next two. For specifics on the organ renovation and the church service at that time, see Rollin Smith, *Saint-Saëns and the Organ* (New York: Pendragon Press, 1992), 25–29.

8 Saint-Saëns's friend and secretary, Jean Bonnerot, put together the first large-scale biography at the composer's request. There, he stressed the composer's frequent haste in writing religious works for performers to learn and rehearse. For example, May, "the month of Mary," required a new piece almost daily, and so, during that month in 1859, Saint-Saëns produced some eighteen French or Latin canticles. Bonnerot laments the disappearance of numerous organ pieces that were improvised but never written down and of vocal pieces that were put to paper but never published (see *C. Saint-Saëns (1835–1921): Sa vie et son oeuvre* (Paris: A. Durand et Fils, 1922), 38–39).

9 This "Ave verum" setting was issued for SATB quartet choir (and later for SATB chorus) and dedicated to Louis Dietsch, Saint-Saëns's colleague at both the Madeleine and the École Niedermeyer. Running only two printed pages, it epitomizes the craftsmanship of these quickly produced miniatures.

10 The *Oratorio de Noël* calls for five soloists (S, Mez, A, T, Bar), SATB chorus, string orchestra with harp and organ, while the grand *Coeli enarrant* requires seven soloists (2S, Mez, A,T, Bar, B), a quartet of baritones (presumably talented chorus members), SATB chorus, and a full Romantic orchestra. Saint-Saëns was interested in bringing dignity to church music, especially in his large works, by referencing tradition (e.g., Bach, plainchant, contrapuntal techniques); however, he also knew, and was occasionally advised by his employers, that the congregation of the Madeleine expected accessible tunes.

11 For a discussion of meanings for the Hymn to Dagon, Act 3, see Ralph P. Locke, "On Music and Orientalism," in *Music, Culture and Society: A Reader*, ed. Derek B. Scott (Oxford: Oxford University Press, 2000), 103–09, here 107. Locke suggests that Saint-Saëns, an anticlericalist, may have "felt hemmed in by the proprieties of bourgeois religiosity" and that "he may have welcomed, or at least unconsciously responded to, the possibility of giving voice to a more sensual and unbuttoned strain of religious feeling."

12 A strong interest in oratorio during the 1870s in Paris is evidenced in several other important works: Massenet's *Marie-Magdeleine* (1874) and *Ève* (1875) and Franck's *Rédemption* (1871, rev. 1874). For a survey of oratorio repertory, see Danièle Pistone, "L'oratorio à Paris de 1870 à 1900," in *Beiträge zur Geschichte des Oratoriums seit Händel, Festschrift Günther Massenkeil*, ed. Rainer Cadenbach and Helmut Loos (Bonn: Voggenreiter Verlag, 1986), 345–56. To provide further context, see Ellis, *Interpreting the Musical Past* (especially Chap. 7 "Baroque choral music"), for her analysis of the meaning and importance of the revival of Handel oratorios in France during the 1870s.

13 See, for example, the highly appreciative commentary of Édouard Noël and Edmong Stoullig, *Les Annales du théâtre et de la musique* (Paris: G. Charpentier, 1877), vol. 2,793.

14 These terrible events irrevocably damaged his marriage and led to a permanent separation from his wife in 1881.

15 This version for alto, mixed chorus and orchestra revisits a text Saint-Saëns set in 1854 but never published (for Mez solo, chorus, saxophone quartet, organ, and string orchestra). This early score was discovered among Saint-Saëns's papers by Yves Gérard at the Château-Musée in Dieppe and premiered there in February 2009.

16 Saint-Saëns led the first performance of this work at the Three Choirs Festival in Gloucester and was not pleased by the reception. His librettist, Herman Klein, hoping that one day the world would come to value the work more, confirms that Saint-Saëns chose to use the forms and approaches of earlier composers

like Handel and Haydn because English appreciation had been responsible for some of their masterpieces ("Saint-Saëns as I knew Him," *The Musical Times* 63, 948 (February 1, 1922): 90–93, here 92).

17 Yves Gérard, CD liner notes, p. 2, in Camille Saint-Saëns, *Requiem. Psaume XVIII.* Chœur Régional Vittoria d'Île de France and Orchestre National d'Île de France, Jacques Mercier, Françoise Pollet, Magali Chalmeau-Damonte, Jean Luc Viala, Nicolas Rivenq. RCA Victor Red Seal/BMG France, BM 600/74321 540502.

18 Saint-Saëns began his publication of short secular choral works with *Sérénade d'hiver* (TTBB), the required piece for the choral competition in Chartres on June 7, 1868.

19 Exposition organizers substituted Rossini's hymn to Napoléon III for performance in the July awards ceremony claiming the cantata was too long and its subtleties unsuitable for the poor acoustics of the Exposition hall. On the other hand, their decision saved the government considerable money (see Demar Irvine, *Massenet: A Chronicle of his life and times* (Portland, OR: Amadeus Press, 1997), 54). As a gesture of reparation to this ardent Republican, the Third Republic finally gave *Les Noces de Prométhée* its official premiere at the 1878 Exposition. For a detailed description/evaluation of the work (requiring soloists, double chorus, and large orchestra), the competition, and the first performance (which was organized by Saint-Saëns himself), see Oscar Comettant, *La musique, les musiciens, et les instruments* (Paris: M. Lévy, 1869), 301–08 (accessed through Google Books). Michel Faure has interpreted *Les Noces de Prométhée* in political and sociological contexts (see *Musique et Société du Second Empire aux Années Vingt* (Paris: Flammarion, 1985), 93–95).

20 Edward Blakeman, "The Correspondence of Camille Saint-Saëns and Paul Taffanel, 1880–1906," *Music and Letters* 63, 1–2 (Jan.–Apr. 1982): 44–58, here 56. Letter of February 18, 1900. Saint-Saëns dedicated the cantata to Taffanel.

21 Saint-Saëns described his lifelong admiration for Hugo in an essay published in 1913; there, he gives details of the genesis of this piece. See "Victor Hugo" (reprinted from *Ecole buissonière*, 1913), 161–66, in *Regards sur mes contemporains*, collected by Yves Gérard (Bernard Coutaz: Arles, 1990).

22 Dennis Shrock, in *Choral Repertoire* (Oxford and New York: Oxford University Press, 2009), 425, describes the homophonic *Calme des nuits* as "one of the most beautiful settings of the Romantic era in France."

23 In his discussion of repertory, Amédée Reuchsel, a student of Fauré, acknowledges Saint-Saëns for "about ten difficult choruses, of which several are well known and of real beauty." He specifically mentions "Les Marins de Kermor," *Les Soldats de Gédéon*, and *Les Titans*. Amédée Reuchsel, *L'Éducation musicale populaire: L'art du chef d'Orphéon* (Fischbacher, Paris, 1906), 108 (accessed via Google Books).

24 Intended for the students in lycées and colleges, this four-square, diatonic chorus has ad lib boys' treble parts as well. Annegret Fauser, "Gendering the nations: The ideologies of French Discourse on Music (1870–1914)," in *Musical Constructions of Nationalism*, ed. Michael Murphy and Harry White (Cork, Ireland: Cork University Press, 2001), pp. 72–103, here 78–79, mentions *À la France* in her discussion of the educational role of music as key to "nationalising French art and to creating both a healthy musical taste and healthy French citizens."

25 Camille Saint-Saëns and Theodore Baker, "Music in the Church," *Musical Quarterly* 2, (1916): 1–8, here 5–6. (A republication of "La Musique religieuse," from *L'Echo de Paris*, 22 June 1912).

26 First performed March 21, 1857.

27 The Kyrie and Credo use a cantus firmus from Henry Du Mont's *Messe Royale* (seventeenth century) while the O Salutaris turns to Abbé Dieudonné Duguet's early nineteenth-century setting. The latter tune can be seen in a harmonized version in Nicola Montani's *The St. Gregory Hymnal and Catholic Choir Book* (Philadelphia: Society of St. Gregory, 1920), 32 (accessed through Google Books).

28 Yves Gérard and Euridyce Jousse, eds., *Lettres de compositeurs à Camille Saint-Saëns*, Letter 310, Franz Liszt, August 4, [18]69, Rome (Lyon: Symétrie, 2009), 392.

29 Using the "O Salutaris" for the Elevation is a practice going back to Louis XII in the Renaissance, though other texts could hold this position, like the "Pie Jesu," "Panis Angelicus," "Ave Maria" or "Ave verum." (See Rollin Smith, *Saint-Saëns*, 55–56.)

30 Rollin Smith, *Saint-Saëns*, Appendix B "Saint-Saëns's Sacred Music" by Louis Vierne (from *Le Guide du concert*, 1914/1922), 225–29, here 226–27.

31 In addition to mixed chorus, the score requires five soloists (S, MS, A, T, Bar), string orchestra plus harp, and organ.

32 Howard Smither, *A History of the Oratorio: The Oratorio in the Nineteenth and Twentieth Centuries*, vol. 4 (Chapel Hill, NC: University of North Carolina Press, 2000), 566–72, here 572.

33 Rollin Smith, *Saint-Saëns*, Appendix B, 227.

34 The bass soloist joins in only for the last thirteen bars (at the text "Pie Jesu").

35 Yves Gérard suggests that supple rhythms and chromaticism give the movement an orientalist flavor but acknowledges that they might also be intended to represent a tortured soul. See CD liner notes, p. 5, in Camille Saint-Saëns, *Requiem. Psaume XVIII*.

36 Georges Servières, "Camille Saint-Saëns," *La Musique française moderne* (Paris: G. Havard, fils, 1897), 318.
37 Jacques Langlois, *Camille Saint-Saëns: Étude technique sur l'artiste et sur son œuvre* (Moulins: Crépin-Lebond, 1934), 70.
38 Georges Servières, *La musique moderne française*, 322.
39 [unnamed correspondent], "Birmingham Musical Festival," *Musical Standard* (September 6, 1879): 143–46 (accessed through Google Books). The article also quotes a similar opinion from the *Birmingham Daily Post*.
40 Stephen Studd, *Saint-Saëns: A critical biography* (Madison and Teaneck, NJ: Fairleigh Dickinson University Press, 1999), 126.
41 Most choral numbers, some with effective fugal writing, fall in the first half of the work, and the sole choral piece for the Harp (no. 6) ends the first half of the ode triumphantly, its tenor solo and chorus urging the righteous to spread the Gospel.
42 Jean Gallois, *Charles-Camille Saint-Saëns* (Sprimont, Belgium: Mardaga, 2004), 224, hypothesizes that this omission may symbolize Saint-Saëns's growing agnosticism "still more enlarged by recent bereavements."
43 Yves Gérard, CD liner notes, pp. 21–22, Camille Saint-Saëns, *La Lyre et la Harpe, Le Déluge*, Chœur Régional Vittoria d'Île de France, Orchestre National d'Île de France, Jacques Mercier, Natalie Dessay, Françoise Pollet, RCA Victor Red Seal/BMG France, 74321 77747 2. Set to the verses of Republican politician and minor poet, Georges Audigier (1863–1925) and written quickly, this nocturne was first performed at the Saint-Saëns festival in Béziers in June 1900, though Saint-Saëns had initially planned a premiere at the Concerts Colonne (he dedicated the score to Colonne, the association's founder and conductor).
44 Gérard, CD liner notes, pp. 21–22.
45 Émile Blémont, "L'inauguration du monument de Molière," in *Théâtre moliéresque et cornélien* (Paris: Alphonse Lemerre, 1989), 245 (accessed through Google Books).
46 I would like to express my gratitude to Sabina Teller Ratner for her suggestions.

Selected Bibliography

Blakeman, Edward. "The Correspondence of Camille Saint-Saëns and Paul Taffanel, 1880–1906," *Music and Letters* 63, 1–2 (Jan.–Apr. 1982): 44–58.

Bonnerot, Jean. *C. Saint-Saëns (1835–1921): Sa vie et son oeuvre*. Paris: A. Durand et Fils, 1922.

Di Grazia, Donna M. "Concert Societies in Paris and their Choral Repertoires *c.*1828–1880." 2 vols. Ph.D. diss., Washington University in St. Louis, 1993.

Ellis, Katharine. *Interpreting the Musical Past: Early Music in Nineteenth-century France*. Oxford: Oxford University Press, 2005.

Faure, Michel. *Musique et Société du Second Empire aux Années Vingt*. Paris: Flammarion, 1985.

Gallois, Jean. *Charles-Camille Saint-Saëns*. Sprimont, Belgium: Mardaga, 2004.

Gérard, Yves. CD liner notes for Camille Saint-Saëns, *La Lyre et la Harpe, Le Déluge*. Chœur Régional Vittoria d'Île de France, Orchestre National d'Île de France, Jacques Mercier, Natalie Dessay, Françoise Pollet, RCA Victor Red Seal/BMG France, 74321 77747 2.

Gérard, Yves. CD liner notes for Camille Saint-Saëns, *Requiem. Psaume XVIII*. Chœur Régional Vittoria d'Île de France and Orchestre National d'Île de France, Jacques Mercier, Françoise Pollet, Magali Chalmeau-Damonte, Jean Luc Viala, Nicolas Rivenq. RCA Victor Red Seal/BMG France, BM 600/74321 540502.

Gérard, Yves and Euridyce Jousse, eds. *Lettres de compositeurs à Camille Saint-Saëns*. Lyon: Symétrie, 2009.

Ratner, Sabina Teller. "Saint-Saëns, Camille," in *The New Grove Dictionary of Music and Musicians*, ed. Stanley Sadie. London: Macmillan, 2001.

Saint-Saëns, Camille (Collected by Yves Gérard). *Regards sur mes contemporains*. Bernard Coutaz: Arles, 1990.

Smith, Rollin. *Saint-Saëns and the Organ*. New York: Pendragon Press, 1992.

Smither, Howard. *A History of the Oratorio: The Oratorio in the Nineteenth and Twentieth Centuries*, vol. 4. Chapel Hill, NC: University of North Carolina Press, 2000.

Studd, Stephen. *Saint-Saëns: A Critical Biography*. Madison and Teaneck, NJ: Fairleigh Dickinson University Press, 1999.

18

GABRIEL FAURÉ

Carlo Caballero

UNIVERSITY OF COLORADO, BOULDER

Choral music occupies an important but not predominant place in Fauré's creative legacy. Besides the Requiem (discussed in Chapter 4 of this volume), his sacred works consist of a short Mass (in two versions), a Benedictus, sixteen extant motets, and five canticles or devotional songs.[1] This body of music dates from between 1863 and 1905. The religious music he published in 1906, in the wake of his resignation from the church of La Madeleine, was the result of a mop-up operation. I have written elsewhere of the relationship between this abrupt closure and Fauré's own lack of personal commitment to Roman Catholicism.[2] One needs to add that not all of the pieces listed above are choral; among the motets, six are solos or duets. It is naturally the choral pieces that most concern us here. Among the five canticles, only the famous *Cantique de Jean Racine* is a partsong. The others are accompanied solos ("Noël" and "En prière"), the sub-genre most appreciated in Parisian churches of Fauré's time, and Christmas carols for unison choir ("Il est né le divin enfant" and "Noël d'enfants") for which Fauré composed attractive accompaniments.[3]

The secular works for chorus are fewer in number. They include *Les djinns*, Op. 12; *Le ruisseau*, Op. 22; *La naissance de Vénus*, Op. 29; Madrigal, Op. 35; Pavane, Op. 50; and the incidental music for *Caligula*, Op. 52. All of these works date from a thirteen-year span between 1875 and 1888, the composer's early middle age.[4] To these we add *Prométhée* (1900), an opera with spoken dialogue that gives a major role to the chorus.

With Fauré, it is logical to think of the sacred and profane choral works separately. In the motets, we meet a composer working for the church under largely utilitarian circumstances and providing compositions more than adequate to his duties, but always practical and modest. They sometimes surprise us for a moment with a delicious detail, but Fauré acted as a professional church musician: he wrote simple pieces that would sound well after a brief rehearsal and that would appeal to the congregation of his parish. They greatly resemble one another in style and vary mostly in the choice of voices and instruments. In the secular domain, however, Fauré's choral music presents almost the opposite picture: a series of experiments, each having no likeness in Fauré's other work, each offering peculiar perspectives on a text or genre.

Sacred Works

Fauré's sacred music owes more to Gounod than to any other composer. We cannot even be certain of the size of this debt, since most of Gounod's vast legacy has been forgotten. With further research, the debt is likely to grow, and a detailed study comparing the religious music of the two composers is needed. In the most general way, Fauré himself once compared his expressive aims with Gounod's in citing the older composer's predilection for expressing "human tenderness" in religious music.[5] But the more one gets to know Gounod's music, the more one finds not merely a sentimental affinity, but specific technical details and approaches that resonate with Fauré's later practice. The famous Introit of Fauré's Requiem, for instance, with its soft, psalmodic chords and slowly plunging bassline, seems to have been modeled on the opening of Gounod's beautiful *Miserere* in C minor (1880), published seven years earlier.[6] Fauré's harmony, to be sure, is often more complicated than Gounod's, as a detailed analysis of the previous comparison would make clear. But Fauré found most of the stylistic premises he needed for his own sacred music in Gounod. For a less direct comparison, but a more comprehensive one, the Sanctus of the Requiem brings together many of the qualities he learned from Gounod: faith in sustained triadic harmony; beautiful melodies verging on sweetness; endlessly renewable figuration unafraid of monotony; and modern voice-leading with sometimes unusual sevenths. The Hosanna in excelsis shows particularly well how Fauré made Gounod's solemn simplicity his own: the music is entirely diatonic and consists of a repeating cycle of five chords, none of them a dominant, many with sevenths. Over these chords, the chorus sings only five different pitches, mostly in unison, and the trumpet and horns play 1–5–1 in unison. This passage, seemingly made of nothing, is almost inexplicably thrilling. Fauré simply sets a wheel of tonic and subdominant harmony in motion and slowly turns it through five revolutions from *fortissimo* to *pianissimo*. Fauré's fondness for the flat seventh as a mixolydian inflection rather than as a clear V of IV also can be traced to Gounod, at least in part. Example 18.1a–b compares a passage from Fauré's Sanctus (in E-flat) to a passage in Gounod's canticle *D'un cœur qui t'aime* (1882, in D major). While the lowered seventh degree is expressed differently in the two passages, in neither of them does it move down to the subdominant in the classical manner.

Finally, Fauré seems to have developed one of his most distinctive melodic traits out of Gounod's style. Many are those unforgettable codas and retransitions where Fauré reduces his melodic material to two or three notes that rock back and forth over repeating or subtly changing harmonies. The emotion may be one of ecstatic peacefulness or gently charged tension. The final flute solo of the Pavane is a well-known example; so is the Pie Jesu of the Requiem. The phrase "sempiternam Requiem" is set in just this way (sung on the notes A and G) before the return of the first section and again in the coda (on F and E-flat, then F and G). Such whole-tone oscillations and melodic

EXAMPLE 18.1a   Fauré, Requiem, Sanctus, mm. 11–13.

EXAMPLE 18.1b   Gounod, *D'un cœur qui t'aime*, mm. 72–74.

cycling are found in Gounod's music very early on, as we may see from a dream-like passage (see Example 18.2) in his double-chorus setting of Racine's "D'un cœur qui t'aime" (1851, in C major, musically unrelated to the setting mentioned above). Over a dominant seventh harmony in third inversion, the upper voices rock quietly from C to D for three measures. A surprising move down to the major submediant (A major rather than the sudominant F in first inversion) unfolds a second patch of circular harmony that seems delighted to go nowhere.[7] Both these points of stasis foreshadow typical Fauréan moments like those in the Pie Jesu.

Despite this continuation and personal development of elements in Gounod's style, Fauré's sacred music—always excepting the Requiem—does not surpass Gounod's achievement in either originality or intrinsic beauty. Gounod, with twenty-one extant masses and innumerable shorter pieces, was obviously a far more ambitious composer of sacred music than Fauré. But even if we constrain the comparison to the smaller boundaries of Fauré's body of work, his motets and canticles cannot match Gounod's for diversity of style or expressive range. Gounod tried out every modern and historicizing style he could command and was willing to go against the ingrained habits of his era: he wrote *a cappella* works in an age of accompanied music; he experimented with double choirs, theatrical idioms, Gregorian cantus firmi, and neo-Palestrinan polyphony. Fauré moved within a much smaller compass: his motets are always instrumentally accompanied, usually homophonic, and neither craftily historicizing nor daringly modern. They are practical, well-made pieces, sometimes intriguing, sometimes merely routine.

Two of Fauré's important pieces of sacred music were written before he began his professional life as a church musician. The motet *Super flumina Babylonis* (1863) for mixed chorus and orchestra remains unknown, while the *Cantique de Jean Racine* (1865) is one of his best-loved choral pieces. Both were composed for the annual composition prize at the École Niedermeyer, where *Super flumina* received a "very honorable mention" and the *Cantique* won first prize.[8] *Super flumina*, which Fauré never published, is surprising in a number of ways: the score calls for a larger orchestra than any other sacred work by Fauré: double woodwinds, four horns, three trombones, and strings with cellos divisi; it is also his longest setting of a single sacred text. Details of the instrumentation serve to remind us that French orchestras at mid-century still serenely preserved eighteenth-century habits: Fauré calls for horns in E and A and two clarinets in C (the key of the work is A minor).

EXAMPLE 18.2 Gounod, *D'un cœur qui t'aime* (ver. with acc. by piano or organ), mm. 91–97.

EXAMPLE 18.2 continued.

That the upper three choral parts are written in C-clefs likewise reminds us of the highly traditional nature of Fauré's training at the École Niedermeyer, where the study of early music from plainchant to the late Baroque was part of the standard curriculum.

The large-scale form is ternary, with two extended *fortissimo* climaxes, one at the end of the first section ("Et qui abduxerunt nos") and one building from the end of the middle section at "Si non proposuero Jerusalem" with harmonies and an ostinato rhythm foreshadowing the Libera me of the Requiem. Both the scale and the length of these climaxes are unusual for Fauré's choral music, and it is a bit surprising that the quietistic Fauré set the entire psalm, not only the opening lament that attracted so many Renaissance composers, but also the final verses, seething with vengeance. He responded to this psalm of exile with striking dynamic contrasts of very quiet and very loud sections. The eighteen-year-old composer felt free to draw on archaic, romantic-expressive, and orientalizing musical vocabularies. This varied and accomplished work, which I have never heard performed, seems worthy of revival.[9]

Fauré's setting of the *Cantique de Jean Racine*, a vernacular hymn by the consummate poet of French classicism, has almost nothing in common with the Latin psalm written two years earlier. Racine's poem is sumptuous in sound yet heartfelt in its direct plea for divine blessing. The same may be said of Fauré's musical setting. Compared to *Super flumina*, the part-writing has become even more elegant and the harmonic rhythm and phrasing more shapely, responding to the text with gentle crests of energy. Fauré gradually builds choral density and then draws back; during these choral silences, when the accompaniment re-emerges alone, one senses how perfect the pacing of the composition is. There is nothing here that Mendelssohn or Mozart would disown, and much they would have loved. And yet from the sound of the very first interval (a major seventh) we already hear Fauré's personal voice. This particular dissonance (C against the bass tonic D-flat) is so typical because it functions at once as a fleeting appoggiatura and as a harmonic sound: an ornament to the tonic arpeggio becomes part of the arpeggio, then withdraws. Fauré exploits this ambiguity throughout the piece. The idea of a "non-harmonic" tone that takes on contrapuntal importance, or a figuration that warps into genuine countermelody, becomes a central compositional technique for Fauré, as it had been for Chopin.

At the École Niedermeyer, Fauré studied Renaissance polyphony by masters such as Palestrina and Lasso; the *Cantique* honors that tradition but blends it seamlessly into a modern, homophonic texture. Fauré was always more interested in blending old with new than with pursuing technical virtuosity for its own sake; he had a perhaps exaggerated fear of academicism. Nonetheless, one may see a classical approach to polyphony in the staggered entries from bass to soprano, alternating rising minor thirds and fourths with each entry of the four choral voices (mm. 13–22), or the stretto-like sequence of alternating entries on rising fourths and fifths at "qui la conduit" (mm. 51–53, see Example 18.3). Fauré's treatment of the musical reprise beginning at "Ô Christ sois favorable," also based on rising fourths and fifths, is a discreet tour de force: after a beautifully elided reprise of the first section (m. 59) the music changes harmonic direction and is unexpectedly enriched by new points of imitation (mm. 65–71, rising fourths and fifths in bass and tenor). As the texture becomes more contrapuntal in conception, the harmonic pacing relaxes correspondingly until the climactic tonic chord in measure 72 is approached. The art of these measures is emblematic of the piece as a whole: just as the musical technique is hidden, the intensity of feeling is inward, not emphatic.

After a series of positions as a church organist, first in Rennes (1866–70) and then in Paris, Fauré began a long period of employment at La Madeleine, first as a substitute organist for Saint-Saëns (1874), then as choirmaster (1876) and finally chief organist (1896). Jean-Michel Nectoux has neatly summarized the circumstances and performance practices surrounding the music Fauré wrote for these services:

EXAMPLE 18.3 Fauré, *Cantique de Jean Racine*, mm. 51–53.

The majority of his motets and his two harmonizations of popular *noëls* were written for the soloists and choir of the church of La Madeleine . . . where Fauré conducted a choir of around thirty boys (sopranos and altos), complemented by, at most, ten men's voices (tenors, baritones and basses) . . . He composed quite a number of pieces intended to display the talents of the Madeleine's professional soloists. . . . In the works for mixed chorus, too, solo parts are very often to be found (*Tu es Petrus*, the three settings of *Tantum ergo*, *Sancta Mater*, *Messe basse*).[10]

Nectoux also explains that even though Fauré designated parts for women's voices and mixed choir in his motets when they were published (so as to make them available to secular performance), the works "had in fact been conceived originally for the exclusively male children's and adults' voice of the Madeleine."[11] Fauré showed no particular attachment to one timbre or the other, and in choosing either choristers or women for the upper parts, according to local needs, a choral director treats such works both artistically and historically. Fauré's designation of some solo parts for either soprano or tenor, as well as the equal status of different instrumental arrangements of the accompaniment (only some of which survive in complete form), reflects a similar attitude of flexibility inherited from pre-romantic aesthetics.[12]

Fauré's motets fit into a well-developed nineteenth-century tradition of French liturgical music. The three hymns "O salutaris hostia," "Ave verum corpus," and "Tantum ergo," along with the prayer "Ave Maria," seem to have been the most popular religious texts for polyphonic setting in nineteenth-century France. Fauré set the "Ave Maria" four times and the "Tantum ergo" three, but his surviving output is too small to be representative. Saint-Saëns, who set "Ave Maria" ten times, "O salutaris" eight, and "Ave verum corpus" six, offers a typical distribution for a working church composer in this period. Gounod seems to have loved the "O salutaris" particularly, but we lack a complete list of his works. All three of the hymns named above belong to the Adoration of the Blessed Sacrament in the context of the Mass. This is a significant commonality: we may infer that this was the point in the liturgy where chapelmasters were expected to provide original music. In local French uses, these hymns were sometimes actually sung in place of the Benedictus.

When we see how many times church musicians set the same texts to music, we should be reminded that Fauré (like Saint-Saëns, Gounod, and Dubois) was providing music on demand and did not necessarily seek to surpass himself with each attempt at setting a particular text. We may assume that he reused these settings regularly but also that many other settings do not survive, and that most were written quickly. One cannot, however, assume that only the *best* settings survive. Fauré never published a beautiful *Ave Maria* in F (*c*.1894), which Nectoux rediscovered in storage at La Madeleine in the 1980s. This duo for tenor, baritone, and organ is close to the *Messe basse* in style and might just be Fauré's finest motet.[13] It is certainly superior to the treacly setting in B minor (1877/1906), also a duo, which Fauré took the time to revise and publish as Op. 93. In any event, Fauré's only truly choral "Ave Maria" setting is an early work in A major for male chorus (TTB and organ, 1871). Brevity, simplicity, and a strong choral sound distinguish this motet. To a style reminiscent of the processional choruses in nineteenth-century opera, Fauré brings a series of more personal harmonic deviations. The quiet fervor of this chorus in 9/8 is almost rustic and perhaps took inspiration from its alpine setting: it was written to celebrate the ascent of Mont Saint-Bernard by the students of the École Niedermeyer, which had moved to Switzerland during the Commune.[14] This *Ave Maria*, like the one in F major, was only published posthumously. Whether Fauré left some of his better pieces in the drawer because he misjudged them, or whether he merely misplaced them, is unknown.

Fauré's motets generally avoid strongly demonstrative emotions. The results of such emotional discretion range from the exquisite poetry of the *Messe basse* for women's voices[15] to the merely pleasant blandness of the *Sancta mater* in A major (n.d., SATB and soloists). The level of musical interest in motets like *Ecce fidelis servus*, Op. 54 (1889, STBar trio) falls somewhere in between. Here, a simple but attractive melody is complicated with a brief hint of canonic writing, then blossoms into a richer middle section at "Justus germinabit." The *Tantum ergo* in A major, Op. 55 (before 1891, SATBB, T solo) is one of the most memorable of the motets yet seems ordinary once we compare it to the In paradisum of the Requiem, of which it is slightly reminiscent. Still, we may cite the passage in Example 18.4 (mm. 35–39) from this *Tantum ergo* as emblematic of what makes his motets distinctive. The prismatic harmonic palette here is uniquely Fauré's.

Fauré's unusual title "Messe basse" probably refers to a definition of a "low mass" as any mass sung to *musica* (newly composed music) rather than *cantus* (plainchant).[16] Was the self-effacing title an ironic bow to the rigor of Pope Pius X's recent *Motu proprio*, or merely a casual idiosyncrasy on Fauré's part? With only four polyphonic settings, Fauré's *Messe basse* is one movement shorter than even a *messe brève*. The Kyrie and Benedictus, both in A-flat major, are written for solo soprano and women's chorus in an almost responsorial arrangement, while the Sanctus and Agnus Dei, both in G major, are choral and homophonic. The work is fundamentally idyllic, even bucolic, and this character is probably explained by its origins in the French countryside. For when Fauré published the *Messe basse* in 1906, he drew all but its Kyrie from an unpublished *Messe des pêcheurs de Villerville* (*Mass of the Fishermen of Villerville*, 1881) also for women's voices, but without soli. This earlier work had been composed jointly with André Messager during a summer holiday in the Norman village of Villerville as a fundraiser for its Fishermen's Association. Messager wrote the Kyrie and—

EXAMPLE 18.4 Fauré, *Tantum ergo*, op. 55, mm. 35–39.

EXAMPLE 18.4   continued.

EXAMPLE 18.4 continued.

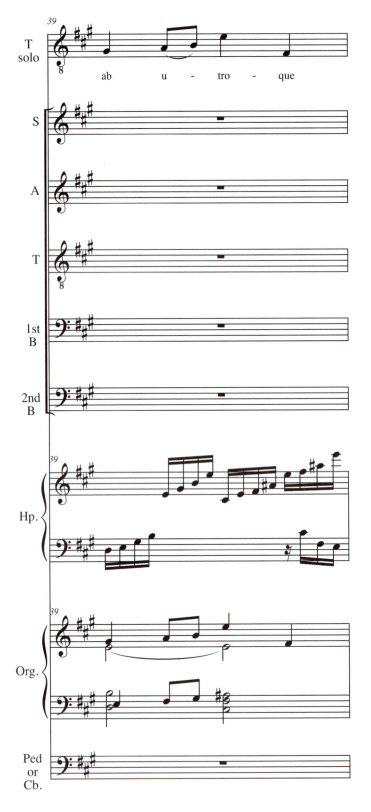

in place of a Benedictus—an O Salutaris, while Fauré composed the Gloria, Sanctus, and Agnus Dei. For the first performance in 1881, a harmonium and violin provided the only accompaniment, but for a revival the next year the Mass was arranged for a small orchestra.[17] The *Messe des pêcheurs* is a delightful composition from start to finish, brightly orchestrated (chiefly by Messager), and thanks to Nectoux's edition, now revived and recorded. Its rustic informality sets it apart from any other mass of the late nineteenth century.

When Fauré returned to his three mass movements twenty-five years later, he touched up the Sanctus and Agnus Dei, sometimes quite significantly, and he used the calm "Qui tollis" at the center of the Gloria as the basis for the Benedictus while leaving the rest of the Gloria in the drawer. To these three revised settings he added a new Kyrie in a typically seductive, legato style.[18]

Secular Works

Fauré's first secular chorus was a setting of Victor Hugo's "Les djinns" ("The Jinn" or "The Winged Demons," 1875, SATB). In this remarkable poem from *Les Orientales*, Hugo increases the length of verses from strophe to strophe, each time adding one syllable and working from disyllabic to decasyllabic verse and back again in a typical display of virtuosity. The *crescendo* and *decrescendo* that control the dynamic form of Fauré's setting, along with a gain and relaxation in rhythmic activity, parallels not only the form of the poem but also its meaning (the silence of the town at night, the descent of the demons, the central prayer that restores safety, the scattering of the demons, and silence again). The constant, extremely brisk tempo prevents any particular cognizance of the versification once the lines reach a length of six syllables, and thus Fauré avoids any prosodic pedantry. Fauré also emphasizes the arch form by returning to the initial theme and texture at measure 97 (when the verse returns to four-syllable lines). The driven harmonic style of *Les djinns* owes something to Saint-Saëns, and perhaps more to German Romanticism: never again would Fauré so favor the "haunted" diminished-seventh harmony of the Weber–Schumann tradition. Kœchlin called the piece "something of a freak,"[19] and while the style is not immediately recognizable as Fauré's, *Les djinns* is a rather wonderful piece. It comes off equally well with solo piano or orchestral accompaniment, and the poem is breathtaking. How many French choral pieces, too, include a prayer to Mohammed ("Prophète, si ta main me sauve," m. 67)—let alone one sincere enough to make us forget the orientalist fantasy of the context? Fauré sets this stirring prayer at the center of the piece, dividing up the male half of the choir in hymn-like homophony and supporting them with trombones.

La naissance de Vénus (The Birth of Venus, 1881), a "mythological scene" for mixed choir (SATB), soli, and orchestra (or piano), is one of Fauré's least-known works, yet, at over 20 minutes, it is his second longest choral composition and his most richly orchestrated. The piece was commissioned by Antonin Guillot de Sainbris for his Société Chorale d'Amateurs. Fauré's piano part seems orchestrally conceived, but according to Nectoux the cantata was repeatedly performed with piano accompaniment until Fauré orchestrated it in 1895.[20] Fauré's imaginative scoring strikes me as integral to the success of this highly coloristic music. In order to paint the imagery of Paul Collin's rather static poem, the composer calls for double woodwinds, four horns, two trumpets, three trombones, timpani, two harps, and strings. To form an appreciation of the work one must accept from the outset that it is wholly ornamental in conception. Venus is born from the waves; Jupiter invites her to join the gods on Mount Olympus. Nothing else happens in this secular cantata: once one reads the title, the plot is almost over. Furthermore, while we hear a great deal from the Nereids and from Jupiter, we hear nothing at all from Venus herself. The ode is meant to limn her reflected glory. Despite this indirectness, the apparition of Venus after the first chorus is actually the most dramatic moment in the score: a long, purely orchestral passage and the closest Fauré ever came to writing a tone poem. Fauré's imagination seems to have traveled from the Aegean coast to another habitat of the goddess, the Venusberg. The twisting sequences and coloristic orchestration have their starting point in the great pantomime scene that opens the second version of Wagner's *Tannhäuser*. In contrast, the orchestral introduction, which begins in a delightful harmonic mist, is not far from the style of Fauré's Ballade, Op. 19, while the chorus of Nereids anticipates the music for the Oceanides in *Prométhée*. The choral writing throughout is sonorous, with more frequent subdivision of choral lines than in Fauré's other works.

When Fauré published the incidental music he wrote for the revival of Alexandre Dumas's play *Caligula* (Paris, Odéon, 1888), he did not transform it into a purely orchestral suite; he retained all four numbers for women's chorus. The composite nature of this score has perhaps kept it from becoming better known.[21] If "César a fermé la paupière" is the prize of the score, so brief but magical, "De roses vermeilles" has been underrated by Nectoux, who complains that the imitative writing makes the words mostly unintelligible (a strange complaint to make of a round).[22] In fact, one understands as much of the words as necessary to grasp the joyful sentiments of the outer sections of the chorus. Fauré wanted the sopranos and mezzo-sopranos acoustically separated for a stereophonic effect, and the beauty of this canon makes one wish Fauré had exploited imitative polyphony more often in choral writing.[23] This final pair of choruses (omitting the long *mélodrame* before the first) should be taken up by chamber choirs with a nimble pianist. The earlier numbers all require the pomp or color of the surrounding orchestral setting. But even in the orchestral context, a large choir is not needed or even appropriate, as Fauré's orchestration is light, and nineteenth-century performances seemed to have used only about six women on each part.[24]

Among the shorter secular choruses, the Madrigal, Op. 35 (1883), and Pavane, Op. 50 (1887), might be seen as a pair. Both are composed for four-part choir (SATB) with piano or orchestral accompaniment, and both are in the minor mode. Other resemblances run deeper: both take up genres of the distant past, both set ironic, madrigalesque texts about the tribulations of love and courtship, and both, in doing so, oppose the men's and women's voices as a reflection of poetic content. Irony also characterizes Fauré's attitude toward his historical models; in both cases he freely mixes a late nineteenth-century style with touches preserved from earlier music. The Madrigal, to be sure, has little to do with Renaissance music, but the pairing of voices, sometimes overlapping in imitation (mm. 11–18, mm. 56–61), casually recalls the imitative texture of sixteenth-century partsongs.[25] The final section in D major, so meltingly beautiful, tinged with modal harmonies, allows the tenors to ascend to their high register, *pianissimo*, and finally weaves all four parts together in a unified expression of the text.

Of the two works, the Pavane shows the deeper connection to early music. The phrasing matches the traditional seventeenth-century step of the pavane, and at the same time Fauré uses (not too obviously) the late Renaissance tradition of the descending tetrachord as a guiding structure for the bass. The famous main tune, of course, is one of Fauré's most ravishing, and while its mode is sometimes aeolian, sometimes minor, its style belongs firmly to the late nineteenth century. Though the Pavane is best known as a work for orchestra alone, the original *ad libitum* chorus adds a striking expressive element to the score and has recently come back into performance. The choral style, particularly the way the men and women describe and deplore each other's dancing and flirting in a sometimes *parlando* style, comes right out of French opera.[26] Most important, the sense of detachment between the choir and the orchestra is not merely a result of the poem coming to the music late in the process; it is a deliberate aesthetic effect that should be exploited in performance. The Pavane was composed at the same time as the song "Clair de lune" (1887), and their resemblance is heuristic. Both pieces create a feeling of nostalgia by detaching the text from an instrumental accompaniment in the form of an antique dance. Just as the instrumental music (the pavane) begins and continues independently of the chorus, the piano part of "Clair de lune" (a minuet) is often out of phase with the vocal line, which never carries the minuet tune itself but only collects fragments here and there as it goes its own way. The disjunction of the voice or voices from a social dance suggests a poetic effect of alienation. Both these pieces from 1887 capture an intense nostalgia for a bygone world of courtiers and gallant liaisons, an *ancien régime* almost out of time and mind.[27]

Fauré's little known "tragédie lyrique" *Prométhée* (1900) is not a traditional opera and presents opportunities to the choral director. In its conception for an outdoor venue on the Mediterranean, the Arènes de Béziers, the work engaged over 400 instrumentalists and 200 choral singers, as well as solo singers and speaking actors.[28] The score comprises a variety of preludes, choruses, and melodramas, as well as airs and ensembles for the solo singers. *Prométhée* is by a far stretch Fauré's most monumental work. In writing for a large open-air venue, he adopted a deliberately block-like approach to musical construction and remarked to one of his collaborators, "This music must almost be written in *display type*!"[29] Example 18.5 gives some idea of what he meant. Fauré knew that half the singers recruited to the Béziers festival were not trained musicians, and so he confined his usual harmonic complexity to the orchestral parts. While some of the choruses have three-part textures, many are written in unison and octaves, splitting into thirds or fifths at cadences. Here the choral director with an eye on the rich orchestral writing may see the virtues in Fauré's simplicity. However, the final chorus of the work, which changes texture frequently and includes passages in eight-part harmony, shows Fauré's perhaps unsuspected capacity for epic grandeur.

A full theatrical revival of this work might be a long time coming; meanwhile there are options for the concert hall. The music for the first act could be performed separately, as a sort of Prometheus cantata for chorus and soli with symphony orchestra, perhaps drawing selectively on the spoken dialogue for a more theatrical presentation.[30] More modestly, the three choruses of Oceanides in Act 3 (nos. 2–4) make a choice excerpt for women's choir and orchestra: they run together in a smooth sequence, require no solo singers, and, most important, offer some of the most seductive music Fauré ever wrote.

In the context of Fauré's career, the sublime Requiem, Op. 48, is almost an anomaly. It became one of his most popular works, but it is not, in the context of his choral productions, a representative one. In discussing the Requiem with Louis Aguettant, Fauré mused, "Perhaps instinctively I sought to break loose from convention. . . . I wanted to do something different."[31] The composer understated his achievement; in beauty and emotional intensity, the Requiem surpasses all his other choral works. Though at first he passed it off as an occasional liturgical mass for La Madeleine (and thereby availed himself of its musical resources), in depth of feeling and musical subtlety it goes beyond his other compositions for the church (including later ones) to a degree that would be difficult to comprehend if we did not suspect a different artistic ambition behind the Requiem, one perhaps closer to the Fauré of the chamber music and songs. In light of such differences, it is appropriate that the *Requiem* is treated in detail in chapter 4.

In discussing the secular choruses, I have not resisted the temptation to praise complexity. In doing so, however, works with passages of polyphonic interest or rich texture come to the fore; unison writing or simpler textures are only "rescued" in critical acts of special pleading. The preference for complexity or richness in choral textures is a modern one, and probably shared by many readers of this book. On reflection, however, it seems possible that Fauré and some of his contemporaries may have placed as much value on the sound of voices doubled or massed in octaves or thirds as on polyphonic intricacy, at least in accompanied choral music, and that the modern

EXAMPLE 18.5   Fauré, *Prométhée*, Act 1, scene 1, at reh. 9 (piano–vocal score).

EXAMPLE 18.5 continued.

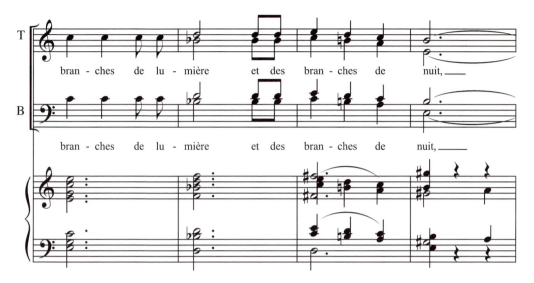

bran - ches   de   lu - mière   et des   bran - ches   de   nuit, ____

bran - ches   de   lu - mière   et des   bran - ches   de   nuit, ____

tendency to demote such textures to a second rank creates a false understanding, opening a gap in the history of choral art. While this chapter does not answer this specific responsibility to history, actual musical performances can realign our understanding of means and effect more persuasively than words.

Notes

1 I follow the terminology of Fauré's time: regardless of number of voices or instrumental accompaniment, "motets" are sacred pieces in Latin; "canticles" are in the vernacular.

2 Carlo Caballero, *Fauré and French Musical Aesthetics* (Cambridge: Cambridge University Press, 2001), 170–98.

3 Fauré's religious music has recently been gathered together in a single volume: Gabriel Fauré, *Musique religieuse*, edited by Jean-Michel Nectoux (Stuttgart: Carus, 2005). This edition is number 70.301 in the Carus catalogue and replaces the earlier volume, 70.300. The new Carus edition has every advantage: high editorial standards, a critical apparatus, current availability on the market, multiple versions of the same works, and near completeness. Nectoux also published here for the first time two newly discovered works by Fauré, a Benedictus in B-flat major and an Ave Maria in F. For reasons of copyright, three works are absent from this volume: *Super flumina Babylonis*, the *Messe des pêcheurs de Villerville*, and the Requiem. Nectoux's editions of these works (with co-editors for the latter two) have been published separately by Durand, Heugel, and Hamelle, respectively.

4 *Le ruisseau* is omitted from the discussion below because of constraints on length. Fauré's Prelude to *La Passion* (1890, SATTB and large orchestra) is also worth mentioning. Part of a larger project of incidental music for a passion play by Edmond Haraucourt, the Prelude is eighty-five measures long and was published for the first time by Sylvia Kahan as an appendix to her article, "Fauré's Prelude to *La Passion* (1890): A Re-examination of a Forgotten Score," in *Regarding Fauré*, ed. Tom Gordon (Amsterdam: Gordon and Breach, 1999), 239–72.

5 Louis Aguettant, "Rencontres avec Gabriel Fauré" [interview, July 7, 1902], *Études fauréennes* 19 (1982): 4. I have discussed Fauré's relationship to the religious music of his time, including his high opinion of Gounod, in *Fauré and French Musical Aesthetics*, 175–92.

6 *Miserere pour 4 voix soli et chœur, avec orgue (ad libitum)* (Paris: H. Lemoine, n.d.). The initial position of the minor tonic triad (fifth in the treble) followed by a bass descent through the tetrachord are especially striking similarities. There is also, later, a curious treble ascent from E-flat to F to G-flat in both works, and Gounod and Fauré adopt the same striking harmonization to the first two notes: E-flat in root position to F$^{4/2}$ (compare Fauré, mm. 13–14, to Gounod, mm. 9–10, though the latter is separated by a fermata). The two passages diverge when they harmonize the G-flat differently. I wish to thank Dr Geoffrey

Webber of Gonville and Caius College, Oxford, for sending me a copy of Gounod's *Miserere* at short notice. My understanding of this work also owes much to his fine recording of it on Centaur CRC 2848 (Centaur Records, 2007).

7 Gounod ultimately restores the expected IV[6] (built on the same bass note, A) seven beats beyond the printed example. Indeed, Example 18.2 hardly does the fluidity of Gounod's composition justice, as the whole passage beginning at m. 91 only achieves resolution with an arrival on a half cadence in m. 101.

8 Jean-Michel Nectoux, *Gabriel Fauré: les voix du clair-obscur*, 2nd ed. (Paris: Fayard, 2008), 646–47, 696–97. Both are written for mixed chorus (SATB).

9 I wish to thank Jean-Michel Nectoux for lending me a copy of Fauré's manuscript, held at the Bibliothèque Nationale de France (BnF Musique MS 17781). Printed performing materials of *Super flumina Babylonis* were produced for the first time by Éditions Durand in 1997 but are available for rental only. Ironically, it is easier to examine the composer's autograph manuscript (thirty-six pages) in Paris than to obtain the printed materials from Boosey & Hawkes.

10 Nectoux, Foreword to Gabriel Fauré, *Musique religieuse*, 13.

11 Ibid.

12 On the richer instrumentation of sacred music on festive occasions and the partial survival of Fauré's alternative versions, see ibid., 13, 14.

13 Parts for harp and cello survive in Fauré's hand, and Nectoux postulates that we are missing the remaining parts of an arrangement of the work for harp, string quintet, and organ (Nectoux, "Apparat critique," in Fauré, *Musique religieuse*, 183).

14 Ibid., 178.

15 As with so many other choral works by Fauré, the voicing of the *Messe basse* is not strictly defined. Fauré's title page, in the autograph manuscript as in the first edition (Heugel), indicates a work "pour voix de femmes, soli et chœur, avec accompagnement d'orgue (ou harmonium)." The first and third movements have braces marked merely "solo" and "chœur"; the purely choral movements (Sanctus and Agnus Dei), however, indicate "1ers Soprani" and "2mes Soprani." Given that the second part is indeed lower in tessitura, dipping to A below middle C, and given that Fauré was not strict about voicing or substitution, the lower part might just as well be designated for alto or mezzo-soprano, according to the women's voices available.

16 André Cœuroy, "La musique religieuse," in *Cinquante ans de musique française de 1874 à 1925*, ed. Ladislas Rohozinski (Paris: Librairie de France, 1925), vol. 2, 149–50 (italics mine); and see Caballero, *Fauré and French Musical Aesthetics*, 183–84.

17 The orchestra consists of flute, oboe, clarinet, and double string quintet; the harmonium provides a sort of "continuo" role in both versions. The women's chorus on both occasions seems to have numbered no more than nine voices. See Jean-Michel Nectoux, Preface to *Messe des pêcheurs de Villerville: pour chœur de femmes et orchestre de chambre*, by Gabriel Fauré and André Messager, piano-vocal score by Odette Gartenlaub (Paris: Heugel, 2001), iv, n. 1.

18 Nectoux, in his edition of the *Musique religieuse* (p. 14), hypothesizes that for this purpose Fauré dug up an older Kyrie (perhaps composed in the 1880s, like the *Messe des pêcheurs*) that does not otherwise survive. The proposal is plausible, but it seems equally plausible that the Kyrie of the *Messe basse* was newly composed. Certainly the more concentrated dissonances and harmonic changes in the Kyrie show traces of the later Fauré, revising if not composing anew.

19 Charles Kœchlin, *Gabriel Fauré*, tr. Leslie Orrey (London: Dennis Dobson, 1946), 26.

20 Nectoux, *Gabriel Fauré*, 160.

21 For the relationship of the incidental music to the published play, see Alexandre Dumas, *Théâtre complet* (Paris: Michel Lévy, 1864), vol. 4, 216, 289–90, 293–94, 298–99. The choral numbers correspond exactly to those passages in Dumas's text labeled for "Le Coryphée" and set off in smaller type.

22 Nectoux, *Gabriel Fauré*, 199.

23 Gabriel Fauré, *Correspondance*, ed. Jean-Michel Nectoux (Paris: Flammarion, 1980), 302.

24 A remarkable photograph of a rehearsal of *Caligula* in Brussels in 1889 shows nine women in the chorus; d'Indy conducts while Fauré looks on; see *Lettres intimes*, ed. Philippe Fauré-Fremiet (Paris: La Colombe, 1951), plate 27. This information is, of course, descriptive, not prescriptive. See Nectoux, *Gabriel Fauré*, 659, for chronological data on the Brussels performance.

25 Kœchlin (*Gabriel Fauré*, 26) observed another allusion to the past: Fauré's opening melody quotes the first strain of the Lutheran chorale "Aus tiefer Not schrei ich zu dir" ("In deepest need I cry to Thee"), which appears in J. S. Bach's cantata BWV 38. The allusion to this dismal liturgical text was surely a private joke: Fauré composed the Madrigal as a *wedding gift* to his friend and sometime student at the École Niedermeyer, André Messager. Nectoux, *Gabriel Fauré*, 162, notes that Bach himself adapted this theme as the subject of the Fugue in D-sharp minor (BWV 853) in *The Well-Tempered Clavier*, book 1. On closer consideration, Fauré's source was probably the Fugue, as he seems to have worked from its rhythms, and

the pitch levels of subject and answering melody in the Madrigal are the same as in the Fugue (dropped a half step, of course, but Bach's D-sharp minor subject and answer may be read off the page in D minor).

26 I believe Fauré's piece stems from a theatrical tradition whose immediate predecessor is the Pavane (no. 12) from Paladilhe's grand opera *Patrie* (1886). Also in F-sharp minor, also built on a descending tetrachord, Paladilhe's Pavane has gone unnoticed as a model for Fauré's. I first presented a history of the "revived" pavane, which includes at least a dozen pieces going back to Saint-Saëns's *Etienne Marcel* (1877–78), in "Ballet and the Secret of Style," a colloquium at the University of British Columbia (September 21, 2006). Under the title "Of Pavanes and Passepieds," it forms a chapter of my forthcoming book, *French Music and the Imagination of Classicism.*

27 The idea that these three pieces belong to a similar stylistic domain finds confirmation in historical programming: on April 30, 1892, the Madrigal, "Clair de lune," and Pavane were performed together at a concert of the Société Nationale de musique under the patronage of Winnaretta Singer (Nectoux, *Gabriel Fauré,* 661).

28 The instruments included two large bands, a symphony orchestra, and a "curtain" of thirteen harps on a raised platform just in front of the stage. The men in the chorus were recruited from the local working class, for the conception of the Béziers Festival was populist and regionalist. See Kœchlin, "Le Théâtre," *La revue musicale* 4 (October 1, 1922): 35, n2, and Nectoux, *Gabriel Fauré,* 264–65, 286, and plate 22.

29 Nectoux, *Gabriel Fauré,* 289. "Display type" refers to the families of fonts used in headlines and advertising.

30 The printed libretto containing all the text is not difficult to find, nor is the piano-vocal score. But obtaining the orchestral materials is problematic because, as with much stage music, they were never engraved. The original version for multiple orchestras exists only in two manuscript exemplars; Roger-Ducasse's arrangement for standard symphony orchestra, too, was never published but rented by Hamelle in manuscript. A photocopy of Roger-Ducasse's score and parts may reportedly still be obtained from Éditions Alphonse Leduc.

31 Louis Aguettant, "Recontres avec Gabriel Fauré," 4.

Selected Bibliography

Aguettant, Louis. "Rencontres avec Gabriel Fauré" [interview, July 7, 1902], ed. Jean-Michel Nectoux, *Études fauréennes* 19 (1982): 3–7.

Boulanger, Nadia. "La musique religieuse," *La revue musicale* 4, 11 (Oct. 1922): 104–11.

Caballero, Carlo. *Fauré and French Musical Aesthetics.* Cambridge: Cambridge University Press, 2001.

Fauré, Gabriel. *Correspondance,* ed. with essays by Jean-Michel Nectoux. Paris: Flammarion, 1980. In English as *Gabriel Fauré, His Life through Letters,* ed. Jean-Michel Nectoux, trans. J. A. Underwood. London and New York: M. Boyars, 1984.

——. *The Correspondence of Camille Saint-Saëns and Gabriel Fauré: Sixty Years of Friendship,* ed. Jean-Michel Nectoux, trans. J. Barrie Jones. Aldershot, England, and Burlington, VT: Ashgate, 2004

——. *Gabriel Fauré: A Life in Letters,* trans. and ed. J. Barrie Jones. London: B. T. Batsford, 1989.

——. *Lettres intimes,* ed. Philippe Fauré-Fremiet. Paris: La Colombe, 1951.

Jost, Peter. "*Les Djinns* und die Chormusik seiner Zeit," in *Gabriel Fauré: Werk und Rezeption,* ed. Peter Jost. Kassel: Bärenreiter, 1996, 102–13.

Kahan, Sylvia. "Fauré's Prelude to *La Passion* (1890): A Re-examination of a Forgotten Score," in *Regarding Fauré,* ed. Tom Gordon. Amsterdam: Gordon and Breach, 1999, 239–72.

Kœchlin, Charles. *Gabriel Fauré,* trans. Leslie Orrey. London: Dennis Dobson, 1946.

——. "Le Théâtre," *La revue musicale* 4 (October 1, 1922): 226–41.

Nectoux, Jean-Michel. *Fauré.* 2nd ed. Paris: Seuil, 1995.

——. Foreword and critical apparatus to *Musique religieuse,* by Gabriel Fauré. Stuttgart: Carus, 2005.

——. *Gabriel Fauré: A Musical Life,* trans. Roger Nichols. Cambridge and New York: Cambridge University Press, 1991. The most up-to-date version of this biography is the following French edition: *Gabriel Fauré: les voix du clair-obscur.* 2nd ed. Paris: Fayard, 2008.

——. Preface to *Messe des pêcheurs de Villerville: pour chœur des femmes et orchestre de chambre,* by Gabriel Fauré and André Messager, piano-vocal score by Odette Gartenlaub. Paris: Heugel, 2001.

Orledge, Robert. *Gabriel Fauré.* Rev. ed. London: Eulenburg Books, 1983.

Phillips, Edward R. *Gabriel Fauré: A Guide to Research.* New York: Garland, 2000.

Italy

19

A TALE OF SURVIVAL

Choral Music in Italy

Francesco Izzo

University of Southampton

There was a time when composers of music considered it a greater success to do well in a mass, in a psalm, [or] in a hymn, than in entire operas. [Perhaps this success was because these composers] were moved by true religious feeling or they expected [sacred] compositions to be less subject to the caprices of fashion; or because of [these works'] more learned style (almost inadmissible in dramatic music) and because they do not repeat themselves many times in a row, as it usually happens in operas, [which] saves them from becoming too common and trivial. At that time every Italian school produced very celebrated masters, who were and still are models for all nations, to the great honor of our homeland.

Then there came another time when sacred music fell into total discredit, and the title of *maestro da chiesa* was held as the equivalent of [an] inept composer, without inspiration, without knowledge. It was then enough for [a musician] to have composed a mass that one no longer wished to hear him in the theater; and conversely, one sent to the church those who no longer knew how to please onstage. A few exceptions were made only for those who clothed sacred words with music [that was] all theatrical, or [who] adapted [such words] without any regard to some aria or favorite duet from this or that serious or comic opera.[1]

Composer and critic Raimondo Boucheron wrote this passage as an introduction to his detailed review of Gaetano Donizetti's *Ave Maria* and *Miserere*, published with great prominence in the January 28, 1844 issue of the *Gazzetta musicale di Milano*, an emerging but already authoritative music journal issued by the Milanese music publisher Ricordi. In it and in other writings published in the *Gazzetta*, Boucheron joined a chorus of writers who, during the course of the nineteenth century, discussed the rise, fall, and resurrection of sacred music.[2] The bleak picture he describes in the second paragraph not only predisposes the reader to welcome the news that the state of sacred music was improving (thanks to the recent appearance of Rossini's *Stabat Mater* as well as Donizetti's latest efforts), but it also reveals a gloomy state of affairs for choral music, reflected to a significant degree in the historiography of Italian music to the present day. John Rosselli, for example, in a chapter emblematically subtitled "The Centrality of Opera," eloquently disposed of church composers in early nineteenth-century Italy in terms analogous to those employed by Boucheron 150 years earlier: "to be a *maestro di cappella* represented security or a fall-back position for those not markedly successful in the theatre. Opera was king, and could keep good musicians fully employed."[3]

At the time of publication of his review, Boucheron was eagerly seeking to be appointed *maestro di cappella* to Milan's renowned Duomo. He finally obtained the position in 1847 and held it until his death in 1876, becoming one of the most representative figures of mid-century sacred music in Italy. (As we shall see, in 1869 he was among those chosen to pay tribute to Rossini in a collective Requiem Mass.) In the progression highlighted in his article, from a past golden age of Italian sacred music through a phase of decadence and (finally) to the dawn of a new era of splendor, one might well read not only an objective criticism of the current state of affairs, but also a way for Boucheron to market himself as being at the forefront of a group of musicians devoted to the regeneration of sacred music.

Boucheron's concern was well founded, however, and could equally apply to other choral genres. Amidst the general decline of sacred music in nineteenth-century Europe, as the prestige and economic power of religious institutions and conservatories gradually but inexorably decreased, the case of Italy is indeed an extreme one. While in other European countries the rise of amateur choral singing compensated to an extent for the widespread decline of religious institutions and their musical chapels, in Italy that was not the case; sacred choral music very much remained something one listened to, rather than something one could actively make. Furthermore, nineteenth-century Italy, like most other Catholic regions, lacked an established tradition of congregational singing, and never had a composer like Mendelssohn, who undertook the twofold mission of reviving choral masterpieces from the past and creating ambitious large-scale choral works that aimed to rival the prestige of contemporary operatic composition. With the exception of important churches that maintained professional musical chapels beyond the Napoleonic period and through most of the nineteenth century, choral music-making in Italy was associated to an overwhelming extent with the opera house. In all likelihood, the first Italian choral composition that will come to the mind of the early twenty-first-century reader will be the celebrated chorus, "Va, pensiero" in Giuseppe Verdi's *Nabucco* (1842); and while many will be familiar with the choral masterpieces produced by prominent opera composers (first and foremost Gioachino Rossini's *Stabat Mater* and Verdi's *Messa da Requiem*), most will be inclined to regard these as exceptional episodes in a music world under the despotic rule of opera.

Such an inclination is as understandable as it is mistaken. Indeed, there can be no doubt that the music marketplace was dominated to a high degree by the production and consumption of opera, and that the tale of non-operatic choral music in nineteenth-century Italy is to a significant extent a tale of survival. Composers who achieved success with their operas enjoyed remarkable financial prosperity, whereas the same could not be said for full-time church musicians, whose positions granted them secure income but not wealth. The case of Saverio Mercadante (1795–1870) is emblematic: toward the end of his tenure as *maestro di cappella* at San Gaudenzio's Cathedral in the northwestern Italian city of Novara (1833–40), he received a fee four times his annual salary from the cathedral for writing a single new opera. Even so, he held on to his church position until he was offered an even more prestigious permanent appointment as director of the Naples Conservatory. Peace of mind may have been a factor in keeping him in Novara, but there were probably other motives as well. Despite the fact that the spiritual, social, and cultural supremacy of the church was generally declining, in mid-century Italy a position at a leading musical chapel still carried not only financial security, but also prestige, and provided composers with the opportunity to write not only for the stage, but also for the church—an endeavor Mercadante and most of his contemporaries regarded as thoroughly worthwhile. To be sure, Mercadante was hardly the only prominent opera composer to seek employment as *maestro di cappella* while successfully pursuing an operatic career. In 1833, when Mercadante's predecessor Pietro Generali left vacant the post at Novara, several composers at the height of their fame applied to replace him, including Carlo Coccia (who eventually succeeded Mercadante in 1840) and Gaetano Donizetti.

Throughout the nineteenth century, then, most non-operatic choral music was written for the church. Other venues and occasions, however, provided opportunities to compose for chorus. Formal studies in composition at any major Italian institution (beginning with the Milan, Bologna, and Naples conservatories) typically included the requirement to write choral works in a learned style to develop a student's proficiency in counterpoint. Oratorios, albeit detached from the strictly devotional contexts in which they originated, were still sporadically composed by prominent composers and became unexpectedly fashionable toward the end of the century, thanks in large part to the overwhelming success of Lorenzo Perosi's early oratorios (discussed later in this chapter). And in secular contexts, celebratory cantatas and hymns (including patriotic hymns composed during the period of struggle for Italian political independence and unification known as the Risorgimento) remained popular genres into the second half of the century.

Churches and Church Music

The Novara Cathedral stands out as an institution that consistently employed prominent opera composers. It was, however, only one of numerous Italian churches that maintained prestigious musical chapels during the nineteenth century. Other important churches in major Italian cities also boasted an honored tradition of sacred music-making, such as the Duomo in Milan, the Basilica of Saint Mark's in Venice, San Petronio in Bologna, and Saint Peter's and other churches in Rome, as well as the cathedrals of smaller, mostly Northern towns like Novara, including the Basilica of Santa Maria Maggiore in Bergamo, and the cathedrals of Vigevano and Casale Monferrato. In addition to a *maestro di cappella*, each of these institutions employed a choir, and could also provide additional singers, instrumentalists, and sometimes an orchestra.[4]

The choral works composed for these and other important churches, often written for solo voices, four-part chorus, and orchestra, testify to the high level of professionalism and impressive forces available. The choral output of Simon Mayr, *maestro di cappella* at Santa Maria Maggiore in Bergamo, includes highly ambitious large-scale compositions such as a monumental *Gran Messa di Requiem* in G minor (1819) that, in its size at least, represents an important antecedent to Verdi's Requiem, and well deserves to be heard today.[5] Mercadante's works composed during the 1830s for Novara include numerous choral masses, mass movements, hymns, and motets. And prominent composers who did not hold church positions welcomed any opportunity to write ambitious choral compositions for religious festivals or events. Donizetti's remarkable compositions reviewed by Boucheron are good cases in point, and so is his heartfelt *Messa da Requiem per la morte di Vincenzo Bellini* (1835), which, together with Mayr's, stands out as the finest Requiem Mass from early nineteenth-century Italy.

It cannot be denied that in a musical culture dominated by opera there was significant overlap between opera and church music. (And this, of course, is by no means unique to the nineteenth century.) Boucheron's censure of those who set sacred texts to operatic music, however, should not lead us to believe that the quest for a distinctly sacred musical style was either non-existent or unsuccessful. A glimpse into the problems faced by those who wished to compose sacred music in early nineteenth-century Italy can be gathered from Gioachino Rossini's *Messa di Gloria* written in Naples in 1820 when the composer was at the height of his operatic activity and fame.[6] In this admirable composition, which consists of nine movements, the composer drew significantly on the experience and expectations derived from his work and success as an opera composer. At the same time, he was able to distinguish clearly between secular and sacred styles and to use a vocabulary appropriate for the church. Neapolitan listeners accustomed to Rossini's operatic idiom must have felt right at home with the Christe eleison for two solo tenors, the Laudamus te for soprano, or the tenor aria Qui tollis that includes the highly virtuosic, cabaletta-like Qui sedes. Those same

EXAMPLE 19.1   Rossini, *Messa di Gloria*, Kyrie, mm. 1–14. Source: *Messa di Gloria*. Critical edition by Martina Grempler. Works of Gioachino Rossini. Kassel, Basel, London, New York, Praha: Bärenreiter-Verlag, forthcoming. Piano reduction by the author. Reproduced by permission.

EXAMPLE 19.1   continued.

listeners, however, may have been surprised (pleasantly, I like to believe) by the distinctly sacred character of the choral sections of the *Messa*. Upon hearing the austere introduction of the Kyrie eleison, for example, with its harmonic progressions that obscure the tonic key for several measures, finally reaching the dominant of E-flat major as the chorus enters in *pp*, they could not have failed to notice how the composer had achieved a result radically different from that of his operatic *introduzioni* (see Example 19.1). The same goes for the triumphant opening of the Gloria, and especially for the impressive double fugue Cum sancto spiritu that concludes the *Messa*. As Jesse Rosenberg has shown, Rossini probably entrusted another composer, Pietro Raimondi, who was particularly admired for his mastery of contrapuntal techniques, to write this ambitious final movement.[7] As we shall see, fugues and other contrapuntal techniques were deployed as indicators of sacredness in numerous works throughout the century.[8]

In 1880, another renowned composer created a large-scale sacred work that has enjoyed some fortune in recent years. The composer was the young Giacomo Puccini, whose operatic success was still distant into the future, and the work, performed for the first time in Lucca on July 12, 1880, was another Mass, recently marketed under the improper title of *Messa di Gloria* (in fact Puccini set the entire Mass Ordinary), but called *Messa a 4 voci con orchestra* by the composer. Exactly sixty years separate this juvenile effort by Puccini from Rossini's *Messa di Gloria*, and yet, the problems involved with the musical setting of the Mass seem remarkably similar to those dealt with by Rossini. While Puccini at the time was hardly as experienced as Rossini had been in 1820, he was indeed intimately conversant with the operatic idiom of his time, and probably inclined to please listeners who were familiar with and keen on that idiom. Thus, it comes as no surprise that here too we encounter sections that sound operatic to the hilt. Upon hearing the festive opening of the Gloria, for example, Puccini aficionados will immediately recognize the character of lively crowd scenes in the composer's early operas (such as in Act 1 of *Manon Lescaut* or Act 2 of *La bohème*), and the youthful exuberance of the Gratias agimus for solo tenor strongly foreshadows the passionate outbursts of Cavaradossi and other young lovers in Puccini's operas.[9] At the same time, Puccini's familiarity with the distinctive features of mid-century sacred choral music is just as apparent; for example, in the solemn and restrained Credo, in the deeply meditative Et incarnatus for solo tenor and chorus, or in the chorale-like beginning of the Sanctus, all of which showcase proficient part writing and soberly orchestrated accompaniments. As in Rossini's *Messa di Gloria*, the Cum sancto spiritu is set as a four-part choral fugue in which Puccini deployed impressive contrapuntal skills. A particularly fascinating instance of Puccini merging sacred and secular in the same movement is the Qui tollis, intoned by the basses in unison in a manner strongly reminiscent of the stirring choruses in Verdi's early operas (see Example 19.2). Rather than dwelling uniquely on the appeal of this soaring melody, however, after a few measures Puccini introduced a contrasting episode on the words "Miserere nobis," in which the chorus sings in four parts, characterized by a more subdued melodic profile and by a sparse use of imitation.[10]

In recent decades, Rossini's *Messa di Gloria* and Puccini's *Messa a 4 voci* have circulated only to a limited extent in live performances and in recordings, and for better or worse their success hardly compares to that enjoyed by the operas of the same composers. This, and the fact that Puccini's piece did not appear in print until 1951 and Rossini's *Messa* was rediscovered only in 1968, speaks volumes for the status of nineteenth-century Italian sacred music in the canon.[11] Indeed, a great deal of that music exists only in manuscript, and lies undiscovered and unperformed in conservatory libraries and in church archives. As Fabrizio Della Seta has wisely warned, it is unlikely that systematic research into these repositories will bring to light a massive quantity of unknown masterpieces, but the quality of many compositions is indeed impressive.[12]

A unique opportunity to explore the work of important composers of sacred music at mid-century comes from the *Messa per Rossini*, a collaborative Requiem Mass planned by Giuseppe Verdi for a public performance in memory of Gioachino Rossini to take place on the first anniversary of his death in 1869. Following Verdi's passionate call for such a collective musical commemoration, a committee was formed at the Milan Conservatory, and nominated suitable composers to be entrusted with writing individual movements of the Mass. As the committee publicly announced, among those chosen were not only celebrated opera composers (beginning with Verdi himself, who famously contributed the Libera me that eventually became the cornerstone of his own *Messa da Requiem*), but also "i maestri delle cappelle più rinomate" (the *maestri* of the most renowned chapels),[13] including Mercadante (who had to decline due to his poor health), Carlo Coccia, Boucheron, Alessandro Nini (Mayr's successor at Bergamo), Gaetano Gaspari (from Bologna's San Petronio), Antonio Buzzolla (from Saint Mark's in Venice), and Antonio Cagnoni

EXAMPLE 19.2　Puccini, *Messa*, Gloria, mm. 206–13. Source: *Messa a 4 voci*. Edited by Dieter Schickling. Stuttgart: Carus-Verlag, 2004. Reproduced by permission.

(who had served at Vigevano's Duomo).[14] The *Messa per Rossini* was completed but ultimately remained unperformed, and several of its composers reused their contributions in different contexts. Its music, however, survived intact, and received a great deal of scholarly attention during the 1980s, culminating in the publication of its score and in performances and recordings conducted by Helmuth Rilling in 1989.[15]

The purpose for which the *Messa per Rossini* was assembled is by all means an exceptional one, and it is likely that the composers involved felt the pressure and realized the opportunities implicit in such circumstances, making every possible effort to rise to the occasion. Thus, though the music it contains may not be representative of the style and conventions commonly encountered in church music of that time, it is undoubtedly indicative of the high level of competence of the composers who took part in the effort, and probably of others who held similar posts. Considered as a whole, the remarkably appealing score once more conveys the unavoidable tension that derives from the combination, clash, or overlap of methods and devices conventionally associated with sacred music with others that are undeniably operatic. The opening movement by Buzzolla, entirely scored for chorus and full orchestra, combines a double fugue in the Kyrie with homophonic passages and with a chant-like "Te decet hymnus." What the piece may lack in dramatic intensity (especially if compared to the corresponding section in Verdi's own Requiem Mass) is compensated for by the refined harmonization of chorale-like passages and by the effectiveness of its uniformly somber mood. This is one of several movements in the *Messa per Rossini* that deliberately steers clear of anything that might suggest comparisons with operatic practice. The same goes for Carlo Coccia's fugal Amen that concludes the Dies irae sequence, whereas the Lacrimosa by the same author, albeit scored *a cappella*, is far less austere, and shows the influence of contemporary popular styles.[16] Boucheron's Confutatis places the solo bass in great prominence, and is in fact highly operatic in its text treatment (note the solo passages at the end of each section); the chorus hardly succeeds in keeping at bay the soloist's virtuosic impulse. The four-part offertory (Domine Jesu) by Gaetano Gaspari is even more indebted to contemporaneous opera, and is one of the least distinguished portions of the Mass.

A unique case is the music provided for the *Messa per Rossini* by Pietro Platania, a pupil of Pietro Raimondi who, at forty-one, was the youngest of the participants in the project. His Sanctus, showcasing a variety of contrapuntal techniques combined with an impressively sophisticated harmonic language, reveals him to be an assured writer of choral music, whose work might well warrant greater fortune in the present day.[17] That Platania never held a position as *maestro di cappella* is indicative of the increasing difficulties in the production of choral music in post-unification Italy. The prestige and financial means of churches that for the first two-thirds of the century had provided support and opportunities for many distinguished composers declined significantly following the annexation of the Papal States to the Kingdom of Italy in 1870s, and their musical chapels either became drastically smaller (often resulting in choruses being available only on special occasions, if at all) or dissolved completely. Thus, the opportunities for professional composers to produce new church music with chorus became few and far between as the 1900s approached, and so did professional performances of existing music. Anyone who is accustomed to today's musical activities (or lack thereof) in the same cathedrals that employed the most accomplished *maestri di cappella* of the nineteenth century knows that the likelihood of hearing competently performed choral music during a liturgical function is remote at best.

The Permanence of Rossini's *Stabat Mater*

The sacred choral music discussed thus far, including the exceptional *Messa per Rossini*, is by definition occasional. These and most other church compositions originated either in close connection with specific occasions or celebrations, or to fulfill the ordinary requirements of a full-time position as *maestro di cappella*. In this context, the popular choral compositions of Rossini's maturity stand out as remarkable exceptions: prior to Verdi's Requiem, no other Italian choral composition can lay the same claim to extensive circulation and lasting fame as Rossini's *Stabat Mater* (1841). Although the work originated in France, the impact it had on Italian musical life and the rapidity with which it was appropriated as an icon of national culture was most remarkable. A measure of the attention it commanded comes from the number of editions published in a timely fashion by Ricordi. The Milanese firm issued a piano–vocal score in December 1841 (in advance of the world premiere in Paris) and vocal parts for chorus and soloists in March 1842, followed by orchestral parts and a full score in July of the same year. In the fall came several arrangements, including Henri Herz's piano transcription in September and an arrangement for accordion with piano accompaniment in December.[18]

Of course, the amount of attention devoted to the *Stabat Mater* by critics and audiences alike had to do not only with the intrinsic musical qualities of the piece or in the way it was perceived in regard to its genre, but especially with the fact that this composition marked Rossini's return into the public eye after more than a decade-long silence (his last opera, *Guillaume Tell*, had been premiered in 1829), at a point where many expected his retirement to be permanent. The first Italian performance of the *Stabat Mater* at Bologna's San Petronio on March 18, 1842, with a stellar cast of singers under the musical direction of none other than Donizetti, was undoubtedly a salient musical event in that year. The Bolognese performance was preceded by the enthusiastic news and reports of the world premiere at the Théâtre Italien in Paris just two months earlier, and went down in history as one of the turning points in nineteenth-century Italian choral music. The Bolognese periodical *Teatri arti e letteratura*, which only rarely discussed non-operatic music, provided extensive coverage of the preparations and rehearsals of the *Stabat Mater*, and its editor, Gaetano Fiori, wrote a raving review immediately after the premiere ("a half hour before midnight," as indicated next to the front title) that was published in a special issue of the journal the very next day. The following passage sums up Fiori's perception of the work:

> Here is art's true progress: because, whereas before this work sacred music was nothing more than a succession of melodies or a mad invention of motives that invited you not to pray but to amuse yourself, in the future it will be, according to the subject, either sad or glorious, joyful and rejoicing, but it will never invite you to merriness or good humor; it will always keep its religious and venerable character. For this the *Stabat Mater* by Rossini will serve as a model.[19]

Fiori had long been partial to Rossini, and his enthusiasm on this particular occasion comes as no surprise. The points in common between this passage and Boucheron's review cited at the beginning of this chapter are obvious. Indeed, to praise the sacredness of sacred music was commonplace in mid-century Italian music criticism, and Fiori must have felt that the most effective strategy to favor Rossini's cause was to emphasize the merits of a composer who had found a way to write in a manner befitting the church rather than the theater. This is the point that was stressed repeatedly, not only in Fiori's writings but also in other favorable reviews of the *Stabat Mater*.[20] Not all reactions to the appearance of this work were as positive, however. Just as Fiori had praised the composition for its distinctly sacred character, others blamed Rossini for the theatrical excess of his setting of the sequence.[21] If one turns to the music itself, it is easy to find support for both perspectives: more than in any other score of nineteenth-century Italian sacred choral music, one is confronted with elements drawn from two different and yet significantly overlapping spheres. Compared to Rossini's earlier *Messa di Gloria*, however, the sacred and secular elements are not merely juxtaposed from one movement to the next, but effectively blended in each of them. Even in the more operatic-sounding passages, the careful listener or performer will easily detect indicators of religiosity in the harmonic idiom, vocal writing, and orchestration: the numbers involving the participation of the chorus, in particular, successfully convey the religious character invoked by Fiori.

The initial number, "Stabat Mater," is a case in point. Just as Rossini began the Kyrie of the *Messa di Gloria*, the orchestral opening here similarly conceals the tonic key until the first root-position G-minor triad is sounded, some sixteen bars into the piece. The remainder of the prelude is tinged with dramatic premonitions, but as soon as the chorus starts singing, we are as far removed from opera, as basses, tenors, and sopranos sing the opening words of the sequence *sotto voce* and in imitation, the soprano line concluding the first phrase with two highly expressive suspensions on the word "dolorosa" (see Example 19.3). Furthermore, throughout the movement, Rossini is particularly attentive to the meaning of individual words and images, as at the phrase "dum pendebat Filius" ("where the Son was hanging," mm. 58–61), market by a sudden *fortissimo* as chorus and soloists sing each syllable in unison on a sustained *d*.

Characteristics strongly suggestive of the sacred context also appear elsewhere. Following three numbers for the soloists, a particularly striking choral effect comes at the beginning of the chorus and recitative "Eja, Mater" (no. 5, "O Mother"), entirely scored *a cappella*. The prayerful tone of the text prompts hieratic, almost chant-like music in the introductory passage sung in unison by the basses, and certainly remembered by Verdi as he wrote the trial scene in *Aida* (see Example 19.4). In the celebrated "Inflammatus" for soprano and chorus (no. 8), the soloist's forceful delivery of the first few lines over an active orchestral accompaniment in sextuplets, foreshadowing "Cortigiani, vil razza dannata" in Verdi's *Rigoletto* (composed in the same key of C minor), gives way to four choral statements of the words "in die judicii" ("on the day of judgment"). The choral intervention effectively mitigates the vehemence of the soprano prompting the transition to the contrasting section in the relative major "Fac me Cruce custodiri," sung in alternation between soloist and chorus. Lastly, in the majestic choral finale (no. 10), the magnificent fugal section "In sempiterna" is introduced by three *fortissimo* orchestral chords setting the tonic key of G minor, each followed by the word "Amen" sung by the whole chorus.

Until we learn much more about widespread trends in early nineteenth-century sacred choral music, any assessment of the genre, conventions, and original traits of Rossini's *Stabat Mater* will have to be regarded as provisional. What is certain, though, is that no other sacred choral composition occupies a similar place in mid-century Italy, and that its impact during the years that followed its appearance was unparalleled. While its influence may have extended well beyond the sacred sphere (as I have hinted in the brief discussions of "Eja, Mater" and "Inflammatus"), Rossini had at last become a force to be reckoned with in the realm of choral music that was not originally intended for the stage. The public success of his *Stabat Mater* continues to the present day.

Music Education, Learned Style, and *Stile Antico*

In light of the impressive essay in counterpoint in the final number of the *Stabat Mater*, the following remarks, which Rossini reportedly uttered during the summer of 1841 and which François-Joseph Fétis published the same year in an article in the *Revue et Gazette musicale de Paris*, will sound either falsely modest or utterly laughable: "[Rossini] again spoke of the insufficiency of his scholastic training as rendering him unable to write for the Church and declared that he no longer had the spirit to return to the study of the elements of fugue and counterpoint."[22] The composer may well have been speaking tongue in cheek (although his words may shed light retrospectively on the reasons why he chose to engage Raimondi to compose the fugue in the *Messa di Gloria*), but the idea of a close connection between formal training and the ability to compose church music is an

EXAMPLE 19.3   Rossini, *Stabat Mater*, Stabat mater, mm. 32–41. Source: *Stabat Mater*. Piano-vocal score. Milan: Ricordi, PN 49182. Reproduced by permission.

EXAMPLE 19.4 Rossini, *Stabat Mater*, Eja mater, mm. 1–13. Source: *Stabat Mater*. Piano-vocal score. Milan: Ricordi, PN 49182. Reproduced by permission.

important one. The numerous fugues encountered in sacred music throughout the century, often appearing at crucial points within large-scale works (for example, at the conclusion of a multi-section movement or of a whole composition), stand as a reminder that the use of a "learned" style carried a close association with sacred music. This is perfectly in line with the established belief—expressed by Padre Martini in the previous century and broadly shared by composers of sacred music in nineteenth-century Italy—that contrapuntal complexity helped to keep the mind of the listener free from the temptations of the senses.[23]

Thus, if the use of fugue and other contrapuntal techniques served well the needs of church music, the study and composition of sacred works provided composers-in-training with the opportunity to practice those techniques beyond a sheer theoretical framework, and to create actual performable works that often gave them their first opportunities for public exposure. Students of composition, and particularly those trained in the classical school of the Naples Conservatory or other institutions (including the conservatories at Bologna and Milan), typically produced significant quantities of choral music in learned style as part of their education. Again, the example of Mercadante is emblematic: during his conservatory years at Naples, he wrote a number of sacred works. Around the same time, Vincenzo Bellini produced numerous sacred compositions during his studies, first in Catania and then at the Real Collegio di Musica in Naples, including sacred hymns and several mass settings. After his operatic career took off in the mid-1820s, however, Bellini never turned to sacred music again.

The high level of music-making at many church chapels was closely connected to the prestige of the educational institutions connected to them. Conservatories throughout the peninsula often worked with local musical chapels, seeking to obtain engagements and commissions for their most talented students. At Bergamo, Simon Mayr could benefit from the joint directorship of the chapel at Santa Maria Maggiore and the Lezioni Caritatevoli di Musica, a free music school he had founded in 1805. The latter provided choir boys and instrumentalists for performances in Santa Maria Maggiore. Among the Lezioni Caritatevoli's students was the young Donizetti, pupil of Mayr's from 1806 to 1814, who during those years developed an acquaintance with and sincere interest in sacred music that lasted for the rest of his life. If the example of Mayr proved extraordinarily influential for Donizetti the opera composer, he was probably even more so for Donizetti the composer of sacred music; the young composer gained further exposure and opportunities to write in the learned style under the guidance of Stanislao Mattei, *maestro di cappella* at San Petronio and professor of composition at the Liceo Musicale in Bologna.

In these and other educational institutions, the notion of "learned style" referred essentially to the principles of eighteenth-century counterpoint and fugue exemplified in the theoretical writings of Johann Joseph Fux and in the compositions and treatises of a selected number of Italian masters. In the minds of early nineteenth-century Italian musicians, such a style carried forward the honored but essentially abstract tradition of Renaissance polyphony. It was only in limited instances and contexts that composers actively sought to revive the compositional style and the actual music of Palestrina, Allegri, and other Italian masters from the sixteenth and seventeenth centuries. It is well known that during a visit to Rome in 1830, Felix Mendelssohn had the opportunity to hear the choir of the Sistine Chapel and expressed his disappointment at what he perceived to be their inappropriate use of ornamentation, inaccuracy of intonation, and cuts.[24] Of course, Mendelssohn's negative reaction expresses to a large extent the clash between his idealistic expectations against long-lived yet changing traditions and practical approaches to performance in Italy, of which he could have no awareness and little understanding.

In fact, Rome was the one place in Italy where the tradition of Renaissance sacred polyphony continued to survive throughout the nineteenth century. It is in that city, and in the specific context of the papal choir and its activities, that concrete scholarly interest in Palestrina and his music awakened in the early 1800s, largely thanks to the efforts of Giuseppe Baini, a stern guardian of the Catholic Church and its musical traditions from 1814 (when he became general administrator of the college of papal singers) until his death in 1844.[25] As a composer, Baini left a number of works that idealistically attempted to reinstate Renaissance polyphony as a living compositional practice, but these did not circulate outside St. Peter's. It is his work as a scholar that left a lasting mark, especially his monumental two-volume monograph on Palestrina[26] and his *Raccolta di musica sacra* (1841–46), a seven-volume collection that made a large number of compositions by Palestrina and his contemporaries available for the first time in a modern edition. Whereas Baini's own compositions circulated only within the circles of sacred music in the Vatican basilica, others expressed a developing interest in Renaissance polyphony in their music, including Francesco Basili, the director of the Milan Conservatory, who infamously went down in history as the administrator who denied admission to the young Giuseppe Verdi. Among other works, Basili composed an ambitious and admirable *Miserere*, a setting for four-part unaccompanied mixed chorus that circulated widely, was published by Ricordi in 1828, and ultimately earned him the position of *maestro di cappella* at Saint Peter's in Rome in 1837.

Although by no means comparable to the revival of the choral works by Bach and Handel elsewhere in Europe, the recovery of Renaissance polyphony promoted by Baini, Basili, and a few others in the early part of the century left a mark on Italian musical culture. When the Accademia di Santa Cecilia began its public concert seasons in Rome on February 2, 1895, for example, the program was devoted in large part to music by Palestrina.[27] The interest in musical traditions and repertories from the past (including not only Renaissance polyphony, but also seventeenth- and early eighteenth-century choral music) became evident also in important compositional experiences of the Italian *fin de siècle*, including Lorenzo Perosi's oratorios (to which we will turn at the conclusion of this chapter), and Verdi's sacred works composed between the late 1880s and the late 1890s and grouped together as *Quattro pezzi sacri* in the 1898 Ricordi edition.

It is worth pointing out that the term "sacred" used in the Ricordi edition comes to acquire a broad meaning, and applies equally to established Latin religious texts featured in three of the four pieces—the *Ave Maria*, the *Te Deum*, and the *Stabat Mater*—and to Dante's Italian poetry—the famous passage from the *Paradiso* in which St. Bernard addresses the Virgin Mary—that Verdi chose for the fourth piece in the set. In the entire collection, Verdi went a long way toward expressing his admiration of Renaissance polyphony, writing in a style that emphasizes the text both at the structural level and in the meaning of individual words and concepts. Pierluigi Petrobelli has convincingly shown that the piece for four-part women's chorus based on Dante and popularly known as *Laudi alla Vergine Maria* (a title Verdi had nothing to do with) draws not only on Palestrina, but also on the madrigalists, "in that the composer never failed to develop in musical imagery the suggestions offered by the poetic text."[28] Indeed, there is far more than the *a cappella* scoring that expresses Verdi's homage to earlier traditions of choral music: the poetic form is mirrored musically in the regular placement of a cadence at the end of each tercet, the use of imitation is sparse and is always intended to emphasize specific details in the poetry, and a mood of serene asceticism pervades the entire piece. Nothing illustrates Verdi's unassuming approach and sincere nod to the national tradition of the *stile antico* better than the straightforward homophonic delivery of the opening lines, where the emphasis is entirely on the text and on the rarified texture of the four-part female ensemble (see Example 19.5).

Celebratory Choral Music: Hymns and Cantatas

The quest for stylistic identity that characterizes so much sacred music in nineteenth-century Italy is all but absent in secular genres that developed in close connection with opera. Indeed, the countless celebratory hymns and cantatas composed for various occasions throughout the century are overtly and uncritically operatic. To get a good sense of what this repertory stood for musically, one need only look at Mercadante's *L'arte che pria divisi* and *Ridente e fausto già sorge il sole*, two wholesome choral cantatas performed in 1818 in Naples to celebrate holidays and occasions involving members of the nobility. The latter, for instance, composed for the name day of the Duchess of Noja, opens with a festive chorus in 3/8 that rings every bit as operatic as any *introduzione* by Rossini or his contemporaries. And as in any *introduzione*, the chorus rapidly gives way to solo numbers and a duet for specific characters—Mercurio and Partenope in this case—that occupy the central portion of the cantata. The chorus then returns for a concluding number.[29] For a young composer like Mercadante, commissions such as these were easier to come by than contracts with opera houses, and represented important professional opportunities; these cantatas allowed him to gain invaluable visibility and experience in dramatic composition, and their success was probably among the factors that earned him his first operatic commission the following year.

An exceptionally ambitious celebratory choral composition is Rossini's *Cantata in onore del Sommo Pontefice Pio IX*, first performed on January 1, 1847 to celebrate the recently elected new pope. Compared to Mercadante's youthful essays and other small-scale choral cantatas, this work stands out for its monumental size, by all means commensurate to the exceptionality of the occasion. Stylistically, however, this work bears much in common with other celebratory compositions, showing a substantial identity with the forms and melodic style of early nineteenth-century opera. Rossini, who had experienced severe health problems and thus agreed to compose the piece reluctantly, drew on passages from his operas *Armida*, *Ricciardo e Zoraide*, and *Le Siège de Corinthe* for five movements of the cantata, effectively producing one of the most striking examples of recomposition of his career.[30]

While most occasional choral compositions in pre-unification Italy were composed in honor of members of the ruling classes, important exceptions came in the form of patriotic hymns, composed in large numbers during the revolutions of 1848–49 or shortly after the unification of Italy in 1861.

EXAMPLE 19.5 Verdi, *Laudi alla Vergine Maria*, mm. 1–8. Source: *Quattro pezzi sacri*. Piano-vocal score. Milan: Ricordi, PN 101729. Reproduced by permission.

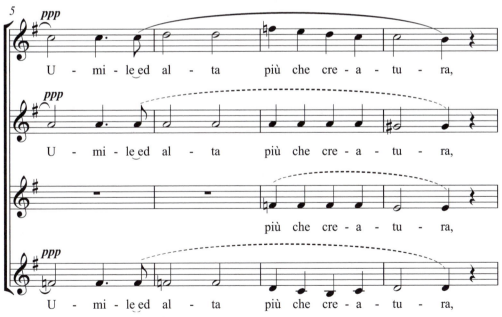

Of course, the social function of these compositions is the diametrical opposite of the celebration of powerful absolute rulers. Musically, too, patriotic hymns tend to shift away from the operatic mode of expression of celebratory cantatas (inclusive of virtuosic parts for solo singers, rich orchestrations, and such), and toward a more popular idiom that privileges simple melodies sung by a chorus, either in unison or plainly scored in parts, often with a simple piano accompaniment and sometimes with no accompaniment at all. Verdi's short but poignant *Inno popolare* ("Suona la tromba"), for example, written in 1848 at the instigation of Giuseppe Mazzini to poetry by Goffredo Mameli, was scored for unaccompanied three-part male chorus (TTB), and numerous patriotic hymns for chorus in unison with piano accompaniment appeared in print during the revolutionary years.[31] The titles of these pieces are as predictable as the contents of their poetry, rooted in the spirit of the Risorgimento: *Il canto di guerra degli italiani* (War Song of the Italians), *Gl'italiani redenti* (The Italians Redeemed), *Alla bandiera italiana* (To the Italian Flag), *L'indipendenza*, and so forth. And their authors were only rarely well-known opera composers like Verdi; rather, they were mostly voice teachers, song composers, and even church musicians (including Boucheron, whose *Canto del milite lombardo* was published by Ricordi in 1848).

As Philip Gossett has shown, the patriotic compositions produced in 1848–49 were strictly connected to their own socio-historical context, and their circulation was limited, or even outright prohibited once the Austrians regained political control over North-Eastern Italy and reinstated their strict censorial practices. Publishers who printed patriotic hymns during the revolutions of these years were sometimes forced to destroy their plates.[32] The patriotic hymns that appeared after the unification, however, enjoyed somewhat better fortune, and among them stands the only other occasional composition of Verdi's maturity. In 1861, Verdi was invited to represent the newly liberated and unified Italy at the 1862 London International Exhibition. Rather than producing a one-dimensional patriotic composition celebrating the glorious conclusion of the War of Italian Independence or exalting the national identity of the newborn country, the composer created a grand *Inno delle nazioni* (Hymn of the Nations) for solo tenor, chorus, and full orchestra, in which the plural "nations" is the operative word. The closing portion of the piece, which skillfully combines "God Save the Queen" and the "Marseillaise" with the song "Fratelli d'Italia" (which was destined to become the Italian national anthem),[33] expresses his political message with sparkling clarity: having achieved unity and independence, Italy now stood on a par with the other great European nations.[34] It goes without saying that Verdi carefully avoided any musical references to the Austrian empire.

Italy after the Unification and at the *Fin de Siècle*

The decline of musical chapels and church music in post-unification Italy was counterbalanced by the rise of music professionalism outside of the church. Opera houses, of course, maintained their prominence in Italian musical life, but numerous concert organizations were established during the final decades of the century, with positive ramifications for the performance of choral music. While the often-cited performance of Haydn's *The Creation* that took place at the Teatro dei Filodrammatici in Milan in April 1834 under the direction of the young Verdi could be regarded as an unusual occurrence in the early part of the century, as the *fin de siècle* approached opera houses and symphonic institutions included large-scale choral compositions in their programs with increasing frequency. Compositions from the classical period, particularly Haydn and Mozart, were heard with some regularity, and audiences were introduced to more recent masterpieces, albeit sometimes with considerable delay. The Italian premiere of Berlioz's *La Damnation de Faust*, for example, took place at the Teatro Argentina in Rome as late as February 19, 1887, performed by the Società Orchestrale Romana conducted by Ettore Pinelli. The Italian translation was published by the

Milanese publisher Sonzogno, whose firm had an active role in promoting this event and subsequent Italian performances of the same work.[35] Also in post-unification Rome, the Accademia Filarmonica Romana organized performances of Mendelssohn's *St. Paul* and Beethoven's *Die Ruinen von Athen* (the incidental music, which included choral numbers). In this context, while the composition of new choral music for the church inexorably declined in quantity, a non-operatic choral repertory was gradually established in the concert hall. Of course, that repertory came to include sacred compositions by Italian composers such as Rossini's *Stabat Mater* and Verdi's Requiem.

Rossini's *Petite Messe solennelle* made its way into Italian concert life against this backdrop. Anything but petite in size—it lasts nearly two hours—this Mass is the unsurpassed achievement of Rossini's late years. Its title expresses the witty modesty with which the composer regarded the piece. Indeed, at the end of the autograph score he left the following cheeky inscription: "Dear God. Here it is, finished, this poor little Mass. Have I written sacred music [musique sacrée] or damned music [sacrée musique]? I was born for opera buffa, you know it well! Little science, some heart, that's all. Be blessed, then, and grant me a place in Paradise."[36] Composed in Paris in 1863 and premiered the following year at the consecration of the private chapel of the Parisian Count and Countess Alexis and Louise Pillet-Will, the original version of the piece (of which two variants exist) was scored for twelve solo voices—four soloists and a chorus of eight—two pianos, and harmonium. In 1867 Rossini prepared a second version for four soloists, chorus, and orchestra, and it is the latter that made its way to Italy and received a great deal of attention soon after the composer's death. The Italian premiere took place at Bologna's Teatro Comunale on March 23, 1869. Roberta Marvin has demonstrated how the performance of the *Petite Messe solennelle* in Bologna took special significance as a celebration not only of Rossini's genius, but also of the Italian musical past, all the more so because Bologna had become a stronghold for foreign (especially German) music in Italy.[37] On the day of the performance, a local newspaper heralded that "Bologna, the native musical city of the Pesarese swan, will celebrate in this way the force of the genius in front of whom all foreigners are obliged reverently to genuflect."[38]

Not everyone, Italian or foreigner, genuflected to Rossini's final masterpiece: the reception of the Bologna performance, in fact, was rather mixed. The piece, however, made its way into the repertory and has continued to enjoy deserved success to the present day.[39] Its music constitutes an extraordinarily effective synthesis of respect for past traditions with a modern idiom. On the one hand, Rossini produced his finest essay in counterpoint (and some of the most impressive contrapuntal writing of the late nineteenth century) in the magnificent double fugue Cum sancto spiritu. The composer who almost a half a century earlier had subcontracted the analogous passage of his *Messa di Gloria* to Raimondi now stood tall in his mastery of fugal writing. On the other hand, he used an abundance of chromaticism and a highly complex harmonic vocabulary, while maintaining his undefiled melodic vein. The spectacular opening of the Credo, with its striking harmonic progressions, forceful delivery of the opening words of the profession of faith, and chromatic inflections, seamlessly flows into a delightfully melodic and diatonic passage at the words "Patrem omnipotentem." The entire movement plays on the combination of these elements.

It is remarkable that a piece conceived for an intimate private occasion ultimately would become a staple of late nineteenth-century choral literature. Other Italian choral compositions from this period followed a reverse path, originating as important commissions for prestigious concert institutions but ultimately failing to establish themselves. At the turn of the century, it was becoming customary for the Accademia di Santa Cecilia and other venues to commission new choral works from both emerging and renowned Italian composers. An important tradition was established at the Accademia Filarmonica Romana as well, which from 1878 to 1927 was entrusted with the regular commission of new Requiem masses to be performed at the Pantheon in memory of

King Victor Emmanuel II and other deceased Italian royalty. Twenty-three new masses resulted from this endeavor, including works by Edoardo Mascheroni, Riccardo Zandonai, and Ildebrando Pizzetti. Particularly appealing is a conservative but deeply emotional Requiem (1895–96) by Giovanni Sgambati, which was used repeatedly at royal funerals well into the twentieth century.

The most relevant phenomenon in *fin-de-siècle* Italian choral music, and one of the most striking aspects of the culture of the time, is the sudden rebirth and overwhelming success of the oratorio. Before proceeding further, it is worth calling again on Boucheron to try to understand the ambiguous status of the oratorio at mid-century:

> Between sacred music and opera there are the oratorios, which are at times woven into true operas, and at times as simple cantatas; they come closer either to one genre or to the other depending on whether they are destined for the theater or not.[40]

Boucheron's words, this time taken from his *Filosofia della musica*, are once again on point. Indeed, as the 1800s dawned over an Italian peninsula mostly under Napoleonic influence and with religious institutions in decline, the oratorio as an institution faced substantial difficulties. Oratorios in Rome, including the Vallicella, continued their activities well into the nineteenth century, but musical performances at those venues typically resembled concerts of sacred music rather than the dramatic genre that had originated in those spaces.[41] As the institution of the oratorio declined, the term came to be used broadly not only to define operas on a sacred subject, such as Rossini's *Mosé in Egitto*, Donizetti's *Il diluvio universale*, and even Verdi's *I lombardi alla prima Crociata* or Saint-Saëns's *Samson et Dalila*, but also to describe the practice of performing operas "in forma di oratorio," meaning concert performances without sets or costumes. During the early and middle part of the century, however, oratorios were composed sporadically in the context of the activities of musical chapels. Simon Mayr produced several in Bergamo; at Novara, Mercadante composed the intimate and poignant *Le sette ultime parole di Nostro Signore*, scored for soloists and four-part chorus (SSTB) with string accompaniment, which was published by Ricordi and reviewed favorably by Boucheron and others.[42]

It is only with the extraordinary rise of Lorenzo Perosi's star, however, that the oratorio returned into the fore of Italian culture. Born in 1872 in Tortona, Perosi studied at the conservatories of Rome and Milan, and he held posts as *maestro di cappella* at St. Mark's in Venice and, from 1898, at the Sistine Chapel. He was ordained priest in 1895. His first four oratorios, *La passione di Cristo secondo San Marco*, *La trasfigurazione di Cristo*, *La risurrezione di Lazzaro*, and *La risurrezione di Cristo*, were composed over a remarkably short period of time and premiered between 1897 and 1899. They took audiences and critics by storm, earning the young composer sensational fame in Italy and at the international level, and Ricordi rushed to publish their piano-vocal scores, a rare occurrence for works in this genre.[43] Perosi composed ten more oratorios in the twentieth century, but none of them paralleled the exploits of the earlier works. By the mid-1910s his career was unsettled by severe mental problems, and by the time of his death in 1956 his compositions were regarded (as they are today) more as curiosities than as living masterpieces. Some of them, however, especially the early oratorios and shorter mass settings and choral pieces, have withstood the test of time, and are still effective in performance. Particularly worth mentioning in this respect are compositions for three-part male chorus (TTB) with organ or harmonium accompaniment, including a *Messa da Requiem* published by Ricordi (1898) and *Missa Davidica* (*c*.1894).[44]

The greatest merit of Perosi's early oratorios is that they presented a successful alternative to the opera-influenced style of other compositions in the same genre. Perosi returned to the origins of the oratorio in seventeenth-century Rome as represented in the work of Carissimi. He used Latin texts, often employed a narrator (labeled *Storico* in his scores), and assigned an important narrative

EXAMPLE 19.6 Perosi, *La risurrezione di Cristo*, Part 1, mm. 781–93. Source: *La risurrezione di Cristo*. Piano-vocal score. Milan: Ricordi, PN 102440. Reproduced by permission.

EXAMPLE 19.6 continued.

function to the chorus as well. True to the doctrines established in Counter-Reformation Rome and to the end-of-century trends, he generally avoided complex contrapuntal writing, preferring homophonic textures and, at times, unison singing. Within the limits imposed by these general principles, Perosi employed contemporary techniques; for example, he wrote each part of his oratorios as a musico-dramatic continuum and refrained from adopting number subdivision or closed sections. His orchestral accompaniments are rich, and the emphasis on the brass section reveals a debt to latest trends in Italian and German opera. Indeed, his idiom reflects an impressive variety of influences, from chant to Renaissance polyphony, Wagner, and *verismo* opera. Such variety is evident in the choral passages of *La risurrezione di Cristo* (1899), perhaps the most effective

EXAMPLE 19.7 Perosi, *La risurrezione di Cristo*, Part 2, mm. 561–68. Source: *La risurrezione di Cristo*. Piano-vocal score. Milan: Ricordi, PN 102440. Reproduced by permission.

EXAMPLE 19.7 continued.

of the early oratorios. The wistful "Vere Filius Dei erat iste," for example, shows Perosi's ability to compose in four parts with an eye to eighteenth-century style, but with a trombone accompaniment that produces a striking sound when combined with the all-male chorus. Conversely, the short "Domine, recordati sumus" contains a passage in unison with an evocative chant-like melody (see Example 19.6). And in Part 2, the news of the resurrection of Christ is trumpeted by an immensely sentimental "Alleluia" chorus that may well strike the modern listener as mannered and naive, but that is dramatically successful in its context (see Example 19.7).

Taken at face value, *La risurrezione* expresses exactly what one would expect: hope, faith, jubilation. But as the nineteenth century waned, it is tempting to read in it the celebration not only of the resurrection of Christ, but also of the return to life of a genre in which, only a few years earlier, scarcely anyone would have put any trust. Even more broadly, the previously mentioned "Alleluia," along with other uplifting choruses in Perosi's other oratorios, may well be regarded as

EXAMPLE 19.7 continued.

a celebration of the survival of choral traditions that, albeit subjected to constant pressure and negotiation during the course of a century overwhelmingly dominated by opera, remained alive and approached the dawn of a new century with renewed vigor.

Notes

1 "Vi fu un tempo in cui i maestri compositori di musica riputavano maggior gloria il ben riuscire in una messa, in un salmo, in un inno, che non in intiere opere teatrali; ossia che mossi fossero da vero affetto religioso; ossia che prevedessero essere tali composizioni men soggette ai capricci della moda; e perché la loro più dotta fattura, quasi inammissibile nella musica drammatica, e pel non ripetersi tante volte di seguito, siccome avviene dei melodrammi, le salva dal divenire troppo comuni e triviali. In quel tempo ogni scuola italiana produsse celeberrimi maestri, i quali furono e tutt'ora sono modelli a tutte le nazioni, a grande onore della patria nostra.

Venne poi un altro tempo in cui la musica sacra cadde in un totale discredito, e il titolo di maestro da Chiesa fu tenuto equivalere a scrittore inetto, senza vena, senza sapere. Bastava allora che uno avesse composto una messa perché non si volesse più sentirlo in teatro, e viceversa si mandava alla chiesa quegli che più non sapeva piacere sulla scena. Solo veniva fatta qualche eccezione a favore di quelli i quali vestivano le sacre parole di musica tutta teatrale, o le adattavano senza alcun riguardo a qualche aria o duetto favorito di tale o tal altro dramma serio o buffo." Raimondo Boucheron, "Musica Sacra: Il *Miserere* e l'*Ave* Maria di Donizetti: Pensieri," *Gazzetta musicale di Milano* 3, 4 (January 28, 1844): 13.

2 In Carl Dahlhaus's words, "the decline and regeneration of church music was a constant topic of discussion." *Nineteenth-Century Music*, trans. J. Bradford Robinson (Berkeley: University of California Press, 1989), 178.

3 John Rosselli, "Italy: The Centrality of Opera," in *The Early Romantic Era: Between Revolutions, 1789 and 1848*, ed. Alexander L. Ringer (Englewood Cliffs, NJ: Prentice Hall, 1991), 161.

4 Another important institution for the production and performance of sacred music was the Cappella Palatina in Naples. Detailed information on its activities and personnel is found in Rosa Cafiero and Marina Marino, "La musica della Real Camera e Cappella Palatina di Napoli fra restaurazione e unità d'Italia. II: Organici e ruoli (1815–1864)," *Studi musicali* 38 (2009), 133–206.

5 A CD recording is available (Agorà Musica AG 131.2). No modern edition exists. The full score was published in the nineteenth century as *Gran Messa da Requiem in partitura del celebre Giovanni Simone Mayr* (Milan: Calcografia Cogliati e Crivelli, n.d.).

6 Common in eighteenth-century Naples, the so-called "Messa di Gloria" is a mass setting consisting of only the first two sections of the Mass Ordinary: Kyrie and Gloria. In addition to Rossini's setting, another nineteenth-century example is Pietro Raimondi's *Messa di Gloria* performed in Palermo in 1836.

7 Jesse Rosenberg, "Rossini, Raimondi e la *Messa di Gloria* del 1820," *Bollettino del Centro Rossiniano di Studi* 35 (1995): 85–102.

8 A critical edition of Rossini's *Messa di Gloria* prepared by Martina Grempler is forthcoming in the Works of Gioachino Rossini series published by Bärenreiter. A few recordings of the piece exist, including one conducted by Neville Mariner with the Academy of St. Martin of the Fields and a group of distinguished soloists (Philips 434 132–2).

9 Mosco Carner remarked that the "Gratias agimus" "might almost have been written for Des Grieux [in *Manon Lescaut*] or Rodolfo [in *La bohème*]." *Puccini: A Critical Biography*, reprint (New York: Holmes and Meier, 1992), 329.

10 Two modern editions of Puccini's *Messa* exist, one published under the improper title of *Messa di Gloria* (New York: Mills Music, 1951) and the other, considerably more accurate and enriched with additional materials, published as *Messa a 4 voci*, edited by Dieter Schickling (Stuttgart: Carus, 2004). Various recordings of the piece are available, including a recent performance of the London Symphony Orchestra and Chorus conducted by Antonio Pappano with soloists Roberto Alagna and Thomas Hampson (EMI CD 5 57159 2).

11 On the discovery of Rossini's work, see Philip Gossett, "Rossini in Naples: Some Major Works Recovered," *Musical Quarterly* 54 (1968), 316–340; here 331–340.

12 Fabrizio Della Seta, *Italia e Francia nell'Ottocento*, Storia della musica a cura della Società Italiana di Musicologia 9 (Turin: EDT, 1993), 21–23.

13 *Gazzetta musicale di Milano* 24, 19 (May 9, 1869), 170. Cited in *Messa per Rossini: La storia, il testo, la musica*, ed. Michele Girardi and Pierluigi Petrobelli (Parma and Milan: Istituto Nazionale di Studi Verdiani and Ricordi, 1988), 64.

14 See Girardi, "I compositori della 'messa' per Rossini," in *Messa per Rossini*, 151–60.

15 The complete score of the *Messa per Rossini* was published by Ricordi in 1988. A complete recording conducted by Helmuth Rilling dates from the same year and is available on CD (Hänssler Classic; 91.549). A facsimile of Verdi's autograph score of his contribution to the setting, the Libera me that served as the basis for Verdi's own *Requiem*, was published by the Istituto Nazionale di Studi Verdiani in 1988.

16 Julian Budden has noted how the melody in the "Lacrimosa" seems to be reminiscent of a Neapolitan song. "Il linguaggio musicale della 'Messa' per Rossini," in *Messa per Rossini*, 101–10.

17 In addition to his contribution to the *Messa per Rossini*, Platania composed numerous choral works, including a *Requiem* for Victor Emmanuel II (1878) and a monumental setting for six four-part choruses and orchestra of Psalm LXVII ("Exsurgat Deus"). These and other works were published in the nineteenth century by Ricordi in Milan and other firms.

18 See *Il catalogo numerico Ricordi 1857 con date e indici*, ed. Agostina Zecca Laterza (Rome: Nuovo Istituto Editoriale Italiano, 1984), *passim*.

19 "Qui consiste il vero progresso dell'arte; poiché dove prima di questo lavoro la musica sacra o non era che una successione di cantilene o una matta invenzione di motivi che non ad orare ma a spassarsi t'invitavano, in avvenire sarà, conforme l'argomento, ora mesta, ora gloriosa gaudiosa e giubilante, ma

non t'inviterà mai alla gioia o all'allegria; serberà sempre il suo carattere religioso e venerando. A ciò servirà di modello lo STABAT MATER di Rossini." *Teatri arti e letteratura*, 944 (March 18, 1842): 25–29.

20 A comprehensive list of early Italian reviews of Rossini's *Stabat Mater* is found in Marco Spada, "Francesco Rangone e la *Narrazione* sullo Stabat Mater a Bologna con altri documenti," *Bollettino del Centro Rossiniano di Studi* 19 (1989): 43–46.

21 Almost a century earlier, Padre Martini had criticized Pergolesi for exactly the same reasons, claiming that he had set the *Stabat Mater* in the same style as *La serva padrona*. See Richard Will, "Pergolesi's *Stabat Mater* and the Politics of Feminine Virtue," *Musical Quarterly* 87 (2004), 602.

22 Cited in Herbert Weinstock, *Rossini: A Biography* (New York: A. Knopf, 1968), 211.

23 Giambattista Martini, *Esemplare . . . di contrappunto* (Bologna 1774), vol. 2, 266–67. See also Jesse Rosenberg, "Notes on Raimondi's 'Triple Oratorio'," in *Ottocento e oltre: Scritti in onore di Raoul Meloncelli*, ed. Francesco Izzo and Johannes Streicher (Rome: Editoriale Pantheon, 1993), 322.

24 John Butt, "Choral Music," in *The Cambridge History of Nineteenth-Century Music*, ed. Jim Samson (Cambridge: Cambridge University Press, 2002), 225–26.

25 Baini and his work in Rome are discussed in Richard Boursy, "Historicism and Composition: Giuseppe Baini, the Sistine Chapel Choir, and *Stile Antico* Music in the First Half of the 19th Century," Ph.D. diss., Yale University, 1994.

26 *Memorie storico-critiche della vita e delle opere di Giovanni Pierluigi da Palestrina, cappellano-cantore, e quindi compositore della cappella pontificia, maestro di cappella delle basiliche Vaticana, Lateranense e Liberiana, detto il principe della musica*, 2 vols. (Rome: dalla Società tipografica, 1828).

27 Guido M. Gatti, "The Academy of St. Cecilia and the Augusteo in Rome," *Musical Quarterly* 8 (1922): 326–27.

28 Pierluigi Petrobelli, "On Dante and Italian Music: Three Moments," *Cambridge Opera Journal* 2 (1990): 219–49; here 239.

29 The autograph score of *Ridente e fausto già sorge il dì*, kept in the Naples Conservatory library (I-Nc) is accessible online through the recently established portal of the Biblioteca Digitale Italiana (www.bibliotecadigitaleitaliana.it).

30 Rossini's *Cantata* for Pius IX received its first modern performance in 1992, and appeared in print in critical edition in 1997. For further information see Mauro Bucarelli's introduction to Gioachino Rossini, *Cantata in onore del Sommo Pontefice Pio IX*, ed. Mauro Bucarelli, Series II, vol. 6 of *Edizione critica delle opere di Gioachino Rossini* (Pesaro: Fondazione Rossini, 1996). Important background information on the origins of the piece is found in Stefano Alberici, "Rossini e Pio IX alla luce di documenti inediti dell'Archivio Segreto Vaticano," *Bollettino del centro rossiniano di studi* 1–2 (1977): 5–35.

31 A piano accompaniment for Verdi's *Inno popolare* was prepared by Achille Graffigna and is included in Giuseppe Verdi, *Hymns/Inni*, Series IV of *Works of Giuseppe Verdi*, ed. Roberta M. Marvin (Milan: Ricordi; and Chicago: University of Chicago Press, 2007).

32 Philip Gossett has recently examined this repertory in depth, emphasizing the musical and cultural continuity from the operatic choruses of the 1840s by Verdi and others. See his "Le 'edizioni distrutte' e il significato dei cori operistici nel Risorgimento," *Saggiatore musicale* 12 (2005): 339–87; English trans., "'Edizioni distrutte' and the Significance of Operatic Choruses during the Risorgimento," in *Opera and Society in Italy and France from Monteverdi to Bourdieu*, ed. Victoria Johnson, Jane F. Fulcher, and Thomas Ertman (Cambridge: Cambridge University Press, 2007), 181–242.

33 "Fratelli d'Italia" is a quintessential Risorgimento poem, and was set to music by Michele Novaro.

34 The genesis of the *Inno delle nazioni* is discussed in great detail in Roberta M. Marvin's introduction to Giuseppe Verdi, *Hymns/Inni*, Series IV of *Works of Giuseppe Verdi* (Milan: Ricordi; and Chicago: University of Chicago Press, 2007).

35 Just as with late-nineteenth-century opera, it was common for publishers to be actively involved in the organization of performances of choral music.

36 Cited in Philip Gossett, "Rossini, Gioachino," in *Grove Music Online, Oxford Music Online*, http://www.oxfordmusiconline.com/subscriber/article/grove/music/23901pg7 (accessed August 2, 2009).

37 Roberta M. Marvin, "La *Messa solenne* di Rossini: La sua prima esecuzione in Italia," *Bollettino del Centro rossiniano di studi* (2001): 37–82. An abridged version in English is "Commercial Intrigue, National Identity, and the Italian Premiere of Rossini's *Petite Messe solennelle*," *Nineteenth-Century Studies* 18 (2004): 117–38.

38 Cited in Marvin, "Commercial Intrigue," 125.

39 A new critical edition by Patricia B. Brauner and Philip Gossett, containing both versions for two pianos and harmonium, was recently published in the Works of Gioachino Rossini (Kassel: Bärenreiter, 2009). This edition provides small choral ensembles with an exceptional opportunity to perform a key masterpiece from a reliable score. The exhaustive introduction by the editors provides detailed information on the genesis, composition, and early reception history of the *Petite Messe Solennelle*.

40 "Fra la musica sacra e la teatrale sonovi gli oratorii i quali ora tessuti in veri melodrammi, ora in semplici cantate piuttosto all'un genere che all'altro si accostano secondo son destinati al teatro o no." Raimondo Boucheron, *Filosofia della musica o estetica applicata a quest'arte* (Milan: Ricordi, 1842), 128.

41 Domenico Alaleona, *Studi su la storia dell'oratorio musicale in Italia* (Turin: Fratelli Bocca editori, 1908), 287–89. On the decline of the oratorio in nineteenth-century Italy, see also Giorgio Mangini, "'Dove son? Dove corro?' Echi ottocenteschi della Passione," *Musica e storia* 9 (2001): 245–63.

42 See John Allitt, "Mayr's *La Passione*," *Journal of the Donizetti Society* 1 (1975): 294–313.

43 The exploit of Perosi's first oratorios was the object of a great deal of critical writings, including Agostino Cameroni's timely book, *Lorenzo Perosi ed i suoi primi quattro oratorii* (Bergamo: Frat[elli] Bolis Editori, 1899).

44 Perosi's choral music was published extensively during the composer's lifetime. Numerous editions (including ones for these two works) are now in the public domain and accessible through the Petrucci/ IMSLP Music Library (http://imslp.org/wiki/Category:Perosi,_Lorenzo).

Selected Bibliography

Alaleona, Domenico. *Studi su la storia dell'oratorio musicale in Italia*. Turin: Fratelli Bocca editori, 1908.

Alberici, Stefano. "Rossini e Pio IX alla luce di documenti inediti dell'Archivio Segreto Vaticano," *Bollettino del centro rossiniano di studi* 1–2 (1977): 5–35.

Allitt, John S. "Mayr's *La Passione*," *Journal of the Donizetti Society* 1 (1975): 294–313.

Baini, Giuseppe. *Memorie storico-critiche della vita e delle opere di Giovanni Pierluigi da Palestrina, cappellano-cantore, e quindi compositore della cappella pontificia, maestro di cappella delle basiliche Vaticana, Lateranense e Liberiana, detto il principe della musica*, 2 vols. Rome: dalla Società tipografica, 1828.

Bellotto, Francesco, ed. *Giovanni Simone Mayr: L'opera teatrale e la musica sacra. Atti del Convegno Internazionale di Studio 1995*. Bergamo: Comune di Bergamo, Assessorato allo Spettacolo, 1997.

Boucheron, Raimondo. "Musica Sacra: Il *Miserere* e l'*Ave* Maria di Donizetti: Pensieri," *Gazzetta musicale di Milano* 3, 4 (January 28, 1844): 13.

Boursy, Richard. "Historicism and Composition: Giuseppe Baini, the Sistine Chapel Choir, and *Stile Antico* Music in the First Half of the 19th Century," Ph.D. diss., Yale University, 1994.

Butt, John. "Choral Music," in *The Cambridge History of Nineteenth-Century Music*, ed. Jim Samson. Cambridge: Cambridge University Press, 2002, 213–36.

Cafiero, Rosa and Marina Marino. "La musica della Real Camera e Cappella Palatina di Napoli fra restaurazione e unità d'Italia. I: Documenti per un inventario (1817–1833)," *Studi Musicali* 19 (1990): 133–92.

——. "La musica della Real Camera e Cappella Palatina di Napoli fra restaurazione e unità d'Italia. II: Organici e ruoli (1815–1864)," *Studi musicali* 38 (2009): 133–206.

Cameroni, Agostino. *Lorenzo Perosi ed i suoi primi quattro oratorii*. Bergamo: Frat[elli] Bolis Editori, 1899.

Carner, Mosco. *Puccini: A Critical Biography*. Reprint. New York: Holmes and Meier, 1992.

Della Seta, Fabrizio. *Italia e Francia nell'Ottocento*, Storia della musica a cura della Società Italiana di Musicologia 9. Turin: EDT, 1993.

Gatti, Guido M. "The Academy of St. Cecilia and the Augusteo in Rome," *Musical Quarterly* 8 (1922): 323–45.

Girardi, Michele and Pierluigi Petrobelli, eds. *Messa per Rossini: La storia, il testo, la musica*. Parma and Milan: Istituto Nazionale di Studi Verdiani and Ricordi, 1988.

Gossett, Philip. "Le 'edizioni distrutte' e il significato dei cori operistici nel Risorgimento," *Saggiatore musicale* 12 (2005): 339–87; English trans., "'Edizioni distrutte' and the Significance of Operatic Choruses during the Risorgimento," in *Opera and Society in Italy and France from Monteverdi to Bourdieu*, ed. Victoria Johnson, Jane F. Fulcher, and Thomas Ertman. Cambridge: Cambridge University Press, 2007, 181–242.

——. "Rossini in Naples: Some Major Works Recovered," *Musical Quarterly* 54 (1968): 316–40.

Mangini, Giorgio. "'Dove son? Dove corro?' Echi ottocenteschi della Passione," *Musica e storia* 9 (2001): 245–63.

Marvin, Roberta M. Introduction to Giuseppe Verdi, *Hymns/Inni*, Series IV of *Works of Giuseppe Verdi*. Milan: Ricordi; and Chicago: University of Chicago Press, 2007.

——. "La *Messa solenne* di Rossini: La sua prima esecuzione in Italia," *Bollettino del Centro rossiniano di studi* (2001): 37–82. Abridged English version, "Commercial Intrigue, National Identity, and the Italian Premiere of Rossini's *Petite Messe solennelle*," *Nineteenth-Century Studies* 18 (2004): 117–38.

Petrobelli, Pierluigi. "On Dante and Italian Music: Three Moments," *Cambridge Opera Journal* 2 (1990): 219–49.

Rosenberg, Jesse. "Notes on Raimondi's 'Triple Oratorio'," in *Ottocento e oltre: Scritti in onore di Raoul Meloncelli*, ed. Francesco Izzo and Johannes Streicher (Rome: Editoriale Pantheon, 1993).

——. "Rossini, Raimondi e la *Messa di Gloria* del 1820," *Bollettino del Centro Rossiniano di Studi* 35 (1995): 85–102.

Spada, Marco. "Francesco Rangone e la *Narrazione* sullo Stabat Mater a Bologna con altri documenti," *Bollettino del Centro Rossiniano di Studi* 19 (1989): 5–46.

Weinstock, Herbert. *Rossini: A Biography*. New York: A. Knopf, 1968.

Will, Richard. "Pergolesi's *Stabat Mater* and the Politics of Feminine Virtue," *Musical Quarterly* 87 (2004): 570–614.

Zecca Laterza, Agostina, ed. *Il catalogo numerico Ricordi 1857 con date e indici*. Rome: Nuovo Istituto Editoriale Italiano, 1984.

Northern Europe

20

BRITAIN AND IRELAND

James Garratt

UNIVERSITY OF MANCHESTER

In Britain and Ireland in the nineteenth century, choral singing dominated musical life to an extent matched in few other periods and places. Lacking a strong native tradition of opera or instrumental music, it was choral genres—from the mighty oratorio to the convivial glee—that were the touchstone for musical values and the composer's craft. The cultural contexts in which choral music flourished varied greatly, yet much of it was conceived for the moment, destined for one-off performance at a music festival, civic ceremony, or informal gathering. As some contemporaries candidly acknowledged, it was the activity of collective singing rather than the presentation of musical works that was the predominant concern of such events. Describing the realm of choral festivals and oratorios as "the only national school of music we possess," one critic from the 1890s conceded its weaknesses while celebrating the unique significance of this tradition:

> The majority of these productions may be of the nature of occasional music; the commonplace of the age, and of little value to the world at large, but even then they are useful to us. Chorus-singing is the one thing that we do more, and perhaps better, than any nation in the world. We must have something new to sing. Our provincial festivals, which multiply yearly, are the direct cause of a great deal of music being written, and, on the whole, adequately performed. It must, therefore, be in this direction that any greatness that is to fall to our lot will come upon us.[1]

These are prophetic words, given that the most illustrious product of this tradition, Elgar's *The Dream of Gerontius* (1900), was soon to receive its premiere. Yet the very success of that work seemingly confirms the picture of ephemeral mediocrity painted above. Casting into obscurity the other oratorios of its composer, let alone those of his contemporaries, *Gerontius* is the sole concert-length choral work of the period to have a firm place in the modern repertory. This fact should not lead us to assume that all other such pieces are merely of historical interest. Several nineteenth-century oratorios, such as Arthur Sullivan's *The Light of the World* and *The Golden Legend*, and Hubert Parry's *Job*, have been successfully revived in recent years, while many shorter concert works for choir and orchestra, such as Parry's *Blest Pair of Sirens*, have never left the repertory. Plenty of other such works, as we will see, also deserve the attention of modern performers. Much church music of the Victorian age retains a place within Anglican services in Britain, Ireland, and further afield, while John Stainer's *The Crucifixion*, in spite of the critical invective that it once attracted, is still sung by choirs throughout the English-speaking world at Passiontide. In addition, a number of unaccompanied secular partsongs from the period remain popular, particularly those of Elgar, Parry, and Sullivan.

Overall, however, the choral music of this period continues to be overlooked, not only when measured against the music of the first half of the twentieth century, but also in comparison with the public interest and scholarly attention lavished on Victorian painting and architecture. This neglect may stem primarily from shifts in taste, or from the disappearance of the institutions for which it was written. But given that more generally, the music of this period continues to find a ready public, it is surely the subject matter and texts of these works that presents the biggest obstacle to their revival. Indeed, some of these works seem irretrievable for modern performers and listeners. In a few cases, bombastically patriotic librettos are to blame, making even major works such as Elgar's *Caractacus* unappealing (the recent flurry of scholarly books and articles critiquing such compositions has served, if anything, to highlight their lack of viability for performance today).[2] More often, it is not bigotry or vainglorious bluster that discourages the revival of Victorian choral works, but rather the strangeness of their subjects and, in particular, the stilted nature of their texts. Even listeners well versed in biblical history, after all, will probably be stumped by the subjects of Frederick Arthur Gore Ouseley's *The Martyrdom of St. Polycarp* or Parry's *Judith, or The Regeneration of Manasseh*. The problems multiply where works with secular subjects are concerned; given that nineteenth-century poetry is now also largely foreign territory, who would be attracted to works—plucked at random from Novello's catalogue *c.*1900—such as *The Lady of Shalott, Boadicea, The Black Knight,* or *King René's Daughter*?

Plenty of people, one might think, given that the Pre-Raphaelite paintings inspired by similar poems and themes continue to draw a large public. Indeed, such art is testimony enough that the sometimes fanciful and recondite subjects of nineteenth-century secular oratorios, cantatas, and partsongs need not preclude their revival. The mannered and stilted nature of some Victorian verse is a more serious impediment than obscure subject matter, and it is no coincidence that many of the most enduring choral pieces of the age draw on other sources: Milton, Shakespeare, Whitman, and Nietzsche. But if some nineteenth-century texts are over-extended, metrically rigid, archaic in idiom, and constrained in expression, others are impressively direct and vivid. Sometimes, too, the strength of the music can pierce through a poem's weaknesses and lay bear the emotional core of the subject; such is the case with *Gerontius*, whose popularity surely owes little to the gothic excesses of John Henry Newman's poem.[3] All of which suggests that while much of this music may well be ephemeral or unexceptional, there is still plenty of interest to reward sympathetic musicians and listeners.

Sacred Oratorios and Other Large-Scale Religious Works

In the nineteenth century, the majority of large-scale choral works, sacred and secular, were written for performance by massed choirs at regional music festivals. Whether staged in large industrial centers like Birmingham or small cathedral cities such as Hereford or Norwich, these events were crucial to the cultural aspirations and self-image of a community. The scale and scope of music festivals varied considerably, yet in each case choral singing was placed at the heart of a nexus of social, ethical, educative, and economic goals; as one observer noted in the 1820s, the newly fashionable "grand musical festivals" served to "benefit charity, advance the interests of trade by the circulation of money in the districts where they occur, rouse public spirit, and increase individual enjoyment."[4]

The character and ingredients of these events, and of the broader cultivation of choral music in the nineteenth century, represent a combination of two earlier models: the Three Choirs Festival, which took place annually from around 1715 in either Gloucester, Hereford or Worcester; and the Handel Commemorations held in Westminster Abbey between 1784 and 1791.[5] The programs of the Three Choirs Festival had consisted initially of short sacred pieces, although oratorios, in particular *Messiah*, were increasingly included from the second half of the eighteenth century. It was the Handel Commemorations, however, that initiated the tradition of monumental performances of this oratorio, drawing on over 500 singers and players in 1784, and double that in 1791.[6] While the singers for the Handel Commemorations and Three Choirs Festival were drawn from all-male professional choirs, the regional music festivals that mushroomed in the nineteenth century were the preserve of amateur mixed-voice choruses. In spite of this crucial change, these festivals in other respects perpetuated the values and tastes of their eighteenth-century precedents. They too centered around the lionization of Handel and massed performances of *Messiah*; indeed, in the 1810s and 1820s it was often the sole large-scale work to be performed in full. Most regional festivals were three-day events, sandwiching the central oratorio performance with lengthy miscellaneous concerts. The encyclopedic scale and scope of the latter are evident from the opening concert of the Birmingham Grand Musical Festival of 1826, which featured

> a grand selection of Sacred Music, in the course of which will be introduced a new sacred drama, the music from *Joseph* the celebrated composition of Méhul; and a selection from the great work of Graun, the *Tod Jesu*. The performance will commence with the *Overture to Esther*, newly arranged, for the purpose of introducing the various wind instruments. It will also comprise portions of the *Requiem* of Mozart; *The Creation*; *Thanksgiving*; *Revelation*; the celebrated scene from *Jephtha*; a variety of concerted pieces from Handel, Beethoven, Leo &c. interspersed with favourite airs by the principal singers.[7]

As this description suggests, only a small proportion of music performed in early nineteenth-century music festivals was by contemporary British or Irish composers (here represented by choruses from oratorios by two Dublin-based composers, Sir John Stevenson's *Thanksgiving* and John Smith's *The Revelation*). Although newly composed oratorios were sometimes given, the slim possibility of repeat performances gave composers little incentive to produce them. Ever since the Handel Commemorations, commentators such as William Jackson argued that the "taste for Handel"—and particularly for his *Messiah*—was at the expense of more recent music: "there are numbers of Composers in England who may be very worthy of notice, if they had the advantage of a public exhibition. These are prevented from shewing their abilities, by the idea that Handel alone can compose Oratorios, Anthems, &c. or that no one else can equal, much less excel, what he has done in that class of Music."[8]

The consequence, as Howard Smither notes, was that only a small number of new oratorios were composed in the first half of the nineteenth century—a mere seven to thirteen per decade.[9] The Handelian stranglehold was not simply a matter of performance statistics. Rather, new oratorios were expected to conform with Handel's models in virtually all aspects of content, idiom, and structure. In the early nineteenth century, the cultivation of Handelian elements owes more to a classicizing impulse—the elevation of his procedures to the level of immutable norms—than to antiquarianism. The dominant British musical figure of the first third of the nineteenth century, the composer William Crotch, epitomizes this perspective. Viewing himself as a bulwark against declining musical taste, Crotch urged young composers, like their counterparts in the other arts, to remain true to the exemplars of the great masters. In Crotch's *Lectures on Music* (1831), Handel's oratorios emerge as the highest summit of musical achievement and worthiest model, rendering all else "limited and humble" in comparison:

His airs, duets, trios, and other vocal pieces, form the great mass of our vocal music to English words. . . . But for oratorio choruses his pre-eminence is still more indisputable. For learning, pathos, and sublimity, what choruses equal them? Hear them worthily rendered, as at Westminster Abbey, with a band of 1000 performers, and the most magnificent choruses of modern authors appear, by comparison, light and puerile.[10]

Given this perspective, it is not surprising that Crotch's own oratorios owe much to Handel's model. Yet *Palestine* (1811), the most important British work in the genre from the first sixty years of the nineteenth century, is no pallid homage to an earlier age. Some movements, to be sure, immediately and intentionally point to Handelian prototypes. But Crotch's veneration of Handel as the master of every style encouraged him to cultivate a similar breadth and variety, drawing on a wide range of contemporary and earlier idioms. For Crotch, the oratorio was an omnigenre, combining the best features of all other forms of music; accordingly, he argued that composers should not simply follow the sublime style of Handel's choruses but rather synthesize "all the styles, preserving their due order."[11] *Palestine*, as a result, resembles the miscellaneous festival programs mentioned above, drawing together elements of all the religious music that received his approval, from the music of Tallis to Haydn's *The Creation*.

Crotch's loyalty to the Handelian tradition resounds at the opening and the close of the work. As with several other nineteenth-century oratorios,[12] *Palestine*'s opening instrumental movement takes the French overture style as its point of departure, although here the tonic minor to major plan adapts this idiom to contemporary expressive parameters. In another Handelian gesture shared with many German and British oratorios of this period, Crotch treats the work's conclusion as an opportunity to display his contrapuntal mastery, employing a pair of fugal movements ("Worthy the Lamb" and "Hallelujah, Amen") in an unabashed emulation of *Messiah*. Many of the other choruses and arias also point to Baroque models, some again through the use of choral declamation in the manner of Handel's *Zadok the Priest* ("He comes! but not in regal splendour drest"), others through ground bass ("Reft of thy sons" and "To him were known"), and others through their ritornello structures and rhetoric ("Triumphant race"). Yet the majority of choruses and, in particular, solo ensemble numbers are in more modern idioms. A good example is the quartet "Lo! star-led chiefs"—still sung today as an Epiphany anthem in British cathedrals—whose attractive, fluent part-writing is characteristic of *Palestine* as a whole (see Example 20.1).

Palestine is unusual among nineteenth-century religious oratorios in departing from the textual model of *Messiah*. Instead of being compiled from biblical passages—the defining feature in the Victorian age of works bearing the description "sacred oratorio"—Crotch derived his libretto from a poem by the cleric and hymn writer Reginald Heber (author of the well-known hymn "Holy, holy, holy"). If Heber's account of the history of Palestine is circuitous, his language is splendid and vivid, making it an ideal stimulus for Crotch's colorful text-setting. As both the music and Crotch's writings attest, he was particularly drawn to the air and chorus "In frantic converse," which contains a line that chimed with his affinity to the music of the past: "Strange shapes he views, and drinks with wond'ring ears / The voices of the dead, and songs of other years." In his *Lectures on Music*, Crotch was to cite Heber's phrase in describing the "pure sublimity" of a Litany by Thomas Tallis.[13] Tallis's piece, edited and published by Crotch in 1807, was evidently in his mind when setting this phrase in *Palestine*, since he imitates the striking modal progression at the opening of the Litany as well as its alternation of recitation and choral response (see Example 20.2).[14] Given the modern chromaticism prevalent elsewhere in the movement, Crotch's intention is not to replicate an earlier idiom; rather, he succeeds in creating an eerie evocation of the simultaneous tangibility and remoteness of past times. Similarly impressive moments abound in

EXAMPLE 20.1 Crotch, *Palestine*, no. 26, mm. 43–6.

EXAMPLE 20.2   Crotch, *Palestine*, no. 18, mm. 45–53.

Palestine, and the work as a whole (as well as individual choral movements such as "Then on your tops" and "Be peace on Earth") deserves revival.

If *Palestine* does not deserve to be dismissed, in Nigel Burton's phrase, as a "magnificent ruin," the same cannot be said of other British oratorios from the first half of the nineteenth century.[15] Small wonder, therefore, that Mendelssohn's oratorios, and in particular *Elijah* (first performed at the Birmingham Musical Festival in 1846), were to find such favor in Britain, and to serve as the major catalyst for the revival of the genre. For the generation of composers born at around the time *Palestine* was premiered—William Sterndale Bennett, George Macfarren, and Henry Smart—Mendelssohn was to prove both a defining influence and an incentive for musical reform. Oratorio formed a key part of this agenda, and in a manifesto from 1852, Macfarren inveighed against "the supposed necessity to imitate Handel" that he considered to have shaped British oratorios prior to *Elijah.*[16] Arguing that the genre had become a byword for sterile academicism, he condemned the notion that oratorio and church music should be stuck in the past and cut off from developments in secular music. For Macfarren, the emulation of Mendelssohn was infinitely preferable to such staleness and irrelevance: "Music produced under such influence must be more genial and even more spontaneous than any composed in designed imitation of the mannerisms of an age with which we have now little or nothing in sympathy, since, as the course of education and the external circumstances that induced the style peculiar to that age have passed away, we can now only imitate the mannerisms, never identify ourselves with the style."[17]

Emblematic of the academicism eschewed by Macfarren is Ouseley's *The Martyrdom of St. Polycarp* (1854). Boasting eight-voice choruses and an elaborate fugal "Amen" in the best Handelian manner, this work, in common with other nineteenth-century oratorios, shows numerous signs of its origin as a doctoral degree exercise. But other aspects of its libretto and music reveal it to be the first of the wave of British oratorios to be modeled on *Elijah*: a Chorus of Pagans, an angelic trio similar to "Lift thine eyes," a quasi-chorale in the manner of "Cast thy burden upon the Lord" and "The Lord is God", and an effective solo Prayer resembling "Lord God of Abraham." In addition to taking individual movements from *Elijah* as templates, Ouseley's oratorio draws more broadly on Mendelssohn's *religioso* idiom: that is, the amalgam of slow-moving chords, regular phrases, diatonic writing and simple dissonance treatment characteristic of Mendelssohn's liturgical music and, by extension, of the slow movements of many of his instrumental works too. This idiom was to have a defining impact on Victorian religious music, and its presence can be felt in works as varied as Sullivan's *The Lost Chord* and Elgar's *Gerontius*.

If Ouseley's oratorio must be regarded as a historical curio, the same is not the case with the music of Macfarren himself or of Bennett, Mendelssohn's greatest British contemporary. Both composers achieved success in the genre relatively late in their careers, yet aimed to reinvigorate it, fusing Mendelssohn's model with their own innovations. Bennett's *The Woman of Samaria*, first performed at the Birmingham Musical Festival in 1867, was described by its composer as a sacred cantata rather than an oratorio, in part because of its relative brevity, and in part to reflect its adherence to Bach's rather than Handel's model. Bennett had conducted the first British performance of the *St. Matthew Passion* in 1854 and, like that work, *The Woman of Samaria* opens with a chorus based on a chorale cantus firmus. The inclusion of a German chorale melody ("Nun freut euch lieben Christen g'mein") in an English religious work signals Bennett's intentions, as does the polyphonic treatment which it is given; outside the chorale cantatas of Mendelssohn, there are few nineteenth-century pieces to rival this one as a re-creation of Bach's idioms. Bennett turns to the same model for the theological crux of the work, the Chorus of the People "Now we believe," set as a succinct double fugue. The most important Bachian aspect of the work, however, is its Passion-like treatment of narrative. The role of the narrator is shared by the alto and bass soloists, a curious maneuver designed to ensure that the direct speech of Jesus (also a bass) is indistinguishable from the preceding narration. At this time, British composers were still reluctant to court controversy by treating Jesus as a dramatic protagonist, although such qualms were soon to fade. In the case of *The Woman of Samaria*, this approach to the portrayal of Jesus reflects a more pervasive lack of drama; the rather talky Gospel incident that it recounts is devoid of action, and there are few nineteenth-century oratorios whose librettos and music are so remote from opera.

The use of narrators and of hitherto neglected Gospel scenes was to become increasingly popular over the 1870s and 1880s, and in many ways Bennett's *The Woman of Samaria* initiated the subgenre of church oratorio that culminated in Stainer's *Crucifixion*. Translating elements of Bach's Passions into a Victorian guise, Bennett popularized the use of hymn texts in oratorios; one of his cantata's most attractive and accessible movements, often performed separately in the nineteenth century, is a setting of the hymn "Abide with me" to an original melody. Another movement still sometimes heard today in church and cathedral services is the unaccompanied quartet "God is a spirit" (see Example 20.3). This little movement offers a combination of elements of the romantic partsong, Mendelssohn's *religioso* idiom and the homophonic church style of Crotch and his generation. Its combination of simplicity and charm proved highly popular and stimulated many imitations:

EXAMPLE 20.3 Bennett, *The Woman of Samaria*, no. 12, mm. 22–34.

notable examples include "God so loved the world" from Stainer's *Crucifixion*, "Yea, though I walk" from Sullivan's *The Light of the World*, and "Blessed are they which are persecuted" from Macfarren's *St. John the Baptist*.

The latter Macfarren work, on a libretto compiled by the organist and composer Edwin George Monk, was the earliest and most successful of the composer's oratorios. Although well received at its premiere at the Bristol Musical Festival in 1872, the piece was rejected by the body that originally commissioned it (the Gloucester committee of the Three Choirs Festival) on the grounds that its libretto contained material unsuitable for performance in a cathedral.[18] As we will see, this was by no means the only Victorian oratorio to fall foul of the puritanical attitudes of cathedral clergy. Monk's libretto is worth exploring further, since it exemplifies the Victorian practice of assembling texts from a host of seemingly unconnected biblical verses. This approach, modeled on *Messiah* and *Elijah*, helped librettists to overcome deficiencies in their source material, enabling brief biblical narratives to be expanded, contextualized, and interpreted. A less sympathetic account of this procedure was given in a satirical commentary on oratorio construction from 1887:

You took your subject—any subject, provided it was a name mentioned in the bible; say Methusaleh, for instance. Well, Methusaleh didn't do anything in particular; he only lived to an age which all the commentators have vainly tried to soften. So you took your Cruden's Concordance (saved you the expense of a librettist, don't you know), and looked up all the references to age, and life, and death, and all that sort of thing; and if that were not enough, you padded it out with copious extracts from the psalms. Thus you could have your work of any required length.[19]

Using this approach, Monk was able to insert authentic biblical texts into the mouths of his protagonists (Herod's brief speeches, for example, are drawn from Ecclesiastes, Job, Deuteronomy, Esdras, Judges, and Proverbs, as well as the Gospels). Even so, the exchange of biblical adages between characters tends to make for stilted and labored dialogue. In addition, the retention of the language of the King James Bible is something of a mixed blessing, as is particularly evident in Herod's limp response to Salome's demand for the head of John the Baptist: "I am exceeding sorry."

In spite of Macfarren's repudiation of Handelian imitation and academicism, the first choral movement of *St. John the Baptist* contains an energetic fugue. Other features characteristic of the mid-Victorian oratorio are a choral march, an unaccompanied female chorus for the words of God—an approach popularized by Mendelssohn's *St. Paul*—and a chorale (an attractive fugal setting of the hymn tune Hanover). Unusual for this period, though increasingly common at the end of the century, is Macfarren's cultivation of continuous dramatic scenes rather than discrete movements (following his librettist, however, he divides the work into twenty-four numbers). This approach also has its origins in Mendelssohn's *Elijah*, where movements are sometimes linked through pivot chords or more subtle transitional passages; in Macfarren's work, such techniques, and sometimes simply the instruction "attacca," serve to create much larger dramatic units.

No less important is the fluid interchange between characters and textures that Macfarren achieves in individual numbers. This is attained largely through a declamatory arioso texture, derived in part from Mendelssohn and in part from mid-nineteenth-century opera. Earlier, Macfarren had bristled at this idiom in reviewing Henry Hugh Pierson's oratorio *Jerusalem* (1852), arguing that "this character of composition may be much more interesting to an author than the usual style of recitative, but it restrains, to a great extent, the singer, and is by no means easily appreciable by an audience."[20] By the time he came to compose his own first oratorio, Macfarren's attitude had clearly changed, and the use of declamatory arioso enabled him to move as far in the direction of dramatic dialogue as his libretto would allow. Indeed, in places he attempts to go still further in the direction of dramatic realism, particularly in the movements which simultaneously evoke Salome's dance and the reactions of Herod and his courtiers to it. This dramatic impulse, together with the fluent handling of dialogue and efforts in the direction of through-composition, make the work an important precursor of the works of Parry and Elgar, as well as of the subgenre of dramatic oratorio pioneered by Alexander Mackenzie (*The Rose of Sharon*, 1884) and Charles Villiers Stanford (*Eden*, 1891).[21]

Two composers of the next generation, Sullivan and Stainer, were to achieve a degree of popularity that eluded Bennett and Macfarren. Indeed, works such as *The Lost Chord* and *The Crucifixion* are still today synonymous with Victorian religiosity. Of Sullivan's three oratorios, the one that best fits this image is *The Light of the World* (1873), inspired by another star in the firmament of Victorian religious art, William Holman Hunt's eponymous painting (1851–56). Composed for the Birmingham Musical Festival, Sullivan's setting of scenes from the life of Christ has forty-two separate numbers; its protracted nature, as well as its sequence of Gospel tableaux ("Bethlehem," "Nazareth: In the Synagogue," "Lazarus," "The Way to Jerusalem," "Jerusalem" and "At the Sepulchre") unavoidably bring to mind elephantine Hollywood epics such as George Stevens' *The*

Greatest Story Ever Told (1965). This parallel is more than skin-deep, since the use of earlier religious art and music in Stevens's film—at once reverential and referential—has much in common with Sullivan's approach to his subject.

As with Liszt's oratorio *Christus*, premiered in the same year as *The Light of the World*, Sullivan's oratorio juxtaposes echoes of the church music of earlier periods with wholly modern stylistic resources. While the stylistic contrasts in *The Light of the World* are less extreme than in *Christus*, it is Sullivan's work that seems less cohesive and convincing. Perhaps the reason is not so much Sullivan's nods in the direction of chant and Renaissance *falsobordone* but rather his work's relationship to more recent religious music. Part of the first tableau, "Bethlehem," for instance, recomposes the Nativity scene from St. Luke's Gospel in a way that willfully invites comparison with Handel's *Messiah*; perhaps the best cinematic parallel here is not *The Greatest Story Ever Told* but Gus Van Sant's remake of *Psycho*. What the work reveals most clearly, however, is the extent to which Mendelssohn's style remained the default oratorio idiom even for composers who elsewhere displayed strong artistic personalities. Many of the choral movements, such as "I will pour my spirit" and "Doubtless thou art our father," offer fluent yet characterless exercises in Mendelssohn's manner, reflecting how the conventions of the Victorian oratorio stifled even its most creative exponents.

While Sullivan's secular oratorio *The Golden Legend* (discussed below) lays greater claim to modern revival, some of the individual numbers of *The Light of the World* are attractive and worth the attention of modern performers. The opening movement "There shall come forth a rod" is impressively vigorous, while the *a cappella* six-voice chorus "The Lord is risen" strikingly anticipates the unaccompanied pieces of Sullivan's younger contemporaries Parry and Stanford. It is in the orchestral and solo movements, however, that Sullivan's own personality most consistently comes to the fore, particularly in the more expansive and operatic numbers such as "Refrain thy voice" and "When the son of man."

Operatic elements abound too in the large-scale choral works of Stainer, three of which deserve attention here: *The Daughter of Jairus*, *St. Mary Magdalen*, and *The Crucifixion*. This may seem surprising, given Stainer's background: as a distinguished scholar of late medieval music, organist of London's St Paul's Cathedral, and a product of Ouseley's tutelage, one might expect his religious music to take an academic or historicist approach. Such was not the case. Stainer swiftly distanced himself from Ouseley's Crotch-inspired conservatism, aiming instead for stylistic freedom, moderate progressivism, and a broad appeal in his church compositions and oratorios.[22]

These traits are certainly evident in his sacred cantata *The Daughter of Jairus*, in spite of the external constraints that attended its creation. This work was composed for the Three Choirs Festival of 1878, which was the first time the event had been held in Worcester since the notorious "Mock Festival" of three years earlier; at that festival, as a result of pressure from conservative clerics, oratorio concerts had been entirely expunged.[23] Stainer's work was designed to forestall such problems, being of a length that made it performable within an extended cathedral service rather than a concert. Although shorter than Bennett's *The Woman of Samaria*, the latter work evidently served as the model for the textual and musical structure of *Jairus*. In line with his desire to communicate to the broader public, Stainer's cantata has a more dramatic and arresting biblical incident at its heart: Christ's raising of a young girl from the dead. Such a subject was guaranteed to appeal to a culture preoccupied with childhood innocence, mortality, and divine power and grace; for the composer, more mundanely, it provided an opportunity to evoke widely contrasting emotions within a brief scene.

Perhaps the contrasts in the libretto were too great, since in spite of Stainer's best efforts, he cannot entirely offset the maudlin character of the verses his friend H. Joyce interpolated within the biblical narrative ("Sweet tender flower, / Born for an hour, / Now by Death's cold hand stricken"). Much of the rest of the work, however, is fresh and effective, in particular the overture and the substantial tenor solo "My hope is in the everlasting." As in Bennett's *The Woman of Samaria*, the penultimate movement sets a hymn, "Love divine! all love excelling," as a lyrical duet (Stainer's more familiar melody for this text was composed a decade later). It is here that Stainer comes closest to the simple yet expressive melodic and harmonic idiom of *The Crucifixion*. The final movement, in a rare nod to Handelian textures and gestures, is cast as a slow introduction and fugue; the latter, fluent and engaging, remains true to the clarity and directness characteristic of the work as a whole.

Stainer's work as the rehearsal organist for the Royal Albert Hall Choral Society ensured a familiarity with a wide range of modern oratorios by British and continental composers.[24] It is therefore not surprising that *Jairus* exhibits the concern for cohesiveness and continuity evident in the works of contemporaries like Macfarren. Much of the central portion of the work is conceived as a single unit, unified by recurring melodies and transitions between the numbers. These techniques are developed further in Stainer's largest work, the oratorio *St. Mary Magdalen*, composed five years later for the 1883 Gloucester Three Choirs Festival. Here, Stainer employs several recurring themes, largely as means to add cohesion to the work's extensive passages of declamatory writing. If these features suggest Wagner, Stainer's handling of them owes more to Gounod's *La Rédemption*, a work he had come to know intimately the previous year while rehearsing its London premiere.

The preference for female subjects suggested by *Jairus* and *St. Mary Magdalen* is unusual for Victorian oratorio but not for the art of this period in general. Many Pre-Raphaelite painters were similarly attracted to mute "holy virgins" and "fallen Magdalens," to quote the chapter headings of Jan Marsh's book on their work.[25] The female characters in such paintings are defined by the male protagonists who share their canvases or back-narratives; similarly, Stainer's two female "heroines" are both bystanders within their own stories. There the parallels between Stainer's characters end, however, since in contrast to the passive, speechless title character of *The Daughter of Jairus*, Mary is positively loquacious. Most of her words stem not from the Bible but from the librettist, Rev. William John Sparrow Simpson, and it was presumably the zealous young curate rather than Stainer who chose to devote the opening scene to Mary's repentance. Mary's opening number "Ah, woe is me" is an important example of the Victorian fascination with "redeeming" fallen women; as in the moments of self-scrutiny captured in Victorian paintings of this subject, Sparrow Simpson's Mary is tormented by memories of childhood purity as well as by the hopelessness of her situation:

> Ah, what am I? —Once heaven so blue and golden
> Glowed with its sunshine o'er my guiltless brow;
> Once—I remember it as ages olden—
> I lived a sinless child: what am I now?
> Ah, God, I perish! tangled in distresses,
> Sunk in the mire, yet deeper still I sink.
> Never shall the Mary of the braided tresses
> Find mercy, leaning o'er this dreadful brink.

Such lines may seem to justify the denigration that Sparrow Simpson's librettos have received from generations of British musical commentators.[26] But even here, his virtues as well as vices are evident. Immediacy and clarity are not characteristics often encountered in the texts of nineteenth-century oratorios and cantatas; what Stainer surely valued in Sparrow Simpson's verse was its simple, vivid expressivity. Some of his end-rhymes slip into bathos, as in *The Crucifixion* when "dark and murderous blot" is paired with "one redeeming spot". But, as singers of *The Crucifixion* will attest, many of Sparrow Simpson's rhyming couplets have a pithy, memorable quality that has helped rather than hindered the work's continuing popularity:

> Who can be like Thee?
> Pilate high in Zion dwelling,
> Rome with arms the world compelling,
> Proud though they be?
>
> . . .
>
> Glory and honour:
> Let the world divide and take them;
> Crown its monarchs and unmake them;
> But thou wilt reign.

St. Mary Magdalen is an uneven work, reliant in places on the stock formulas of the oratorio after Mendelssohn—like *Elijah*, the work includes a bass recitative interpolated into the overture, an unaccompanied quasi-chorale, and an angelic trio. In addition, the hymn-like character of much of the choral writing seems rather meager within the monumental frame of the Victorian oratorio. Within the more concentrated context of *The Crucifixion*, however, this feature becomes one of the work's greatest strengths, epitomizing how it offers, as one contemporary reviewer put it, a "singularly happy union of artistic feeling with simplicity."[27]

Intended for a church choir (that of Marylebone Parish Church) rather than massed festival forces, *The Crucifixion* (1887) dispenses with the orchestra in favor of the organ. The composer described the work as a "meditation on the sacred Passion" rather than a cantata or oratorio, a phrase that reflects the importance of free poetry within the work as well as its relation to the Passions of Bach. In addition to the use of congregational hymns, *The Crucifixion* exhibits a range of other affinities with Bach: in the trial scene (no. 2) the words of Jesus are set as accompanied recitative, and Stainer even echoes the word-painting in the *St. John Passion* ("Then the high priest rent his clothes"). What is most striking, however, is the telescoped nature of this scene; Jesus's arrest, trial, and scourging are accomplished within a mere forty-five measures. The decision to focus the work entirely on the crucifixion itself reflects the principal model for the libretto: Part One of Gounod's *La Rédemption*. Like Gounod, Stainer represents the procession to Calvary through an instrumental march, and counterpoints this with contrasting material in the voices. While Gounod juxtaposes his march with plainchant, Stainer superimposes fanfare-like material for choir ("Fling wide the gates") onto the reprise of his A-minor march. The ensuing choral march in C major is one of the highlights of the work, climaxing on a bold dominant thirteenth chord. But the construction of the movement as a whole is no less impressive, the varied themes enabling Stainer to trace the constantly shifting sentiments of the text.

This pared-down approach is characteristic too of the solo movements, many of which are entirely through-composed. Perhaps the best of these, "King ever glorious," exemplifies Stainer's approach, being constructed out of short contrasting units unified by two recurring passages. Just one of the movements seems to miss the mark, a peculiar piece for the tenor ("So thou liftest thy divine petition") that resembles an operatic love duet. It is the choral movements, however, that are surely responsible for the work's popularity. "God so loved the world," the unaccompanied biblical dicta at the heart of *The Crucifixion*, was published separately during Stainer's lifetime and is often still performed on its own today. The most impressive chorus, however, is the substantial "From the throne of his cross." Here, a textual and melodic refrain, "Is it nothing to you, all ye that pass by," serves to unify a varied and expressive musical journey, made all the more remarkable for the simple homophonic textures out of which it is constructed.

The fifteen or so years separating *The Crucifixion* from Elgar's *The Apostles* (1903) mark the zenith of the Victorian cantata and oratorio, and of the massed choirs and festivals that sustained their production. At the same time, the tensions between the oratorio tradition and the impulses of artistic progressives were becoming increasingly marked. The most vociferous musical commentator of the day, the dramatist, critic and perfect Wagnerite George Bernard Shaw, inveighed repeatedly against the oratorio, considering it to epitomize the banality and complacency of British musical life.[28] Similarly, for the leading composers of the period—Elgar, Parry, and Stanford—the oratorio tradition was as much a source of frustration as of success; all three eventually renounced the genre, and in later life Elgar was to dismiss his cultivation of it as "the penalty of my English environment."[29] With some notable exceptions, the next generation of British composers—Samuel Coleridge-Taylor, Frederick Delius, Gustav Holst, and Ralph Vaughan Williams—were largely to abandon the biblical oratorio in favor of fresher literary and musical stimuli.

The oratorios of Elgar, Parry, and Stanford present remarkably varied solutions to the challenge of reconciling their own personalities and impulses with the conventions of the genre. Parry's solution in his three Old Testament works *Judith* (1888), *Job* (1892) and *King Saul* (1894) was to strive to revitalize the Mendelssohnian orientation of the oratorio through a creative engagement with the music of the distant past. The largest of these works, *Judith*, offers telling examples of the strengths and weaknesses of this approach, as well as exemplifying the broader problems involved in reviving this repertory. The libretto of *Judith*, penned by Parry himself, presents a striking case of how the genre's conventions could function as an artistic straitjacket. Aside from being overextended, Parry's libretto suffers through its similarity with *Elijah*, seemingly inviting comparison with Mendelssohn's work. As in *Elijah*, the story revolves around a clash between Jews and pagans, the latter's noisy worship of the god Moloch recalling the choruses in praise of Baal in Mendelssohn's oratorio. These parallels are underscored by structural and stylistic similarities, particularly in the fugue "It is the god's decree" and the genteel ensuing chorus "Hail, Moloch, hail!" (Act I scene i).

As if to distract attention from the work's relationship to Mendelssohn, Parry assiduously cultivates references to a range of earlier styles. Such eclecticism was no stranger to the Victorian oratorio, yet the sheer extent of Parry's historicism is surprising. Consider, for example, the Intermezzo between Acts I and II, which offers an assured and convincing replication of Bachian idioms (see Example 20.4). No less startling is the aria "God breaketh the battle" from Act II, where it is Handel's heroic vein that is tapped. Other movements, such as the opening chorus from Act II, combine Baroque gestures with modern expressive parameters (the first choral entry of this movement recalls "Herr, unser Herrscher" from the *St. John Passion*). While these and other movements deserve reviving, one passage of *Judith* has been heard regularly since its premiere: the solo ballad "Long since in Egypt's plenteous land," better known today as the hymn tune Repton ("Dear Lord and Father of Mankind"). This melody gains substantially from being heard in its original context, where it is subtly varied for each verse and complemented by instrumental interludes.

While Parry's oratorios were derided by Shaw, the critic was more sympathetic to the work of his fellow Dubliner Stanford. Responding positively to the Wagnerian elements within Stanford's dramatic oratorio *Eden*, Shaw praised it as "ingenious and peculiar" in contrast to the studied mediocrity of most oratorio manufacture.[30] Stanford's oratorio is of considerable historical significance, not least because of the many ways in which it prepared the ground for Elgar's *Gerontius*. Yet, as Paul Rodmell argues, it is by far "the strangest piece Stanford ever wrote."[31] In part, its oddness stems from Robert Bridges's outlandish libretto, which offers a whirlwind tour of heaven and hell as well as Eden, in episodes with subtitles such as "Chorus of impatient fiends awakening Satan from his sleep," "The praise of Satan," and "Vision of plague, famine, and diseases." Such vividly

EXAMPLE 20.4 Parry, *Judith*, Intermezzo, mm. 36–41.

dramatic subjects surely required a composer at the top of his game. But Stanford went to such trouble constructing a series of new musical personalities for this work that his authentic voice is seldom at the fore. Much of the opening section presents large stretches of unaccompanied modal writing in the Palestrina style, which for Stanford was essential to evoking the speech of the angels. Yet other portions of the work offer Wagnerian echoes, recalling the opening of Act III of *Götterdämmerung* (no. 15), Klingsor's entrance in *Parsifal* (no. 7), and Donner's "Heda! Hedo!" from *Das Rheingold* (no. 27). Stanford's own voice does assert itself in places: no. 25 "We come, O Muse of delight" is an attractive triple-time chorus with a bass ostinato, bringing to mind his later anthem "Ye Choirs of New Jerusalem." But in spite of such passages and the popularity of the composer, a modern performance of *Eden* is surely an unlikely event.

Of Elgar's four religious oratorios, three are based on biblical episodes. The earliest of them, *The Light of Life* Op. 29, composed for the Worcester Three Choirs Festival in 1896, resembles Bennett's *The Woman of Samaria* and Stainer's *The Daughter of Jairus* in length, subject matter and level of musical interest. As the relatively high opus number indicates, it dates from Elgar's late thirties, by which time he had several large-scale compositions behind him. Of these, however, only the *Serenade for Strings* has remained in the repertory; as this suggests, *The Light of Life* is the work of a highly experienced composer who was only just beginning to find a truly personal voice. It is a moot point whether this process was hastened by Elgar's industrious work on oratorio commissions in the mid- and late 1890s, given the constraints and conventions of the medium. Certainly, *The Light of Life* has its share of passages that are anonymous or routine. It also suffers as a result of Edward Capel Cure's libretto, which manages to treat its central incident—Jesus's healing of a blind man—both unsympathetically and undramatically.

If the whole does not reach the level of Elgar's secular choral works from the same period, *The Light of Life* contains some attractive individual movements. It opens with a splendidly effective orchestral "Meditation" that seems to have outgrown its context; in many ways, this movement can be seen as the missing link between the preludes of *Parsifal* and *Gerontius*. But there is little trace of the latter in the solo vocal portions of the work. A charming surprise, after several movements in a dogged *religioso* idiom, is the duet "Doubt not thy Father's care" for chorus or soloists; ushered in by an unpretentious canonic theme, the piece seems to breath the folk song-like air of Brahms's *Zigeunerlieder*. Elgar deploys several of the familiar ingredients of Victorian oratorio to good effect in the solo and chorus "He went his way therefore," where a fugue to the text "the wisdom of their wise men shall perish" serves as an emblem of unthinking dogmatism. The composer saves the best till last, and the final movements, Jesus's solo "I am the good shepherd" and the chorus "Light of the world," both offer fine examples of the *nobilmente* idiom which Elgar inherited from Parry.

Elgar's original title for *The Light of Life*, *Lux Christi*, was suppressed by his publisher Novello, fearful of the impact that a perceived Roman Catholic tendency might have on sales figures. Such sentiments did not impede the favorable reception of *Gerontius*, even though some portions of its libretto required retouching for performances in Protestant cathedrals.[32] The immediate success of the work reflects the universality of its subject—an old man's contemplation of the afterlife—as well as the quality of the music. Part One of the work, portraying the final hours of Gerontius, surely marks the culmination of the Victorian oratorio, combining several of its familiar elements with a panoply of Wagnerian techniques. Here, as in *The Light of Life*, references to earlier styles (a *stile antico* unaccompanied "Kyrie" and the chant "Noe from the waters") are dramatically moti- vated, and rather than padding out Part One with extraneous choruses, Elgar gives full weight to portraying the emotional state of his protagonist in his final moments. Many listeners, whether or not they are Catholic, find the posthumous events narrated in Part Two to be less persuasive, in spite of the vivid and imaginative nature of much of the orchestral and vocal writing. Elgar's picture of purgatory is gripping, to be sure, yet arguably no more profound than the hellish and apocalyptic visions in Stanford's *Eden*. All in all, perhaps, Part Two of *Gerontius* offers a disconcerting marriage of magnificent music and gaudy melodrama, as if Poe's "The Facts in the Case of M. Valdemar" had been composed as a grand opera.

Following the completion of *Gerontius*, Elgar envisaged composing a trilogy of biblical oratorios on the scale of Wagner's *Der Ring des Nibelungen*. While Elgar finished two of these works, *The Apostles* and *The Kingdom* (premiered, respectively, at the Birmingham Festival in 1903 and 1906), he abandoned plans for the third, *The Last Judgement*, although he toyed with the idea of taking it up again throughout the rest of his life.[33]

Elgar followed Wagner's lead by serving as his own librettist, compiling his texts from biblical passages at the same time as working on the music. This approach might suggest that little thought went into the librettos, yet one of the most impressive features of *The Apostles* is Elgar's assured, subtle and often thought-provoking treatment of narrative. While he sometimes relies on conventional devices to introduce his biblical tableaux (such as the use of narrators and recitative), he shows considerable ingenuity in coming up with fresh ways of presenting familiar stories. One example is Jesus's calming of the storm, which is framed within a monologue in which Mary Magdalene repents her sins. What is striking about this approach is how Elgar, like an arthouse auteur, revels in the ambiguities he creates: what begins as a vision conjured up by Mary's troubled conscience turns into a vivid portrayal of a concrete event. It is in passages like this that Elgar's extraordinary ambition for the genre comes to the fore. His most audacious stroke involves a similar kind of metamorphosis: transforming Judas's lament for the betrayal of Jesus into a narrative of the crucifixion. Chronicling Jesus's death from the perspective of Judas is startling enough, but Elgar's boldest move is to imply a parallel between them (as a result of another striking narrative shift, the death of Judas is followed by the words "Truly this man was the son of God").[34]

Such literary and theological subtleties may suggest a cerebral work, yet nothing could be further from the truth. Indeed, one reason why the neglect of *The Apostles* is so puzzling is its capacity to make a powerful first impression. By this stage of his career, Elgar was well familiar with the needs of festival performers and audiences; as a result, the work is replete with vivid tone-painting (most famously, the thirty pieces of silver in "The Betrayal"), colorful instrumental effects and forceful moments of drama. At the core of the work, however, is Elgar's textually and musically rich characterization of Judas, Mary Magdalene, John, and Peter. While introduced in the previous number, their characters are first developed in Section Two, "By the wayside." Here, in a movement resembling the opening scene of Monty Python's *Life of Brian*, Jesus's recitation of the Beatitudes is juxtaposed with his disciples' conflicting interpretations of his words, emphasizing from the start Judas's revolutionary zeal. This combination of different layers of utterance is found throughout the work, often underscored by quasi-spatial contrasts; in the final chorus, for example, Elgar's vocal forces are divided into two groups, "In Heaven" and "On Earth." It is in Judas's extended final soliloquy that this approach proves most effective. Divided into two sections, "The temple" and "Without the temple," Elgar traces Judas's final actions and thoughts as the dour Old Testament verses of the temple singers add to his guilt and hopelessness.

It was evidently the very human characters of Judas, Mary Magdalene, and Peter that attracted Elgar to composing the work; the history of the early church, the avowed subject of his projected trilogy, turned out to hold less attraction for him. The problem with *The Kingdom*, which contains movements as fine as anything in Elgar's other oratorios, is not only that its protagonists are less interesting but that the work is far less character-driven. It begins and closes with protracted portrayals of the disciples at prayer, and overall it gives the impression of being a hugely extended contemplative anthem rather than an oratorio. While portions of *The Kingdom*, especially its fine prelude, have always found admirers, the work as a whole surely has considerably less appeal to performers and listeners than *The Apostles*.

Church Music and Quasi-Liturgical Music

With the exception of the Catholic Elgar, most of the composers encountered earlier in this chapter were major figures in Anglican church music as well as oratorio. These musical traditions were distinct in some key respects, the former sustained by professional, all-male cathedral and collegiate choirs, and the latter by amateur mixed-voice choral societies. Yet the interchange of institutions and personalities was such that the boundaries between church music and oratorio were fluid. Popular movements from oratorios were habitually taken up by church choirs, and from at least the time of Bennett's *The Woman of Samaria*, composers and publishers approached the oratorio with this in mind. Works such as Stainer's *Crucifixion* belong in both camps, while many smaller-scale compositions that are now a firm part of the cathedral repertory, such as Parry's *Hear my words, ye people*, were originally intended for massed voices and festival use.

In spite of this interchange, there are important differences between the histories of nineteenth-century church music and oratorio. Crucially, while almost all oratorios still of interest today date are from the last third of the century, the most productive phase in church music was significantly earlier. Indeed, the common notion of an English musical renaissance post-1870 fits uneasily with church music, in spite of the enduring interest of the compositions of individual figures such as Stanford.

As in oratorio, two dominant tendencies—one moderately progressive, the other historicist in orientation—were at work within nineteenth-century Anglican church music. The relationship between them has sometimes been viewed as if it were a clash between doggedly opposed camps: a conflict between conservative conceptions of the "church style," such as that expounded by William Crotch, William Horsley, and other judges of the Gresham Prize, and the innovative, unconstrained approach of composers such as Samuel Sebastian Wesley.[35] While Crotch and Wesley did indeed represent polarized conceptions of church music, the majority of composers owed something to both these tendencies, cultivating a range of different approaches in their church compositions. Indeed, some of the staples of the repertory, such as Thomas Attwood Walmisley's Evening Service in D minor (*c*.1855), are gloriously eccentric in their stylistic orientation. Walmisley's setting of the Magnificat combines passages in a lilting post-classical idiom with *stile antico* cantus firmus techniques; in addition—as if to prove its ecclesiastical credentials—it boasts basslines appropriated from the seventeenth-century French composer Henry Du Mont.

Early nineteenth-century composers for the Anglican Church inherited a narrow selection of genres and idioms from their predecessors. Multi-sectioned canticles and anthems in a sub-Handelian idiom were still the order of the day around 1800, as the church music of John Clarke-Whitfeld attests (*A Morning and Evening Service, with Six Anthems in Score*, Cambridge [1800]). A sharp contrast to this hidebound traditionalism is provided by Thomas Attwood, a pupil of Mozart who enjoyed a successful career as a theatre composer before becoming organist of St Paul's Cathedral in London. Attwood's best anthems are concise, melodious pieces cast in a single movement, an idiom modeled on Mozart's *Ave verum*. Most are strophic or ternary in organization and technically simple: perhaps the most attractive examples are the hymn setting *Come, Holy Ghost*, and two other triple-time pieces, *Teach me, O Lord* and *Turn thee again, O Lord*. The straightforward nature of these compositions surely reflects performance practices in the early nineteenth century: such music would have been learned on the job rather than rehearsed, and the simple vocal lines would have been heavily ornamented even in choral passages. Some of Attwood's anthems have more elaborate writing for the lower voices, such as *O God, who by the leading of a star*, yet in all the role of the organ is largely limited to doubling the voices.

Some of the anthems of Samuel Sebastian Wesley, such as *O Lord my God*, have a similar scope and idiom to those of Attwood. But most are on an altogether grander scale, and in some cases completely outgrew their liturgical context; in spite of their quality, church performances of his lengthiest anthems and of the Service in E are rare events. Grandson of the hymn writer Charles and son of the composer Samuel, S. S. Wesley's church music seemingly unites the spiritual fervor of the former and the contrapuntal craftsmanship of the latter. Both qualities are in evidence in his most substantial anthem *O Lord, thou art my God*, a five-movement work submitted as his degree exercise for the Oxford D. Mus. in 1839. Beginning, unusually for Wesley, with a lengthy organ introduction, the first movement offers an imposing combination of eight-part counterpoint and harmonic expressivity; particularly impressive, and characteristic of the composer, is the way that the fugue theme "For thou hast been a strength" emerges from out of the contrapuntal texture. Following a bass aria of ritornello construction, the central movement is a declamatory chorus whose idiom is close to that of Spohr's church music (perhaps the inspiration for this eight-voice anthem was Spohr's imposing Mass for Double Choir). After a contrasting verse section for smaller forces, the anthem concludes with another monumental fugue. In spite of Wesley's masterful counterpoint, the most distinctive element of his music is the breadth and purposefulness of its harmonic movement. In this work and other large-scale anthems such as *Let us lift up our heart*, Wesley pioneered the *nobilmente* idiom of slow-moving seventh chords and suspensions that, in the hands of his admirers Parry and Elgar, was to become so emblematic of English music (see Example 20.5).

Several of Wesley's short full anthems, such as *Thou wilt keep him in perfect peace* and *Wash me throughly*, perfectly distill his broad and dignified style into a form accessible to amateur church choirs. A more lyrical vein is tapped in his solo movements, and several of his anthems, such as *Blessed be the God and Father* and *O give thanks unto the Lord*, include solo middle movements in a Mendelssohnian idiom. The first of these two works, composed shortly after Wesley became organist of Hereford Cathedral in 1832, is one of his most popular works and well deserves a closer look. At its heart is a mellifluous section for treble soloist and treble chorus, whose immediacy and freshness are enhanced by its subtle rhythmic construction, unpredictably alternating three- and four-measure phrases (see Example 20.6). No less impressive is its use of choral recitative: a key aspect of Wesley's style, belying the notion that he was uninterested in the niceties of word-setting. In addition to the declamatory opening chorus, Wesley introduces recitative for the work's penultimate section, responding to the text "For all flesh is as grass" with a poignant directness.

Such music found little favor with Crotch and the Gresham Prize committee, who in 1832 rejected one of the greatest of Wesley's large-scale anthems, *The wilderness and the solitary place*.[36] Crotch's view of the church style, like his conception of oratorio, was grounded on exemplars from the distant past. In this sphere, however, his stance was more rigid, aiming at the exclusion of any elements redolent of secular or newfangled genres: "let the young composer study the productions of the sixteenth and seventeenth centuries, in order to acquire the true church style, which should always be sublime and scientific, and contain no modern harmonies or melodies."[37] Little of Crotch's own church music has remained in the repertory, although several of his *stile antico* pieces are worth reviving for their texts alone ("Methinks I hear the full celestial choir, / thro' heaven's high dome, their awful anthem raise"). The anthems and services of several prominent composers of the next generation, in particular Ouseley and John Goss (Attwood's successor as organist of St. Paul's), ensured that such viewpoints continued to have a significant impact on English church music; in Ireland, thanks to the long-serving organist of Dublin's Christ Church Cathedral, Robert Stewart, such ideals were upheld for the rest of the century.[38]

For Crotch and his followers, the church music of the sixteenth and seventeenth centuries served as a model for some but by no means all of their own compositions; as with their German Protestant contemporaries, it was primarily in works for penitential seasons and somber occasions that they turned to the strict church style.[39] Ouseley's other compositions draw on more recent idioms, and the short full anthems *Lord, I call upon thee* and *From the rising of the sun* both resemble the succinct

EXAMPLE 20.5 S. S. Wesley, *O Lord, thou art my God*, mm. 101–07.

EXAMPLE 20.6 S. S. Wesley, *Blessed be the God and Father*, mm. 92–104.

idiom of Mendelssohn's homophonic choruses such as "He that shall endure to the end" from *Elijah*. Some of Goss's more popular pieces are in a similar style, while his Christmas anthem *Behold, I bring you good tidings* offers an effective fusion of Handelian structure and Victorian hymnody. Other works present a very different idiom. Ouseley's conception of church music reform, embodied in St. Michael's College, Tenbury, the model institution he founded and bankrolled, centered on English church music from Byrd to Purcell; it is the latter whose style is emulated in Ouseley's own works with a historicist bent. His eight-part unaccompanied anthem *O Saviour of the world* replicates aspects of Purcell's dissonance treatment in its final bars, while in other pieces he went considerably further: the anthem *How goodly are thy tents* is replete with hemiolas, false relations and clashing anticipation notes, resulting in a surprisingly close imitation of Purcell's style. Goss's cultivation of earlier idioms was less mannered, yet he too turned to Baroque gestures for his most solemn effects. *If we believe*, composed for the funeral of the Duke of Wellington in 1852, draws on the rhythmic freedom and harmonic subtlety of *stile antico* polyphony in its opening part (see Example 20.7); Goss offers an effective updating of this style, however, by casting the consolatory final section in the tonic major.

The historicist leanings of Crotch and his successors found little sympathy with Stainer, who repudiated the compositional cultivation of "bygone styles" in an 1874 address "On the Progressive Character of Church Music."[40] Even while under Ouseley's tutelage, as assistant organist of St. Michael's College, Tenbury, Stainer had departed significantly from his mentor's model. *I saw the Lord* for double choir and organ, composed for the choir of St. Michael's when Stainer was just nineteen, is surely the Victorian anthem *par excellence*, combining flair and technical assurance with a bold new dramatic idiom. The generous scale of the work, use of double choir and aspects of its style, in particular the handling of the fugal entries in the final section, point to Wesley's influence. But in other respects, this vision of the apocalypse owes little to earlier English church music. Stainer's style is bolder harmonically than Wesley's, as witness the confident alternation of tonic minor and major at the opening and at the climax "And the house was filled with smoke." The most impressive aspect of the piece, however, is its dramatic conception, which is most evident in the entry of the chorus of seraphim in the striking key of F-sharp minor and later, when this material is pitted against the fugal theme in the final section. Much of Stainer's later output of anthems, conceived on an altogether smaller scale for the lucrative parish church market, fails to live up to the promise of this work. Yet its colorful and dramatic idiom was imitated by cathedral composers well into the twentieth century.

As with Stainer's *I saw the Lord*, Stanford's most influential compositions for the church service were written at the start of his career. The *Morning, Evening, and Communion Service in B-Flat*, Op. 10, composed and published in 1879 while Stanford was organist at Trinity College, Cambridge, had a lasting impact on Anglican church music, elevating the canticles to a level of artistic significance commensurate with that of the anthem. Crucial to this development was his introduction of a new symphonic approach to form, motivic manipulation, cyclic unity, and the treatment of the organ; no less important was the confidence and clarity of Stanford's idiom. The "Te Deum," the largest movement of the cycle, quickly became established as a festival piece, and was performed with a new introduction at the coronation of Edward VII in 1902. Most frequently performed today, however, are the "Magnificat" and "Nunc dimittis," which within the overall scheme serve respectively as scherzo and slow movement.[41] The enduring popularity of these pieces is immediately understandable, given their assurance and brevity, qualities that by no means preclude subtlety (consider in particular the harmonic sophistication of the central section of the Magnificat); also noteworthy, as in so much of Stanford's vocal music, is the imaginative text-setting. Both movements close with citations of the Dresden Amen, one of several musical devices Stanford employs to give unity to the cycle as a whole.

EXAMPLE 20.7 Goss, *If we believe*, mm. 12–21.

Such references to the church music of the past are not typical of Stanford's liturgical compositions with English texts. Another notable exception, however, is the Service in F Op. 36 from 1889, whose antiphonal approach and optional accompaniment, as one reviewer put it, "might have been inspired by Birde, Tallis, or any of the old English fathers of harmony."[42] Stanford's interest in sixteenth-century music is also apparent in his Latin Three Motets Op. 38 from the same year, written not for the Catholic liturgy but for the choir of Trinity College, Cambridge. It is not hard to see why these pieces have remained highly popular with choirs, since each inhabits its own fresh and distinctive musical terrain. The third piece of the set, *Coelos ascendit hodie*, for double choir, is terse and direct, while the effortless polyphony of the second, *Beati quorum via*, conceals considerable artistry. It is the first of the motets, *Justorum animae*, that makes the most profound impression, rivaling the contemporary *a cappella* pieces of Bruckner for harmonic boldness and richness of texture.

As with Stanford's motets, most of the other Latin sacred works from this period that have remained in the repertory were not composed for the Catholic service. A handful, such as the popular setting of the carol *In dulci jubilo* by the antiquarian and eccentric Robert Pearsall, were historicist flights of fancy. Composed in 1833 in Munich, where Pearsall became acquainted with the church music reformer and composer Caspar Ett, *In dulci jubilo* was intended to evoke the naive religiosity of the medieval world: "fancy it sung by a single-hearted and uncorrupted congregation of peasants in their Xmas-eve procession and I am sure you will appreciate it. Such melodies cannot be composed now-a-days. They were the emanations of a pure and sincerely religious spirit and this spirit is now no more."[43] Other Latin compositions of this period were destined for music festivals, supplementing the masses by figures such as Hummel, Weber, and Spohr that were propagated by the Catholic organist, composer, and publisher Vincent Novello. Throughout the nineteenth century, there remained little demand for home-grown works in Latin, and Ethel Smyth's mighty Mass in D (1891) is unusual in this and other respects. Exhibiting an impressive armory of Germanic symphonic and contrapuntal techniques, the Mass seemingly shakes its fist at the conventionality and isolationism of the British choral tradition. Yet there is something impersonal about its Brahmsian idiom, particularly in comparison with Smyth's later works. A similar charge could be leveled at another important Latin composition from the same year, Parry's *De profundis* for soprano, chorus, and orchestra. As with Smyth's Mass, Parry's three-movement work is distinguished by attractive choral writing, much of it in twelve parts, and would reward sympathetic performers. Yet it is of less interest than other of his works on a similar scale, such as *Blest Pair of Sirens* (1887), whose splendid *nobilmente* style has often been viewed as inaugurating an English musical renaissance.

Few Catholic liturgical compositions from the nineteenth century have remained in the repertory, aside from Elgar's youthful motets *Ave verum corpus*, *Ave Maria*, and *Ave maris stella*. Such lyrical pieces show no trace of the impact of the German Cecilian reform movement, which scarcely touched Catholic church music in Britain until the early twentieth century (in Ireland, however, Cecilianism found an energetic advocate in the cleric and composer Heinrich Bewerunge).[44] Little Catholic liturgical music of note had been composed in Britain in the century preceding Elgar's motets, with the exception of the works of Novello and more particularly Samuel Wesley; until 1791, the public celebration of mass was illegal in England, and Catholic musical activity was thus largely restricted to the chapels of foreign embassies in London. (It was for the chapel of the Portuguese embassy that much of the sacred music of both Novello and Wesley was written.) Wesley's two largest works with Latin texts, the *Missa de Spiritu Sancto* (1784) and the concerted psalm setting *Confitebor tibi, Domine* (1799) would have been too lengthy for liturgical use; the first was a presentation piece dedicated to Pope Pius VI following Wesley's conversion to Catholicism, while the second also had no immediate prospect of performance.[45] The Italian Baroque idiom of these works is condensed into a more practical format in Wesley's *Exultate Deo* and his best-known work *In exitu Israel*. No less attractive are his unaccompanied *stile antico* motets, the best of which are *Ostende nobis Domine*, *Ecce panis angelorum*, and *Omnia vanitas*.

Secular Choral Music

Like their religious counterparts, large-scale secular choral works such as oratorios, cantatas, and ballads with orchestral accompaniment were in general intended for massed mixed choruses and music festivals. But many forms of secular choral music were conceived for very different types of organizations, some of which were new (such as the working men's choirs that grew up in the second half of the nineteenth century in industrial areas), while others had emerged in the eighteenth century (such as the gentlemen's catch and glee clubs that flourished in London, Dublin, and other large cities). The repertory of some choirs, then as now, centered on arrangements of popular songs, hymns, and operatic choruses. But a vast output of pieces were composed especially for such organizations: in 1886, William Barrett estimated that 25,000 glees and partsongs had been published, while many times that figure surely circulated in manuscript.

A rigid distinction between the glee, the madrigal, and the partsong did not exist in this period, although each term carried different connotations. In 1852, one observer noted, "the glee, as a species of English composition, no longer has any active existence, and may now almost be said to be extinct."[46] A few decades earlier, it remained the unchallenged focal point of social part-singing. Cultivated by professional musicians, typically cathedral lay clerks together with female guest singers or boy choristers for the top part, glees were convivial pieces designed to impress on their first hearing. Accordingly, many glee clubs demanded that their members be able either to sing from sight or demonstrate sufficient mastery of counterpoint to compose their own works.[47] Early nineteenth-century glees, such as John Wall Callcott's *Rosabelle* and *Melrose* (both settings of excerpts from Walter Scott's *The Lay of the Minstrel*), consist of a patchwork of contrasting sections, with alterations in mood, tempo, and texture every few bars. The sectional nature of such pieces was prompted by the impulse to project individual lines of text; often, key words are underlined by more florid writing, an approach that led composers to prefer poems with varied and colorful imagery. The glees of the 1820s and 1830s, by figures such as William Horsley and Thomas Forbes Walmisley, retain the sectional nature of their precursors as well as a significant element of independence in the voices; Horsley's *Come, gentle Zephyr* and *Come follow me*, and Walmisley's *Music, all powerful* are attractive examples.[48] Yet many compositions bearing the description glee are homophonic strophic songs, with little to distinguish them from the Romantic partsongs that became popular in the second quarter of the nineteenth century.

The nineteenth-century English madrigal is a surprising development, since elsewhere in Europe compositional historicism was in general limited to sacred music. As with the latter, however, the composition of madrigals was prompted by a sense of declining musical values, representing an attempt to recapture a golden age. In 1811, the London Madrigal Society launched a prize competition for the best composition in the manner of the sixteenth-century madrigal, "each part to contain a certain melody either in figure or in imitation; a melody harmonised will be inadmissible."[49] As this instruction indicates, the madrigal was elevated as a bulwark against the supposed decline of polyphonic singing; some entries to the competition, such as Samuel Wesley's *O sing unto mie Roundelaie*, adopt a studiedly old-fashioned manner, but do not replicate elements of the historical madrigal.

The best-known nineteenth-century madrigals are those of Pearsall, who was a founding member of the Bristol Madrigal Society in 1837. In addition to producing sixteenth-century pastiches such as the eight-part *Lay a garland* (1840), Pearsall ventured back even further in time with his "ante-madrigal" *Who shall win my lady fair*, in a curious parallel to the art of the Pre-Raphaelites, Pearsall aimed here to recapture the Tudor partsong idiom that came before the Italianate madrigal.[50] The compositional revival of the madrigal should not be thought of as an eccentricity limited to Wesley and Pearsall, however. Even fully paid-up purveyors of Romantic Victoriana, such as Joseph Barnby, ventured into the realm of the madrigal, or rather, the balletto, with his *Whilst youthful sports*. Well worth reviving, too, is T. A. Walmisley's elegantly polyphonic setting of Isabella Jane Towers's poem "Sweete floweres, ye were too faire" (1839); in spite of occasional passing chromaticisms, this work offers a fresh and convincing recreation of its models (see Example 20.8).

By the end of the 1850s, even Pearsall's choir had largely abandoned the madrigal in favor of choral partsongs in Mendelssohn's vein.[51] The popularity of Mendelssohn's partsongs inspired British composers such as Bennett (*Come live with me*) and Macfarren (*Orpheus, with his lute*) to produce attractive strophic songs in a similar idiom. Perhaps the most beguiling of all Romantic partsongs are those of the next generation, in particular Sullivan's *The long day closes* and Barnby's *Sweet and low* (see Example 20.9), whose simple voice-leading and sparing use of chromatic harmony make the music a fine match for Tennyson's lullaby. Most English Romantic partsongs, like their German prototypes, fall into subgenres such as the lullaby, serenade, and ballad, and this is one of the elements that encouraged composers to remain close to the simplicity of folk song. In the late nineteenth century, however, composers such as Parry, Elgar, and Charles Wood pushed the genre in the direction of the more refined art song; good examples of this tendency are Parry's *There rolls the deep* and Elgar's *My love dwelt in a northern land*. While the artistic merits of these pieces are considerable, there was surely some loss involved in nudging the partsong away from what one earlier commentator aptly described as the "department of social harmony"; a world in which "glees and part-music, without the trouble of accompaniment, or even of music-books, can be often got up *extempore* to enliven any party of pleasure, boat excursion, or country jaunt."[52]

Large-scale secular choral works, uncommon prior to 1870, fall for the most part into two categories: historical scenes and dramas, often set in the Middle Ages, and patriotic pieces of various shades. The enduring Victorian enthusiasm for the age of chivalry ensured the production of a large number of ballads and cantatas with medieval settings, many of which have creaky plots, impenetrable poems, and lackluster music. But two large-scale pieces are well worth exploring: Sullivan's *The Golden Legend* and Elgar's *The Black Knight*, both settings of texts by the American poet Henry Wadsworth Longfellow. Completed in 1886, a year after the premiere of *The Mikado*, Sullivan's cantata received more public and critical acclaim than any other British choral work of the nineteenth century. A glance at the plot—which occupies literary terrain midway between Schumann's *Szenen aus Goethes Faust* and Liszt's *Die Legende von der heiligen Elisabeth*—may make that success seem hard to fathom. But Joseph Bennett's libretto does an effective job of cutting down Longfellow's poem to manageable proportions, and the vivid, widely contrasting scenes offer considerably more scope to the composer than most Victorian oratorio librettos. In addition, Sullivan's skills as a musical dramatist enabled him to infuse even some of the most awkward passages of the libretto with charm and conviction.

Like Elgar's oratorios, for which it is arguably the most important precursor, Sullivan's *The Golden Legend* makes the best of the genre's capacity to conjure up the mystical and supernatural while balancing these traits with human pathos. The prologue, pitting the choir and bells of Strasbourg Cathedral against the attacking forces of Lucifer and his demons, elicits a full-blooded and colorfully orchestrated symphonic response; here, Sullivan presents an effective characterization of the opposed forces, as well as giving a musical form to the mischievous malevolence of his demonic protagonist. The other great set piece for choir and soloists is Scene III, in which the

EXAMPLE 20.8 Walmisley, *Sweete floweres, ye were too faire*, mm. 40–53.

EXAMPLE 20.9 Barnby, *Sweet and low*, mm. 1–10.

mortally sick Prince Henry and his retinue, journeying to Salerno, meet a group of pilgrims among whom Lucifer is concealed. Such a scenario brings to mind a host of the stock devices of grand opera and Sullivan is not shy in deploying them: tarantella rhythms, chant-like material for the pilgrims, and the use of quasi-spatial collage and montage effects reminiscent of the pilgrims' chorus in Act I scene iii of *Tannhäuser*. Sullivan's approach to the scene, and in particular to setting Lucifer's sardonic commentary, is however highly engaging. The chorus plays relatively little role in the rest of the work, with the exception of two numbers that can effectively be performed separately. The first of these is the Evening Hymn "O gladsome light" from Scene II, a quasi-liturgical movement that was swiftly taken up for church use, eclipsing Sullivan's anthems in popularity. The second is the work's rather patchy Epilogue, whose stylistic contrasts point to the tensions between Sullivan and the conventions of the oratorio; the hymn-like sections for unison voices tap a popular vein, while the central fugal section is as wooden as its text ("The deed divine / Is written in characters of gold / That never shall grow old").

Elgar's *The Black Knight*, while the earliest of his large-scale secular choral works, is arguably the most attractive to modern performers. It is a choral ballad in the manner of Schumann's works in the genre; in contrast to Schumann, however, Elgar assigns the roles of narrator and the different characters entirely to the chorus, dispensing with soloists. Although *The Black Knight* inhabits the same chivalric world as *The Golden Legend*, it is an altogether darker piece, whose macabre story closely resembles that of Poe's "The Masque of the Red Death." Considered in itself, the plot is unpromising: Death, personified in the character of a mysterious knight, visits a castle and claims a series of victims, culminating in the children of the king. But Longfellow's verse (adapted from a poem by Johann Ludwig Uhland) sketches this scenario with artful strokes, providing Elgar with the opportunity to create a cantata that is subtle and touching as well as genuinely creepy. The first scene evokes the proud swagger of the castle's inhabitants in a chorus resembling the opening movement of the Organ Sonata in G, Op. 28. The appearance of the Black Knight, to a theme that echoes the diabolical opening of Act II of *Parsifal*, rapidly destabilizes this world. Following the death of the king's son, the castle's residents, like children whistling in the dark, attempt to keep their spirits up through madrigals and dancing, only for the latter to be transformed into an eerie dance of death; Elgar's Neapolitan-inflected slow waltz provides a fine foil for the text "Danc'd a measure weird and dark." The expansive final scene is the most impressive, tracing the rapidly changing moods prompted by the fading and death of the children, and recapitulating some of the earlier themes along the way. It is the work's combination of symphonic sweep and dramatic refinement that make it well worth reviving today.

In Elgar's other secular choral works, such subtleties are often displaced by patriotic and imperialist bluster. The years between Queen Victoria's diamond jubilee (1897) and the coronation of Edward VII (1902) brought forth a mountain of occasional pieces celebrating the empire and its values, yet Elgar's commitment to the production of such music went well beyond the norm. Scholars may well debate whether the epilogues to *The Banner of Saint George* (1897) and *Caractacus* (1898) exhibit jingoistic, chauvinistic forms of nationalism or rather affirm a noble vision of *pax Britannica*.[53] But even Elgar's apologists would have to admit that these and similar works can never reenter the repertory; even in the case of *Caractacus*, the splendor of the music cannot offset the toe-curling awfulness of H. A. Acworth's verses:

> On – though the world desert you,
> On – so your cause be right;
> Britons, alert! and fear not,
> But gird your loins for fight.
> And ever your dominion
> From age to age shall grow
> O'er peoples undiscovered,
> In lands we cannot know;
>
> . . .
>
> For all the world shall learn it –
> Though long the task shall be –
> The text of Britain's teaching,
> The message of the free;
> And when at last they find it,
> The nations all shall stand
> And hymn the praise of Britain,
> Like brothers, hand in hand.

Not all compositions inspired by patriotism can be dismissed so readily, as is evident from the works of Stanford. Of a series of choral pieces celebrating Britain's seamanship and naval heroes, the most striking is the choral ballad *The Revenge: A Ballad of the Fleet* (1886). Recounting the gallant exploits of the Elizabethan captain Sir Richard Grenville and the crew of the *Revenge*, the text, by Stanford's friend Alfred, Lord Tennyson, enabled the composer to capitalize on his strengths: responding vividly to the shifting moods of the text, creating musical structures that complement poetic ones, and composing pithy and memorable vocal lines. Judging by the sales figures—over 120,000 vocal scores were sold in the years prior to 1914[54]—choirs loved the dramatic nature of the work, reveling in taking on the roles of the different protagonists as well as relishing Stanford's colorful text-setting and the 'nautical' touches in the orchestration.

In addition to hymning English heroes, Stanford wrote patriotic choral music of a different hue. Following hot on the heels of his opera *Shamus O'Brien* (1895), Stanford composed a choral ballad, *Phaudrig Crohoore*, also to a poem by his fellow Dubliner J. Sheridan Le Fanu. As in *The Revenge*, the folk song-like text of *Phaudrig Crohoore* elicited a boisterous setting, with the composer's authentic voice to the fore. But in an episode emblematic of the moralistic atmosphere of some British choral societies, Le Fanu's text was rejected by a number of choirs in Lancashire and Yorkshire for being lewd and blasphemous.[55] Such objections, bizarrely, were prompted by the following innocuous lines (mm. 45–49): "An' there wasn't a girl from thirty-five under, / Divil a matter how cross / But he could get round her." While Stanford managed to prevent his publisher from censoring these lines, the work never gained anything approaching the popularity of *The Revenge*; for modern choirs able to approach Le Fanu's Anglo-Irish dialect unselfconsciously, it would make a lively and effective concert piece.

Toward an Unknown Region

In the years around 1900, composers, frustrated by the moribund nature of the Victorian oratorio, increasingly turned to different forms and to more exotic textual material. *Phaudrig Crohoore* reflects both moves, as do works such as Delius's *Appalachia* (1903) and *A Mass of Life* (1905), Samuel Coleridge-Taylor's *Kubla Khan* (1905) and *A Tale of Old Japan* (1911), and Holst's *Choral Hymns from the Rig Veda* (1912). Of the works that reflect this tendency, by far the most popular at the time was Coleridge-Taylor's *Scenes from the Song of Hiawatha*, a portmanteau work consisting of *Hiawatha's Wedding Feast* (first performed in 1898 at the Royal College of Music in London), *The Death of Minnehaha* (premiered at the North Staffordshire Festival in 1899), and *Hiawatha's Departure* (commissioned and performed by the Royal Choral Society in 1900). While performances of the trilogy, and in particular *Hiawatha's Wedding Feast*, were common until the mid-twentieth century, the work seems to have sunk without trace over recent decades. For the most part, this neglect stems from the fall from grace of Longfellow and suspicion of his brand of exoticism. But part of the blame also lies with the work itself, since no matter how varied and subtle Coleridge-Taylor's approach, he is not able wholly to offset the monotonous effect of Longfellow's rigid four-trochee lines; indeed, the principal theme, which recurs rather too often, serves to underscore this problem (see Example 20.10). Within the context of late nineteenth-century choral music, however, the work's freshness was striking. One feature that differentiates it from earlier works is its uncluttered and artless nature; Coleridge-Taylor's simple choral style jettisons much of the conventional afflatus of the oratorio. In addition, rather than ponderously doubling the chorus, the orchestra has an independent role, flitting in and out of the texture.

Another breath of fresh air from America, the poetry of Walt Whitman, came to be emblematic of the concerns of the new generation; indeed, somewhat surprisingly, it became the most important textual source for composers seeking to move beyond the conventions of the Victorian oratorio tradition. While composers as varied as Holst, Cyril Scott, and Percy Grainger produced musical responses to Whitman, it was works by Delius (*Sea Drift*, 1904) and Vaughan Williams (*Toward the Unknown Region*, 1907; and *A Sea Symphony*, 1903–09) that were to redefine British choral music.

EXAMPLE 20.10 Coleridge-Taylor, *Hiawatha's Wedding Feast*, mm. 121–28.

The shortest of these works, Vaughan Williams's *Toward the Unknown Region*, resembles an artistic manifesto, casting aside dogma and convention to embrace the future, even in the absence of spiritual and musical certainties—as Whitman wrote, "all is a blank before us". Not that the slate is entirely blank: the imprint of Parry's *Blest Pair of Sirens* can be heard in Vaughan Williams's choral textures and harmonic language, while the shadow of Part Two of Elgar's *Gerontius* forms a background to the visionary climax. But the striking modal opening of *Toward the Unknown Region* surely heralded a new future for British choral music, albeit one in which past and present would continue to be fused intimately together.

Notes

1 "E.D.R.," "English Music," *Musical Times* 35 (1894): 592.
2 See, for example, Jeffrey Richards, *Imperialism and Music: Britain 1876–1953* (Manchester: Manchester University Press, 2001), 44–88; and Laura Upperton, "Patriotic Vigour or Voice of the Orient? Re-reading Elgar's *Caractacus*," in *Music and Orientalism in the British Empire, 1780s–1940s: Portrayals of the East*, ed. Martin Clayton and Bennett Zon (Aldershot, England: Ashgate, 2007), 165–88.
3 For a harsher take on Newman's poem, see Robin Holloway, "The Early Choral Works," in *The Cambridge Companion to Elgar*, ed. Daniel Grimley and Julian Rushton (Cambridge: Cambridge University Press, 2004), 63–64.
4 Anon., "Grand Musical Festivals," *The Quarterly Musical Magazine and Review* 8 (1826): 263.
5 Howard E. Smither, *A History of the Oratorio*, 4 vols. (Chapel Hill, NC: University of North Carolina Press, 1977–2000), vol. III, 215–17, vol. IV, 274–75.
6 Donald Burrows, *Handel: Messiah* (Cambridge: Cambridge University Press, 1991), 48; John Butt, "Choral Music," in *The Cambridge History of Nineteenth-Century Music*, ed. Jim Samson (Cambridge: Cambridge University Press, 2001), 216.
7 Anon., "Musical Festivals," *The Quarterly Musical Magazine and Review* 8 (1826): 259–60.
8 William Jackson, *Observations on the Present State of Music in London* (London, 1791), 29, as quoted in Eva Zöllner, "Zur Geschichte des englischen Oratoriums im frühen 19. Jahrhundert," *Händel-Jahrbuch* 44 (1998): 140.
9 Smither, *A History of the Oratorio*, vol. IV, 288.
10 William Crotch, *Substance of Several Courses of Lectures on Music, Read in the University of Oxford and in the Metropolis* (London: Longman, Rees et al., 1831), 127, 124–25.
11 Ibid., 78.
12 Smither, *A History of the Oratorio*, vol. IV, 321.
13 Crotch, *Lectures on Music*, 82.
14 Crotch's edition of Tallis's Litany is discussed in Suzanne Cole, *Thomas Tallis and his Music in Victorian England* (Woodbridge and New York: Boydell Press, 2008), 34.
15 Nigel Burton, "Oratorios and Cantatas," in *The Blackwell History of Music in Britain*, vol. 5: *The Romantic Age 1800–1914*, ed. Nicholas Temperley (Oxford: Blackwell, 1988), 215.
16 G. A. Macfarren, "Jerusalem, An Oratorio, by Henry Hugh Pierson," *Musical Times* 5 (1852): 51.
17 Ibid.
18 Smither, *A History of the Oratorio*, vol. IV, 340. Such objections are surprising in this case, given that the libretto, including Salome's purportedly lascivious song "I rejoice in my youth" (*Ecclesiastes* ch. 11, v. 9), is entirely derived from the Bible.
19 Anon., "The Way we write our Oratorios. By one of the Unperformed," *Musical World* 65 (1887): 829, as quoted in Smither, *A History of the Oratorio*, IV, 302–03.
20 Macfarren, "Jerusalem, An Oratorio," 52.
21 For a reappraisal of Mackenzie's work, see Duncan James Barker, "Mackenzie's *The Rose of Sharon*: Continental Prima Donna or Norfolk Lass," in *Nineteenth-Century British Music Studies*, ed. Jeremy Dibble and Bennett Zon (Aldershot, England and Burlington, VT: Ashgate, 2002), 101–13.
22 Jeremy Dibble, *John Stainer: A Life in Music* (Woodbridge and New York: Boydell, 2007), 71–72.
23 Smither, *A History of the Oratorio*, vol. IV, 266.
24 Dibble, *Stainer*, 204–05.
25 Jan Marsh, *Pre-Raphaelite Women: Images of Femininity in Pre-Raphaelite Art* (London: Weidenfeld and Nicolson, 1987).
26 See Janet Hopewell, "Stainer's Librettist, W. J. Sparrow Simpson," *Musical Times* 124 (1983): 255–56.
27 Anon., Review of *The Crucifixion, Musical Times* 28 (1887): 174–75.

28 Smither, *A History of the Oratorio*, vol. IV, 299–300.
29 Eric Fenby, *Delius as I Knew Him* (Cambridge: Cambridge University Press, 1981), 124, as quoted in Byron Adams, "Elgar's Later Oratorios: Roman Catholicism, Decadence and the Wagnerian Dialectic of Shame and Grace," in *The Cambridge Companion to Elgar*, 81.
30 George Bernard Shaw, "Stanford's 'Irish' Symphony" (1893), *G.B.S. on Music* (London: Penguin, 1962), 131.
31 Paul Rodmell, *Charles Villiers Stanford* (Aldershot, England and Burlington, VT: Ashgate, 2002), 158.
32 Smither, *A History of the Oratorio*, vol. IV, 382.
33 Adams, "Elgar's Later Oratorios," 103–05.
34 On Elgar's characterization of Judas, see Charles Edward McGuire, "Elgar, Judas, and the Theology of Betrayal," *19th-Century Music* 23/3 (2000): 236–72.
35 The Gresham Prize, funded by the philanthropist and church music reformer Maria Hackett, was awarded annually from 1831 for the best church anthem or service (see Nicholas Temperley, "Cathedral Music," *The Romantic Age*, 188).
36 Ibid., 194.
37 Crotch, *Lectures on Music*, 77–78.
38 Barra Boydell, "'A Bright Exception to the General Rule'? Musical Standards at Christ Church Cathedral Dublin in the Early Nineteenth Century," in *Nineteenth-Century British Music Studies*, ed. Jeremy Dibble and Bennett Zon (Aldershot, England and Burlington, VT: Ashgate, 2002), 57–58.
39 See James Garratt, *Palestrina and the German Romantic Imagination: Interpreting Historicism in Nineteenth-Century Music* (Cambridge: Cambridge University Press, 2002), 98–109, 131.
40 Nicholas Temperley, "Ancient and Modern in the Work of Sir John Stainer," in *Nineteenth-Century British Music Studies*, ed. Peter Horton and Bennett Zon (Aldershot, England and Burlington, VT: Ashgate, 2003), 109.
41 Rodmell, *Stanford*, 68–73; see also Jeremy Dibble, *Charles Villiers Stanford: Man and Musician* (Oxford and New York: Oxford University Press, 2002), 104–5.
42 Anon., Review of Charles Villiers Stanford's Service in F, *Musical Times* 30 (1889): 744.
43 Robert Pearsall, letter of 7 May, 1833 to H. T. Ellacombe, as presented in William Barclay Squire, "Letters of Robert Lucas Pearsall," *Musical Quarterly* 5/2 (1919): 267.
44 Harry M. White, "Toward a History of the Cecilian Movement in Ireland," in *Irish Musical Studies*, ed. Gerard Gillen and Harry M. White, vol. II (Blackrock: Irish Academic, 1993), 78–107.
45 Samuel Wesley, *Confitebor tibi, Domine*, ed. John Marsh, *Musica Britannica* 41 (London: Stainer and Bell, 1978), xiii–iv.
46 Thomas Forbes Walmisley, *A Collection of Glees, Trios, Rounds, and Canons* (London, 1826), preface; E. Holmes, "English Glee & Madrigal Composers. No. VI," *Musical Times* 5 (1852): 3.
47 Percy M. Young (ed.), *The English Glee* (New York: Oxford University Press, 1990), viii.
48 Horsley's two glees were later presented as supplements to the *Musical Times* 3 (1848): 53–55, and 11 (1860): 369–72; Walmisley's glee and most of the other partsongs discussed below are presented in Paul Hiller (ed.), *English Romantic Partsongs* (Oxford: Oxford University Press, 1986), which offers a wide-ranging selection of pieces in all three genres.
49 Nicholas Temperley, "Domestic Music in England 1800–1860," *Proceedings of the Royal Musical Association* 85 (1958–9): 45–46.
50 Edgar Hunt, "Robert Lucas Pearsall," *Proceedings of the Royal Musical Association* 82 (1955–6): 84.
51 Ibid., 85.
52 Holmes, "English Glee & Madrigal Composers," 4.
53 Richards, *Imperialism and Music*, 51.
54 Rodmell, *Stanford*, 119.
55 Dibble, *Stanford*, 264–65.

Selected Bibliography

Adams, Byron. "Elgar's Later Oratorios: Roman Catholicism, Decadence and the Wagnerian Dialectic of Shame and Grace," in *The Cambridge Companion to Elgar*, ed. Daniel Grimley and Julian Rushton. Cambridge: Cambridge University Press, 2004, 81–105.

Anon. "Musical Festivals," *The Quarterly Musical Magazine and Review* 8 (1826): 257–62.

Anon. "Grand Musical Festivals," *The Quarterly Musical Magazine and Review* 8 (1826): 263–95.

Anon. Review of *The Crucifixion*, *Musical Times* 28 (1887): 174–75.

Anon. Review of Charles Villiers Stanford's Service in F, *Musical Times* 30 (1889): 744.

Barclay Squire, William. "Letters of Robert Lucas Pearsall," *Musical Quarterly* 5, 2 (1919): 264–97; 6, 2 (1920): 296–315.

Barker, Duncan James. "Mackenzie's *The Rose of Sharon*: Continental Prima Donna or Norfolk Lass," in *Nineteenth-Century British Music Studies*, ed. Jeremy Dibble and Bennett Zon. Aldershot and Burlington: Ashgate, 2002, 101–13.

Benoliel, Bernard. *Parry before "Jerusalem": Studies of his Life and Music with Excerpts from his Published Writings*. Aldershot and Brookfield: Ashgate, 1997.

Boydell, Barra. "'A Bright Exception to the General Rule'? Musical Standards at Christ Church Cathedral Dublin in the Early Nineteenth Century," in *Nineteenth-Century British Music Studies*, ed. Jeremy Dibble and Bennett Zon. Aldershot and Burlington: Ashgate, 2002, 46–58.

Burrows, Donald. *Handel: Messiah*. Cambridge: Cambridge University Press, 1991.

Burton, Nigel. "Oratorios and Cantatas," in *The Blackwell History of Music in Britain*, vol. 5: *The Romantic Age 1800–1914*, ed. Nicholas Temperley. Oxford: Blackwell, 1988, 214–41.

Butt, John "Choral Music," in *The Cambridge History of Nineteenth-Century Music*, ed. Jim Samson, 213–36. Cambridge: Cambridge University Press, 2001.

Cole, Suzanne. *Thomas Tallis and his Music in Victorian England*. Woodbridge and New York: Boydell Press, 2008.

Crotch, William. *Substance of Several Courses of Lectures on Music, Read in the University of Oxford and in the Metropolis*. London: Longman, Rees et al., 1831.

Dibble, Jeremy. *Charles Villiers Stanford: Man and Musician*. Oxford and New York: Oxford University Press, 2002.

——. *John Stainer: A Life in Music*. Woodbridge and New York: Boydell, 2007.

Garratt, James. *Palestrina and the German Romantic Imagination: Interpreting Historicism in Nineteenth-Century Music*. Cambridge: Cambridge University Press, 2002.

Holmes, E. "English Glee & Madrigal Composers. No. VI," *Musical Times* 5 (1852): 3–6.

Holloway, Robin. "The Early Choral Works," in *The Cambridge Companion to Elgar*, ed. Daniel Grimley and Julian Rushton. Cambridge: Cambridge University Press, 2004, 63–80.

Hopewell, Janet. "Stainer's Librettist, W. J. Sparrow Simpson," *Musical Times* 124 (1983): 255–56.

Hunt, Edgar, "Robert Lucas Pearsall," *Proceedings of the Royal Musical Association* 82 (1955–6): 75–88.

Macfarren, G. A. "Jerusalem, An Oratorio, by Henry Hugh Pierson," *Musical Times* 5 (1852): 51–59.

McGuire, Charles Edward. "Elgar, Judas, and the Theology of Betrayal," *19th-Century Music* 23, 3 (2000): 236–72.

Marsh, Jan. *Pre-Raphaelite Women: Images of Femininity in Pre-Raphaelite Art*. London: Weidenfeld and Nicolson, 1987.

"E.D.R." "English Music," *Musical Times* 35 (1894): 592–96.

Richards, Jeffrey. *Imperialism and Music: Britain 1876–1953*. Manchester and New York: Manchester University Press, 2001.

Rodmell, Paul. *Charles Villiers Stanford*. Aldershot and Burlington: Ashgate, 2002.

Shaw, George Bernard. *G.B.S. on Music*. London: Penguin, 1962.

Smither, Howard E. *A History of the Oratorio*, 4 vols. Chapel Hill, NC: University of North Carolina Press, 1977–2000.

Temperley, Nicholas, "Domestic Music in England 1800–1860," *Proceedings of the Royal Musical Association* 85 (1958–59): 31–47.

——. "Cathedral Music," in *The Blackwell History of Music in Britain*, vol. 5: *The Romantic Age 1800–1914*, ed. Nicholas Temperley. Oxford: Blackwell, 1988, 171–213.

——. "Ancient and Modern in the Work of Sir John Stainer," in *Nineteenth-Century British Music Studies*, ed. Peter Horton and Bennett Zon. Aldershot and Burlington: Ashgate, 2003, 103–18.

White, Harry M. "Toward a History of the Cecilian Movement in Ireland," in *Irish Musical Studies*, ed. Gerard Gillen and Harry M. White. Blackrock: Irish Academic, 1993, vol. II, 78–107.

Zöllner, Eva. "Zur Geschichte des englischen Oratoriums im frühen 19. Jahrhundert," *Händel-Jahrbuch* 44 (1998): 139–45.

21

THE NORDIC WORLD

Scandinavia and Finland

Harald Herresthal

Norges musikkhøgskole, Oslo, Norway

At the beginning of the nineteenth century there were two kingdoms in Scandinavia: Sweden and Denmark. Iceland, Greenland, and the Faroe Islands belonged to the twin kingdom of Denmark–Norway, and Finland belonged to Sweden. The professional musical life in the seventeenth and eighteenth centuries, therefore, was related to the courts in Stockholm and Copenhagen, which imported singers and musicians from Italy, France, and Germany. Throughout the eighteenth century, German orchestra conductors and composers played an important role at the Scandinavian courts, and many musicians from the German-speaking areas under Danish rule worked as musicians and organists in both the cities and the countryside. This picture changed very little in the first half of the nineteenth century, although the political turmoil and development of national states created a stronger need for indigenous musicians and composers. In many cases, the immigrant musicians took the first steps toward giving each Scandinavian country their own characteristic national music.

Great political upheavals in the century's first two decades not only influenced the political situation, but also played an important role in each country's musical development. In 1809, Sweden had to cede Finland to Russia; in return, Denmark had to cede Norway to Sweden (1814). In union with Sweden, Norway maintained cultural contact with Denmark, but the will and the need to show that Norway was a country with its own identity and culture soon made itself evident and became an important driving force for Norwegian artists. In Finland, student patriotism created major problems for the Russian authorities, and by the end of the century there was a growing wish in Finland for independence.

Church Music

To understand the development of choir music in Scandinavian churches in the nineteenth century we have to know some background. In the first part of the sixteenth century, the Scandinavian kings established Lutheran state churches in their countries, and from that period the German Lutheran liturgy and hymns were introduced. In the cities, the Mass was sung in Latin by cathedral school choirs; in the rural countryside, however, the liturgy was replaced by hymns in the region's native language. Many of the hymn texts were translations from German, but soon hymns in native languages were also composed; these were often sung to local folk tunes or were transformed versions of German melodies.[1]

Around 1800, boys enrolled in Latin schools were no longer obliged to sing at church services, and in the following years a new school system was created. As early as 1790, the German choral conductor, Johann Abraham Peter Schulz (in Copenhagen) had pointed out the weakness of hymn singing in churches in Denmark. He put forward concrete suggestions for improvement, and in 1799 the teaching of "proper harmony singing" was introduced in Danish schools. The idea spread rapidly to the rest of Scandinavia, and two-, three- or four-part singing of hymns became a central part of the curriculum in public schools. For most of the century, church choirs were made up of men and boys; only toward the end of the 1800s could boys be replaced by young ladies.

Choral Music and Scandinavism

As a fruit of the period of Enlightenment, a new human ideal developed in Europe. The Swiss pedagogue Johann Heinrich Pestalozzi, who was inspired by Rousseau's ideas on education, wanted a school for all children in the community. Singing and playing music should not be reserved for the privileged classes only; rather, it should play a key role as part of the people's spiritual, moral, and religious development. These thoughts are based on Plato's writings and Greek formation ideals, which came to be crucial for the development of choral singing. Through singing, the love of country should be awoken and cultivated.

European men's choirs had their origins in the liberation and education movements of the nineteenth century, and the Nordic world was no exception. Throughout the century, students were at the heart of political change, and early on they used songs to get their message out. Sweden was the first country where they spread radical thoughts about freedom. One of the earliest such occasions was at Uppsala University in 1792, when students sang popular songs by the famous Swedish troubadour Carl Michael Bellman (1740–95). Musical influences came especially from the student communities in Germany; Scandinavian writers and composers also played an important role not only in expressing the people's longing for freedom, but also in the overall national awakening and the development of cultural institutions.

In 1808, the *directores musices* at Uppsala University, J. C. H. Haeffner, founded the first organized student choir. Their first performance took place that autumn, when the retired marshal Klingspor was recognized for his participation in the Swedish-Russian War. Finland fell into Russian hands the following year despite the heroic fighting of the Swedish troops. The Finnish students studying in Uppsala at the time took this singing tradition with them when they returned to Finland in 1820 to continue their studies at the University of Turku.

Until a catastrophic fire destroyed most of Turku in 1827, the students there were a constant disturbing element for the Russian authorities, and this political opposition was particularly reflected in the student choir. In May 1827, it was banned from singing in public places for fear that their songs would incite the rest of the population. The great fire that September gave the Tsar a welcome excuse to move the university to Helsinki. In this way, he hoped to gain better control over the opponents of the regime.

In Norway, students also used singing as a weapon in their fight for freedom. After Sweden lost Finland to the Russians, it was given Norway as compensation and as a reward for participating in the war against Napoleon and Denmark. Before that time, however, Norway had managed to acquire one of Europe's most liberal constitutions. In 1824, when the students wanted to celebrate the constitution's tenth anniversary (May, 17), King Carl Johan perceived this as a celebration of the royal election of the Danish Prince Frederick. Fearing Norwegian nationalism, the king instituted a ban on students singing national songs in public places on that day and used all means available to silence them. The Norwegian students, in turn, suddenly realized the power their singing had, and on the same day five years later (May 17, 1829), they joined many other people in the streets of Christiania (now Oslo) and in the main market place in defiance of the authorities. The resulting conflict, known as the "market battle" was one of the most significant confrontations in Norway against the Swedish king. It was no longer possible to stop the rise of nationalism or to deny these national celebrations of May 17, a national day that is still observed annually with great fanfare, including much singing of patriotic songs.

By the 1830s, this form of choral singing began to flourish throughout the Nordic world. In Helsinki, the German composer Fredrik Pacius established the all-male student choir, the Akademiska Sångföreningen (1838). In Sweden, student singers in Uppsala met with competition from a similar student ensemble founded at Lund University in 1831, the Lunds Studentsångförening, led by the composer Otto Lindblad.

The change in the political climate between Sweden and Denmark in the 1830s made it possible for Swedish and Danish students to meet across the border, and in 1838 and 1839 the first joint meetings took place in Copenhagen. The beautiful four-part singing of the student choir from Lund caused such a sensation that the Danes were inspired to organize their own choir. Two of the most popular songs were Lindblad's *Vintern rasat ut* (The Winter cooled off, 1839) and Otto Westermark's *Kung Karl den unge hjälte* (King Karl, the young hero, 1823). The content of the latter was a typical expression of the anti-Russian mood that prevailed at such gatherings. In 1842, the Uppsala students were invited to take part in the collaboration; at the same time inquiries were also made to see if it would be possible to invite the Finnish and Norwegian students.

Behind these ideas there was the dream of a united Nordic people, a concept that was expressed even more strongly in 1843, as students from Copenhagen and Lund went to Uppsala. These students envisioned a future Nordic association that could promote common national interests. The Finnish-Swedish composer Bernhard Crusell's song *Nordens Enhet* (The Nordic Unity), to a text by the Danish poet Carl Ploug, stands as a symbol of what became the ultimate goal of Scandinavism. In that same year, the Skandinavisk Samfund (the Scandinavian Society) was founded in Copenhagen with the aim of promoting social and literary relations between the Scandinavian nations, but it was such a clear political move that the Danish King Christian VIII chose to prohibit it. In the following years, several new Scandinavian societies were founded, but with less radical programs. Still, the Scandinavian student meetings provided an opportunity for the participants to become familiar with each other's songs and singing traditions. At the same time they were inspired and competed to improve the quality of their own songs.

The students in Norway were initially skeptical of the political idea of the Nordic countries as a political association, as they considered Scandinavism to be an attack on the freedom the Norwegian Constitution gave Norway in relation to Sweden. However, Norway still had strong cultural ties to Denmark and the students in Christiania had nothing against fraternization in a cultural sense. Thus, they attended the 1845 gathering in Copenhagen, and from that experience their support of Scandinavism and their desire for fraternization and cohabitation between nations grew.

Although Scandinavism eventually lost its importance due to continuing political and territorial conflicts in the region, Scandinavian students continued to meet each other across their respective borders, and a new milestone was reached when the Russian Tsar Alexander II allowed the Finnish student singers to participate for the first time in the meeting in 1875.

Historically, Finland had political problems not only in relation to Russia. Like Norway, which still had Danish as its official written language in the 1800s, there were many Finns whose mother tongue was Swedish. As Finnish nationalism grew, however, a native Finnish language emerged that could not be understood by the other Scandinavians. From the perspective of choral music, the Swedish and Finnish-speaking groups split and formed their own choral societies, which initially seemed devastating in terms of both quality and cohesion.

Concert Life and Repertoire: Student and Worker Choruses

The interest in choral singing that had been stirred up by student gatherings such as those in Uppsala in 1843 and Copenhagen in 1845 set the stage for the creation of numerous new choirs in Norway. Three such ensembles were founded in quick succession by the noted Norwegian choral conductor Johan Diderik Behrens: the Norwegian Student Choral Society (Den norske Studentersangforening, 1845), a choral society for the mercantile association (Handelsstandens Sangforening, 1847) and another for the craftsmen's guild (Håndverkersangforeningen, 1848). Similarly, the other Scandinavian countries founded choral societies as sub-units of various professional associations.

Political and territorial hostilities continued throughout the Nordic world, as they did elsewhere in Europe at mid-century. From these struggles, new social groups emerged that demanded better living conditions. When the Scandinavian students met in Christiania in 1851, they were greeted by 2,000 members of the workers' union: the socialist movement of the Norwegian politician and musician Marcus Thrane had formed the first choir for workers the previous year as part of a larger public educational program. A similar development occurred in the other Scandinavian countries, and soon there were male choirs everywhere, in the military, in hunting clubs, in Christian societies, and in all the existing clubs, unions, and associations. The repertoire sung by these ensembles consisted of patriotic songs, drinking songs, hunting songs, chorales, folk tunes, spring songs, and serenades depending on the social profile of the different male choirs.

The 1845 student meeting in Copenhagen also inspired Behrens to arrange national song festivals held in various places throughout Norway. A characteristic feature of the Norwegian male choir movement was that the meetings and festivals were not reserved just for student choirs from the middle classes, but also included participation by craftsmen associations. In connection with these festivals, Behrens also formed a festival choir that was composed of members from all the male choirs in Christiania. In this way, the different classes of society agreed on a common musical goal. This development was quite unique and remarkable compared with what was happening in the other Scandinavian countries at the time, and it marked an important step toward creating a more democratic society.

The song collections by the Swedish troubadour Carl Michael Bellmann, *Fredmans epistlar* (1790) and *Fredmans sånger* (1791), formed a joint Nordic repertoire for these groups. Bellmann's poems were politically harmless and dealt with things that mostly were attractive to the students. Patriotic songs were also an important repertoire for such choirs, however, and each country created its own national song tradition. Choirs commissioned and performed songs written by their country's leading poets and composers, such as August Söderman's *Ett bondbröllop* (A Peasant Wedding, 1868), a favorite of Swedish men's choirs. Large collections of choral music were published with works from the Renaissance to the Romantic period, as well as arrangements of folk music.

The latter part of the century also saw the creation of international music festivals. In 1867, for example, a singing contest was arranged in connection with the *Exposition universelle* in Paris. The student choir in Uppsala, the Studentkårs Allmänna Sångförening, competed with two selections, Gunnar Wennerberg's the still-popular *Hör oss, Svea* (Listen to us, Svea, 1853) and *Brudefærden i Hardanger* (The Bridal Procession in Hardanger) by the Norwegian composer Halfdan Kjerulf. Their performance attracted considerable attention and the group ended up being awarded first prize. The following day it performed several Scandinavian songs at a concert in the opera house, including two Finnish songs by Pacius: *Suomis sång* (Song of Finland, 1854) and *Vårt land* (Our country, 1848), which became the Finnish national anthem (*Oi maamme Suomi, synnyinmaa*). Kjerulf's *Brudefærden i Hardanger* was received with such enthusiasm that it was immediately translated into French and performed by French choirs.

This positive international reception acted as an inspiration, and at the next *Exposition universelle* in 1878, students from Uppsala and Christiania joined forces to form a huge choir. For the exhibitions in 1889 and 1900, however, Norway focused strongly on its own musical tradition as a political demonstration of Norway as an independent country within the Sweden–Norway Union.

Scandinavian student choirs also participated in the first Nordic music festival in Copenhagen in 1888. Although male choirs were a significant part of the festival, philharmonic choirs played a more prominent role. The purpose of these Nordic music festivals was to present the best contemporary music from each country. Rather than writing for student ensembles, composers increasingly preferred to compose music for philharmonic societies, which used professional musicians in the orchestra and which had larger mixed-voice choirs capable of performing more demanding music.

Concert Life and Repertoire: Philharmonic and Oratorio Choirs

In the first part of the eighteenth century, the nobility and the middle classes in Copenhagen and Stockholm had their own music societies. The amateurs and music lovers of high society performed instrumental music, arias, and choruses from operas and singspiels, passion music, cantatas, and incidental music. In the nineteenth century, however, different types of music societies were formed in many other Scandinavian cities. Usually these started as ordinary concerts in private houses, but when the salons became too small, the concerts were moved to a hall or private theater. The next step was to form a society where talented amateurs from the bourgeoisie could perform songs, piano music, chamber music, and larger works for mixed choir and orchestra. When a society needed a large orchestra, they had to invite or engage professional musicians from the church or theater, or from a military band, to play the instruments that the amateurs could not. The orchestra was composed of men almost exclusively. Female members played the piano or could participate as solo singers, if they were skilled enough; otherwise, they sang in the choir. The growing number of such societies increased the demand for composers to produce secular cantatas and oratorios for soloists, mixed choirs, and orchestra; many of these works were performed at university jubilees, royal anniversaries or funerals, and other high-profiled occasions.

Private music societies were run by enthusiastic individuals, and their viability was dependent on the effort and commitment of their members. Among the more significant of these groups was the Harmonic Society (Harmoniska sällskapet, 1820) in Stockholm, which had an orchestra of forty musicians and a choir of 120 singers; the Music Society (Musikforeningen, 1836) in Copenhagen; and Det Musikalske Lyceum in Christiania, which was replaced in 1846 by the Philharmonic Society (Det philharmoniske Selskab). In Finland, Turku and Helsinki also had music societies, and in 1846 Pacius founded the first symphony orchestra in Helsinki; it also had a choir. The repertoire of these symphonic choirs was largely the same: large-scale works from the Baroque, Classical, and Romantic periods.

In 1850, Copenhagen's Musikforeningen received a boost, when Niels Gade became its director. Gade had been the assistant conductor of the Gewandhaus orchestra in Leipzig under Felix Mendelssohn and, as head of the music scene in Copenhagen, tried to build up a similar tradition. With the Musikforeningen he performed many of the choral–orchestral masterworks, including the first performance in Scandinavia of Bach's *St. Matthew Passion* (1875).

In Stockholm, the composer Ludvig Norman founded the Nya harmoniska Sällskapet (The New Harmonic Society) in 1860 with 100 choral singers; six years later he replaced the amateur musicians in the orchestra with players from the Hovkapellet. Similar changes were made in Christiania's Philharmoniske Selskab, which consisted of amateurs and some hired musicians from the theater orchestra and the military band. When Edvard Grieg founded Christiania's Musikforeningen in 1871, he also engaged professional musicians for the orchestra.

There are many similarities between these Nordic music societies in terms of repertoire. All of them performed works by Bach, Handel, Haydn, Mozart, Beethoven, Mendelssohn, and Schumann. More importantly, though, since the leading composers of each country conducted these groups, their concerts frequently featured new music.

A typical trait of Romanticism was the increasing interest in music from the Renaissance and Baroque. Many Scandinavian music societies performed Handel's oratorios because they were inspired by the unbroken performance tradition these works enjoyed in England, and by the late 1870s, Bach's choral works began to be performed. In connection with the rediscovery of Renaissance and Baroque masterpieces, a number of choral societies emerged with the purpose of performing great church music. Many of these choirs, such as the Cæciliaforeningen founded in Christiania in 1879 by the composer and oratorio singer Thorvald Lammers, were large and performed Romantic *a cappella* music for mixed choirs, as well as the great oratorios of the Baroque and Romantic periods.

Concert Life and Repertoire: Smaller Ensembles

Although male choirs played a central role in Nordic choral music-making throughout the nineteenth century, several women's choirs were also founded in the century's last two decades. At the same time, the interest in music for smaller, unaccompanied mixed choirs was growing. This development inspired composers to write choral pieces that are still regarded as highlights in the Scandinavian repertoire, the most familiar of which today outside of Scandinavia is the Swedish composer Wilhelm Stenhammar's *Tre körvisor* (1890). Other noteworthy works, which fall outside the chronological scope of this chapter, include Oskar Lindberg's *Pingst* (At Whitsuntide, 1911) and *Stjärntändningen* (Light the stars, 1922), and David Wikander's *Kung Liljekonvalje* (King Lily of the Valley, 1946) and *Förvårskväll* (An evening in early spring, *c.*1950). Hugo Alfvén's adaptations of Swedish folk songs, all arranged after 1900, also have a special place in the Swedish choir tradition.

An interest in Renaissance vocal polyphony led to the creation of a number of small nineteenth-century madrigal and motet choirs. The Danish composer Henrik Rung (1807–72) was one of the first in Scandinavia to perform the masses and motets by Palestrina—he performed the *Stabat Mater* as early as 1841 in Copenhagen—and he started the first Cæcilia Society in 1851 with the specific goal of performing choral music from the Italian Renaissance. Rung's work was continued after his death by his son Frederik, who started his own madrigal choir in 1887. This interest in Renaissance polyphony in the style of Palestrina continued into the twentieth century.

Finally, there was a close correlation between the organ movement, choral movement and worship renewal within Scandinavian churches. What particularly interested Nordic music scholars and composers was the relationship between Gregorian chant and the Nordic medieval melodies, and the revival of music from the Middle Ages influenced some Scandinavian composers. Late examples can be found in the *a cappella* works of the Swedish composer Otto Olsson (*Sex latinska hymner*, 1919) and the Danish composer Carl Nielsen (*Tre motetter*, 1929).

Composers and Selected Works

Among the leading Nordic composers of nineteenth-century choral music are Niels Gade, J. P. E. Hartmann, Peter Erasmus Lange-Müller, and Carl Nielsen from Denmark; Halfdan Kjerulf, Friedrich August Reissiger, and Edvard Grieg from Norway; Gunnar Wennerberg, Prince Gustaf, Jacob Axel Josephson, and Otto Lindblad from Sweden; and Jean Sibelius from Finland.

Denmark

Niels Gade (1817–90) was one of the most important Danish musicians in the nineteenth century, noted throughout the Nordic world as well as in England and Germany for his talents both as a conductor and as a composer. He was at the height of his career when he composed *Elverskud* (The Elf-king's Daughter, 1854). A work for soloists, mixed chorus, and orchestra, *Elverskud* has remained the most important choral work from Danish Romanticism due to its use of Nordic colors and its medieval tone. Based mainly on two of Denmark's most famous medieval ballads, with some additions by Gade himself, the work has a simple, uncomplicated structure with an easily understandable mixture of narrative and action. The cantata is divided into three main sections each of which is divided into three subdivisions, and the music alternates between lyrical and dramatic episodes with the choir taking an active part in the drama that unfolds.

Eight years before he wrote *Elverskud*, Gade composed *Comala* (1846), another large work for soloists, mixed chorus, and orchestra, this one inspired by Ossian poetry. After 1850, he composed several other major choral works including the cantatas *Baldurs drøm* (Baldur's Dream, 1857), *Korsfarerne* (The Crusaders, 1866), *Kalanus* (1869), *Zion* (1874), *Psyke* (1882), and *Der Strom* (The River, 1889). Smaller choral works of note are *Frühlingsbotschaft* (1858) to a poem by Emmanuel Geibel and the beautiful and evocative *Ved solnedgang* (At sunset, 1863) to the poem of the Norwegian poet Andreas Munch. Although best known for his symphonic works, Gade's *Fünf Gesänge* Op. 13 (1846) for unaccompanied four-part choir is one of the best examples of his gifts as a composer of small-scale choral works.

Johann Peter Emilius Hartmann (1805–1900) is one Denmark's most important nineteenth-century composers of choral music. His main large choral work, *Vølvens spådom* (The Prophecy of the Völva, 1872) for male choir and orchestra, is based on a text from the elder Eddaic poem. Hartmann also composed a number of special cantatas for the royal family and motets for church services; one of the most significant of these is *Quando corpus morietur* (1850) for three soloists, choir, and strings. Another significant work is Hartmann's collection of ten *Religiøse og folkelige Digte*, Op. 86 (Religious and popular poems, 1888). Fine examples of his many popular student songs include *Sulamith og Solomon* (Sulamith and Solomon) and *Flyv fugl* (Fly bird).

Another important choral composer from the Danish Romantic period (despite a relatively small output of works) was Peter Erasmus Lange-Müller (1850–1926). His *Tre Salmer*, Op. 21 (Three Psalms, 1883) for mixed choir and orchestra is one of his most inspired works on a larger scale. Of his works for unaccompanied chorus, his Serenade *Kornmodsglandsen ved Midnatstid* (Summer lightning, 1879) for male voices must be mentioned, as well as his *Tre Madonnasange*, Op. 65 ("Ave maris stella," "Madonna over bølgerne" ["Madonna over the waves"], and "Salve Regina," 1900) for mixed chorus, which are considered to be some of the most beautiful *a cappella* works in Danish music history.

Like his countryman Niels Gade, Carl Nielsen (1865–1931) is primarily known as a composer of instrumental music, but he also wrote a substantial number of vocal works. Although his output for chorus is small, these works are masterpieces. The earliest of his choral efforts is *Hymnus amoris* (1897), a work in praise of love and a description of its power. Written for soloists, chorus, and orchestra, it was composed after Nielsen studied the music of Palestrina. The text was Nielsen's own, based on the work of the Axel Olrik, which the composer translated into Latin because he thought that the Danish text would give the work a more personal air than he wished.

The rest of Nielsen's music for accompanied chorus was composed after the turn of the century; among these the most noteworthy are *Søvnen* (Sleep, 1904) on a poem by John Jørgensen, and *Fynsk Foraar* (Springtime on Funen, 1921), which includes characteristics from Danish folk tunes. *Tre motetter*, Op. 55 ("Afflictus sum," "Dominus regit me," "Benedictus Dominus," 1929), for varying combinations of unaccompanied voices, reflect Nielsen's neo-Classical style and had a great stylistic influence on later Danish *a cappella* works.

Norway

The strongest representatives of nineteenth-century choral music in Norway are Halfdan Kjerulf (1815–68), Friedrich August Reissiger (1809–83), and Edvard Grieg (1843–1907). Kjerulf is regarded as the creator of the Norwegian lied, but he was also important in the male choir movement. In 1845, he became the first conductor of the Norske Studentersangforening founded by Behrens, and he composed a large number of works and arrangements for them. Additionally, he wrote many others for his own male-voice quartet, which bore his name. *Brudefærden i Hardanger* (1848) with a text by Andreas Munch, belongs to Kjerulf's most well-known works for male choir. It differs from most of his other works written for male chorus in terms of its complexity. Traditional rhythms from Norwegian folk dances—the halling and gangar—that are found in the second part were an important reason why this work became so popular. Today it remains as a symbol of the national Romantic breakthrough in Norway. Other popular male choruses by Kjerulf include *Norges Fjelde* (Norwegian Mountains, 1853) to a poem by Henrik Wergeland; he also arranged a large number of songs from France, Germany, Italy, and England for male chorus. In the 1860s, he composed works for mixed voices, including *Aus der Jugendzeit* and *Tanzlied aus Tyrol*, both of which were published for the first time in connection with a recent edition of his complete works.[2]

The German-born Reissiger came to Norway in 1840 as the choir and orchestra conductor at the Christiania Theater; at that point in his career he had already published a wide range of choral music, as well as songs and works for piano. During his stay in Christiania, he founded a vocal institute comprising 120 singers. With the help of musicians from the theater orchestra, Reissiger performed the oratorios of Graun, Haydn, and Mendelssohn, as well as his own Requiem on the occasion of King Carl Johan's death in 1844. From 1850 until his death, he worked as organist and director of several male choirs in Halden, a town located on the Swedish border in southeast Norway. During this period he composed more than sixty works for male choirs. Of these *En sangers Bøn* (A Singer's Prayer, 1865) and *Olav Trygvason* (1864) are two of the best known.

Apart from the *Dona nobis pacem* (1862) for mixed chorus, Grieg's engagement with choirs and choral music began in the late 1860s, once he settled down in Christiania as a piano teacher and conductor of the Philharmonic Society. When that society was disbanded, Grieg organized several subscription concerts for choir and professional orchestra until 1871, when he formed the Musikforeningen (The Music Society), a predecessor of the Oslo Philharmonic Orchestra. With these societies, Grieg performed cantatas and oratorios by Handel, Mendelssohn, and Schumann, as well as by contemporary Scandinavian composers.

Grieg composed several special choral works for anniversaries and the unveilings of monuments; one such work is the *Holberg* cantata (1884) for unaccompanied male chorus. In this work we notice more of the technique he learned during his time in Leipzig rather than folk-tune inspired melodies. From a historical view, the musical style is very interesting; unfortunately, the text is too closely connected with the bicentennial celebration of the eighteenth-century Norwegian writer Ludvig Holberg's birth in 1684 to be appropriate for performances not linked to that occasion. More important are his arrangements of melodies from L. M. Lindeman's folk-tune collections. These melodies inspired Grieg to compose exciting, challenging music that eventually became part of the standard repertoire for Norwegian male choirs.

The rediscovery of the rich cultural heritage from Norwegian antiquity and the Middle Ages contributed to the increasing patriotism in Norway. As a sign of this development, Grieg created one of his most patriotic and stirring works, *Landkjenning* (Land-sighting) for baritone, male choir, orchestra, and organ Op. 31 (1873). The text, from the poet Bjørnstjerne Bjørnson's drama *Arnljot Gelline*, depicts in dramatic fashion Olav Trygvason's impression of nature's grandeur as he came from England to Norway's coast to become the Norwegian king. Grieg's use of the chorus as both a dramatic and a narrative element presages its similar treatment in the music for Ibsen's drama *Peer Gynt* (1875).[3] Also deserving mention is *Foran Sydens kloster* (In front of a southern convent, 1871), for women's chorus (with soloists) and orchestra.[4]

That Grieg was critical of the Norwegian clergy and their strict religious practices might be a reason why he did not contribute to the renewal of church music. Thanks to his fascination for religious folk tunes, however, he nevertheless arranged some songs with religious texts, including the popular folk tune *Den store hvite flokk*; these songs were published in the *Album for mandssang* Op. 30 (Album of male choir songs, 1878). Grieg's *Ave maris stella* (SSAATTBB arrangement, 1898) is perhaps his most well-known and frequently performed work for unaccompanied mixed voices outside of Scandinavia. It is not this work, however, but his last composition, *Fire Salmer*, Op. 74 (Four Psalms, 1906), a veritable and unsurpassed masterpiece, that is Grieg's most significant *a cappella* choral work, and the one most frequently performed in Norway today. The melodies are from Lindeman's folk-tune collections, and the harmonies are as daring as one hears in his piano works *Norwegian Folk Songs* Op. 66 (1897) and the *Slåtter*, Op. 72 (Peasant dances, 1903). Around the time Op. 74 was composed, Norwegian church music was very conservative and retrospective; thus, Grieg's settings represent something quite exceptional in church music, and also place considerable technical demands on the singers. With its colorful sounds and bold chords, *Fire Salmer* anticipated the musical style of Scandinavian choral works in the twentieth century.

Sweden

A much-beloved Swedish composer with the student community in Uppsala was Gunnar Wennerberg (1817–1901). Mostly self-taught, Wennerberg composed patriotic works for male choirs to his own original texts. Works like *Frihet bor i Norden* (Freedom is living in Scandinavia, 1847), *Stå stark, du ljusets riddarvakt* (Stand strong, you knight guard of the light, 1848), *Hur länge skall Norden* (How long shall the Nordic countries, 1848) and *O Gud, som styrer folkens öden* (O God who rules the people's destiny, 1849) were almost more popular than *Gluntarne*, his immortal collection of duets for male voices and piano. In the 1860s, Wennerberg was mainly concerned with publishing a collection of psalms for soloists and mixed choir with piano. These are spiritual songs in a simple form with melodies based on simple triads that avoid chromaticism. Wennerberg's surprisingly confident, stylish feeling made these songs popular in Christian congregations throughout nineteenth-century Scandinavia.

Another composer who should be mentioned in connection with choral singing in Sweden, is King Oscar I's second son, Prince Gustaf (1827–52). Several of the royal children were musical and participated in male vocal quartets; such involvement gave prestige to choral singing in the Swedish society. Gustaf was known as "the song prince," and by 1846 he had already had success with the spring song, *Glad så som fågeln* (Happy as the bird). His other noteworthy choral songs include *I rosens doft* (In the fragrance of the rose), for which he composed both the text and melody, and *Sjungom studentens lyckliga dag* (Sing about the happy student days), which has remained a highlight within this genre.

Jacob Axel Josephson (1818–80) was influential both as a conductor in Uppsala and as a choral composer. As leader and conductor of the Filharmoniska Sällskap (Philharmonic Society) and the university orchestra, he performed all the major choral works from the Classical and Romantic periods. In 1853, he took over directorship of the Orphei Drängar and turned it into an outstanding men's chorus. He wrote several songs that remain in the repertoire today; of special mention among these are *Vårt land* (Our country, 1850), *Stärnorna tindrar* (The stars are shining, 1852), and *Vårliga vindar draga* (Spring breezes propel, 1850). He also composed cantatas and church music, including his well-regarded Requiem, also for men's voices.

In Lund, Otto Lindblad (1808–64) led the students' singing movement from 1830. He began by having the Lund University Student Singing Society (Lunds Studentsångförening) sing songs by Spohr, Friedrich Kuhlau, Mendelssohn, Rossini, and Meyerbeer, but gradually he began to compose for the ensemble himself. Among his more than seventy works for male choirs *Til skogs en liten fågel flög* (To the forest a little bird flies), *Ångbåtssång* (Steamboat Song) and *Orpheus sjöng* (Orpheus is singing), remain popular with student male choruses in Sweden.

Finland

Because Finland had been subject to Swedish rule for years, its official language was Swedish, and even after the country became a grand duchy under the Russian Empire in 1809, the Swedish language and culture continued to be important there. Still, the patriotic currents in Europe also affected the developments in Finland, which little by little tried to advance its cultural independence. As in Norway, the first step was to promote the original language of the country, Finnish, which is a Finno-Ugric (Uralic) language rather than a Germanic language like Danish, Norwegian, and Swedish. After the national epic *Kalevala* was published in 1835, Finnish also began to be used more and more in the literary medium, and toward the end of the nineteenth century, it made its way into the theater, visual art, and music.

In 1882, Helsinki saw the creation of its own music conservatory, as well as the first professional symphony orchestra in the Nordic world. The following year the first Finnish-language choir was formed at the university, the Helsinki University Chorus (Ylioppilaskunnan Laulajat). The male choir movement was expanding across the region, and just as in the other Nordic countries, this choir became an important promoter of the growing patriotic feeling in the people. This ensemble formed the core of the male chorus Jean Sibelius (1865–1957) used when he held the premiere of *Kullervo* (1892), an important early symphonic work for two soloists, male chorus, and orchestra that embodied Finnish culture both musically and in its use of Finnish texts from *Kalevala*.[5] Although *Kullervo* was Sibelius's breakthrough work as a symphonist, there is no doubt that the vocal movements were the reason why the music was so well received.

The following year he began to compose a series of *a cappella* works for the choir, which from now on became the leading choir to perform Sibelius's choral music for men's voices. One of the most significant examples from the period are the six partsongs Op. 18 (1893–1901), which include many of the most popular Finnish songs for male choirs. Some of the texts used are taken from the Finnish language folk epics *Kalevala* and *Kanteletar*; he also used poems by the author Aleksis Kivi, who wrote the first novel in the Finnish language. Additionally, Sibelius wrote works for male or mixed choir (rarely for women's choir), some with soloists and some requiring orchestral accompaniment. One of the most famous of these works is *Rakastava* (The Beloved, 1894), a work he originally composed for unaccompanied male voices but later arranged several times, including one version for mixed voices.

The music Sibelius wrote for choir and orchestra around the turn of the century such as *Tulen synty* (The origin of fire, 1902) for baritone, male choir, and orchestra that was composed for the opening of the Finnish National Theater, is on a scale that makes them equal to the many symphonic poems Sibelius composed during the same period. At this time the tension between the Finnish and Russian authorities was increasing, and Sibelius used this occasion to highlight his anti-Russian position by using a *Kalevala* poem for *Tulen synty* in an allegorical way as a protest.[6] The patriotic song *Isänmaalle* (To the Fatherland), on a poem by Paavo Cajander, had similar national significance and was published in different choir versions, first for mixed chorus (1900) and later arranged for men's voices (1908). The purpose of these works and many others (*Finlandia* among them, of course) was to encourage patriotism, and through these efforts Sibelius's music became a unifying symbol in the years before Finland declared its independence in 1917.

Notes

1 Singing also played an important role in Methodist, Baptist, Pentecostal, the Salvation Army, and other Christian revival movements that were also allowed to establish congregations during the second half of the century.
2 Nils Grinde, *Halfdan Kjerulfs samlede verker*, bd. 1–5 (Oslo: Musikhuset A/S, 1977–98).
3 A noteworthy choral moment in *Peer Gynt* is the harmonized Pentecost hymn, "Velsignede morgen" ("Oh Blessed Morning") that is sung near the end of the play; just as in Solveig's famous Cradle song ("Solveigs vuggevise"), which immediately follows it, this hymn contains one of the most beautiful melodies Grieg ever wrote.
4 *Foran Sydens kloster* and *Landkjenning* were the forerunners of Bjørnson's and Grieg's collaborative opera project, *Olav Trygvason*. The opera was never more than a fragment, but in the first three stages Grieg completed, the choir plays a central role. These were revised, orchestrated, and published in 1889.
5 A native Swedish speaker, Sibelius learned Finnish as a second language; according to a member of the chorus, Sibelius had to run rehearsals in Finnish, Swedish, and German to communicate with all the participants involved. See Andrew Barnett, CD booklet for *Kullervo* (BIS-CD-1215, Lahti Symphony Orchestra, Helsinki University Chorus; Osmo Vänskä, conductor; 2000), 3.
6 The text was so controversial that in the beginning Sibelius used the title *Siell' laulavi kunigatar* (There the queen is singing).

Selected Bibliography

The principal publishers of Nordic choral music at present are: Edition Wilhelm Hansen (Denmark; http://www.ewh.dk/), Norsk Musikforlag (Norway; http://www.norskmusikforlag.no), Norsk Korsenter AS (Norway; http://www.norskkorsenter.com/templates/home.asp), Gehrmans musikförlag (Sweden; http://www.gehrmans.se/), Sulasol (Finland; http://www.sulasol.fi/en/sheet/), and Fennica Gehrman (Finland; http://www.fennicagehrman.fi/sheet.php).

Andersson, Greger, ed. *Musik i Norden*. Stockholm: Musikaliska akadamien, 1997.

Foster, Beryl. *Edvard Grieg: The Choral Music*. Aldershot, England: Ashgate, 1999.

Herresthal, Harald. *Med spark i gulvet og quinter i bassen. Musikalske og politiske bilder fra nasjonalromantikkens gjennombrudd*. Oslo: Universitetsforlaget, 1993.

Jonsson, Leif. *Ljusets riddarvakt. 1800–talets studentsång utövad som offentlig samhällskonst*. Ph.D. diss. Uppsala University, 1990.

Lysdahl, Anne Jorunn Kydland. *Studentersang i Norge på 1800–tallet*. Oslo: Solum, 1995.

Musikken i Sverige. Den nationella identiteten 1810–1920. Ed. Leif Jonsson. Stockholm: Fisher and Co., 1992.

Norges musikkhistorie. Vols. 2 and 3. Ed. Arvid Vollsnes. Oslo: Aschehoug, 2000 and 1999.

Schiørring, Nils. *Musikens Historie i Danmark*, Vols. 2 and 3. København: Politikens Forlag, 1978.

Tawaststjerna, Erik. *Sibelius*. Vol. 1: 1865–1905. Trans. Robert Layton. Berkeley: University of California Press, 1976.

Eastern Europe

22

EASTERN EUROPE

Introductory Thoughts

Barbara Milewski

Swarthmore College

Any discussion of Eastern European choral music of the nineteenth century holds unique challenges. How do we discuss distinct national choral music traditions born and nurtured in an age of multiethnic empires and against the backdrop of shifting boundaries and socio-political realities? And how do our present-day geopolitical conceptions of modern countries such as Poland, the Czech Republic, Hungary, and Russia shape our understanding of these vibrant but culturally distant nineteenth-century choral traditions? Decades after communism's collapse, our knowledge of the region's choral music is fragmentary at best, a consequence, in large part, of a half century of Cold War politics, language barriers, and limited scholarly exchange. It is thus important for us to approach these choral developments not only on their own terms—that is, as the unique products of both empire building and national striving, and the myriad ways such agendas more often than not intersected—but also as formative musical contributions that now culturally define autonomous (and far more homogenous) Eastern European nations today.

Beyond these rather global concerns, there are the more immediate difficulties of registering the specific political conditions that fostered each of the four national choral traditions touched on in this chapter. At the end of the eighteenth century, Poland, then known as the Polish-Lithuanian Commonwealth, was divided among Russia, Prussia, and Austria, and eradicated from the map of Europe, creating distinct socio-cultural circumstances that differentiated choral music development in each of the three foreign-controlled territories during the nineteenth century. At the same time, Hungary and the Czech lands of Bohemia and Moravia were subject to Habsburg imperial authority and tolerated (to lesser or greater extents) Austro-German cultural hegemony, with only the Dual Monarchy of Austria-Hungary bringing domestic self-rule to Hungary in 1867. And while Russia was not subject to foreign political dominance, attempts to move away from a century of Western musical influence and establish a choral music practice based on indigenous Russian vocal traditions paralleled nationalist impulses in other parts of Eastern Europe.

Then there is the matter of geographic place names. The shift from national strivings in the nineteenth century to full-fledged, independent national identities in the twenty-first—not to mention the various geopolitical realities of the twentieth century in between—has rendered an Eastern Europe defined over time in multiple languages, its cities still known to us today by names that bear the traces of shifting national boundaries, and periods of foreign occupation. For the purpose of these chapters focusing on Eastern Europe, then, we have provided place names as they were most commonly used in the nineteenth century, followed by modern-day place designations, that is, names one would encounter more recently, or if traveling the region today.

Despite the unique geopolitical and socio-cultural circumstances that prevailed upon different developing choral traditions across Eastern Europe, generally speaking we can see some common trends. With the exception of the Polish territories, all-male choirs dominated the Eastern European choral music landscape until the last quarter of the century, when women's and mixed choirs began to flourish alongside them. Public sacred concerts, ever more popular in the regions under discussion here as the century progressed, allowed for sacred choral works to be heard in extra-liturgical settings (as was the case in other parts of Europe). Finally, socio-political changes after the revolutions and reforms of the 1860s led to the emergence of greater numbers of vibrant choral music societies that, though largely amateur, did an enormous service to the development and advancement of separate national choral traditions.

23

POLAND

Barbara Milewski

SWARTHMORE COLLEGE

Polish choral music during the course of the nineteenth century developed rather modestly and haphazardly due to varying forms of political and cultural repression imposed by the partitioning powers. Early in the century, music societies were established either to support the performance quality of sacred music, or more generally to improve musical life in urban centers of former Poland: most notably Warszawa (Warsaw); Cracow or Kraków (then as now the terms have been used interchangeably) and Lemberg (Lwów, Lviv) in the Galician region of the Austrian Empire; and Prussian-ruled Danzig (Gdańsk), Posen (Poznań) and Łódź. These efforts, however, were characteristically isolated and at times short lived.[1] With the rise of choral societies in numerous urban and provincial locales across the territories in the second half of the century, however, and especially in its last two decades, concerts of religious music increased not only in churches, but also in other venues, as did the performance of secular vocal music, bringing a more vibrant musical culture to many parts of the dissolved Polish-Lithuanian Commonwealth.[2]

Throughout the century, Warsaw, Poland's former capital, maintained its status as the center of Polish musical life. There, already during the first half of the century, composers such as Józef Elsner (1769–1854; Chopin's teacher) and Karol Kurpiński (1785–1857) made valuable contributions to Polish opera, as well as to other vocal genres, including choral music. Among Elsner's more note-worthy sacred choral works is his ambitious oratorio, *Passio Domini Nostri Jesu Christi*, Op. 65 (1835–37) for fourteen solo voices, three mixed choirs, and orchestra; it was intended to replace the *Stabat Maters* of Pergolesi, Haydn, and Peter von Winter that were frequently performed on Good Friday.[3] Arranged in four parts, with Latin texts taken from the gospels of Saint Matthew and Saint Mark, the Book of Psalms, and religious hymns, Elsner includes twenty-seven musical numbers, using one women's and two mixed choirs to represent angels, Christians and Jews, respectively. A late-classical style prevails, though there are moments, especially the Marsz żałobny (Funeral March) to begin Part IV and the operatic Finale, that display early Romantic musical sensibilities.[4]

Like Elsner, Kurpiński wrote a number of secular cantatas, often to nationalist texts meant to preserve a sense of Polish identity by underscoring the nation's more illustrious past. He also wrote numerous patriotic songs, among them *Warszawianka* (The Song of Warsaw, 1831) and *Marsz Obozowy* (Camp March, 1831), both battle cries composed in response to the November Uprising of 1830–31. Originally scored for soloist, mixed choir, and orchestra, these songs exist today in various choral arrangements, a testament to their unwavering popularity as expressions of Polish nationalism.

Stanisław Moniuszko's (1819–72) vocal compositions dominated the second half of the century. Though his choral works remain overshadowed by his operatic achievements, Moniuszko himself preferred to compose cantatas: "The most tempting form for me is not opera but rather the cantata, which has over opera an incalculable superiority on every account. It is time to examine the extent to which opera is nothing but a resolute absurdity."[5] Of particular note are his secular cantatas *Widma* (The Phantoms) composed sometime before 1859, and *Sonety krymskie* (Crimean Sonnets, 1867), both settings of texts by the important nineteenth-century Polish poet Adam Mickewicz for solo voices, mixed choir, and orchestra. Active in the Roman Catholic religious life of Vilna (Wilno, Vilnius), where he lived before taking up post as director of Polish productions at the *Wielki* Theater in Warsaw in 1858, Moniuszko also wrote the four cantata-like *Litanie ostrobramskie* (The Ostra Brama Litanies, 1843–55), settings of Latin Marian texts for solo voices, mixed choir, and orchestra in honor of the Ostra Brama Madonna.[6] Though designed for the small scale of the chapel in which the shrine is housed, and composed with amateur performers in mind, the Litanies nonetheless impress by the richness of their musical invention, notably Litany III (dedicated to Gioachino Rossini) and Litany IV where they adopt a more dramatic tone, ambitious harmonic language, and a cohesive design. And while Litany II alone reveals a folk-inspired directness, all four strike the listener as intimate confessions of Moniuszko's deeply held religious faith. Given their beauty and accessible style, they certainly merit wider performance outside of Poland.[7]

Moniuszko also wrote numerous songs for mixed, women's and men's choirs that achieved widespread popularity. But it was the songs he wrote for voice and piano accompaniment, published within a twelve-volume series titled *Spiewniki domowy* (Songbooks for Home Use), that frequently served in various choral arrangements as the basis for repertoire performed by Polish choral societies across the Russian, Prussian, and Austrian territories.[8]

Such choral music societies did much to popularize ensemble singing. The first Polish choral organizations, modeled after German singing societies and decidedly of a patriotic character, were formed in the 1860s in the Prussian-occupied Wielkopolska region including Posen, but these efforts were variously limited by inadequate skill, repertoire, organization or public support.[9] By the last quarter of the century, however, a substantially greater number of societies sprang up in the region and, indeed, in other parts of former Poland. In the Grand Duchy of Posen, amateur Polish church and secular choirs served as a defense against Bismarck's *Kulturkampf* campaign begun in 1870.[10] Among secular choral organizations, arrangements of folk songs, real or invented, were highly favored. Also programmed were compositions by Moniuszko, Kurpiński, and lesser-known Polish composers such as Bolesław Dembiński (1833–1914), Ignacy Feliks Dobrzyński (1807–67), Stanisław Niewiadomski (1859–1936), and Zygmunt Noskowski (1846–1909). Men's, women's, and mixed church choirs, like their secular counterparts, often performed Polish repertoire alongside compositions by foreign composers, most often Haydn, Rossini, Mendelssohn, and Mozart. Significantly, there were also many German Protestant church choirs, which until the last decade of the century were more numerous and skilled than virtually any Polish Catholic church choir.

In Austrian-controlled Polish Galicia, Lemberg and Cracow were major centers of choral music activity. Lemberg in particular boasted the men's "Lutnia" society founded in 1880. Its success inspired numerous imitations, most notably in Warsaw in 1886 under Piotr Maszyński's direction, where a women's choir was also formed and, with the men's, occasionally performed mixed choir repertoire.[11] Russian-controlled Łódź was home to the Jewish Hazomir Choral Society founded in 1899 and successfully directed first by Joseph Rumshinsky, then Zavel Zilberts and others. Modeled after secular Polish choral groups and established to strengthen a secular Jewish cultural identity, the mixed choir performed a wide-ranging repertoire of Handel, Haydn, and Mendelssohn oratorios; Mozart's and Cherubini's Requiems performed either in the original language or translated into Yiddish; arrangements of Jewish folk songs; and at least one work by Moniuszko.[12]

In summary, Poland's status as a partitioned country greatly hampered musical development of any sort, especially after 1830. What music-making there was, therefore, was invariably dominated by concepts of nationalism. In the realm of choral compositions and arrangements, this meant that regardless of whether or not texts could communicate patriotic sentiments unequivocally, folk-inspired musical elements such as lydian fourths and mazurka and polonaise dance rhythms further marked works as distinctly Polish. Moreover, the desire to sustain Poland culturally motivated the creation of Polish choral music societies that promoted works by Polish composers. Thus despite the challenges of lost independence, one can find noteworthy contributions to a distinctly Polish choral music tradition, one born of revolutionary and patriotic songs arranged for choirs,[13] religious works written in Latin and the vernacular, and secular cantatas giving voice to rousing nationalist sentiments penned by some of Poland's most famous nineteenth-century poets.

Notes

1 See Jolanta T. Pekacz, *Music in the Culture of Polish Galicia: 1772–1914* (Rochester: University of Rochester Press, 2002), 124–43; Barbara Zakrzewska-Nikiporczyk, "Działalność wielkopolskich chórów kościelnych w latach 1870–1918" [The Activities of *Wielkopolska* Church Choirs During the Years 1870–1918], *Muzyka* 22, 3 (1977): 62; Halina Goldberg, *Music in Chopin's Warsaw* (Oxford and New York: Oxford University Press, 2008), 257–73.

2 No comprehensive study of nineteenth-century Polish choral music in either Polish or English exists that encompasses all of the partitioned territories. For a detailed examination of choral music in the Prussian territories see, Barbara Zakrzewska-Nikiporczyk, "Działalność wielkopolskich chórów kościelnych w latach 1870–1918," and Barbara Zakrzewska-Nikiporczyk, "Z dziejów polskiego świeckiego ruchu śpiewaczego w Wielkim Księstwie Poznańskim" [On the History of the Polish Secular Choral Movement in the Grand Duchy of Poznań] *Muzyka* 24, 2 (1979): 95–112. For a very fine summary of music-making in Polish Galicia see, Pekacz, *Music in the Culture of Polish Galicia: 1772–1914*; and for a thorough treatment of the activities of choral music societies in Russian-controlled Poland, and specifically Warsaw see, Irena Chomik, "Warszawskie Towarzystwo Śpiewacze 'Lutnia' w latach 1886–1914 [The Warsaw Choral Society '*Lutnia*' During the Years 1886–1914], *Szkice o kulturze muzycznej XIX w.* [Essays on Nineteenth-Century Musical Culture], ed. Zofia Chechlińska, (Warsaw: Państwowe Wydawnictwo Naukowe, 1971), 163–317.

3 Alina Nowak-Romanowicz, *Józef Elsner*, (Kraków: Polskie Wydawnictwo Muzyczne, 1957), 227–28.

4 Nowak-Romanowicz, *Józef Elsner*, 229–39. Nowak-Romanowicz argues that the Marsz żałobny is stylistically modeled after the "Marcia funebre" of Beethoven's Third Symphony. When the piece was first performed on 20, 22 and 25 June 1838 in Warsaw's Lutheran Church of the Holy Trinity (the church was among the most musically active sites in the city at the time), the piece involved no fewer than 400 musicians and was directed by Kurpiński. Later, the piece was dedicated to Tsar Nicolas I. In addition to this most monumental work, Elsner wrote three modest oratorios, and over 80 offertories, graduals and hymns. Of his 33 masses, nine are written in the vernacular, including a folk mass. The composer also wrote numerous secular cantatas, mostly for state and private celebrations, but the vast majority of these compositions are now lost. For a catalog of works see, Nowak-Romanowicz, *Józef Elsner*, 265–326.

5 Letter from Moniuszko to Józef Ignacy Kraszewski as cited in Józef Reiss, *Najpiękniejsza ze wszystkich jest muzyka polska: szkic historycznego rozwoju na tle przeobrażeń społecznych z licznymi przykładami muzycznymi i z 50 ilustracjami* [The Most Beautiful of All is Polish Music: A Study of Its Historical Evolution against the Backdrop of Social Transformations with Numerous Musical Examples and 50 Illustrations], (Kraków: T. Gieszczykiewicz, 1946), 147.

6 The Ostra Brama icon of the Virgin Mary, which dates from the seventeenth century, is housed in a small chapel located in the last remaining city gate of Vilnius; it is one of the most important symbols of the city. The cult of the Ostra Brama Madonna, begun after the partitions, lives on among Poles, Lithuanians, and Belorussians, and is venerated by Roman and Greek Catholics and Orthodox alike.

7 Scores for this and other works of Polish choral music can be obtained through *Polskie Wydawnictwo Muzyczne* (PWM) in Kraków: http://www.pwm.com.pl.

8 Zakrzewska-Nikiporczyk, "Z dziejów polskiego świeckiego ruchu śpiewaczego w Wielkim Księstwie Poznańskim," 109, and Chomik, "Warszawskie Towarzystwo Śpiewacze 'Lutnia' w latach 1886–1914," 293–310.

9 Chomik, "Warszawskie Towarzystwo Śpiewacze 'Lutnia' w latach 1886–1914," 167. Of course, societies for the performance of sacred music, such as the St. Cecilia Society, already existed in Warsaw earlier in

the century, and more ambitious performances during Holy Week of works by Haydn and Mozart, involving both amateurs and professionals, were not uncommon. There were also numerous choirs in existence before this time. But choral music societies organized by Poles for the express purpose of singing not only well-known Classical repertoire but also secular Polish repertoire did not arise until the second half of the century.

10 The term *Kulturkampf* (cultural struggle) was first applied in Bismarck's Prussia to efforts to suppress the Catholic Church. The policy soon after came to embrace the struggle against the Polish minority in Prussian Poland, with Poles becoming subject to ever-greater socio-cultural repressions.

11 Chomik, "Warszawskie Towarzystwo Śpiewacze 'Lutnia' w latach 1886–1914," 168–77.

12 See Joseph Rumshinsky, *Klangen Fun Mayn Lebn* [Sounds from My Life] (New York: Biderman, 1944), 194–98; Joshua Jacobson, "Choirs," in *Encyclopedia Judaica*, ed. Fred Skolnik and Michael Berenbaum (Detroit: Thomas Gale, 2007), 2nd ed., vol. 4, 662.

13 See Jan Prosnak, "Powstanie styczniowe w muzyce 1863–1963" [The January Uprising in Music 1863–1963], *Muzyka* 8, 1–2 (1963): 127–69.

Selected Bibliography

Chechlińska, Zofia, ed. *Szkice o kulturze muzycznej XIX w.* [Essays on Nineteenth-Century Musical Culture], vols. 2, 4. Warsaw: Państwowe Wydawnictwo Naukowe, 1973, 1980.

Chomik, Irena. "Warszawskie Towarzystwo Śpiewacze 'Lutnia' w latach 1886–1914" [The Warsaw Choral Society '*Lutnia*' During the Years 1886–1914], in *Szkice o kulturze muzycznej XIX w.* [Essays on Nineteenth-Century Musical Culture], vol. 1, ed. Zofia Chechlińska. Warsaw: Państwowe Wydawnictwo Naukowe, 1971, 163–317.

Goldberg, Halina. *Music in Chopin's Warsaw*. Oxford and New York: Oxford University Press, 2008.

Jacobson, Joshua. "Choirs," in *Encyclopedia Judaica*, 2nd ed., vol. 4, ed. Fred Skolnik and Michael Berenbaum. Detroit: Thomas Gale, 2007, 662.

Nowak-Romanowicz, Alina. *Józef Elsner*. Kraków: Polskie Wydawnictwo Muzyczne, 1957.

——. *Klasycyzm 1750–1830. Historia muzyki polskiej*, vol. 4, ed. Stefan Sutkowski. Warsaw: Sutkowski Edition, 1995.

Pekacz, Jolanta T. *Music in the Culture of Polish Galicia: 1772–1914*. Rochester: University of Rochester Press, 2002.

Prosnak, Jan. "Powstanie styczniowe w muzyce 1863–1963" [The January Uprising in Music 1863–1963]. *Muzyka* 8 (1963): 127–69.

Przybylski, Tadeusz. *Karol Kurpiński*. Warsaw: Państwowe Wydawnictwo Naukowe, 1980.

Reiss, Józef. *Najpiękniejsza ze wszystkich jest muzyka polska: szkic historycznego rozwoju na tle przeobrażeń społecznych z licznymi przykładami muzycznymi i z 50 ilustracjami* [The Most Beautiful of All is Polish Music: A Study of Its Historical Evolution against the Backdrop of Social Transformations with Numerous Musical Examples and 50 Illustrations]. Kraków: T. Gieszczykiewicz, 1946.

Rumshinsky, Joseph. *Klangen Fun Mayn Lebn* [Sounds from My Life]. New York: Biderman, 1944.

Strumiłło, Tadeusz. *Szkice z polskiego życia muzycznego XIX wieku* [Essays on Polish Musical Life of the Nineteenth Century]. Małe Monografie Muzyczne [Short Musical Monographs], vol. 5, ed. Stefania Łobaczewska. Kraków: Polskie Wydawnictwo Muzyczne, 1956.

Zakrzewska-Nikiporczyk, Barbara. "Działalność wielkopolskich chórów kościelnych w latach 1870–1918" [The Activities of *Wielkopolska* Church Choirs During the Years 1870–1918]. *Muzyka* 22 (1977): 61–73.

——. "Z dziejów polskiego świeckiego ruchu śpiewaczego w Wielkim Księstwie Poznańskim" [On the History of the Polish Secular Choral Movement in the Grand Duchy of Poznań]. *Muzyka* 24 (1979): 95–112.

24

THE CZECH LANDS

Bohemia and Moravia

Judith Mabary

UNIVERSITY OF MISSOURI, COLUMBIA

For a major portion of its history, the choral tradition of Bohemia and Moravia—the area known today as the Czech Republic[1]—was most vibrant in its sacred repertoire. Under the patronage of Charles IV (1316–78), choristers at the Cathedral of St. Vitus in Prague numbered 150.[2] In the sixteenth century, members of the working class are reported to have been able to join the church choirs in singing music in several parts.[3] Yet dominated for much of their existence by foreign powers, the Czech lands failed to achieve a distinctive voice until the mid-1800s when a prevailing spirit of dissatisfaction with political leadership based in Vienna led to numerous manifestations of national pride in the arts.

Forecasting this emergence was Jakub Jan Ryba (1765–1815). Among approximately 100 masses, including several written in Czech, is his still popular folk-tinged *Česká mše vánoční* (Czech Christmas Mass, 1796) for soloists, mixed chorus, orchestra and organ.[4] Jan Antonín Kozeluch (1738–1814), the great contrapuntalist, contributed approximately 400 sacred works, many of which were completed during the last thirty years of his career, while serving as choirmaster for Prague's St. Vitus Cathedral, the most coveted church position in Bohemia. The sacred repertoire was expanded further in the conservative masses and partsongs of Václav Jan Tomášek (1774–1850) and Jan August Vitašek (1770–1839), the latter of whom succeeded Kozeluch as choirmaster at St. Vitus. All of these composers adopted the tradition of Mozart to some degree in their works, representing a continuation of the Classical style into the nineteenth century. Deserving special mention are Tomášek's Requiem in C minor, Op. 70 (1820), for four soloists, chorus, and orchestra, which the composer himself considered successful in satisfying the most stringent artistic demands of the genre and worthy to take its place among even the most well-known Requiems,[5] and Vitášek's *Hymnus pastoralis Adeste fideles* for bass solo, mixed chorus, strings, and organ with *ad libitum* flute, bassoon, and two horns.[6]

More progressive, reflecting characteristics of the late musical style of Mozart as well as those of Beethoven and Schubert, was the music of Jan Václav Voříšek (1791–1825), who, at the end of his career, served as court organist in Vienna. Intended for performance by the court choir, his Mass in B-flat major, Op. 24 (1824) for soloists, mixed chorus, and orchestra achieved such popularity that it was programmed regularly for much of the nineteenth century. While clearly indebted to the late classical style, Voříšek writes with melodic and harmonic invention, rich in thirds and sixths, and sprinkled with imitative counterpoint, resulting in a satisfying and effective work that deserves a place in the present repertoire.

Throughout Europe, a crucial performance force for new music in the 1800s resided in the growing number of choral societies, and in this respect Bohemia and Moravia followed suit. Although the Prague Hlahol was among the most important of the Bohemian choral groups in the nineteenth century, it was by no means the first. Founded in 1861, this ensemble joined the ranks of numerous other Bohemian and Moravian choral societies with similar artistic goals that focused on providing performance opportunities for amateur singers.[7] Among the earliest of these organizations was the Cecilská hudební jednota (Music Union of St. Cecilia) founded in 1803 in the town of Wildenschwert (Ústí nad Orlicí).[8] Many years later, in 1840, the Žofínská akademie (Žofín Academy) and the Cecilská jednota (St. Cecilia Union) were organized in Prague, the latter group with as many as 120 members in its adult men's chorus plus a boys' choir that numbered sixty.[9] Many towns to the west and east witnessed the formation of societies in the coming years: Slavoj (1856) in Chrudim, Dobroslav (1858) in Kollin (Kolín), Hlahol (1860) in Nimburg (Nymburk), and Hlahol (1862) in Pilsen (Plzeň). Similarly in Moravia, the capital city of Brünn (Brno) was home to some of the most important organizations of amateur singers of this period, among them the Beseda brněnská (1860) established by Pavel Křížkovský, a leading figure in joining Moravian folk tradition with choral music, and Svatopluk (1868), which in the mid-1870s boasted the young Leoš Janáček as its choirmaster.

Naturally, the enthusiasm for choral singing manifested in these emerging, mostly all-male societies increased the demand for new music. Answering the call frequently fell to the groups' conductors. Karel Bendl (1838–97), one of the most popular composers of his day, wrote the majority of his choral works for the Prague Hlahol, which he directed from 1865 to 1877. In addition to the Czech-language repertory, he also programmed pieces by German and French composers, including Ambroise Thomas, Gounod, Mendelssohn, Liszt, and Wagner.[10] For a short period, Bendl served as president of the Jednota zpěváckých spolků českoslovanských (Union of Czech Choral Societies), which by 1950, its final year, had a membership of 12,568 (7,381 men and 5,187 women).[11]

Brno-based Pavel Křížkovský (1820–85), founder of the Männergesangverein in 1848 and the Beseda brněnská (which he conducted from 1860 to 1863), was a dedicated nationalist, promoting vocal music set to texts in his native Czech language. Among the most popular of his many choral compositions was *Utonulá* (The Drowned Maiden, 1848, rev. 1860) for male chorus. In this work, a tranquil folk-like melody is skillfully supported by consonant lower voices—the resulting harmonies elegantly beautiful in their simplicity—so that even when dissonant clashes and minor inflections required by the text intrude, they fail to disrupt the prevailing serenity of the work.

As was the case with many composers from the Czech lands, Křížkovský was attracted to the folk music of Moravia, and particularly to the work being conducted by František Sušil, as a basis for his unaccompanied male choruses.[12] Křížkovský's choral works impacted even the most iconic of Czech composers, Bedřich Smetana (1824–84), who admitted that it was only after becoming familiar with Křížkovský's scores that he understood the true significance of folk melody.[13]

Smetana's position as the standard bearer of Czech national identity in music gains support not only from his operas, but also from his choral works, many of which were written for the Prague Hlahol. More at home in German, the official language of his homeland, than in his native Czech, Smetana's first choral excursions were settings of German and Latin texts. By 1862, however, with the completion of *Tři jezdci* (The Three Riders), an unaccompanied work for male chorus, he shows a growing confidence in setting the vernacular. Of his subsequent thirteen choral works, eight are scored TTBB, continuing to reflect the vibrant Czech tradition of the male choral ensemble. Certainly one of his greatest contributions to this repertoire is the large-scale *Píseň na moři* (Song of the Sea, 1877), written to a text by Vítězslav Hálek (1834–74), whose lyric poetry, aimed at realism and anchored in nature, was especially popular during his lifetime. With its demanding narrative for male chorus, divided into several contrasting episodes depicting both the excitement and the loneliness of a sea voyage, *Píseň na moři* was considered too virtuosic for Prague's amateur singers. It has subsequently attained recognition, however, as among the best works in the Czech choral literature. Among Smetana's more intimate works are the three choruses for female voices (*Sbory trojhlasné pro ženské hlasy*; SSA) completed in 1878: *Má hvězda* (My Star) with its ethereal harmonies and subdued dynamics, *Přiletěly vlaštovičky* (Return of the Swallows) exuding the rhythmic vitality of a carefree dance, and *Za hory slunce zapadá* (The Sun Sets behind the Mountain) with its air of subdued restraint.

Though much of his career lies in the twentieth century, Leoš Janáček (1854–1928) also made significant contributions to the nineteenth-century choral repertoire. A student of Křížkovský at the Augustinian Monastery in Brno, Janáček was greatly influenced in his early works by his teacher's style and commitment to folk tradition. Among the choruses in which this indebtedness is evident, in part via the gentle contours of folk-like melodies, are *Oráni* (Plowing, 1873), *Válečná* (War Song, 1873), *Nestálost lásky* (The Fickleness of Love, 1873), *Osamělá bez útěchy* (Alone without Comfort, 1874), all written while Janáček was serving as choirmaster for Svatopluk, a choral society of working-class men. The seriousness with which these amateur singers regarded their responsibility to the group is evident in Janáček's commendation: "nowhere have I found such devotion, diligence, love and assiduousness among singers."[14] In 1876, Janáček was selected as choirmaster for the men's choral society Beseda brněnská. In only a few months, he expanded the group into a mixed chorus with singers from the monastery and students from the Slovanský ústav ku vzdělání učitelů (Teachers' Training Institute), amassing as many as 250 voices and a sizable orchestra for performances of large-scale classic works.[15] In addition to extending the repertoire to include selections such as Mozart's Requiem (1878) and Beethoven's *Missa solemnis* (1879), he also championed his friend Dvořák (programming the *Stabat Mater* in 1882 and *Svatební košile* [The Spectre's Bride] in 1888) as well as his own new works.[16]

This overview mentions only a few of the more prolific and influential contributors to nineteenth-century Czech choral music. Yet many of those omitted are, nonetheless, integral to the complete story, including František Doubravský (1790–1867), a church musician in northern Bohemia whose numerous sacred works for his congregation reveal the typical "small-town Kapellmeister laboring in the Czech lands during the first half of the century";[17] Jan Bedřich Kittl (1806–68), whose unaccompanied male choruses display a patriotic tone at a key point in Bohemia's struggle for national recognition; the Prague-based Jan Malát (1843–1915), with his numerous and very popular choral arrangements of folk songs that added significantly to the repertoire for amateur ensembles; and Josef Bohuslav Foerster (1859–1951), also based in Prague, whose early settings of Czech texts for male voices in the late nineteenth century represent only the first of a career total of over three hundred choral works.

The indisputable zenith of choral music from this region flows from the pen of Antonín Dvořák. So great is his importance that a separate chapter (Chapter 25) is devoted to his contributions. Yet, though his choral works are the most well-known outside the Czech lands and deserve recognition as among the best this region has to offer, it is important to remember that the soil from which they grew and drew inspiration was indisputably fertile.

Notes

1 In the nineteenth century, what we now call the Czech Republic was divided into two distinct countries: Bohemia, with Prague as its provincial capital, and Moravia, with its corresponding seat of government in Brünn (Brno). Both Bohemia and Moravia were part of the Austro-Hungarian empire, with legislative oversight centered in Vienna. The Hungarian portion of the empire counted Slovakia among its holdings until 1918, when the regions of Bohemia, Moravia, and Slovakia joined to become the single nation of Czechoslovakia.

2 Rosa Newmarch, *The Music of Czechoslovakia* (New York: Da Capo Press, 1978), 6.

3 Jindřich Hantich, *La Musique Tchéque* (Paris, 1907) as reported in Newmarch, *The Music of Czechoslovakia*, 8.

4 Ryba's Christmas Mass is classified as a pastoral Mass, not unrelated to the pastorella. The pastorella is similar to a cantata, with sections for soloists and chorus to orchestral accompaniment. The subject matter is more confined, however, focusing on the pastoral elements of the Christmas story, particularly the response of the shepherds and peasants to the star of Bethlehem and the birth of the Christ child. The score for Ryba's Mass is currently available in a piano reduction from Editio Bärenreiter Praha. In 1973, Editio Supraphon, the publishing arm of which has since been purchased by Bärenreiter, issued an orchestral version of the work. This version is not included in the present Bärenreiter catalog but may be acquired from various libraries through interlibrary loan.

5 Václav Jan Tomášek. *Vlastní životopis Václava Jana Tomáška* (Prague: Topičova edice, 1941), 213. The score for this work is not commercially available; however, copies from the early 1800s are listed in the library catalogs of several academic centers, including the British Library and Columbia University in New York. The piece was first published by the firm of Marco Berra under the title *Hymni in sacro pro defunctis cantari soliti* (ibid., 214).

6 The scores to Vitášek's works are almost entirely confined to libraries. *Hymnus pastoralis Adeste fideles*, however, is still available for purchase from Dr. J. Butz Musikverlag (http://www.butz-verlag.de/).

7 The fervor of choral singing spread quickly. According to Sayer, Bohemia had 655 male, female, and mixed choral societies by 1888. See Derek Sayer, *The Coasts of Bohemia: A Czech History* (Princeton: Princeton University Press, 1998), 104.

8 The Cecilská hudební jednota was an officially organized extension of the musicians used regularly in secular performances in the previous century.

9 Stanislav Pecháček, *Česká sborová tvorba 1800–1950* (Prague: Universita Karlova v Praze, Pedagogická fakulta, 2002), 288.

10 Gracian Černušák, Bohumír Štědroň, and Zdenko Nováček, eds., *Československý hudební slovník*, vol. 1 (Prague: Státní hudební vydavatelství, 1963), 78.

11 Černušák et al., *Československý hudební slovník*, 288. Bendl served as president from 1890 to 1891.

12 Many Czech composers, including Dvořák, Janáček, Josef Bohuslav Foerster, Vitěžslav Novák, and Bohuslav Martinů, continued this trend of folk-based partsongs. Sušil's seminal collections of folk tunes and texts began in 1835 with his *Moravské národní písně* (Moravian folk songs) and were greatly expanded with volumes that were completed in 1840 and 1859.

13 Brian Large, *Smetana* (New York: Praeger Publishers, 1970), 122.

14 Jaroslav Vogel, *Leoš Janáček*, rev. edn., ed. Karel Janovický (New York: W. W. Norton & Company, 1981), 47.

15 Vogel, *Leoš Janáček*, 59–60.

16 Vogel indicates that Dvořák was the main composer represented in the Beseda's repertoire, going so far as to state that not a single concert failed to include one of his works (Vogel, *Leoš Janáček*, 77).

17 Nick Strimple, *Choral Music in the Nineteenth Century* (New York: Amadeus Press, 2008), 123.

Selected Bibliography

Books

Bartoš, František, comp. *Smetana ve vzpomínkách a dopisech* [Smetana in Remembrances and Letters]. Prague: Státní nakladatelství krásné literatury, hudby a umění, 1954.

Černušák, Gracian, Bohumír Štědroň, and Zdenko Nováček, eds., *Československý hudební slovník* [Dictionary of Czechoslovak Music], 2 vols. Prague: Státní hudební vydavatelství, 1963–1965.

Černý, Jaromír, Jan Kouba, Vladimír Lébl, Jitka Ludvová, Zdeňka Pilková, Jiří Sehnal, and Petr Vít. *Hudba v českých dějinách od středověku do nové doby* [Music in Czech History from the Middle Ages to the Present]. Prague: Editio Supraphon, 1989.

Large, Brian. *Smetana*. New York: Praeger Publishers, 1970.

Newmarch, Rosa. *The Music of Czechoslovakia*. London: Oxford University Press, 1942. Reprint. New York: Da Capo Press, 1978.

Očadlík, Mirko and Robert Smetana, eds. *Československá vlastivěda* [An Encyclopedia of Czechoslovakia]. Part 9, *Umění* [The Arts]. Vol. 3, *Hudba* [Music]. Prague: Horizont, 1971.

Pecháček, Stanislav. *Česká sborová tvorba 1800–1950* [Czech Choral Works 1800–1950]. Prague: Universita Karlova v Praze, Pedagogická fakulta, 2002.

Sayer, Derek. *The Coasts of Bohemia: A Czech History*. Princeton: Princeton University Press, 1998.

Simeone, Nigel, John Tyrrell, Alena Němcová, and Theodora Straková. *Janáček's Works: A Catalogue of Music and Writings of Leoš Janáček*. Oxford: Clarendon Press, 1997.

Smolka, Jaroslav. *Smetanova vokální tvorba* [Smetana's Vocal Works]. Dílo a život Bedřicha Smetany, vol. 2. Prague: Editio Supraphon, 1980.

Strimple, Nick. *Choral Music in the Nineteenth Century*. New York: Amadeus Press, 2008.

Tomášek, Václav Jan. *Vlastní životopis Václava Jana Tomáška* (Autobiography of Václav Jan Tomášek). Prague: Topičova edice, 1941.

Valový, Evžen. *Sborový zpěv v čechách a na moravě* [Choral Singing in Bohemia and Moravia]. Brno: Universita J. E. Purkyně, 1972.

Vogel, Jaroslav. *Leoš Janáček*. Rev. ed. Ed. Karel Janovický. New York: W. W. Norton, 1981.

Scores

The principal publishers of Czech choral music at present are the Czech Radio Publishing House (http://www.rozhlas.cz/nakladatelstvi/english); Editio Bärenreiter Praha (http://www.sheetmusic.cz/); and Schott Music Panton (http://www.panton.cz/).

Janáček, Leoš. *Muzské sbory I* [Male Choruses I]. Complete Critical Edition. Series C, vol. 1. Ed. Leoš Faltus and Petr Oliva. Kassel: Bärenreiter, 1983. In Czech, German, and English.

Křížkovský, Pavel, Vilém Steinman, and Jan Racek. *Skladebné dilo* [Compositions]. Monumenta musicae Bohemicae, vol. 1: Skladby písňové, sborové a kantátové (Songs, Choruses, and Cantatas). Prague: Melantrich, 1949. In Czech.

Ryba, Jakub Jan. *Czech Christmas Mass* [Česká mše vánoční] for solo voices, mixed choir, and piano. Piano reduction. Prague: Editio Bärenreiter Praha, 2004. In Czech and German.

Smetana, Bedřich. *Sborové skladby* [Choral Works]. Prague: Museum Bedřicha Smetany v Praze, Státní nakladatelství krásné literatury, hudby a umění, 1956. In Czech.

Tomášek, Václav Jan. *Hymni in sacro pro defunctis cantari soliti* [Requiem in C minor, op. 70]. Score and four parts. Prague: M. Berra [c. 1825].

Vitášek, Jan August. *Adeste fideles: hymnus pastoralis* für Solobass, SATB, 2 Violinen, Viola, Violoncello, Bläser (ad lib.) und Orgel. Sankt Augustin: J. Butz Musikverlag, 2005.

Voříšek, Jan Hugo. *Missa in B-flat: Missa solemnis*, op. 24. Musica antique Bohemica. Series II, vol. 15. Prague: Editio Supraphon, 1997.

Recordings

Janáček, Leoš and Pavel Křížkovský. *Janáček / Křížkovský: Choirs*. Q VOX Quartet. Arco Diva compact disc UP 0068-2 231 DDD FP.

Janáček, Leoš. *Leoš Janáček: Male Choruses*. Prague Philharmonic Choir. Joseph Veselka. Supraphon compact disc SU 3022-2 211.

Ryba, Jakub Jan. *Czech Christmas Mass*. Choir and Orchestra of the Czech Madrigalists. František Xaver Thuri. Naxos compact disc 8.554428.

Smetana, Bedřich. *Czech Song, Choruses*. Czech Philharmonic Chorus, Prague Radio Chorus, Prague Symphony Orchestra, and others. Supraphon compact disc SU 3040-2 211.

Voříšek, Jan Václav. *Symphony in D; Mass in B-Flat*. Czech National Symphony Orchestra, Patrice Michaels, William Watson, Tami Jantzi, and Paul Freeman. Cedille Records compact disc 00000 058.

25

ANTONÍN DVOŘÁK

Alan Houtchens

TEXAS A&M UNIVERSITY

Antonín Dvořák (1841–1904) was exceedingly reluctant to express his ideas about philosophical matters or explain his creative processes beyond making statements like "I only write music and let it speak for itself."[1] On one occasion, however, he articulated in writing a private creed, one that seems to have guided him in his personal life as well as in his activities as a creative artist. Without necessarily prioritizing them, he listed three principles that should transcend all others: *láska* (love), *Bůh* (God), and *vlast* (homeland).[2] His notion of *láska* embraced an affection for and charity toward all humankind, without regard for station, birth, ethnicity, religious belief, or political doctrine. He strove to encompass the whole of humanity in much of his music, but perhaps nowhere more eloquently than in his works for the "first musical instrument," the human voice. These works range from folk ballads narrating the pains of unrequited love to the sacred Latin rite of the Roman Catholic Mass. Unfortunately, many of them are unknown because Dvořák has been viewed primarily as a composer of chamber and orchestral instrumental works even though, in terms of sheer number of notes, he cultivated vocal and instrumental music in nearly equal measure.

Dvořák's greatness as an artist partly lies in the fact that, while he maintained very strong patriotic sentiments for Bohemia and his Czech heritage in keeping with the concepts of *vlast* (homeland) and *vlastenectví* (love for one's homeland; patriotism), his compositions are not so constrained by the more politically and ideologically oriented, highly charged, and chauvinistic notions of *národ* (nation) and *národnost* (nationality) as to make them incomprehensible or uncommunicative to non-Slavic peoples. To appropriate an apt metaphor used by the eminent scholar Michael Beckerman, Dvořák was able to put on and take off nationalism like a mask as the occasion suited him.[3] Being very sensitive to fluctuations in public taste and attentive to critical reviews of his compositions, he was instinctively motivated by healthy doses of pragmatism and even opportunism.

The commonly held perception of Dvořák as a purely nationalist composer therefore must be abandoned. He was thoroughly conversant throughout his career with the progressive aesthetics and musical techniques of the so-called New German composers—principally Wagner, Liszt, and Berlioz.[4] For a variety of reasons, however, he began to cultivate a separate musical speech during the 1870s that would be perceived as being Slavic and, more particularly, Czech. The results are noticeable less with regard to harmonic procedure than in a new sense of rhythmic animation; a simpler, more lyrical, and more clearly articulated melodic phraseology influenced by folk music; a new preference for lighter, more transparent textures; and a more streamlined manner of unifying single movements or entire multi-movement works by combining techniques found in both art and folk musics.

Enriching his progressive compositional style by infusing elements drawn from central European folk musics was a logical way for Dvořák to gain notoriety and acceptance simultaneously among his countrymen and among broader European and international audiences. In part, he was responding to the social, political, and cultural milieu of Prague at the time. By 1860, increased migration to the Bohemian provincial capital from the countryside reversed the population figures in favor of Czech speakers over German speakers. In addition, both Germans and Czechs throughout the Bohemian crown lands campaigned during the 1860s and 1870s for more control over their own economic, judicial, cultural, and educational affairs. When the Hungarian nobility were granted extraordinary concessions by the Habsburg government with the *Ausgleich* of 1867, Bohemians felt slighted and began pursuing the agendas of the nascent national revival movement with even greater vigor.

The conflict between Germans and Czechs on purely nationalistic grounds, which began festering during the early 1870s, reached an apex only in the last decade of the century. For the Czechs, the most important tangible cultural manifestation of a new and growing national identity, based primarily on language, was the Czech National Theatre, which was built exclusively through private subscriptions and public donations. A fire gutted its interior shortly after its completion in 1881, but money to rebuild it was raised in the same manner within the span of just two years, and its opening fostered an outpouring of new plays, operas, and other artistic works in the Czech language to which Dvořák contributed his full share.

It is indicative of Dvořák's deep attachment to his roots—to his native Czech language, the landscape of Bohemia, and the rural and urban Habsburg culture into which he was born and schooled—that his very first preserved choral work is *Hymnus z básně Dědicové Bílé hory* for mixed chorus and orchestra, Op. 30.[5] It is a setting of the final stanzas of Vítězslav Hálek's poem *The Heirs of White Mountain,* which marks the centuries-long subjugation of Bohemia by Habsburg monarchs following the Battle of White Mountain in 1620 and encourages Bohemians to wake up to a new awareness of country and nation. Another indication of Dvořák's patriotism is the fact that the majority of his partsongs and smaller choral works are either settings of folk-song texts taken from Czech, Moravian, and Slovakian collections or of poems penned by significant Czech writers. Otherwise, his interest in cultures outside the Austro-German orbit led him to Lithuanian and Irish texts in Czech translation. During his tenure as Director of the National Conservatory of Music of America in New York City, he also completed two works in English for soloists, mixed chorus, and orchestra: the cantata *The American Flag,* Op. 102 (1893) and an arrangement of Stephen Foster's *Old Folks at Home* (1894).

The American Flag is a thoroughly delightful setting of several rather prosaic stanzas of verse written around 1815 by Joseph Rodman Drake in response to the United States' victory over England in the War of 1812. In his patriotic poem, which had become a classic of its kind in America by the end of the century, Drake instructs the national bird, the American bald eagle, to guard and protect the flag; he then assures members of the various fighting forces that the flag will always be their guide in the defense of freedom. Dvořák's music for the lines directed toward the cavalry is especially noteworthy for its bounce, lightness, and witty—almost satirical—turns of phrase. The piece is not very far removed in musical style from turn-of-the-century Viennese operettas or the works of Gilbert and Sullivan or Victor Herbert, who was a member of the faculty of the National Conservatory under Dvořák's leadership.

In Bohemia, Dvořák found ready venues for establishing himself as a composer of vocal music among the many amateur and professional choral societies that were as numerous throughout the region by the 1870s as *Singvereinen, Singakademien,* and *Männerchoren* were in Austria proper and the neighboring German states. He composed most of his thirty-two partsongs and smaller choral works expressly for one or another of these choral societies. Prominent among them were those conducted by his close friends Karel Bendl (Hlahol in Prague), Leoš Janáček (Beseda brněnská, Brno Choral Society), and Josef Zubatý (Lukes Choral Society, Prague).[6]

Dvořák's partsongs are mainly grouped into eight sets, each containing from three to five songs. With the single exception of *V přírodě* (Amid nature, 1882), they were composed within the brief span of two years, from February 1876 to December 1878. The majority are written for TTBB men's chorus, some *a cappella,* others with piano accompaniment. They do not depart markedly in musical style from those of Schubert, Felix Mendelssohn, or Schumann; or, closer to home, from those of Alois Jelen, Pavel Křížkovský, Karel Bendl, Bedřich Smetana, and Josef Leopold Zvonař or Josef Foerster, the last two of whom taught at the Institute for the Cultivation of Church Music in Prague, the organ school where Dvořák received most of his early professional training. Composed mainly for amateur or semi-professional singing groups, these partsongs are vocally grateful and prevailingly homophonic.

Dvořák's contributions to this genre include a few truly excellent pieces that stand out because of their rhythmic vitality (often achieved through the use of off-beat accents and hemiola), their colorful combinations of diatonic and chromatic chords, and their unusual harmonic relationships. Among the most noteworthy are "Úmysl milenčin" ("The sweetheart's resolve") and "Kalina" ("The Guelder rose") in the collection *Kytice z českych národních písní,* Op. 41 (Bouquet of Czech folksongs, 1877/1898); "Pomořané" ("Dwellers by the sea") and the more folksy "Hostina" ("The sparrow's party") in *Pět sborů pro mužké hlasy na texty litevských národních písní,* Op. 27 (Five partsongs for male voices on Lithuanian folksong texts, 1878); and two songs included in *Sborové pisně pro mužké hlasy* (Partsongs for men's voices, 1877), the hauntingly disturbing "Milenka travička" ("Lover-Poisoner") and the humorously ironic "Ja jsem huslař" ("I am a fiddler," poem by Adolf Heyduk). A high level of artistry is not always maintained, however, and the texts are not always treated properly with regard to musical declamation. For example, in his first set of partsongs, *Čtyři sbory pro smíšené hlasy,* Op. 29, for mixed voices (1877), a real gem like "Nepovím" ("I will not say"), with its lush and occasionally unusual harmonies, is followed by "Opuštěný" ("The forsaken one"), which contains some awful mistakes in declamation even though Dvořák seems to have tried to avoid them by frequently changing meter.[7]

In at least two noteworthy instances, Dvořák returned to the music of one of his partsongs for inspiration in creating a later composition. "Já jsem huslař" (mentioned above) serves as the basis for his Symphonic Variations, Op. 78 (1877), where Dvořák explores more fully the unusual harmonic nuances and, above all, the rhythmic and textural features of the partsong. In the second significant instance of self-borrowing, music taken from the inspiringly patriotic *Píseň Čecha* (Song of a Czech) for TTBB men's chorus reappears in his Cello Concerto in B minor, Op. 104 (1894–95). Dvořák most likely began composing the partsong sometime in 1877 but left it unfinished after setting only three stanzas of František Jaroslav Vacek-Kamenický's five-stanza poem. The principal four-note motif of the partsong, presented in inversion and with a slightly different rhythm, serves as the germinal melodic idea in the first movement of the concerto; then in the coda of the last movement, the solo cello sings the original form of the melody, now in the minor mode (compare Examples 25.1, 25.2, and 25.3).

This connection between the Cello Concerto and *Píseň Čecha,* which hitherto has been overlooked by scholars, lends support to the commonly held supposition that certain passages in all three movements of the concerto (but especially in the coda of the third) reflect Dvořák's nostalgia and homesickness at a time when he may have felt isolated and uneasy amidst the hustle and bustle of New York City.[8] The first stanza of *Píseň Čecha* is a paean to Bohemia, while the sentiments expressed in the third stanza bring together precisely Dvořák's trinity of animisms: *láska, Bůh, and vlast:*

EXAMPLE 25.1 Dvořák, *Píseň Čecha*, mm. 1–4.

EXAMPLE 25.2 Dvořák, Cello Concerto, Op. 104, first movement, mm. 1–6.

EXAMPLE 25.3 Dvořák, Cello Concerto, Op. 104, third movement, mm. 489–93.

First stanza:

Kde můj je kraj, kde má je vlast? Where is my land, my motherland?
To jméno má největší slast! The name that sounds the sweetest!
Není to blud, není to klam, It is no chance, no illusion either,
zemi českou za vlast že mám. that Bohemia should be my motherland.

Není země jako země,	There is no other such land,
hlas přírody mluví to ke mně,	here the voice of nature speaks to me,
a srdce mé volá splesem,	and my heart responds with joy,
v Čechách že já jen doma jsem.	that only in Bohemia do I feel at home.

Third stanza:

Zde jsem se učil Boha znát,	Here I learned to know the Lord,
co dítě otcem svým ho zvát;	while still a child to call Him Father;
zde můj vzděláván byl rozum	here my mind was trained at school,
a zde je můj otcovský dům.	and here is my family home.
Na něj oko mé rádo patří,	The sight of it is so dear to my eye,
zde sestry mé, moji tu bratři;	here my sisters dwell, here are my brothers;
mně touha lásky táhne sem;	the attraction of love draws me here;
u nich tu já jen doma jsem.	only among them do I feel at home.

Dvořák was deeply spiritual and devoutly religious, though he eschewed the ritual and overtly pompous trappings of the Roman Catholic Church.[9] The personal God invoked in the first two lines of Vacek-Kamenický's third stanza also animates the small-scale sacred piece *Žalm 149*, Op. 79 (1888), the Czech text of which is taken from the Kralice Bible.[10] The depth of Dvořák's religious devotion is most gloriously revealed, however, in a series of large-scale compositions for soloists, mixed chorus, and orchestra on Latin texts: *Stabat Mater,* Mass in D major, Requiem, and *Te Deum.*

The Mass in D major, Op. 86 (1887, revised 1892[11]) and the more flamboyant *Te Deum*, Op. 103 (1892) are occasional pieces on a smaller scale, but they nevertheless deserve to be performed more frequently than has been the case. The Mass satisfied a commission from Josef Hlávka, a highly respected architect and the first President of the Czech Academy of Arts and Sciences in Prague, for a piece to be performed during the ceremony consecrating a small chapel newly constructed on his estate at Lužany. The *Te Deum* was composed to mark the 400th anniversary of the discovery of America by Christopher Columbus; its first performance was conducted by Dvořák at Carnegie Hall in October 1892. *Stabat Mater*, Op. 58 (1877) is rather static and monolithic, partly because its musical discourse is reflective rather than dramatic, and partly because the weight of each of the ten movements is achieved through considerable repetition of text in order to fit a grandiose symphonic design. Minor keys prevail, but welcome relief comes with a set of four shorter and livelier movements in major modes (nos. 5–8), the last of which, "Fac, ut portem Christi mortem," is a deceptively simple-sounding, stunningly beautiful duet for the soprano and tenor soloists.

The most imposing of Dvořák's large-scale choral works is the Requiem in B-flat minor, Op. 89 (1890). At the height of his compositional powers, Dvořák created an edifice that is monumental in scope yet structurally taut and unflaggingly compelling. Although his earlier works certainly are masterfully orchestrated, the Requiem reveals a new, painterly sound world foreshadowing that of Gustav Mahler, most notably in the integration of solo voices and gorgeous choral writing, in his virtuoso writing for the strings, and in colorful splashes of woodwind and brass timbres that include remarkable solo or obbligato parts for English horn, bass clarinet, French horn, and trumpet.

The Requiem, which premiered at the Birmingham Triennial Music Festival in October 1891, is the last of several major vocal and instrumental works Dvořák composed to satisfy commissions from various performance organizations in England. The British public first became attracted to his choral music in March 1883, when Joseph Barnby conducted the *Stabat Mater* at the Royal Albert Hall in London. This perfomance was so successful that Dvořák was invited to conduct the work himself in London and Worcester one year later. During the years 1884–86, 1890–91, and 1896, he traveled nine times to England for the purpose of attending, and often conducting, concerts featuring his own choral and orchestral works. In May 1885, for example, he conducted a third, substantially revised version of his patriotic *Hymnus z básně Dědicové Bílé hory* in London and had it published with this dedication: "With feelings of deep gratitude to the English People." Three months later, in August 1885, Dvořák's multi-movement choral ballad *Svatební košile,* Op. 69 (The wedding shirts, known more commonly as *The Spectre's Bride*[12]) was performed during the Birmingham Festival (under the composer's direction), along with other major newly commissioned choral works that included Gounod's dramatic sacred oratorio *Mors et vita* (whose *La Rédemption* had met with great success at the previous festival in 1882) and Stanford's *The Three Holy Children.*[13]

Svatební košile is based on the Czech poet Karel Jaromír Erben's poem about a young maiden who is lured to her grave by Death disguised as her deceased lover.[14] The bass-baritone soloist and the chorus in the work both serve the function of narrator / commentator / witness, while the soprano and tenor soloists take on the roles of the maiden and the spectre. Although Dvořák called it a choral ballad, *Svatební košile* is operatic in style and structure, and is highly reminiscent of his grand operas *Vanda* and *Dimitrij.* Operatic features include its substantial overture, its demanding solo vocal parts and masterful integration of soloists and chorus, the prominence of full-textured choral writing, and the grouping of its nineteen individual tableau-like set pieces into three acts that are situated in scenes corresponding to those of the ballad.[15]

When the organizers of the Leeds Music Festival requested a large-scale choral work to be performed the following year, Dvořák turned once again to Czech legend in composing *Svatá Ludmila* for SATB soloists, mixed chorus, and orchestra, Op. 71 (1886). Unlike *Svatební košile,* this story is based on actual historical events. During the last half of the ninth century, both the Roman and the Byzantine Churches sent missionaries into Bohemia and Moravia to convert the various Slavic peoples. Duke Bořivoj I of the Přemyslid dynasty and his wife Ludmilla embraced Christianity and, according to legend, were baptized by Methodius, who helped establish a Slavic rather than Latin liturgy in the region.[16] At the beginning of the third part of *Svatá Ludmila,* which focuses on their baptism, Dvořák presents the words and melody of the medieval Old Slavonic / Czech liturgical chant "Hospodine, pomiluj ny!" ("Lord, have mercy on us!") in an exquisite hymn-like setting. The original chant, a plea for peace and prosperity in the Czech lands, is a trope on the Greek invocation "Kyrie eleison." For the work's grand finale, Dvořák incorporates it once again into the musical fabric of a marvelous neo-Baroque vocal / instrumental concerto—with a fleeting obeisance to similar grand moments in Beethoven's Ninth Symphony and *Missa solemnis*— that very nearly matches the jubilant, majestic, and electrifying quality of Bach's "Et resurrexit" from his Mass in B minor (a performance of which preceded that of *Svatá Ludmila* by twenty-four hours at the festival). The celebration marking the ascendancy of Christianity over paganism in *Svatá Ludmila* reaches its climax as all the vocal forces sing the supplication "Dej nám všem hojnost, pokoj v naší zemi" ("Grant unto us all bountifulness and peace in our Czech lands") one last time *pianissimo* in the *alla breve* style conventionally reserved for such momentous moments, followed by the phrase "Kyrie eleison" *fortissimo* in familiar style (homorhythmically).

By choosing the subject of St. Ludmilla's conversion, Dvořák figured that he would be able not only to accommodate the request of the Leeds Festival committee for a "substantial" sacred work (the first performance lasted three and a half hours), but also to nurture his image as a Czech composer both at home and abroad. After hearing Gounod's and Stanford's compositions at the Birmingham Festival the year before, and after becoming further acquainted with similar works that had especially pleased the organizers and audiences at earlier Birmingham and Leeds festivals— Mendelssohn's *Elijah* (1846), Max Bruch's *Das Lied von der Glocke* (1879, libretto after Schiller), and Niels Gade's cantatas *Zion* (1874, libretto by Gade and Carl Andersen) and *Psyke* (1882, libretto by Andersen), to name the most important—Dvořák was ready to exceed all expectations. This meant, of course, providing a substantial but by no means preponderant amount of music for mixed chorus;[17] it also meant (or so he thought) that the work should exhibit stylistic traits and compositional processes reflecting an appreciation of late Baroque music, mainly that of Handel as filtered through the venerable vocal works of Mendelssohn, of course, but also of composers like Haydn, Gluck, and Brahms.[18]

Sváta Ludmila manifests some truly marvelous features, most notably an atmospheric brief orchestral introduction followed by a male-voice chorus equal to anything of this kind found in Gluck's operas or Haydn's secular oratorios, and many gorgeous choral numbers and masterfully crafted vocal solos and ensembles. Nevertheless, critics at the time tended to treat the work unkindly, complaining that it was too long and not sacred enough (meaning it was not biblical in nature); that the libretto was in Czech rather than Latin and was poorly fashioned; and that the music conformed too much to the Handelian / Mendelssohnian mold.[19]

The libretto was penned by the Czech poet Jaroslav Vrchlický, who later supplied the text for Dvořák's last choral piece, *Slavnostní zpěv* (Festival Song), composed for mixed chorus and orchestra (1900) to celebrate the seventieth birthday of his good friend and legal advisor, Dr. Josef Tragy,[20] as well as the libretto for his last opera, *Armida* (1903). Alluding to the melody of a well-known sacred folk song, "Tisickráte pozdravujem Tebe" ("We greet you a thousand times"), the charming *Slavnostní zpěv* begins with a passage headed "Springtime of Youth" recognizing the power and joy of music. A humorous section labeled "Longing for the Art of Music: Studies in Counterpoint" presents a purposefully elementary three-part exercise in counterpoint, and another marked "Murmur of the Waves of Vltava" evokes in sound the great river that runs through Bohemia. Heard music (*musica instrumentalis*), unheard music (*musica humana,* the music of the soul), and the divine music of the spheres (*musica mundana*) are glorified in a section involving some very nice choral writing where one or more of the four principal voice parts are occasionally divided. Throughout, Tragy's virtues and deeds are described in such a general way that they might apply just as well to the composer himself, who led a group of students at the Prague Conservatory in the first performance. It was Dvořák's last appearance as a conductor, a fitting moment for someone who, indeed, had served beyond measure *láska, Bůh,* and *vlast* through music.

Notes

1 Dvořák quoted in Joseph J[an] Kovařík, "Dr. Dvořák As I Knew Him," *Fiddlestrings,* 1, 8 (1924): 4.

2 Antonín Dvořák, letter to Alois Göbl dated December 31, 1884, in *Antonín Dvořák: Korespondence a dokumenty,* ed. Milan Kuna, Ludmila Bradová, et al. (Prague: Editio Supraphon, 1987), vol. 1, 462.

3 Michael Beckerman, "The Master's Little Joke: Antonín Dvořák and the Mask of Nation," in *Dvořák and His World,* ed. Michael Beckerman (Princeton: Princeton University Press, 1993), 134–54. See also Beckerman, *New Worlds of Dvořák* (New York: W. W. Norton, 2003), 10–16.

4 In 1859, Franz Brendel published an article in the *Neue Zeitschrift für Musik* in which he famously singled out Wagner, Liszt, and Berlioz as the principal representatives of a "New German School," even though only Wagner was actually German by birth. Brendel had succeeded Robert Schumann as chief editor of that highly influential journal in 1845.

5 Dvořák's works are conventionally identified using two numbering systems: opus numbers assigned by Dvořák or his publishers to indicate (with some very important exceptions) the order of composition, and numbers prefaced by the letter *B,* refering to Jarmil Burghauser's carefully researched chronology in *Antonín Dvořák Thematický katalog* (Prague: Bärenreiter Editio Supraphon, 1996). Thus, the three versions of *Hymnus z básně Dědicové Bílé hory,* which date from 1872, 1880, and 1884, are catalogued by Burghauser as B27, B102, and B134.

6 Hlahol, founded in Prague in 1861, was one of the first of many Bohemian choral societies formed for the purpose of championing the music of Czech composers and performing works in Czech, Moravian, or Slovak. Its motto was "Zpěvem k srdci, srdcem k vlasti" (roughly translated, "Song for the Heart, Heart for the Homeland"). The word *hlahol* means "ring," the sound of something that is resounding.

7 In his defense, it should be noted that principles governing the setting of Czech words to music had not yet been established, just as rules concerning Czech pronunciation and grammar were not yet codified. Rightly believing that they had the tools and the talent necessary to create literary works equal to anything written in the major European languages, Czech philologists and literati worked intently even up to the end of the nineteenth century on developing their language further, issuing language dictionaries, and building up a body of respectable works. Their efforts were yet another manifestation of the Czech national revival movement. Many of the faults in Czech declamation found in Dvořák's early partsongs may be attributed to his familiarity with, and initial adoption of, German musical phraseology, and even into the 1880s he seems to have felt more comfortable treating German rather than Czech texts.

8 Foremost among recent studies of the Cello Concerto is Jan Smaczny's *Dvořák: Cello Concerto* (Cambridge: Cambridge University Press, 1999).

9 Otakar Dvořák's comments concerning his father's piety make for especially interesting reading. See his *Antonín Dvořák, My Father* (Spillville, IA: Czech Historical Research Center, 1993), 105–07.

10 The first version of this setting of the 149th Psalm was written for TTBB and orchestra in 1879; Dvořák later arranged it for mixed chorus and orchestra in 1888 and published it as Op. 79. The first Czech translation of the Bible, called the Kralice Bible, was produced by the counter-Reformation *Unitas Fratrum* during the sixteenth century.

11 The first version of the Mass is for mixed chorus with organ accompaniment; the revised version is for SATB soloists (or semi-chorus), mixed chorus, organ, and orchestra.

12 The title *Spectre's Bride* was suggested by Alfred Littleton of the publishing firm Novello, Ewer & Co. As was customary in Great Britain for works in languages other than English or Latin, an English translation was used in performing *Svatební košile,* as well as *Svatá Ludmila* at the Leeds Festival in 1886.

13 Due to some rather sordid personal and legal entanglements, Gounod was unable to attend the festival, so the newly appointed principal conductor of the Festival, Hans Richter, conducted the premiere (and a reprise two days later) of *Mors et vita,* as well as Stanford's work. This was just one of very many times since the year 1875 that Dvořák's and Hans Richter's paths crossed. Although Richter was a disciple of Wagner and Liszt—for example, he conducted the first performance at Bayreuth in 1876 of Wagner's complete *Ring* cycle—he championed the works of many composers not in their orbit. He played a significant role in introducing Dvořák's music to a wider public in Austria and England, where he held major conducting posts, and everywhere else he appeared as guest conductor. Dvořák dedicated his Symphony no. 6 in D major, Op. 60 (1880) to him.

14 Variations of this tale appear in the folklore of nearly every European culture, and it figures prominently in late eighteenth- and nineteenth-century literature, the visual arts, and music. One of the earliest and best-known treatments, Gottfried August Bürger's *Lenore* (1773), helped establish a form of verse cultivated especially by German writers (among them Goethe and Schiller) in which fantastical, macabre, and supernatural events, sagas, wonder tales, and legendary exploits are related in a dramatic *Sturm und Drang* manner while still involving a prominent narrative element.

15 Dvořák titled the overture *předehra* (overture), a term generally reserved for operatic works, then added the term *introduzione* at a later date, probably in preparation for publication.

16 Although she was unsuccessful in her attempt to Christianize her people, Ludmila was canonized for her efforts and became the patron saint of Bohemia. Bořivoj and Ludmila's grandson was Václav I, known as "Good King Wenceslaus."

17 After looking over what Dvořák was prepared to show the Leeds committee of his score at the beginning of 1886, the publisher Alfred Littleton, who was an ardent champion of Dvořák's music in England, responded with these comments: "It seems to us that the soloists (except the soprano) will have very little to do; and it is certainly unfortunate that the tenor has so little to do. I do not think [Edward] Lloyd would agree to sing the part at all." Letter to Dvořák dated February 4, 1886, in *Korespondence* (1997), vol. 6, 73. By the time the rest of *Svatá Ludmila* was completed, the issue of the apportionment of music among the performing forces was not raised again.

18 During the course of his early musical training and performance experience, Dvořák was exposed to the styles and compositional practices of Renaissance and Baroque music, especially church music, to a much greater extent than is generally realized, so he was already well prepared to satisfy these expectations. In two important articles, Jan Smaczny has laid the groundwork for further consideration of how Dvořák appropriated earlier musical styles and techniques to enrich his own forward-looking compositional practice: "Dvořák and the *Seconda Pratica*," in *Antonín Dvořák 1841–1991,* ed. Milan Pospíšil and Marta Ottlová (Prague: Ústav pro hudební věd České republiky, 1994), 271–80; "Dr. Dvořák Steps Off his World of Baroque Certainty: Dvořák and Early Music," in *The Work of Antonín Dvořák (1841–1904): Aspects of Composition—Problems of Editing—Reception,* ed. Jarmila Gabrielová and Jan Kachlík (Prague: Academy of Sciences of the Czech Republic, 2007), 310–23.

19 An excellent discussion of *Svatá Ludmila's* reception history in England may be found in Jitka Slavíková's

Dvořák a Anglie [Dvořák and England] (Prague: Paseka, 1994), 115–17. It is interesting to note that Alfred Littleton, upon learning of Dvořák's intention to treat something drawn from Czech history, issued this strongly worded advisory: "In order to make a *certain success* with the English public, it is, I think, of the *utmost importance* that the subject should be taken from the *Bible*." Letter to Dvořák dated March 31, 1885, in *Korespondence a dokumenty* (1997), vol. 6, 25. Part of the failure for the libretto to impress may be ascribed to the fact that the English translation provided by Reverend John Troutbeck, as also his earlier translation of the libretto of *Svatební košile,* is fundamentally unacceptable. The modern critical editions of both works use English translations newly prepared by John Clapham.

20 Tragy was a prominent lawyer, composer, organist, and Vice-President of the Prague Conservatory of Music. Dvořák had resumed his duties as Professor of Compostion at the Conservatory in 1895, after resigning his post in America.

Selected Bibliography

Beckerman, Michael, ed. *Dvořák and His World.* Princeton: Princeton University Press, 1993.

——. *New Worlds of Dvořák: Searching in America for the Composer's Inner Life.* New York: W. W. Norton, 2003.

Burghauser, Jarmil. *Antonín Dvořák Thematický katalog.* Prague: Bärenreiter Editio Suprahon, 1996.

Clapham, John. *Antonín Dvořák: Musician and Craftsman.* London: Faber and Faber, 1966.

——. *Dvořák.* London and New York: W. W. Norton, 1979.

Döge, Klaus. *Dvořák: Leben—Werke—Dokumente.* 2nd rev. ed. Zürich: Atlantis Musikbuch-Verlag, 1997.

Dvořák, Antonín. *Antonín Dvořák: Letters and Reminiscences.* Ed. Otakar Šourek. Trans. Roberta Finlayson Samsour. Prague: Artia, 1954.

——. *Korespondence a dokumenty.* Ed. Milan Kuna, Ludmila Bradová, et al. 10 vols. Prague: Editio Supraphon, 1987–2004.

Dvořák, Otakar. *Antonín Dvořák, My Father.* Spillville, IA: Czech Historical Research Center, 1993.

Houtchens, Alan. "Some Interconnections between *Vanda* and other Works by Dvořák," in *Dvořák-Studien,* ed. Klaus Döge and Peter Jost. Mainz: B. Schott's Söhne, 1994, 65–75.

Hurwitz, David. *Dvořák: Romantic Music's Most Versatile Genius.* Pompton Plains, NJ: Amadeus Press, 2005.

Jirak, James Edwin. "The Partsongs of Antonín Dvořák: Background and Analysis." D.M.A. diss., University of Northern Colorado, 1996.

Kovařík, Joseph J[an]. "Dr. Dvořák As I Knew Him." *Fiddlestrings* 1, 8 (1924): 4.

Philippi, Daniela. *Antonín Dvořák, Die Geisterbraut / Svatební košile op. 69; Die heilige Ludmilla / Svatá Ludmila op. 71: Studien zur "großen Vokalform" im 19. Jahrhundert. Mainzer Studien zur Musikwissenschaft,* vol. 30. Tutzing: Hans Schneider, 1993.

——. "Dvořák and the Development of Oratorio in the Nineteenth Century," trans. Luis Grilo and Graham Melville-Mason. *Czech Music* (Journal of the Dvořák Society for Czech and Slovak Music) 18, 1 (Summer 1993): 45–57; "Dvořák und die Entwicklungen oratorischer Formen im 19. Jahrhundert," in *Dvořák-Studien,* ed. Klaus Döge and Peter Jost (Mainz: B. Schott's Söhne, 1994), 147–55.

Robertson, Alec. *Dvořák.* Master Musicians Series. Rev. ed. London: J. M. Dent & Sons, 1964.

Slavíková, Jitka. *Dvořák a Anglie* [Dvořák and England]. Prague: Paseka, 1994.

Smaczny, Jan. "Dr. Dvořák Steps Off his World of Baroque Certainty: Dvořák and Early Music," in *The Work of Antonín Dvořák (1841–1904): Aspects of Composition—Problems of Editing—Reception,* ed. Jarmila Gabrielová and Jan Kachlík. Prague: Academy of Sciences of the Czech Republic, 2007, 310–23.

——. "Dvořák and the *Seconda Pratica,*" in *Antonín Dvořák 1841–1991,* ed. Milan Pospíšil and Marta Ottlová, 271–80. Prague: Ústav pro hudební věd České republiky, 1994.

——. *Dvořák: Cello Concerto.* Cambridge: Cambridge University Press, 1999.

——. "Dvořák's *Cypresses:* A Song Cycle and its Metamorphoses," in *Dvořák-Studien,* ed. Klaus Döge and Peter Jost. Mainz: B. Schott's Söhne, 199, 47–64.

Šourek, Otakar. *Život a dílo Antonína Dvořáka* [The Life and Works of Antonín Dvořák]. Rev. eds. 4 vols. Prague: Hudební matice Umělecké besedy, 1955–57.

Strimple, Nick. *Choral Music in the Nineteenth Century.* Milwaukee: Amadeus Press, 2008.

——. "The Choral Works: Te Deum and *The American Flag,*" in *Dvořák in America, 1892–1893,* ed. John C. Tibbetts. Portland, OR: Amadeus Press, 1993, 193–201.

26

HUNGARY

Paul A. Bertagnolli

University of Houston

The sterling international reputation that Hungary's professional, church, academic, and amateur choirs have earned for pure intonation, clear diction, and linguistic versatility since the advent of Kodály's method during the early twentieth century is scarcely new. As early as 1483 a papal emissary reported the chapel of King Matthias's Italian-born wife, Queen Beatrice, exceeded the standards of the recently founded Sistine Chapel.[1] Although the Ottoman occupation (1526–1699) decimated Hungary's cultural institutions, the Habsburgs gradually rebuilt them after expelling Turkish forces and suppressing Ferenc Rákóczy's insurrection (1703–11). Further upheavals divided the "long" nineteenth century into three periods that affected Hungarian choral music and music-making. First was the period of Austrian hegemony, which waned slightly after Joseph II died in 1790 but ultimately endured until at least 1825, when the Hungarian Diet addressed urgent socio-economic problems. Next was the nationalistic Reform Era (1825–67), which saw attempts to rejuvenate Magyar culture, notwithstanding the disruptive Revolution of 1848–49. Last were the years following the Compromise of 1867, which revived Austro-German impulses that would last until the outbreak of the First World War.[2]

During the first quarter of the nineteenth century, and in some locales until even later, Austrian Habsburg aristocrats and their Hungarian allies continued to enlist musicians from throughout the empire to revitalize courts, episcopates, and county seats, just as they had prior to 1800. Voluminous Esterházy archives assembled between 1727 and 1846 in the city of Tata, for example, preserve choral works by 171 composers, largely Austrians, Germans, Italians, and Bohemians, but only seven of verifiably Hungarian origin.[3] These and other foreign-born, cosmopolitan composers perpetuated Viennese Classicism's choral traditions as codified by Mozart, the Haydn brothers, Beethoven, and their contemporaries. Thus, in masses written for cathedrals in Pozsony (Preßburg, modern-day Bratislava), Buda, and Pécs (Fünfkirchen),[4] three church composers whose music was widely disseminated—the Bohemians Georg Druschetzy (1745–1819) and Franz Novotni (1749–1806) and the Austrian Georg Lickl (1769–1843)—observed numerous Viennese conventions, including using symphonic movement forms and *longa* and *brevis* distinctions (such as the Dona ut Kyrie[5]), associating specific lines of text with readily distinguished musical characters or topoi (for example, imbuing the Et incarnatus est with a mood of pathos or the Benedictus with pastoral qualities), and scoring certain passages specifically for soloists, ensembles, chorus, and obbligato instruments.[6] At Pest's venerable Parish Church (Belvárosi plébániatemplom), 130 works by Joseph Bengraf (1745–91), the Würzburg-born *regens chori* (choirmaster), were continuously performed from 1776 until forty years after his death,[7] an achievement the Moravian contrapuntist Henrik Klein (1756–1832) matched in Pozsony.

Among Viennese Classicism's Hungarian-born propagators, György Arnold (1781–1848) was *regens chori* and municipal music director—a dual occupation common among emerging middle-class, native musicians—in provincial Szabadka (Subotica). His choir at the Cathedral of Saint Theresa of Avila (A Szabadkai Szent Teréz Székesegyház), enlarged by giving boy sopranos free lessons, sang offertories he based on popular operatic melodies by Mozart, Grétry, and Weigl. Antal Richter (1802–54) likewise wrote numerous liturgical and civic works in Győr (Raab), an episcopal city that regularly commemorated its struggles against Turkey. More typically, however, Arnold's contemporaries developed vicissitudinous careers, teaching aristocratic children, writing occasional pieces such as name day cantatas, and working or publishing abroad, as did Ferenc Kéményi (1763–1802), who notably produced a Mass for male voices "in Hungarian style," János Spech (1767–1836), and János Fusz (1777–1819).

Resisting Austrian dominance, choirs that formed at Calvinist colleges in Debrecen, Sárospatak (Potok am Bodroch), and other Protestant centers between 1728 and 1811 maintained post-Reformation vernacular traditions. Their *melodária* (songbooks) preserve monophonic and polyphonic hymns (mostly translated Geneva Psalms) and songs for funerals or public festivities, supplemented between 1780 and 1830 by four-part settings of student tunes and Hungarian folk songs. This repertoire, featuring tenor melodies and textures that expanded to as many as eight parts through fauxbourdon-like doublings, established the nineteenth-century choral movement's foundation.

The Reform Era's moderate proponents, likewise opposing Germanization, urged Hungary's fragmented regions—the Habsburg north and west, the Ottoman-conquered south, and Transylvania—to act as a nation in developing economic, social, and cultural institutions. New music schools and private or civic societies quickly outshone short-lived precursors, despite imperial restrictions against public organizations. Conservatories or other specialized music schools opened in Kolozsvár (Klausenburg, present-day Cluj-Napoca, 1819), Pest (a singing school, or *énekiskola*, 1829), Árad (1833–34), and, after 1860, in Debrecen and elsewhere. Pesti Musikai Intézet (Pest's Music Institute, 1818–22) was founded earlier than counterparts established during the 1820s in Veszprém (Weißbrunn), Pozsony, Sopron (Ödenburg), and Kassa (Kaschau, present-day Košice), but the city boasted no enduring association until 1836, when the Pestbudai Hangászegy-stület (Pest-Buda Musical Association), modeled on Vienna's Gesellschaft der Musikfreunde, began sponsoring orchestral concerts in the National Museum's assembly hall. In 1840, the society opened its own *énekiskola* expressly to train the substantial number of singers required for its performances of large-scale choral works, a goal achieved when seventy-three students initially enrolled.[8] Similar church, volunteer, or social groups spread musical culture and an agreeable, homophonic repertoire nationwide. A society in Pécs, for instance, claimed thirty-eight singers and 346 supporting members by 1862.[9] Five years later an amateur choral association (*dalárda*) inaugurated a Hungarian federation comparable to the French *orphéons* with a chapter in Árad.

Leading Reform Era composers wrote choral music for such societies, but they usually concentrated on nationalistic operas, songs, and instrumental music. Three representative composers nonetheless illustrate contemporaneous choral trends. Ferenc Erkel (1810–93), the creator of Hungarian national opera and the Budapest Philharmonic's founding director (1853), composed seventeen choral works.[10] Just two bear religious associations, *Litánia* (1822–25), now lost, and *Buzgó kebellel* (With Fervent Breast, 1875), commemorating the centennial of the Belvárosi katolikus templom (the Catholic Parish Church) in Gyula. Prior to 1867, Erkel wrote occasional pieces, including a tribute to the educational reformer Johann Heinrich Pestalozzi (1846), a greeting to Emperor Franz Joseph (1852), and an impressive funeral chorus for men's voices (1856).[11] This latter work, *Gyászkar*, would be performed at four significant funeral services over the next several decades: for the renowned Hungarian statesman István Széchenyi (1860), for Erkel's fellow composer Robert Volkmann (1883), for Erkel himself, and for the revolutionary Lajos Kossuth (1894). After the Compromise of 1867, however, he provided a dozen largely unaccompanied men's choruses for annual festivals. Erkel's most famous choral work is Hungary's national anthem, *Hymnusz* (1844) for mixed voices and orchestra, written as nationalism approached its zenith.

Mihály Mosonyi (1815–70), born Michael Brand in Boldogasszonyfalva (Frauendorf, also known as Frauenkirchen), began publishing music under his Hungarian name in 1859. Primarily a symphonist and pianist, he was also the Reform Era's foremost choral composer. His five masses and a dozen smaller sacred pieces, most of which are worthy of revival, respect evolving Viennese conventions, incorporating romantic melodicism and chromatic harmonies, but later favoring continuous four-part textures over episodic counterpoint. Surpassing contemporary standards, numerous homophonic men's choruses—some folk-like, others patriotic—feature daring harmonies and sometimes observe Hungarian speech rhythms (e.g., *A dalárda* [The Choral Society], 1844). Several occasional works honor well-known Hungarians, but Mosonyi's preeminent choral work, *A tisztulás ünnepe az Ungnál 886-ik esztendöben* (Purification Festival at the River Ung in 886, 1859) bolstered the spirit of nationalism a decade after the Revolution's collapse. Narrating the hardships Hungary's Árpád founders overcame, the cantata also epitomizes nineteenth-century Hungarian choral style (see Example 26.1).[12] After an orchestral introduction, the chorus proclaims, "The god of war fights for us," with imposing block chords, weak-beat accents, and a prominent augmented second in the uppermost voice. Then, as the chorus repeats the phrase, "God helps the oppressed and strikes the oppressor," persistent dotted rhythms, parallel thirds, and chromatic neighbor tones evoke the Hungarian *verbunkos* style,[13] whereupon repeated chords and a melodic ascent achieve a grandiose, heroic effect.

In contrast, Robert Volkmann (1815–83) remained a Germanophile even though he left Saxony in 1841 and spent almost all of his remaining years in Pest (save a Viennese sojourn from 1854 to 1858). He held nationalist sympathies but never learned Hungarian or set Hungarian texts, instead catering to Pest's German-speaking community. Of thirty largely generic partsongs (e.g., the very popular *Schlummerlied*, Op. 76, 1876; and *Jagdlied*, Op. 30/6, 1856), ten for mixed, women's, or children's choruses exploit more diverse forces than the period's ubiquitous repertoire for men's choruses. Volkmann's liturgical and spiritual works, several completed while he served as *regens chori* at Pest's Reformed Jewish Temple (e.g., *Gottes Güte*, 1848–49),[14] encompass wider moods, from light fluidity (Mass No. 1 in D major, Op. 28, 1843; *Osanna domino deo*, Op. 47, 1864) to solemn grandeur (Mass No. 2 in A-flat major, Op. 29, 1852; *Vertrauen auf Gott*, Op. 38b, 1859). Tinged with archaisms, his lovely unaccompanied motet *Weihnachtslied aus dem 12. Jahrhundert*, Op. 59 (1867) remained an Advent favorite at Leipzig's Thomaskirche decades after his death.[15] When the Országos Magyar Királyi Zeneakadémia (National Hungarian Royal Music Academy) opened in 1875, Volkmann's appointment as composition professor reflected both his prominence in Pest's musical circles and Germanophilia's post-Compromise resurgence.

Defeat in the Austro-Prussian War (1866) obliged Austria to allow Hungary to form a parliament and govern internal affairs. Austro-Hungarian equality, however, was nominal: Emperor Franz Joseph became Hungary's king, and his ministers controlled vital common departments (Foreign Affairs, Finance, Defense). Serious Hungarian composers often succumbed to cosmopolitan pressures, whereas others satisfied bourgeois demand for "Hungarian" fantasies, "gypsy" arrangements, and csárdás-style salon music. The Budapest Philharmonic's repertoire between 1853 and 1903 mirrored these conditions: of 992 performances of 511 compositions, 786 were devoted to works by foreigners, but only 206 to works by Hungarians, and just nineteen works involved chorus.[16] Evincing another Germanic encroachment, Hungarian Baptist congregational choirs, whose

EXAMPLE 26.1 Mosonyi, *A tisztulás ünnepe az Ungnál 886-ik esztendöben*. Excerpt: "The god of war fights for us!"

EXAMPLE 26.1 continued.

EXAMPLE 26.1 continued.

"spirited" manner of performance attracted attention from Catholic and Calvinist Hungarians accustomed to more staid church choirs, sang in German from 1874, when Baptists established a continuous presence in Hungary, until 1889, when the first Hungarian-language Baptist choir formed in Szada.[17] Most Hungarian Baptists, however, continued to sing in German well into the 1890s, when the first important Hungarian-language hymnals were published.[18]

Otherwise, earlier practices survived after 1867. Sacred music by Mátyás Engeszer (1812–85), Gyula Beliczay (1835–93), who synthesized Baroque and Hungarian styles, and Sándor Bertha (1843–1912) perpetuated German Romanticism. Homophonic, often folk-like works for men's and mixed choruses proliferated—sometimes in awkward Hungarian translations of German poems—thanks to Beliczay, Franz Doppler (1821–83), Károly Huber (1828–85), Vienna-based Karl Goldmark (1830–1915), Gyula Erkel (1842–1909), Ödön Mihalovich (1842–1929), and Gyula Major (1858–1925). Rather exceptional were full-scale oratorios by Károly Aggházy (1855–1918), whose *Rákóczi* (1905) recalls faded nationalist glories, and Hans Koessler (1853–1926), whose *Triumph der Liebe* (1897), like his psalm settings, is vocally idiomatic, if occasionally virtuosic. But these achievements scarcely gained the local popularity, international recognition, and lasting reputation of choral works by Hungarian music's prodigal son, Franz Liszt, whose choral works are discussed in the next chapter.

Notes

1 László Dobszay, *A History of Hungarian Music*, trans. Mária Steiner ([Budapest]: Corvina, 1993), 39.
2 Systematic musicological investigations of nineteenth-century Hungarian choral music have been under-taken only recently, leaving the field in its preliminary stages. Large portions of the repertoire (especially part songs and cantatas) were occasional in nature, circulated in manuscript, and were never published. Even some important pieces were published in limited editions now held only by archives or large libraries. Editing and printing these scores is accordingly a task awaiting scholars of Hungarian music. Nevertheless, many nineteenth-century Hungarian choral works have been recorded on the Hungaroton label (often in performances based on manuscript or archival sources) and are now widely available through the Naxos Music Library.

3 Tallies derive from Kornél Bárdos, *A tatai Esterházyak zenéje, 1727–1846* [The Musical Life of the Esterházy Family in Tata, 1727–1846] (Budapest: Akadémiai Kiadó, 1978), 78–241.

4 The complexities of Hungary's changing borders often created multilingual place names. Cities in the Austrian-dominated north and west typically bore Hungarian and German place names during the eighteenth, nineteenth, and early twentieth centuries. In Transylvania (formerly part of Hungary but now falling largely within Romania's borders), two names likewise prevailed and are sometimes still current, as is likewise true in several Slavic-language areas that once comprised Hungarian territories. In Transdanubia and the Ottoman-conquered south, however, Hungarian names were more commonly known in the West, though Turkish nomenclature naturally developed. Some town names developed only minor, easily recognized spelling variants in several languages. Historical sources such as letters and newspapers often use just one place name, creating confusion for later readers. Consequently, multiple names are included in this chapter when appropriate.

5 The *Dona ut Kyrie* practice is one whereby the opening music of the Kyrie recurs in the call for peace ("dona nobis pacem") that concludes the Agnus Dei.

6 Zoltán Farkas, "Die Missa solemnis im Schaffen dreier Komponisten-Generationen in Ungarn: Istvánffy – Druschetzky – Lickl," in *Anton Bruckner: Tradition und Fortschritt in der Kirchenmusik des 19. Jahrhunderts*, ed. Friedrich Wilhelm Riedel (Sinzig: Studio Verlag, 2001), 155–88.

7 Ágnes Sas, "Bengraf, (Johann) Joseph," *Grove Music Online. Oxford Music Online*, http://www. oxfordmusiconline.com/subscriber/article/grove/music/02685 (accessed July 3, 2011).

8 Mária Eckhardt, "Liszt's 125-Year-Old Academy of Music: Antecedents, Influences, Traditions," *Studia Musicologica* 42, 1–2 (2001): 111.

9 Dobszay, *A History of Hungarian Music*, 160.

10 Amadé Németh, *Ferenc Erkel: sein Leben und Wirken*, trans. Hannelore Weichenhain (Budapest: Corvina Kiadó, 1979), 202–03.

11 The titles of these pieces are *Kar Ének Pestalozzi Emlékünnepére* (*Chorus for the Pestalozzi Commemoration Day*) for mixed chorus with organ or harmonium accompaniment, to a text by an unknown author; *Ferenc József Császárt üdvözlő ének* (*Greeting Song for Emperor Franz Joseph*), to a text by Deinhardstein; and *Gyászkar* (*Mourning Chorus*), also known from its opening line of text as *A halálnak éjszakája* (*The Night of Death*), to a text by an unknown author. For the titles of additional works, see Németh, *Ferenc Erkel*, 202–03.

12 János Káldor, "Michael Mosonyi, 1815–1870" (Ph.D. diss., Universität Leipzig, 1936), 22–24.

13 Pieces in *verbunkos* style typically divide into two sections, the *lassú* and the *friss*. The slow to moderate *lassú* normally features improvisatory tempo modifications, dotted or double-dotted rhythms, thick textures, and highly ornamented melodies often doubled in thirds. The multi-sectional *friss* is livelier and often virtuosic. In both sections accents regularly shift to weak beats. Originally an instrumental idiom, *verbunkos* style ultimately pervaded all types of nineteenth-century Hungarian music, including songs, operas, and choral works.

14 Hans Volkmann, *Robert Volkmann: sein Leben und seine Werke* (Leipzig: Hermann Seemann Nachfolger, 1903), 40. Hans Volkmann does not otherwise identify the temple where his ancestor worked, nor do other sources even refer to Volkmann's temple service. But before 1848 the moderate Reform Temple of the Hesed Ne'urim Association was transferred from the House of the "White Goose" ("Fehér Lud") to the so-called Orczy Temple (also known as the "Large Temple"), following the dissolution of most other private and association temples in 1830. A new Temple of the Reform Society occupied the Valero House from 1848 to 1852, coinciding with the time of Robert Volkmann's employment.

15 Ibid., 122.

16 Kálmán Isoz, *L'histoire de la Société Philharmonique Hongroise, 1853–1903* (Budapest: Victor Hornyánszky, 1903), 23–39. Only nineteen of the 511 works involved a chorus, which routinely comprised the Philharmonic Society's own choir, plus members of Budapest's numerous choral societies, the chorus of the Royal Hungarian Opera, and, occasionally, church choirs. Four of the nineteen choral works derived from operas by Erkel (who conducted the Philharmonic from 1853 to 1875) and Wagner, with selections from *Tannhäuser* performed most frequently; the fifteen non-operatic choral works were by J. S. Bach (Mass in B minor, *St Matthew Passion*, an otherwise unidentified "Pentecost Cantata"), Beethoven (Symphony No. 9 in D minor, *Choral Fantasy* in C minor, Op. 80), Berlioz (*Roméo et Juliette*, *Grande Messe des morts*), Goldmark (Psalm 113), Liszt (*Eine Faust-Symphonie*, *Eine Symphonie zu Dantes Divina Commedia*, *Sainte Cécile*, *Zur Säkularfeier Beethovens*), Mozart (an otherwise unidentified "Grand Chorus"), Schubert (Mass No. 6 in E-flat major, D. 950), and Wagner (*Das Liebesmahl der Apostel*). Thus, the only Hungarian-born choral composers featured on the Philharmonic's programs were Erkel, Goldmark, and Liszt, of whom only the first actually made his career in Hungary.

17 Jenő Bányai, *A magyarországi Baptista egyházzene története* (Budapest: Baptista Kiadó, 1996), 112. See also Aubrey Wayne Barrett, Jr. "A Study of the Choral Music Tradition in the Hungarian Baptist Churches" (D.M.A. Thesis, University of Iowa, 1992), 17–18.

18 Barrett, "Choral Music Tradition," 19. *Enekek keresztyén vasárnapiiskolák számára* (*Christian Sunday School Songs for the Young*) had appeared as early as 1876, but included only thirty-one didactic songs. The first Hungarian-language hymnbook, *Kis zsoltárok* (*Little Psalter*, 1893) comprised 250 four-part hymns, mostly translated from German sources. *Sion énekei* (*Songs of Zion*, 1896) is usually considered the first genuinely Hungarian hymnbook.

Selected Bibliography

The most useful resource for scores of choral music by Hungarian composers is Editio Musica Budapest (http://www.emb.hu/), the leading publisher of all types of music in Hungary. EMB succeeded Magyar Kórus, which was founded in 1931 and was active until 1950, when it was nationalized.

Balázs, István. *A Musical Guide to Hungary*. Trans. Mária Steiner. Budapest: Corvina Books, 1992.

Bárdos, Kornél. *A tatai Esterházyak zenéje, 1727–1846*. Budapest: Akadémiai Kiadó, 1978.

Barrett, Aubrey Wayne, Jr. "A Study of the Choral Music Tradition in the Hungarian Baptist Churches: Its History, Leadership, Literature, Personnel, and Practice, including an Anthology of Representative Choral Works." D.M.A. Thesis, University of Iowa, 1992.

Bodolai, Zoltán. *The Timeless Nation: The History, Literature, Music, Art, and Folklore of the Hungarian Nation*. 4th ed. Sydney: Hungaria Publishing Company, 1978.

Csuka, Béla. *Kilenc évitized a Magyar zeneművészet szolgálatában*. Budapest: A Filharmóniai Tarsaság, 1943.

Dobszay, László. *A History of Hungarian Music*. Trans. Mária Steiner. Trans. revised by Paul Merrick. [Budapest]: Corvina, 1993.

Eckhardt, Mária. "Liszt's 125-Year-Old Academy of Music: Antecedents, Influences, Traditions," *Studia musicologica* 42, 1–2 (2001): 109–32.

Farkas, Zoltán. "Die Missa solemnis im Schaffen dreier Komponisten-Generationen in Ungarn: Istvánffy – Druschetzky – Lickl," in *Anton Bruckner: Tradition und Fortschritt in der Kirchenmusik des 19. Jahrhunderts*, ed. Friedrich Wilhelm Riedel. Kirchenmusikalische Studien, no. 7. Sinzig: Studio Verlag, 2001, 155–88.

Halmos, Endre. *Die Geschichte des Gesang-Musikunterrichts in Ungarn: unter besonderer Berücksichtigung des Einflusses aus dem deutschsprachigen Kulturbereich*. Stuttgart: Franz Steiner Verlag Wiesbaden, 1988.

Haraszti, Émile. *La musique hongroise*. Paris: Henri Laurens, 1933.

Isoz, Kálmán. *L'histoire de la Société Philharmonique Hongroise, 1853–1903*. Budapest: Victor Hornyánszky, 1903.

Káldor, János. "Michael Mosonyi (1815–1870)." Ph.D. diss., University of Leipzig, 1936.

Káldy, Gyula. *A History of Hungarian Music*. London: William Reeves, 1902; New York: Haskell House Publishers Ltd., 1969.

Kodály, Zoltán, and Dénes Bartha. *Die ungarische Musik*. Budapest: Danubia, 1943.

Legány, Dezső. *A magyar zene krónikája: zenei művelodésünk ezer éve dokumentumokban*. Budapest: Zeneműkiadó Vállalat, 1962.

Mona, Ilona. "Erste musikalische Analyse der 'Graner Messe' von Ferenc Liszt," *Studia musicologica* 29, 1 (1987): 343–51.

Németh, Amadé. *Ferenc Erkel: sein Leben und Wirken*. Trans. Hannelore Weichenhain. Budapest: Corvina Kiadó, 1989.

Sas, Ágnes. "The Life and Works of János Fusz," *Studia musicologica* 40, 1–3 (1999): 19–58.

Sonkoly, István. "Die Vertonungen von Texten deutscher Dichter des 19. Jahrhunderts in Ungarn. *Német filológiai tanulmányok* [Arbeiten zur deutschen Philologie] 19 (1990): 25–38.

Szabolci, Bence. *A Concise History of Hungarian Music*. Trans. Sára Karig. Trans. revised by Florence Knepler. Budapest: Corvina; London: Barrie and Rockliff, 1964.

Szabolcsi, Bence, and Miklós Forrai, eds. *Musica Hungarica*. Budapest: Editio Musica Budapest, 1965.

Szőnyiné Szerző, Katalin. "Mihalovich Ödön zeneműveinek jegyzéke," *Magyar zene* 4 (1979): 374–90.

Vavrinecz, Veronika. *Richter Antal (1802–1854), élete és működése*. Győr: Szkarabeusz Kiadó, 2003.

Vigué, Jean, and Jean Gergely. *La musique hongroise*. Paris: Presses universitaires de France, 1959.

Volkmann, Hans. *Robert Volkmann: sein Leben und seine Werke*. Leipzig: Hermann Seemann Nachfolger, 1903.

Volkmann, Hans. *Robert Volkmann*. Musiker-Biographien, no. 33. Leipzig: Philipp Reclam, [1915].

27

THE CHORAL MUSIC OF FRANZ LISZT

Paul A. Bertagnolli

University of Houston

Liszt shared much in common with other late eighteenth- and early nineteenth-century choral composers born in Hungary's Austrian-dominated regions. Raised by German-speaking parents in the western Burgenland, the prodigy trained abroad, studying intensively with Czerny and Salieri in Vienna (1822–23), and intermittently until 1827 with Paër and Reicha in Paris, where he adopted lifelong French cultural manners. Like peers who remained in Hungary, Liszt composed Catholic liturgical music and occasional secular works, typically for men's choral societies. He sometimes employed nationalistic idioms in sacred and secular genres. And some major works remained unpublished during his lifetime or were printed in limited editions.

Unlike compatriots who served as choirmasters or concentrated on operas, songs, or instrumental music, however, Liszt forged a multifaceted, cosmopolitan career. He successively became Europe's unrivaled piano virtuoso (1830–47), a controversial *Kapellmeister* in Weimar (1848–61), and a cloistered Roman abbé (1861–68). After emerging from monastic seclusion, he retraced a pattern of pilgrimage almost annually from 1869 until his death in 1886, invigorating Hungarian musical life every spring, holding summer-long master classes in Weimar, and composing and meditating in Rome during falls and winters. Fame and versatility afforded Liszt unique opportunities to cultivate a vast array of choral compositions that has been surveyed chronologically, generically, and at various levels of detail.[1] Accordingly, my discussion first offers a cursory overview of this vital yet largely unfamiliar portion of Liszt's *œuvre* and then samples works from each phase of his career, emphasizing their representative styles, typical compositional techniques, and potential for performance.

Liszt wrote approximately 113 choral works whose style, length, and performing forces vary tremendously.[2] Of sixty-four sacred works, only eleven are large scale, comprising three oratorios, two masses, three psalm settings, and three cantatas, and requiring orchestra, soloists, and (usually) mixed chorus. Most of the remaining sacred compositions are brief motets and simple chant or chorale harmonizations, notably excepting three masses and several multi-movement scores based on Catholic doctrines. Intended for simple devotional services, these shorter works normally employ mixed or men's choruses, though a handful are for women's or children's voices. Their modest, occasionally *ad libitum* organ accompaniments are sometimes supplemented with brass and percussion parts. Several others are *a cappella* or feature piano only, while twenty either exist in multiple versions with different accompaniments or their scores contain alternative accompaniments.[3] Latin prevails in two-thirds of the sacred works, the rest featuring German, French,

Italian, or polylingual texts. Editions of Liszt's sacred music are readily available, excluding several unpublished works and early versions of pieces whose successors achieved wider circulation.[4]

Forty-nine secular works present a contrasting picture. Of seventeen compositions with orchestra, only six cantata-like scores are genuinely large scale; eight of the shorter pieces last 10 to 15 minutes, while three comprise briefer civic or patriotic tributes. Six of these orchestrally accompanied scores feature mixed chorus, nine call for men's voices, and two use ensembles that differ with the version of the piece. Thirteen require soloists, usually men. The thirty-two remaining secular works are for men's chorus, except for two versions of *Morgenlied* that respectively call for children's and women's voices. Even the most ambitious of these *Männerchöre* lasts less than 9 minutes.[5] Twelve *a cappella* settings join ten with piano, three with other instruments (trumpets and timpani, brass orchestra, and organ), and seven with accompaniments that vary in different versions of the piece.[6] German prevails in these secular works; just two are in French and four in Hungarian. Because Liszt often composed secular pieces for specific occasions or performing groups, some of them remained unpublished during his lifetime or were printed in limited editions. Rare copies of several important scores are consequently available today only in research libraries, though this situation is gradually improving. Overall, however, Liszt's secular music remains difficult to access.

Early Works

Liszt began writing choral music in 1841, while concertizing in Germany, and tackled twenty-seven secular and six sacred works during his virtuoso years.[7] The secular compositions often reveal generic attributes of the *Männerchor*: forms are largely strophic; light imitation periodically enlivens four-part, tenor-dominated homophony; and lyrics about patriotism, love, nature, and drinking feature authors ranging from Liszt's amateur acquaintances to illustrious poets, including Goethe, Schiller, and Heine.[8] Perhaps more often than in similar repertoire by contemporaries such as Mendelssohn, Schumann, and Marschner, Liszt's harmonies incorporate daring enharmonic modulations, chromatic mediant relationships, and altered chords—traits Liszt simplified when he revised a dozen partsongs during the early 1860s after having conducted numerous choirs.[9] But otherwise his efforts in the genre rarely illustrate his compositional evolution or the factors that stimulated it.

Such is certainly not the case with *Le forgeron*, a cantata for tenor, bass, and men's chorus conceived with piano accompaniment during Liszt's Iberian tour in 1845 and orchestrated in 1848.[10] The piece simultaneously reflects Liszt's enduring belief in art's capacity to transform society and illustrates three quintessentially Lisztian compositional techniques, as will be seen in the description below. Its libretto is by Abbé Félicité de Lamennais, a charismatic, socialist utopian whose vision of universal liberty and preoccupation with the welfare of growing industrial classes had started influencing Liszt profoundly in 1833.[11] The cantata embodies these concerns by vividly depicting the struggles of exploited ironworkers, just as *Lyon*, a piano piece written in 1834 and dedicated to Lamennais, had supported striking silk weavers. The text accordingly imparts that the ironworkers, though denied nature's benefits and burdened with family obligations, will overcome pain and achieve a better future, aided by divine love and courage.

Le forgeron exploits the characteristically Lisztian compositional technique of thematic transformation, whereby musical materials are substantially varied in successive presentations to suit dramatic contexts that are typically elucidated in a text or, in instrumental music, a program. This familiar process is admittedly less fully realized in the cantata than in many later Weimar choral and instrumental scores, but it nonetheless allows Liszt to portray the ironworkers in various psychological states. Helping to explain the correlation between thematic treatment and emotional affect is a schematic reduction of *Le forgeron*'s ritornello-like structure: I^{a}ABACADAEA. An instrumental introduction (I^a) prefigures the motivic content of a refrain (A) that usually appears in the tonic (E minor), although it sometimes recurs in other keys, modulates in the manner of a transition, or punctuates contrasting episodes.

The introduction's principal motive, consisting merely of the first three pitches of an ascending E-minor scale, seemingly offers little potential for transformation. But because it is repeated conspicuously with thick chordal support in the opening measures and recurs in the bassline beneath suspenseful tremolos as the introduction draws to a close, it is memorable enough to undergo recognizable variation as the cantata unfolds. In the first refrain, the men's chorus insistently declaims the motive with dotted rhythms, repeated notes, and triadic leaps, all suggesting a fanfare-like, martial character consistent with the ironworkers' militantly reiterated exhortation, "Le fer est dur, frappons, frappons!" ["The iron is hard, let's strike, let's strike!"] As the first episode begins (B), a tenor solo subjects the three-note motive to rising sequential statements, augmenting its rhythmic values, eliminating its repeated notes, and restoring its smooth, scalar contour. The resulting *cantabile* melody again aptly matches the tenor's sentiments as he admires a sunrise. But when the ironworkers reply that the sun's beauty is not for them, hunger's slaves, the motive regains its martial character. The tenor duplicates his earlier motivic strategies in the second episode (C), extolling the pleasures of a breeze that caresses flowers and rustles reeds at the water's edge. The choral response, however, differs. When the ironworkers feel the breeze on their brows, they rejoice in seeing the sun and erupt in thick, major-mode homophony whose lines preserve the scale motive. In the third episode (D), the chorus interjects agitated, increasingly shorter fragments of the motive into a dramatic recitative for tenor and bass soloists, urging them to remain courageous, despite their harsh working conditions. The sobering recognition of their plight prompts solidarity among the ironworkers: in the final episode (E), they begin each phrase of their sustained, unison, major-mode melody with ascending sequences of the three-note motive, proclaiming today's pain will yield to a better future. A final refrain, now in E major and replete with fanfares based on the motive's dotted rhythms, confirms the ironworkers will be victorious in their struggles. Thus an ostensibly nondescript yet malleable motive occurs in varied contexts, tracing a path that leads the ironworkers from militant defiance, through nature's consolations, agitation, and unity, to inevitable triumph.

Liszt's motivic processes scarcely achieve such large-scale goals autonomously, but instead interact with other stylistic features, especially accompanimental patterns and harmony. These features often converge to define topics, or commonly recognized correlations between musical styles and affects.[12] As already noted, *Le forgeron*'s refrain exploits variants of a martial topic to suggest conflict and victory. The refrain's accompaniment also anticipates famous examples of operatic "anvil music" with an ostinato that imitates hammer strokes. The cantata's introduction and dramatic recitative embody a lament, a topic Liszt often cultivated by embellishing tremulous diminished seventh chords with descending half-step appoggiaturas.[13] And the second episode's *cantabile* tenor solo expands into a nocturne with a *bel canto* melody and arpeggiated accompaniment—a topic Liszt frequently associated with nature's stasis and attendant spiritual peace.[14] Such topics, along with the narrative sequences they routinely create, imbue the choral music of the avant-gardist Liszt with a vividly "programmatic" character less frequently encountered in the works of more classically oriented nineteenth-century composers such as Mendelssohn and Brahms. Topics would also attain fuller development later in Liszt's career.

Le forgeron's final quintessentially Lisztian trait is that third-related harmonies predominate in all of its episodes. Both tenor solos modulate from G major to D-flat major, respectively a minor third above and below the tonic, though the keys are directly related by a bold tritone. When the chorus joins the tenor in the second episode, an enharmonic mode change from D-flat to C-sharp minor is followed by a half-step shift to C major, a major third below the tonic. In the ensuing refrain, the chorus modulates conventionally from C minor to E-flat major, but in the third episode the rapid-fire choral punctuations of the soloists' recitative occur first in A minor and then modulate from D-flat to F major—keys outlining an augmented triad. The last episode proceeds from C minor homophony to antiphonal exchanges in A-flat major, thus balancing the earlier excursion to C major with the key an enharmonically spelled major third above the tonic. This balanced structuring of thirds is encapsulated in the final refrain's succession of three major keys, A-flat, C, and E, which explicitly articulates the arch-Lisztian tonal plan based on an augmented triad.

The cantata's pervasive, rapidly executed tertian modulations exceeded tonal norms for moderately scaled choral works of the early and mid-nineteenth century composed by many of Liszt's contemporaries—notably including Schubert, Spohr, Hummel, and Mendelssohn[15]—and may have consequently challenged the local amateur choristers who typically performed his early choral music. Indeed, it was precisely such modulations that Liszt would later simplify in revising a dozen *Männerchöre* during the early 1860s, as previously noted. Tonal factors may have accordingly informed Liszt's reservations about the cantata's performance, which he was reluctant to authorize unless he could supervise rehearsals.[16] Modern choristers, accustomed to "Wagnerian" chromaticism that developed during the 1850s, may find the score's tonal peregrinations less imposing. Liszt's reservations should accordingly not discourage the occasional revival of *Le forgeron* or overshadow the appeal of its social message, tonal variety, effective solo and tutti contrasts, and vigorous accompaniment.

Liszt's first surviving sacred choral work, an *Ave Maria* in B-flat major for mixed chorus and organ *ad libitum* (1842),[17] exemplifies a style frequently adopted in his later sacred music. It originated, Liszt recalled, as an experimental imitation of sixteenth-century masters, especially Palestrina and Lassus, whose works he studied after hearing the Sistine Chapel perform them while living in Rome in 1839.[18] Thus the first of Liszt's numerous "Ave Maria" settings embodies principles that eighteenth-century composers had sporadically cultivated in opposing Baroque church music's secularization and would proliferate after the reform-driven Cecilian movement's founding in 1868.

A hallmark of Lisztian scores that emulate antique styles is their cultivation of a three-stage process: formal sections begin with static, repetitive passages; textures, rhythms, harmonies, and dynamics grow increasingly animated; and the return of a simple yet different type of stasis emphasizes important textual sentiments through understatement. This process shapes the setting of the *Ave Maria*'s first sentence. Initially each vocal line repeats "Ave Maria" on one pitch, with successive entrances tiered in descending thirds that imply a somber minor mode (F–D-flat–B-flat–G-flat). Every line observes piano dynamics and steady dactylic rhythms. As the salutation continues in the brighter major mode ("Ave Maria, gratia plena"), slightly more animated lines adopt minimal motion to form tonic and dominant chords above a tonic pedal. Only the sopranos embellish an upward leap with an emotive escape tone, a signature dissonance in Liszt's sacred music.[19] Animation increases in ensuing expansive phrases ("gratia plena"), thanks to livelier, arpeggiated, antiphonal part writing and a rapidly traversed circle of fifths that departs unexpectedly from D major (D–g–c–F–B-flat). Another energetic surge heralds the Lord's presence ("Dominus tecum") with incisive dotted rhythms; antiphonal exchanges between the tenors and divisi sopranos, altos, and basses; a strong plagal cadence in a new local tonic, G major; and the first accents and first *forte* markings in the score. The setting then retreats from this forceful stance, reverting to a static, subdued style that underscores the intimacy of the miraculous revelation that Mary, blessed among all women, bears Jesus in her womb. Liszt achieves an introspective quality simply, with *sotto voce* dynamics, totally unanimous homophony, and unbroken quarter-note rhythms. This moment is remarkable—and contrasts with all that has preceded it—because the harmonies pass through marvelously remote, unanticipated keys (A-flat–F–C–c) to arrive at an augmented sixth chord that reinstates D as the dominant of G major.[20] Liszt accordingly emphasizes the text's most important and most personal sentiment thus far with great subtlety.

Liszt typically achieved such poignancy when subjects were personally significant, especially in prayers to the Virgin or familial patron saints. The *Ave Maria*'s ending, for example, illustrates his lifelong preoccupation with mortality,[21] although its effectiveness is best perceived in context, in relation to preceding passages. Duplicating the earlier three-stage process, the second sentence's setting varies old material before presenting a new denouement. In the varied passages, harmonies are altered, the emotive escape tone is elaborated, and multiple appeals to Mary ("Sancta Maria, mater Dei") erupt in the far-removed key of F-sharp major, emphasized by *forte* dynamics, accents, and the sopranos' highest pitch in the entire score (F-sharp). Precipitous downward octave leaps in every vocal part collapse into a prolonged silence. When Mary is repeatedly asked to pray for sinners ("ora pro nobis peccatoribus"), a varied sequence of the foregoing events ends a third lower, in D major. Such tumult would normally comprise a dramatic climax, a work's culmination. For Liszt, however, it merely focuses attention on the prayer's crux, when the supplicant specifies the hour of death as the desired moment for Mary's intercession ("et in hora mortis nostrae"). Exquisite understatement again emphasizes a single, quiet utterance of this crucial plea with a tempo change from *Andante con moto* to *Quasi adagio*, completely unanimous homophony, low tessitura in all voices, the score's only *marcato* indication, and prolonged, mournful, B-minor chords. Maintaining the intimate mood, three sustained, plagal "Amens" softly restore the tonic and resolve the formerly dissonant escape tone as a suspension. Other small motets evince similarly rewarding contrasts and nuances and deserve to be programmed more frequently.

Works from Weimar

The twenty-eight choral works associated with Liszt's Weimar period divide equally between secular and sacred genres. Most of the secular scores are occasional works for male chorus,[22] written during Liszt's tenure as *Kapellmeister* to commemorate Weimar's legacy as the center of the German Enlightenment, when court aristocrats patronized Goethe, Schiller, and Herder.[23] The most significant among them exemplify *Zukunftsmusik* (music of the future), an avant-garde style Liszt, Wagner, and the New German School's lesser-known members developed during the 1850s.[24] *Zukunftsmusik*'s characteristics—continuous forms, cyclical references, thematic transformation, intense chromaticism, sequential constructions, programs illustrated with mimetic figuration, declamatory vocal lines, and elaborate orchestration—challenged performers, audiences, and critics upon their inception.[25]

Two such works merit special attention. *An die Künstler* (1853–57), based on excerpts from Schiller's magnificent ode, exhorts artists to preserve human dignity, freedom, and unity through their work. This subject resonated deeply with Liszt, eliciting rapt choral meditations characterized by slow-moving, chromatic mediant harmonies, upwardly striving melodic sequences, and unison responses that drift into remote keys. The setting's second half, however, is prosaically martial in tone and subordinates the men's chorus to four male soloists led by a Heldentenor. While the idealistic 13-minute score is a strenuous work, it would fittingly introduce performances of the most celebrated Schiller-inspired composition, Beethoven's Ninth Symphony.

The second especially meritorious occasional work has been hailed by several scholars as Liszt's "most important" large-scale secular choral composition, though it, too, raises practical concerns for modern performances.[26] In the summer of 1850, Liszt composed eight choruses as incidental music for Herder's *Der entfesselte Prometheus*, a play revived for a festival honoring Weimar's philosopher-cleric. For later concert presentations of the choruses, however, Liszt replaced Herder's play with a condensed spoken narration suiting nineteenth- but not twenty-first-century tastes.

Moreover, the condensed narration closely juxtaposes the choruses, producing a disjointed sequence of disparate topics—three laments, two hymns, a storm, a pastorale, and a drinking song. A purely practical consideration is that the full score of the Herder choruses was printed in two limited editions whose rare copies are preserved in only a few research libraries. Fortunately, all of the preceding issues do not impede the independent concert performance of the most appealing and readily available fourth movement: the *Schnitter-Chor* (Chorus of Reapers).

Even when the public rejected *Zukunftsmusik*, the beguiling *Schnitter-Chor* was encored frequently, published separately in multiple formats, and programmed independently throughout Germany, in international capitals, and in a host of important musical centers as far flung as Boston and Cincinnati.[27] Herder's charming lyrics depict the reapers engaging in three activities: they thank Ceres, the goddess of the harvest, for seedlings, fertile crops, and invigorating bread; they observe that the seeds they had sowed as larks warbled sprouted as nightingales sang; and as they head homeward they joyfully sing love songs. The first two of these delightful Arcadian actions are matched by the myriad musical traits of a pastoral topic, including drones, static tonic and dominant harmonies, repetitive rhythms, pentatonic melodies, evocations of birdcalls, echo effects, and solos for woodwinds, especially the bagpipe-like oboe. These pastoralisms recede when the reapers' thoughts turn from nature to human actions (their songs), a juncture marked by the onset of an enchanting waltz (another human activity).

The *Schnitter-Chor*'s naive text belies a sophisticated, characteristically Lisztian formal process. Increases in textural density, called "structural crescendi" by Márta Grabócz,[28] articulate formal sections and generate climaxes within and among them. Structural crescendi, which involve both the number of textural layers and the activity within them, govern the *Schnitter-Chor*'s instrumental introduction and three choral sections based on the reapers' threefold activities (A, thanking Ceres; A', observing birdcalls; B, singing love songs). A structural diminuendo shapes the instrumental coda. The first choral section clearly illustrates the process. As divisi tenors hail Ceres, they statically intone the root and third of the A–major tonic triad, leaping upward to the third and fifth only once in their first phrase and to the dominant triad's pitches at the end of the second. Altos and sopranos echo the tenors, transposing both phrases to the dominant. When the reapers thank Ceres for seedlings and fertile crops, the choral texture expands to five parts, and the altos enliven hitherto completely homorhythmic part writing with an independent line featuring wide leaps and passing tones. Intensifying the reapers' gratitude for invigorating bread are a further expansion to six choral parts, an independent tenor line, melodic ornaments for the sopranos, and enough chromaticism to modulate to C major. The section's accompaniment, a verbatim repetition of the introduction, enhances the chorus's structural crescendo, subjecting three motives—a drone permeated by hemiola, an arpeggiated figure saturated with neighbor tones, and a lively scale broken by occasional leaps—to incremental changes in doubling, register, and scoring. Ensuing formal sections generate even larger structural crescendi by adding more and increasingly active layers. Combining an attractive pastoral surface with underlying formal control, the six-minute *Schnitter-Chor* deserves frequent performance.

The fourteen Weimar sacred works constitute a mixed lot. Small-scale, modestly accompanied motet-like pieces broadly resemble the previously discussed *Ave Maria* in style, except for a collection of harmonized plainchants. Five large-scale, orchestrally accompanied scores, in contrast, apply *Zukunftsmusik* principles to sacred genres. The result in mixed-voice treatments of Psalms 13, 18, and 96 is that grandiose, occasionally bombastic sentiments find welcome relief in intimate vocal solos.[29] Liszt's first oratorio, *Die Legende von der heiligen Elisabeth* (1857–62), likewise illustrates New German precepts.[30] Its crucial solo roles unfold largely in the arioso style of Wagner's *Tannhäuser* and *Lohengrin*. As in these two operas, its three acts are continuous, avoiding conventional divisions into self-contained numbers. Similarly, motives and tonalities that are associated with characters or actions recur in a cyclical, almost leitmotivic fashion. Equally untraditional is that *Elisabeth*'s hagiographic libretto presents isolated episodes in the titular Hungarian saint's life instead of a continuous plot.[31] Compensating for these generic unorthodoxies are many attractive choral passages, including a rousing hunters' song, a crusaders' hymn, and the angelic "Miracle of the Roses." Such passages, together with the nationalistic subject and attendant coloring,[32] account for *Elisabeth*'s lasting popularity in Hungary.

Liszt's *Missa solennis* eschews *Elisabeth*'s idiosyncrasies to observe time-honored conventions, even while epitomizing *Zukunftsmusik*. It was commissioned in 1855 by the eminent Hungarian cleric János Scitovszky for the dedication of a newly rebuilt cathedral in Esztergom (Gran), the Catholic Church's seat in Hungary.[33] The building's construction eradicated architectural remnants of the Turkish occupation (when the original cathedral had been destroyed) and thereby boosted Hungarian nationalistic morale after the calamitous 1848 Revolution. The Mass's sensationally enthusiastic reception by 4,000 spectators during the reconsecration ceremony in August 1856 and its successful repetition in Pest a month later allayed suspicions among Liszt's aristocratic friends and the Esztergom clerics that religion and *Zukunftsmusik* were incompatible.[34]

Three conventions of symphonic-style masses are obvious in the score. First, the topics of its movements, though vivid, fall within generic norms: a somber Kyrie; a festive, martial Gloria with a mournful "Qui tollis" section; a stately Credo punctuated by sorrowful and celebratory interludes;[35] an ethereal Sanctus; a serene Benedictus; and an anguished Agnus Dei. Second, is the use of four soloists (SATB) at traditional points in the text ("Christe eleison," "Quoniam tu solus Sanctus," and "Et incarnatus est," among others). Finally, the choral writing is pervasively homophonic, except in fugues that Liszt added after the premiere as customary conclusions to the Gloria and Credo.

Zukunftsmusik principles are likewise threefold. The orchestra expands to include harp and extra woodwinds, brass, and percussion. Cyclical form and thematic transformation link many of the Mass's sections, underscoring connections among similar textual sentiments or emphasizing tenets of faith of special importance to Liszt.[36] And multiple passages illustrate the quintessentially New-German principle of maximally smooth voice leading, whereby chord tones move not according to standard root progressions, but rather by the smallest possible intervals, normally major and minor seconds, to form new harmonies.[37]

This principle is illustrated by the Credo's "descendit de coelis et incarnatus est" (Examples 27.1a and 27.1b). Christ's descent from heaven is accompanied by falling arpeggios whose roots move entirely in thirds (D–b– G–E-flat). Common chord tones are retained in some voices, while changing chord tones move in other voices only by half or whole steps. Unusual first and second inversions result, obscuring harmonic functions that would be clearer if traditional, bassline-driven root movements were observed. Although a tritone breaks the third descent, maximally smooth voice leading prevails as the soprano announces Christ's incarnation above dominant seventh and six-four chords related by more unusual root movements of thirds and fourths (A–C-sharp–F-sharp–B–F-natural). The principle also applies when the chorus joins the soprano, forming chords whose roots alternate in major seconds (F-sharp–G-sharp, now a tritone removed from the tonic). The entire passage's unorthodox root movements and omnipresent second-inversion chords suspend functional tonality, matching textual revelations with astonishing, ethereal harmonies that are enhanced by a shimmering orchestral texture of lightly articulated woodwinds and ten divisi solo violins. The excerpt supports Liszt's claim that his Mass had been "more *prayed* than composed."[38]

EXAMPLE 27.1a Maximally smooth voice leading in the Credo from Liszt's *Missa solennis zur Erweihung der Basilika in Gran*, mm. 83–103.

EXAMPLE 27.1a   continued.

EXAMPLE 27.1a continued.

EXAMPLE 27.1b Voice reduction of Example 27.1a.

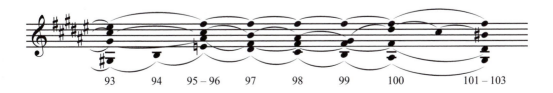

Late Works

After settling in Rome in 1861, Liszt composed only nine secular choral works. Although six are occasional pieces, three reflect Liszt's personal interests: Schubert, whose music he performed and transcribed; the historic Wartburg Castle in Eisenach, where the oratorio *Elisabeth* is set; and a poem by Longfellow, who visited Liszt in Rome in 1868. Of seven orchestrally accompanied scores, only three (all for mixed chorus) aspire to a large scale: *Zur Säkularfeier Beethovens* (1869–70), a cantata written for the centennial of Beethoven's birth; the *Wartburg Lieder* (1872–73), a set of character studies; and the delightfully zany Longfellow setting *Die Glocken des Strassburger Münsters* (1874–75), which narrates Satan's fall from a belfry. Liszt composed just two *Männerchöre* after 1861, verifying his reduced secular output.

In contrast, Liszt wrote three times as many sacred compositions during his later years as he had in Weimar, reflecting intensified religious convictions and his entry into minor ecclesiastical orders in 1865. Of forty-three late works, five require mixed chorus and orchestra: *Cantico del Sol di San Francesco* (1862), a baritone solo with modest choral contributions; the *Ungarische Krönungsmesse* (1866–69), performed during Austrian Emperor Franz Joseph's coronation as King of Hungary; *Cantantibus organis* (1879), written for the dedication of a Palestrina monument in Rome; and two oratorios, *Christus* (1855–72)[39] and *Die Legende vom heiligen Stanislaus* (1863–85). Many of the remaining works are short, minimally accompanied or *a cappella* motets, though compelling full-length scores include the Palestrina-style *Missa choralis* (1859–65), the lugubrious Requiem (1867–68) for male voices, and three tributes to Catholic doctrines: *Via Crucis* (1876–79), *Septem Sacramenta* (1878–84), and *Rosario* (1879). Liszt's post-Weimar choral compositions embrace many diverse styles, some already cultivated, others new, as two extraordinarily different works demonstrate.

Christus resembles *Elisabeth* in that its hagiographic libretto emphasizes pivotal moments in Christ's life over narrative linearity. It nonetheless differs significantly: its ascetic texts were drawn from biblical and liturgical sources; and its music renounces proto-Wagnerian continuity, leit-motivic cyclicism, and arioso singing style. Instead, fourteen discrete movements range widely in style. Several elaborate pieces based on cantus-firmus style counterpoint require six soloists, children's, women's, and mixed choruses, and a very large orchestra; other intimate movements feature only the chorus and organ; and three long but effective movements are entirely or almost entirely orchestral. Additionally, the musical language is variously tonal, modal, purely diatonic, or highly chromatic. Such stylistic diversity is conducive to the performance of separate movements, a practice Liszt observed during the oratorio's long genesis until its complete premiere in 1873.[40] Presenting individual movements would also circumvent several "logistical and financial problems standing in the way of regular performance" of the complete work.[41]

The "Stabat Mater speciosa" (movement 3, SATB divisi with modest organ accompaniment) especially suits independent performance. Its attractive text, an obscure medieval poem Liszt probably encountered in French monographs on Franciscan authors,[42] describes Mary joyfully contemplating her Son in the manger and implores her to fill believers' hearts with an understanding of Christ. An accessible musical idiom makes the movement a perfect companion for pieces in *tintinnabuli* style, whose "rigorously limited" materials and "strict organizational principles" are espoused by composers such as Arvo Pärt.[43]

Rigorous limitations take several forms. Liszt's setting scrupulously observes trochaic meter in all of the poem's twenty-three tercets, producing hypnotically repetitive rhythms that are hallmarks of *tintinnabuli* style (see Example 27.2). The initial harmonic progression, spanning the first three tercets (twenty-three measures), inserts only one secondary dominant into a string of chords whose roots fall exclusively in thirds from the tonic (G major) until all diatonic chords have sounded. Maximally smooth voice leading, achieved through rigorously limited intervallic motion, again

EXAMPLE 27.2   Maximally smooth voice leading and series of root movements in descending thirds in "Stabat Mater speciosa" from Liszt's *Christus*.

EXAMPLE 27.2 continued.

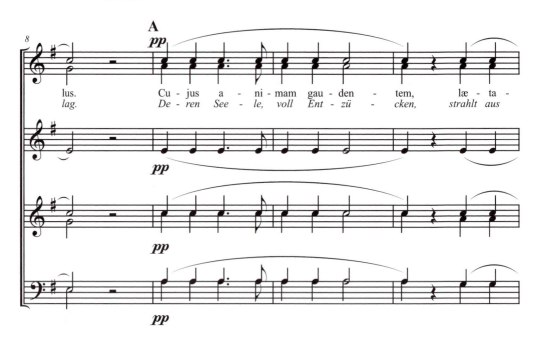

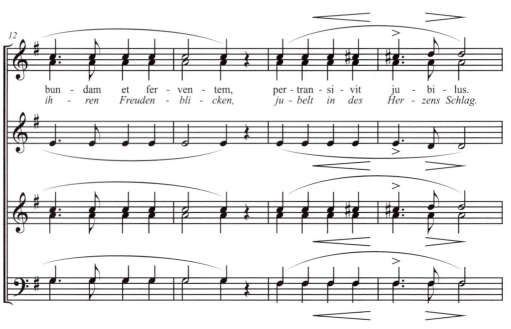

EXAMPLE 27.2 continued.

Part I (First Half)		Part II (Second Half)		
T1, T2, T3	strictly trochaic	T15	a	medieval bar form
T4	lilting refrain	T16	a	
		T17	B	
T5, T6, T7	strictly trochaic	T18	a	medieval bar form
T8	lilting refrain	T19	a	
		T20	B	
T9, T10	*ppp*			
	angelic interruption			
T11, T12, T13	strictly trochaic	T21		unique, departs from previous rigor
T14	lilting refrain	T22		unique, most freely melodic tercet
		T23		unique, reverts to austerity
[T = Tercet]				

FIGURE 27.1   Strict Organization of the "Stabat Mater speciosa" (Liszt, *Christus*, movement 4).

prevails. Dynamics are subdued. And in the first half of the piece, comprising fourteen tercets, unison, syllabic declamation is relieved only three times by a lilting, lullaby-like refrain whose short melismas are sporadically dispersed among the vocal lines.

Strict organization is likewise apparent (see Figure 27.1). The movement's first half is divided into three groups of three strictly trochaic tercets, each followed by the lilting refrain. Between the second and third groups, two additional trochaic tercets, marked *ppp*, distinguish the moment when angels' voices interrupt Mary's contemplation. In the second half, two sets of three tercets observe medieval bar form (aaB), but each of the three final tercets is set uniquely. This departure from all the preceding limitations and strictness constitutes a formal liberation that seemingly correlates with the feeling of freedom that the supplicant expresses in the penultimate and most melodious tercet, when asking for protection through Christ's birth, God's holy word, and His grace. The final tercet reverts to earlier austerity. Thus, the movement twice temporarily abandons rigor and strictness to emphasize portions of the prayer that Liszt ostensibly thought were crucial.

Ten months after *Christus* was premiered, Liszt declared his one remaining musical ambition was "to hurl [his] spear into the unlimited realm of the future."[44] Lisztians agree his late works achieved this goal through austerity and harmonic novelty, as *Via Crucis* illustrates. This set of terse, subjective reflections on the fourteen Stations of the Cross, for mixed choir, soloists, and organ or piano, was finished in 1879, but it remained unperformed until 1929. The 40-minute score gained a secure foothold in concert venues only after its publication in 1936.

Station XI ("Jesus wird ans Kreuz geschlagen") epitomizes the work's uncompromising nature (see Examples 27.3a and 27.3b). Unison men's voices are restricted to just five pitches within the compass of a tritone, and they repeat only one word, "Crucifige," six times in militant, dotted rhythms. The accompaniment's *fortissimo*, weak-beat chords define no clear tonality and elude triadic classification unless a G-sharp pedal point is ignored. Instead, maximally smooth voice leading culminates in an excruciating tone cluster for solo keyboard—a graphic representation of nails piercing Christ's flesh. Spare octaves lacking tonal orientation conclude a shocking vignette that encapsulates the Station's violence.[45]

Via Crucis realizes Liszt's futuristic ambition in another way. Like works of polystylistic composers ranging from Ives to Schnittke, this haunting piece evokes a remote past and portrays irony, estrangement, isolation, and grief by embracing myriad idioms and quoting familiar music. Its ascetic miniatures attain these ends by juxtaposing monophonic and harmonized plainchants, Protestant chorales, Renaissance-style polyphony, operatic recitative, crucial keyboard interludes, and Lisztian musical symbols, notably the "Cross motive"[46] that pervades his sacred music—a collage engendering modality, tonality, whole-tone scales, tone clusters, and ultimately, atonality. These borrowings and tonal-motivic idiosyncrasies not only attest to Liszt's highly personal and deeply felt approach to a subject central to his Catholic faith, but also reward thoughtful interpretation.

Liszt's entire choral *œuvre*, like *Via Crucis*, encompasses enormous variety, as even a cursory sampling demonstrates. Some styles correlate broadly with his career's phases: the largely conventional *Männerchor* idiom is basically associated with his virtuoso and Weimar periods, while grandiose *Zukunftsmusik* scores are essentially Weimar products. In contrast, the proto-Cecilian Palestrina style leads uninterruptedly from Liszt's experiments of the 1840s to his late, rigorously limited,

EXAMPLE 27.3a Liszt, *Via Crucis*, Station XI ("Jesus wird ans Kreuz geschlagen")

EXAMPLE 27.3a continued.

EXAMPLE 27.3b Voice reduction of Example 27.3a.

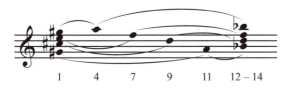

austerely futuristic settings. The typically Lisztian techniques discussed in this chapter, however, know few chronological boundaries. Among recurrent, personally significant subjects, Liszt's devotion to the Virgin and social consciousness are paramount; these remain constant regardless of the vicissitudes of the composer's career. His output, though occasionally idiosyncratic, will nonetheless benefit from advocates who can realize its value by studying individual works in the contexts of Liszt's biography, social and religious history, and performance traditions. Such attention from scholars and performers alike would recover the conspicuous riches of one of the nineteenth century's most opulent yet sorely neglected choral legacies.

Notes

1 Chiefly see Paul Merrick, *Revolution and Religion in the Music of Liszt* (Cambridge: Cambridge University Press, 1987), 7–266; Dolores Pesce, "Liszt's Sacred Choral Music," in *The Cambridge Companion to Liszt*, ed. Kenneth Hamilton (Cambridge: Cambridge University Press, 2005), 223–48; Michael Saffle, "Sacred Choral Works," and Kristin Wendland, "Secular Choral Works," in *The Liszt Companion*, ed. Ben Arnold (Westport: Greenwood Press, 2002), 335–63, 365–91; Robert Collet, "Choral and Organ Music," in *Franz Liszt: The Man and his Music*, ed. Alan Walker (London: Barrie & Jenkins, 1970), 318–49.

2 The number varies depending on several factors: Liszt made choral arrangements of works that he and other composers had originally conceived as instrumental or solo vocal compositions; in setting the same text multiple times, he often produced pieces that differ radically, but in other cases are merely slightly varied arrangements for men's, women's, and mixed choruses; and several large-scale scores whose components were performed and published separately at early stages in their compositional evolution were eventually assembled as one composition. For the most comprehensive, reliable catalogue of Liszt's choral music, see Rena Charnin Mueller and Mária Eckhardt, "Liszt, Franz: Works," *Grove Music Online, Oxford Music Online*, http://www.oxfordmusiconline.com/subscriber/article/grove/music48265 (accessed April 29, 2011). The total I use here does not count the same work twice if Mueller and Eckhardt list it separately under pieces accompanied by orchestra and keyboard, nor does it include lost or incomplete works other than the unfinished oratorio, *Die Legende vom heiligen Stanislaus*, now partially available in Paul Allen Munson, ed., *St. Stanislaus: Scene 1, Two Polonaises, Scene 4*, Recent Researches in the Music of the Nineteenth and Early Twentieth Centuries, vol. 26 (Madison, WI: A-R Editions, 1998). To the resulting total I have added only the miniature motet cycle *Zwölf alte deutsche geistliche Weisen*, some of whose constituent numbers were published separately or in other larger works during Liszt's lifetime. (Mueller and Eckhardt catalogue two of the twelve *Weisen* separately; four are included in *Via Crucis*.)

3 Alternative accompaniments usually involve chordal instruments: harmonium may replace organ, or harp may replace piano. In several cases, however, several orchestral instruments may replace chordal instruments.

4 Much of Liszt's sacred music was collected and published in *Franz Liszts musikalische Werke*, ed. Ferruccio Busoni, Peter Raabe, et al. (Leipzig: Breitkopf & Härtel, 1907–36). Commercially available reprints from this set of collected works, of both large- and small-scale sacred compositions, have been issued by such familiar North American and Western European companies as Kalmus, Bärenreiter, Gregg International Publishers, and Belwin Mills, the latter firm offering miniature study scores of forty small-scale pieces. A handful of works that are not available from these standard publishers are accessible in Editio Musica Budapest's handsome editions.

5 Appropriately illustrating the concision of Liszt's *Männerchöre* is the forty-two-measure setting of Goethe's epiphanic *Über allen Gipfeln ist Ruh'*. Longer are settings of Friedrich Rückert's *Ständchen*, Hoffmann von Fallersleben's rousing *Vereinslied*, Franz Schober's rumination on Goethe's last words (*Licht, mehr Licht*), and Lamennais's *Arbeiterchor* (in Philipp Kaufmann's German translation).

6 The usual difference involves a choice between *a cappella* performance and a piano's largely *colla parte* support.

7 Liszt accepted his appointment as *Kapellmeister* in "extraordinary service" to the Weimar court in 1842, but toured six more years before settling there and assuming official duties.

8 For details, see Wendland, "Secular Choral Works," 369–81, and James Thomson Fudge, "The Male Chorus Music of Franz Liszt" (Ph.D. diss., University of Iowa, 1972).

9 Liszt began revising these partsongs in the late 1850s, but did not complete the revisions or publish the new versions until the early 1860s. See a letter that the Viennese conductor Johann Herbeck received from Liszt on January 12, 1857 in La Mara [Marie Lipsius], ed., *Letters of Franz Liszt*, trans. Constance Bache, 2 vols. (New York: Haskell House, 1968), vol. 1, 313–15.

10 Editio Musica Budapest published István Szelényi's piano edition in 1961.

11 Merrick, *Revolution and Religion*, 7–25.

12 Regarding Liszt's use of topics, see Márta Grabócz, *Morphologie des œuvres pour piano de Liszt: influence du programme sur l'évolution des formes instrumentales* (Budapest: MTA Zenetudományi Intézet, 1986); Constantin Floros, "Die Faust-Symphonie von Franz Liszt: Eine semantische Analyse," in *Franz Liszt*, Musik-Konzepte: Die Reihe über Komponisten, vol. 12, ed. Heinz-Klaus Metzger and Rainer Riehn (Munich: Edition Text + Kritik, 1980), 42–87; and Keith T. Johns, *The Symphonic Poems of Franz Liszt*, ed. Michael Saffle, Franz Liszt Studies Series, no. 3 (Stuyvesant, NY: Pendragon Press, 1997).

13 Regarding funereal topics in Liszt's music, see Grabócz, *Morphologie*, 39, 53, 91, 98–9.

14 Regarding this specific form of pastoralism, see Grabócz, *Morphologie*, 94.

15 Schubert obviously used many mode changes, but the enharmonic and third-related modulations in the masses and partsongs tend to be more isolated than is the case here—and they are usually the most dramatic modulations of an entire piece, movement, or section. Spohr's chromaticism, and Hummel's, is on the surface (i.e., decorative), not in the root movements or in the overall tonal plan (i.e., not structural), and Mendelssohn's third-related modulations within movements are isolated or emphatic.

16 See Liszt's letter of April 28, 1845 to Lamennais in La Mara, ed. *Letters of Franz Liszt*, vol. 1, 44. The letter does not indicate precisely why Liszt expressed this attitude, though his reservations seem to have been directed at musical conditions in Paris. He merely stated that music, unlike a painting or a novel, "has to be performed, and very well performed, too, to be understood and felt. Now the performance of a chorus of the size of that is not an easy matter in Paris, and I would not even risk it without myself conducting the preliminary rehearsals." Later, well into his Weimar years, Liszt offered several reasons for such reservations about his music in general or other works in particular, all relating to his belief that his music was difficult to understand and to perform.

17 Liszt's first composition of any kind, a *Tantum ergo* completed in Vienna under Salieri's supervision, is lost. The autograph of the *Ave Maria* is signed Paris, July 1, 18..; 1842 is the only plausible year when Liszt is known to have been in Paris in July.

18 See Liszt's letter of January 27, 1855 in Wilhelm von Csapó, ed., *Franz Liszts Briefe an Baron Anton Augusz, 1846–1878* (Budapest: Franklin-Verein, 1911), 51–52.

19 See Pesce, "Liszt's Sacred Choral Music," 225.

20 Until this juncture, harmonic movement is largely conventional: a mode change; a circle of fifths (admittedly from an unexpected point of departure that may nonetheless be heard as a tonicization of the relative minor); and a forceful modulation to Liszt's quintessential chromatic mediant key. A-flat and F major are quite unanticipated in the local context of G major. A-flat is also distant from the global tonic, B-flat major.

21 See Alan Walker, *Franz Liszt*, vol. 1, *The Virtuoso Years (1811–1847)*, rev. ed. (Ithaca, NY: Cornell University Press, 1987), 61–62, 117, 132.

22 Only the *Prometheus* choruses require mixed forces. The *Chor der Engel aus Goethe's 'Faust'* exists in versions for men's, women's, and mixed choruses, and two contrafacta (*Mit klingendem Spiel* for children, *Morgenlied* for women) use different texts for the same music.

23 Only five of Liszt's Weimar secular works were unrelated to his position's duties: *Titan* (unpublished), the *Ungaria-Kantate*, the two contrafacta, and *Das deutsche Vaterland II*, dedicated to students in six German-speaking cities.

24 See Gerhard J. Winkler, "Zum Sozialstatus der Zukunftsmusik: Franz Liszt in Weimar," in *Bruckner Symposion: Kreativität und Gesellschaft—Die materielle und soziale Situation des Künstlers*, ed. Theophil Antonicek et al. (Linz: Anton-Bruckner-Institut, 2004), 89–96.

25 For representative accounts of the reception of the New German School and *Zukunftsmusik* during Liszt's lifetime and beyond, see Alan Walker's "The War of the Romantics," in *Franz Liszt*, vol. 2, *The Weimar Years (1848–1861)* (Ithaca, NY: Cornell University Press, 1989), 338–67; and Richard Taruskin's "Midcentury: The New German School; Liszt's Symphonic Poems; Harmonic Explorations," in *The Oxford History of Music*, vol. 3, *The Nineteenth Century* (Oxford: Oxford University Press, 2005), 411–22. For additional investigations of the polemic and practical objections that orchestral and choral musicians, conductors, critics, and Liszt's opponents made against *Zukunftsmusik* in general and against the *Prometheus* choruses in particular, see Paul A. Bertagnolli, "A Newly Discovered Source for Franz Liszt's *Chöre zu Herder's 'Entfesseltem Prometheus*,'" *Journal of Musicology* 19, 2 (May 2002): 138–56; and Paul A Bertagnolli, "Franz Liszt's *Prometheus* Music" (Ph.D. diss., Washington University in St. Louis, 1998), 64–136.

26 Derek Watson names the choruses as "Liszt's most important secular choral work" in *Liszt* (New York: Schirmer Books, 1989), 291–92. Seconding Watson's assessment are Rainer Kleinertz, "Liszts Ouvertüre und Chöre zu Herders Entfesseltem Prometheus," in *Liszt und die Weimarer Klassik*, ed. Detlef Altenburg, Weimarer Liszt Studien, no. 1 (Laaber: Laaber-Verlag, 1997), 155–78; and Peter Raabe, *Franz Liszt*, vol. 2, *Liszts Schaffen*, rev. ed. (Tutzing: Schneider, 1968), 134.

27 The *Schnitter-Chor* was issued by the Leipzig firm of C. F. Kahnt in full and vocal scores for mixed chorus and in arrangements for women's chorus, piano four-hands, and solo piano. For a detailed reception history of the *Prometheus* choruses, including separate discussion of the *Schnitter-Chor*, see Bertagnolli, "A Newly Discovered Source for Franz Liszt's *Chöre zu Herder's 'Entfesseltem Prometheus*,'" 125–70.

28 Grabócz, *Morphologie*, 128. Structural crescendi are common in Liszt's piano, orchestral, and choral compositions.

29 Partisans of Liszt's psalms include Saffle, "Sacred Choral Works," 348, who attributes their infrequent performance to technical difficulty, instrumentation, and monumental scale, and Pesce, "Liszt's Sacred Choral Music," 226–28, who focuses on their many striking features.

30 I include *Elisabeth* among the Weimar works because Liszt composed most of it between 1857 and 1861, though he did not complete it until 1862. Its premiere occurred in Pest in 1865.

31 For a compelling discussion of this aspect of *Elisabeth*, see Paul Allen Munson, "The Oratorios of Franz Liszt" (Ph.D. diss., University of Michigan, 1996), 32–43.

32 *Elisabeth* contains Hungarian plainchants, but they are not treated in an "antique" manner. They are instead absorbed into the prevailing New-German idiom.

33 As early as 1846, then Bishop Scitovszky had asked Liszt to compose a Mass to reconsecrate the cathedral in Pécs, but construction delayed the project.

34 Merrick relates that Liszt's friend Count Leo Festetics wrote to the newly elevated Cardinal Scitovszky, communicating reservations about "allowing *Zukunftsmusik* into the Church." The cardinal then wrote to Liszt, claiming the Mass could not be performed because the Esztergom choir was too small and the Mass was rumored to last two and a half hours. (It actually lasted only forty-five minutes during the second performance in Pest. The rumor is nonetheless a good illustration of the controversy, intrigue, and resistance that often surrounded Liszt's Weimar-period music.) Liszt replied that the choir's size was adequate and that the Mass lasted only an hour. The cardinal then suggested it should be presented months after the reconsecration ceremony. Plans for the premiere resumed only after Liszt countered Cardinal Scitovszky's objections, raised several of his own, and received Baron Anton Augusz's support. See Merrick, *Revolution and Religion*, 110.

35 The "Et incarnatus est," for example, observes the eighteenth-century pathos convention mentioned in my introduction to Hungarian choral music appearing earlier in this volume.

36 The return of the opening of the Kyrie at the end of the Agnus Dei merely replicates the *Dona ut Kyrie* practice mentioned in the introduction to Hungarian choral music. Regarding the Mass's other, more distinctive cyclical recurrences, see Merrick, *Revolution and Religion*, 112–19; Pesce, "Liszt's Sacred Choral Music," 229–30; and William Drabkin, "Beethoven, Liszt, and the Missa solemnis," in *Franz Liszt and the Birth of Modern Europe: Music as a Mirror of Religious, Political, and Aesthetic Transformations*, ed. Michael Saffle and Rossana Dalmonte, Analecta Lisztiana, no. 3 (Hillsdale, NY: Pendragon Press, 2003), 237–52.

37 The principle also applies to large-scale tonal organization. See Richard Cohn, "Maximally Smooth Cycles, Hexatonic Systems, and the Analysis of Late-Romantic Triadic Progressions," *Music Analysis* 15, 1 (March 1996): 9–40.

38 See Liszt's letter of June 2, 1855 to Carl Gille in Franz Liszt, *Franz Liszts Briefe*, ed. La Mara, 8 vols. (Leipzig: Breitkopf & Härtel, 1893–1905), vol.1, 241.

39 Liszt first planned to write *Christus* in 1853, began composing portions of it in 1855, declared it finished in 1866, but added two additional movements in 1867 and 1868. See Merrick, *Revolution and Religion*, 182–83.

40 Movement 6 (The Beatitudes) was performed in Weimar in 1859. Movements 6 and 7 (The Beatitudes and Pater noster) were published separately in 1861 and 1864. Movement 3 ("Stabat Mater speciosa") was performed in Rome in 1866. Part I, comprising movements 1–5 and known as the "Christmas Oratorio," was given a "trial performance" in Rome in 1867 and performed in Vienna in 1871. The full score was published in 1872, a year before the Weimar premiere. See Walker, *Franz Liszt*, vol. 3, *The Final Years, 1861–1886*, (Ithaca: Cornell University Press, 1996), 256.

41 See Walker, "Liszt, Franz," *Grove Music Online, Oxford Music Online*, http://www.oxfordmusiconline. com/subscriber/article/grove/music48265 (accessed April 24, 2011). Walker cites as problems the oratorio's length (3.5 hours without authorized cuts), its large performing forces, and the need for an offstage women's chorus. He nonetheless observes that *Christus* can make an "overwhelming" impression "when properly presented in a spacious church by devoted interpreters."

42 The "Stabat Mater speciosa," a Latin hymn, is not liturgical, though its form resembles that of the sequence. Like the more familiar "Stabat Mater dolorosa," it was once attributed to Jacopone da Todi (*c.*1230–1306), but is now thought to be the work of an anonymous Franciscan parodist. A later source for Jacopone's poems (1495) preserves it, but otherwise it remained unknown until Antoine-Frédéric Ozanam and Emile Chavin de Malan transcribed it in monographs respectively published in 1852 and 1855. See Günther Massenkeil, "Das weihnachtliche *Stabat Mater* in dem Oratorium *Christus* von Franz

Liszt," in *Artes liberales: Karlheinz Schlager zum 60. Geburtstag*, ed. Marcel Dobberstein (Tutzing: Schneider, 1998), 283–89.

43 Stephen Wright, "Arvo Pärt (1935–)," in *Music of the Twentieth-Century Avant-Garde*, ed. Larry Sitsky (Westport, CT: Greenwood Press, 2002), 359.

44 See Liszt's letter of February 9, 1874 to Princess Carolyne Sayn-Wittgenstein in La Mara, ed. *Franz Liszts Briefe*, vol. 7, 57–58.

45 The accompaniment's pitches (in the entire movement) are restricted to a so-called "gypsy" scale with two augmented seconds (A–B-flat–C-sharp–D–E–F–G-sharp–A). After Hungary's defeat in the Revolution of 1848–49, Liszt often associated this scale type with mournful subjects or death, notably in threnodies he wrote in 1877, when he was working on *Via Crucis*. These threnodies were published in 1882 as part of his collection of character pieces for solo piano, *Années de pèlerinage, Troisième année*. The voices add one pitch, B-natural, to the movement's pitch collection.

46 The "Cross motive," deriving from the plainchant *Crux fidelis*, comprises an ascending major second followed by an ascending minor third. It often appears in Liszt's sacred choral music when the Cross is mentioned and in programmatic instrumental compositions with religious associations. Liszt sometimes varied its intervals or inverted their order. For an extensive discussion of the motive, see Merrick, *Revolution and Religion*, 94, 103, 146–47, 156–59, 256–57, 263–64, 268–72, 284–85, 287–91, 293–95, 307–8.

Selected Bibliography

Bertagnolli, Paul A. "A Newly Discovered Source for Franz Liszt's *Chöre zu Herder's 'Entfesseltem Prometheus'*," *Journal of Musicology* 19, 2 (May 2002): 125–70.

Collet, Robert. "Choral and Organ Music," in *Franz Liszt: The Man and his Music*, ed. Alan Walker. London: Barrie & Jenkins, 1970, 318–49.

Domokos, Zsuzsanna. "Liszt's Church Music and the Musical Traditions of the Sistine Chapel," in *Franz Liszt and the Birth of Modern Europe: Music as a Mirror of Religious, Political, and Aesthetic Transformations*, ed. Michael Saffle and Rossana Dalmonte. Analecta Lisztiana, no. 3. Hillsdale, NY: Pendragon Press, 2003, 25–46.

Drabkin, William. "Beethoven, Liszt, and the 'Missa solemnis'," in *Franz Liszt and the Birth of Modern Europe: Music as a Mirror of Religious, Political, and Aesthetic Transformations*, ed. Michael Saffle and Rossana Dalmonte. Analecta Lisztiana, no. 3. Hillsdale, NY: Pendragon Press, 2003, 237–52.

Fudge, James Thomson. "The Male Chorus Music of Franz Liszt." Ph.D. diss., University of Iowa, 1972.

Hamburger, Klára. "Program and Hungarian Idiom in the Sacred Music of Liszt," in *New Light on Liszt and His Music: Essays in Honor of Alan Walker's 65th Birthday*, ed. Michael Saffle and James Deaville. Analecta Lisztiana, no. 2. Franz Liszt Studies Series, no. 6. Stuyvesant, NY: Pendragon Press, 1997, 239–51.

Kinder, Keith William. "Sacred Choral Music with Winds," *Journal of the World Association for Symphonic Bands and Ensembles* 2 (1995): 5–31.

Loos, Helmut. "Franz Liszts Graner Festmesse," *Kirchenmusikalisches Jahrbuch* 67 (1983): 45–59.

Massenkeil, Günther. "Das weihnachtliche *Stabat Mater* in dem Oratorium *Christus* von Franz Liszt," in *Artes liberales: Karlheinz Schlager zum 60. Geburtstag*, ed. Marcel Dobberstein. Tutzing: Schneider, 1998, 283–89.

Merrick, Paul. *Revolution and Religion in the Music of Liszt*. Cambridge: Cambridge University Press, 1987.

Minor, Ryan. "Prophet and Populace in Liszt's Beethoven Cantatas," in *Liszt and his World*, ed. Christopher Gibbs and Dana Gooley. Princeton: Princeton University Press, 2006, 113–65.

Munson, Paul Allen. "The Oratorios of Franz Liszt." Ph.D. diss., University of Michigan, 1996.

Orr, Lee N. "Liszt, *Christus*, and the Transformation of the Oratorio," *JALS: The Journal of the American Liszt Society* 9 (June 1981): 4–18.

Pesce, Dolores. "Liszt's Sacred Choral Music," in *The Cambridge Companion to Liszt*, ed. Kenneth Hamilton. Cambridge: Cambridge University Press, 2005, 223–48.

Saffle, Michael. "Sacred Choral Works," in *The Liszt Companion*, ed. Ben Arnold. Westport, CT: Greenwood Press, 2002, 335–63.

Walker, Alan. *Franz Liszt*. 3 vols. Ithaca, NY: Cornell University Press, 1983–96.

Wendland, Kristin. "Secular Choral Works," in *The Liszt Companion*, ed. Ben Arnold. Westport, CT: Greenwood Press, 2002, 365–91.

28

RUSSIA

Vladimir Morosan

Musica Russica

The art of choral singing in Russia—in this context, this includes the modern-day nations of Ukraine and Belarus[1]—developed historically along a path that was markedly different from other European nations, both Eastern and Western.[2] Although by the turn of the nineteenth century, choral part-singing had become relatively widespread there, it did not represent a natural phenomenon from either a sociological or a cultural standpoint. The various private *kapellas* that were started by wealthy nobility in imitation of the Imperial Court Chapel were a response to Russian high society's taste for elaborate imported music in the Italianate style. But neither the style of performance nor the repertoire sung by such choirs[3] had any connection to the two types of indigenous Russian vocal ensemble music: church chants and village folk songs. Only as the nineteenth century progressed did the seeds planted by foreign musicians a century earlier combine with the emerging national consciousness in musical thinking. Fuelled by the social and educational reforms of Tsar Alexander II in the 1860s, the union of assimilated foreign skills and native Russian music-making traditions produced an extraordinary renaissance of choral music that began in the last two decades of the nineteenth century and spilled over into the twentieth, only to be cut off by the cataclysmic fracturing of all artistic and cultural life brought about by the Communist Revolution of 1917.

While the nineteenth century witnessed a steady broadening in the base of social and economic support for musical institutions such as orchestras, opera theaters, and public concert societies, choral music prior to the social reforms of the 1860s remained confined to a large extent to the realm of church choirs and theater choirs. Church choirs fall into three different categories, depending on their economic status. At the top echelon of state-supported choirs were the Imperatorskaya pridvornaya pevcheskaya kapella (Imperial Court Chapel) and the Moskovskii sinodal'nyi khor (Moscow Synodal Choir), which sang services in the Uspensky Sobor (Dormition Cathedral) of the Moscow Kremlin. Archepiscopal choirs attached to diocesan cathedrals were supported by diocesan treasuries. Some monasteries and convents had organized choirs, although generally speaking, monastic singing was on a very low level in the nineteenth century. Completing this category of government- or church-supported[4] choirs were those groups connected to theological academies and seminaries, and military regiment choirs. With the exception of convent choirs, all of these ensembles were staffed by men alone, or boys and men.[5] The use of boys' voices dates back to at least the seventeenth century, and choirs such as the Imperial Chapel and the Moscow Synodal Choir continued to be staffed by boys and men right up to the 1917 Revolution. The

Imperial Chapel in the late eighteenth and nineteenth centuries provided instruction on various instruments to its charges in order to staff the Imperial orchestra, but naturally this did not affect liturgical performance practice, since all Orthodox church music is unaccompanied.

The second major category of Russian choirs included those supported by private individuals—wealthy nobility for their own household chapels—or by choral entrepreneurs, whose choirs were primarily commercial enterprises in large cities. Essentially, these were large contingents of men and boys who were hired out for singing in various churches, as well as for such occasions as weddings and funerals.

The final principal category of choral ensemble, amateur church choirs, comprising members of the middle-class bourgeoisie who belonged to a particular (mainly urban) parish, began to appear at the end of the eighteenth century but became widespread only toward the end of the nineteenth century. After the emancipation of the serfs in 1861 and the growth of city industry, similar choirs were organized in villages and factory towns, often as part of efforts to bring culture and musical educations to the masses. These groups became known as folk choirs because they comprised commoners from the peasant or worker class; however, they sang the same repertoire as the other church choirs described above.[6] Often, such folk choirs functioned together with choirs at a local elementary or secondary school, since the school singing teacher was also the church precentor.

An important role in the growth of choral culture in Russia was played by public sacred concerts, in which sacred choral works were presented in an extra-liturgical setting. The first such concert took place in Moscow in 1864, and the phenomenon grew throughout the 1870s and 1880s. Historical concert series given in the late 1880s and early 1890s by Alexander Arkhangelsky's Choir in St. Petersburg, and (later) in Moscow by the Moscow Synodal Choir in the late 1890s, exposed the public to the history and evolution of sacred choral music both in Europe and in Russia. These concerts were the first opportunities Russian audiences had to hear such Western choral masterpieces as Palestrina's *Missa Papae Marcelli*, as well as early unison Russian chants and Russian choral polyphony from the Baroque period, which by then had been thoroughly forgotten. Sacred concerts stimulated numerous Russian composers to create new works, which resulted in the enormous blossoming of the sacred choral repertoire in the late nineteenth and early twentieth centuries. Between 1897 and 1917 the Moscow Synodal Choir alone gave no fewer than sixty-two concerts, premiering close to one hundred works.

Independent, non-institutional choral societies whose main interest lay in secular choral singing as a cultural pursuit were practically non-existent in Russia before Alexander II's reforms of the 1860s, chiefly because a meeting of a choral society was considered an assembly, permission for which had to be obtained on every occasion from the local police. In 1862, immediately after the reforms, the Besplatnaya muzykal'naya shkola (Free Musical School), which included choral singing, was founded in St. Petersburg by Mily Balakirev and Gavriil Lomakin, and later involving Rimsky-Korsakov as well. The amateur Russian Choral Society was formed in 1878 in Moscow. Another group, Besplatnyi khorovoi klass I. A. Mel'nikova (I. A. Melnikov's Free Choral Class), was established in 1890 in St. Petersburg under the direction of Fyodor Bekker. These choral societies stimulated the composition of secular choral partsongs and folk-song arrangements, which were relative latecomers to the Russian choral repertoire.

Non-institutional professional choirs,[7] which were organized primarily as secular business enterprises were also late in developing in Russia. One of the two most prominent groups of this kind was Khor A. A. Arkhangel'skogo (A. A. Arkhangelsky's Choir) in St. Petersburg, an ensemble of some 120 voices, many of whom earned their income by contracting to sing in various churches by dividing themselves into small ensembles of four to eight singers. In the early 1880s, Arkhangelsky was also the first to introduce women's voices, supplementing and eventually replacing boys' voices into what initially was an all-male choir. The other prominent professional choir was Dmitry Agrenev-Slaviansky's Cappella, which gave close to 15,000 concerts over the course of four decades beginning in 1868, many of them in foreign countries. Although Westerners reacted enthusiastically to Agrenev-Slaviansky's performances, which featured stage sets, costumes, and other aspects of showmanship, most Russian critics agreed that neither his selection of repertoire nor his manner of performance embodied the best traditions of Russian music.

Although much of Agrenev-Slaviansky's repertoire was billed as folk songs, the singing of his choir was a far cry from the singing of actual village peasant choirs, with their distinctive age-old traditions of collective heterophonic singing. This type of choral singing did not capture the attention of academic musical circles until the first two decades of the twentieth century, when Mitrofan Piatnitsky brought a group of peasant singers to Moscow for the purpose of performing their authentic choral songs in a concert setting. Organized and often state-supported folk choirs were chiefly a phenomenon of the Soviet era, which witnessed the suppression or disbanding of most, if not all, pre-revolutionary institutional church choirs.

In the final analysis, the two Russian choirs that dominated Russia's choral culture of the nineteenth century were the Imperial Court Chapel in the first half of the century, an exceptional choral ensemble whose reputation spread throughout Europe and garnered accolades from such visiting luminaries as Robert Schumann and Hector Berlioz,[8] and the Moscow Synodal Choir from the late 1800s to 1917. Most of the Russian choral repertoire, in which sacred music predominates by a ratio of about four to one, was created with these two ensembles in mind, and it is within these two ensembles that the highest traditions of Russian choral performance were cultivated and embodied. Of these two ensembles, the Moscow Synodal Choir was both the primary catalyst and the beneficiary of the rise of the New Russian Choral School, which included such composers as Tchaikovsky, Kastalsky, Ippolitov-Ivanov, Gretchaninoff, Rachmaninoff, Nikolsky, Chesnokov, and Victor Kalinnikov, among others. Their essential contributions to the Russian choral repertoire will be discussed in the next chapter.

Notes

1 Russia, Ukraine, and Belarus together represent the three main branches of Eastern Slavs.
2 A detailed account of the historical development of vocal ensemble and choral singing in Russia is found in Vladimir Morosan, *Choral Performance in Pre-Revolutionary Russia*, 2nd ed. (Madison, CT: Musica Russica, 1996), esp. 3–36.
3 Just as the Imperial Chapel gave rise to less accomplished, provincial imitators, the style of music brought by foreign *Kapellmeisters* to the St. Petersburg Court spawned numerous imitative sacred choral compositions, most of them anonymous, bearing such whimsical attributions or subtitles as "birdie" (*ptichka*), "down from the attic" (*s cherdaka*), "a merry song" (*vesiolaya*). The musical level of these home-based creations was beneath criticism, to say nothing of their lack of propriety for church use. The appointment in 1816 of Imperial Chapel Director Dmitri Bortniansky as censor for church music was an attempt to eradicate this low-brow repertoire and to raise the quality of polyphonic compositions in the new Western European style.
4 Since the Russian Orthodox Church under the reforms of Peter I was essentially relegated to the status of a government department, one can consider these church choirs to be government supported.
5 Although there has never been any canonical prohibition in the Eastern Orthodox Church against women singing during worship services, the same cannot be said about tonsured readers or chanters, whose role was initially to lead the congregation in worship; that role, since it was potentially a step to higher orders, was reserved for men. More problematic was the pious custom, which can still be observed in tradition-minded parishes today, of having men and women stand in church separately—the men on the right, opposite the icon of Christ on the *iconostasis*, and the women on the left, opposite the icon of the Virgin Mary. Only with the breakdown of such traditional sensibilities in the 1880s did it become possible for men and women to stand and sing together in a mixed-gender choir.
6 These types of folk choirs should not be confused with authentic village folk choirs that were first brought to the concert stage by Mitrofan Piatnitsky in the early 1900s, and became the basis for Soviet-era folk ensembles.

7 During this time, choirs were considered professional if they supported their singers in some way, either by paying their singers or by providing living accommodations and meals along with a stipend for singing.

8 The Imperial Chapel began its rise to excellence in the second half of the eighteenth century. Already in the 1760s, the visiting Italian maestro Baldassare Galuppi remarked: "Un si magnifico coro mai non io sentito in Italia." [I have not heard such a magnificent choir in all Italy]. (Quoted in Jakob von Stählin, "Nachrichten von der Musik in Russland" in *Haygold's Beylagen zu dem unveränderten Russland* (St. Petersburg: n.p., 1767–68); Russian translation in *Russkaya muzykal'naia gazeta* 11 (1902): 322–25.) Under the leadership of Italian-trained Bortniansky (1751–1825), who became Director in 1796, the Imperial Chapel increasingly participated in extra-liturgical concert performances of Western European oratorios and cantatas, including Handel's *Messiah*, Haydn's *The Creation* and *The Seasons*, Mozart's Requiem and *Davidde penitente*, and Cherubini's requiems and masses; additionally, it gave the world premiere of Beethoven's *Missa solemnis* in 1824. (For an account of Schumann's and Berlioz's comments, see Morosan, *Choral Performance*, 82).

29

RUSSIAN CHORAL REPERTOIRE[1]

Vladimir Morosan

MUSICA RUSSICA

Russian choral repertoire in the nineteenth century must be considered against the background of the historical development of vocal ensemble singing in the lands of the Eastern Slavs. The Christianization of Kievan Rus' in AD 988—the geographical region that roughly corresponds to modern-day Russia, Ukraine, and Belarus—marked the beginning of systematically cultivated musical art, which occurred almost entirely within the realm of liturgical worship. Initially coming from Byzantium, sacred liturgical music in its most fundamental form—unison chant (termed *znamenny*) with possible elements of diaphony, evidence for which has only recently been set forth[2]—was the prevailing type of ensemble singing for the first five or six centuries following the Christianization of Rus'. The development of notated organum-like polyphony (termed *strochny* and *demestvenny*) is documented in fifteenth- and sixteenth-century manuscripts, displaying characteristics not unlike indigenous Georgian polyphony. Throughout all this time, the repertoire of liturgical chant adhered strictly to the canon of the Orthodox[3] liturgy, and its performance did not involve any type of instrumental accompaniment or support.

Although there is no evidence that any type of secular artistic ensemble singing developed at Russian princely courts, in the realm of folk music-making the Eastern Slavs exhibited a very strong predilection for collective rather than individual performance. Russian folk music, existing primarily as an oral tradition, abounded with a vast array of lyric, calendar, and ritual songs, marking the seasons, events, and vicissitudes of agrarian life, that by all evidence were performed by groups of unaccompanied voices singing in improvised heterophony ("countervoice" polyphony).

These two factors—the centuries-old cultivation of exclusively vocal liturgical chant and a strong tradition of collective secular folk singing—constituted the fertile environment into which the Eastern Slavs received Western European-style polyphonic part-singing beginning in the seventeenth century. Initially adopted by Orthodox churches in Southwestern Rus' (modern-day Ukraine and Belarus) as a countermeasure against Roman Catholic expansionism via the *unia*,[4] part-singing was brought to Muscovy and Northern Russia in the mid-seventeenth century by traveling ensembles of Ukrainian singers, some of whom were undoubtedly trained in Poland. The new style of singing found favor with the Tsar and the Patriarch, as well as among the upper-class layers of society, and very quickly it obscured the unison *znamenny* chant and *strochny* polyphony in favor of elaborate Baroque-style works, which, nevertheless, continued to be sung *a cappella* and very often with one voice on a part.[5] This initial rapid acceptance of musical styles imported from points west, which antedated Peter I's westernizing reforms by several decades, and began a steady trend of importing musicians to Russia from Western Europe that lasted to the very end of the eighteenth century.

By the turn of the nineteenth century, then, the repertoire of choral music in Russia existed in several distinct and rarely interacting stylistic streams. The most visible style was the polyphonic part-singing cultivated at the Imperial Court Chapel and its imitators among the private *kapellas* maintained by members of the nobility. Essentially, this was the current style of Viennese classicism, known among Russians as "the Italian style" because virtually all of its practitioners were Italian composers and conductors who had been invited to serve at the Imperial Court to produce operas and to supply instrumental music for court functions. Several of these Italians, most notably Baldassare Galuppi (1706–85) and Giuseppe Sarti (1729–1802), tried their hand at composing choral music on texts of the Russian Orthodox Church.[6] In doing so, they employed the *stile antico* prevalent in Europe at the time, but of necessity restricted their writing to music for unaccompanied voices. The majority of the works in this style were new compositions called sacred choral concertos (discussed in greater detail below), although some liturgical hymns of the Ordinary were also composed in this style.[7]

The second stylistic stream was represented by liturgical chant, which continued to constitute the backbone of Orthodox worship music; it was used for the numerous festal, daily, and seasonal Propers, as well as for hymns of the Ordinary. From the time harmonic part-singing had become the norm in the middle of the seventeenth century, the vast repertory of chant had been harmonized, initially in a somewhat modal homophonic style resembling Renaissance motets (which came to be known as the *partesny* style, from the Latin *partes*), but then increasingly took on a more contemporary harmonic vocabulary until it was codified as the Imperial Court Chant in the 1840s by Alexei L'vov (1798–1870).[8]

The third stylistic stream of Russian choral music—the indigenous heterophonic folk song as sung by village peasant choirs—continued its existence in the rural countryside, having little interaction with the two streams of sacred choral music throughout much of the nineteenth century. There are only occasional reports of trained composers taking any note of village choral singing, and what they heard found its way into some of the choruses in Alexander Borodin's *Prince Igor* (most notably, the opening "Chorus of the Settlers") and in Modest Musorgsky's *Boris Godunov* and *Khovanshchina*. Only toward the very end of the nineteenth century did the choral folk song begin to influence the choral compositional style of such composers as Nikolai Rimsky-Korsakov, as well as those who taught at the Moscow Synodal School of Church Singing.

Sacred Music

The most prominent choral genre in Russia at the turn of the nineteenth century was the sacred choral concerto, an extended composition for a choir of unaccompanied voices (boys and men), sometimes involving incidental solos. Lasting anywhere from 5 to 10 minutes, sacred concertos were intended to be sung during the Divine Liturgy at a point of no liturgical action, when the clergy were partaking of Holy Communion in the Altar[9] immediately before the Communion of the faithful. Occasionally, texts of sacred concertos were taken from feast-day Propers, and it is possible that such concertos were actually sung during that point in the festal Vespers or Matins. Much more often, however, the texts were freely selected by the composer from the psalms. In terms of musical structure, sacred concertos typically contained several sections or distinct movements, often in contrasting keys and tempos. The texture was also varied, usually tending toward animated homophony, with occasional passages of pure homophony and, more rarely, systematically worked out imitative polyphony; a few formal fugues can be found in the repertory, usually in concluding movements.[10]

The most prominent and prolific composer of the classical-era sacred choral concerto was Dmitri Bortniansky (1751–1825), who composed thirty-five concertos for single chorus, ten concertos for double chorus, and fourteen concerto-like settings of *Tebe Boga hvalim* (We praise Thee, O God [Te Deum laudamus]).[11] Although he was trained in Italy and was thoroughly versed in the musical language he learned there, Bortniansky had a sense of reverence for the Orthodox liturgy and understood the bounds of good taste that should not be exceeded in sacred choral music intended for the church. Not only did many of his works become staples of the Russian Orthodox Church repertoire throughout the nineteenth and twentieth centuries, he also served as the sole censor for all published church music for the Russian Orthodox Church from 1816 until his death, a tenure of nearly ten years.

Sacred choral concertos were also composed by Bortniansky's contemporaries: Maksim Berezovsky (1745–77), Stepan Degtiarev (1766–1813), Stepan Davydov (1777–1825), and Artemy Vedel (*c*.1767–1808). Berezovsky, who also studied in Italy, but whose suicide cut short his promising musical career, composed a brooding, intense work titled *Ne otverzhï mene vo vremia starosti* (Do not reject me in my old age) that is alternately dramatic and lyric, featuring rich contrapuntal writing; it is his best-known sacred concerto. Degtiarev, who spend most of his life as a serf of the Sheremetev family—they were patrons of the musical arts and maintained a well-known private chapel choir throughout the nineteenth century—composed four especially well-known concertos that continue to be heard in Russian churches to this day: *Dnes' Hristos v Vifleyeme* (Today Christ is born in Bethlehem) and *Nebo i zemlia* (Heaven and earth) for the feast of the Nativity, *Dnes' vsiaka tvar'* (Today all creation rejoices) for Paschaltide, and *Preslavnaya dnes'* (All the nations have beheld wondrous things) for Pentecost. He is also the likely composer of *Griadi, griadi, ot Livana nevesto* (Come forth, come forth, O bride from Lebanon), a setting of a non-liturgical text that is sung at Russian weddings at the entrance of the bride. Davydov trained at the Imperial Chapel and later became a prominent theater conductor. Although his sacred concertos are less known than those of his contemporaries, his writing is marked by its clarity and elegance of structure; his *Obnovliaysia, novïy Iyerusalime* (Be renewed, O new Jerusalem), composed to be sung at the consecration of a new church, is representative of his best writing. Rounding out this group is Vedel, a student of Count Potemkin's *maestro di cappella* Giuseppe Sarti who spent most of his life in Ukraine, but whose choral works were popular throughout the Russian Empire. Vedel's best-known sacred concerto is *Na rekakh Vavilonskikh* (By the waters of Babylon), a complex and dramatic work that features extensive melismatic passages inspired by Ukrainian lyric folk motifs.[12]

The sixty years following Bortniansky's death in 1825 were a time of extreme conservatism in the sphere of Russian sacred choral repertoire. Bortniansky's successors to the Directorship of the Imperial Chapel—Fyodor L'vov (from 1825 to 1836), his son Alexei L'vov (from 1837 to 1861) and Nikolai Bakhmetev (from 1861 to 1883)—projected their powers of censorship so effectively that during their combined tenure, fewer than twenty titles besides Alexei L'vov's and Bakhmetev's own compositions and arrangements were added to the list of approved works. These works were produced entirely by composers affiliated with the Imperial Chapel; the censorship process was so intimidating that those not connected with the Chapel did not bother to submit their works for consideration. This situation undoubtedly explains why composers of the nascent Russian nationalist school such as Alexander Dargomyzhsky, Alexander Serov, Borodin, and Musorgsky did not write anything for the Russian Orthodox church.[13]

Alexei L'vov contributed only five large-scale sacred concertos to the repertoire and these have remained largely unknown. However, he also wrote several freely composed settings of various Lenten texts that enjoyed wide popularity in nineteenth-century Russia, although they do not fit the more traditional mold of the sacred concerto established by Bortniansky. The best of these include *Predstoyashche krestu* (Standing before the Cross), *Uyazvennuyu moyu dushu* (My wounded soul), *Vizhd' moyu skorb' i bolezn'* (Behold my sorrow and sickness), and *Vizhd' tvoya prebezzakonnaya dela* (Behold your acts of iniquity), each of which is written in a colorful Romantic harmonic language and containing a high degree of emotion.

The sacred choral concerto repertoire was enriched by new compositions only after the demise of the Chapel's censorship in 1883. The most prolific contributor at this time was Alexander Arkhangelsky (1846–1924), whose works in this genre number approximately twenty.[14] These concertos tend to be on a smaller scale than Bortniansky's, having a single movement and a single affect, and are usually infused with strong emotional content and employ a Romantic harmonic vocabulary; only his *Blazhen razumevayay na nishcha i uboga* (Blessed is he that considers the poor and lowly) approaches the scope of a Bortniansky concerto.

The emotionally charged style of the sacred choral concerto pioneered by Alexei L'vov and Arkhangelsky was carried on most vividly by Pavel Chesnokov (1877–1944), whose prolific compositional output of more than 400 sacred choral works is about evenly divided between free compositions (some of which are choral concertos) and chant arrangements. While his chant arrangements tend to employ a more austere modal style, his sacred concertos use a colorful harmonic vocabulary, intense dynamic contrasts, and forceful homorhythmic text declamation for dramatic effect. Chesnokov also composed concerto-like liturgical works for solo voice with choral accompaniment; these were premiered by some of the most prominent operatic singers of his day in extra-liturgical concert settings.

The Moscow Synodal School of Church Singing and its choir, which sang services in Russia's national cathedral—the Cathedral of the Dormition in the Kremlin—were fundamentally reformed in 1886. Peter Tchaikovsky, who had on many occasions expressed concern about the future direction of Russian church music, was among the members of the new Supervisory Council that recommended the appointment of the talented conductor Vasily Sergeevich Orlov to head the choir, as well as Tchaikovsky's former student at the Moscow Conservatory, Alexander Kastalsky, to the faculty; the triumvirate was completed in 1889, with the appointment of Stepan Smolensky as Director of the School.

Smolensky, who also read lectures on liturgical chant at the Conservatory next door, would prove to be a guiding star to an entire generation of choral composers, among the first of whom was the young Sergei Rachmaninoff (1873–1943). In 1893, shortly after graduating from the Conservatory, Rachmaninoff chose to make his first composition in the choral genre a sacred concerto: *V molitvah neusïpayushchuyu Bogoroditsu* (The Theotokos, ever-vigilant in prayer, 1893).[15] This work was in the well-established multi-movement form of a Bortniansky concerto, and may have been loosely patterned upon Vedel's concerto on the same text, with which Rachmaninoff may well have been acquainted through church attendance. While there are many traditional features in Rachmaninoff's youthful opus, it already foreshadows the expressive depth and originality that would characterize his later works.

Tchaikovsky had drawn the attention of the Russian musical world to the vast repository of indigenous chants from Russia's traditional musical heritage with his *All-Night Vigil* of 1881. But Smolensky, who was more of a musicologist than a composer,[16] encouraged those around him to look beyond the latter-day Kievan and Russian "Greek" chants favored by Tchaikovsky to the more melodious *znamenny* chants. By analyzing the old neumatic notation, he unveiled the centonic[17] structure of the chants, assembled from small melodic kernels known as *popevki*[18] in accordance with the requirements of a given liturgical text. Like the rediscovery of ancient techniques and materials of iconography, this approach amounted to a radically different compositional technique for composers who were attempting to define a new national style of choral writing, one that was better suited to the genuine ethos of Orthodox worship and that was organically connected with the traditional Russian Orthodox chant melos.

Smolensky was of the opinion that neither Western European harmony nor counterpoint were suitable for the creation of new sacred choral works for the Russian Orthodox liturgy. Rather, he advocated an indigenous Russian approach, one that drew upon the counter-voiced polyphony of the Russian peasant folk song and the melodic style of Russian church chants wedded to the liturgical text. Smolensky termed this hitherto unidentified technique "kontrapunktika," the salient features of which may be identified as follows:

- the admissibility of parallel voice leading (in fifths, fourths, and octaves),
- a constantly changing number of voices in the choral texture, expanding from the usual four to as many as eight and contracting to only two or a unison,
- the possibility of a single melodic line with a drone (the texture of chant with an ison characteristic of Byzantine chant performance), and
- formal structures that are word-related, rather than determined by purely musical relationships of periods and phrases.[19]

The first composers to apply Smolensky's principles, including the technique of composing new quasi-chant melodies for sacred concertos (for which, by definition, there could be no pre-existing chant melodies) were Kastalsky (1856–1926) and Alexander Gretchaninoff (1864–1956). Kastalsky broke ground in 1897 with his fourth sacred opus, *Miloserdiya dveri* (Open to us the doors),[20] a non-liturgical devotional prayer to the Virgin, while Gretchaninoff followed suit with his two concertos Op. 19 published in 1899, *Volnoyu morskoyu* (Beneath the waves of the sea) and *Voskliknite Ghospodevi* (Make a joyful noise).[21] By constructing new, extended musical themes out of pre-existing melodic material, composers such as Kastalsky, Gretchaninoff, and those who followed them were able to expand greatly the proportions, forms, and the expressive content of *all* liturgical hymns they set to music, not just sacred concertos. In contrast to the composers of *partesny* concertos at the turn of the eighteenth century who had somewhat mindlessly applied foreign principles of *concertato* and imitation to Orthodox liturgical texts (with predictably deleterious effect), composers of the New Russian Choral School were finally able to apply the principles of thematic creation and development using the Russian national melodic vocabulary, and to remain within the ethos of Russian Orthodox worship. In this connection, Kastalsky wrote:

> The future of our creative work for the church can . . . be merely surmised, but I felt what its real task should be. I am convinced that it lies in the idealization of authentic church melodies, the transformation of them into something musically elevated, mighty in its expressiveness and near to the Russian heart in its typically national quality. . . . I should like to have music which could be heard nowhere except in a church, and which would be as distinct from secular music as the church vestments are from the dress of the laity.[22]

Several other composers contributed significant works to the sacred choral concerto genre: Mikhail Ippolitov-Ivanov (1859–1935), who wrote primarily in a harmonic style, exemplified by his concerto *Se nïne blagoslovite Ghospoda* (Behold now, bless the Lord), Op. 29/2; Victor Kalinnikov (1870–1927), whose only concerto *Kamo poydu ot Duha Tvoyego* (Where can I go from Thy Spirit?) is, like all his sacred choral works, a laconic gem, in this instance employing some of the most chromatic writing in the repertory of the period; Alexander Nikolsky (1874–1943), whose monumental concerto *Ghospod' votsarisia* (The Lord reigns), Op. 45/7 combines elements of bold unison writing, quasi-chant melodic construction, expressive use of harmony, and brilliant choral effects; and Constantine Shvedoff (1886–1954), whose concerto *Blago yest' ispovedatisia Ghospodevi* (It is good to give thanks to the Lord), Op. 9 contains some of the most systematic imitative writing in all Russian sacred choral literature, using a quasi-chant subject derived from *znamenny* chant motifs.

Although the sacred choral concerto was initially the primary vehicle by which new styles were introduced into the Russian sacred choral repertoire, free compositional approach soon came to be applied to other elements of the Orthodox liturgical repertoire. In the late seventeenth and early eighteenth centuries, composers such as Nikolai Diletsky (*c.*1630–*c.*1680), Vasily Titov (*c.*1650–*c.*1715), and Nikolai Kalashnikov (to name just a few) began writing *Sluzhby Bozhii* (Divine Services), which consisted of polyphonic settings of the Ordinary hymns of the Divine Liturgy, the All-Night Vigil, and other services and festal cycles. In the late eighteenth and early nineteenth centuries, this trend continued, though on a somewhat limited scale, with the work of Berezovsky, Bortniansky, Davydov, and Archpriest Pyotr Turchaninov (1779–1856). In addition, Bortniansky and Turchaninov composed a number of individual settings of Ordinary hymns from the Divine Liturgy of St. John Chrysostom as well as from the Lenten Liturgy of the Pre-Sanctified Gifts. This approach was followed by several other composers, among them Mikhail Glinka (1804–57), the acclaimed "father of national Russian music."[23]

Musical settings of complete services suffered from the restrictive effects of the Imperial Chapel's censorship throughout the middle of the nineteenth century; it was Tchaikovsky who inadvertently broke that iron grip with his *Liturgy of St. John Chrysostom*, Op. 41, which was published in 1878 by P. Jurgenson without the Imperial Chapel's prior approval.[24] Musically there was little that was remarkable or innovative about Tchaikovsky's setting of the Liturgy. Armed with an Orthodox service book, he set the various Ordinary hymns and responses to music of his own invention. The music is in a pleasant homophonic harmonic style, with occasional passages of imitative polyphony, most notably in the Cherubic Hymn, and a fairly elaborate fugato in the Sunday Communion Hymn. He did break new ground, however, by setting to new music almost every unchangeable verse and response of the Divine Liturgy, an approach some critics likened to the way composers treat opera librettos. Every major composer who wrote settings of the Divine Liturgy after the publication of Op. 41—Arkhangelsky, Chesnokov, Gretchaninoff, Ippolitov-Ivanov, Kastalsky, Nikolsky, Rachmaninoff, Shvedoff, and Tcherepnin—essentially followed the same structure Tchaikovsky had used, though most of them also set to music the three opening antiphons: "Blagoslovi, dushe moya" ("Bless the Lord, O my soul"), "Ghospoda, Hvali, dushe moya, Ghospoda" ("Praise the Lord, O my soul"), and "Vo tsarstvii Tvoyem" ("In Thy Kingdom" ; otherwise known as The Beatitudes).

Next to the Divine Liturgy, the most prominent Orthodox service from a musical standpoint is the All-Night Vigil, a concatenation of Vespers, Matins, and First Hour that became particularly widespread in Russia after the fourteenth century. Compared to the Divine Liturgy, the Vigil has fewer hymns than the Ordinary and many more weekly and daily Propers. The only setting of the All-Night Vigil dating from the turn of the century is by Vedel.[25] Only a handful of individual hymn settings from the Vigil were composed during the course of the nineteenth century; it was not until Tchaikovsky published his *All-Night Vigil*, Op. 52 in 1882 that composers turned their attention to this cycle. By basing his *All-Night Vigil* almost entirely on pre-existing chant melodies, Tchaikovsky brought this neglected aspect of the national Russian musical heritage to the attention of composers, thus single-handedly identifying two directions of sacred choral writing—free composition and polyphonic chant arrangement—for the successive generation of composers, most notably Rachmaninoff and his own famous *All-Night Vigil*, Op. 37 (1915).[26]

Besides the Divine Liturgy and the All-Night Vigil, the most musically intense and textually rich area of Russian Orthodox sacred repertoire is connected with the Paschal Cycle: the period from Lent through Pentecost. The most distinctive liturgical service for this part of the liturgical year is the Liturgy of the Pre-Sanctified Gifts,[27] and the first freely composed settings of hymns from this service were by Bortniansky, including his well-known *Da ispravitsia molitva moya* (Let my prayer arise) and *Nïne silï nebesnïya* (Now the powers of Heaven). Bortniansky also wrote several pioneering chant arrangements that remain staples of the church repertoire to this day, including *Chertog Tvoy* (Thy bridal chamber), *Pomoshchnik i pokrovitel'* (A helper and a protector), which is a setting of the Great Penitential Canon of St. Andrew of Crete), and *Angel vopiyashe* (The angel cried out), the Paschal Hymn to the Virgin. Major contributions to the Lenten chant repertoire were also made in the earlier part of the nineteenth century by Turchaninov (his arrangements of *O Tebe raduyetsia, Da molchit vsiakaya plot,* and *Voskresni, Bozhe*), and by Alexei L'vov (*Vecheri Tvoyeya taynïya*).[28] The fact that these works employ a familiar nineteenth-century harmonic vocabulary and a homophonic chorale-like texture has contributed to their ongoing popularity in the West (including in émigré Orthodox church choirs), although they do not represent the stylistic developments of the New Russian Choral School.

The most prominent choral cycle drawn from Lenten texts is Gretchaninoff's *Strastnaya sedmitsa* (Passion Week), Op. 58, which comprises thirteen hymns drawn from various Lenten and Holy Week services. Clearly conceived for concert performance, the scoring is among the richest in the Russian sacred choral repertoire, ranging from four parts to eight-part double chorus, while the formal scope of the musical settings far exceeds typical liturgical service music.

Musical settings of two other liturgical services, the Memorial Service (or *Panihida*) and the Wedding Service, enriched the Russian sacred choral repertoire in the nineteenth century.[29] Chesnokov's unaccompanied *Panihida,* Op. 39, which the composer produced in both mixed and men's choir versions, is richly scored for soloists and chorus in a manner that makes it suitable for both liturgical and concert performance. On the other hand, Kastalsky's Requiem, entitled *Bratskoye pominoveniye* (Fraternal commemoration of the fallen warriors [of the Allied Armies]), which juxtaposed Orthodox, Roman Catholic, and Anglican melodies (to reflect the Allied Forces of the First World War), was conceived solely as a concert work. Initially scored for soloists, chorus, and organ, Kastalsky subsequently expanded it to include orchestral interludes; he later reshaped the work again, turning it into an *a cappella* cycle comprising the hymns of the *Panihida* titled *Vechnaya pamiat' geroyam* (Eternal memory to the heroes). Kastalsky also composed an attractive *Venchanie* (Wedding Service) Op. 32, which frames the hymns of the wedding ceremony with sacred concertos at the beginning and at the end.

A discussion of nineteenth-century Russian sacred choral music would not be complete without mentioning in passing the contributions of several composers who either wrote a small number of sacred works or who did not compose any large-scale choral cycles. Among the members of the Mighty Five, only Nikolai Rimsky-Korsakov (1844–1910) composed a significant number of small-scale sacred choral works—forty in all,[30] while Mily Balakirev (1837–1908) and César Cui (1835–1918) each wrote only a small number of sacred choruses: Balakirev is chiefly known for his chant arrangement of *Angel vopiyashe* (The angel cried out) and his concerto-style composition for the vesting of a bishop, *Svïshe prorotsï* (The prophets proclaimed you from on high); Cui's most representative sacred work, *Velichit dusha moya Ghospoda* (My soul magnifies the Lord), resembles a sacred concerto in its scope and musical content. Several small-scale liturgical choral works, such as *Svete tihiy* (Heavenly light or Gladsome light) by Alexander Kopylov (1854–1911), *Ghospodi, pomiluy* (Lord, have mercy) by Grigorii L'vovsky (1830–94), and *Otche nash* (Our Father) by Anton Arensky (1861–1906), have become extremely well known outside of Russia almost by accident, chiefly through the efforts of Western music publishers or through the repertoire of such émigrés as the Don Cossacks, directed by Moscow Synodal School graduate Serge Jaroff.

Several younger composers who began composing sacred choral music squarely within the nineteenth-century idiom might have gone on to compose significant works in the twentieth century had the 1917 Revolution not abruptly curtailed opportunities to compose, publish, and perform sacred choral music.[31] The Bolshevik takeover forced a number of composers, among them Arkhangelsky, Gretchaninoff, Rachmaninoff, Shvedoff, and Tcherepnin, to emigrate to the West, where the lack of performance opportunities and separation from their homeland severely curtailed their activity in the area of sacred choral composition.

Secular Music

By comparison with sacred music, the volume of Russian secular choral literature is comparatively small. For the first half of the nineteenth century, secular choral music primarily took the form of opera choruses. Only one oratorio is known: Degtiarev's *Minin i Pozharskiy* (1811) named after the two leaders of the Russian volunteer army that liberated Muscovy from the Polish invaders in 1612. In the second half of the century and up to 1917, a greater number of large-scale choral–orchestral secular works appeared as a result of the growing number of civic choral societies founded chiefly in Moscow and St. Petersburg following the social reforms of the 1860s, which contributed to a growing culture-driven concert life there.[32] Some of these compositions were cantata-like works modeled after Western European biblical oratorios: Modest Musorgsky's *Porazhenie Sennacheriba* (The destruction of Sennacherib, 1866) on a text by Byron and *Iisus Navin* (Joshua, 1877); Anton Rubinstein's *Vavilonskoye stolpotvoreniye* (The Tower of Babel, 1869), and Sergei Taneyev's *Ioann Damaskin* (John of Damascus, 1884) and *Po prochtenii psalma* (At the reading of a psalm, 1915); others were works on purely secular themes, such as Tchaikovsky's *Snegurochka* (The snow maiden, 1872; composed as incidental music to Ostrovsky's play) and his anniversary cantata *Moskva* (Moscow, 1883), and Rachmaninoff's cantatas *Vesna* (Spring, 1902) and *Kolokola* (1913), composed on Konstantin Balmont's Russian translation of Edgar Allan Poe's *The Bells*.

The Russian unaccompanied partsong developed slowly in the nineteenth century. Although German immigrants to Russia are known to have established Singakademien and Liedertafeln as early as 1822, there was no parallel development of Russian amateur singing societies until much later in the century, and only in the last quarter of the century did Russian composers begin to produce partsongs in large numbers, finding a wealth of inspiration in the texts of such Russian romantic poets as Pushkin, Lermontov, Polonsky, Balmont, and a host of others, as well as in translations of Schiller, Goethe, and Heine.

By far the most prolific contributors to the partsong repertoire in the second half of the nineteenth and early twentieth centuries were Cui, Taneyev, Gretchaninoff, and Chesnokov.[33] Cui wrote close to seventy secular choral pieces, chiefly romantic choral miniatures, many of which are not yet readily accessible in modern editions. Sergei Taneyev (1856–1915) wrote eighteen partsongs for mixed voices, including the magnificent cycle of twelve choruses, Op. 27 (1909) on texts by Polonsky that grows in contrapuntal complexity, beginning with four voices and expanding to six and eight in the later movements; and nineteen partsongs for men's voices, including a set of sixteen on texts by Konstantin Balmont, Op. 35 (1912). Gretchaninoff wrote close to fifty secular choruses, both accompanied and unaccompanied, for various combinations of voices. Chesnokov wrote close to forty, also for various combinations of voices accompanied and unaccompanied.

Somewhat less voluminous but no less worthy of exploration are the contributions to the secular partsong repertoire by Rimsky-Korsakov (fifteen titles, unaccompanied, among which are some interesting works that use classic contrapuntal techniques); Tchaikovsky (fourteen titles, all but one unaccompanied); Victor Kalinnikov (at least fifteen titles, unaccompanied); and Rachmaninoff (*Panteley-tselitel'* [Panteley the Healer] for unaccompanied mixed voices; and Six Choral Songs, Op. 15 for SA chorus with piano).

One final category of Russian choral literature needs to be mentioned: choral arrangements of folk-song melodies transcribed directly from live performance.[34] One of the earliest efforts in this realm were Musorgsky's Four Russian Folk Songs for men's voices. Numerous similar arrangements were made by Rimsky-Korsakov and Anatoly Liadov (1855–1914), the latter of whom was active in the collection and notation of folk songs in the field. Such arrangements made folk-song material accessible to choral societies that were springing up in urban centers, often preserving the manner in which these melodies were traditionally performed: usually beginning with an opening phrase sung by a soloist, followed by the entrance of the full chorus. The part-writing was also strongly influenced by folk style, even if it did not attempt to reproduce the folk chorus's heterophony in every detail. Among the composers of the New Russian Choral School who arranged folk songs in this way were Gretchaninoff, Kastalsky, Nikolsky, Victor Kalinnikov, and Chesnokov.

Because secular choral music was developed relatively late in nineteenth-century Russia, and because the forces involved in its performance were not of the same stature or level of excellence as the Imperial Chapel or the Moscow Synodal Choir, this area of the repertoire is not as well known. Yet as choral music, these works share many of the same attractive features found in the more familiar sacred works of the New Russian Choral School: rich sonorities, flowing vocal melodies, and a wealth of nuance and color expressing a wide range of human emotions.

Notes

1 Although a number of composers whose works are discussed below lived and composed well into the twentieth century, stylistically their works retained the musical language of the nineteenth century, particularly in the sphere of sacred music. Rather than the somewhat arbitrary "turn of the century," a much more significant watershed for Russian music was the 1917 Bolshevik Revolution. This chapter therefore includes works written up to 1917. (See also Chapter 28 for a brief contextual introduction to choral music in nineteenth-century Russia.)

2 See Anatoly Konotop, *Russkoe strochnoe mnogogolosie XV–XVII vekov* ("Russian Linear Polyphony of the XV–XVII Centuries"), Moscow: Kompozitor, 2005.

3 As used in this chapter, the term "Orthodox" appearing without a modifying adjective refers to the Eastern Orthodox Christian Church in general, whereas the expression "Russian Orthodox" refers more narrowly to the Orthodox Church that began as the Metropolitan See of Kiev (Kyiv) and eventually became the Church of Russia, under the leadership of Moscow.

4 Under the terms of the Brest-Litovsk Union of 1596, Orthodox Christians living in territories under the political control of the Polish-Lithuanian Kingdom accepted the ecclesiastical authority of the Roman Pope, while being allowed to maintain Orthodox liturgical customs, to have married clergy, and so on. This resulted in a schism between the Orthodox and Eastern-rite Catholics, which continues to this day.

5 It is not coincidental that numerous works in the new Baroque style were composed for twelve voice parts, while payment records and other documents identify the personnel of various ensembles as numbering twelve singers.

6 Illuminating details concerning the manner in which Church Slavonic texts were phonetically transliterated for foreign composers at the St. Petersburg Court may be found in Marika Kuzma, "Bortniansky à la Bortniansky: An Examination of the Sources of Dmitry Bortniansky's Choral Concertos," *Journal of Musicology* 14 (Summer 1996): 183–212.

7 The structure of Orthodox services is discussed in varying degrees of detail in Vladimir Morosan, *Choral Performance in Pre-Revolutionary Russia*, 2nd ed. (Musica Russica, 1996), 210–17; Johann von Gardner, *Russian Church Singing*, vol. 1: Orthodox Worship and Hymnography, trans. Vladimir Morosan (Crestwood, NY: St. Vladimir's Seminary Press, 1980); and Paul Meyendorff, "Russian Liturgical Worship," in *Peter Tchaikovsky: The Complete Sacred Choral Works*, in series *Monuments of Russian Sacred Music*, series II. 3 vols. in 1 (Madison, CT: Musica Russica, 1996).

8 Alexei L'vov's compilation, *Obihod prostogo tserkovnogo peniya, pri Visochayshem Dvore upotrebliayemyi* (The Common Chants of Church Singing used at the Imperial Court; known as "the Obihod" in the vernacular), remains in use in many Russian churches to this day, albeit most often transposed and rearranged in close harmony. This harmonized compilation should not be confused with the unison *Obihod notnogo peniia* (The Common Hymns in Staff Notation), which is notated in square notes and in alto clef; this collection was first published by the Holy Synod of the Russian Orthodox Church in 1772 and saw continuous editions until 1909. A reprint of the 1909 edition is available from Holy Trinity Monastery, Jordanville, New York.

9 Every Orthodox church is divided into three sections, corresponding to the three areas of the Old Testament Temple: the Narthex, the Nave, and the Sanctuary or Altar. In Orthodox churches, the Altar is the entire area surrounding the actual altar table; this area is located behind a wall of icons (called an iconostasis), and is visible to worshippers through the Royal Doors during those times of the service when the doors are open, providing, as it were, a glimpse into the "Holy of Holies."

10 See, for example, the final movements of Maksim Berezovsky's concerto *Ne otverzhï mene vo vremia starosti* (Do not reject me in my old age) and Bortniansky's Concerto nos. 32 and 34: *Skazhï mi, Ghospodi* (Lord, make me to know) and *Da voskresnet Bog* (Let God arise).

11 Bortniansky's concertos were published either in his lifetime or shortly after his death; in her study of his concertos, Kuzma established that the plates used to print these concertos shortly after his death were prepared during his lifetime under his supervision. The concertos were later re-published by the Moscow firm of P. Jurgenson in an edition prepared by Tchaikovsky. Kuzma's new edition of the thirty-five concertos for single chorus eliminates Tchaikovsky's numerous editorial "improvements" and restores Bortniansky's music to its original state. See *Dmitry Bortniansky: The Sacred Choral Concertos for Single Chorus*, ed. Marika Kuzma; in ser. *Monuments of Russian Sacred Music*, ser. XIII, vol. 2, San Diego: Musica Russica (forthcoming).

12 Vedel's and Degtiarev's works, which number several dozen each, survived throughout the nineteenth century in manuscript notebooks whose use was expressly forbidden by the Imperial decree that established the Director of the Imperial Chapel's powers of censorship, which was in force from 1816 to 1883. They began to appear in print only in the early 1900s, chiefly in historical anthologies and choral collections published by P. Kireev of St. Petersburg. It is unclear, however, what degree of source verification was employed in compiling these editions, whose character was more commercial than scholarly. As a result, the authorship of many of the works in the collection cannot be established with certainty.

13 Musorgsky is occasionally credited with one apocryphal setting of the Paschal Hymn to the Mother of God, *Angel vopiyashe* (The Angel cried out), but others attribute it to the minor Moscow composer known only by his last name: Uvarov. Throughout the forty-odd years of Alexei L'vov's and Bakhmetev's combined tenure as censors at the Imperial Chapel, only a handful of minor composers wrote choral music for the Orthodox Church; of these, only seven are known with any certainty: Archimandrite Feofan (Aleksandrov) (*c.*1785–1852), Hieromonk Viktor (Vysotsky) (1791–1871), Pavel Vorotnikov (1804–76), Archpriest Mikhail Vinogradov (1809–88), Gavriil Lomakin (1811–85), Priest Vasily Starorussky (1818–71), and Grigory L'vovsky (1830–94). Few of these composers' works were approved by the Chapel's censors; Lomakin's and L'vovsky's works were published only when the censorship was relaxed after 1883.

14 Among the best known of these concertos are *Pomiluy nas, Ghospodi* (Have mercy on us, O Lord), *Pomyshliayu den' strashnïy* (I ponder the fearful day), and *Ghlasom moim ko Ghospodu vozzvakh* (With my voice I cried out to the Lord).

15 Previously, Rachmaninoff had composed a short Latin motet *Deus meus* (1890) as part of his graduation requirements.

16 Smolensky's best-known choral work is his harmonized arrangement of the Paschal Stichera *Da voskresnet Bog* (Let God arise), the same melody that opens Rimsky-Korsakov's *Russian Easter Overture*.

17 From the Latin *cento*, originally referring to the practice of composing poetry of pre-existing material. In music, this term refers to the construction of melodies by combining series of pre-existing pitch patterns or melodic formulae, a technique widely used in Medieval liturgical chants, both Eastern and Western, as well as in non-Western musical theory: the *maqam* of Arabic music, the *raga* of Indian music, and the *pathet* of Indonesian music.

18 The term *popevka* comes from the same root as "to sing" (*pet'*). Thus, a *popevka* can be loosely translated as "a movement of the voice."

19 See Morosan, *Choral Performance*, 231.

20 Kastalsky's other notable works in the concerto genre are *Ne imamï inïya pomoshchi* (We have no other help), Op. 21, and three concertos in his Wedding Service, Op. 32.

21 Gretchaninoff's subsequent sacred concertos include *Vnushi, Bozhe* (Hear my prayer, O God), Op. 26, a vast, multi-movement choral tapestry; *K Bogoroditse prilezhno* (Let us fervently beseech), which he inserts "in place of the Communion Hymn" (*zaprichasten*) in his Liturgy no. 2, Op. 29, and *Blazheni, yazhe izbral* (Blessed are they, whom Thou hast chosen), Op. 44/2, constructed from melodic kernels of Bulgarian chant.

22 A. Kastalsky, "My Musical Career and My Thoughts on Church Music," *The Musical Quarterly* 11, 2 (April 1925): 245.

23 Glinka composed only one important sacred choral work, a Cherubic Hymn. His other two sacred works, a Great Litany, and the Lenten prokeimenon *Da ispravitsia molitva moya* (Let my Prayer Arise), set for a vocal trio, are of limited interest.

24 Mainly because the work was not submitted for his prior approval, the Director of the Imperial Chapel (Bakhmetev) issued orders to have all copies of Tchaikovsky's *Liturgy* confiscated by the police.

Tchaikovsky's publisher sued, and the case went as far as the Russian Senate, which ruled in Jurgenson's favor, thus breaking the stranglehold of the Imperial Chapel upon sacred choral literature.

25 The date of this work is not known, nor was it published in Vedel's lifetime; it appeared in print for the first time in 1902. From the publication it is not clear whether Vedel himself assembled the cycle, comprising thirty-eight numbers, or whether it was compiled by the modern editor, Mikhail Gol'tison.

26 Other All-Night Vigil settings include those by Arkhangelsky (1897), Ippolitov-Ivanov (1907), Semyon Panchenko (1908), Alexander Nikolsky (1909), Gretchaninoff (1912), and Chesnokov (1909 and 1913). These settings were not nearly as all-encompassing as Vedel's thirty-eight numbers; nor were they even as complete as Tchaikovsky's, who, in addition to the unchanging hymns of the Ordinary, included various short responses and several of the elements that change according to the Eight-Tone cycle (the *Octoechos*). Most of these focus on ten to twelve major hymns of the Ordinary. As in the case of the Divine Liturgy, individual hymns for the Vigil were composed by other composers; of these Kastalsky's and Victor Kalinnikov's can be assembled into particularly noteworthy complete or nearly complete Vigil cycles.

27 This service occurs on Wednesdays and Fridays of the six weeks of Lent, and on Monday, Tuesday, and Wednesday of Holy Week.

28 *All creation rejoices in you* (from the Liturgy of St. Basil the Great), *Let all mortal flesh keep silence* and *Arise, O God* (both from the Liturgy of Holy Saturday); and L'vov's *Of Thy mystical supper* (the special Cherubikon and Communion Hymn for Holy Thursday).

29 The Russian Orthodox Church does not have a Requiem Mass comparable to the Roman Catholic tradition. The *Panikhida* or Memorial Service (and its variant, the Burial Service), are a form of Matins that continues to be sung to this day in a basic, four-part harmonization that first appeared in Alexei L'vov's 1848 publication of the Imperial Chapel *Obihod*. In some churches, the burial is preceded by a Memorial Divine Liturgy (*Zaupokoynaya Liturgiya*), which is essentially the same as a regular Liturgy of St. John Chrysostom, except for three special hymns that replace the daily Troparia and Kontakia, and a special Communion Hymn, "Blazheni, yazhe izbral" ("Blessed are they, whom Thou hast chosen"). The only Russian composer to write a setting of a Memorial Liturgy was Arkhangelsky (Op. 15). Settings of the Memorial Communion Hymn "Blazheni, yazhe izbral" were also composed by L'vovsky, Tchaikovsky, Kastalsky, Chesnokov, Shvedoff and Gretchaninoff.

30 See *Nikolai Rimsky-Korsakov: The Complete Sacred Choral Works*, in series *Monuments of Russian Sacred Music*, series III. 3 vols. in 1 (Madison, CT: Musica Russica, 1999).

31 Works such as *Hristos razhdayetsia* (Christ is born) by Priest Georgiy Izvekov (1874–1937), *Blagoslovi, dushe moya, Ghospoda* (Bless the Lord, O my soul, from Op. 1) by Nikolai Tolstiakov (1883–1958), the sacred concerto *Dnes' Hristos* (Today Christ is born) by Belorussian composer Alexei Turenkov (1886–1958), and the array of sacred choruses for mixed and men's chorus published in 1917, on the eve of the Revolution, by Nikolai Golovanov (1891–1953), are indicative of the unrealized potential of their creators.

32 This is discussed in greater detail in the overview of nineteenth-century choral music and music-making in Russia, in Chapter 28.

33 Other than the author's unpublished bibliography, there have been no known studies of the Russian partsong repertoire, nor are there standard reference works that contain complete and accurate listings of the secular choral output of many composers. Thus, some of the information given below awaits further study and refinement.

34 It is not possible here to give a complete listing of the various collections of Russian folk songs. One of the earliest efforts in this realm was Nikolai L'vov and Ivan Prach's *A Collection of Russian Folk Songs*, first published in 1790. A facsimile of the second edition of this work (from 1806) has been edited by Malcolm Brown and published in the series *Classics of Russian Musical Folklore in Facsimile* (UMI Research Press, 1987). The collecting of folk songs began in earnest in the latter half of the nineteenth century, through the pioneering efforts of Tertius Filippov, Fyodor Istomin, Georgiy Dyutch, Yuly Melgunov, Nikolai Palchikov, and Anatoly Liadov, among others. In the early twentieth century, these efforts were continued by Eugenia Lineva and other composers and ethnographers connected with the Musical-Ethnographic Commission of the Moscow University.

Selected Bibliography

The chief source for editions of Russian choral music is the ongoing series *Monuments of Russian Sacred Choral Music*, published by Musica Russica (www.musicarussica.com). All prefatory and critical material is in English and Russian; text underlay in the music is in Roman transliteration and Cyrillic.

Presently, the series includes the following volumes (in order of publication):

One Thousand Years of Russian Church Music: 988–1988. Series I, vol. 1 (1991).
Sergei Rachmaninoff: The Complete Sacred Choral Works. Series IX, vols. 1 and 2 (1995).
Vasily Titov and the Russian Baroque, Selected Choral Works. Series XIII, vol. 1 (1995).
Peter Tchaikovsky: The Complete Sacred Choral Works. Series II, vols. 1, 2 and 3 (1996).
Nikolai Rimsky-Korsakov: The Complete Sacred Choral Works. Series III (1999).
Victor Kalinnikov: The Complete Sacred Choral Works. Series VIII (2001).
Alexandre Gretchaninoff: Collected Sacred Choral Works. Series VII, vol. 2 (2009).

Chesnokov, Pavel. *The Choir and How to Direct It.* Trans. and with intro. by John C. Rommereim. San Diego: Musica Russica, 2010.

Dunlop, Carolyn C. *The Russian Court Chapel Choir, 1796–1917.* Amsterdam: Harwood Academic Publishers, 2000.

Findeizen, Nikolai, Milos Velimirovic, and Claudia Jensen. *History of Music in Russia from Antiquity to 1800.* Bloomington, IN: Indiana University Press, 2007.

Gardner, Johann von. *Russian Church Singing, Vol. 1: Orthodox Worship and Hymnography.* Trans. Vladimir Morosan. Crestwood, NY: St. Vladimir's Seminary Press, 1980.

——. *Russian Church Singing, Vol. 2: History from the Origins to the Mid-Seventeenth Century.* Trans. Vladimir Morosan. Crestwood, NY: St. Vladimir's Seminary Press, 1999.

Gretchaninov, Alexander; Slonimsky, Nicolas (1952). *My Life.* New York: Coleman-Ross Co., 1952.

Jensen, Claudia R. *Musical Cultures in Seventeenth-Century Russia,* in ser. Russian Music Studies, Bloomington, IN: Indiana University Press, 2009.

Kastalsky, Alexander. "My Musical Career and Thoughts on Church Music," trans, S. W. Pring. *Musical Quarterly* 11, 2 (April 1925): 235–35.

Kuzma, Marika. "Bortniansky à la Bortniansky: An Examination of the Sources of Dmitry Bortniansky's Choral Concertos," *Journal of Musicology* 14 (Summer 1996): 183–212.

Morosan, Vladimir. "Folk and Chant Elements in Musorgsky's Choral Writing," in *Musorgsky: In Memoriam, 1881–1981,* ed. Malcolm Hamrick Brown. Ann Arbor: UMI Research Press, 1982, 91–134.

——. *Choral Performance in Pre-Revolutionary Russia.* Ann Arbor: UMI Research Press, 1986. 2nd ed., San Diego: Musica Russica, 1995.

Prokhorov, Vadim. *Russian Folk Songs. Musical Genres and History.* Lanham, MD: Scarecrow Press, 2002.

Swan, Alfred J. *Russian Music and Its Sources in Chant and Folk-Song.* London: J. Baker, 1973.

Zvereva, Svetlana. *Alexander Kastalsky: His Life and Music.* Trans. Stuart Campbell. Aldershot, England: Ashgate, 2003.

The Iberian World

30

THE PHILIPPINES, LATIN AMERICA, AND SPAIN

Walter A. Clark

University of California, Riverside

Introduction

Surveying choral music of the Iberian world during the 1800s requires confronting one outstanding geo-cultural reality of that period: at the beginning of that century—a largely inauspicious one for the Iberian Peninsula—Spanish and Portuguese colonies spanned the globe, though they were concentrated in the Western hemisphere, on the southeastern and southwestern coasts of Africa, and Southeast Asia. Spanish and Portuguese were spoken as a native tongue by millions of people over an immense area. And wherever the Spaniards and Portuguese took their language, they also took their religion; hence, by 1800, choral music associated with the Catholic liturgy was also a global phenomenon, as it had been for centuries. In addition, they brought a tradition of various kinds of musical theater that sometimes included the use of chorus.

Under such circumstances, one would expect a very rich legacy of choral music to examine. Yet, there are daunting obstacles standing in the way of a comprehensive view of choral music over this vast area during the nineteenth century. Among these is the loss or destruction of manuscripts—or at least our failure to recover sufficient numbers of them—that would give us a fuller picture of choral music during this epoch, particularly beyond the Iberian Peninsula. One example is provided by the Church of Bõa Morte in Vila Boa de Goiás, Brazil.[1] Most of its music manuscripts disappeared in a 1921 conflagration. Another comes from a century earlier, in Caracas, Venezuela, in 1806, when church composer José Cayetano Carreño (1774–1836) decided to discard all the "worn out and useless" seventeenth- and eighteenth-century music manuscripts in the cathedral archive and replace them with his own sacred works.[2] This fate would befall many manuscripts from the 1800s as well, especially as a result of changes in the liturgy dictated by Rome.[3]

Of course, if nothing at all had survived, there would be little we could write about now. In fact, a great deal of music *did* survive, but much of it has simply not yet been examined by musicologists, who have in general devoted far more attention to the colonial period. Perhaps this emphasis has arisen from the fact that, in the words of Suzanne Tiemstra, "scholars today think that the music of that era was inferior to that of previous centuries."[4] She made that claim in 1992, but as recently as 2001, Mendoza de Arce reported that in Cuba "the manuscript holdings of several cathedrals and churches around the island have not been inventoried."[5] Such neglect continues to characterize this area of research.

The destruction and disarray of choral music resulted at least in part from the chaos that swept over Iberia and its former colonies in the nineteenth century. In the wake of the Peninsular War against Napoleon (1808–14), Spain and Portugal were left in a parlous state both politically and economically. It would take decades for their musical life to recover, leaving relatively little of any lasting import for us to examine from the first half of the 1800s.

Having gained their independence from the mother country in the early nineteenth century, most of the newly minted nation-states of Latin America would require even longer to achieve the minimum level of stability and prosperity necessary for the establishment of cultural institutions to fill the void left by the collapse of colonial rule and the decline of the church as a patron of art music. Even as the church's wealth and influence declined, however, Italian opera increasingly captured the public's attention in the early decades of the 1800s, eclipsing in popularity other types of music making. Though some Latin American composers assayed opera in the Italian style, the core repertoire was dominated by Rossini, Bellini, Donizetti, and Verdi. Certainly their works entailed choral numbers, but they bore no musical connection to Latin America itself.

The other major region of the Spanish dominion in the nineteenth century, the Philippines, has only relatively recently begun to attract the attention of musicologists; however, what they have found is a flourishing of music, especially for the church. Unlike most of Ibero-America (except Cuba and Puerto Rico), the Philippines retained their colonial status throughout the 1800s, exchanging rather than expelling colonial overlords after Spain's war with the United States in 1898. Of course, Portugal also retained overseas possessions, especially in African areas now known as Angola and Mozambique. But from a musical standpoint, its most important colonial progeny was Brazil, which gained its independence peacefully in 1822.

Proceeding from eastern to western hemispheres, we begin our survey in the Philippine archipelago and then move on to Latin America. Finally, reaching the Iberian Peninsula itself, we will focus on Spain, which provides us with the greatest quantity, quality, and variety of music in the Iberian world of the 1800s.

The Philippines

Though there were numerous churches in the Philippines with a rich tradition of both chant and polyphony, much of this literature was destroyed during the Second World War, especially in Manila, when the old colonial district, Intramuros, was heavily shelled by the Americans while taking the city from Japanese defenders in 1945. The ravages of time and general neglect of manuscripts have also taken a grievous toll, though notable progress is now being made researching and, where possible, recovering this splendid heritage, not only in Manila but also other provinces and islands in the archipelago.[6]

Still, there are as yet insufficient materials available to provide more than a sketch of choral music in the capital city during the final century of Spanish colonial rule, not only in relation to liturgical music but also to theatrical and concert works. The leading U.S. expert on Philippine colonial music, William Summers of Dartmouth College, reports the following:

> Newspapers occasionally mention new choral works, such as a solemn mass by one of the Spanish Franciscans, and new works of a commemorative nature, anthems and the like for the academic ceremonies, term openings, and degree-granting rites, and one famous *velada* for a Dominican Cardinal at the University of Santo Tomas. . . . Along with this is the more irregular information about requiems, and the devotional music sung during novenas and special, elaborate presentations of the rosary. Motets, litanies, and Marian anthems were sung in these rites, and the titles and composers are often given. . . . [However], after ten years of

archival searching in Manila, I have not found any music surviving from the nineteenth century. There clearly was [a lot] of choral music in Manila in the nineteenth century, but truly shockingly, not one page of these historic sources survives.[7]

Summers's observations about musical Manila receive corroboration from Filipina scholar Patricia Brillantes-Silvestre, who tells us tantalizing things about the district of Quiapo:

> Today's Quiapo may seem but a shabby, decrepit shadow of the grand old days of gracious living and genteel music making among *ilustrado* (educated, elite) families emergent in the area in the 1850s. Church music was on a level equal to that of the splendid repertoires of the great Intramuros cathedrals. Vocal and instrumental groups were in great abundance. Quiapo was home to a rousing network of composers, singers, band and orchestra players, music teachers, impresarios, instrument makers and repairers, music merchants, conductors, pianists, music publishers, opera costume designers, and even opera make-up artists.[8]

Thus, if we want to recover actual music from this period, we have to go outside the city to the provinces and islands where it has survived. These locales experienced less destruction, and musicologists are slowly but steadily reconstructing the musical life of the country by examining provincial archives that survived the ravages of time and war.

The chief focus of current research in this area is Marcelo Adonay (1848–1928), one of the major figures in Philippine music of the late 1800s and early 1900s. He was born in Pakil, Laguna, to a farming family with a proclivity for music.[9] When he was eight years old, he began music studies at the San Agustín Church Convent, where he learned piano, organ, and harmony; later, he played violin in the church orchestra and in 1870 became its conductor, a post he held until 1914. He also served as *maestro de capilla* there. He was devoted to the composition and performance of sacred music, conducting Beethoven's *Missa solemnis* in 1887; in 1893, he led his orchestra in a presentation of Spanish composer Hilarión Eslava's *Miserere*. In addition to his contributions as a composer and conductor, Adonay figured prominently as a teacher, privately and at various girls' schools.

Although it lies slightly outside our chronological boundaries, among his finest works is certainly the *Pequeña Misa Solemne sobre Motivos de la Missa Regia del Canto Gregoriano* (for bass soloist, mixed chorus, and orchestra), composed between 1901 and 1903 and premiered at the San Agustín Cathedral in 1904, with Adonay conducting.[10] Like his other sacred works, it does not exhibit the influence of opera so characteristic of religious music elsewhere in the Iberian world of the 1800s; rather, Adonay drew inspiration from chant in giving his works a solemn and reverential character. His skillful textural contrasts and handling of the voices display admirable sensitivity to the text.

Latin America

Certainly a loss of manuscripts and general neglect have also plagued our study of sacred music in Latin America, though by now we have a fairly detailed picture of that literature stretching from the Renaissance to independence. In the early years of the nineteenth century, a rich tradition of sacred-music composition and performance persisted in regions where it had historically been strong, especially the Viceroyalty of Mexico and in Minas Gerais, Brazil. Stylistically, however, this repertoire often belonged to earlier epochs.[11] As Tiemstra observes, "the music of political and commercial centers in Latin America was current with that of Europe in style and form," whereas music in rural areas developed more slowly. In fact, the Baroque style persisted in some areas well into the nineteenth century.[12]

The period from 1810 to 1830 was one of transition for Latin America, during which it cast off colonial rule and struggled to establish its independence economically and culturally, as well as politically. Latin America's struggle for freedom from Spain was just the beginning of this region's difficulties. Carving viable nation-states out of the old Viceroyalties of Mexico, Nueva Granada, Peru, and Río de La Plata was an undertaking that would last through most of the 1800s and absorb the lion's share of economic resources that, in more stable societies, could have been devoted to cultural infrastructure. The establishment of concert organizations (e.g., symphonies and opera companies), building of suitable venues for them (e.g., concert halls and operas houses), and founding of conservatories for training musicians and composers took place only gradually, in many areas not until the twentieth century. Operas were performed by touring companies, and concert life was dominated by recitals of music for small forces, especially piano and voice.

The church, the historic source for most of Latin American choral music up to this time, was greatly weakened by independence and was no longer in a position to support or promote choral music on the scale and at the level it had previously. In addition, the expulsion of the Jesuits in the late eighteenth century, resulting from a 1767 edict by Spanish King Carlos III, meant that in some areas, for instance Paraguay and Argentina, the musical establishments supported by that order were diminished or disappeared altogether; manuscripts were also lost.

In fact, general impoverishment afflicted church music in many areas around 1800. As Mendoza de Arce has noted,

> as a reflection of the times, which witnessed poverty, meager resources, and the invasion of churches by secular music, many cathedral chapels faced difficulties. In 1804 there was not one cleric in Lima who knew how to sing at the *facistol* [a large music stand from which the choir sang]. Around 1800, all Lima cathedral singers were laymen, more concerned with displaying their vocal prowess in an operatic manner than with liturgy. Cathedral archives were reorganized. The anti-Baroque feeling that prevailed among chapelmasters during this period meant that music manuscripts considered unusable were disposed of. Caracas Cathedral's archive was lost.[13]

Indeed, though the use of figured bass persisted in some remote regions, by the 1820s, Viennese classicism was in the ascendant and early Romanticism was gaining ground. In addition to the operatic character of much church music, there was the gradual infiltration of folk and popular styles. As Mendoza de Arce further reports, "High-Peruvian composers Eusebio Moya and Julian de Vargas y Caro, . . . cleverly combined traditional Spanish church music, delightful folkloric themes, and up-to-date Viennese classical instrumental style."[14] Even salon music came to find a stylistic equivalent in many sacred works. In fact, much of the church music from the early decades of the nineteenth century was rather simple, as a result of decreased resources and inadequate training of church musicians.

Yet, despite all this, chapelmasters throughout Latin America continued to compose music, often of high quality, and possessed the resources for its performance. Most of this repertoire remains in manuscript, however, and still requires cataloging, publication, and revival. Still, the recent advances in research summarized below allow us to survey this epoch in more detail than was possible just a few decades ago.

Beyond the confines of the church, there were certainly other outlets for choral music, as Mendoza de Arce explains:

> During the first fifty years of the nineteenth century, Spanish America's rich and varied musical life remained centered on the theatre, which continued to appeal to the aristocracy

and the masses. . . . Even though theatres were nonexistent in such places as Ecuador and Central America until close to mid-century, visiting troupes brought the popular stage genres to those remote areas.[15]

Choral societies based on European models did spring up in some areas and were, in fact, usually founded by European immigrants; predictably, the repertoires of such ensembles were almost exclusively European as well.[16] Like their counterparts in Europe, these societies varied in size depending on local resources and were initially male preserves, though over time, they also came to include female voices.

Below is a brief overview of choral music—sacred, theatrical, and civic—for each of the major regions in Latin America, moving from north to south. This includes the major venues, composers, organizations, works, and developments for each.

Mexico

Mexico had among the most glorious traditions of sacred music in Latin America, stretching back to the late sixteenth century with the works of Hernando Franco (1532–85) and continuing into the Baroque and Classical eras with masterpieces by Juan Gutiérrez de Padilla (c.1590–1664), Francisco López Capillas (c.1615–73), Manuel de Sumaya (c.1678–1755), and Ignacio de Jerusalem (c.1707–69). Antonio Juanas (c.1750–1819), chapelmaster at Mexico City Cathedral (Catedral Metropolitana de la Asunción de María) until 1816, wrote an enormous amount of sacred music, including numerous masses, responsories, Magnificats, psalms, hymns, and Salves, which reside in the Cathedral's archive. Still, in Mendoza de Arce's estimation, "Juanas's music appears to be of uniformly good quality, although he was not adventurous, and accepted no challenges, only composing what was requested of him."[17] Another native composer of considerable gifts was José Mariano Elízaga (1786–1842). A child prodigy, he became third organist of Morelia Cathedral when he was only thirteen. He later became chapelmaster at Mexico City Cathedral. His sacred choral works include Lamentations and responsories, music for Matins, and two masses.[18] Elízaga's sacred music is largely in the Classical style and exhibits an operatic quality, reflecting the enormous popularity of Italian opera in Mexico during the nineteenth century.[19]

Indeed, sacred music was increasingly eclipsed by the growing popularity of opera. These were most often performed by touring companies, especially at the Coliseo in Mexico City, though in 1831 the Teatro Principal initiated an annual season of Italian opera, which featured works by such local figures as Luis Baca (1826–55), Cenobio Paniagua y Vásquez (1821–82), and Melesio Morales (1838–1908). Béhague claims that the opera *Guatimotzin* (1871), by Aniceto Ortega (1823–75), "is generally considered to have been the first serious attempt to incorporate some native elements within the prevailing Italian format. The libretto, which romanticized an Aztec theme, appealed to the nationalist sentiment of the time."[20] These works no doubt contained some choral numbers, but as yet we know little about them.

So precipitous was the decline of the Catholic Church's cultural importance and so pervasive was the influence of secular music in general in the 1800s that church organists often played popular music to entertain the public, even during services. The sacred music of José Ignacio Triujeque, chapelmaster at Mexico City in the 1830s and 1840s, reflects this trend in its genuflections toward the salon and bel canto.[21]

However, Spanish-style *orfeónes* (discussed below), made up of talented amateurs, also caught on in Mexico and included the Águila Nacional. As elsewhere in the Americas, Mexico experienced an influx of German immigrants during the latter half of the nineteenth century. Fleeing political and economic hardships at home, they settled primarily in the Mexico City and northern areas of the country. The German community formed choral organizations for the performance of German-language masterworks by Handel, Mozart, Haydn, Beethoven, and Mendelssohn.[22] Even as church music went into decline during the last half of the century, other types of choral-music organizations came forward to fill the gap. This pattern would be repeated throughout Latin America.

Central America (Guatemala, El Salvador, Honduras, Costa Rica)

Central America was generally plagued by economic underdevelopment, military conflicts, socio-economic disparities, and uprisings provoked by the subjugated status of Native Americans in general. However, there had been a strong tradition of sacred music in many parts of the region, especially Guatemala. In the nineteenth century, sacred works in Latin for mixed choirs and orchestra continued to be composed in that country in particular.

In the early 1800s, the Saenz family produced a number of important figures, including Vicente (1756–1841), a prolific composer of Classical-style *villancicos*; his son Benedicto, Sr. (1780–1831); and his grandson Benedicto, Jr. (1815–57). The latter traveled throughout Europe and wrote a prodigious quantity of church music, for both the Office and the Mass. Yet another Saenz, Francisco Isaac (1816–80), brother of Benedicto, Jr., succeeded him as chapelmaster at Guatemala City Cathedral, though much of his music has been lost.[23]

Guatemalans worked in El Salvador as well, and one of the leading musicians in that country was José Escolástico Andrino (1807–62), chapelmaster at the capital city's cathedral. Spaniards were also represented, especially Santiago Reyes (c.1780–1850), who worked in Honduras. His sacred music often exhibits the influence of folk and popular music. An even more prominent example of the creeping vernacular influence in church music is offered by one Maestro Mora, music director at San José Cathedral in Costa Rica: "A chronicler [called] it wretched, with waltzes and potpourris of operas played with more serious music."[24]

Caribbean (Cuba and Puerto Rico)

Cuba and Puerto Rico remained Spanish colonies until 1898; thus, their cultural trajectory differs somewhat from the other Spanish-speaking areas in Latin America, which gained their independence decades earlier. The Napoleonic Wars and wars of independence throughout Latin America resulted in a surge of immigration to both islands, enhancing their cultural life.[25]

Music of all kinds continued to thrive throughout the 1800s, in churches and concerts halls. In Cuba, Santiago was a major center for musical performance, along with Havana. Italian and French operas were immensely popular, and Santiago composer Laureano Fuentes Matons (1825–98) wrote opera and zarzuela (operetta) as well; in addition, he wrote excellent sacred music.[26] Fuentes Matons's style was rooted in Viennese classicism, and works like his Requiem (1856) reflect the influence of Haydn and Pergolesi.[27]

Musical theater, consisting of both opera and zarzuela, was also popular and featured numbers for chorus and orchestra. In the latter half of the 1800s, choral groups for workers, inspired by the example of Anselmo Clavé in Barcelona (discussed below), achieved popularity in Havana, especially among the Catalan community. The most celebrated of these groups included the Sociedad Catalana y Balear de Beneficencia, with twenty-five male voices, and the Coros Catalanes de Sagua la Grande. Galician immigrants participated in the Orfeón Ecos de Galicia and Glorias de Galicia, sponsored by the Centro Gallego.[28]

Sacred music in Puerto Rico was largely confined to chant until the nineteenth century, when the first Puerto Rican choral works were composed by Domingo Delgado Gómez (1806–56), including a *Misa de la Providencia* (1856), for tenor, bass, mixed choir, and orchestra.[29] Other composers included Felipe Gutiérrez y Espinoza (1825–99), who worked at San Juan Cathedral in Puerto Rico and composed a *Misa en Do mayor*. This same composer wrote three operas, with choral numbers in the Italian style. Another *portoriqueño*, Juan Bautista Alfonseca de Baris (1810–75), was perhaps chapelmaster at Santo Domingo, leaving two masses.[30] The leading local chapelmaster in Santo Domingo was José María Arredondo (1840–1924), who wrote 135 masses. As we have observed, a notable shift in public taste toward opera meant that increasing resources were devoted to the production of musical theater.

Venezuela

Though many composers in Venezuela were Iberian immigrants or of Spanish descent, others were indigenous, black, or mulatto. Juan José Landaeta (1780–1812) was a mulatto from Caracas who wrote a great deal of sacred music, as did José Ángel Lamas (1775–1814), whose *Popule meus* (1811), for soprano and tenor soloists, mixed choir, and orchestra, has taken on nationalistic significance because of its text and the fact that it was composed just before independence. Other notable figures include José Francisco Velázquez, Jr. (1781–1822) and José Antonio Caro de Boesi (1750–1836). A later Caracas composer of prominence was Atanasio Bello Montero (1800–76), whose prodigious output included Lamentations, Misereres, and masses, as well as a Requiem for the 1842 burial of Simón Bolívar in Caracas.[31] The composers who were working in Caracas around 1800 are collectively known as the Chaco School, but their heyday did not survive independence very long.

In fact, Venezuela remained musically underdeveloped until the twentieth century and the reforms of such figures as Juan Bautista Plaza (1898–1965) and Vicente Emilio Sojo (1887–1974), in the realms of composition, performance, and musicology.[32] Of course, there was choral music in the churches during the 1800s, but beyond that venue, choral organizations were slow to develop, and the general level of performance in musical theater was low.[33]

Andes (Chile, Peru, Colombia)

Although it is not clear just how prominently choral numbers figure in the Italianate *La Telesfora*, this was perhaps the first Chilean national opera. It was composed by Bavarian émigré Aquinas Ried (1810–69) in 1846, six years after his arrival in Chile. He also composed a *Missa solemnis* in an operatic style (1844).[34] Ried became one of the leading composers in Chile, but he was not alone in writing sacred music. José Bernardo Alzedo (1788–1878) continued a pattern we observed elsewhere, as a mulatto who became a composer of some prominence. Though his race proved an impediment to becoming a priest, he ascended to the position of chapelmaster at Santiago Cathedral in the same year that Ried's opera premiered. His *œuvre* included passions, motets, hymns, and *villancicos*.[35]

As the result of German immigration mentioned earlier (in the context of Mexico), German choral ensembles sprang up during the last half of the century in many areas of South America. For example, Chile benefited from a prominent German colony that quickly established choral groups of high quality, especially the Deutscher Gesangverein in Santiago and Club Alemán and Jägerchor in Valdivia. Italians were also represented by groups such as the Coral Sociedad Italiana Musical. Their repertoire included a wide range of choral classics as well as numbers from opera.

Along with Mexico, Peru had had the largest and most numerous musical establishments of the Spanish colonies, but after independence these largely disappeared as the church's position deteriorated and popular tastes shifted to opera and salon music.[36] Nonetheless, Lima benefited from the contributions of cathedral organist Melchor Tapia y Zegarra (*c*.1755–1818). His prodigious works list boasts fifteen masses, four Magnificats, and three passions, as well as several psalm settings. Stylistically, his works owe an obvious debt to Mozart.[37] Elsewhere, Colombia's Julio Quevedo Arvelo (1829–97) wrote operas and masses reflecting the pervasive influence of Italian Romanticism.

Rioplatense region (Uruguay, Paraguay, Argentina)

Church music in colonial Uruguay was limited to Montevideo, and the earliest extant composition we have from there is an 1802 *Misa para día de difuntos* (*Mass for the Day of the Dead*) by the Spaniard Fray Manuel Úbeda.[38] Italian opera was hugely popular, and works by Rossini, Bellini, and Donizetti dominated the stage until 1850, after which Verdi reigned supreme. Paraguay lagged behind its neighbor in this regard, and lyric theater took longer to establish itself.[39] Due to the suppression of monastic institutions, "very little is known about the state of sacred music in Asunción del Paraguay during the late colonial and early Republican times due primarily to the disappearance of essential documentation."[40] However, we do know that, in the civic arena, Paraguayans enjoyed performances by the Italian Circolo Corale Filodrammatico Italiano, founded in 1887 by Luis Cavedagni.[41] Like others of its kind, this group sang choral works from the standard repertory and popular operatic choruses, either *a cappella*, accompanied by piano or, on occasion, an orchestra.

Argentina forms something of an exception to the rule stated at the outset of this chapter, which is that there was a decline in music culture in Latin America, especially in the church, in the immediate aftermath of independence, a decline that would not be remedied until well into the century. True, Argentina did not have the flourishing colonial music culture of the Viceroyalties of Peru and Mexico, but newly awakened patriotic fervor and the rise of Buenos Aires as an economic and cultural powerhouse stimulated music to a greater extent than in earlier epochs. Music in churches, opera houses, and philharmonic societies experienced a florescence in the nineteenth century.[42] As elsewhere, opera was increasingly popular, and in 1854 no fewer than thirty operas appeared on the Buenos Aires stage, by both Italian and French composers.[43] Rossini's *Barber of Seville* was done in the capital in 1825, followed by Mozart's *Don Giovanni* two years later.

In fact, a secular spirit dominated the culture, at the expense of sacred music, though there were choirs of indigenous peoples who, trained by the Jesuits in their missions, performed in Buenos Aires and other cities, offering music for the Mass in various churches. Even here, however, Mendoza de Arce notes that "much profane music was played in the churches. For example, a regimental band performed music at the Merced Convent."[44] One should note that the situation relative to church music was not uniformly grim. For instance, the Anglican church Saint John the Baptist of Buenos Aires presented choral masterworks in English, especially Handel's *Judas Maccabeus* and *Messiah*. In 1845, a German choral group made up of immigrants performed Haydn's *Die Schöpfung*.[45] After 1880 there was notable growth in the number and importance of music societies promoting all kinds of music, including choral.[46]

Brazil

Developments in Brazil paralleled those elsewhere in Latin America, with some significant differences. The most important among these is the fact that Brazil was the only country to gain its independence without violence. Portuguese King Dom João VI fled Napoleon's invasion of the Iberian Peninsula in 1808 and re-established his court in the previously underdeveloped Rio de Janeiro, turning it into a European-style metropolis. Portugal's loss was thus Brazil's gain, and this is the main reason we devote little attention to Portugal in this chapter. For, as Béhague pointed out, Rio "became overnight the main center of the huge Portuguese Empire." Brazil was also the largest of the new nations in Latin America, and it had several important centers of music making, principally Rio but also Salvador de Bahia[47] and Minas Gerais.

Minas Gerais had been a very important musical center during the colonial period, owing to its tremendous mineral wealth, but during the 1800s that wealth began to decrease as it produced fewer minerals, and because of political difficulties with the Portuguese rulers in Rio.[48] Even as Minas Gerais declined in prominence, Rio's stature benefited from the presence of the royal family and the resources they devoted to the Royal Chapel. João VI had a preference for lavish religious services, and his chapel employed a large mixed choir and orchestra. Yet, music for the royal court became increasingly secular. "Chapelmasters adapted melodies from the theatre, such as arias, cavatinas, and overtures, to their religious chants, and many composers of religious music cultivated salon forms . . . using contradance or waltz-like rhythms."[49]

The career of the mulatto composer and priest José Maurício Nunes Garcia (1767–1830) is closely connected with the reign of João VI in Rio and with that of his successor, Dom Pedro I.[50] He was the "most distinguished Brazilian composer up to his time"[51] and was appointed master of the Royal Chapel by João VI. Nunes Garcia's prolific output includes a wide variety of sacred genres, especially masses, mostly in the homophonic style of Viennese composers.[52] He organized performances of Mozart's Requiem and Haydn's *The Creation* in Rio, and it is hardly surprising that his own Requiem (SATB, with ATB solos and orchestra) exhibits the marked influence of Mozart's work.

Two other mulatto composers were Rio-born: Damião Barbosa de Araujo (1778–1856), who worked at the Royal Chapel, and Pedro Antônio de Azevedo (c.1780–1840), who was active in Recife. The most distinguished composer of choral music after Nunes Garcia, however, was Antônio Carlos Gomes (1836–96), best known for his Indianist opera *Il Guarany* (1870), which premiered to acclaim at La Scala in Milan.[53] He thus became the first Brazilian composer to establish an international reputation—Verdi praised him as a "true musical genius."[54] He also wrote sacred music, and the fact that he composed his first Mass at age eighteen suggests something of the talent Verdi noted.

Another key development was the genesis of music clubs, which performed a variety of chamber, orchestral, and choral works. Despite its name, The Club Mozart (founded 1867) was not devoted exclusively to Mozart's music. It eventually ceded preeminence to the Club Beethoven (1882). Unlike these two, the Sociedade de Concertos Clássicos was not just an institution intended to delineate social boundaries; rather, its mission was to teach the local public to appreciate classical music.[55] These groups occasionally offered choral music by a variety of eighteenth- and nineteenth-century composers, featuring thirty or more male and female singers, with piano or orchestral accompaniment.

Despite all this activity, the rise of a significant body of Latin American choral music would have to wait for the twentieth century, with the advent of composers capable of writing works of originality and genius, such as Carlos Chávez in Mexico, Alberto Ginastera in Argentina, Heitor Villa-Lobos in Brazil, and Juan Bautista Plaza in Venezuela, among many others.

Spain

During the nineteenth century, the Iberian Peninsula suffered greatly from invasions, civil wars, political instability, economic underdevelopment, illiteracy, poverty, assassinations, and revolutions. Economic reversals in Portugal resulted in the steep decline in the musical life of that nation during the 1800s. As a consequence, it has far less to offer our survey than neighboring Spain, on which we now focus our attention. The latter half of the century witnessed a remarkable resurgence in

Spanish culture, particularly music, giving rise to composers and a body of literature fully worthy of our attention. The situation was different from that in Latin America, where "the loss of the chapel's ability to keep up to date with Spanish church music allowed the musical gap between Europe and the New World to widen."[56] Choral music figures in three main contexts: theatrical, ecclesiastical, and civic.

Choral Music in the Theater

Indigenous musical theater experienced a renaissance in Spain at mid-century with the revival of the zarzuela. The major figure in this development was Francisco Asenjo Barbieri (1823–94), whose 1851 *Jugar con fuego* (To Play with Fire) initiated a golden age of the zarzuela that would last a century. However, choral passages in zarzuela, when they occurred, were generally sung in unison; thus, there is not a significant body of Spanish-language choral music located in the zarzuela that we should examine. Nonetheless, there are two important things connecting the zarzuela to choral music. First, some of these same zarzuela composers played a role in the development of Spanish opera; second, many composers of zarzuela also devoted their creative efforts to writing sacred music.

In response to the overwhelming popularity of French, Italian, and German opera in Spain, toward the end of the century several native composers sought to create *ópera española*, a movement that produced no genuine masterpieces but nonetheless gave rise to several remarkable works, replete with effective choral numbers deserving our attention here. Among the most prominent manifestations of this movement toward *ópera española* were Felipe Pedrell's *Els Pirineus* (1891), Tomás Bretón's *La Dolores* (1891), and Enrique Granados's *María del Carmen* (1898).

However, the only Spanish opera of this period to attract international attention was Isaac Albéniz's *Pepita Jiménez* (1896). Based on an epistolary novel by Juan Valera of the same title (pub. 1874), the book's Andalusian setting gave Albéniz ample scope for deploying his trademark Spanish style. It tells the story of a young seminarian, Don Luis, who falls in love with Pepita Jiménez, a wealthy and fetching young widow. Despite Luis's inner spiritual conflict, the lovers are ultimately united. Premiered in 1896 at the Liceu in Barcelona, *Pepita Jiménez* was subsequently produced in Prague (1897), Brussels (1905), Paris (1923), and Madrid (1964).[57]

One of the most charming and effective numbers in the opera is a "Children's Hymn to the Infant Jesus" (SSAA), evoking the *villancico*, a choral work in a simple vernacular style expressing popular devotion on such important occasions as Christmas and Easter. Although Albéniz composed many striking choral numbers in his various operas, none is more memorable than this. Especially attractive is the use of *bocca chiusa* (closed mouth) (see Example 30.1).

In fact, *Pepita Jiménez* was not Albéniz's first opera. The year before, his *Henry Clifford* premiered at the Liceu in Barcelona (in Italian translation, as *Enrico Clifford*), with a libretto by the Englishman Francis Burdett Money-Coutts, Albéniz's close friend and patron.[58] *Henry Clifford* is set in fifteenth-century England, during the Wars of the Roses. In the first act, Lord Clifford falls at the battle of Towton, and his body is returned to the family estate for burial. The funeral chorus Albéniz composed for this scene is one of his most moving confections and demonstrates a remarkable stylistic range when compared with *Pepita Jiménez* (see Example 30.2). Money-Coutts fashioned the librettos for all three of Albéniz's completed operas, the other being *Merlin* (from the early 1900s), which contains some of the composer's most impressive choral writing.[59]

EXAMPLE 30.1 Albéniz, *Pepita Jiménez*, Act II, scene i, "Children's Hymn to the Infant Jesus," mm. 471–78.

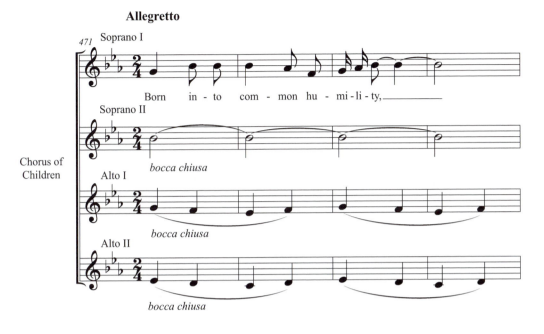

EXAMPLE 30.2 Albéniz, *Henry Clifford*, Act I, scene vi, Funeral Chorus, mm. 77–84.

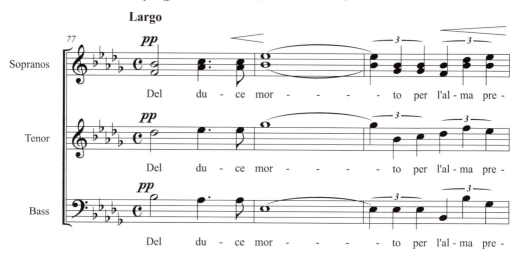

Sacred Choral Music

Napoleon's invasion of Spain and its aftermath did great harm to the church and sacred music. Carlos Aransay sums up the situation:

> [T]he French seized temples, relics and works of art, imposed substantial ecclesiastical tributes, dismantled music chapels, [and] reduced the number of convents by a third. . . . [T]he king, José I, went so far as to suppress all male religious orders (these subsequently reappeared later in the century). In 1836, [three years] after the death of the absolutist monarch and supporter of the French, Fernando VII, minister Juan Álvarez de Mendizábal decreed the confiscation of ecclesiastical assets, the first of many actions that would gradually impoverish the patrimony of the Catholic Church. It was at this stage that some of the most important music chapels and valuable religious traditions and styles disappeared forever. Finally, in 1851 the Church and State signed a Concordat, which reduced the size of music chapels,

abolished schools for child choristers and banned anyone who was not a clergyman from performing music in churches. This last demand meant that a number of professional musicians abandoned sacred music altogether and standards of sacred musical performance worsened dramatically.[60]

Despite all this, there is a surprisingly rich legacy of sacred music from nineteenth-century Spain, and some of the era's leading composers devoted attention to writing it.

Although the first half of the century witnessed Spain's greatest distress as a nation, militarily, politically, economically, and culturally, there were still a few shining lights in musical theater and sacred music. Outstanding among these is Manuel García (1775–1832), the famed tenor who composed many songs and operas. His sacred works include five masses, two Sanctus, a *Salve Regina*, an *In nomine dye amen* [sic], and a *Tibi omnes angeli*, most of them dating from 1812 to 1828. In addition, he wrote a number of secular choral works, with and without accompaniment (either piano or orchestra). However, all remain in manuscript; regrettably, none have yet been published or recorded.[61] The Spanish Basque composer Juan Crisóstomo Arriaga (1806–26), sometimes referred to as the "Spanish Mozart," is another figure worthy of mention, an astoundingly gifted musician who composed sacred music as well as symphonies. He was the author of several sacred works, including a *Stabat Mater*, for two tenors, bass, and orchestra. Among his finest choral works is *O salutaris hostia*, for male chorus (TTB) and string quintet or organ. These very expressive works speak to the composer's affinity for the texts and skill in setting them. Unfortunately, his promising career was cut short by illness.[62]

One of Spain's greatest performer–composers of the early 1800s was certainly the Catalan Josep Ferran Sorts i Muntades (1778–1839), universally known as Fernando Sor. A guitar virtuoso, he established an international reputation as a composer and pedagogue, leaving Spain in 1813 to reside in Paris, London, Moscow, and again Paris, where he died. Though his reputation as a composer rests exclusively on his works for guitar (secondarily for guitar and voice), he also wrote opera, ballet, orchestral music, and a single sacred choral work, *O crux, ave spes unica* (SATB). This merits mention here because it is one of the few works of its kind from that period in Spanish history; it is also a work of very high quality.[63] The somber subject matter brought forth from Sor some of his best melodic inspirations, and the score reveals his familiarity with the harmonic language of Viennese classicism, particularly Mozart's *Ave verum corpus* (see Example 30.3).

In the second half of the nineteenth century, the most prominent composers of choral music included clergyman Hilarión Eslava (1807–78), a prolific composer of sacred works. His first series of three *Motetes al Santísimo*, including *Bone pastor*, *O salutaris hostia*, and *O sacrum convivium* (all SATB, *a cappella*), offers outstanding examples of his musical deliberation and skill. Composer and musicologist Felipe Pedrell (1841–1922) was one of Spain's most important musicians during this time and did seminal research on Spanish Renaissance polyphony, editing the complete works of Tomás Luis de Victoria. As a composer, Pedrell's chief aim was to advance *ópera española*, but he also wrote several sacred choral works, whose solemnity and non-nationalistic character reflect the influence of his musicological endeavors. One of his loveliest works is certainly *A solis ortus* (SATB with organ).

Although *zarzueleros* wrote little of lasting significance in the realm of choral music for their operettas, they often composed sacred choral music of a high caliber as a sort of avocation. For example, zarzuela revivalist Francisco Barbieri composed a lovely *Libera me Domine*. This responsory, for *a cappella* chorus (SATB), was composed in honor of Cervantes and dedicated to the Spanish Royal Academy. At century's end, Tomás Bretón (1850–1923), author of the ever-popular zarzuela *La verbena de la paloma*, wrote a beautiful *Salve montserratina*, for unison choir singing chant and a three-voice female chorus accompanied by organ and double bass.[64] It is dedicated to the famous Catalonia monastery of Montserrat. The greatest composer Spain produced in the 1800s, Isaac Albéniz (1860–1909), was a socialist and atheist. Thus, it comes as something of a surprise that even one sacred work by him has come down to us; yet, he was inspired to compose a setting of Psalm 6 in 1885, on the death of his patron King Alfonso XII.[65] It is a remarkably expressive work exhibiting a fine gift for chromatic nuance and sensitive treatment of the text that reminds one of the sacred works of Liszt and Bruckner.

Unlike his friend and fellow Catalan Albéniz, Enrique Granados (1867–1916) was a devout Catholic and wrote works of heartfelt sincerity. He was seven years Albéniz's junior and achieved

EXAMPLE 30.3 Sor, *O crux, ave spes unica*, mm. 1–13. Edited Michael Fink (London: Tecla Edition, 1980). This excerpt is reproduced courtesy of Brian Jeffrey and Tecla Editions, www.tecla.com.

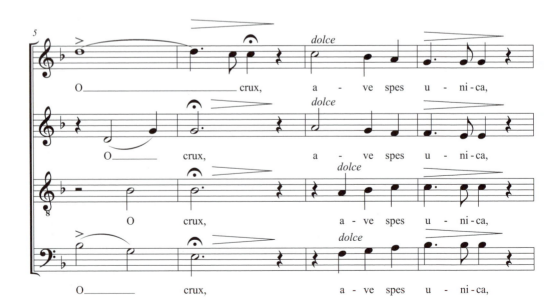

EXAMPLE 30.3   continued.

artistic maturity only in the early twentieth century; nonetheless, he was writing beautiful sacred music already in the late 1800s. The finest of these works is probably his *Salve Regina*, for SATB chorus and organ, dating from 1896.[66] According to Joaquim Zueras Navarro,[67] Granados composed this work at the invitation of Pedrell, who challenged him to write something in the manner of Palestrina, but with organ interludes reminiscent of Antonio de Cabezón (*c.*1510–66) or Juan Bautista Cabanilles (1644–1712). Along with this are touches of chromatic harmony that place the work firmly in the Romantic style. Granados's *Salve Regina* provides delightful contrasts in texture and color, along with a lyric style that, though uninformed by his Spanish manner, nonetheless yields moments of genuine satisfaction (see Example 30.4).

Choral Music for the Masses

The spread of religious skepticism in Spain during the 1800s was connected with political movements, principally socialism and anarchism, that reflected important changes in Spain's economy and demographics. In particular, rapid industrial growth in Catalonia and the Basque country produced a large urban proletariat, a potentially unstable mass of urban poor whose socio-economic condition was a source of concern to the Catalan bourgeoisie, especially in Barcelona. A sincere desire to improve the cultural, intellectual, and moral condition of this group motivated the creation of workers' choruses in mid-century, choruses modeled on French and German prototypes and utilizing pedagogical methods similarly inspired.[68]

Of course, public performance of choral music, especially by civic choruses, was an important socio-cultural phenomenon throughout Europe in the nineteenth century, as discussed elsewhere in this volume. Early in the nineteenth century, choral societies began as a response to several developments: the rise of democracy, the ideals of the Enlightenment, the French Revolution and its embrace of hymns and collective songs, industrialization and the workers' movement, Romantic patriotism, and the increasing access of all classes to music. Spain also witnessed the rise of civic choruses whose purpose was to provide working-class men—and, later, women—with opportu-

EXAMPLE 30.4 Granados, *Salve Regina*, mm. 1–16. Edited by Douglas Riva and Miriam Perandones; published by Editorial Boileau (Barcelona, 2008); editor Yolanda Guasch granted permission to use these measures.

EXAMPLE 30.4   continued.

nities to learn and perform music. However, this movement arrived later in Spain than elsewhere in Europe, beginning around 1850 in Catalonia, specifically Barcelona, a region of the country more progressive and receptive to foreign trends. Because it was among the first areas of Spain to industrialize, there were more workers and hence more singers and societies. The government realized that the choral movement could not only educate and impart moral values to the workers, but also keep them under effective control. Moreover, it provided an arena for cooperation at a time when political and economic problems spread across classes. Not only industrialization but also nationalist–regionalist sentiments played a role in promoting these societies, which often performed arrangements of folk songs.

The two leaders of this movement were José Anselmo Clavé (Josep Anselm Clavé) (1824–74) and Juan Tolosa (1818–unknown). Clavé's aim was to use music for the moral upliftment of the proletariat, not simply to create an ensemble devoted to music for its own sake. Tolosa, influenced by choral groups in France, especially Guillaume-Louis Wilhem's orphéonistes, was first and foremost devoted to an artistic ideal. He used the Wilhem Method of teaching singing (1842) to instruct his choristers and get from them the best possible results.[69]

Clavé established his all-male choral society La Fraternidad on February 2, 1850, and it gave its first performance about six months later. Inspired by the French orpheón movement, with its social and moral goals, the "important thing was not that they sang well, but that they sang at all."[70] Clavé's example resulted in the formation of other *orfeónes*, and within a decade there were no fewer than eighty-five throughout Catalonia, though La Fraternidad remained the leader (at this same time it changed its name to Euterpe). Clavé-like groups for men now sprang up in Spanish cities beyond Catalonia, including Málaga, Sevilla, Granada, Almería, Córdoba, Lugo, Zaragoza, Pamplona, León, Salamanca, Burgos, Valladolid, Pontevedra, Gijon, Coruña, Lugo, Santiago, Vigo, Vitoria, and San Sebastián. In Madrid, La Aurora Orfeónica began in 1863, which soon merged with the Orfeón Artístico Matritense, directed by José Flores Laguna, whose goal was to "give to the lovers of music the ability to dedicate themselves to the study of such a sublime art, without having to spend a lot of money, and without having to abandon their ordinary occupations."[71] Again, it was directed toward men in the working classes. By 1923, there were 561 such groups in Spain, and seventy years later, there were no fewer than 1,320 (in the 1900s, *orfeónes* included women as well as men).

Tolosa formed his most advanced singers into the group Orfeón Barcelonès, which was modeled on the mass choirs of France and Germany. The Orfeón inspired imitators elsewhere in Spain, including Cádiz, Bilbao, and Valencia. While Clavé wanted to spread singing among the working classes, Tolosa wanted to bring musical instruction to all classes, in the pursuit of artistic excellence. In any case, all of these groups were predicated on the belief in the transformative power of music and group singing, "to elevate and ennoble all social classes and impart virtue to the individual."[72]

Clavé and Tolosa were not the only innovators, however. In 1891, Lluis Millet (1867–1941) and Amadeu Vives (1871–1932) established what would become the preeminent choral ensemble in Barcelona, the Orfeó Català. What made the Orfeó distinctive, aside from its musical excellence, was its mission to promote Catalan music in particular, a mission that revealed a regionalist and even separatist slant that was highly political. Not everyone approved of this agenda, and Granados, who assisted in the administration of the Orfeó, said that "They wanted to give a Catalanist political color to the Orfeó, something with which I am not in agreement. To my way of thinking, art has nothing to do with politics."[73] Nonetheless, the political orientation of choral groups was already inherent, though muted, in Clavés's La Fraternidad, with its name's obvious nod to republican ideals. The advent of a limited democratic franchise in Spain during the late 1800s, and the concomitant emergence of various political parties, encouraged the formation of choral groups with overtly political affiliations. The first socialist, republican, and nationalist *orfeónes* arose around

1900. Moreover, regionalist groups, singing arrangements of folklore, were popular in the Basque country, Catalonia, and Galicia. For instance, the newspaper *El Nervión* exhorted the Orfeón Euskeria (1896) to "sing with passion, with emotion, the hymns and songs of our mountains."[74] Of course, all of this dovetailed with the Romantic era's interest in folk culture as well as national and racial essences.

There were also *orfeónes* associated with the Roman Catholic Church, and these performed both chant and sacred polyphony. The outstanding example of this in Barcelona was the Orfeó Català's Capella de Sant Felip Neri, which was made up of men and boys and devoted itself to sacred polyphony. In Madrid, the leading group was the Círculo Católico de Obreros de San José. In fact, assorted chapel choirs and *scholae cantorum* emerged throughout Spain during this period. The formation of workers' choirs devoted to sacred music dovetailed with Leo XIII's 1891 encyclical *Rerum Novarum*, which expressed a genuine concern for the plight of the urban proletariat even as it condemned socialism.

Secular choral groups performed a wide-ranging repertoire that included dances, opera excerpts, salon-style pieces, popular and folk songs, works for chorus and orchestra, and sacred music.

EXAMPLE 30.5 Clavé: *Al Mar (Barcarola á voces solas)*, mm. 1–6.

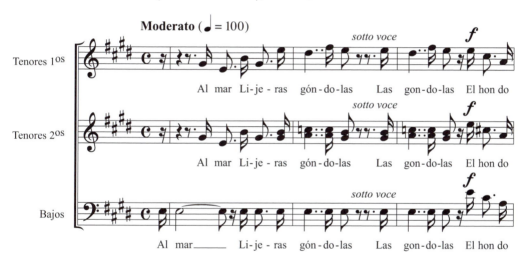

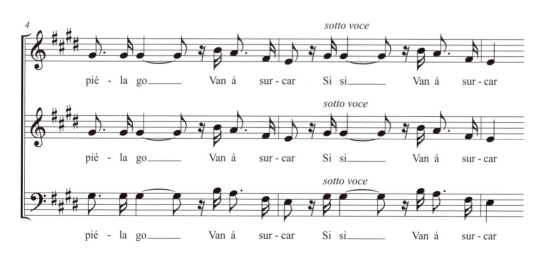

Accompaniment varied, from guitars to piano to orchestra. The choral parts were for low voices, since women were admitted only gradually. When they participated, it was usually in all-female groups. In fact, the first of the *orfeónes* to integrate, the Orfeó Català, did not do so until 1896, though as mentioned above, a mixed choir would be the standard arrangement in the twentieth century.

One should bear in mind that most of the workers had no musical education at all, and many could not read music, instead learning their parts by rote. Clavés's groups in particular sang simple, accessible arrangements. In this respect they resembled the socialist *orfeónes*, who kept their repertoire simple for ideological reasons, especially in their performance of revolutionary hymns such as the *Internationale*. By contrast, Tolosa's ensembles and the Orfeó Català aimed for a higher level of musical accomplishment and sophistication.

A good example of the sort of music that Clavé wrote for his groups is *Al Mar* (*Barcarola á voces solas*),[75] scored for TTB chorus, which charms by its unaffected directness and lack of musical affectation (see Example 30.5).

Conclusion

We have seen that, in regard to the choral music in the Iberian world of the nineteenth century, the rich heritage of the Renaissance and Baroque eras underwent a transformation in response to Romanticism, the collapse of the Iberian empire, and the rise of independent nation-states throughout Latin America. Though the choral riches of this period are not as conspicuous as those that preceded and followed it, they offer one large compensating advantage: numerous opportunities for pioneering research, along with enticing possibilities for publication and performance.

Notes

1 Daniel Mendoza de Arce, *Music in Ibero-America to 1850* (New York: Scarecrow Press, 2001), 520.
2 Ibid., 489.
3 Ibid., 521. For instance, in later years, the liturgical reforms of Pope Pius XII (in the mid-1900s) and then Vatican II (1962–65) often accomplished what fires could not, as music directors chose to destroy the old manuscripts in their collections and focus on newer music that conformed to the changing spirit of the times.
4 In Suzanne Spicer Tiemstra, *The Choral Music of Latin America: A Guide to Compositions and Research* (New York: Greenwood, 1992). This still-useful volume provides a narrative description of the subject (see pp. 7–17 for the nineteenth century), a catalogue of composers and their works, and an extensive listing of anthologies, collections, series, publishers, discography, recording companies, music archives, biographies, and periodicals, as well as useful appendices. Tiemstra's book has been updated and made available online at www.latinamericanchoralmusic.org. It is the only comprehensive index of Latin American composers and their choral music, with approximately 13,000 entries as of this writing.
5 Mendoza de Arce, *Music in Ibero-America to 1850*, 486.
6 An excellent recent study of music in colonial Manila is by David Irving, *Colonial Counterpoint: Music in Early Modern Manila* (New York: Oxford University Press, 2010). See also the recent dissertation on music on the island of Bohol, David Kendall, "Spanish Colonial Liturgical Music in the Philippines: Inventing a Tradition" (Ph.D., diss., University of California, Riverside, 2010). Leading Philippine musicologists participated in *Encuentro Filipino 2008* at the University of California, Riverside, organized by Bill Summers and this author. See the proceedings of this conference in *Diagonal* 4 (2008), http://cilam.ucr.edu/diagonal/issues/2008.
7 Email correspondence with Professor Summers, March 30, 2010.
8 Patricia Brillantes-Silvestre, "Music in The Heart of Manila: Quiapo from the Colonial Period to Contemporary Times: Tradition, Change, Continuity," *Diagonal* 4 (2008). http://cilam.ucr.edu/diagonal/issues/2008/Brillantes-Silvestre2.pdf.
9 Elena Rivera Mirano, ed., *The Life and Works of Marcelo Adonay*, vol. 1 (Diliman, Quezon City: University of the Philippines Press, 2009). This groundbreaking book is not yet widely available. An important and

readily available source of information on the recovery of Adonay's works is to be found in Elena Rivera Mirano, "Finding Marcelo: Reconstructing the Lost Repertoire of a Nineteenth-century Philippine Master," *Diagonal* 4 (2008). http://cilam.ucr.edu/diagonal/issues/2008/Mirano1.pdf. Other useful websites include http://www.nhi.gov.ph/downloads/ca0002.pdf and http://en.wikipilipinas.org/index.php?title=Marcelo_Adonay.

10 This work survives in two versions, one with large orchestra and the other with a small ensemble. Both are reproduced in Mirano, ed., *Marcelo Adonay*, vol. 1. Unfortunately, many of Adonay's works are lost.

11 A remarkable study of music during this transitional period is now available: Craig H. Russell, *From Serra to Sancho: Music and Pageantry in the California Missions* (New York: Oxford University Press, 2009).

12 Tiemstra, *The Choral Music of Latin America*, 7.

13 Mendoza de Arce, *Music in Ibero-America to 1850*, 473.

14 Ibid., 474.

15 Ibid., 453.

16 See the extensive treatment of choral ensembles in Latin America under "Coros" in Emilio Casares Rodicio, ed., *Diccionario de la música española e latinoamericana* (Madrid: Sociedad General de Autores y Editores, 1999), iv, 39–66. This section is organized by country name, in alphabetical order.

17 Mendoza de Arce, *Music in Ibero-America to 1850*, 477.

18 Ibid., 479–80.

19 Gerard Béhague, *Music in Latin America: An Introduction* (Englewood Cliffs, NJ: Prentice-Hall, 1979), 97.

20 Ibid., 98.

21 Mendoza de Arce, *Music in Ibero-America to 1850*, 478.

22 Gloria Carmona, "Coros, X: México," *Diccionario de la música española e latinoamericana*, 56.

23 Salvador Marroquín, "Coros, VIII: El Salvador," *Diccionario de la música española e latinoamericana*, 55.

24 Mendoza de Arce, *Music in Ibero-America to 1850*, 481–82. Perhaps this was a reference to Alejandro Monestel Zamora (1865–1950), also director of the national symphony and conservatory. In Tiemstra's estimation, "His imaginative use of folk elements inspired other nationalistic composers." See Tiemstra, *The Choral Music of Latin America*, 12.

25 Mendoza de Arce, *Music in Ibero-America to 1850*, 484. An excellent resource on this topic is Donald Thompson, *Music in Puerto Rico: A Reader's Anthology* (Lanham, MD: Scarecrow, 2002).

26 Béhague, *Music in Latin America*, 102.

27 Mendoza de Arce, *Music in Ibero-America to 1850*, 485.

28 Marina Rodríguez López, "Coros, VII: Cuba," *Diccionario de la música española e latinoamericana*, 51.

29 See Daniel Mendoza de Arce's article "Domingo Delgado Gómez (1805–56): Puerto Rican Master Composer," in *Latin American Music Review* 16, 2 (Fall 1995): 160.

30 Mendoza de Arce, *Music in Ibero-America to 1850*, 483.

31 Ibid., 488–90.

32 A superb study of Plaza's life and work is now available in Marie Elizabeth Labonville's *Juan Bautista Plaza and Musical Nationalism in Venezuela* (Bloomington: University of Indiana Press, 2007).

33 Felipe Sangiorgi, "Coros, XIV: Venezuela," *Diccionario de la música española e latinoamericana*, 61.

34 Mendoza de Arce, *Music in Ibero-America to 1850*, 463, 499.

35 Ibid., 496.

36 Armando Sánchez Málaga, "Coros, XII: Perú," *Diccionario de la música española e latinoamericana*, 58.

37 Mendoza de Arce, *Music in Ibero-America to 1850*, 495.

38 Béhague, *Music in Latin America*, 56.

39 Mendoza de Arce, *Music in Ibero-America to 1850*, 467.

40 Ibid., 503.

41 Isis de Barcena, "Coros, XI: Paraguay," *Diccionario de la música española e latinoamericana*, 58.

42 See Béhague, *Music in Latin America*, 105.

43 Béhague, *Music in Latin America*, 106. Not surprisingly, the works of Rossini, Donizetti, Mercadante, Verdi, Auber, Halévy, Hérold, and Meyerbeer dominated.

44 Mendoza de Arce, *Music in Ibero-America to 1850*, 500. Indeed, as Tiemstra, *Choral Music of Latin America*, 14, points out: "Picassari conducted the Sociedad Filarmónica in the New World premiere of Beethoven's *Missa solemnis* in 1836."

45 Roberto Britos, "Coros, II: Argentina," *Diccionario de la música española e latinoamericana*, 39.

46 According to Béhague, *Music in Latin America*, 107.

47 See Mendoza de Arce, *Music in Ibero-America to 1850*, 505, for more information on Salvador and its "intense" music scene.

48 Ibid., 509, 516.

49 Ibid., 504.

50 João VI and his wife remained in Brazil until 1821, when they returned to Portugal. Their son, Pedro I,

declared Brazil's independence the following year. His son, Pedro II, ascended to the throne in 1840 and reigned until his abdication in 1889 and declaration of the republic.

51 Béhague, *Music in Latin America*, 85.

52 Mendoza de Arce, *Music in Ibero-America to 1850*, 508.

53 See Cristina Magaldi, *Music in Imperial Rio: European Culture in a Tropical Milieu* (Lanham, MD: Scarecrow Press, 2004), 43–46 and 137 for more on Italian opera in Rio.

54 Béhague, *Music in Latin America*, 113.

55 See Magaldi, *Music in Imperial Rio*, 70–78, for a discussion of these clubs.

56 Mendoza de Arce, *Music in Ibero-America to 1850*, 475.

57 See Walter Aaron Clark, *Isaac Albéniz: Portrait of a Romantic* (Oxford: Oxford University Press, 1999/2002), 136–77, for a detailed examination of this opera. It was published by Breitkopf und Härtel in 1897, and in a revised version in 1904. A vocal score was issued by Max Eschig in 1923. It has recently been revived by Spanish conductor José de Eusebio, directing the Orquesta y Coro de la Comunidad de Madrid, Deutsche Grammophon Gesellschaft, 002894776234, 2006.

58 See ibid., 125–33, for an in-depth examination of this work.

59 Anyone interested in the music of Albéniz must consult the definitive catalog of his works, Jacinto Torres, *Catálogo sistemático descriptivo de las obras musicales de Isaac Albéniz* (Madrid: Instituto de Bibliografía Musical, 2001). Recordings are available of both *Henry Clifford* (José de Eusebio and the Coro y Orquesta Sinfónica de Madrid, Decca 473937-2, 2003) and *Merlin* (José de Eusebio and the Coro y Orquesta Sinfónica de Madrid, Decca, 289467096-2, 2000); *Merlin* is also available on DVD (José de Eusebio and Coro y Orquesta Titular del Teatro Real de Madrid, BBC/Opus Arte DVD, OA 0888D, 2004).

60 Taken from Aransay's liner notes for *O Crux: Spanish Choral Music*, Coro Cervantes, dir. Carlos Fernández Aransay, Guild GMCD 7243. This indispensable CD includes all of the sacred works discussed here, except for Eslava's motet *O salutaris hostia*.

61 For a more detailed listing, see James Radomski, *Manuel García: Chronicle of the Life of a* bel canto *Tenor at the Dawn of Romanticism* (Oxford: Oxford University Press, 2000), 315–18. All the manuscripts are in the Bibliothèque Nationale in Paris.

62 See Arriaga's *Obra completa*, ed. Christophe Rousset (Madrid: Instituto Complutense de Ciencias Musicales, 2006).

63 See Fernando Sor, *O Crux*, ed. Michael Fink (London: Tecla Editions, 1980).

64 On his recording of this work, Aransay uses basses to sing the chant portions and tenors to sing the contralto parts, which are very low (email correspondence, February 4, 2011).

65 *Salmo VI: Oficio de difuntos*, ed. Jacinto Torres (Madrid: Instituto de Bibliografía Musical, 1994). For a discussion of this work, see Clark, *Isaac Albéniz*, 70.

66 Granados's *Salve Regina* has been edited by Douglas Riva and Miriam Perandones and published by Boileau (Barcelona, 2008). This edition includes two other sacred works by Granados: *L'herba de l'amor* ("A Prayer in Gregorian Style for the Virgin of Montserrat") and *Escena religiosa*. The former of these is also featured on the Coro Cervantes CD. For more information about Granados's sacred music, see Walter Aaron Clark, *Enrique Granados: Poet of the Piano* (New York: Oxford University Press, 2006), 146–47.

67 Joaquim Zueras Navarro, "La música religiosa de Enrique Granados," *OpusMusica: Revista de música clasica*, n 48 (September 2010), http://www.opusmusica.com/048/granados.html (accessed September 15, 2010).

68 María Nagore Ferrer, "Coros, I. 1–10: España," *Diccionario de la música española e latinoamericana*, 24. The ensuing discussion is indebted to this source, 23–28.

69 Wilhem (1781–1842) studied at the Paris Conservatoire and later established sight-singing in Parisian schools. He founded all-male choirs throughout France. His Method emphasized singing on fixed Do.

70 Ferrer, "Coros, I. 1–10: España," 24.

71 Ibid., 25.

72 Ibid., 24.

73 Quoted in Pablo Vila San-Juan, *Papeles íntimos de Enrique Granados* (Barcelona: Amigos de Granados, 1966), 78, and cited in Clark, *Enrique Granados*, 74.

74 Ferrer, "Coros, I. 1–10: España," 30.

75 This piece appeared in a complete collection of his works in 1897, edited and published by the composer's daughter, Aurea Rosa Clavé.

Selected Bibliography

Béhague, Gerard. *Music in Latin America: An Introduction*. Englewood Cliffs, NJ: Prentice-Hall, 1979.

Brillantes-Silvestre, Patricia. "Music in The Heart of Manila: Quiapo from the Colonial Period to

Contemporary Times: Tradition, Change, Continuity," *Diagonal* 4 (2008). http://cilam.ucr.edu/diagonal/issues/2008/Brillantes-Silvestre2.pdf.

Casares Rodicio, Emilio, ed. *Diccionario de la música española e latinoamericana.* Madrid: Sociedad General de Autores y Editores, 1999. S.v. "Coros," iv, 39–66.

I: "España," María Nagore Ferrer; II: "Argentina," Roberto Britos; VII: "Cuba," Marina Rodríguez López; VIII: "El Salvador," Salvador Marroquín; X: "Mexico," Gloria Carmona; XI: "Paraguay," Isis de Barcena; XII: "Perú," Armando Sánchez Málaga; XIV: "Venezuela," Felipe Sangiorgi.

Clark, Walter Aaron. *Enrique Granados: Poet of the Piano.* New York: Oxford University Press, 2006/2011.

———. *Isaac Albéniz: Portrait of a Romantic.* Oxford: Oxford University Press, 1999/2002.

Fernández Aransay, Carlos. Liner notes for *O Crux: Spanish Choral Music.* Coro Cervantes, dir. Carlos Fernández Aransay. Guild GMCD 7243.

Irving, David. *Colonial Counterpoint: Music in Early Modern Manila.* Series: Currents in Latin American and Iberian Music. Ed. Walter Aaron Clark. New York: Oxford University Press, 2010.

Kendall, David. "Spanish Colonial Liturgical Music in the Philippines: Inventing a Tradition." Ph.D., diss., University of California, Riverside, 2010.

Labonville, Marie Elizabeth. *Juan Bautista Plaza and Musical Nationalism in Venezuela.* Bloomington: University of Indiana Press, 2007.

Magaldi, Cristina. *Music in Imperial Rio: European Culture in a Tropical Milieu.* Lanham, MD: Scarecrow Press, 2004.

Mendoza de Arce, Daniel. "Domingo Delgado Gómez (1805–56): Puerto Rican Master Composer." *Latin American Music Review* 16, 2 (fall 1995): 154–64.

———. *Music in Ibero-America to 1850.* New York: Scarecrow Press, 2001.

Radomski, James. *Manuel García: Chronicle of the Life of a* bel canto *Tenor at the Dawn of Romanticism.* Oxford: Oxford University Press, 2000.

Rivera Mirano, Elena. "Finding Marcelo: Reconstructing the Lost Repertoire of a Nineteenth-century Philippine Master," *Diagonal* 4 (2008). http://cilam.ucr.edu/diagonal/issues/2008/Mirano1.pdf.

———, ed. *The Life and Works of Marcelo Adonay.* Vol. 1. Diliman, Quezon City: University of the Philippines Press, 2009.

Russell, Craig H. *From Serra to Sancho: Music and Pageantry in the California Missions.* Series: Currents in Latin American and Iberian Music. Ed. Walter Aaron Clark. New York: Oxford University Press, 2009.

Tiemstra, Suzanne Spicer. *The Choral Music of Latin America: A Guide to Compositions and Research.* New York: Greenwood Press, 1992. Updated version available at www.latinamericanchoralmusic.org.

Thompson, Donald. *Music in Puerto Rico: A Reader's Anthology.* Lanham, MD: Scarecrow, 2002.

Torres, Jacinto. *Catálogo sistemático descriptivo de las obras musicales de Isaac Albéniz.* Madrid: Instituto de Bibliografía Musical, 2001.

Zueras Navarro, Joaquim. "La música religiosa de Enrique Granados." *OpusMusica: Revista de música clasica,* n. 48 (September 2010). http://www.opusmusica.com/048/granados.html.

North America

31

THE UNITED STATES

N. Lee Orr

GEORGIA STATE UNIVERSITY

Organized choral singing in the United States grew out of the same impulses that spawned the popular, non-professional singing societies in Germany and England. Unlike the older European model, where for centuries professionals in opera and church dominated music-making, early singing societies in America emerged from the growing democratic spirit of the young republic with enthusiastic amateurs who relished finding their own voice. This republican choral model proved so flexible that it easily adapted to a variety of diverse cultures and community structures. By the end of the nineteenth century, many viewed choral music as the most important musical activity in the country.

This chapter surveys the emergence of organized choral singing in the United States during a period of unprecedented growth and expansion that affected the history of choral music-making in significant ways.[1] In 1800, twenty-five years after the original thirteen Colonies declared their independence, just three new states had been added to the Union, and although the country's western edge extended to the Mississippi River, most of its 5.3 million inhabitants lived near traditional population centers along the eastern seaboard and in the South; just over 894,000 were slaves.[2] By the end of the century, however, nearly seventy-six million people inhabited forty-five states, as the western border stretched nearly three million square miles to the Pacific Ocean.[3] As the century unfolded, technological innovations set a foundation that would eventually transform the country into an economic and military power in the next century. Yet old European ideas and philosophies continued to exert influence on an American culture that remained unsettled as a result of various factors, from disputes with the indigenous peoples (as well as with various foreign governments) over territorial rights in parts of North America, to the increasingly bitter disputes over slavery and states' rights that led the United States to the Civil War.

Choral music flourished throughout the century at least in part due to the ideals of democracy and self-rule, to the growth of the middle class, and to the waves of immigrants that came from points East and West. As citizens realized the old restraining hierarchies had vanished, they increasingly exercised personal freedoms and, as Robert Wiebe put it, "fought to extend the range of these exhilarating new rights in a self-fueling process that propelled the participants as fast and as far as their impulses drove them."[4] This freedom of choice, combined with the significant rise in literacy and education rates, had far-reaching consequences in the development of political, philosophical, religious, and cultural attitudes. In time, the new urban middle class transformed America's social structure, and came to impart considerable cultural authority to choral music as a major factor in the genteel refinement of America. Moreover, the gradual urbanization of the population, combined with spreading religious fervor, brought about a significant increase in the number of choral groups established both inside and outside the church. Directly influencing the growth of choral music as well was the invention of the steam press in 1810 and the rotary printing press in 1843. This development boosted the number of sheets per hour from the low hundreds to the thousands, making music cheaper to produce in large quantities and less expensive to purchase.

As the population grew throughout the century, choral music making came to serve multiple purposes in addition to its role in religious worship. Joining a choir was a way for citizens and new immigrants alike to assimilate into the community. It could also be a way to *preserve* one's specific ethnic and cultural identity, as the emergence of German singing societies (among others) illustrates most directly. Perhaps more significantly, singing in a church choir or a community chorus became a democratic experience, as men and women seized the opportunity to sing what they wanted, with whom they wanted, and where they wanted. For these reasons and many more, singing in an ensemble became a vibrant, socially binding experience in nineteenth-century American culture.

The Post-Revolutionary Period to the 1850s

At the end of the eighteenth century, population density in the United States consisted of a sparse 6.1 people per square mile; small, rural farms owned mainly by white Protestants from Britain and Germany formed a significant part of American commerce. With the acquisition of the vast Louisiana Territory from France in 1803, however, the young nation's population became more diverse, in terms not only of race and ethnicity, but also of language, religion, and culture. Not only did the Louisiana Purchase double the country's size, its newly acquired lands were rich in natural resources that fueled future industrial and economic development.

As the country's physical dimensions expanded, so too did its ability to conduct business. The newly acquired port of New Orleans (secured as part of the Louisiana Purchase) opened up the entire central United States, allowing unlimited access to transport goods freely along the Mississippi River without the threat of blocked access by its previous owners, France or Spain. The completion of the Erie Canal (1825) and the development of the steam locomotive (1829), greatly enhanced the ability to move materials and people at significantly faster speeds. By the 1820s, more than 1,800 miles of turnpikes had been completed, and another 700 were in progress, the most significant of which was the National Road (1811–39), which stretched from Maryland over the Allegheny Mountains into Ohio and (eventually) to Vandalia, Illinois, just short of St. Louis, Missouri. Such improvements led directly to a first wave of economic prosperity, but they also added to the growing political tensions between North and South, especially on the issue of slavery.

Early Church Choirs and Community Singing Societies

Given the importance of religious worship in the thirteen Colonies, it is little surprise that the first efforts at organized singing arose in the Colonial church—mainly Episcopalian, Congregational, and Presbyterian—where the first book of any kind to be published in North America was a metrical psalter, *The Whole Booke of Psalmes* (Cambridge, MA, 1640). Although it would be more than 130 years before the Colonies officially declared their independence from England, democracy and the concept of an open, free society began to take shape early on. Choral singing embodied the developing democratic philosophy, as church choirs, and later singing schools and community choral groups, extended an invitation to sing to anyone within their respective social spheres who wished to join. By the middle of the eighteenth century, self-selected groups of singers came together to learn the rudiments of music and lead congregational psalmody. Eventually, these groups evolved into church choirs: typically men and women singing either in unison or in parts, who gathered for the express purpose of rehearsing and presenting choral music.

Late eighteenth- and early nineteenth-century churches viewed choral music mainly as an embellishment and aid to worship. Congregations only occasionally allowed anthems in the Sunday worship service out of fear that such choral singing would foster an attitude focused more on musical expression than on worshipful reverence, as the following complaint illustrates: "There is a set of Geniuses, who stick themselves up in a Gallery, and seem to think that they have a Priviledge [sic] of engrossing all the singing to themselves; . . . by singing such Tunes, as is impossible for the Congregation to join in."[5]

Unfortunately, these early choirs added little in terms of quality to the music heard during services. Choirs consisted of amateurs who gathered mainly for social purposes and who saw little need to rehearse. Many of these singers were self-taught or were the product of singing schools; few had the training to sing solos or to navigate the complicated lines found in European choral music.[6] Choirs sang from the gallery and rarely used music, as limitations in print technology meant tunebooks were expensive, leaving most singers to sing from memory. Consequently, the ability to read from scores rapidly declined, causing poor performances, as Samuel Gilman recalled in his *Memoirs of a New England Village Choir*:

> Accordingly, in our choir, among the men, the proportion of books was scarcely more than one to four or five performers, so that you might often hear some ardent and confident individual, who was stationed too far from the page to read distinctly, attempting to make out the sentence from his own imagination,—or, when he despaired of achieving that aim, filling up the line with uncouth and unheard of syllables, or with inarticulate sounds.[7]

Initially, ensemble singing outside of the church was often viewed as frivolous. But around the turn of the nineteenth century, singing societies only loosely connected with the church began to appear. Although their membership was comprised mainly of church choir members, these societies focused on the musical experience and music education rather than worship, even though their repertoire remained mostly sacred. Unlike church choirs, which met to sing for Sunday services with little or no rehearsal, members of these new singing societies gathered during the week for vocal training and to perform music for meetings and concerts.

As cultural and religious tensions grew during the first decades of the 1800s, people increasingly turned to secular singing societies as a means for self-improvement and as a way to heighten the quality of the performance experience. These developments brought about a fundamental reform of American choral music, resulting in new hymns, anthems, and service music for the church, and more extended works such as cantatas and oratorios, and shorter works such as partsongs for secular choirs.

The enthusiasm for new hymns and for hymn singing, especially in the growing evangelical denominations, stirred a reaction among northeastern Presbyterian and Congregational reformers, which led to the creation of a new repertoire designed to foster a proper devotional spirit. Thus, sacred music tunebooks published in the Northeast after 1805, such as *The Salem Collection of Classical Sacred Musick* (Salem, 1805) and *The Middlesex Collection of Church Music: or, Ancient Psalmody Revived* (Boston, 1807), quickly began supplanting American pieces with European ones.[8] Their contents immediately differentiated them from American tunebooks, which consisted of music drawn mostly from the 1770s or earlier, by including music that was almost exclusively European in origin. The compilers and composers chose dignified European texts and tunes owing to their refinement as well as their lack of profane allusions, and set them in a "scientifically" correct manner.[9]

In the first four decades of the nineteenth century, the gradual establishment of choral groups outside of the church occurred almost entirely in the Northeast. Nourished by the tradition of singing schools and other later eighteenth-century musical societies, interest in community choral societies began to accelerate.[10] By the time Boston's Handel and Haydn Society was founded in 1815, at least twenty-five musical societies had been formed, including the Massachusetts Musical Society (1807), the Middlesex Musical Society (1807), the Lock Hospital Society (1812), and the Norfolk Musical Society (1814).[11] While larger cities such as Philadelphia and Baltimore saw a few early organizations emerge, virtually none survived longer than a few years and exercised little impact on the later founding of permanent choral groups. Boston's pervasive religious heritage and New York's vibrant economy, however, offered rich cultural soil for the first community choral activity to seed, sprout, and flourish. Two other major events served to encourage these nascent efforts in the first half of the century: the success of Boston's Handel and Haydn Society, and the influence of Lowell Mason's work in Boston and (through disciples such as William Bradbury and George Frederick Root) in New York and elsewhere.

Choral Music in the Northeast to Mid-Century: Boston

The Massachusetts Anti-Theater Law of 1750 stifled most of the professional music throughout the Commonwealth for nearly all of the second half of the eighteenth century, leaving Boston's numerous church choirs and some singing schools as the source for nearly all public musical activity. The Musical Society of Boston, established by English-born William Selby (1738–98) in 1786, somehow skirted the law and performed the first complete oratorio, Samuel Felsted's *Jonah*, for George Washington during his visit to the city in December 1789.[12] The state finally repealed the Anti-Theater Law in 1793, an act that unleashed decades of pent-up music and theater expression.

Boston gained its first important professional musician when George K. Jackson (1757–1822) moved there from New York in 1812. Three years later, he led a concert commemorating Washington's birthday, a performance that proved to be the catalyst for the growing culture of nineteenth-century American singing societies. Exhilarated by the singing and playing at the concert, the performers wanted to continue making music together even though their original purpose for meeting had passed. The audience, having never heard such grand music before, enthusiastically encouraged them to establish a permanent chorus. On April 20, 1815, Gottlieb Graupner, Thomas Webb, Amasa Winchester, and Matthew Parker did just that, founding the Handel and Haydn Society, "for the purpose of improving the style of performing sacred music, and introducing more into general use the works of Handel and Haydn and other eminent composers."[13] The society gave its first concert in Boston's Stone Chapel (the King's Chapel at Tremont and School streets) on Christmas night 1815, with a chorus of ninety male and ten female singers and a paying audience estimated at 1,000, featuring excerpts from Haydn's *The Creation*, the "Hallelujah Chorus" from *Messiah*, and other works. One Boston newspaper asserted the concert "electrified" the crowd.[14]

As Richard Crawford observed, this concert marked a major shift in the status of choral music in America. No longer was leading music in worship the goal around which people came together to sing. Rather, individuals became part of a choir specifically to prepare and present a chosen repertoire conducted by a professional musician in a concert setting. In this way, personal edification now supplanted divine praise. Moreover, organizations made the composers themselves—here Handel and Haydn—the focal point of the musical event. This was in sharp contrast to singing in church, where the music offered was a means to an end of a very different sort. Even more importantly, choral music originally composed for concert use rather than for a service assumed a place of equal importance to the hymn.[15] Boston's Handel and Haydn Society was the first significant American choral group organized with these aims clearly articulated.

Soon, choral societies and church choirs were established throughout Massachusetts (as they were elsewhere in the Northeast).[16] Typical of this growth was the Union Sacred Singing Society, which succeeded the Middlesex Society in 1825. In Essex, north of Boston, the Union Sacred Singing Society's success encouraged other composer-named organizations: the Handel Society (1817), the Haydn Association (1821), and the Mozart Association (1825). Mozart's name was also used briefly for a choral group in Worcester in 1827; similarly, Beethoven's was used for a group in Taunton in 1821. Few of these societies lasted longer than ten or so years largely owing to scarce financial resources, a lack of competent singers (especially women), and little professional leadership. Even so, it was with community choruses such as these that choral music began developing its own legitimate cultural presence apart from religious institutions. Moreover, this choral activity increased the importation and performance of European choral music.[17]

Boston's choral landscape took its next significant step in 1827 with the arrival of Lowell Mason, labeled by many as the most influential American musician in the nineteenth century.[18] Born in Medfield, Massachusetts in 1792 into a musical family, Mason attended a singing school taught by the American composer and teacher Oliver Shaw (1779–1848) and played various instruments. In 1812, he left home for Savannah, Georgia, where he first worked in a dry-goods store, then as a clerk at the Planter's Bank, while also serving as organist and choirmaster at the Independent Presbyterian Church.

In Savannah, Mason assembled his first tunebook, which would serve as the foundation for his career and establish him as the leader of American choral-music reform and music education. He gathered most of the music from other publications, including William Gardiner's *Sacred Melodies from Haydn, Mozart, and Beethoven* (London, 1812–15), which adapted European melodies for English texts.[19] He traveled north in 1821 to show his collection to members of the Handel and Haydn Society; George K. Jackson, the society's organist, put his stamp of approval on the "judicious" selection of tunes declaring that, "It is the best book I have seen published in this country."[20]

With the prominent society's backing, Mason published the first of nearly two dozen editions of his tunebook in 1822 under their name, the *Boston Handel and Haydn Society Collection of Church Music*.[21] What distinguished this tunebook from the many similar ones? First, Mason earned prestige for himself and the tunebook by being associated directly with the Handel and Haydn Society. Second, the book received the imprimatur of two knowledgeable European musicians: Frederick L. Abel and the aforementioned Jackson. Third, Mason aligned the book with a choral ensemble widely regarded as the arbiters of high cultural taste. Perhaps most importantly, Mason's book featured music that had better crafted melodic lines, more purposeful chord progressions, clearer text accentuation, and more satisfying harmonizations compared to the banal anthem materials that constituted some earlier collections. Even when Mason used some of the same tunes other composers had arranged, they sounded better in his new arrangements.

Mason's approach helped to shape Americans' taste for better choral music.[22] The tunebook's success led a group of churches to invite Mason to return to Boston in 1827 to improve their music programs; it was at this time that he became the accepted leader of Boston's musical life. When Mason came to head the Handel and Haydn Society that year, the ensemble was still as much a social group as a musical one, plagued by poor rehearsal and performance attendance by the singers. For years the press decried the inadequate preparation, inconsistent attendance, lack of fundamental musical skills, and overall amateurish spirit that marred their concerts. Society members consisted of unauditioned male singers; women participated by invitation only and few of these were issued.

Mason introduced several fundamental practices into his work with the society that would transform American choral music-making. First, he emphasized the importance of vocal training, and of being able to read music. He recruited more female singers, particularly altos; eventually, singing in four parts rather than three was the norm, though only after much work and controversy.[23] Most importantly, Mason argued that the choir should be a body of singers that rehearsed regularly and strove for excellence—an uncommon idea at the time. He introduced other modern choral practices too, including reserving the melody line for sopranos, improving the overall balance between the male and female voices, eliminating octave doublings, and instilling the choral concepts of proper voice production, blend, and accuracy.

Gradually, the quality of the Handel and Haydn Society rose under Mason's leadership, and the repertoire expanded as well. In December 1827, he conducted Haydn's *The Creation*, and in 1829 he led the group in the first American performance of a complete Haydn Mass (an unspecified setting in B-flat). During Mason's five-year tenure as the group's leader, and in the eighteen years that followed, works by five composers dominated the society's repertoire: Neukomm's *David* (59 performances), Haydn's *The Creation* (36) Handel's *Messiah* (28) and *Samson* (22), Mendelssohn's *Elijah* (15), and Rossini's opera *Moses in Egypt* (29; unstaged) and *Stabat Mater*.[24] In the two decades following Mason's departure, the ensemble's offerings expanded to include complete or partial performances of Handel's *Judas Maccabeus*, Spohr's *God, Thou Art Great* and *Last Judgment*, Romberg's *Transient and Eternal*, Neukomm's *Hymn of the Night*, Mendelssohn's *St. Paul*, and Donizetti's *The Martyrs* (unstaged). All told, the society presented 300 performances between 1830 and 1850, all of which were accompanied by an orchestra that varied from fifteen to twenty-five professional and volunteer players.[25]

Mason retired as president and musical director of the Handel and Haydn Society in 1832 to devote himself full time to music education. He realized in a way no one had before how he could connect sacred and secular music; this realization allowed him to apply the same singing-school techniques previously used for teaching secular music. For the rest of his career he strove to make organized musical participation available to as many Americans as possible, and his efforts left an indelible mark on America's musical culture.[26]

In 1833, Mason, his English émigré associate George James Webb (1803–87), and other spirited community leaders founded the Boston Academy of Music to teach both sacred and secular singing, and to train music teachers.[27] By its second year, the Academy already had 1,700 pupils, an impressive number considering that the total student enrollment in the Boston public schools was 2,200.[28] Soon the academy's 200-voice adult choir surpassed the Handel and Haydn Society in excellence, largely owing to stricter auditions and better musical leadership.

During the academy's early years, Mason published his *Manual of the Boston Academy of Music for Instruction in the Elements of Vocal Music on the System of Pestalozzi* (1834); that it enjoyed eleven more printings by 1861 attests to its popularity as a method for music education. He also began publishing tunebooks with secular music, the first of which was *Selections for the Choir of the Boston Academy of Music* (1836). Mason and Webb also organized a four-day music convention in 1836, held at the Odeon Theater, for the purpose of making music education available to people of all ages.[29] The first gathering drew just fourteen church musicians, but within fifteen years the annual event, named The National Musical Convention from 1840 onward, reportedly attracted more than 1,000.

The Academy of Music legitimized secular music in a culture that previously valued only sacred choral music. Encouraged by its success and that of the Handel and Haydn Society, other societies were established throughout New England.[30] Few of these groups functioned for more than eight or ten years, but while they existed, they tapped into the community's love of choral music and inspired future generations to create ensembles of their own.

Choral Music in the Northeast to Mid-Century: New York

Choral music took somewhat longer to come of age in New York than it did in Boston. With its economic vibrancy, entertainment diversity, and tolerant religious politics, the history of organized singing societies in the city is strewn with oft-repeated unstable yet enthusiastic beginnings, inept organization, fractious and petty bickering, and brutally partisan critiques in the press. When ensembles dissolved, displaced singers formed into new societies, only to see them fizzle out just as ingloriously.

The choral musical fare in New York, like Boston, consisted invariably of sacred music concerts given at the city's numerous churches by amateur local singers, often for charitable causes. They typically presented exceedingly long, mixed programs of vocal solos, small vocal ensembles, and choruses consisting of short- to medium-length sacred works: hymns, psalms, anthems by Lowell Mason and Oliver Shaw, as well as excerpts from well-known oratorios by Handel, Haydn, Mozart, and Beethoven.

The first efforts at serious choral performance began with the arrival of professionally trained immigrant musicians such as George K. Jackson in 1801 and Samuel Priestly Taylor (c.1779–1875) in 1806, both of whom advocated the performance of European choral literature. Jackson failed in his attempts in the first decade of the 1800s to interest New Yorkers in music of a more serious nature and went off in a huff, moving first to Hartford, and then to Boston in 1812 where, as we have already seen, he found success with the Handel and Haydn Society. Taylor, on the other hand, founded a singing school in New York in 1813 whose students undoubtedly participated in his "grand oratorio" of March 8, 1814, where they joined with local players to present lengthy portions from Haydn's *The Creation* and Handel's *Messiah* at the Church of Saint-Esprit. Two years later, a group of 150 amateurs sang excerpts from *Messiah* and *Israel in Egypt* at St. Paul's Church. Many of these singers became members of the newly established New York Handel and Haydn Society, which presented its first concert in 1818, only to disappear from the historical record three years later.

In 1823, two new choral organizations appeared, the New York Choral Society and the New York Sacred Music Society, the latter of which became the most influential musical institution in the 1830s. Composed of defectors from the Zion Church choir, who resigned over a dispute with the church vestry, the Sacred Music Society had one of the first balanced choral ensembles in the country with a membership of seventeen men and thirteen women.[31] The group presented New York's first complete performance of *Messiah* on November 18, 1831, with seventy-three singers and an orchestra of thirty-eight players. They performed an impressive number of other premieres in New York over the next twenty years, including the first American performances of Mendelssohn's oratorios, *St. Paul* in 1838 (two years following its Düsseldorf premiere) and *Elijah* in 1847 (just one year after its Birmingham premiere). They also gave performances of the first oratorio written in America, Charles Edward Horn's *Remission of Sin* (composed in 1835 specifically for the society), as well as the 1846 premiere of the first oratorio written by an American-born composer, John Hill Hewitt's *Jephtha's Rash Vow*.[32]

The late 1830s saw a brief flourishing of additional New York singing societies as well as impermanent groups that appear briefly in the records only to disappear just as quickly. Professional-quality performances still eluded most groups owing to the lack of experienced singers and trained conductors. The Academy of Sacred Music, founded in 1835 by Thomas Hastings (1784–1872), made its concert debut in 1837 at the Broadway Tabernacle. The group gave what was probably the American premiere of Pergolesi's *Stabat Mater* at the Catholic Chapel on December 28, 1837.[33] A massed group of various choirs joined together with Hastings's Academy at the Tabernacle the following December for an event billed as the "Great Union Performance of Sacred Music." In 1839, the academy repeated the Union Concerts twice, joined by thirty-one other choirs—reportedly involving some 900 singers—in a program consisting largely of American works by Mason, Elam Ives, Jr., S. B. Pond, and Charles Zeuner. For its part, the now well-established Sacred Music Society announced the presentation of five complete oratorios at the Tabernacle with a chorus of 200 and an orchestra of sixty for its 1839–40 season: *Messiah, St. Paul, The Creation, The Seasons* and the first New York performance of the oratorio *David* by the popular Austrian composer Sigismund Neukomm.

In the 1840s, these and other established choral groups began experiencing their first significant musical competition with the increase of instrumental and operatic concerts being performed by the wave of European virtuosos and foreign singers that had recently arrived in New York (and elsewhere). Soon, most of the choral groups that had once had a presence in the city's concert life began to disappear, reducing the main source of serious choral concerts to a handful of ensembles, including the short-lived New York Vocal Society. On January 19, 1844, 400–500 people attended this ensemble's debut at Washington Hall in an all-secular program consisting of English and (a few) Italian madrigals and glees—a "notoriously neglected repertoire" as one reviewer reportedly observed—and later that spring they presented the first New York performance of Mendelssohn's *Forty-Second Psalm*.[34] A spirited rivalry developed in the middle of the decade between the Sacred Music Society and a new group, the American Musical Institute, which presented Haydn's *The Seasons*, Carl Lowe's *The Seven Sleepers*, Mendelssohn's *St. Paul*, Beethoven's *The Mount of Olives*, and Felicien David's *The Desert* in 1846, its first formal season.[35] For its part, the Sacred Music Society's offerings that same year included Handel's *Messiah* and *Samson*, Hewitt's *Jephtha's Rash Vow* and Lowe's *The Seven Sleepers*. One year later, the Institute announced its premiere of Mendelssohn's *Elijah* on November 9, 1847; not to be outdone, the Sacred Music Society scooped the Institute by scheduling their own performance of *Elijah* one day earlier. Despite this rather captivating rivalry, competition for audiences from New York's rapidly diversifying concert scene had a negative effect on both groups, and by 1848, both ceased to exist, a significant loss as it reduced concerts of sacred music to modest events at local churches.[36]

Other Trends before Mid-Century

Several other kinds of choral music-making also had their origins in the late eighteenth and first half of the nineteenth centuries. The tradition of amateur glee singing, organized on English models, appeared in New York and Boston soon after the American Revolution; the first such ensembles included New York's Columbia Anacreonic Society (1795), and later, Boston's Junior and Senior Glee Clubs (*c.*1820s), and Apollo Club (1824–26); the Handel and Haydn Society likely sang glees as well. Soon glee clubs arose in cites and towns across the region, such as the Salem Glee Club in Salem Massachusetts (1832), where Mason was a member. Additionally, leading musicians published numerous collections specifically for glee clubs, many of which were reissued numerous times; these included George James Webb's *The American Glee Book* (1841); Isaac Baker Woodbury's *Glees for the Million* (multiple volumes, 1844–46), Woodbury and Thomas Hastings's *The Chorus Glee Book* (1850), Mason's *The Gentlemen's Glee Book* (1841), and Mason and Webb's three joint publications, *The Boston Glee Book* (1838), *The Vocalist* (1844), and *The Glee Hive* (1851). As American choral music embraced the new romantic musical style, the glee's simply harmonized, homophonic style underwent a stylistic transformation, merging with the partsong (discussed below), the generic name given to these works after mid-century.

Following the American Revolution, additional different types of sacred music developed as pioneers migrated into the South and Midwest, especially to Ohio, Missouri, Virginia, West Virginia, Tennessee, Kentucky, North and South Carolina, and Georgia. With few established churches and even fewer ordained ministers, these settlers gradually developed a frontier Christianity expressed periodically in days-long camp meetings. Gradually, a new American revivalist movement emerged—part of the so-called Second Great Awakening—espoused by various new brands of Baptists, Methodists, and, later, Pentecostals. The songs sung at these camp meetings included "camp-meeting spirituals," consisting of easily memorized, repetitive phrases that typically included hallelujahs (or similar tag lines) and refrains, sung to melodies that were improvised and derivative of familiar folk melodies.

Also part of the early nineteenth-century American "spiritual song" tradition in these regions was the emergence of shape-note hymnody. This repertoire—so called because of the specific note shapes assigned to each solmization syllable—combined folk hymns and spirituals from the oral tradition with the body of psalms and hymn tunes, fuging tunes, set-pieces, and anthems from the earlier New England repertoire. Melodies were harmonized in three or four parts consisting of many open fifths and fourths, giving the music a distinctive, archaic sound.

Early nineteenth-century shape-note singing took place at singing conventions, non-denominational gatherings held monthly or annually, and frequently not connected to worship. Being untrained musicians, singers could sing as loudly or softly as they wished; treble and tenor voices usually doubled each other at whatever octave was comfortable. The resulting sound was apparently unrefined, full-throated, possibly nasal, and certainly fiery.

In 1801 in Philadelphia, William Little and William Smith published the first widely successful shape-note tunebook, *The Easy Instructor*, using the four-syllable "fasola" solmization; the collection went through many editions into the 1820s.[37] Other tunebooks soon appeared, including *Wyeth's Repository of Sacred Music, Part Second* (Harrisburg, Pennsylvania, 1813), and numerous other publications from the Shenandoah Valley region, St. Louis, and Cincinnati. Additionally, Virginian Ananias Davisson published the first Southern shape-note tunebook, which was specifically intended for camp meetings and revivals, with his *Kentucky Harmony* (Harrisburg, Virginia, 1816, with four subsequent editions issued by 1826) and his *Supplement to the Kentucky Harmony* (1820, plus two subsequent editions).

Two tunebooks securely planted shape-note hymnody in the Deep South: William Walker's *The Southern Harmony and Musical Companion* (New Haven, Connecticut, 1835) and Benjamin Franklin White and Elisha J. King's *The Sacred Harp* (Philadelphia, 1844). Walker's *Southern Harmony*, compiled in Spartanburg, South Carolina, was the first Southern shape-note collection to be distributed nationally; it reportedly sold 600,000 copies by 1866. Included in it was perhaps the most enduring of all Southern folk hymns, "Amazing Grace," which had first appeared in *The Virginia Harmony* (1831). White and King's *The Sacred Harp* was compiled in Hamilton, Georgia; it went through three revisions and a number of editions under White's supervision and has never been out of print.[38]

From Mid-Century to c.1900

It should be clear from the preceding discussion that the most active centers for organized choral music in the first half of the nineteenth century were in the Northeast. As America moved through the century's second half, however, this activity spread as a direct result of the unprecedented advances in technology that energized the nation, some of them financed from wealth acquired during the California Gold Rush. The influx of huge numbers of immigrants between 1850 and the turn of the twentieth century, many of them Catholics and Jews, was principally responsible for the nation's exploding population and increasing diversity: Germans, Irish, French, British, Mexicans, Chinese (many as laborers in the West), Poles, Italians, Russians, and others from Northern, Central, Southern, and Eastern Europe—all bringing their unique cultural heritage with them. Although Congress had abolished the importation of slaves from Africa and the West Indies in 1808, interstate and inter-territory slave trade was still actively practiced at mid-century, especially (but not exclusively) in the South until the end of the Civil War in 1865.

The most significant advances to directly impact choral music and choral music-making in the second half of the century were those in communication and transportation. The telegraph, initially developed in the United States in the 1840s, connected the east and west coasts by 1861; the transatlantic cable was installed just five years later. Just as important was the completion of the first transcontinental railroad in 1869, joining the Union Pacific and Central Pacific rail lines to link the nation from the Atlantic to the Pacific oceans. The aggressive growth of the rail system brought the Second Industrial Revolution to most of the country and made a mass market possible for the first time in American history. Although agricultural production still exceeded industrial output by $500 million in 1870, by 1900, manufactured goods would surpass agricultural products $13 billion to $4.7 billion.[39]

More important for the rise of choral music was the shift from a rural, agrarian society to a modern urban one. At the eve of the Civil War, only one American in six lived in cities with populations over 8,000, and only nine cities had more than 100,000 inhabitants.[40] In the succeeding forty years, however, urban population expanded seven times as the overall population grew from 34.1 million in 1860 to an astonishing 76.2 million in 1900.[41]

Such technological and cultural transformations further stimulated interest in choral music across the country, and choral activity began to be organized and institutionalized in new ways. As music education spread musical literacy, the antebellum singing school disappeared, supplanted by secular choral groups based in the community; many of these ensembles reflected a distinctive cultural or ethnic heritage, organizational structures that mirrored the increasingly democratic nature of American life. Increasingly, singers could form groups and choose repertoire and leaders as they wished, free of constraints from a church or other authority. More significantly, the choral movement in the second half of the century produced a vigorous, non-professional musical life that easily outpaced the socially prominent professional concert world in terms of the number of participants, financial support, and social inclusiveness.

In the years following the Civil War in particular, the rise in the number of community and church choirs, combined with cheaper sheet music prices, an attractive new romantic musical idiom, and the strong general interest in choral music, produced an explosion of choral activity across the country that generated a rising demand for choral music. As a writer for the *Musical Record* observed in 1879, "That the knowledge and love of music have prodigiously increased within the last few years cannot be doubted. Thousands now assist in choral societies and go to concerts and operas who a few years ago could only have been tempted to hear the simplest ballads and most common-place pianoforte pieces."[42] Improvements in printed music, including the wide-spread availability of cheaper octavo formats (developed and perfected in the 1840s by Novello in England) and the use of cylindrical offset lithography (1876 by Oliver Ditson in Boston) encouraged this growth, not only because it lowered the price of music by about 800%, but also because it made mass production of the repertoire possible. This was a development that benefited composers and performers alike: more composers were getting published, and each singer had an individual copy of Sunday's anthem rather than having to share a single score among multiple singers.

Community Singing Societies

From mid-century on, choral groups organized along community, ethnic, or social lines took various forms. Among the most widespread were choirs whose repertoire regularly consisted of small-scale works; larger community ensembles that focused on oratorios, cantatas, and larger-scale pieces; and groups created to promote a single ethnic identity.

Small choruses established to perform small-scale works such as partsongs—often called glee, Orpheus, or Apollo clubs—evolved from English and earlier American models. The most prominent and respected of these ensembles was the New York Mendelssohn Glee Club, which started in 1866 with eight singers; within two years it numbered twenty-four. A visit by this group to Boston in April 1871 led to the founding of the Boston Apollo Club with fifty-two men. Similar groups modeled after New York's club followed soon thereafter, including Philadelphia's Orpheus Club (1872), Chicago's Apollo Musical Club (1872; women were admitted in 1876), and the Brooklyn Apollo Club (1877).[43]

Glee clubs (usually all-male, but not exclusively so) were also an important part of college and university choral music-making between 1850 and 1900. A group of students founded the Harvard Glee Club in 1858 to sing glees and partsongs, making it the oldest collegiate group specifically named "glee club" in the United States.[44] The University of Michigan's Glee Club (1859) and the Yale Glee Club (1861) soon followed suit, as did other collegiate glee clubs established both at Ivy League schools such as the University of Pennsylvania (1862), Cornell (1868), Columbia (1873), and Princeton (1874), and in regions other than the Northeast, including at the University of Virginia (1871), The Ohio State University (1875), the University of Illinois (1886), and the University of California, Berkeley (c.1890). By the early 1890s, similar groups also appeared at small liberal-arts colleges including at Amherst, Mount Holyoke, Smith and Williams Colleges in Massachusetts, and at Pomona College in Claremont, California.[45]

After the Civil War, newly established black schools and universities formed choirs that introduced American and European audiences to arranged versions of the black spiritual. The most significant of these was the Fisk Jubilee Singers, founded in 1871 as a touring ensemble by the school's music professor, George L. White, to raise funds for the financially strapped Fisk University in Nashville, Tennessee.[46] The original touring group consisted of nine singers (several of whom were former slaves) and a pianist. After some difficult early experiences, the Jubilee Singers began achieving success when the widely popular minister of Brooklyn's Plymouth Congregational Church, Henry Ward Beecher, endorsed the group. They came to national prominence in 1873 with their appearance at Patrick Gilmore's colossal World Peace Jubilee in Boston, marking the first time black singers participated in a major American musical event. The group toured throughout the United States and in Europe from 1871 to 1878, giving concerts in England (where they famously sang for Queen Victoria), Germany, Holland, Sweden, Switzerland, and France.

The Fisk Jubilee Singers opened up a new era of American music. As Richard Crawford explained, the group used black spirituals to build a bridge between the foreign world of Southern slaves and Northern white Protestants.[47] The singers' skin color, the newness of the music, and the style of their performance, was mitigated by their upper-middle-class clothing and genteel presentation, as well as by the comfortable atmosphere of the church and meeting houses in which they sang. White took the spirituals he had learned from his students and cast them into restrained concert-style works that were familiar to white audiences. An equally important repository of spirituals was Theodore Seward's published collection of arranged works titled *Jubilee Songs: As Sung by the Jubilee Singers of Fisk University* (1872 and 1884), in which most of the original dialect, rhythmic irregularities, and unusual harmonies had been removed.[48]

Sandra Graham has discovered a dozen or more groups modeled after the Fisk ensemble, including the noted Hampton Singers (from the Hampton Institute of Virginia), the Tennesseans, the Jackson Jubilee Singers, the Wilmington Jubilee Singers, the North Carolinians, Sheppard's Colored Jubilee Singers, the Alabama Jubilee Singers, and others.[49] Other black choral groups formed outside of academia at the end of the nineteenth and beginning of the twentieth centuries. These included a number of ensembles founded in Washington D.C. such as Henry J. Lewis's Amphion Glee Club (1891), the all-female Treble Clef Club (1896), the Washington Permanent Chorus (1899), the Coleridge-Taylor Choral Society (1901), and the Burleigh Choral Society (1903).[50] As Eileen Southern notes, similar groups soon sprung up in other major cities with large black communities, most notably in Chicago, which boasted at least four important choral groups including the Choral Study Club (1900) and the Umbrian Glee Club (1908), and in Philadelphia, where The People's Choral Society (1908), which may have had one of the early modern gospel choral sounds, grew out of the East Calvary Methodist Episcopal Church.[51]

The last half of the nineteenth century also saw the formation of many choral societies organized specifically to perform large-scale choral works with orchestra. Emulating English models, these oratorio societies appeared in nearly every large city. One such group was the Mormon Tabernacle Choir, founded in Salt Lake City, Utah in 1847 by the newly arrived Mormons. Among the most well-known choral ensembles west of the Mississippi River, it is still considered one of America's major choruses today. Many other oratorio choruses imitated Boston's Handel and Haydn Society by naming themselves after European composers, including Milwaukee's Beethoven Society (1843); Chicago's Mozart Society (1849), Mendelssohn Society (1858), and Beethoven Society (1873); Atlanta's Beethoven Society (1872) and Rossini Club (1876); Philadelphia's Mendelssohn Club (1874); and Pittsburgh's Mozart Club (1879).

Perhaps the best-known nineteenth-century ensemble of the large oratorio society type was the New York Oratorio Society, established in 1873 by Leopold Damrosch (1832–85) and featuring a repertoire that rivaled many European choral groups. Included on their programs were some standard works such as *Messiah*, but they also offered a host of others not often programmed by other American ensembles, including Liszt's *Christus*, Schumann's *Das Paradies und die Peri*, Bach's *St. Matthew Passion*, Berlioz's *Grande Messe des morts* and *Roméo et Juliette*, and Elgar's *The Dream of Gerontius*.[52] By the end of the century, the ensemble's membership fluctuated between 400 and 600 singers, and they had given the American premier of at least seven oratorios and two concert performances of operas.

The growing number of German immigrants arriving in the United States during the 1840s brought with them their tradition of singing. Nearly every town with a substantial German population established a *Männerchor*, an all-male singing society; some larger metropolitan areas such as New York seemed to have one every few blocks.[53] The Philadelphia Männerchor (1835) was the first formally established German male chorus; it was followed in quick succession by the Baltimore Liederkranz (1836) and the Cincinnati Deutscher Gesangverein (1838 or 1839). In New York, the Deutsche Liederkranz was organized in 1847; seven years later it had a rival: the Männergesangverein Arion (1854), formed by discontented members of the Deutsche Liederkranz. From the 1850s on, increasing numbers of German émigrés spread across the country forming large German-American communities in Milwaukee, St. Louis, Chicago, Cincinnati, Cleveland, and Indianapolis, as well as in smaller towns, where they established social singing groups; larger communities in the far west also record the existence of male German singing societies, including Los Angeles and Denver.

Musically, *Männerchöre* were often the most professional musical organizations in the community; this was particularly true in the Midwest. Most groups were led by professional musicians (many of whom had been trained in Europe); in the larger cities, some of the most prominent names in music conducted *Männerchöre*, including Leopold Damrosch, Theodore Thomas, and Heinrich Zoellner. These groups epitomized musical populism with their blend of musical and social functions, their open approach to membership, and their method of governing themselves along strictly democratic lines by electing officers, establishing by-laws, and voting on procedures. Likewise, the repertoire proved just as inclusive, ranging from lighter, traditional folk music to professional concerts of the finest German choral works by Beethoven, Schumann, Schubert, and others.

The popularity of the German singing societies stimulated enormous interest in secular choral music in the United States. Even though *Männerchöre* were men's singing societies, women were sometimes invited to sing mixed choral repertoire; occasionally women were allowed to join as full-fledged members, expanding the groups into large mixed choral societies. Some local societies took part in large Sängerfests, where, like similar choral festivals in England, France, and Germany, multiple choirs assembled to sing for and with each other. Although the earliest such affairs in Philadelphia (1837) and Baltimore (1840s) were small, many were not, and the ability to travel easily and relatively quickly by train had a direct effect on the growth of such gatherings. Cincinnati hosted the first extended Sängerfest in 1849; the following year the Philadelphia Männerchor hosted a similar one with groups from various locations in the Northeast. Both festivals became annual events and grew in popularity with each successive year. By 1870, the Cincinnati Festival hosted nearly 2,000 male singers;[54] three years later, the first Cincinnati May Festival took place, with a mixed chorus of 800 and an orchestra of 100, under the direction of the noted German conductor Theodore Thomas. These efforts led organizers to establish a permanent May Festival Chorus in 1880; the festival and chorus still exist today. Ensembles with other Old World connections also formed around the country. Welsh immigrants who settled in Pennsylvania and Ohio, and later in Wisconsin and Kansas, held annual *eisteddfodau* (choral conventions), and by the end of the century Welsh choirs routinely presented full oratorios in concert.[55] Scandinavian choirs prospered in Minneapolis; Irish, Hungarian, Czech, and Italian choirs appeared in Cleveland; Polish choirs in Buffalo.

Singing festivals were not exclusive to choirs linked to specific nationalities. Boston held some of the largest and most notable festivals of the century.[56] The Handel and Haydn Society presented the first of its many festivals in 1857 with six concerts under the direction of Carl Zerrahn, each featuring 600 singers; audiences heard three oratorios—*The Creation, Elijah,* and *Messiah*—as well as various other pieces. In May 1865, the society celebrated their fiftieth anniversary with a week-long festival repeating the same three oratorios plus selections from *Israel in Egypt.* The success of the event was the catalyst for a recurring festival held every three years from 1868 to 1883.

Also in Boston, the popular Irish-American bandmaster Patrick Gilmore (1829–92) organized the first of his massive festivals, the first in June 1869 with over 11,000 performers (singers and instrumentalists combined), with 100 firemen dressed in bright red playing anvils in Verdi's "Anvil Chorus," with firing cannons and ringing church bells.[57] Another Gilmore extravaganza, this one in June 1872, involved a chorus numbering an astonishing 20,000 singers plus 2,000 in the orchestra.[58] Participating choral groups received bound copies of the music for the festival, all works that came to define the core repertoire for many nineteenth-century American choral groups: excerpts from Haydn's *The Creation,* Handel's *Messiah* and *Judas Maccabeus,* Mendelssohn's *Elijah* and *St. Paul,* Rossini's *Moses in Egypt* and *Stabat Mater,* and the so-called Twelfth Mass spuriously attributed to Mozart.

New York was also an important location for large choral festivals, with the earliest dating from the 1840s. By the 1880s, similar events were being held across the country. Among these, specific mention should be made of Theodore Thomas's significant undertakings with his traveling orches-tra: his 1882 tri-city festival in New York, Cincinnati, and Chicago, for example, and his famous "Ocean to Ocean" festival tour (1883), with stops in thirty cities, including Baltimore, Pittsburg, Memphis, St. Louis, San Francisco, Salt Lake City (with the Mormon Tabernacle Choir), and Des Moines, Iowa. Also at this time, the musically active Moravian community in Bethlehem, Pennsylvania, which had hosted local choral festivals for singers from neighboring towns beginning in the 1830s, expanded their efforts with such notable offerings as the first American performance of Bach's *St. John Passion* (1888) and *St. Matthew Passion* (1892). These concerts were the precur-sors to the Bethlehem Bach Festival, which was established in 1900 and still runs today.[59]

Church Choirs after 1850

From the 1850s on, the rapidly growing choral activity and the rise of music education improved the quality of church choirs as well as community-based ensembles. Changes in the formats of sacred music publication, in the character and use of church organs, in the state of volunteer choirs, and in the use of so-called quartet choirs did much to shape this development.

No consistent pattern existed in the placement, function, and organization of church choirs. In some churches, the singers clustered near the clerk's desk; in others, they occupied the gallery over the narthex; and in others still, they sang from the front of the church behind the pulpit. Well into the 1830s and 1840s, composers had continued to compile and publish tunebooks following a tradition already many decades old; these anthologies contained a miscellany of hymns, psalm settings, and anthems drawn from various sources and composers, European and American. By the 1850s, though, more diverse formats for sacred music publications were being explored. The quality of singing by church choirs, which at mid-century still consisted of volunteer singers rather than paid professionals, rarely rose above the mediocrity of the music found in these tunebooks, and musically untrained singers led by equally untrained conductors produced dismaying musical results. Thomas Hastings, now a leading church musician in New York, left a telling account of this sorry state of affairs in his *History of Forty Choirs* (1854). Writing with obvious despair, he described how even in large churches the gallery choir was "so feeble, so inefficient, and so ill-ordered, as scarcely to deserve the name. Instead of leading in the exercise, they were overpowered by voices below, that would drag at a fearful distance behind them."[60]

As churches grew dissatisfied with how their choirs sounded, those that could afford them began installing organs and hiring professional singers, one singer on each part, to form quartet choirs. From the 1840s on, the number of congregations using professional singers began increasing rapidly, influenced by Italian opera and a desire for a more expressive tone in the service.[61] A survey in 1861 of over 130 New York City churches revealed seventy-two had solo or double quartets. Of seventeen Roman Catholic parishes, fourteen used quartets, as did twenty-four of thirty-one Episcopal churches; the historic Grace Church on lower Broadway was especially esteemed for the music sung by its quartet under the direction of its English organist George Washburne Morgan.[62] Yet, only seven of twenty-four Presbyterian churches employed quartets, while twelve had volunteer choirs; the Church of the Puritans, Rutgers Church, The Riverside Church, West Presbyterian Church, and the Scotch Presbyterian Church, however, used only solo singers. Eight of the eleven Dutch Reformed congregations used professionals, and nearly every Congregational church and Reformed Jewish synagogue seems to have had a professional quartet; Methodist and Baptist churches, however, relied more heavily on volunteers. By the 1880s, churches in other growing urban areas emulated this trend seen in New York, and by the 1890s, most large churches in bigger cities such as Atlanta, San Francisco, St. Louis, and Chicago had professional quartets.

As quartets grew more fashionable, a few musicians began to produce collections with music that capitalized on the skills of these singers. One of the earliest was Henry Wilson's *Quartettes of the Christ Church Collection of Sacred Music* (1851), which consisted of arrangements of European compositions and a few short anthems and services by Wilson himself. Other popular collections included Henry Wellington Greatorex's *A Collection of Psalm and Hymn Tunes, Chants and Anthems* (1851), William King's *The Grace Church Collection* (1852), George Kingsley's *Templi Carmina* (1853, 1861), and Adolph Baumbach's *Sacred Quartetts; A Collection of Pieces for the Opening and Close of Service* (1862).

Repertoire Trends: Smaller Choral Genres

As choral music became cheaper and easier to produce in the 1840s and 1850s, publishers were able to meet the demand for appealing, less taxing music for small volunteer choirs that could be easily learned by all. These publications consisted of sentimental gospel-style pieces on simple texts with repetitive melodies and uncomplicated rhythms. Most of this music was written by composers employed by publishing firms, who frequently used familiar, transparent formulas in their new compositions, or who simplified and shortened older works from the classical repertoire so they could be sung by groups with limited skills. Generally resisting romantic trends in harmony and melody, these mostly simple, chordal works with syllabically set texts tended to be sectionalized, with variety achieved through contrasting moods, tempos, and meters. Anthems of this type typically featured solo voices alternating with the full choir, and minimal accompaniment.[63]

The poor quality of much of this music drew sharp criticism from musicians seeking higher standards in American musical life. Music educators from the first half of the century had succeeded in instilling a love of music in many, but had developed little discriminating taste. Raymond Seely spoke for many when he upbraided church members for their musical indifference, "when they, in some instances, rest contented with, or allow of music in the house of God, which would be hissed at a public concert, hooted at the evening serenade, and secretly laughed at in the parlor."[64]

The major catalyst for improving the situation in the second half of the century began when Dudley Buck (1839–1909) returned from Europe in 1862 and began composing anthems in the new romantic style he had encountered there.[65] Buck was arguably the finest of a new generation of American composers of choral music who had come of age following the Civil War.[66] He was the first to write anthems that could stand on their own merits, and they became exemplars of Victorian sacred music. A native of Hartford, Connecticut, Buck spent two years at the Leipzig Conservatory and a year each in Dresden and Paris before returning to America, first as organist at the North Congregational Church in Hartford, and later (after a short stay in Chicago) at the New England Conservatory in Boston, and at Holy Trinity Church in New York.

Buck had a knack for composing music that held popular appeal without sacrificing artistic substance. By 1873, his output included more than eighty published pieces, some of which appeared in two seminal compilations of church music—*Motette Collection* (1864) and the *Second Motette Collection* (1871)—and others published in octavo format. His own contributions to the 1864 *Motette Collection* made him the first successful American composer to synthesize the quartet tradition with that of the standard volunteer choir by including both quartet and full-chorus passages in the same anthem, and he did so in a romantic musical idiom new to the practice of American sacred music. He also wrote the first artistically satisfying music for both volunteer and professional choir singers, resulting in a body of emotionally expressive anthems. Two of his most popular anthems, *Rock of Ages* and the iconic *Festival Te Deum*, remained popular well into the twentieth century.

Initially, Buck's church music found its most immediate welcome in the Episcopal Church and in the larger, urban Methodist, Congregational, and Baptist churches due to the growing influence of the Oxford Movement from England, which led a gradual move toward a more elaborate, richer liturgy.[67] His popular musical style was mainly taken up by his pupils, the most important being Harry Rowe Shelley (1858–1947, who had served as Buck's accompanist and successor as director of the Brooklyn Apollo Club), Raymond H. Woodman (1861–1943), and William H. Neidlinger (1863–1924).[68] However, it was Horatio Parker (1863–1919), perhaps the most distinguished American composer of the later nineteenth century, who inherited Buck's mantle as the most important anthem composer in the decades surrounding the turn of the twentieth century. Trained in Germany (with Josef Rheinberger) as well as America (with George Whitfield Chadwick and others), Parker served as organist and choirmaster at various churches in New York and later, Boston, including at the Church of the Holy Trinity. He held Yale's Battel Professorship in music theory from 1894, and later became dean of its School of Music. His anthems equaled the best English church music, as indicated by Novello's publication of some of his works.[69] One of his finest efforts, *The Lord is My Light*, demonstrates a depth and musical mastery not seen before in American church music, with its compelling unison passages, vigorous organ accompaniment, and dynamic melodic writing.

Brief mention should be made of the sacred music of Charles Ives (1874–1954). Although most of his choral music, such as *The Harvest Home Chorales* and *Psalm 67*, is in a modernist experimental style that places it outside this study, the pre-modernist sacred choral works that he composed for the solo quartet choir in the years 1893–1902 stand squarely in the high Victorian anthem tradition he absorbed during his study with Buck and Shelley. These include the *Easter Carol*, *Crossing the Bar*, and *Turn Ye, Turn Ye*, all written for the choir at the Center Church on the Green in New Haven, where he was organist from 1894 to 1896.[70]

Among the small choral genres sung outside of the church during the last half of the nineteenth century, the partsong became the most popular, gaining prominence on choral programs beginning in the 1860s.[71] A direct outgrowth of the German *Männerchor* and the English glee traditions, the partsong was typically a piece for two or more voices without independent accompaniment. These works rarely departed from a straightforward ternary, modified strophic, or rondo-like design, featuring a homophonic and homorhythmic texture. Early nineteenth-century partsongs involved uncomplicated strophic settings that seldom strayed from a Mendelssohnian transparency and harmonic vocabulary, with close part writing and occasional augmented sixths or diminished sevenths for effect. Later works, however, show the influence of more recent European music with their expanded scope, luxuriant chromaticism, increased number of voice parts, expanded ranges, and more complex counterpoint. Composers drew upon an immense body of poetry for these works, ranging from the highest literary figures such as Shakespeare, Tennyson, Browning, Burns, and Kipling, to contemporary writers whose reputations soon evaporated. Among favorite American authors were Longfellow, Lowell, Whitman, and Lanier.

Many contemporary American composers wrote partsongs, including Dudley Buck, Amy Beach, George Chadwick, Arthur Foote, William Wallace Gilchrist, Henry Hadley, Margaret Ruthven Lang, Edward MacDowell, John Knowles Paine, and Horatio Parker.[72] Buck's later partsongs contain a contrapuntal sophistication seen in few other works of the period; for example, his *The Signal Resounds from Afar* (Op. 92/5), which he called a "vocal march in canon-form," employs a chorale cantus firmus as well as a double canon. Chadwick's early partsongs include gentle works with titles such as *In a China Shop* and *Mary's Lullaby* (both from 1910). Foote creates an uncommonly effective partsong cycle in his *Flower Songs*, Op. 49, a set of six works for women's voices with varied groupings of voices and piano. Among the few Victorian works in the genre that remain on choral programs today are some of Edward MacDowell's partsongs; his *Two Northern Songs*, Op. 43 and the haunting, eight-part *Barcarole*, Op. 44 (both from 1890), represent some of the finest American works written in this genre.

Repertoire Trends: Larger Choral Genres

With no royal court or long-standing artistic heritage to define the nation's culture and character, Americans found their beliefs and aspirations, as well as significant events from their relatively brief history as a country, voiced in a steady flow of extended works—the popular cantata and oratorio in particular—written by American composers for community choral societies, church choirs, festival choruses, college choirs, and *Männerchöre* that sprang up in the second half of the century. Many such works are imbued with religious concepts, cast in the codes of stories about Christopher Columbus, the Pilgrim Fathers, the Puritans, Native Americans, or other American legends. Running through virtually all of them are two prominent themes from nineteenth-century American life: Christian Romanticism, which echoed the English Romantic writers' insistence that man could be understood most fully only through religious thinking and writing, and American Triumphalism, the overriding conviction that the American way of life and its philosophies were superior to those of other peoples and nations.

The earliest American cantatas were composed in Boston, New York, and Philadelphia during the eighteenth century as cantata odes (or "libretto odes"), a genre based on English models (specifically those of Henry Purcell), containing solos, duets, and a few choruses.[73] The nineteenth-century American cantata, however, was less a case of genuine evolution from this prototype than one of simply appropriating a term that served to contrast it with the other principal extended-work genre of the day: the oratorio. Ultimately, the difference between nineteenth-century American cantatas and oratorios, then, comes down to subject matter and length.[74] Typically, works designated as cantatas are shorter than oratorios, the former lasting from 10 minutes to one hour in performance (seldom more), the latter lasting from one to three hours. While oratorios are usually based on religious themes, cantatas depict either sacred or secular subjects. The structural forms of both genres reflect that of the traditional Mendelssohnian oratorio, with choral writing that intermingles solo and ensemble work.[75] The majority of cantatas and oratorios are for mixed chorus, though some were written for male voices only; works for women's voices alone are rare.

Five composers dominate the early history of the nineteenth-century American cantata: John Hill Hewitt (1801–90), William Henry Fry (1813–64), William Bradbury (1816–68), George Frederick Root (1820–95), and George Frederick Bristow (1825–98). The most influential of these was Root, whose first work, *The Pilgrim Fathers* (1854, with a text by the prominent gospel hymnist, Fanny J. Crosby) set the tone for the genre with its story of the Pilgrims' religious faith and their successful encounter with the Wampanoag tribe in the spring of 1621. More important, however, was Root's second work, *The Haymakers* (1857). Calling the piece an "operatic cantata," Root combined elements of the reformed American hymn tune, the English glee, and the Mendelssohnian oratorio. With its progressive harmonic idiom and skillful treatment of rural American life, it contains uncommon dramatic power for a mid-century American work.[76]

Although these early cantatas remain almost completely unknown today, they enjoyed considerable popularity at the time. Root conducted *The Haymakers* twenty times during its first year in circulation and it remained popular into the 1870s; a revised edition appeared as late as 1904.[77] Another successful early effort was William Bradbury's most important choral work, *Esther the Beautiful Queen* (1856, on a text compiled by Chauncey Cady), which sold some 255,000 copies between 1856 and 1866.[78]

The popularity of the cantata in the United States after the Civil War mirrored its similar status in Europe; even a cursory bibliographical search reveals an astonishing number of cantatas written and published during the period.[79] This was democratic music at its richest (in more ways than one), if not always its finest, in that the music was meant for everyone to sing and appreciate, even if much of it was never more than merely Victoriana. Now average citizens could sing choral music that, although only slightly more difficult than the traditional psalm tunes and simple anthems sung in church, seemed (and often was) more sophisticated. Such experiences were thrilling to be sure, and kept choir members eager for more.

The prominent musicians of the period, Paine, Frederick S. Converse, Chadwick, Charles W. Cadman, Henry Hadley, Parker, Deems Taylor, Victor Herbert, and Buck all contributed significantly to this genre, as they busily turned out the kind of music on which American choral societies thrived. Of these, Buck's efforts again deserve special mention for producing some of the finest examples of the American Victorian cantata, many of which remained popular for nearly half a century.[80] His cantatas succeeded in part owing to his texts, which served as metaphors for America's civil religion of freedom, expressed in stories that forged the central allegories of national life. Moreover, they articulated the noble, Christian, and heroic light in which a large number of Americans viewed themselves. *The Legend of Don Munio* (1874) for mixed voices, soloists, and orchestra, was the most popular of Buck's three large-scale secular cantatas; it was the first published cantata by an American scored for orchestra. Another important cantata, one that is a superb example of Buck's work in this genre, was his *Centennial Meditation of Columbia*, composed for the 1876 Centennial Exhibition in Philadelphia on a text by the Southern poet, Sidney Lanier. Other popular late nineteenth-century American cantatas are George Frederick Bristow's *The Pioneer, A Grand Cantata* (1872), Frederick Grant Gleason's *The Culprit Fay* (1879), Chadwick's *The Viking's Last Voyage* (1881), Paine's *The Nativity* (1883), Foote's *The Wreck of the Hesperaus* (1887–88), Gilchrist's *The Legend of Bended Bow* (1888), and Parker's *Dream-king and His Love* (1891).

The oratorio proved less popular than the cantata in the United States owing to its longer length, more operatic style, and less relaxed formality.[81] As a result, American choral societies produced no significant demand for newly-composed American oratorios compared to those by English and German composers. That said, American composers wrote a number of important oratorios, especially towards the end of the century when performing groups were larger and their musical abilities more advanced. According to Howard Smither, just twelve extended works were labeled oratorios by their American composers at the time of the Civil War; by 1900, however, that number grew to 47.

American oratorios from the period reflected the subjects, style, and structure of English and German oratorios such as Handel's *Messiah* and Mendelssohn's *St. Paul* and *Elijah*. Most were divided into two large parts, some three. While the traditional "number oratorio" consisting of discrete movements dominated these American works, an increasing flexibility appears toward the end of the century as composers began imitating developments in their English and German counterparts by writing in a more continuous style with individual numbers grouped into larger sections connected by uninterrupted orchestral music. Librettos were taken from the Bible rather than newly written verse; these were divided nearly equally between Old and New Testament subjects. As noted earlier in this chapter, the first known oratorio by an American-born composer is *Jephtha's Rash Vow* (1845), a somewhat quaint work by John Hill Hewitt that is clearly intended for amateurs. Of considerably more significance is the cycle of four Old Testament oratorios completed around 1890 by Horace Wadham Nicholl: *Adam, Abraham, Isaac,* and *Jacob*. Although these works were never performed, they elicited a certain amount of comment as the most ambitious cycle of oratorios composed to that point. The cycle is historically significant not only because of his monumentality, but also for its modernity, including the use of Wagnerian-style leading motives.[82]

More general oratorio subjects also followed European models such as Paine's ambitious *St. Peter* (1870–72). This work represents one of the best American oratorios in the biblical tradition, with its lyrical solo writing, use of chorales, and heavy reliance on the chorus in the style of Mendelssohn. Paine was the first American composer whose extended works held up comfortably in comparison to the music of European composers, as demonstrated by the inclusion of *St. Peter* in the offerings of the Handel and Haydn Society; after the work's premiere in Portland, Maine in 1873, the well-respected Boston ensemble presented it during their Third Triennial Festival in May 1874 to wide acclaim.

Perhaps the best and most well-known example of the non-biblical American oratorio is Horatio Parker's *Hora Novissima*, written for the Church Choral Society of New York in 1893. It differs from many contemporary oratorios with its contemplative text, drawn from Bernard of Cluny's long satirical poem *De contemptu mundi* ("Scorn of the World"). Parker employs an understated motif of a perfect fourth to unify the work's eleven discrete numbers. The impressive choral writing offers considerable variety and power, including one extended *a cappella* passage, while its single quartet and four arias provide lyrical contrast.[83] It is one of the few nineteenth-century American extended choral works that continues to be performed today, albeit infrequently, and it surely merits more frequent hearings.

In concluding this discussion of large-scale genres, three other American composers whose choral outputs included works in various large and small choral genres deserve brief mention.

Brooklyn-born George Frederick Bristow, was the first American composer to write well-crafted, substantial works in the European art-music tradition; these included operas, symphonies, two oratorios, an extensive Mass in C (1885), and a grand national *Ode* (1856). His oratorio *Daniel*, which premiered in December 1867, is a dramatic retelling of three stories found in the Book of Daniel, featuring arias that display operatic virtuosity, and dramatic choruses that are powerfully enhanced by symphonic writing.[84] Similarly noteworthy from this part of the century is Paine's Mass in D for mixed chorus, solo quartet, orchestra, and organ. Paine conducted the Gloria, Benedictus, Agnus Dei, and Dona nobis pacem on Harvard Commemoration Day in 1865 with a sixty-voice chorus and twenty-five-piece orchestra; two years later he led a performance of the complete work at the Singakademie in Berlin, where it met with warm reviews.[85] This two-hour work consists of eighteen numbers, and apparently was the first extended choral composition by an American-born composer to be performed in Europe, where it was also published. Modeled on the choral works of Bach and the Viennese classicists, the Mass goes beyond mere craftsmanship to genuine inspiration, and stands apart from many other late century large choral works owing to Paine's imaginative counterpoint, formal clarity, lyricism, skillful orchestration, and original musical ideas.

Amy Beach (1867–1944) was the first American woman to gain recognition as a professional performer and composer. She wrote a number of major choral works between 1885 and 1910, including the symphonic Mass in E-flat, the *Festival Jubilate* for the dedication of the Woman's Building of the World's Columbian Exposition in 1893 in Chicago, and the *Song of Welcome* for the Trans-Mississippi Exposition in 1898. Her most popular compositions, each composed after the turn of the century, were the secular choral work *The Chambered Nautilus* (1907) and two sacred pieces, *Let This Mind be in You* (1924) and the Expressionist *The Canticle of the Sun* (1928), which remained in the repertory of church choirs for years.

The choral music heard in nineteenth-century America is difficult to summarize in a few descriptive words; the length of the period in question, coupled with the massive changes in America that took place during that time, make most generalizations difficult. Nevertheless, it bears noting that the rich variety of types of choral music heard throughout the century paralleled the growing diversity of the nation itself. Even in the most conservative programming situations, many choral concerts presented much more than a never-ending presentation of the same core works: *Messiah*, *The Creation*, *Elijah*, to name the three most popular (and most frequently cited here). One sees in the records of choral music-making in nineteenth-century America not only a dedication to presenting European masterworks, but also a commitment to new works by American composers reflecting the contemporary ideals of American life. Although the musical language and texts give much of the repertoire a dated quality, a circumstance that accounts for much of the repertoire being forgotten today, choral music continued to hold a prominent place in American concert life throughout the century, and set a foundation for the next 100 years, when it would continue to flourish.

Notes

1 The main sources used for this historical introduction are the *Encyclopedia of American Cultural History*, vol. 1, s.v. Part Two, "The Revolutionary Era and the Early Republic"; Part Three, "Overview. Antebellum, Civil War and Reconstruction: 1838–1877"; Part Four, "Overview. Commercial and National Consolidation: 1878–1912"; *Encyclopedia of the United States in the Nineteenth Century*, vol. 1, s.v. "Preface": vol. 2. "Nineteenth Century"; and Robert H. Wiebe, *The Opening of American Society from the Adoption*

of the Constitution to the Eve of Disunion (New York: Vintage Books, 1985), 129–67. Because white Protestants of European descent dominated free American society during most of this time, this chapter presents a picture that reflects the influences of these European roots. Consequently, the rich history of other traditions such as the music of African slave communities before the Civil War and of freed African Americans (after 1868), or of rural country communities of southern Appalachia, to pick just two of the most obvious examples, are not covered at length.

2 http://www2.census.gov/prod2/decennial/documents/1800-return-whole-number-of-persons.pdf, initial table.

3 *Fourteenth Census of the United States* (Washington: Government Printing Office, 1921), 14, 20, 24.

4 Wiebe, *The Opening of American Society*, 146.

5 Quoted in Nym Cooke, "Sacred Music to 1800," in *The Cambridge History of American Music* ed. D Nicholls (Cambridge: Cambridge University Press, 1998), 90.

6 Singing schools consisted of a series of local regular meetings, usually held one or two nights a week for no longer than two or three months, for instruction in basic singing and note reading; both men and women were welcome to attend. First established in the eighteenth century mainly in New England, these schools were the first American choral groups to emerge outside of the church.

7 Samuel Gilman, *Memoirs of a New England Village Choir, with Occasional Reflections from a Member*, 2nd ed. (Boston: Benjamin H. Greene, 1834), 35.

8 "'Ancient Music' and the Europeanizing of American Psalmody, 1800–1810" in *A Celebration of American Music: Words and Music in Honor of H. Wiley Hitchcock*, ed. Richard Crawford, R. Allen Lott, and Carol J. Oja (Ann Arbor: The University of Michigan Press, 1990), 225–55.

9 Music that was described as "scientific"—a term regularly used at the time in contrast to music that was merely "artful" (Richard Crawford, *America's Musical Life: A History* (New York: W. W. Norton, 2001), 142)—meant it used correct harmony, careful voice leading, and accurate rhythmic notation. These are characteristics more frequently seen in European psalmody and hymns, rather than in music composed early on in America, which was considered to be less polished.

10 Donald Nitz, "Community Musical Societies in Massachusetts to 1840" (D.M.A. diss., Boston University, 1964), 404–05; and Howard E. Smither, *A History of the Oratorio*, vol. 4, (Chapel Hill, NC, and London: University of North Carolina Press, 2000), 391. Stoughton, Massachusetts appears to have established the first organizations in America not officially connected to a church: Ye Olde Musical Society (1762) and the Old Stoughton Musical Society (1786). Other early societies included the Musical Society in Newburyport (1774), the Aretinian Society, Boston (1782), and the Singing Club of Harvard College (1789). The last decade of the century saw at least nine other societies appear.

11 Charles Hamm, *Music in the New World* (New York and London: W. W. Norton, 1983), 99–100; Charles Callahan Perkins and J. S. Dwight, eds, *History of the Handel and Haydn Society, of Boston, Massachusetts* (1883–93; reprint, New York: Da Capo Press, 1977), 29; Smither, *A History of the Oratorio*, vol. 4, 391–92.

12 *Jonah*'s premiere the previous year in New York marked the first complete performance of an oratorio in America. (Smither, *A History of the Oratorio*, vol. 4, 401–02.)

13 Perkins and Dwight, *History of the Handel and Haydn Society*, 38, n. 2.

14 Ibid., 44–5; Crawford, *America's Musical Life*, 293.

15 Crawford, *America's Musical Life*, 295–96.

16 At least 100 community musical societies existed in Massachusetts alone between 1774 and 1840 (Nitz, "Community Musical Societies," 231, 264–93).

17 Ann Yardley, "Choirs in the Methodist Episcopal Church, 1800–1860," *American Music* 17, 1 (Spring 1999): 39–64.

18 Hamm, *Music in the New World*, 163, asserts that Mason "had as much impact on the musical life of nineteenth-century America as any other person."

19 Crawford, *America's Musical Life*, 141.

20 Perkins and Dwight, *History of the Handel and Haydn Society*, 81–82.

21 Carol A. Pemberton, *Lowell Mason. His Life and Work* (Ann Arbor, MI: UMI Research Press, 1985), 36–38; Crawford, *America's Musical Life*, 141–42.

22 Perkins and Dwight, *History of the Handel and Haydn Society*, 142; Crawford, *America's Musical Life*, 140; Elwyn A. Wienandt and Robert H. Young, *The Anthem in England and America* (New York: The Free Press, 1970), 235–36.

23 Eric Paul Paige, "Musical Organizations in Boston: 1830–1850" (Ph.D. diss., Boston University, 1967), 42–43. The status of women in the choir remained in dispute throughout Mason's five-year tenure with the group. When he arrived, he found that few women could read music or sing an independent melody line. Thus, a group of male tenors called "soprano leaders" typically sang the soprano part an octave lower while the women followed at pitch. Mason found this effect "disagreeable."

24 Ibid., 51.

25 Smither, *A History of the Oratorio*, vol. 4, 397–99.

26 Crawford, *America's Musical Life*, 139–40.

27 Harry Eskew et al., "Lowell Mason," *Grove Music Online* (accessed August 30, 2010).

28 Paige, "Musical Organizations in Boston: 1830–1850," 329–36.

29 Pemberton, *Lowell Mason. His Life and Work*, 87–89.

30 William James Thompson, "Music and Musical Activities in New England, 1800–1838" (Ph.D. diss., George Peabody College for Teachers, Nashville, 1962), 74–149.

31 Smither, *A History of the Oratorio*, vol. 4, 403.

32 Vera Brodsky Lawrence, *Strong on Music. The New York Music Scene in the Days of George Templeton Strong*. Vol.1. *Resonances. 1836–1849* (Chicago and London: University of Chicago Press, 1988), xxxv–xxxvii, 10, 56, 397; Smither, *A History of the Oratorio*, vol. 4, 403.

33 Lawrence, *Strong on Music*, xxxv–xxxvii, 43–53.

34 Ibid., 237.

35 In *Strong on Music* 1, Lawrence states the American Musical Institute was founded by George Loder and Henry Meiggs (p. 372; see also see pp. 364, 372–73); Smither, *A History of the Oratorio*, vol. 4, 404, names Henry C. Timm as the group's founder.

36 Lawrence, *Strong on Music* 1, 305–07, 397–400.

37 A seven-shape system, which eventually succeeded this four-shape one, was the notation of the white gospel hymnody that emerged in the last quarter of the nineteenth century.

38 The two best sources on *The Sacred Harp* are Kiri Miller, *Travelin' Home: Sacred Harp Singing and American Pluralism* (Urbana: University of Illinois Press, 2008) and Buell Cobb, *The Sacred Harp. A Tradition and Its Music* (Athens: University of Georgia Press, 1978). "Amazing Grace" also appeared later in many other tunebooks under the names "Harmony Grove" and "New Britain."

39 *Historical Statistics of the United States. Colonial Times to 1970*. Bicentennial edition (Washington, DC: Bureau of the Census, 1976), 482, 699.

40 Ibid., 11–12.

41 http://www.census.gov/population/www/documentation/twps0029/tab04.html (accessed September 7, 2010).

42 *Musical Record*, 31 (May 3, 1879): 66.

43 Mark Clague, "Choral Music," http://encyclopedia.chicagohistory.org/pages/286.html (accessed September 1, 2010). See also www.orpheusclub.org.

44 "History of the Harvard Glee Club": http://www.harvardgleeclub.org/info/history (accessed August 9, 2009).

45 For a discussion of the pre-history of many of these groups, see Arnold R. Thomas, "The Development of Male Glee Clubs in American Colleges and Universities" (Ed.D. diss., Columbia University, 1962), 48, 57–59, 63–64. Other sources include *New Grove Dictionary of American Music* s.v. "Glee"; and B. E. Lindsay, "The English Glee in New England, 1815–1845" (Ph.D. diss., George Peabody College for Teachers, 1966). See also the histories posted on individual ensemble websites.

46 The information included in this paragraph relies heavily on the following sources: Geneva H. Southall, "Jubilee Singers," *Grove Music Online* (accessed September 10, 2010), and Eileen Southern, *The Music of Black Americans. A History*, 3rd ed. (New York: W. W. Norton, 1997), 227–31. See also Dena J. Epstein, "Black Spirituals: Their Emergence into Public Knowledge," *Black Music Research Journal*, 10, 1 (Spring, 1990): 58–64.

47 Crawford, *America's Musical Life*, 419–20.

48 Another significant and popular early publication was Thomas Fenner's *Cabin and Plantation Songs as Sung by the Hampton Students* (1874).

49 Sandra J. Graham, "The Fisk Jubilee Singers and the Concert Spiritual: The Beginning of an American Tradition" (Ph.D. diss., New York University, 2001), 309–36.

50 Katherine K. Preston, "Washington, D.C.," *Grove Music Online* (accessed September 10, 2010); see also Jacqueline Moore, *Leading the Race* (Charlottesville: University Press of Virginia, 1999), and Reid Badger, *A Life in Ragtime: A Biography of James Reese Europe* (Cambridge: Oxford University Press, 1995).

51 Southern, *The Music of Black Americans*, 294–96.

52 Irving Kolodin et al., "New York: Choral Societies," *Grove Music Online* (accessed September 10, 2010) and Henry E. Krehbiel, *Notes on the Cultivation of Choral Music and the Oratorio Society of New York* (New York: Edward Schuberth, 1884). See Krehbiel for a list of the society's concert programs from 1873 to 1884; see also the ensemble's website: http://www.oratoriosocietyofny.org/history.html.

53 Suzanne Gail Snyder, "The *Männerchor* Tradition in the United States: A Historical Analysis of Its Contribution to American Culture" (Ph.D. diss., University of Iowa, 1991), 1–20; William Osborne, *American Singing Societies and Their Partsongs* (Lawton, OK: American Choral Directors Association, 1994), 3–18. According to Snyder, more than 900 German singing societies are known to have existed in America by the middle of the twentieth century.

54 Snyder, "The *Männerchor* Tradition in the United States," 140–41.

55 Linda Poly, "Welsh Choral Music in America in the Nineteenth Century" (Ph.D. diss., The Ohio State University, 1989).

56 Smither, *A History of the Oratorio*, vol. 4, 414–26; New Grove Dictionary of American Music, s.v. "Choral Music."

57 Hamm, *Music in the New World*, 308–11.

58 Numbers from the Patrick Gilmore Collection materials on the University of Maryland's Special Collections online site for the American Bandmasters Association Research Center; see www.lib.md.edu/PAL/SCPA/ABA/Gilmore/Gilmore.html (accessed August 13, 2010); see also *New Grove Dictionary of American Music* s.v. "Chorus (i)"; Smither, *A History of the Oratorio*, vol. 4, 419 lists slightly smaller numbers: 17,000 singers and 1,500 players.

59 For a thorough investigation of Moravian music and music-making in America—centered principally in communities in Pennsylvania and North Carolina—and its influence from the middle of the eighteenth century on, see Nola Reed Knouse, ed., *The Music of the Moravian Church in America* (Rochester, NY: University of Rochester Press, 2008).

60 Thomas Hastings, *The History of Forty Choirs* (1854; reprint, New York: AMS Press, 1976), 162.

61 Stanley Robert McDaniel, "Church Song and the Cultivated Tradition in New England and New York," (D.M.A. diss., University of Southern California, 1983), 362–68; Paul Allwardt, "Sacred Music in New York City, 1800–1850" (D.S.M. diss., Union Theological Seminary, 1950), 9–12; Robert Stevenson, *Protestant Church Music in America* (New York: W. W. Norton, 1966), 112–14.

62 John Ogasapian, *Church Music in America, 1620–2000* (Macon, GA: Mercer University Press, 2007), 193, and *Dwight's Journal of Music*, 18/23 (March, 1861), 396. By 1895, *Nickerson's Illustrated Musical and Church Choir Directory of the City of New York* listed sixty Baptist churches, fifty of which maintained professional vocalists.

63 Ogasapian, *Church Music in America, 1620–2000*, 203–05. The first serial publication of church choir music, *The Parish Choir*, appeared in 1874, followed in 1892 by John P. Vance's *The Choir Herald,* which contained anthems in each month's issue. Two years later Edmund S. Lorenz founded the music-publishing dynasty with his *Choir Leader*. With Vance's death in 1897, Lorenz bought *The Choir Herald*; in 1913, Lorenz added a periodical with easier music, *The Volunteer Choir*.

64 Raymond Seely, lecture to the American Musical Convention (1845) as cited in Wienandt and Young, *The Anthem in England and America*, 306.

65 The major twentieth-century writings on Buck include William K. Gallo, "The Life and Church Music of Dudley Buck (1839–1909)" (Ph.D. diss., Catholic University of America, 1968); James R. Hall, "The Vocal Music of Dudley Buck" (M.A. thesis, University of North Carolina, 1951); N. Lee Orr, *Dudley Buck* (Champaign-Urbana: University of Illinois Press, 2008); "Dudley Buck: Leader of Lost Tradition," *The Tracker* 38 (Fall, 1995): 10–20. More information may be found in *Brainard's Biographies of American Musicians*, ed. E. Douglas Bomberger (Westport, CT, and London: Greenwood Press, 1999), 47–50; Frances Hall Johnson, *Musical Memories of Hartford* (Hartford: Witkowers, 1931), 2–16; Ralph McVety Kent, "A Study of Oratorios and Sacred Cantatas Composed in America Before 1900" (Ph.D. diss., University of Iowa, 1954); Peter Lutkin, *Music in the Church* (Milwaukee: Young Churchman Company, 1910), 252–53; and in Wienandt and Young, *The Anthem in England and America*, 330–37.

66 This talented group, including James Cutler Dunn Parker, Charles C. Converse, W. Eugene Thayer, and George E. Whiting, had all been born in or near the century's fourth decade, though none achieved the prominence Buck did.

67 Linda Jane Clark. "Music in Trinity Church, Boston, 1890–1900: a Case-Study in the Relationship Between Worship and Culture" (S.M.D. thesis, Union Theological Seminary, 1973).

68 Like Buck, Shelley was prolific and popular, evidenced by the engaging tunefulness of his anthems, especially works such as *The King of Love My Shepherd Is* (1886), which continues to be sung today.

69 Wienandt and Young, *The Anthem in England and America*, 342–43.

70 His most important sacred cantata, *The Celestial Country*, also appeared at the end of this period, taking as its model Buck's quartet-choir cantata style found in the five sacred cantatas Buck published during the 1890s. See Gayle Sherwood, "'Buds the Infant Mind': Charles Ives's *The Celestial Country* and American Protestant Choral Traditions," *19th-Century Music* 23 (Fall, 1999): 163–89.

71 Any discussion of the American partsong must begin with William Osborne's *American Singing Societies and Their Partsongs*, cited above, and Judith Blessard, "Partsong," *Grove Music Online* (accessed June 3, 2008). For a list of partsongs by ten of the most important composers, see Osborne, 69–92.

72 Osborne, *American Singing Societies and Their Partsongs*, 49–66.

73 The major sources for the cantata and oratorio in the United States include the following: Smither, *A History of the Oratorio*, vol., 4; Thurston J. Dox, *American Oratorios and Cantatas: A Catalog of Works Written in the United States from Colonial Times to 1985,* 2 vols., (Metuchen, NJ: Scarecrow Press, 1986); Jacklin

Talmage Bolton, "Religious Influences on American Secular Cantatas, 1850–1930" (Ph.D. diss., University of Michigan, 1964); H. Earle Johnson, "Longfellow and Music," *American Music Research Center Journal* 7 (1997), entire issue; George Putnam Upton, *The Standard Cantatas: Their Stories, Their Music, and Their Composers, A Handbook*, 6th ed. (Chicago: A. C. McClurg, 1897); Maurice Allen Jones, "American Theater Cantatas: 1852–1907" (Ph.D. diss., University of Illinois at Urbana-Champaign, 1975); Ralph McVety Kent, "A Study of Oratorios and Sacred Cantatas Composed in America before 1900" (Ph.D. diss., University of Iowa, 1954); Irving Lowens, *The Choral Music of America Before the Civil War* (New York: New York Public Library, 1958); Peter Lutkin, "The Larger Choral Groups and Preeminent Choral Leaders since 1876," *Music Teachers National Association, Proceedings* 23 (1928): 81–100; Jacklin Bolton Stopp, "The Secular Cantata in the United States: 1850–1919," *Journal of Research in Music Education* 17, 4 (Winter 1969): 388–98; David P. DeVenney, *Nineteenth Century American Choral Music: An Annotated Guide* (Berkeley, CA: Fallen Leaf Press, 1987); Suzanne G. Snyder "The *Männerchor* Tradition in the United States: A Historical Analysis of Its Contributions to American Music Culture"; and Dan Hardin and N. Lee Orr, *Choral Music in Nineteenth Century America: A Guide to the Sources* (Metuchen, NJ and London: Scarecrow Press, 1999).

74 It is even more difficult (and probably of little use) to distinguish between the choral cantata and similar choral works called odes or ballads, or works having no generic title at all. The term "oratorio," which proved just as fluid (especially in the first half of the century), had a dual meaning at the time: it not only signified a genre but was also used as a synonym for concert of sacred music. This last usage gradually disappeared after mid-century.

75 Malcolm Boyd, "Cantata: The Cantata since 1800," *Grove Music Online* (accessed June 3, 2008); and Smither, *A History of the Oratorio*, vol. 4, 251.

76 Crawford, *The American Musical Landscape: The Business of Musicianship from Billings to Gershwin* (Berkeley: University of California Press, 1993), 170–71.

77 George F. Root, *The Haymakers*, ed. Dennis R. Martin, Recent Researches in American Music, vols. IX and X (Madison: A-R Editions, 1984), vii–x.

78 *Esther, the Beautiful Queen*, ed. Juanita Karpf, Recent Researches In American Music 38 (Madison, WS: A-R Editions, 2000): ix–xiii. See also Karpf, *William Bradbury's Social Music: Making Music Accessible in the Nineteenth Century* (Lanham, MD: Scarecrow Press, forthcoming), part II, chapters 6–9.

79 Stopp gives the cantatas she consulted on pp. 395–98 in her article "The Secular Cantata in the United States: 1850–1919," cited above. There were four main American publishers: G. Schirmer in New York, Arthur P. Schmidt and Oliver Ditson in Boston, and John Church in Cincinnati.

80 Buck finished an extended choral work nearly every other year from 1872 to 1989; he would eventually write six secular cantatas for mixed chorus, beginning with *Festival Hymn* in 1872, plus an additional six for male chorus concluding with *Paul Revere's Ride* in 1898.

81 Much of this discussion of the nineteenth-century American oratorio is based on Smither's thorough survey and assessment in the fourth volume of his *A History of the Oratorio*, pp. 383–506.

82 Ibid., vol. 4, 448, 463.

83 For a thorough discussion of Parker's work, see ibid., vol. 4, 493–506.

84 Ibid., vol. 4, 472–3; George Frederick Bristow, *The Oratorio of Daniel*, Op. 42, ed. David Griggs-Janower, vol. 34, *Recent Researches in American Music* (Madison: A-R Editions, Inc., 1999).

85 The first complete American performance did not take place until 1972. John C. Schmidt, *The Life and Work of John Knowles Paine* (Ann Arbor, MI: UMI Research Press, 1980), 63–64, 69–74, 416–23.

Selected Bibliography

Allwardt, Paul. "Sacred Music in New York City, 1800–1850." D.S.M. diss., Union Theological Seminary, 1950.

Badger, Reid *A Life in Ragtime: A Biography of James Reese Europe*. New York: Oxford University Press, 1995.

Bolton, Jacklin Talmage. "Religious Influences on American Secular Cantatas, 1850–1930." Ph.D. diss., University of Michigan, 1964.

Clark, Linda Jane. "Music in Trinity Church, Boston, 1890–1900: A Case-Study in the Relationship Between Worship and Culture." S.M.D. thesis, Union Theological Seminary, 1973.

Cobb, Buell. *The Sacred Harp. A Tradition and Its Music*. Athens: University of Georgia Press, 1978.

Cooke, Nym. "Sacred Music to 1800," in *The Cambridge History of American Music*. Cambridge: Cambridge University Press, 1998.

Crawford, Richard. "'Ancient Music' and the Europeanizing of American Psalmody, 1800–1810." *A*

Celebration of American Music: Words and Music in Honor of H. Wiley Hitchcock. Ann Arbor: The University of Michigan Press, 1990.

———. *America's Musical Life: A History.* New York: W. W. Norton, 2001.

DeVenney, David. *Varied Carols. A Survey of American Choral Literature.* Westport, CT: Greenwood Press, 1999.

———. *Nineteenth Century American Choral Music: An Annotated Guide.* Berkeley, CA: Fallen Leaf Press, 1987.

Dox, Thurston J. *American Oratorios and Cantatas: A Catalog of Works Written in the United States from Colonial Times to 1985,* 2 vol. Metuchen, NJ: Scarecrow Press, 1986.

Encyclopedia of American Cultural History, vol. 1.

Encyclopedia of the United States in the Nineteenth Century, vol. 1.

Epstein, Dena J. "Black Spirituals: Their Emergence into Public Knowledge," *Black Music Research Journal* 10, 1 (Spring, 1990): 58–64.

Fourteenth Census of the United States. Washington: Government Printing Office, 1921.

Gilman, Samuel. *Memoirs of a New England Village Choir, with Occasional Reflections from a Member,* 2nd ed. Boston: Benjamin H. Greene, 1834.

Graham, Sandra J. "The Fisk Jubilee Singers and the Concert Spiritual: The Beginning of an American Tradition." Ph.D. diss., New York University, 2001.

The Grove Dictionary of American Music. 2nd ed., ed. Charles Hiroshi Garrett. New York and Oxford: Oxford University Press, forthcoming.

Grove Music Online.

Hamm, Charles. *Music in the New World.* New York and London: W. W. Norton and Company, 1983.

Hardin, Dan and N. Lee Orr. *Choral Music in Nineteenth Century America: A Guide to the Sources.* Metuchen, NJ and London: Scarecrow Press, 1999.

Hastings, Thomas. *The History of Forty Choirs.* 1854; reprint, New York: AMS Press, 1976.

Historical Statistics of the United States. Colonial Times to 1970. Bicentennial edition. Washington, DC: Bureau of the Census, 1976.

Johnson, H. Earle. "Longfellow and Music," *American Music Research Center Journal* 7 (1997).

Jones, Maurice Allen. "American Theater Cantatas: 1852–1907." Ph.D. diss., University of Illinois at Urbana-Champaign, 1975.

Karpf, Juanita. *William Bradbury's Social Music: Making Music Accessible in the Nineteenth Century.* Lanham: MD: Scarecrow Press, forthcoming.

Kent, Ralph McVety. "A Study of Oratorios and Sacred Cantatas Composed in America before 1900." Ph.D. diss., University of Iowa, 1954.

Knouse, Nola Reed, ed. *The Music of the Moravian Church in America.* Rochester, NY: University of Rochester Press, 2008.

Krehbiel Henry E. *Notes on the Cultivation of Choral Music and the Oratorio Society of New York.* Reprint, 1884; New York: AMS Press, 1970.

Lawrence, Vera Brodsky. *Strong on Music. The New York Music Scene in the Days of George Templeton Strong.* Vol. 1. Resonances. 1836–1849. Chicago and London: University of Chicago Press, 1988.

Lindsay, B. E. "The English Glee in New England, 1815–1845." Ph.D. diss., George Peabody College for Teachers, 1966.

Lutkin, Peter. "The Larger Choral Groups and Preeminent Choral Leaders since 1876," *Music Teachers National Association, Proceedings* 23 (1928): 81–100.

McDaniel, Stanley Robert. "Church Song and the Cultivated Tradition in New England and New York." D.M.A. diss., University of Southern California, 1983.

Miller, Kiri. *Travelin' Home: Sacred Harp Singing and American Pluralism.* Urbana: University of Illinois Press, 2008.

Nitz, Donald. "Community Musical Societies in Massachusetts to 1840." D.M.A. diss., Boston University.

Ogasapian, John. *Church Music in America, 1620-2000.* Macon, GA: Mercer University Press, 2007.

Orr, N. Lee. *Dudley Buck.* Urbana and Chicago: University of Illinois Press, 2008.

Osborne, William. *American Singing Societies and Their Partsongs.* Lawton, Oklahoma: American Choral Directors Association, 1994.

Paige, Eric Paul. "Musical Organizations in Boston: 1830–1850." Ph.D. diss., Boston University, 1967.

Pemberton, Carol A. *Lowell Mason. His Life and Work.* Ann Arbor, MI: UMI Research Press, 1985.

Perkins, Charles Callahan and J. S. Dwight, eds., *History of the Handel and Haydn Society, of Boston, Massachusetts.* 1883–93; reprint, New York: Da Capo Press, 1977.

Poly, Linda. "Welsh Choral Music in America in the Nineteenth Century." Ph.D. diss., Ohio State University, 1989.

Schmidt, John C. *The Life and Work of John Knowles Paine.* Ann Arbor, MI: UMI Research Press, 1980.

Sherwood, Gayle. "'Buds the Infant Mind': Charles Ives's *The Celestial Country* and American Protestant Choral Traditions," *19th-Century Music* 23 (Fall, 1999): 163–89.

Smither, Howard E. *A History of the Oratorio*, vol. 4. Chapel Hill, NC, and London: University of North Carolina Press, 2000.

Snyder, Suzanne Gail. "The *Männerchor* Tradition in the United States: A Historical Analysis of Its Contribution to American Culture." Ph.D. diss., University of Iowa, 1991.

Southern, Eileen. *The Music of Black Americans. A History*, 3rd ed. New York: W. W. Norton, 1997.

Stevenson, Robert. *Protestant Church Music in America.* New York: W. W. Norton, 1966.

Stopp, Jacklin Bolton. "The Secular Cantata in the United States: 1850–1919," *Journal of Research in Music Education* 17, 4 (Winter, 1969): 388–98.

Thomas, Arnold R. "The Development of Male Glee Clubs in American Colleges and Universities." Ed. D. diss., Columbia University, 1962.

Thompson, William James. "Music and Musical Activities in New England, 1800–1838." Ph.D. diss., George Peabody College for Teachers, Nashville, 1962.

Upton, George Putnam. *The Standard Cantatas: Their Stories, Their Music, and Their Composers, A Handbook*, 6th ed. Chicago: A. C. McClurg, 1897.

Wiebe, Robert H. *The Opening of American Society from the Adoption of the Constitution to the Eve of Disunion.* New York: Vintage Books, 1985.

Yardley, Ann. "Choirs in the Methodist Episcopal Church, 1800–1860," *American Music* 17, 1 (Spring, 1999): 39–64.

INDEX

Note: Boldface page numbers indicate main discussion. Figures and endnotes have not been indexed (with a few exceptions), nor has the introductory information that precedes the discussion of each masterwork on pp. 43–108. Performing groups are listed alphabetically under "ensembles, societies."